KARL MARX

HIS LIFE AND THOUGHT

KARL MARX
HIS LIFE AND THOUGHT

David McLellan

1817

HARPER & ROW, PUBLISHERS

New York, Evanston, San Francisco, London

FIRST U.S. EDITION

Library of Congress Cataloging in Publication Data

McLellan, David.
   Karl Marx: his life and thought.
   Bibliography: p.
   1. Marx, Karl, 1818–1883.
HX39.5.M26 1974   335.4'092'4 [B]   73-4104
ISBN 0-06-012829-1

Contents

List of Plates

Between pages 178 and 179

The plates are reproduced by permission of the following: 1, Staats-
bibliothek, Berlin; 2 and 14, Dietz Verlag, Berlin; 3–7, 10, 15, 18 and
26, Int. Instituut voor Soc. Geschiedenis, Amsterdam; 9 and 21,
Radio Times Hulton Picture Library; 11 and 13, Marx Memorial
Library; 12, David Heisler, London; 17, 19 and 22, Institut für Marxis-
mus-Leninismus, East Berlin; 20 and 23, Communist Party Headquarters, London; 24, the British Museum; 25, Angelo Hornak,
London. Nos 8 and 16 were taken by the author.

Preface

THERE HAS been no full-scale biography of Marx in English covering all aspects of his life since that of Mehring, first published in the original German in 1918. Two events have occurred since then which justify a fresh attempt: first, there is the publication of the unexpurgated Marx–Engels correspondence – together with numerous other letters relating to Marx's activities; second, several of Marx's crucial writings were published only in the 1930s and considerably alter the picture of his intellectual contribution.

Much writing about Marx has obviously suffered from the grinding of political axes. Clearly it is impossible to pretend to a completely 'neutral' account of anyone's life – let alone Marx's. There is a vast amount of information and commentary on Marx and the very process of selection implies a certain standpoint. What I have tried to do is at least to write *sine ira et studio* and present the reader with a reasonably balanced picture. I have therefore relied considerably on quotation and write from a sympathetically critical standpoint that avoids the extremes of hagiography and denigration.

The book is intended for the general reader; and I have attempted to cover fully the three main facets of Marx's life – personal, political and intellectual. In dealing with this last aspect I have had to include some rather difficult passages, particularly in the latter halves of chapters one and two and the beginning of chapter six. These passages are, however, necessary for an accurate appreciation of Marx as a thinker.

I am grateful to Dr R. D. McLellan, Dr Brian Harrison and Mr C. N. Taylor who read parts of the manuscript and made many helpful suggestions; my particular thanks go to Dr G. M. Thomas whose inimitable sense of style has left its imprint on virtually every page of the book. Remaining deficiencies are certainly not their fault.

122 Old Dover Road,   D. M.
Canterbury,
Kent
December 1972

GERMANY ABOUT 1848

Königsberg
Danzig
HOLSTEIN
MECKLENBURG
Hamburg
HANOVER
Hanover
Berlin
PRUSSIA
NETHERLANDS
Hague
R. Rhine
WESTPHALIA
PRUSSIA
Barmen
Brussels
Cologne
Gotha
Halle
Leipzig
BELGIUM
Bonn
THURINGAN
Jena
Dresden
RHINELAND
STATES
SAXONY
SILESIA
HESSE
Frankfurt
Karlsbad
Trier
Kreuznach
Mainz
Prague
R. Main
Paris
Metz
Nuremburg
Hambach
Toul
BAVARIA
Strasbourg
WURTTEMBURG
Augsburg
Vienna
BADEN
Munich
AUSTRIAN EMPIRE
FRANCE
Basel
Zürich
SWITZERLAND
Lausanne
Geneva
VENETIA

—— German League
▨ Prussia

0   50   100 150 Miles
0   100   200
Kilometres

I

Trier, Bonn and Berlin

I feel myself suddenly invaded by doubt and ask myself if
your heart is equal to your intelligence and spiritual
qualities, if it is open to the tender feelings which here on
earth are so great a source of consolation for a sensitive
soul; I wonder whether the peculiar demon, to which
your heart is manifestly a prey, is the Spirit of God or that
of Faust. I ask myself – and this is not the least of the doubts
that assail my heart – if you will ever know a simple happiness and family joys, and render happy those who surround
you.

Heinrich Marx to his son, *MEGA* I i (2) 202.

I. CHILDHOOD

IT MAY seem paradoxical that Karl Marx, whom so many working-
class movements of our time claim as their Master and infallible guide
to revolution, should have come from a comfortable middle-class
home. Yet to a remarkable extent he does himself epitomise his own
doctrine that men are conditioned by their socio-economic circumstances. The German city in which he grew up gave him a sense of
long historical tradition and at the same time close contact with the
grim realities of the underdevelopment then characteristic of Germany. Thoroughly Jewish in their origins, Protestant by necessity yet
living in a Catholic region, his family could never regard their social
integration as complete. The sense of alienation was heightened in
Marx's personal case by his subsequent inability to obtain a teaching
post in a university system that had no room for dissident intellectuals.

Marx was born in Trier on 5 May 1818. A community of about 15,000
inhabitants, it was the oldest city in Germany[1] and also one of the

---

[1] For further background, see W. Bracht, *Trier und Karl Marx* (Trier, 1947); H.
Monz, *Karl Marx und Trier* (Trier, 1964); H. Hirsch, 'Marxens Milieu', *Études de
Marxologie* (Aug 1965).

loveliest – situated as it was in the Mosel valley, surrounded by vine-yards and luxuriating in an almost Mediterranean vegetation. Under the name of Augusta Treverorum the city had been considered the Rome of the North and served as the headquarters of the most power-ful of the Roman armies. The Porta Nigra, in whose shadow (literally) Marx grew up, and the enormous fourth-century basilica were endur-ing monuments of Trier's imperial glory. In the Middle Ages the city had been the seat of a Prince-Archbishop whose lands stretched as far as Metz, Toul and Verdun; it was said that it contained more churches than any other German city of comparable size. Marx did not only get his lifelong Rhineland accent from Trier: more importantly, his absorbing passion for history originated in the very environment of his adolescence. But it was not just the city of Roman times that in-fluenced him: during the Napoleonic wars, together with the rest of the Rhineland, it had been annexed by France and governed long enough in accordance with the principles of the French Revolution to be imbued by a taste for freedom of speech and constitutional liberty uncharacteristic of the rest of Germany. There was considerable dis-content following incorporation of the Rhineland into Prussia in 1814. Trier had very little industry and its inhabitants were mainly officials, traders and artisans. Their activities were largely bound up with the vineyards whose prosperity, owing to customs unions and outside competition, was on the decline. The consequent unemployment and high prices caused increases in beggary, prostitution and emigration; more than a quarter of the city's population subsisted entirely on public charity.

Thus it is not surprising that Trier was one of the first cities in Germany where French doctrines of utopian socialism appeared. The Archbishop felt himself compelled to condemn from the pulpit the doctrines of Saint Simon; and the teachings of Fourier were actively propagated by Ludwig Gall, Secretary to the City Council, who con-stantly emphasised the growing disparity and hence opposition between the rich and the poor.

Marx was all the more predisposed to take a critical look at society as he came from a milieu that was necessarily excluded from complete social participation. For it would be difficult to find anyone who had a more Jewish ancestry than Karl Marx.[1] The name Marx is a shortened

[1] For detailed research on Marx's genealogy, see B. Wachstein, 'Die Abstammung von Marx', in *Festskrift i anledning of Professor David Simonsens 70-aaroge födseldag* (Copen-

form of Mordechai, later changed to Markus. His father, Heinrich Marx, was born in 1782, the third son of Meier Halevi Marx who had become rabbi of Trier on the death of his father-in-law and was followed in this office by his eldest son Samuel (Karl's uncle) who died in 1827. Meier Halevi Marx numbered many rabbis among his ancestors, who came originally from Bohemia, and his wife, Chage, had an even more illustrious ancestry: she was the daughter of Moses Lwow, rabbi in Trier, whose father and grandfather were also rabbis in the same city. The father of Moses, Joshue Heschel Lwow, had been chosen rabbi of Trier in 1723, corresponded with the leading Jewish personalities of his time and had been widely known as a fearless fighter in the cause of truth. It was said of him that no important decision was taken in the Jewish world without his having first been consulted. The father of Joshue Heschel, Aron Lwow, was also rabbi in Trier and then moved to Westhofen in Alsace where he held the rabbinate for twenty years. Aron Lwow's father, Moses Lwow, came from Lemberg (the German name for Lwów) in Poland, and numbered among his ancestors Meir Katzenellenbogen, head of the Talmudic High School in Padua during the sixteenth century, and Abraham Ha-Levi Minz, rabbi in Padua, whose father had left Germany in the middle of the fifteenth century owing to persecutions there. In fact almost all the rabbis of Trier from the sixteenth century onwards were ancestors of Marx.[1]

Less is known of the ancestry of Karl's mother, Henrietta, but she seems to have been no less steeped in the rabbinic tradition than her husband. She was Dutch, the daughter of Isaac Pressburg, rabbi of Nijmegen. According to Eleanor (Karl's daughter), in her grandmother's family 'the sons had for centuries been rabbis'.[2] In a letter to the Dutch socialist Polak, Eleanor wrote: 'It is strange that my father's semi-Dutch parentage should be so little known ... my grandmother's family name was Pressburg and she belonged by descent to an old Hungarian Jewish family. This family, driven by persecution to Holland, settled down in that country and became known as I have said, by the name Pressburg – really the town from which they came.'[3]

---

hagen, 1923) pp. 277 ff.; E. Lewin-Dorsch, 'Familie und Stammbaum von Karl Marx', *Die Glocke*, IX (Berlin, 1924) 309 ff., 240 ff.; H. Horowitz, 'Die Familie Lwow', *Monatsschrift für Geschichte und Wissenschaft des Judentums*, LXXII (Frankfurt, 1928) pp. 487 ff.

[1] See the genealogical table on p. 459.

[2] Eleanor Marx to Wilhelm Leibknecht, in *Mohr und General* (Berlin, 1965) p. 159.

[3] Eleanor Marx to Henri Polak, in W. Blumenberg, 'Ein unbekanntes Kapitel aus Marx' Leben', *International Review of Social History* (1956).

Marx's father was remarkably unaffected by this centuries-old tradition of strict Jewish orthodoxy. He had broken early with his family, from whom he claimed to have received nothing 'apart from, to be fair, the love of my mother',[1] and often mentioned to his son the great difficulties he had gone through at the outset of his career. At the time of Marx's birth he was counsellor-at-law to the High Court of Appeal in Trier; he also practised in the Trier County Court, and was awarded the title of *Justizrat* (very roughly the equivalent of a British Q.C.). For many years he was President of the city lawyers' association and occupied a respected position in civic society though he confined himself mostly to the company of his colleagues.

Although his beliefs seem to have been very little influenced by his Jewish upbringing, Heinrich Marx's 'conversion' to Christianity was one made solely in order to be able to continue his profession.[2] The Napoleonic laws had given Jews in the Rhineland a certain equality but had attempted to impose strict controls over their commercial practices. On the transference of the Rhineland to Prussia, Heinrich Marx addressed a memorandum to the new Governor-General in which he respectfully requested that the laws applying exclusively to Jews be annulled. He spoke of his 'fellow believers' and fully identified himself with the Jewish community. But the memorandum was without effect. The Jews got the worst of both worlds: in 1818 a decree was issued keeping the Napoleonic laws in force for an unlimited period; and two years earlier the Prussian Government had decided that the Rhineland too should be subject to the laws that had been in force in Prussia since 1812. These laws, while granting Jews rights equal to those of Christians, nevertheless made their holding of positions in the service of the state dependent on a royal dispensation. The President of the Provincial Supreme Court, von Sethe, made an inspection tour of the Rhineland in April 1816 and interviewed Heinrich Marx, who impressed him as 'someone of wide knowledge, very industrious, articulate and thoroughly honest'. As a result he recommended that Heinrich Marx and two other Jewish officials be retained in their posts. But the Prussian Minister of Justice was against exceptions and Heinrich Marx was forced to change his religion to avoid becoming, as

---

[1] Heinrich Marx to Karl Marx, K. Marx–F. Engels, *Historisch-kritisch Gesamtausgabe*, ed. D. Rjazanov and V. Adoratskÿ (Berlin, 1927 ff.) I i (2) p. 242 (hereinafter referred to as *MEGA*).

[2] F. Mehring, *Karl Marx* (London, 1936) p. 3, is mistaken on this point.

von Sethe put it, 'breadless'. He chose to become a Protestant – though there were only about 200 Protestants in Trier – and was baptised some time before August 1817.[1] (It was at this period that he changed his name to Heinrich having been known hitherto as Heschel.)

Marx's mother, who remains a shadowy figure, seems to have been more attached to Jewish beliefs than his father. When the children were baptised in 1824 – the eldest son, Karl, being then of an age to start school – her religion was entered as Jewish with the proviso that she consented to the baptism of her children but wished to defer her own baptism on account of her parents. Her father died in 1825 and she was baptised the same year. Her few surviving letters are written in an ungrammatical German without any punctuation. The fact that her letters even to her Dutch relations were in German suggests that she spoke Yiddish in her parents' home. Being very closely attached to her own family, she always felt something of a stranger in Trier. The few indications that survive portray her as a simple, uneducated, hard-working woman, whose horizon was almost totally limited to her family and home, rather over-anxious and given to laments and humourless moralising. It is therefore quite possible that Henrietta Marx kept alive in the household certain Jewish customs and attitudes.

It is impossible to estimate with any precision the influence on Marx of this strong family tradition. 'The tradition of all the dead generations weighs like a mountain on the mind of the living',[2] he wrote later. Jewishness, above all at that time, was not something that it was easy to slough off. Heine and Hess, both intimate friends of Marx – the one a convert to Protestatism for cultural reasons, the other an avowed atheist – both retained their Jewish self-awareness until the end of their lives. Even Marx's youngest daughter, Eleanor, though only half-Jewish, proclaimed constantly and with a certain defiant pride at workers' meetings in the East End of London: 'I am a Jewess.'[3] The position of Jews in the Rhineland, where they were often scapegoats for the farmers' increasing poverty, was calculated to increase their collective self-awareness. Although civil equality had been achieved under the Napoleonic laws, the inauguration of the Holy Alliance and its policy of the 'Christian state' inevitably involved an anti-semitism

[1] For details, see A. Kober, 'Karl Marx' Vater und das napoleonische Ausnahmegesetz gegen die Juden, 1808', *Jahrbuch des kölnischen Geschichtsverein*, XIV (1932).

[2] K. Marx, 'The Eighteenth Brumaire of Louis Bonaparte', in K. Marx and F. Engels, *Selected Works* (Moscow, 1935), I 247 (hereinafter referred to as *MESW*).

[3] Cf. E. Bernstein, *Die neue Zeit* (1898) p. 122.

on the double count that the religious Jews professed an alien faith
and many claimed to be a separate people. In much of the bitterest
polemic – which Marx engaged in with, for example, Ruge, Proudhon,
Bakunin and Dühring – his Jewishness was dragged into the debate.
Whether Marx himself possessed anti-semitic tendencies is a matter of
much controversy: certainly a superficial reading of his pamphlet *On
the Jewish Question* would indicate as much;[1] and his letters contain
innumerable derogatory epithets concerning Jews;[2] but this does not
justify a charge of sustained anti-semitism. Some students of Marx
believe they have found the key to Marx's whole system of ideas in his
rabbinic ancestry; but although some of his ideas – and even life-style –
have echoes of the prophetic tradition, this tradition itself is more or
less part of the Western intellectual heritage; and it would be too
simplistic to reduce Marx's ideas to a secularised Judaism.[3]

Typically Jewish attitudes were certainly not in keeping with the
general views of Marx's father. According to Eleanor, he was 'steeped
in the free French ideas of the eighteenth century on politics, religion,
life and art'.[4] He subscribed entirely to the views of the eighteenth-
century French rationalists, sharing their limitless faith in the power
of reason to explain and improve the world. In this belief these
French intellectuals tempered the dogmatic rationalism of the classical
metaphysicians like Leibnitz with the British empiricism of Locke
and Hume. They believed that they were capable of showing that
men were by nature good and all equally rational; the cause of
human misery was simply ignorance, which resulted partly from
unfortunate material circumstances and partly from a deliberate
suppression or distortion of the truth by those in authority, whether
civil or religious, in whose obvious interest it was to perpetuate the

---

[1] See the text and comments on pp. 80 ff. below.

[2] See particularly his remarks on Lassalle, pp. 322 ff. below.

[3] This problem has given rise to a large literature that is interesting in its specu-
lations, but sparse in convincing conclusions. In English the two best studies are:
S. Bloom, 'Karl Marx and the Jews', *Jewish Social Studies* (1942), and E. Silberner, 'Was
Marx an Antisemite?', *Judaica* (1949). At greater length there is a study which
draws on all the available – and sometimes unavailable – evidence to demonstrate Marx's anti-semitism and pathological Jewish self-hate in A. Künzli's *Karl
Marx. Eine Psychographie* (Vienna, 1966). From the opposite point of view, A. Massiczek
in *Der Menschliche Mensch: Karl Marx's jüdischer Humanismus* (Vienna, 1968) argues that
all the positive elements in Marx's humanism came from his Jewish upbringing.
A good all-round discussion of the literature is H. Lamm, 'Karl Marx und das
Judentum', in *Karl Marx 1818–1968* (Mainz, 1968).

[4] Eleanor Marx, 'Karl Marx', *Die neue Zeit* (1883) p. 441.

deceptions under which mankind laboured. One of the chief means of destroying this state of affairs was education; another was change in material conditions.

His surviving letters show that Heinrich Marx was indeed, in the words of his grand-daughter Eleanor, 'a real Frenchman of the eighteenth century who knew his Voltaire and Rousseau by heart'.[1] His religion was a shallow and moralising deism: Edgar von Westphalen, Karl Marx's future brother-in-law, described Heinrich Marx as a 'Protestant à la Lessing'.[2] His outlook on life is well summed up in the advice he gave to Karl: 'A good support for morality is a simple faith in God. You know that I am the last person to be a fanatic. But sooner or later a man has a real need of this faith, and there are moments in life when even the man who denies God is compelled against his will to pray to the Almighty . . . everyone should submit to what was the faith of Newton, Locke and Leibnitz.'[3]

Heinrich Marx was also closely connected with the Rhineland liberal movement. He was a member of a literary society, the Trier Casino Club, founded during the French occupation and so called from its meeting place. The liberal movement gained force after the the 1830 Revolution in France, and the Club held a dinner in 1834 (when Karl was sixteen) in honour of the liberal deputies from Trier who sat in the Rhineland Parliament. This dinner – part of a campaign for more representative constitutions – was the only one held in Prussia, though many such were held in non-Prussian areas of Germany. Although Heinrich Marx was extremely active as one of the five organisers of this political dinner, the toast he eventually proposed was characteristically moderate and deferential. The nearest he got to the demands of the liberals was effusively to thank Frederick William III, to whose 'magnanimity we owe the first institutions of popular representation'. He ended: 'Let us confidently envisage a happy future, for it rests in the hands of a benevolent father, an equitable king. His noble heart will always give a favourable reception to the justifiable and reasonable wishes of his people.'[4] Several revolutionary songs were then sung and a police report informed the Government that Heinrich

[1] Eleanor Marx to Wilhelm Liebknecht, in *Reminiscences of Marx and Engels* (Moscow' n.d.) p. 130.

[2] Quoted in B. Nicolaievsky and O. Maenchen-Helfen, *La Vie de Karl Marx* (Paris, 1970) p. 19.

[3] Heinrich Marx to Karl Marx, MEGA I i (2) 186.

[4] The speech is reprinted in H. Monz, *Karl Marx und Trier*, p. 88.

had joined in the singing. The dinner caused anger in government circles, and this anger was increased by a more radical demonstration two weeks later, on the anniversary of the founding of the Casino Club, when the 'Marseillaise' was sung and the Tricolor brandished. The Prussian Government severely reprimanded the provincial governor and put the Casino Club under increased police surveillance. Heinrich Marx was present at this second demonstration but this time refrained from joining in the singing: he was no francophile and hated what he termed Napoleon's 'mad ideology'.[1] Although his liberal ideas were always tempered by a certain Prussian patriotism, Heinrich Marx possessed a sympathy for the rights of the oppressed that cannot have been without influence on his son.[2]

The Marx family had enough money to live fairly comfortably. Heinrich's parents had been poor and, although his wife brought a fair dowry, he was a self-made man. The building in which Marx was born was a finely constructed three-storey house with a galleried courtyard.[3] However, Heinrich rented only two rooms on the ground floor and three on the first floor, in which he housed seven people as well as exercised his legal practice. Eighteen months after Karl's birth, the family bought and moved into another house in Trier, considerably smaller than the previous one, but comprising ten rooms – and with a cottage in the grounds.[4] The family had two maids and also owned a vineyard near the city. Nevertheless the low income tax paid by Heinrich Marx and some of his remarks in letters to his son (he urged Karl to send several of his letters together by parcel post as it was cheaper) suggest that there was not much money to spare.[5]

There were nine children in the Marx family of whom Karl was the third; but the eldest, Moritz David, died aged four the year after Karl's birth so that Karl occupied the position of elder son. He had an elder sister, Sophie, to whom he seems to have been particularly attached during his childhood; she later married a lawyer and lived in Maast-

[1] Heinrich Marx to Karl Marx, *MEGA* I i (2) 205.

[2] See further, H. Monz, 'Die rechtsethischen und rechtspolitischen Anschauungen des Heinrich Marx', *Archiv für Sozialgeschichte* (1968).

[3] The house, then Brückengasse 664, now Brückenstrasse 10, has recently been turned into a museum and library with numerous photographs, first editions and originals of Marx's manuscripts.

[4] It is now an optician's shop, Simeonstrasse 8, in the main street beside the Porta Nigra.

[5] For more details, see H. Monz, 'Die soziale Lage der elterlichen Familie von Karl Marx', in *Karl Marx 1818–1968*.

richt in Holland. Marx's two younger brothers both died early from tuberculosis, as did two of his sisters. Of the two remaining sisters, Louise married a Dutchman, Juta, and emigrated with him to Cape-town, and Emilie married an engineer and lived in Trier. Most of the little information about Marx's childhood comes from these sisters, who told their niece, Eleanor, that as a child Marx was 'a terrible tyrant of his sisters, whom he would "drive" as his horses down the Markusberg in Trier at full speed – and worse, would insist on their eating the "cakes" he made with dirty dough and dirtier hands. But they stood the "driving" and ate the "cakes" without a murmur, for the sake of the stories Karl would tell them as a reward for their compliance.'[1]

Up to the age of twelve Marx was probably educated at home. For the subsequent five years 1830–5 he attended the High School in Trier which had formerly been a Jesuit school and then bore the name Frederick William High School. Here he received a typically solid humanist education. The liberal spirit of the Enlightenment had been introduced into the school by the late Prince-Elector of Trier, Clement Wenceslas, who had adopted the principles of his famous predecessor Febronius and tried to reconcile faith and reason from a Kantian standpoint. In order to combat the ignorance of the clergy he turned the school into a sort of minor seminary. It sank to a very low level under the French occupation, but was reorganised after the annexation of the Rhineland and recruited several very gifted teachers.[2] The chief influence in the school was its headmast, Hugo Wyttenbach, Karl's history teacher and a friend of the Marx family. He had made a favourable impression on Goethe as 'an adept of Kantian philosophy',[3] and took part in the founding of the Casino Club. After a big demon-stration at Hambach in favour of freedom of the Press in 1832, Wytten-bach was put under police observation and the school was searched: copies of the Hambach speeches and anti-government satire were found in the possession of pupils. As a result of the Casino affair of 1834, Karl Marx's fourth year at the school, the mathematics teacher was accused of materialism and atheism, and the Hebrew teacher of having joined in the revolutionary songs. Wyttenbach himself was

[1] Eleanor Marx, 'Karl Marx. A few Stray Notes', in *Reminiscences of Marx and Engels*, p. 251.

[2] Cf. C. Grünberg, *Archiv für die Geschichte des Sozialismus und der Arbeiterbewegung* (1926) pp. 239 f.

[3] J. Goethe, *Die Campagne des Frankreichs*, 25 Oct 1792.

threatened with dismissal, but in the end a reactionary co-headmaster, Loehrs, was appointed to counteract the prevalent liberalism. Karl Marx's attitude here can be gauged by the complaint addressed to him by his father that he and another pupil had made themselves conspicuous by deliberately slighting Loehrs when they left the school by taking their leave of all the teachers except him.[1]

Among Karl Marx's fellow pupils, four-fifths were Catholics and most were of lower-middle-class origin, the sons of farmers and artisans. Karl is said to have been 'both loved and feared by his fellow pupils, loved because he was always ready for boyish pranks and feared for the ease with which he composed satirical verses and lampoons against his enemies'.[2] In a letter to Engels much later, he spoke disparagingly of the 'denseness and age' of the 'country bumpkins who were preparing themselves for the Catholic seminary and for the most part lived on stipends'.[3] Marx formed no lasting friendships at school, though he was to develop an affection for one of his contemporaries, his future brother-in-law Edgar von Westphalen, whom Edgar's sister Jenny described as 'the idol of my childhood and youth'.

The academic level of the pupils was not high, and half of them failed their final examination. Intellectually Marx was above average though not outstanding, being equal eighth in a class of thirty-two. He was one of the youngest in his class, whose average age, when they left the school, was around twenty. The school put most emphasis on languages, and Marx's Latin and Greek verse were good, his Religion satisfactory, his French and Mathematics weak, and his History (strangely) weakest of all.[4] The earliest surviving documents in Marx's hand are the three essays he wrote for his Abitur, the German school-leaving examination. The essay in Latin on the Emperor Augustus is uninteresting. The one on Religion, however, and the one for German composition showed more individuality; both were filled with idealism and an enthusiasm for the development of one's personality to the full by eschewing power and glory and working with self-sacrifice for the good of humanity as a whole. The theme of the religious essay was 'a demonstration, according to St John's Gospel, chapter 15, verses

---

[1] Cf. Heinrich Marx to Karl Marx, MEGA I i (2) 186.

[2] Eleanor Marx in Progress (London, May 1885).

[3] Marx to Engels, in K. Marx and F. Engels, Werke (Berlin, 1956 ff.), xxxiv 87 (hereinafter referred to as MEW).

[4] See C. Grünberg, 'Marx als Abiturient', Archiv für die Geschichte des Sozialismus und der Arbeiterbewegung, xi (1925) pp. 424 ff.

1-14, of the reason, nature, necessity and effects of the union of believers with Christ'.[1] Marx began by saying that History, 'the great teacher of mankind', showed us that, from antiquity onwards, human nature had always tried to raise itself to a higher morality. 'Thus the history of mankind teaches us the necessity of union with Christ. Also when we consider the history of individuals, and the nature of man, we immediately see a spark of the divine in his breast, and enthusiasm for the good, a striving after knowledge, a desire for truth.'[2] Although these natural instincts were overlaid by sinful desires, the union of believers with Christ could overcome these and afford a 'happiness which the Epicurean in his simple philosophy and the more profound thinker in the furthest depths of knowledge seek in vain, which only one bound unconditionally and childlike to Christ, and through him to God, can know, and which makes for a finer and more elevated life'.[3]

The essay was written with considerable pathos and rather sugary piety, but had a basically rational structure, explaining how the advent of Christianity was necessary for the full moral development of humanity. Marx had a very distant and colourless deistic conception of God – akin to that of his father and to that of the Pastor Josef Küpper who gave religious instruction at the school and had confirmed Marx in March 1834. Küpper was also in charge of the small Protestant parish in Trier and a friend of Heinrich Marx. He was particularly interested in ethical questions, and his approach to religion, strongly influenced by Kant, held that it was the best means of educating men to a 'true humanity'. Küpper based his teaching on the person of Christ and on the Bible and, being strongly influenced by rationalist elements, avoided any sectarianism.[4] Marx's essay very much reflected the approach of his teacher, who praised it – though he also made the justifiable comment that 'the essence of the union in question is not dealt with and the reason for it only dealt with from one aspect'.[5]

The German composition, entitled 'Reflections of a Young Man on the Choice of a Career', showed more originality.[6] Marx's theme was

[1] First published in *MEGA* I i (2) 171 ff.
[2] *MEGA* I i (2) 171.   [3] *MEGA* I i (2) 174.
[4] Further on Küpper, see W. Sens, *Karl Marx. Seine irreligiöse Entwicklung* (Halle, 1935) pp. 13 f.
[5] *MEGA* I i (2) 174.
[6] First published in *MEGA* I i (2) 164 ff. Translated in *Writings of the Young Marx on*

that, though man's choice of a career could not be completely arbitrary, yet it was the freedom of choice that distinguished him from animals. One should not be carried away by ambition or quick enthusiasm: what was important was to take the opportunity offered of working in the service of humanity while avoiding being carried away by abstract truths. The essay ended with an impassioned declaration of faith in the value of a life sacrificed for the good of mankind.

In theme and structure, the essay is much the same as those of Marx's fellow pupils. Its underlying ideas are those of the humanist ideal of the German Enlightenment and classical period – the full development of the individual and the full development of the community of mankind being interdependent.[1] There is no trace in Marx's essay of a transcendental God: the words of God, nature and creation are interchangeable and the process of history is an immanent one. Marx began his essay:

> Nature has assigned to the animal the sphere of its activity, and the animal acts calmly within it, not striving beyond, not even surmising that there is another. To man, too, the deity gave a general goal, to improve mankind and himself, but left it to him to seek the means by which he must attain this goal, left it to him to choose the position in society which is most appropriate and from which he can best elevate both himself and society. This choice offers a great advantage over other creatures but at the same time is an act which can destroy man's entire life, defeat all his plans, and make him unhappy.[2]

To every person there had been allotted his own purpose in life, a purpose indicated by the 'soft but true' interior voice of the heart. It was easy to be deluded by ambition and a desire for glory, so close attention was necessary to see what one was really fitted for. Once all factors had been coolly considered, then the chosen career should be eagerly pursued. 'But we cannot always choose the career for which we believe we have a vocation. Our social relations have already begun

---

Philosophy and Society, ed. L. Easton and K. Guddat (New York, 1967) pp. 35 ff. (hereinafter referred to as Easton and Guddat).

[1] For striking parallels between Marx's essay and Rousseau's *Émile*, see the detailed commentary in G. Hillman, *Marx and Hegel* (Frankfurt-am-Main, 1966) pp. 33 ff.

[2] *MEGA* I i (2) 164; Easton and Guddat, pp. 35 f.

to form, to some extent, before we are in a position to determine them.'[1] This sentence has been hailed as the first germ of Marx's later theory of historical materialism.[2] However, the fact that human activity is continuously limited by the prestructured environment is an idea at least as old as the Enlightenment and the Encyclopedists. It would indeed be surprising if even the germ of historical materialism had already been present in the mind of a seventeen-year-old school-boy. It would be a mistake to think that, in his early writings, Marx was raising questions to which he would later produce answers: his later work, coming as it did after the tremendous impact on him of Hegel and the Hegelian School, contained quite different questions – and therefore quite different answers. In any case, the subsequent passages of the essay, with their mention of physical or mental deficiencies, show that Marx here merely means that when choosing a career one should consider one's circumstances.

Marx then went on to recommend that a career be chosen that conferred on a man as much worth as possible by permitting him to attain a position that was 'based on ideas of whose truth we are completely convinced, which offers the largest field to work for mankind and approach the universal goal for which every position is only a means: perfection'.[3] This idea of perfectibility was what should above all govern the choice of a career, always bearing in mind that

> The vocations which do not take hold of life but deal, rather, with abstract truths are the most dangerous for the youth whose principles are not yet crystallised, whose conviction is not yet firm and unshakeable, though at the same time they seem to be the most lofty ones when they have taken root deep in the breast and when we can sacrifice life and all striving for the ideas which hold sway in them.[4]

Here, too, commentators have tried to discover an embryo of Marx's later idea of the 'unity of theory and practice'.[5] Once again, this is to read into Marx's essay much more than is there. All that Marx meant

---

[1] *MEGA* I i (2) 165; Easton and Guddat, p. 37.

[2] See, for example, F. Mehring, *Karl Marx*, p. 5; A. Cornu, *Karl Marx et Friedrich Engels* (Paris, 1955) I 64.

[3] *MEGA* I i (2) 166; Easton and Guddat, p. 38.

[4] *MEGA* I i (2) 166 f.; Easton and Guddat, pp. 38 f.

[5] Cf. A. Cornu, op. cit., I 65; G. Mende, *Karl Marx' Entwicklung vom revolutionären Demokraten zum Kommunisten*, 3rd ed. (Berlin, 1960) p. 26.

is that the sort of profession that deals with abstract ideas should be approached with special circumspection, for 'they can make happy him who is called to them; but they destroy him who takes them overhurriedly, without reflection, obeying the moment'.[1] The problem was above all a practical one and not at all posed in terms of theories.

The essay ended with a purple passage revealing a pure, youthful idealism:

> History calls those the greatest men who ennoble themselves by working for the universal. Experience praises as the most happy the one who made the most people happy. Religion itself teaches that the ideal for which we are all striving sacrificed itself for humanity, and who would dare to gainsay such a statement?

> When we have chosen the vocation in which we can contribute most to humanity, burdens cannot bend us because they are only sacrifices for all. Then we experience no meagre, limited, egotistic joy, but our happiness belongs to millions, our deeds live on quietly but eternally effective, and glowing tears of noble men will fall on our ashes.[2]

The essay was marked by Wyttenbach, who qualified it as 'fairly good' and praised Marx for being rich in ideas and well organised, though he rightly criticised Marx's 'exaggerated desire for rare and imaginative expressions'.[3]

The enthusiasm for excessive imagery and the love of poetry that Marx was to display in his first years at the university were heightened by his friendship with Baron von Westphalen who was a third important influence on the young Marx in addition to his home and school. Ludwig von Westphalen was twelve years older than Heinrich Marx, being born in 1770 into a recently ennobled family. His father, Philip von Westphalen, an upright, straightforward and extremely capable member of the rising German middle class, had been private secretary to the Duke of Brunswick during the Seven Years War, had given essential help to his master in several military campaigns culminating in the battle of Minden, and was consequently ennobled by George III of England. During the war he had married a Scottish noblewoman,

---

[1] *MEGA* I i (2) 167; Easton and Guddat, p. 39.
[2] Ibid.   [3] *MEGA* I i (2) 167.

Jeanie Wishart, who had come to Germany to visit her sister, whose husband, General Beckwith, commanded the English troops. Jeanie Wishart was descended from the Earls of Argyll and brought with her, among other things, the crested silver that Marx and Jenny later had so many occasions to pawn.[1] The youngest of their sons, Ludwig von Westphalen, inherited the liberal and progressive views of his father: after the defeat of Prussia he entered the civil service of the Napoleonic kingdom of Westphalia and then became Vice-Prefect of the town of Salzwedel in North Saxony. His first wife, who had given him four children, having died, he married Caroline Heubel, the daughter of a horse trainer.

Ludwig and Caroline had three children, the eldest being Jenny, born in 1814 – two years before they were to move to Trier where he was transferred (and slightly downgraded) as city counsellor: he was not fully in agreement with the policies of the new Prussian Government and it was thought that his liberal views would be more at home in the ex-French Rhineland. The Westphalens moved into a fine house quite near to that of the Marxes,[2] though they were by no means a rich family.[3] As Heinrich Marx and Ludwig von Westphalen were both in the city's legal service and members of the small Protestant community, it was natural that they should become friends. Jenny became very intimate with Sophie Marx and the families were in constant contact. The Baron, now over sixty, developed a particular affection for Karl. He was an extremely cultured man, spoke English as well as he spoke German, read Latin and Greek without difficulty and particularly liked romantic poetry. Eleanor Marx wrote that Baron von Westphalen 'filled Karl Marx with enthusiasm for the romantic school and, whereas his father read Voltaire and Racine with him, the Baron read him Homer and Shakespeare – who remained his favourite authors all his life'.[4] The Baron devoted much of his time to the young Marx, and the two went for intellectual walks through the 'wonderfully picturesque hills and woods' of the neighbourhood.

[1] On the family tree in general, see Mehring, 'Die von Westphalen', Die neue Zeit, x (1891–2) 481 ff.

[2] That Marx married 'the girl next door' is a widespread, but unfortunately inaccurate, impression.

[3] Cf. the very small inheritance left by Jenny's mother in 1856. For this and other details, see H. Monz, 'Unbekannte Kapitel aus dem Leben der Familie Ludwig von Westphalen', Archiv für Sozialgeschichte (1968).

[4] Eleanor Marx, 'Karl Marx', Die neue Zeit (May 1883) p. 441.

As well as being a man of culture, the Baron was keen on progressive political ideas and interested Marx in the personality and work of the French utopian socialist Saint-Simon.

Heinrich Marx approved of his son's attachment to the Baron and admonished him: 'You have good fortune such as is given to few young people of your age. On the first important stretch of life you have found a friend, and a very worthy one, older and more experienced than yourself. It will be the best test of your character, spirit and heart, indeed of your morality, if you can keep your friend and be worthy of him.'[1] Marx's gratitude for the Baron's friendship was such that in 1841 he dedicated his doctoral thesis to him in a most effusive manner:

> Forgive me, my dear fatherly friend, for prefacing an unimportant work with a name so beloved as yours: but I am too impatient to await another opportunity of giving you a small proof of my love. May all who have doubts of the power of the spirit have, like myself, the good fortune to admire an old man who has kept his youthful impulses and who, with wise enthusiasm for the truth, welcomes all progress. Far from retreating before the reactionary ghosts and the often dark sky of our time, you have always been able, inspired by a profound and burning idealism, to perceive, behind the veils that hide it, the shrine that burns at the heart of this world. You, my fatherly friend, have always been for me the living proof that idealism is no illusion, but the true reality.[2]

II. STUDENT DAYS

In October 1835, at the early age of seventeen, Marx left home for the university. His whole family turned out at four o'clock in the morning to see him off on the steamer that took sixteen hours to travel down the Mosel to Coblenz, where the following day he took a further steamer down the Rhine to Bonn; on the third day he registered himself as a student in the Law Faculty at the University of Bonn. The enthusiasm for romanticism that Baron von Westphalen had aroused in Marx – thus supplanting to some extent the Enlightenment rationalism of home and school – was increased by the year spent at Bonn. The city itself was scarcely larger than Trier. But the university

[1] Heinrich Marx to Marx, *MEW*, Ergsbd. [suppl. vol.] I 617.
[2] *MEGA*, I i (2) 7.

– with 700 students – served as the intellectual centre of the Rhineland; the dominant outlook there was thoroughly romantic and the most popular lectures (which Marx attended) were those given by the old A. W. Schlegel on philosophy and literature. In general, politics was little discussed: the university, like most in Germany, had experienced a wave of free speech and anti-government activity in the early 1830s, but this had been thoroughly suppressed. Marx began the year with great enthusiasm for his work, putting himself down for nine courses, which he subsequently reduced to six on his father's advice, three of which were on literary subjects. His first end-of-term report said that he followed all six courses with zeal and attention. The second term, however, following an illness from overwork at the beginning of 1836, he reduced the number of courses to four and gave much less time to formal studies.

His father continually complained of his son's inability to keep his family informed of his activities: on his arrival in Bonn he left them three weeks without news and then produced only two short letters in three months. He was also spending much more money than his family could afford – a lifelong characteristic. During the first semester, Marx shared a room with a highly respected philosophy student from Trier (who had entered the university a year earlier), became one of the thirty members of the Trier Tavern Club and was soon one of its five presidents. The activities of the club were largely confined to drinking and Marx entered so fully into the spirit that he found himself imprisoned by the university for 'disturbing the peace of the night with drunken noise'[1] – though only for twenty-four hours; and the university 'prison' was far from uncomfortable as the friends of the condemned man had the right to come and help him pass the time with beer and cards. During 1836 rivalry broke out in the university between the students from Trier and the young Prussian aristocrats in the Borussia-Korps. Sometimes it degenerated into open fighting and in August 1836 Marx was wounded above the left eye in a duel. He was also denounced to the university authorities for having 'been in the possession of forbidden weapons in Cologne',[2] but the investigation petered out.

When not drinking and duelling, Marx spent most of his time writing poetry and joined a club of like-minded students. The club probably had political overtones: one of its members was Karl Grün,

---

[1] *MEGA* i i (2) 194.   [2] Ibid.

one of the future founders of 'true' socialism; it was under police surveillance, and had contacts with other university poetry clubs that were similarly suspect. In his rare letters home Marx was in the habit of enclosing specimens of his compositions which his father found quite incomprehensible. On being asked to bear the cost of their publication, he warned his son that 'although I am very pleased with your poetical gifts and have great hopes of them, I would be very sorry to see you cut in public the figure of a minor poet'.[1] Well before the end of the academic year Heinrich Marx decided that one year at Bonn was quite enough and that his son should transfer to the University of Berlin.

Before Marx set out for Berlin, however, another problem arose: 'Scarcely was the wild rampaging in Bonn finished,' Heinrich Marx wrote to him during the summer vacation of 1836, 'scarcely were your debts paid – and they were really of the most varied nature – when to our dismay the sorrows of love appeared.'[2] Jenny and Karl had been friends from earliest childhood. Jenny, with her dark auburn hair and green eyes, was widely noticed in Trier and had even been chosen as Queen of the Ball. The young Marx, who later described himself as 'a really furious Roland',[3] was an insistent suitor: there had been an understanding between them before Marx left for Bonn and in the summer of 1836 this was turned into a formal engagement. By the standards of the time, the engagement was an extremely unusual one: Marx was only eighteen, Jenny was four years older, and there was also a certain difference in social status. At first only Marx's parents, and his sister Sophie – who had acted as go-between for the lovers – were let into the secret. Jenny's father gave his consent in March 1837. Marx's parents were not (initially at least) very keen on the match; and the pair had also to sustain 'years of unnecessary and exhausting conflicts'[4] with Jenny's family. Marx later denied vehemently his son-in-law's statement in a newspaper that the opposition from the Westphalens was based on anti-semitism,[5] and it is more likely that the conflicts arose from the generally reactionary attitudes of some members of that family.

[1] Heinrich Marx to Marx, *MEW*, Ergsbd. i 621.
[2] Heinrich Marx to Marx, *MEW*, Ergsbd. i 638.
[3] Eleanor Marx, 'Remarks on a letter by the Young Marx', *Reminiscences*, p. 256.
[4] Marx to A. Ruge, in K. Marx, *Early Texts*, ed. D. McLellan (Oxford, 1971) p. 59 (hereinafter referred to as *Early Texts*).
[5] Marx to Jenny Longuet, *MEW* xxxv 241 f.

His taste for romanticism and poetry increased by his successful if still semi-secret wooing, Marx left Trier in October 1836 for Berlin. The capital city was in almost total contrast to Bonn. Engels later graphically recalled the Berlin of the time 'with its scarcely formed bourgeoisie, its loud-mouthed petty bourgeoisie, so unenterprising and fawning, its still completely unorganised workers, its masses of bureaucrats and hangers-on of nobility and court, its whole character as mere "residence" '.[1] Berlin was, indeed, a very rootless city with no long-established aristocracy, no solid bourgeoisie, no nascent working class. With over 300,000 inhabitants it was nevertheless the largest German city after Vienna, and possessed a university three times the size of that in Bonn and totally different in atmosphere. Ten years earlier the student Feuerbach had written to his father: 'There is no question here of drinking, duelling and pleasant communal outings; in no other university can you find such a passion for work, such an interest for things that are not petty student intrigues, such an inclination for the sciences, such calm and such silence. Compared to this temple of work, the other universities appear like public houses.'[2]

We are exceptionally well informed about Marx's first year in Berlin (where he was to remain four and a half years) thanks to his one surviving letter to his father written (by candlelight, during the early hours of the morning) in November 1837. It is an extraordinarily intimate letter in which he retails at great length the spiritual itinerary of his last year.

> When I left you [he began] a new world had just begun to exist for me, the world of love that was at first drunk with its own desire and hopeless. Even the journey to Berlin which would otherwise have charmed me completely, exciting in me an admiration for nature and inflaming me with a zest for life, left me cold and, surprisingly, even depressed me; for the rocks that I saw were not rougher, not harsher than the emotions of my soul, the broad cities not more full of life than my blood, the tables of the inns not more overladen and their fare not more indigestible than the stocks of fantasies that I carried with me, nor, finally, was any work of art as beautiful as Jenny.[3]

[1] F. Engels, quoted in *Karl Marx, Dokumente seines Lebens* (Berlin, 1970) p. 80.
[2] *L. Feuerbach in seinen Briefwechsel und Nachlass*, ed. K. Grün (Leipzig, 1876) I 183.
[3] K. Marx, *Early Texts*, p. 2.

As soon as he reached Berlin he reluctantly made a few necessary visits and then completely isolated himself in order to immerse himself in science and art. The writing of lyric poetry was his first concern;

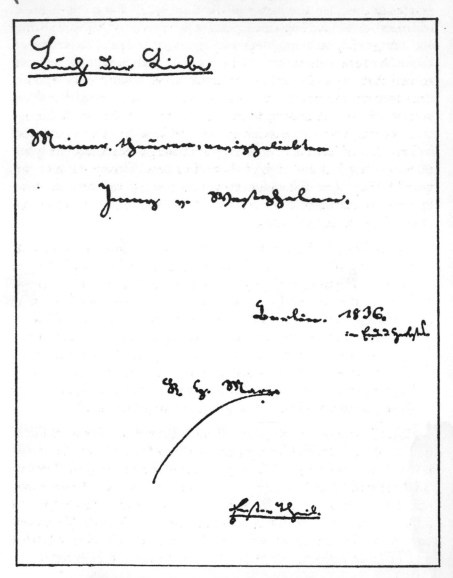

Marx's present to Jenny von Westphalen on his arrival in Berlin. The text reads: '*Buch der Liebe. Meinen teuren ewiggeliebten Jenny von Westphalen. Berlin, 1836, am Ende des Herbstes.*' Translation: 'To my dear, eternally loved Jenny von Westphalen. Berlin, 1836, at the end of the autumn.'

at least, as he himself put it, it was 'the pleasantest and readiest to hand'.[1] IIis poems written while he was in Bonn and those written during the autumn of 1836 in Berlin have not survived. The latter were written in three books entitled 'Book of Love, Part 1 and 2' and 'Book of Songs' – all three being dedicated to Jenny von Westphalen who, according to Sophie Marx, 'wept tears of delight and pain'[2] on receiving them. She kept them carefully all her life, though her daughter Laura related that 'my father treated those verses with scant respect; each time that my parents spoke of them, they laughed outright at these youthful follies'.[3] According to the social-democrat historian Mehring, these poems, with one exception, were all love lyrics and romantic ballads. He had had the opportunity of reading them before the great majority were lost and judged them 'formless in every sense of the word'.[4] They were full of gnomes, sirens, songs to stars and bold knights, 'romantic in tone without the magic proper to romanticism'.[5] They were, said Marx,

> in accordance with my attitude and all my previous development, purely idealistic. My heaven and art became a Beyond as distant as my love. Everything real began to dissolve and thus lose its finiteness, I attacked the present, feeling was expressed without moderation or form, nothing was natural, everything built of moonshine; I believed in a complete opposition between what is and what ought to be and rhetorical reflections occupied the place of poetic thoughts, though there was perhaps also a certain warmth of emotion and desire for exuberance. These are the characteristics of all the poems of the first three volumes that Jenny received from me.[6]

Most of the few surviving poems are those written during the first half of 1837, together with fragments of a dramatic fantasy and a comic novel. Marx tried to publish some of these poems and sent them to Adelbert von Chamisso, editor of the annual *Deutscher Musenalmanach*, but the issue had already gone to press. Although dedicated to his father, the poems were not much to his taste and Heinrich Marx even encouraged his son to attempt an ode which 'should glorify Prussia and afford an opportunity of praising the genius of the Monarch . . .

[1] Ibid.
[2] Sophie Marx to Karl Marx, *MEGA* I i (2) 211.
[3] Laura Lafargue to Franz Mehring, in F. Mehring, *Aus dem literarischen Nachlass von K. Marx, F. Engels, F. Lassalle* (Stuttgart, 1902) I 25.
[4] F. Mehring, op. cit., I 26.   [5] Ibid.   [6] *Early Texts*, pp. 2 f.

patriotic, emotional and composed in a Germanic manner'.[1] Marx's models, however, were Heine, Goethe and Schiller, and his verses contained all the well-known themes of German romanticism, with the exception of political reaction and nationalism. They were full of tragic love and talk of human destiny as the plaything of mysterious forces. There was the familiar subjectivism and extreme exaltation of the personality of the creative artist isolated from the rest of society, while seeking, at the same time, for a community of like-minded individuals. As a result of his love for Jenny,

> With disdain I will throw my gauntlet
> Full in the face of the world,
> And see the collapse of this pigmy giant
> Whose fall will not stifle my ardour.
>
> Then I will wander godlike and victorious
> Through the ruins of the world
> And, giving my words an active force,
> I will feel equal to the creator.[2]

Other poems display a longing for something infinite and a love of death à la Novalis, while still others consist entirely of a dream world of mystical imagination. To the aesthetic idealism of these poems was added a series of typically romantic ironical attacks on 'Philistines', people like doctors and mathematicians, who followed utilitarian professions based on an ordered and rational approach to problems.

To help him in his composition, Marx had copied out large extracts from Lessing's *Laokoon*, Solger's *Erwin*, and Winckelmann's *History of Art*. Marx's habit of making excerpts from all the books he was reading (and sometimes adding comments of his own) stayed with him all his life, and those notebooks that remain form a valuable guide to the development of his thought.[3] He also wrote a few chapters of a comic novel, 'Scorpion and Felix', in the style of Sterne and then gave that up to compose the first scene of 'Oulanem', a contemporary comic thriller whose hero was a feeble copy of the ageing Faust. 'Oulanem', too, never got beyond an immensely long first act which contained frenzied reflections on love (in all its forms), death, destruction and

[1] Heinrich Marx to Karl Marx, *MEGA*, I i (2) 204.
[2] *MEGA* I i (2) 50.
[3] See M. Rubel, 'Les Cahiers d'études de Karl Marx (1840–1853)', *International Review of Social History* (1957).

eternity.[1] Finally there was an interesting series of epigrams on Hegel, whom Marx accused of being arrogant and obscure. In the first epigram, he says:

Because my meditations have discovered the highest of things and
   also the depths,
I am as crude as a god and cloak myself in darkness as he does,
In my long researches and journeys on the wavy sea of thought,
I found the word and remain firmly attached to my find.[2]

The second epigram had the same theme, opening:

I teach words that are mixed up in a devilish and chaotic mess.[3]

The most interesting was the last epigram:

Kant and Fichte like to whirl into heaven
And search there for a distant land,
While my only aim is to understand completely
What – I found in the street.[4]

The point of this epigram is totally misunderstood if it is taken to be Marx himself speaking.[5] As in the former epigrams, it is 'Hegel' who is speaking, criticised by Marx, the subjective romantic, for being too attached to day-to-day reality. The whole tenor of Marx's poems makes this an obvious criticism of Hegel, and it was a common one among romantic writers.

   In general Marx's first contact with Berlin University brought about a great change in the views he had expressed in his school-leaving essay. No longer was he inspired by the thought of the service of humanity and concerned to fit himself into a place where he might best be able to sacrifice himself for this noble ideal; his poems of 1837, on the contrary, reveal a cult of the isolated genius and an introverted concern for the development of his own personality apart from the rest of humanity.[6]

[1] There is a translation in *The Unknown Marx*, ed. R. Payne (London, 1972).
[2] *MEGA* I i (2) 41.   [3] Ibid 42.   [4] Ibid.
[5] This is the interpretation of, for example, W. Johnston, 'Marx's verses of 1836–7', *Journal of the History of Ideas* (Apr 1967) p. 261; also of E. Kamenka, *The Ethical Foundations of Marxism* (London, 1962) p. 20, and of S. Avineri, *The Social and Political Thought of Karl Marx* (Cambridge, 1968) p. 8.
[6] For a lengthier discussion of Marx's poems than, perhaps, they merit, see A. Cornu, *Karl Marx et Friedrich Engels* (Paris, 1955) pp. 74 ff.; R. Payne, *Marx* (London, 1968) pp. 59 ff.; P. Demetz, *Marx, Engels and the Poets* (Chicago, 1967) pp. 47 ff. These

Marx's penchant for romantic poetry was undoubtedly increased by the strain of his relationship with Jenny and the uncertainty of his future. While their engagement was still a secret from her parents, she refused to correspond with her fiancé at all. 'I have gained the complete confidence of your Jenny,' Heinrich Marx wrote to his son, 'but the good, kind girl is continually tormenting herself, she is afraid of hurting you, of making you overstrain yourself, etc., etc. She is oppressed by the fact that her parents know nothing or, as I think, don't *want* to know anything. She cannot understand how she, who considers herself to be such a rational being, could let herself get so carried away.' He advised his son to enclose a letter for Jenny 'full of tender, devoted sentiment . . . but taking a clear view of your relationship' and definitely 'not a letter distorted by the fantasies of a poet'.[1]

Eventually it was decided that Marx should send a letter to the Baron declaring his intention and should give his own family a week's notice of its arrival so that his father could do his best to secure a favourable reception. Jenny herself, even when the engagement was accepted by her father, continued to be extremely apprehensive, being already past the age when most girls of her class were married. 'She has the idea', Heinrich Marx reported, 'that it is unnecessary to write to you . . . But what does that matter? You can be as certain as I am (and you know that I am hard to convince) that even a Prince would not be able to steal her affections from you. She is attached to you body and soul. . . .'[2] Jenny herself explained her state of mind:

> That I am not in a condition to return your youthful romantic love, I knew from the very beginning and felt deeply even before it was explained to me so coldly, cleverly and rationally. Oh, Karl, my distress lies precisely in the fact that your beautiful, touching passionate love, your indescribably beautiful descriptions of it, the enrapturing images conjured up by your imagination, that would fill any other girl with ineffable delight, only serve to make me anxious and often uncertain. If I gave myself over to this bliss, then my fate would be all the more frightful if your fiery love were to die,

---

essentially immature literary efforts should not be taken as evidence of Marx's capacities in this field; on the contrary remarks scattered throughout his later writings show that he had the ability to be a first-class literary critic.

[1] Heinrich Marx to Marx, *MEW*, Ergsbd. 1 624.

[2] Ibid., 632.

and you were to become cold and unwilling. . . . You see, Karl, that is why I am not so completely grateful, so thoroughly enchanted by your love as I ought to be; that is why I am often mindful of external things, of life and reality, instead of holding fast, as you yould like, to the world of love, losing myself in it and finding there a higher dearer spiritual unity with you enabling me to forget all other things.[1]

Occasionally even Heinrich Marx began to regret that he had sanctioned the engagement and was full of sound advice that his son was obviously not in a position to follow:

> Your exalted and exaggerated love cannot bring back peace to the person to whom you have entirely given yourself and you run the contrary risk of entirely destroying her. Exemplary conduct, a manly and firm desire rapidly to raise yourself in the world without thereby alienating people's goodwill and favour: this is the only way of creating a satisfactory state of affairs and of both reassuring Jenny and raising her in her own eyes and those of the world . . . She is making an inestimable sacrifice for you and gives evidence of a self-denial such as only cold reason can fully appreciate. . . . You must give her the certainty that in spite of your youth you are a man who merits the respect of the world and can earn it.[2]

Under the impact of his father's advice and the general atmosphere of the university, Marx's romantic period did not survive long. Poetry, even during his first year at Berlin, was not his only concern. He also read widely in jurisprudence and felt compelled to 'struggle with philosophy'.[3] In the Berlin Law Faculty, the progressive Hegelian standpoint was represented by Eduard Gans, whose lectures Marx attended during the first term. Gans was a baptised Jew, a liberal Hegelian who in his brilliant lectures elaborated on the Hegelian idea of a rational development in history by emphasising particularly its libertarian aspects, and the importance of social questions. Gans approved of the French Revolution of 1830, advocated a British style of monarchy, was impressed by the ideas of Saint-Simon and was eager to find solutions to overcome 'the struggle of the proletarians with

---

[1] Jenny von Westphalen to Marx, quoted in L. Dornemann, *Jenny Marx* (Berlin, (1969) p. 41.
[2] Heinrich Marx to Marx, *MEGA* I i (2) 198.
[3] *Early Texts*, p. 3.

the middle classes'.[1] The opposing school of thought, known as the Historical School of Law, was represented by Karl von Savigny, whose lectures Marx also attended. The Historical School claimed to find the justification for laws in the customs and traditions of a people and not in the theoretical systems of lawgivers. This point of view linked law closely to history but had necessarily reactionary overtones in that it looked to the past to reinforce its principles of organic development.[2] There being no open political discussion in the Prussia of that time, the conflict between the principles of the French Revolution and those of the reaction that succeeded it was fought out in such disputes as then existed in the Law Faculty.

It is not, therefore, surprising that Marx should have been led, through his legal studies, to engage in philosophical speculation. The two were, in his mind, closely connected and he tried to work out a philosophy of law. He prefaced this with a metaphysical introduction and the whole grew to a work of three hundred pages before he gave it up. The particular problem which he was unable to overcome in the metaphysical introduction was the conflict between what is and what ought to be, 'the hallmark of idealism which gave rise to its dominating and very destructive features and engendered the following hopelessly mistaken division of the subject-matter: firstly came what I had so graciously christened the metaphysics of law, i.e. first principles, reflections, definitions distinct from all actual law and every actual form of law – just as you get in Fichte, only here more modern and with less substance'.[3] It was precisely this gap between what is and what ought to be that Marx later considered to have been bridged by the Hegelian philosophy. Marx's second objection to the metaphysical system he had constructed was its 'mathematical dogmatism'. According to Marx, the systems of Kant and Fichte, which were the inspiration for his own ideas at this time, were open to this objection: they were abstract systems that, like geometry, passed from axioms to conclusions. In contrast, 'in the practical expression of the living world of ideas in which law, the state, nature and the whole of philosophy consist, the object itself must be studied in its own development, and arbitrary divisions must not be introduced'.[4] Marx then outlined the

---

[1] E. Gans, *Rückblicke auf Personen und Zustände* (Berlin, 1836) pp. 99 ff. Further on Gans, see H. Reissner, *Eduard Gans. Ein Leben im Vormärz* (Tübingen, 1965).

[2] Cf. the very thorough article, H. Jaegar, 'Savigny et Marx', *Archives de la Philosophie du Droit* (1967).

[3] Marx to Heinrich Marx, *Early Texts*, p. 3.   [4] Ibid.

complicated *schema* of his philosophy of law that comprised the second part of his treatise. The main reason for his dissatisfaction with this classification seems to have been that it was essentially empty – a desk, as he put it, into whose drawers he later poured sand.

When he got as far as the discussion of private material law, he realised that his enterprise was mistaken:

At the end of material private law I saw the falsity of the whole conception (whose outline borders on the Kantian but when elaborated veers completely away), and it again became plain to me that I could not get by without philosophy. So I was forced again with a quiet conscience to throw myself into her arms, and composed a new basic system of metaphysics at the end of which I was forced to realise the perversity of this and that of all my previous efforts.[1]

This brought Marx to the end of his first semester and he sought refuge from his philosophical problems in writing the poetry discussed above:

At the end of the term I again sought the dances of the Muses and the music of the Satyrs and in the last volume that I sent you the forced humour of 'Scorpion and Felix' and the misconceived fantastic drama of 'Oulanem' are shot through with idealism which finally changes completely, dissolving into purely formal art which has no objects to inspire it and no exciting progress of ideas.[2]

But this activity, while revealing what poetry could be, at the same time made it impossible for Marx to continue: 'These last poems were the only ones in which suddenly, as though at the touch of a magic wand – oh! the touch was at first shattering – the kingdom of true poetry glittered opposite me like a distant fairy palace and all my creations dissolved into nothingness.'[3]

Not surprisingly this period of intense intellectual activity in several fields, often involving his working through the night, ended in a period of severe illness. Marx seems to have suffered quite severely from the tendency to tuberculosis that killed so many of his family: the following year his military service was put off 'because of weakness of the lungs and periodical vomiting of blood'. And in 1841 his military obligations were cancelled for good and he was declared completely

[1] Ibid., p. 6.   [2] Ibid.   [3] Ibid.

invalid 'owing to the sensitivity of his lungs'.[1] His doctor advised a change of scene and Marx went to the village of Stralow just outside Berlin. Here his views underwent radical change: 'A curtain had fallen, my holy of holies was rent asunder and new gods had to be installed. I left behind the idealism which, by the way, I had nourished with that of Kant and Fichte, and came to seek the idea in the real itself. If the gods had before dwelt above the earth, they had now become its centre.'[2]

Previously Hegel's conceptual rationalism had been rejected by Marx, the follower of Kant and Fichte, the romantic subjectivist who considered the highest being to be separate from earthly reality. Now, however, it began to seem as though the Idea was immanent in the real. Previously Marx had 'read fragments of Hegel's philosophy, but I did not care for its grotesque and rocky melody'.[3] Now he had to resolve his spiritual crisis by a conversion to Hegelianism – a conversion that was as profound as it was sudden. It was probably the most important intellectual step of Marx's whole life. For however much he was to criticise Hegel, accuse him of idealism, and try to stand his dialectic 'on its feet', Marx was the first to admit that his method stemmed directly from his Master of the 1830s.

Hegelianism was the dominant philosophy in Berlin where Hegel had held the chair of Philosophy from 1818 until his death in 1831. Building on the centrality of human reason propounded by Kant, Hegel had united into a comprehensive system the themes of German idealist philosophy and in particular the philosophy of Fichte and Schelling: immanence, development and contradiction. 'The great merit of Hegel's philosophy', wrote Engels, 'was that for the first time the totality of the natural, historical and spiritual aspects of the world were conceived and represented as a process of constant transformation and development and an effort was made to show the organic character of this process.'[4] Hegel started from the belief that, as he said of the French Revolution, 'man's existence has its centre in his head, i.e. in Reason, under whose inspiration he builds up the world of reality'. In his greatest work, the *Phänomenologie*, Hegel traced the development of mind or spirit, reintroducing historical movement

---

[1] Quoted in H. Monz, *Karl Marx und Trier*, pp. 133 f.
[2] Op. cit., p. 7.
[3] Marx to Heinrich Marx, *Early Texts*, p. 7.
[4] F. Engels, 'Socialism, Utopian and Scientific', in *MESW* II 162.

into philosophy and asserting that the human mind can attain absolute knowledge. He analysed the development of human consciousness, from its immediate perception of the here and now to the stage of self-consciousness, the understanding that allows man to analyse the world and order his own actions accordingly. Following this was the stage of reason itself – understanding the real, after which spirit – by means of religion and art – attained absolute knowledge, the level at which man recognised in the world the stages of his own reason. These stages Hegel called 'alienations', in so far as they were creations of the human mind yet thought of as independent and superior to the human mind. This absolute knowledge is at the same time a sort of recapitulation of the human spirit, for each successive stage retains elements of the previous ones at the same time as it goes beyond them. This movement that suppresses and yet conserves Hegel called *Aufhebung*, a word that has this double sense in German. Hegel also talked of 'the power of the negative', thinking that there was always a tension between any present state of affairs and what it was becoming. For any present state of affairs was in the process of being negated, changed into something else. This process was what Hegel meant by dialectic.[1]

Faced with the manifest attraction of this philosophy, Marx began to clarify his ideas by writing – a procedure he had adopted before and would adopt many times later. He produced a twenty-four-page dialogue entitled 'Cleanthes, or the Starting Point and Necessary Progress of Philosophy'. For this purpose he acquainted himself with natural science, history and a study of the works of Schelling. This dialogue ended with Marx's conversion to Hegelianism: 'My last sentence was the beginning of Hegel's system and this work which had caused one endless headache . . . this my dearest child, reared by moonlight, like a false siren delivers me into the arms of the enemy.'[2] Thus Marx had gone through the same evolution as classical German philosophy itself, from Kant and Fichte through Schelling to Hegel.

This process of giving up his romantic idealism and delivering

---

[1] It is obviously impossible to give an adequate account of the ideas of so complex a thinker in so short a space. Two good recent books in English dealing with Hegel's philosophy in general are J. N. Findlay, *Hegel: A Re-examination* (London, 1958), and W. Kaufmann, *Hegel* (New York, 1965). See also H. Marcuse, *Reason and Revolution* (New York, 1941) and the more analytic approach in J. Plamenatz, *Man and Society* (London, 1963) II 129 ff.

[2] Marx to Heinrich Marx, *Early Texts*, p. 7.

himself over to 'the enemy' was an extremely radical and painful one for Marx. He described its immediate results:

> My vexation prevented me from thinking at all for several days and I ran like a madman around the garden beside the dirty waters of the Spree 'which washes souls and makes weak tea'. I even went on a hunting party with my landlord and rushed off to Berlin and wanted to embrace every street-loafer I saw. . . . My fruitless and failed intellectual endeavours and my consuming anger at having to make an idol of a view that I hated made me ill.[1]

His conversion to Hegel was completed firstly by a thorough reading of Hegel: while sick he 'got to know Hegel, together with most of his disciples, from the beginning to end'; and secondly, by joining a sort of Hegelian discussion group: 'through several gatherings with friends in Stralow I obtained entrance into a graduate club among whose members were several university lecturers and the most intimate of my Berlin friends, Dr Rutenberg. In the discussions here many contradictory views appeared and I attached myself ever more closely to the current philosophy which I had thought it possible to escape'.[2] This club, which met regularly in a café in the Französische Strasse and subsequently in the houses of its members, was a hard-drinking and boisterous company and formed the focal point of the Young Hegelian movement.

The Young Hegelians' attack on the orthodoxies of their time started in the sphere of religion – a much safer area than politics. Here Hegel's legacy was ambiguous. Religion, together with philosophy, was for him the highest form of man's spiritual life. Religion (and by this Hegel, who remained a practising Luteran all his life, meant Protestant Christianity which he considered the highest and final form of religion) was the return of the Absolute Spirit to itself. The content of religion was the same as that of philosophy, though its method of apprehending was different. For whereas philosophy employed concepts, religion used imagination. These unsatisfactory imaginings afforded only a fragmentary and imprecise knowledge of what philosophy comprehended rationally. But religion could be linked to philosophy by means of a philosophy of religion, and Hegel considered that the particular dogmatic contents of the religious imagination

---

[1] Op. cit., p. 8.   [2] Ibid.

were necessary stages in the development of Absolute Spirit. The philosophy of religion interpreted at a higher level both naïve faith and critical reason. Thus Hegel rejected the view of the eighteenth-century rationalists that religion did inadequately what only science was competent to do; in his eyes, religion (or his philosophical interpretation of it) fulfilled man's constant psychological need to have an image of himself and of the world by which he could orientate himself.[1]

Although in the years immediately following Hegel's death his school was united and supreme in the German universities, by the late 1830s it had already begun to split into two wings on the subject of religion. Whereas the conservative wing of the school held to the slogan that 'the real is the rational' and saw nothing irrational in the traditional representation of religion, the radical wing opposed the conservatives' complacency with a dissastifaction that meant it wanted to destroy the dogmas enshrined in religious representations that were now said to be outdated. These representations all had to be judged by a progressive reason, not one which, as Hegel had said, only 'paints grey with grey' and thus merely recognised what already existed. For the Master had also said that an age comprehended in thought was already in advance of its time, and the radicals drew the conclusion that the comprehension of religion already modified even its content, while its form became a pure myth. This debate started with the publication of David Strauss's *Life of Jesus* in 1835. Having failed to extract a picture of the historical Jesus from the gospel narratives, Strauss presented these narratives as mere expressions of the messianic idea present in primitive Christian communities, myths that were never intended to be taken as real historical narratives. It was quite natural that Young Hegelian discussion should at first be theological: most members of the Hegelian school were interested in religion above all; and the attitude of the Prussian Government made politics an extremely dangerous subject for debate. Yet granted the Establishment of the Church in Germany and the close connection between religion and politics, it was inevitable that a movement of religious criticism would swiftly become secularised into one of political opposition. It

[1] For Hegel's views on religion, see K. Barth, *From Rousseau to Ritschl* (London 1959) pp. 268 ff.; P. Asveld, *La Pensée religieuse du jeune Hegel* (Paris, 1953); A. Chappelle, *Hegel et la Religion*, 2 vols. (Paris, 1964); K. Lowith, 'Hegel and the Christian Religion', in *Nature, History and Existentialism* (Evanston, Ill., 1966) pp. 162 ff.

was as a member of this rapidly changing movement, which had its centre in the Berlin Doctors' Club, that Karl Marx first began to work out his views on philosophy and society.

According to one of the members of the Doctors' Club, 'in this circle of aspiring young men, most of whom had already finished their studies, there reigned supreme the idealism, the thirst for knowledge and the liberal spirit, that still completely inspired the youth of that time. In these reunions the poems and essays that we had composed were read aloud and assessed, but the greatest part of our attention was devoted to the Hegelian philosophy....'[1] Of Marx's more intimate friends in the club, Adolph Rutenberg had recently been dismissed as a teacher of geography and now earned his living as a journalist; Karl Köppen was a history teacher who later became an acknowledged expert on the origins of Buddhism. Köppen published in 1840 *Frederick the Great and his Opponents*: dedicated to Marx, the book was a eulogy of Frederick and the principles of the Enlightenment.[2] The leading light in the club was Bruno Bauer, who had been lecturing in theology at the university since 1834 and was to be Marx's closest friend for the next four years.[3] One of his contemporaries described him as follows: 'His pointed nose, with sharp bone, juts out boldly, his forehead is high and domed, and his mouth delicately shaped; his figure is almost Napoleonic. He is a very decided man who, under a cold exterior, burns with an inner fire. He will not brook any opposition and will sooner be a martyr to his own convictions.'[4] Bauer's special field was New Testament criticism where he made a lasting contribution.

Marx himself seems to have been a lively and central figure in the club. Edgar Bauer (Bruno's brother) gave the following description of Marx in a satirical poem on club members:

But who advances here full of impetuosity?
It is a dark form from Trier, an unleashed monster,
With self-assured step he hammers the ground with his heels
And raises his arms in full fury to heaven
As though he wished to seize the celestial vault and lower it to earth.

---

[1] M. Ring, *Erinnerungen* (Berlin, 1898) I 113 f.
[2] On Köppen, see H. Hirsch, *Denker und Kämpfer* (Frankfurt, 1955).
[3] On Bauer, see D. McLellan, *The Young Hegelians and Karl Marx* (London, 1969) pp. 48 ff. Also E. Barnikol, *Bruno Bauer: Studien und Materialen* (Assen, 1972).
[4] Varnhagen von Ense, *Tagebücher* (Leipzig, 1861) I 341.

In rage he continually deals with his redoubtable fist,
As if a thousand devils were gripping his hair.[1]

Köppen called his friend 'a true arsenal of thoughts, a veritable
factory of ideas' and remarked that Bruno Bauer's *The Christian State in
our Time* – the first directly political article of the Young Hegelians –
drew largely on Marx's ideas.[2] Meanwhile his life-style, which was in
keeping with the studied bohemianism of the Doctors' Club, led
Marx to become more and more estranged from his family. While his
mother merely recommended moderation in his consumption of
wine, coffee and pepper, the long 'confession' of November 1837
prompted a very tart reply from his father:

> Alas, your conduct has consisted merely in disorder, meandering in
> all the fields of knowledge, musty traditions by sombre lamplight;
> degeneration in a learned dressing gown with uncombed hair has
> replaced degeneration with a beer glass. And a shirking unsociability
> and a refusal of all conventions and even all respect for your father.
> Your intercourse with the world is limited to your sordid room,
> where perhaps lie abandoned in the classical disorder the love letters
> of a Jenny and the tear-stained counsels of your father. . . . And do
> you think that here in this workshop of senseless and aimless
> learning you can ripen the fruits to bring you and your loved one
> happiness? . . . As though we were made of gold my gentleman-son
> disposes of almost 700 thalers in a single year, in contravention of
> every agreement and every usage, whereas the richest spend no
> more than 500.[3]

In fact, the final report on Marx's university career declared that he
had 'several times been sued for debt', and he had changed his address
at least ten times during his five-year stay.

His family ties were further loosened by the death of his father in
May 1838. In spite of their disagreements, Marx always retained a
strong affection for his father: 'he has never tired of talking about
him', wrote Eleanor, 'and always carried an old daguerreotype photograph of him. But he would never show the photo to strangers,

---

[1] E. Bauer and F. Engels, 'The Triumph of the Faith', *MEW*, Ergsbd. II 301.
[2] K. Köppen to Marx, *MEGA* I i (2) 257.
[3] Heinrich Marx to Marx, *MEW*, Ergsbd. 637 ff.

because, he said, it was so unlike the original.'[1] On Marx's death, Engels laid the photograph in his coffin. The death of Heinrich Marx naturally reduced the income of the Marx family quite considerably. It also led to increased difficulties with the von Westphalen family, some of whom seem to have snubbed Henrietta Marx completely.[2] At the same time Marx's interests began to turn definitely from law to philosophy. Although in his letter of November 1837 he had written to his father about the possibility of his becoming an assistant judge, he began now more and more to opt out of the formal aspects of the university. Gans died in 1839 and during his last three years in Berlin Marx only attended two courses: one on Isaiah given by Bruno Bauer and another on the drama of Euripides. Marx had entirely given up the writing of poetry and when he wished to present more poems to Jenny in 1839 he very sensibly copied some out from two anthologies that had recently appeared.

With the diminishing lack of support from his family, the choice of a career became all the more pressing, and the academic world seemed to offer the most immediate prospect of effective action. 'It would be stupid', Bruno Bauer wrote to him, 'if you were to devote yourself to a practical career. Theory is now the strongest practice, and we are absolutely incapable of predicting to how large an extent it will become practical.'[3] At the beginning of 1839 Marx decided to start work on a doctoral dissertation with a view to getting a university post as lecturer in philosophy – preferably at Bonn to which Bauer, increasingly under attack for his radical views, had been moved by the Ministry of Education. Throughout 1839 and early 1840 Marx was busy reading and making excerpts for use in his thesis. The general heading he gave to these notes was 'Epicurean Philosophy'. At the same time he was reading Hegel, Aristotle, Leibnitz, Hume and Kant, and his pre-liminary notes were very wide-ranging, dealing with such subjects as the relationship between Epicureanism and Stoicism, the concept of the sage in Greek philosophy, the views of Socrates and Plato on religion and the prospects of post-Hegelian philosophy.

Marx's choice of subject was influenced by the general interest that the Young Hegelians (particularly Bauer and Köppen) had in post-Aristotelian Greek philosophy. There were two reasons for this

---

[1] Eleanor Marx, 'Remarks on a Letter by the Young Marx', *Reminiscences*, p. 257.
[2] See her long letter of complaint in *MEGA* I i (2) 242 ff.
[3] B. Bauer to Marx, *MEGA* I i (2) 250.

interest: firstly, after the 'total philosophy' of Hegel the Young Hegelians felt themselves in the same position as the Greeks after Aristotle; secondly, they thought that the post-Aristotelian philosophies contained the essential elements of modern thought: they had laid the philosophical foundations of the Roman Empire, had profoundly influenced early Christian morality and also contained rationalist traits of the eighteenth-century Enlightenment. For Marx, too, the Stoic, Sceptic and Epicurean philosophies were 'prototypes of the Roman mind, the form in which Greece emigrated to Rome'.[1] They were 'such intense and eternal beings, so full of character, that even the modern world has to allow to them their full spiritual citizenship'.[2] 'Is it not remarkable', Marx continued in the Introduction to his thesis, 'that after the philosophies of Plato and Aristotle, which extend to universality, new systems appear which do not refer back to these rich intellectual figures but look further back and turn to the simplest schools – in regard to physics, to the philosophers of nature, and in regard to ethics, to the Socratic school?'[3] In short, Marx's choice of subject was designed to throw light on the contemporary post-Hegelian situation in philosophy by the examination of a parallel period in the history of Greek philosophy.

Marx's preliminary notes for the thesis were rather obscure, partly because they were only personal notes and partly because they were often couched in the vividly metaphorical language characteristic of the Young Hegelians who saw themselves living in a general atmosphere of crisis and impending catastrophe. Bruno Bauer, for example, with whom Marx kept up a constant correspondence while he was composing his thesis, wrote in 1840: 'our epoch becomes more and more terrible and beautiful'.[4] Or again: 'The catastrophe will be terrible and must be great. I would almost say that it will be greater and more horrible than that which heralded Christianity's appearance on the world scene.'[5] The most interesting passage in Marx's notes was one where he dealt with the philosophical climate following on the world-philosophy of Hegel. Philosophy, he claimed, had now arrived at a turning point: 'like Prometheus who stole fire from heaven and began to build houses and settle on the earth, so philosophy, which

[1] K. Marx, 'Doctoral Dissertation', in N. Livergood, Activity in Marx's Philosophy (The Hague, 1967) p. 64.
[2] Ibid.   [3] Ibid.   [4] B. Bauer to Marx, MEGA i i (2) 236.
[5] Ibid., 241.

has so evolved as to impinge on the world, turns itself against the world that it finds. So now the Hegelian philosophy.'[1] Marx believed that Hegel's philosophy had, by its very completeness and universality, become unreal and opposed to the world which continued to be divided. Thus philosophy itself had become split: 'The activity of this philosophy appears, too, to be rent asunder and contradictory; its objective universality returns into the subjective forms of the indivi-dual minds in which it has its life. Normal harps will sound beneath any hand; those of Aeolus only when the storm strikes them. But we should not let ourselves be misled by the storm that follows a great, a world-philosophy.'[2] 'Anyone', Marx continued, 'who did not under-stand this necessary development had to deny the possibility of continuing to philosophise after such a total system: to such a man the appearance of Zeno or Epicurus after such a thinker as Aristotle would be incomprehensible.'

What was needed was a fundamental change of direction:

> In such times half-formed spirits have the opposite view to real com-manders. They believe that they can make good their losses by reducing and dividing their forces and make a peace treaty with real needs, whereas Themistocles, when Athens was threatened with destruction, persuaded the Athenians to quit their city completely and found a new Athens on another element, the sea.[3]

Marx went on to say that in such a period two alternatives presented themselves: either to imitate feebly what had gone before or to undertake a really fundamental upheaval:

> Nor should we forget that the period that follows such catastrophes is an iron one, happy if it is marked by titanic struggles, lamentable if it is like the centuries that limp behind the great period of art and busy themselves with imitating in wax, plaster and copper what sprang from Carrara marble like Pallas Athene from the head of Zeus, father of the gods. But those periods are titanic that follow a total philosophy and its subjective forms of development, for the division that forms its unity is gigantic. Thus the Stoic, Epicurean and Sceptic philosophies are followed by Rome. They are unhappy and iron for their gods are dead and the new goddess has as yet only the obscure form of fate, of pure light or of pure darkness.[4]

[1] K. Marx, 'Doctoral Dissertation', in *Early Texts*, p. 19.
[2] Ibid., p. 20.   [3] Ibid.   [4] Ibid.

In the preface to the thesis itself Marx briefly outlined previous, mistaken interpretations of Epicurus's philosophy and mentioned the insufficiency of Hegel's treatment of the period. He then added a paean in praise of the supremacy of philosophy over all other disciplines, and in particular over theology. To prove his point, Marx quoted Hume: 'Tis certainly a kind of indignity to philosophy, whose sovereign authority ought everywhere to be acknowledged, to oblige her on every occasion to make apologies for her conclusions, and justify herself to every particular art and science, which may be offended at her. This puts one in mind of a king arraign'd for high treason against his subjects.'[1] Thus Marx made his own the Young Hegelian criticism of the Master's reconciliation of philosophy and religion. He continued:

As long as a single drop of blood pulses in her world-conquering and totally free heart, philosophy will continually shout at her opponents the cry of Epicurus: 'Impiety does not consist in destroying the gods of the crowd but rather in ascribing to the gods the ideas of the crowd.' Philosophy makes no secret of it. The proclamation of Prometheus: 'In one word – I hate all gods' is her own profession, her own slogan against all gods of heaven and earth who do not recognise man's self-consciousness as the highest divinity. There shall be none other beside it.[2]

This 'self-consciousness' was the central concept of the philosophy that the Young Hegelians, and Bruno Bauer in particular, were elaborating. For them, man's self-consciousness developed continually and realised that forces it had thought separate from itself – religion, for example – were really its own creation. Thus the task of self-consciousness and its principal weapon, philosophical criticism, was to expose all the forces and ideas that stood opposed to the free development of this human self-consciousness.[3]

This enthusiasm for the philosophy of self-consciousness was reflected in the body of the thesis where Marx criticised the mechanistic determinism of Democritus by contrasting it with the Epicurean ethic

---

[1] *MEGA* I i (1) 10; the quotation is from Hume's *Treatise of Human Nature*, ed. L. Selby-Biggs (Oxford, 1888) p. 250.

[2] K. Marx, 'Doctoral Dissertation', in *Early Texts*, p. 13.

[3] See in particular on this, C. Cesa, 'Bruno Bauer e la filosofia dell' autoscienza (1841–1843)', *Giornale Critico della Filosofia Italiana*, I (1960); D. McLellan, *The Young Hegelians and Karl Marx*, pp. 48 ff.

of liberty.[1] A native of Abdera in Thrace, writing at the end of the fifth century B.C., Democritus, summed up, in his theory of atoms and the void, the previous two hundred years of Greek physical speculation. Epicurus taught more than a century later in an Athens marked by the general social chaos of the post-Alexandrine epoch and was concerned to supply principles for the conduct of individuals.[2] Marx began his account of the relationship of the two philosophers with a paradox: Epicurus held all appearances to be objectively real but at the same time, since he wished to conserve freedom of the will, denied that the world was governed by immutable laws and thus in fact seemed to reject the objective reality of nature. Democritus, on the other hand, was very sceptical about the reality of appearance, but yet held the world to be governed by necessity. From this Marx concluded, rightly, that Epicurus's physics was really only a part of his moral philosophy. Epicurus did not merely copy Democritus's physics, as was commonly thought, but introduced the idea of spontaneity into the movement of the atoms, and to Democritus's world of inanimate nature ruled by mechanical laws he added a world of animate nature in which the human will operated. Marx thus preferred the view of Epicurus for two reasons: firstly, his emphasis on the absolute autonomy of the human spirit freed men from all superstitions of transcendent objects; secondly, the emphasis on 'free individual self-consciousness' showed one the way of going beyond the system of a 'total philosophy'.

It was above all this liberating aspect of Epicurus that Marx admired. A few years later in *The German Ideology* he called Epicurus 'the genuine radically-enlightened mind of antiquity',[3] and often referred to him in similar terms in his later writings. This enthusiasm for Epicurus was also seen in the appendix (to the thesis) which attacked Plutarch and particularly his treatise entitled 'It is impossible to live happily by following the principles of Epicurus';[4] taking each of Plutarch's arguments separately, Marx demonstrated that the opposite conclu-

[1] Marx's preference seems to have depended simply on his contrasting their moral philosophies; as a philosopher and a natural scientist, Democritus is by far the more profound and original thinker.

[2] See further B. Farrington, *The Faith of Epicurus* (London, 1967) pp. 7 f.

[3] *MEGA* I v 122.

[4] This appendix does not survive, but can be reconstructed from the preliminary notes: see *MEGA* I i 31; D. Baumgarten, 'Uber den "verloren geglaubten" Anhang zu Karl Marx' Doktordissertation', in *Gegenwartsprobleme der Soziologie*, ed. Eisermann (Potsdam, 1949).

sion followed. Although now it makes rather dry reading and often interprets the ideas of the ancients in an inappropriately subtle Hegelian perspective, Marx's thesis was a profoundly original work. One of those best qualified to judge has written that 'it is almost astonishing to see how far he got considering the materials then available'.[1]

During these years Marx was not only concerned with writing his thesis. The other projects he was engaged in similarly reflected the Young Hegelian climate and the discussions in the Doctors' Club. He had planned to edit a literary review and was much encouraged, 'since, through the agency of Bauer, who plays a leading role among them, and of my colleague Dr Rutenberg, all the aesthetic celebrities of the Hegelian School have promised to contribute'.[2] But the only result of Marx's literary endeavours was the appearance of two short poems in the Berlin review *Athenaeum* in 1841: these poems were his first published work. In early 1840 Marx was co-operating with Bruno Bauer in editing Hegel's *Philosophy of Religion* and was thinking of writing a similar book himself. He also considered giving a course of lectures at Bonn attacking Hermes, a Catholic theologian who had tried to reconcile religion and Kantian philosophy; like all his plans at the time, he discussed the project at length with Bruno Bauer. By the summer of 1840 Marx had finished a book on the subject and sent the manuscript to Bauer enclosing a letter to a publisher, but the book was not in fact published, and Bauer wrote to Marx about the covering letter: 'Perhaps you might write in such terms to your washerwoman, but not to a publisher from whom you are asking a favour.'[3] At the same time Marx had the idea of writing a farce entitled *Fischer Vapulans* using it as a vehicle to attack *Die Idea der Gottheit*, K. P. Fischer's philosophical attempt to justify theism. Marx was also much concerned with logical problems and wanted to devote a work to dialectic: he took extensive notes on Aristotle and discussed the question in letters to Bauer; he proposed writing a criticism of the contemporary philosopher Trendelenburg and demonstrate that Aristotle was dialectical whereas Trendelenburg was only formal.

Meanwhile Bauer was full of good advice on how to finish his 'stupid examination' and join him in Bonn. He had already written to

[1] C. Bailey, 'Karl Marx and Greek Atomism', *The Classical Quarterly* (1928).
[2] Marx to Heinrich Marx, *Early Texts*, p. 9.
[3] B. Bauer to Marx, *MEGA* i i (2) 244.

Marx in 1840: 'You can tell Gabler [Professor of Philosophy in Berlin] of your interests and he will be all the more enthusiastic and delighted with the examination when he learns that another Hegelian is now getting a chair.'[1] And a year later he was writing: 'In any event see that Ladenberg [Rector of the University of Berlin] smoothes the way for you. Get him to write here on your behalf and anticipate all the sorts of intrigues that there could be. See, too, if you cannot win over Eichhorn [Minister of Culture].'[2]

Thus encouraged, Marx duly submitted his thesis in April 1841, but not to the University of Berlin: instead, he sent it to Jena, one of the small universities which 'greatly facilitated the gaining of the title of Doctor'.[3] In fact, Jena held the record in the production of Doctors of Philosophy. The whole affair was managed by Wolff, Professor of Literature there, a friend of Heinrich Heine and an acquaintance of Marx, who had probably informed him of the situation inside the Faculty at Jena. Marx was immediately granted his degree *in absentia* on 15 April 1841.

III. JOURNALISM

As soon as his thesis was accepted, Marx began a very restless year which was finally to culminate in his adopting journalism as a career in mid-1842. His search for a secure means of earning his livelihood led him to commute between Trier, Bonn and Cologne, never remaining for very long in any one place. He began many projects but – true to his previous life-style – finished none of them.

After six weeks at his parents' home in Trier, Marx moved to Bonn to pursue his academic career in the company of Bruno Bauer. To obtain a lectureship, the university statutes required a dissertation in addition to a doctoral thesis, so Marx began to revise his thesis for publication and also extend it in 'a longer dissertation, in which I will present in detail the cycle of Epicurean, Stoic and Sceptical philosophy in relation to all Greek Speculation'.[4] He also appended two extended notes to his thesis.

The first of the substantial notes that Marx added to his thesis at the end of 1841 was directed primarily against Schelling, who had just been summoned to Berlin by Frederick William IV in order to 'root out the

[1] B. Bauer to Marx, in *Karl Marx, Dokumente seines Lebens*, p. 100.   [2] Ibid.
[3] K. Kautsky, quoted in *Karl Marx, Dokumente seines Lebens*, p. 97.
[4] K. Marx, 'Doctoral Dissertation', in N. Livergood, op. cit., p. 61.

dragon-seed of Hegelianism'.[1] In his lectures entitled 'The Philosophy of Revelation', Schelling drew a distinction between a negative and purely rational philosophy, and a positive one whose real content was the evolution of the divine in history and as it was recorded in the various mythologies and religions of mankind. Schelling's lectures were accompanied by much publicity and at first attracted wide attention: Engels, Kierkegaard and Bakunin were all present at his inaugural lecture. The reaction of the Hegelians was strong and Marx's not least: his technique here was to contrast what Schelling was then saying with his earlier writings, and point out the disparity between his dogmatic Berlin lectures and his earlier belief in the freedom of speculation. Marx went on the claim that Hegel had inverted the traditional proofs for the existence of God and thereby refuted them. For Marx, either the proofs for the existence of God were tautologies or they were 'nothing but proofs for the existence of an essentially human self-consciousness and elaborations of it'.[2] Marx finished his note – with its strange mixture of post-Hegelian philosophy and the simple rationalism of the Enlightenment – by quoting two more passages from the early Schelling: 'If you presuppose the idea of an objective God, how can you speak of laws that reason independently creates, for autonomy can only be ascribed to an absolutely free being?' 'It is a crime against humanity to conceal principles that are communicable to everyone.'[3]

The second note appended to the thesis takes up the themes already treated in the passage in the preliminary notes on the future of philosophy after Hegel's total system, and elaborates for the first time (though still in a very idealistic manner) the notions of the abolition of philosophy and praxis that were to be so central to his later thought.[4]

At the same time as extending his thesis by means of these rather theoretical discussions, Marx was engaged in more immediate and polemical projects – mostly in collaboration with Bruno Bauer whose

[1] Frederick William IV to Bunsen, in Chr. von Bunsen, *Aus seinen Briefen* (Leipzig, 1869) II 133.

[2] K. Marx, *Early Texts*, p. 18.

[3] Ibid., p. 19.

[4] Both these ideas were derived from a small book with the mysterious title *Prolegomena to Historiosophy* published by a Polish Count, August von Cieszkowski in 1838. On the book and its influence on the young Hegelians, see further D. McLellan, *The Young Hegelians and Karl Marx*, pp. 9 f.

increasing difficulties with the government authorities seemed to be jeopardising the prospective university careers of both of them. For Bauer was engaged in writing his *Criticism of the Synoptic Gospels*, a work which denied the historicity of Christ and portrayed the gospels as mythical inventions. Since March 1841 the two men had planned to found a review entitled *Atheistic Archives*, which would take as its foundation Bauer's gospel criticism.[1] Certainly Marx's atheism was of an extremely militant kind. Ruge wrote to a friend: 'Bruno Bauer, Karl Marx, Christiansen and Feuerbach are forming a new "Montagne" and making atheism their slogan. God, religion, immortality are cast down from their thrones and man is proclaimed God.'[2] And Georg Jung, a prosperous young Cologne lawyer and supporter of the radical movement, wrote to Ruge: 'If Marx, Bruno Bauer and Feuerbach come together to found a theological-philosophical review, God would do well to surround Himself with all His angels and indulge in self-pity, for these three will certainly drive Him out of His heaven.... For Marx, at any rate, the Christian religion is one of the most immoral there is.'[3]

These plans came to nothing, however. Instead, Bauer published anonymously in November what purported to be an arch-conservative pietist attack on Hegel, entitled *The Trump of the Last Judgement on Hegel the Atheist and Anti-Christ*. Under the cover of attacking Hegel, this tract was designed to show that he was really an atheist revolutionary. Marx may well have collaborated with Bauer in writing *The Trump. . .* , and some indeed thought it was their joint work. At any rate they certainly intended jointly to produce a sequel, to be called *Hegel's Hatred of Religious and Christian Art and his Destruction of all the Laws of the State*. Marx therefore began to read a series of books on art and religion. Bauer had finished his part in December 1841, but he had to publish it without his collaborator's contribution: in December 1841 Marx was obliged to return to Trier where Baron von Westphalen had fallen seriously ill. Until his father-in-law's death on 3 March 1842, Marx stayed in the Westphalen house and helped, as Bauer put it, to 'lighten the days' of the dying man. March was a bad month for Marx: not only did he lose his closest friend and supporter in the Westphalen household, but his hopes of a university career were

[1] Cf. *MEGA* I i (2) 152.
[2] A. Ruge, *Briefwechsel und Tageblätter*, ed. P. Nerrlich (Berlin, 1886) I 239.
[3] *MEGA* I i (2) 261 f.

shattered when Bauer was deprived of his teaching post on account of his unorthodox doctrines. While in Trier Marx had already composed an article which he sent to Arnold Ruge who edited the *Deutsche Jahrbücher*.

Ruge, who was to be a close colleague of Marx's for the next two years, was also an exile from university teaching; being refused a chair owing to his unorthodox views, he resigned from the university and devoted himself entirely to journalism. For this he was admirably suited: he was a man of independent means, and although having no very original mind, he wrote quickly and well and had a very wide range of contacts.[1] In 1838 he started the *Hallische Jahrbücher* which soon became the leading periodical of the Young Hegelians. Although during the early years the contributions to the *Hallische Jahrbücher* had in general addressed themselves to an enlightened Prussian state, by 1840 overtly political articles were beginning to follow on religious ones – a logic implicit in the notion of the 'Christian state'. As a result the *Jahrbücher* was banned in Prussia in June 1841 and moved to Dresden, where it appeared under the title *Deutsche Jahrbücher*.[2] During 1840 the Berlin Young Hegelians had begun to write for it, and by the middle of 1841 Bauer had become a regular contributor.

Marx had already been introduced to Ruge by his Berlin friend Köppen, himself a frequent contributor. The article Marx sent to Ruge in February 1842 (together with a covering letter offering to review books and put all his energies at the service of the *Deutsche Jahrbücher*) dealt with the new censorship instruction issued by Frederick William IV in December 1841. Frederick William IV had succeeded to the Prussian throne the year before and the Young Hegelians had expected a liberalisation to ensue. The new king certainly shared with the bourgeoisie a hatred of regimented bureaucracy: his ideal was paternalistic government. He agreed with the bourgeoisie's claim to express their opinions in Parliament and the press, and even emphasised in the censorship instruction 'the value of, and need for, frank and loyal publicity'. Since, however, what the bourgeoisie wanted to campaign for was not a romantically paternalist society, a collision was inevitable. In his article, entitled 'Comments on the latest Prussian Censorship Instruction', Marx exposed the inconsistencies of the new

[1] On Ruge, see further W. Neher, *Arnold Ruge as Politiker und Politischer Schriftsteller* (Heidelberg, 1933).
[2] See further D. McLellan, *The Young Hegelians and Karl Marx*, pp. 11 ff.

censorship regulations that were supposed to relax the prevailing ones. Since they forbade attacks on the Christian religion and penalised offences against 'discipline, morals and outward loyalty', he considered that the 'censorship must reject the great moral thinkers of the past – Kant, Fichte, Spinoza, for example – as irreligious and violating discipline, morals and social respectability. And these moralists start from a contradiction in principle between morality and religion, for morality is based on the autonomy of the human mind whereas religion is based on its heteronomy.'[1] Further, the new regulations were inimical to good law in so far as they were directed at 'tendencies' and 'intentions' as much as acts. For Marx, this was to create a society in which a single state organ regarded itself as the sole possessor of reason and morality, whereas 'an ethical state reflects the views of its members even though they may oppose one of its organs or the government itself'.[2] He was thus beginning to draw liberal democratic conclusions from Hegel's political philosophy.

Marx's article was a masterpiece of polemical exegesis, demonstrating the great pamphleteering talent in the style of Boerne that he was to exhibit throughout his life. All his articles of the Young Hegelian period – and, to a lesser extent, many of his later writings – were written in an extremely vivid style: his radical and uncompromising approach, his love of polarisation, his method of dealing with opponents' views by reductio ad absurdum, all led him to write very antithetically. Slogan, climax, anaphora, parellelism, antithesis and chiasmus (especially the last two) were all employed by Marx – sometimes to excess. In the event, the authorities would not pass this particular article of his (it eventually appeared in February 1843 in Switzerland in Anekdota, a collection of articles suppressed by the Prussian censhorship and issued in book form by Ruge).

Finding 'the proximity of the Bonn professors insufferable',[3] Marx moved to Cologne in April 1842 with the intention of at least writing something that would find its way into print. While in Bonn he had made several visits to Cologne where he found much pleasure in champagne and discussions about Hegel. Jenny wrote to him: 'My dark little savage, how glad I am that you are happy, that my letter exhilarated

[1] K. Marx, 'Comments on the latest Prussian Censorship Instruction', *Early Texts*, pp. 29 f.
[2] K. Marx, op. cit., *Writings of the Young Marx*, p. 80.
[3] Marx to Ruge; *MEW* xxvii 401.

you, that you long for me, that you live in well-papered rooms, that you have drunk champagne in Cologne, that there are Hegel clubs there, that you have dreamed and, in short, that you are my darling, my own dark little savage.'[1] But the high life in Cologne turned out to be too much for him as 'the life here is too noisy and good boisterous friends do not make for better philosophy'.[2] So Marx returned to Bonn where he was able to relax with Bauer. 'Marx has come back here,' his friend wrote: 'Lately we went out into the open country to enjoy once again all the beautiful views. The trip was marvellous. We were as gay as ever. In Godesberg we hired a couple of donkeys and galloped on them like madmen around the hill and through the village. Bonn society gazed at us as amazed as ever. We halloed and the donkeys brayed.'[3] But their ways soon parted for good when Bauer went to Berlin to try and get his dismissal rescinded. Marx meanwhile continued with his journalism. At the end of April he already had four articles to propose to Ruge. His visits to Cologne did not only consist in drinking champagne: he was gradually becoming involved in the city's liberal opposition movement, an involvement in practical politics that eventually led to his breaking with the Young Hegelians and taking over the editorship of the *Rheinische Zeitung*. In spite of Jenny's warning against getting 'mixed up' in politics (an activity she described as 'the riskiest thing there is'),[4] it was an almost inevitable step for a young Rhineland intellectual of progressive views.

The political atmosphere in the Rhineland was quite different from Berlin: Rhineland-Westphalia, annexed by France from 1795 to 1814, had had the benefit of economic, administrative and political reforms. What had before been 108 small states were reorganised into four districts; feudalism was abolished, and various administrative anomalies – as regards the political, juridical and financial systems – were eliminated. The corporations and customs barriers were done away with, much could be exported to France and producers were protected against competition from England. Expansion, led by the textile industry, was so rapid that by 1810 the Prefect of the Ruhr plausibly claimed that it was the most industrial region in Europe. The majority of progressive figures in Germany of that time came from the Rhine-

---

[1] Jenny von Westphalen to Marx, *MEW*, Ergsbd. I 641.
[2] Marx to Ruge, *MEW* XXVII 402.
[3] *Briefwechsel zwischen Bruno und Edgar Bauer* (Charlottenburg, 1844) p. 192.
[4] Jenny von Westphalen to Marx, *MEW*, Engsbd. I 641.

land: the leaders of the liberal opposition, and many future activists in the 1848 revolutions, and poets such as Heine and Boerne.

One of the focal points of this political activity was the 'Cologne Circle' – the Rhineland's more down-to-earth equivalent of the Doctors' Club – which Marx joined as soon as he established himself in Bonn. In many ways the central figure of the Cologne Circle was Georg Jung who had also been a member of the Berlin Doctors' Club. He quickly became Marx's closest friend in the Circle, whose other members included individuals such as the financiers Camphausen and Hansemann, both future Prime Ministers of Prussia, the industrialists Mevissen and Malinckrodt, and a large number of young intellectuals such as Moses Hess, who had perhaps the best claim to have introduced communist ideas into Germany. It was natural that the Circle should welcome the idea of a newspaper to propagate their doctrines. Already in 1840 a paper with the title *Rheinische Allgemeine Zeitung* had been founded by a group who considered that the *Kölnische Zeitung* did not adequately defend their social and economic interests. When it was evident that this paper would soon become bankrupt, Georg Jung and Moses Hess persuaded leading rich liberals of the Rhineland, including Camphausen, Mevissen and Oppenheim, to form a company which bought out the *Rheinische Allgemeine Zeitung* (in order to avoid having to renegotiate a concession) and republished it from 1 January 1842 under the title *Rheinische Zeitung*.[1] The sub-heading of the paper was 'For Politics, Commerce and Industry', and its declared object was to defend the interests of the numerous Rhineland middle class whose aims were to safeguard the Napoleonic *Code Civil* and the principle of equality of all citizens before the law, and ultimately to bring about the political and economic unification of all Germany – aspirations that necessarily led them to oppose Prussia's religious policies and semi-feudal absolutism.

The holding company of the *Rheinische Zeitung* had no lack of money and started with a share capital of over 30,000 thalers. They were, however, unlucky in their initial choice of editors. Moses Hess had taken the leading part in founding the paper and had consequently expected to be appointed editor; but the financial backers did not want a revolutionary in the editorial chair. Their chief aim was to campaign for measures that would help the expansion of industry and com-

[1] Further details on the background of the *Rheinische Zeitung* can be found in E. Silberner, *Moses Hess* (Leiden, 1966) pp. 91 ff.

merce, such as an extension of the customs unions, accelerated railway construction and reduced postal charges. So the shareholders offered the editorship first to the protectionist economist Friedrich List and then (when he was forced to decline for health reasons) to Hoeffken, editor of the *Augsburger Allgemeine Zeitung* and a follower of List. Swallowing his pride, Hess accepted a post as sub-editor with special reference to France. Renard, Oppenheim and Jung were appointed directors. Since Oppenheim and particularly Jung had been converted by Hess to Young Hegelian radicalism, friction soon developed between them and Hoeffken. He refused to accept articles from the Berlin Young Hegelians and was obliged to resign (on 18 January 1842) – declaring himself 'no adept of neo-Hegelianism'.[1]

Hoeffken was replaced by Rutenberg, brother-in-law of Bruno Bauer. He was supported by Marx, who had taken part in discussions on the organisation of the paper since September of the previous year. The new appointment made the authorities so anxious as to the tendency of the paper that suppression was suggested by the central Government; but the President of the Rhineland province, fearing that this would create popular unrest, only promised closer supervision.

From the start Marx enjoyed a great reputation in the Cologne Circle. Jung said of him that 'Although a devil of a revolutionary, Dr Marx is one of the most penetrating minds I know.'[2] And Moses Hess, a man of generous enthusiasm, introduced him to his friend Auerbach as follows:

> You will be pleased to make the acquaintance of a man who is now one of our friends, although he lives in Bonn where he will soon be lecturing. He made a considerable impression on me although our fields are very close; in brief, prepare to meet the greatest – perhaps the only genuine – philosopher now alive, who will soon . . . attract the eyes of all Germany. . . . Dr Marx . . . will give medieval religion and politics their *coup de grâce*. He combines the deepest philosophical seriousness with the most biting wit. Imagine Rousseau, Voltaire, Holbach, Lessing, Heine, and Hegel fused into one person – I say fused not juxtaposed – and you have Dr Marx.[3]

[1] *Rheinische Briefen und Akten*, ed. Hansen, I 315.
[2] G. Jung to A. Ruge, *MEGA* I (2) 261.
[3] M. Hess to A. Auerbach, in M. Hess, *Briefwechsel*, ed. E. Silberner (The Hague, 1959) p. 80.

Marx had already been asked in January by Bauer why he did not write for the *Rheinische Zeitung*; and in March, pressed by Jung, he began to transfer his major effort from Ruge's journal to that newspaper.[1] One of his first contributions, though it was not published until August, was a criticism of the Historical School of Law. Written in April 1842, this article was occasioned by the appointment of Karl von Savigny as Minister of Justice, who was expected to introduce into the legal system the romantic and reactionary ideas of the new king. Thus it was indirectly an attack on the institutions of the Prussian 'Christian state'. The Historical School of Law had just published a manifesto in honour of their founder Gustav Hugo (1764–1844), who held that historical existence was the prime justification of any law. Marx's main point was that this position forced Hugo to adopt an absolute scepticism which deprived him of any criterion of judgement. Against this position Marx employed a rationalism based on Spinoza and Kant, both of whom refused to equate the positive with the rational: 'Hugo desecrates everything that is sacred to lawful, moral, political man. He smashes what is sacred so that he can revere it as an historical relic; he violates it before the eyes of reason so that he can later honour it before the eyes of history; at the same time he also wants to honour historical eyes.'[2] In short, the Historical School of Law had only one principle – 'the law of arbitrary power'.[3]

At the same time as writing the attack on Hugo, Marx decided to devote a series of article to the debates of the Rhineland Parliament that had held a long session in Düsseldorf in mid-1841. He originally proposed a series of five articles on the debates, of which the first was to be the one written in early April and entitled 'Debates on the Freedom of the Press and on the Publication of the Parliamentary Proceedings': the other four were to deal with the Cologne Affair, the laws on theft of wood, on poaching and 'the really earthy question in all its vital extent, the division of land'.[4] But the only articles to be published were those on the freedom of the Press and the theft of wood. In the parliamentary debates on the freedom of the Press, Marx found that the 'characteristic outlook of each class' was 'nowhere

[1] On Marx's articles for the *Rheinische Zeitung* in general, see A. McGovern, 'Karl Marx's first political writings: the *Rheinische Zeitung* 1842–43', *Demythologising Marxism*, ed. F. Adelmann (The Hague, 1969).

[2] *Writings of the Young Marx*, p. 98.

[3] Ibid., p. 105.

[4] Marx to A. Ruge, *MEGA* I i (2) 278.

more clearly expressed than in these debates'. The speakers did not regard freedom as a natural gift to all rational men; for them it was 'an individual characteristic of certain persons and classes'.[1] Such an attitude was incapable of drawing up any laws to govern the Press. Marx went on to criticise in particular the feudal romanticism of the Prussian regime, and developed ideas on evasion and projection that later turned into a full theory of ideology:

> because the real situation of these gentlemen in the modern state bears no relation at all to the conception that they have of their situation; because they live in a world situated beyond the real world and because in consequence their imagination holds the place of their head and their heart, they necessarily turn towards theory, being unsatisfied with practice, but it is towards the theory of the transcendent, i.e. religion. However, in their hands religion acquires a polemical bitterness impregnated with political tendencies and becomes, in a more or less conscious manner, simply a sacred cloak to hide desires that are both very secular and at the same time very imaginary.
>
> Thus we shall find in our Speaker that he opposes a mystical/ religious theory of his imagination to practical demands ... and that to what is reasonable from the human point of view he opposes superhuman sacred entities.[2]

Marx finished by outlining the part laws should play in the state: 'A Press law is a true law because it is the positive existence of freedom. It treats freedom as the normal condition of the Press. . . .'[3] Marx went on to draw conclusions about the nature of law in general: 'Laws are not rules that repress freedom any more than the law of gravity is a law that represses movement . . . laws are rather positive lights, general norms, in which freedom has obtained an impersonal, theoretical existence that is independent of any arbitrary individual. Its law book is a people's bible of freedom.'[4] In this case it was nonsense to speak of preventive laws, for true laws could not prevent the activities of man, but were 'the inner, vital laws of human activity, the conscious mirror of human life'.[5] This article, the first Marx ever published, was greeted enthusiastically by his friends: Jung wrote to

[1] K. Marx, 'Debates on the Freedom of the Press', *MEW* I 34.
[2] K. Marx, 'Debates on the Freedom of the Press', *Early Texts*, pp. 35 f.
[3] K. Marx, *MEW* I 57.   [4] Ibid., 58.   [5] Ibid.

him that 'your article on the freedom of the Press is superb',[1] and Ruge wrote in similar vein: 'your commentary in the paper on the freedom of the Press is marvellous. It is certainly the best that has been written on the subject.'[2]

Marx was all the more eager to earn a living through journalism as he quarrelled definitively with his mother at the end of June 1842 and was deprived of all financial help from his family. 'For six weeks', he wrote, 'I had to stay in Trier because of a new death and the rest of the time was wasted and upset through the most disagreeable of family controversies. My family has put difficulties in my way which, despite their own prosperity, subject me to the most straitened circumstances.'[3] This quarrel was so violent that Marx left the family house in the Simeonstrasse and put up in a nearby guest house. He remained in Trier until the wedding of his sister Sophie and in mid-July left for Bonn where he could devote himself uninterruptedly to journalism.

In spite of the tense atmosphere in Trier, Marx had found time while there to compose another major contribution to the *Rheinische Zeitung*. By June 1842 the paper's radical tone provoked its large rival, the *Kölnische Zeitung*, into launching an attack on its 'dissemination of philosophical and religious views by means of newspapers',[4] and claiming in a leading article that religious decadence involved political decadence. Marx believed the reverse to be true:

> If the fall of the states of antiquity entails the disappearance of the religions of these states, it is not necessary to go and look for another explanation, for the 'true religion' of the ancients was the cult of 'their nationality', of their 'State'. It is not the ruin of the ancient religions that entailed the fall of the states of antiquity, but the fall of the states of antiquity that entailed the ruin of the ancient religions.[5]

Marx went on to defend the right of philosophy – 'the spiritual quintessence of its time' – to comment freely on all questions, and finished his article with an outline of the ideal state according to modern philosophy, that is, Hegel and after.

[1] G. Jung to Marx, *MEGA* I i (2) 275.
[2] A. Ruge to Marx, *MEGA* I i (2) 276.
[3] Marx to A. Ruge, *MEW* XXVII 405.
[4] K. Marx, 'The leading Article of the *Kölnische Zeitung*', *MEGA* I i (2) 233.
[5] K. Marx, *Early Texts*, p. 38.

But if the previous professors of constitutional law have constructed the state from instincts either of ambition or sociability or even from reason, but from the individual's reason and not social reason, the profounder conception of modern philosophy deduces the state from the idea of the all. It considers the state as the great organism in which juridical, moral and political liberties must be realised and in which each citizen, by obeying the laws of the state, only obeys the natural laws of his own reason, human reason. *Sapienti sat.*[1]

Finally, Marx welcomed the idea of the clash of parties, another favourite Young Hegelian topic: 'Without parties there is no development, without division, no progress.'[2]

On his return to Bonn in July 1842, Marx began to be drawn more and more into the organisation of the *Rheinische Zeitung*, owing mainly to the incompetence of the alcoholic Rutenberg, whom Marx declared himself ashamed to have suggested for the job. Simultaneously with his closer involvement with the paper came signs of increasing disagreement with his former Berlin colleagues. They had formed themselves into a club known as the *Freien*, which was the successor to the old Doctors' Club. The *Freien* were a group of young writers who, disgusted with the servile attitude of the Berliners, lived a style of life whose aim was in many respects simply *épater les bourgeois*. They spent a lot of their time in cafés and even begged in the streets when short of money. The intransigence of their opposition to established doctrines, and particularly to religion, was causing public concern. Their members included Max Stirner, who had published atheist articles in the *Rheinische Zeitung* as a prelude to his supremely anarcho-individualistic book *The Ego and His Own*; Edgar Bauer (Bruno's brother), whose fervent attacks on any sort of liberal political compromise were taken up by Bakunin; and Friedrich Engels, who was the author of several polemics against Schelling and liberalism.

Marx, however, was against these public declarations of emancipation, which seemed to him to be mere exhibitionism. In view of the Young Hegelians' association with the *Rheinische Zeitung* he also feared that the articles from Berlin might give his rival editor Hermes a further opportunity of attacking the paper. Marx was writing for a business paper in the Rhineland where industry was relatively

---

[1] Ibid., p. 42.　　　[2] K. Marx, *MEGA* I i (2) 250.

developed, whereas the *Freien* were philosophising in Berlin where there was little industry and the atmosphere was dominated by the government bureaucracy. He was therefore in favour of supporting the bourgeoisie in the struggle for liberal reform, and was against indiscriminate criticism. It was indeed on his own advice that the publisher of the *Rheinische Zeitung*, Renard, had promised the President of the Rhineland that the paper would moderate its tone – particularly on religious subjects.[1]

The attitude of the *Freien* raised the question of what the editorial principles of the *Rheinische Zeitung* ought to be. Accordingly at the end of August, Marx wrote to Oppenheim, whose voice was decisive in determining policy, virtually spelling out his own proposals for the paper, should the editorship be entrusted to him. He wrote:

If you agree, send me the article [by Edgar Bauer] on the *juste-milieu* so that I can review it. This question must be discussed dispassionately. General and theoretical considerations on the constitution of the state are more suitable for learned reviews than for newspapers. The true theory must be expanded and developed in relation to concrete facts and the existing state of affairs. Therefore striking an attitude against the present pillars of the state could only result in a tightening of the censorship and even in the suppression of the paper . . . in any case we are annoying a large number, perhaps even the majority, of liberals engaged in political activity who have assumed the thankless and painful task of conquering liberty step by step within limits imposed by the Constitution, while we, comfortably ensconced in abstract theory, point out to them their contradictions. It is true that the author of the articles on the *juste-milieu* invites us to criticise, but (1) we all know how the Government replies to such provocations; and (2) it is not sufficient to undertake a critique . . . the true question is to know whether one has chosen an appropriate field. Newspapers only lend themselves to discussion of these questions when they have become questions that closely concern the state – practical questions. I consider it absolutely indispensable that the *Rheinische Zeitung* should not be directed by its contributors but on the contrary that *it* should direct *them*. Articles like these afford an excellent opportunity of showing

[1] Cf. *MEGA* I i (2) 281 ff.

the contributors the line of action to follow. An isolated writer cannot, like a newspaper, have a synoptic view of the situation.[1]

In mid-October, as a result of this letter, Marx, who had already effectively been running the paper for some months, was made editor-in-chief.

Under Marx's editorship, the circulation of the paper more than doubled in the first months. His personality was so predominant that the censorship official could call the organisation of the paper simply 'a dictatorship of Marx'.[2] In the last months of 1842 the *Rheinische Zeitung* began to acquire a national reputation. Robert Prutz, himself a contributor and later a prominent liberal politician, subsequently wrote of the paper:

All the young, fresh, free-thinking or (as the friends of the government complained) revolutionary talent that Prussia and Germany possessed took refuge here. Fighting with a great variety of weapons, now earnest, now mocking, now learned, now popular, today in prose, tomorrow in verse, they formed a phalanx against which the censorship and police struggled in vain. . . .[3]

And the editor appears to have been no less impressive than the paper. Mevissen left the following vivid description of Marx at this time:

Karl Marx from Trier was a powerful man of 24 whose thick black hair sprung from his cheeks, arms, nose and ears. He was domineering, impetuous, passionate, full of boundless self-confidence, but at the same time deeply earnest and learned, a restless dialectician who with his restless Jewish penetration pushed every proposition of Young Hegelian doctrine to its final conclusion and was already then, by his concentrated study of economics, preparing his conversion to communism. Under Marx's leadership the young newspaper soon began to speak very recklessly. . . .[4]

In his first task as editor, however, Marx showed himself very circumspect: he was faced with accusations of communism brought against the *Rheinische Zeitung* by the *Augsburger Allgemeine Zeitung*, probably inspired by Hoeffken, one-time editor of the *Rheinische Zeitung*, who had

[1] Marx to Oppenheim, *MEGA* I i (2) 280.
[2] *Karl Marx: Dokumente seines Lebens*, p. 117.
[3] R. Prutz, *Zehn Jahre* (Leipzig, 1856) II 359 ff.
[4] G. Mevissen, in H. von Treitschke, *Deutsche Geschichte im Neunzehnten Jahrhundert* (Leipzig, 1905) v 201.

already attacked the *Rheinische Zeitung* in March for printing an article by Bruno Bauer. The basis for the accusation was that in September the *Rheinische Zeitung* had reviewed two articles on housing and communist forms of government, and that in October it had reported a conference at Strasbourg where followers of Fourier had put forward their ideas. All these items had been written by Hess. In his reply, Marx criticised the Aubsburg paper for trying to neglect what was an important issue, but denied that the *Rheinische Zeintung* had any sympathy with communism:

> The *Rheinische Zeitung*, which cannot even concede theoretical reality to communistic ideas in their present form, and can even less wish or consider possible their practical realisation, will submit these ideas to thorough criticism. If the *Augsburger* wanted and could achieve more than slick phrases, the *Augsburger* would see that writings such as those by Leroux, Considérant, and above all Proudhon's penetrating work, can be criticised only after long and deep study, not through superficial and passing notions.[1]

But these notions had to be taken seriously, for ideas were very powerful:

> Because of this disagreement, we have to take such theoretical works all the more seriously. We are firmly convinced that it is not the practical effort but rather the theoretical explication of communist ideas which is the real danger. Dangerous practical attempts, even those on a large scale, can be answered with cannon, but ideas won by our intelligence, embodied in our outlook, and forged in our conscience, are chains from which we cannot tear ourselves away without breaking our hearts; they are demons we can overcome only by submitting to them.[2]

This reply reflected the general policy of the *Rheinische Zeitung*, which certainly treated poverty as a social and not merely a political question, but which did not see the proletariat as a new social class but only as the innocent victim of bad economic organisation.

It was not among the German working classes that socialist ideas either originated or initially took root. Germany was only just beginning to become an industrialised country, and industrial workers

---

[1] K. Marx, 'Communism and the *Augsburger Allgemeine Zeitung*', *Early Texts*, pp. 47 f.
[2] K. Marx, op. cit., p. 48.

were far from being the majority of the population. They did not have sufficient organisation and, being mostly ex-artisans, were nostalgic for the past rather than revolutionary. Socialist ideas were spread by a party of the intellectual élite, who saw the proletarian masses as a possible instrument of social renewal. French utopian socialism began to have an influence inside Germany during the 1830s.[1] In Trier itself (where Marx was born), Ludwig Gall spread Fourierist ideas; but in Berlin the poems of Heine and the lectures of Gans gained a wider audience. The first book by a native German communist was *The Sacred History of Mankind*, written by Moses Hess, who had picked up communist ideas after running away to Paris from his father's factory in Cologne.[2] The book was mystical and meandering, but contained quite clearly the idea of the polarisation of classes and the imminence of a proletarian revolution. Hess went on to convert Engels to communism and published much covert communist propaganda in the *Rheinische Zeitung*. A year later a tailor, Wilhelm Weitling, active in the expatriate German workers' association in Paris and Switzerland, published a booklet entitled *Mankind as it is and as it ought to be*. It was a messianic work which defended, against the rich and powerful of the earth who caused all inequality and injustice, the right of all to education and happiness by means of social equality and justice.

The book which most helped to spread knowledge of socialism was Lorenz von Stein's inquiry, *The Socialism and Communism of Present-Day France*. It was due to Stein's book that socialism and communism (the terms were generally used interchangeably in Germany at this time) began to attract attention in 1842. Commissioned by the Prussian Government, Stein had conducted an investigation into the spread of French socialism among German immigrant workers in Paris; though the author was far from sympathetic to socialists, his published report helped enormously to spread information about and even generate enthusiasm for their cause.[3] The climate of opinion in Cologne was particularly favourable to the reception of socialist ideas: the Rhineland liberals (unlike their Manchester counterparts) were very socially-conscious and considered that the state had far-reaching duties towards society. Mevissen, for example, had been very struck when visiting England by the decrease in wages, and had become converted

[1] See E. Butler, *The Saint-Simonian Religion in Germany* (Cambridge, 1926).
[2] On Hess, see E. Silberner, *Moses Hess*.   [3] On Stein, see p. 97 below.

to Saint-Simonianism during a stay in Paris. In the offices of the *Rheinische Zeitung* social questions were regularly discussed at the meetings of a group (founded by Moses Hess) which was effectively the editorial committee of the paper. Its members also included Jung, and the future communists Karl d'Ester and Anneke. It met monthly, papers were read, and a discussion followed among the members, who did not necessarily share the same political viewpoint but were all interested in social questions. Marx joined this group when he moved to Cologne in October 1842.[1]

The interest aroused in social questions by these seminars was heightened, for Marx, by his study of socio-economic conditions in the Rhineland. In his first important article as editor (the fourth in the planned series of five dealing with the debates in the Rhineland Parliament), he discussed the more stringent laws recently proposed in regard to thefts of timber. The gathering of dead wood had traditionally been unrestricted, but the scarcities caused by the agrarian crises of the 1820s and the growing needs of industry led to legal controls. The situation had become unmanageable: five-sixths of all prosecutions in Prussia dealt with wood, and the proportion was even higher in the Rhineland.[2] So it was now being proposed that the keeper be the sole arbiter of an alleged offence and that he alone assess the damages.

Marx discussed these questions from a legal and political standpoint, without much social and historical detail, and claimed that the state should defend customary law against the rapacity of the rich. For some things could never become the private property of an individual without injustice; moreover, 'if every violation of property, without distinction or more precise determination, is theft, would not all private property be theft? Through my private property, do not I deprive another person of this property? Do I not thus violate his right to property?'[3] Marx here used the language of Proudhon, but not his spirit, for he confined himself to strict legal grounds. Men's social relationships would become 'fetishes' – dead things that maintained a secret domination over living men; the natural relationships of domination and possession were reversed, and man was determined

---

[1] See J. Hansen, *Gustav von Mevissen* (Berlin, 1906) I 264 ff.

[2] See H. Stein, 'Karl Marx and der Rheinische Pauperismus', *Jahrbuch des kölnischen Geschichtsvere ins*, XIV (1932).

[3] K. Marx, 'Debates on the Law on Thefts of Wood', *Early Texts*, p. 49.

by timber, because timber was a commodity that was merely an objectified expression of socio-political relationships. Marx maintained that this dehumanisation was a direct consequence of the advice given by the *Preussische Staats-Zeitung* to lawgivers: 'that, when making a law about wood and timber, they are to think only of wood and timber, and are not to try to solve each material problem in a political way – that is, in connection with the whole complex of civic reasoning and civic morality'.[1] Marx concluded his article by comparing an independent observer's impression that wood was the Rhinelanders' fetish with the belief of the Cuban savages that gold was the fetish of the Spaniards.

This article illustrated Marx's growing interest in socio-economic realities. It stuck in his mind as a turning point in his intellectual evolution. As he himself wrote later: 'In the year 1842–3, as Editor of the *Rheinische Zeitung*, I experienced for the first time the embarrassment of having to take part in discussions on so-called material interests. The proceedings of the Rhineland Parliament on thefts of wood, and so on . . . provided the first occasion for occupying myself with the economic questions.'[2] Engels, too, said later that he had 'always heard from Marx, that it was precisely through concentrating on the law of thefts of wood and the situation of the Mosel winegrowers, that he was led from pure politics to economic relationships and so to socialism'.[3]

The Rheinische Zeitung's growing success, together with its criticism of the Rhineland Parliament, so annoyed the Government that the President of the province wrote in November to the Minister of the Interior that he intended to prosecute the author of the article on theft of wood. Relations had already been strained by the publication in the *Rheinische Zeitung* in October of a secret government project to reform the divorce law, the first of Frederick William IV's measures to 'christianise' the law. The paper followed up this exposure with three critical articles, the third of which (in mid-December) was by Marx. He agreed that the present law was too individualistic and did not take into account the 'ethical substance' of marriage in family and children. The law still 'thinks only of two individuals and forgets the family'.[4]

---

[1] K. Marx, *MEGA* I i (1) 304.
[2] K. Marx, 'Preface to A Critique of Political Economy', *MESW* I 361 f.
[3] Engels to R. Fischer, *MEW* xxxix 466.
[4] K. Marx, 'On a Proposed Divorce Law', *MEGA* I i (1) 317.

But he could not welcome the new proposals – for it treated marriage not as an ethical, but as a religious institution and thus did not recognise its secular nature.

By the end of November the break between Marx and his former Berlin colleagues was complete. Matters came to a head with the visit of Ruge and the poet Herwegh to Berlin, where they wished to invite the *Freien* to co-operate in the founding of a new university. Ruge (who was always a bit of a Puritan) and Herwegh were revolted by the licentiousness and extravagant ideas of the *Freien*. According to Ruge, Bruno Bauer, for example, 'pretended to make me swallow the most grotesque things – e.g. that the state and religion must be suppressed in theory, and also property and family, without bothering to know what would replace them, the essential thing being to destroy everything'.[1] On 25 November Marx made his position clear to everyone by publishing a report from Berlin whose essential points were taken from a letter sent by Herwegh to the *Rheinische Zeitung*. The break proved final and Marx justified his action as follows in a letter sent a few days later to Ruge:

> You know that every day the censorship mutilates our paper so much that it has difficulty in appearing. This has obliged me to suppress quantities of articles by the *Freien*. I allowed myself to annul as many as the censor. Meyen and Co. sent us heaps of scrawls pregnant with world revolutions and empty of thought, written in a slovenly style and flavoured with some atheism and communism (which these gentlemen have never studied). . . . I declared that I considered the smuggling of communist and socialist ideas into casual theatre reviews was unsuitable, indeed immoral, and a very different and more fundamental treatment of communism was required if it was going to be discussed at all. I then asked that religion be criticised more through a criticism of the political situation, than that the political situation be criticised through religion. For this approach is more suited to the manner of a newspaper and the education of the public, because religion has no content of its own and lives not from heaven but from earth, and falls of itself with the dissolution of the inverted reality whose theory it is.[2]

The furore caused by the publication of the draft law on divorce had

[1] A. Ruge, *Briefwechsel und Tageblätter*, ed. P. Nerrlich (Berlin, 1886) i 290.
[2] Marx to A. Ruge, *MEW* xxvii 412.

increased governmental pressure on the *Rheinische Zeitung* and Marx found that more and more of his time was taken up in dealing with censorship officials. 'The *Rheinische Zeitung*', wrote Engels, 'managed almost always to get through the most important articles; we first of all fed smaller fodder to the censor until he either gave up his of own accord or was forced to do so by the threat: in that case the paper will not appear tomorrow.'[1] Until December 1842 the censorship was exercised by an official so crass that he was said to have censored an advertisement for a translation of Dante's *Divine Comedy* saying that divine things were no fit subject for comedy. He was frequently not astute enough to note what it was important to censor and, on being reprimanded by his superiors for his negligence, was wont to approach his daily task with the words: 'now my livelihood is at stake. Now I'll cut at everything'.[2] Blos related a story told him by Marx about the same official. 'He had been invited, with his wife and nubile daughter, to a grand ball given by the President of the Province. Before leaving he had to finish work on the censorship. But on precisely this evening the proofs did not arrive. The bewildered censor went in his carriage to Marx's lodging which was quite a distance. It was almost eleven o'clock. After much bell-ringing, Marx stuck his head out of a third-storey window. "The proofs!" bellowed the censor. "Aren't any!" Marx yelled down. "But— !" "We're not publishing tomorrow!" Thereupon Marx shut the window. The censor, thus fooled, was at a loss for words. But he was much more polite thereafter.'[3]

In January 1843, Marx published a piece of research on poverty that was to be his last substantial contribution to the *Rheinische Zeitung*. The Mosel wine-farmers had suffered greatly from competition after the establishment of the *Zollverein*. Already the subject of considerable public outcry, their impoverishment prompted a report in November 1842 from a *Rheinische Zeitung* correspondent whose accuracy was at once questioned by von Schaper, the President of the Rhineland Province. Judging the correspondent's reply unsatisfactory, Marx prepared to substantiate the report himself. He planned a series of five articles. In the event, only three were written and only two were published before the *Rheinische Zeitung* was banned. Comprising a mass of detail to justify his correspondent's assertions, the two published

---

[1] F. Engels, 'Karl Marx', *MEW* xix 97.
[2] Marx to Engels, *MEW* xxxiv 60.
[3] W. Blos, in *Mohr und General* (Berlin, 1965) p. 352.

articles were largely instrumental, in Marx's view, in the suppression of the paper. The conditions in the Mosel valley were due to objectively determined relationships:

> In the investigation of political conditions one is too easily tempted to overlook the objective nature of the relationships and to explain everything from the will of the person acting. There are relationships, however, which determine the actions of private persons as well as those of individual authorities, and which are as independent as are the movements in breathing. Taking this objective standpoint from the outset, one will not presuppose an exclusively good or bad will on either side. Rather, one will observe relationships in which only persons appear to act at first.[1]

To remedy these relations, Marx argued, open public debate was necessary: 'To resolve the difficulty, the administration and the administered both need a third element, which is political without being official and bureaucratic, an element which at the same time represents the citizen without being directly involved in private interests. This resolving element, composed of a political mind and a civic heart, is a free Press.'[2]

Marx must already have had the impression that the days of the *Rheinische Zeitung* were numbered. On 24 December 1842, the first anniversary of the relaxed censorship, the *Leipziger Allgemeine Zeitung*, one of the most important liberal newspapers in Germany, published a letter from Herwegh protesting against the fact that a newspaper he had hoped to edit from Zürich had been forbidden in Prussia. In reply, Herwegh was expelled from Prussia and the *Leipziger Allgemeine Zeitung* was suppressed; on 3 January 1843, under pressure from Frederick William IV, the Saxon Government suppressed the *Deutsche Jahrbücher*; and on 21 January the Council of Ministers presided over by the King decided to suppress the *Rheinische Zeitung*. Marx wrote to Ruge:

> Several particular reasons have combined to bring about the suppression of our paper: our increase in circulation, my justification of the Mosel correspondent which inculpated highly placed politicians, our obstinacy in not naming the person who informed us of

[1] 'On the Distress of the Mosel Wine-Farmers', *MEGA* I i (1) 360; Easton and Guddat, pp. 144 f.
[2] 'On the Distress of the Mosel Wine-Farmers', *Writings of the Young Marx*, pp. 145 f.

the divorce law project, the convocation of the parliaments which we would be able to influence, and finally our criticism of the suppression of the *Leipziger Allgemeine Zeitung* and *Deutsche Jahrbücher*.[1]

In addition, the Tsar had personally protested to the Prussian Government against anti-Russian articles in the *Rheinische Zeitung*. Marx had offered to resign earlier in the hope of saving the paper, but the Government's decision was final.[2] The date picked for the final issue of the paper was 31 March 1843, but the censorship was so intolerable that Marx preferred to resign on 17 March. In a declaration published in the newspaper Marx said that his resignation was due to 'the present state of the censorship',[3] though later he ascribed it to the desire of the shareholders to compromise with the government.[4]

During the last few months, Marx had certainly been the main force behind the paper. By the end of December its circulation had mounted to 3500. On 18 March the censor, Saint-Paul, wrote: 'Today the wind has changed. Yesterday the man who was the *spiritus rector*, the soul of the whole enterprise, finally resigned. . . . I am well content and today I have given to censoring scarcely a quarter of the time that it usually took.'[5] Marx's views were certainly strongly held. Saint-Paul wrote that 'Marx would die for his views, of whose truth he is absolutely convinced'.

The decision to suppress the *Rheinische Zeitung* came as a release: 'The Government', he said, 'have given me back my liberty.'[6] Although he was still writing, he was certain that his future lay abroad: 'In Germany I cannot start on anything fresh; here you are obliged to falsify yourself.'[7] His decision to emigrate was already taken: the only remaining questions were when and where.

---

[1] Marx to A. Ruge, *MEW* xxvii 414.
[2] On this aspect, see further B. Nicolaievsky and O. Maenchen-Helfen, *La Vie de Karl Marx*, pp. 76 f.
[3] Karl Marx, 'Declaration', *MEW* i 200.
[4] Marx to Engels, *MEW* xxxii 128.
[5] *Rheinische Briefen und Akten*, ed. Hansen, i 496.
[6] Marx to A. Ruge, *MEW* xxvii 415.
[7] Ibid.

2

Paris

We are going to France, the threshold of a new world. May
it live up to our dreams! At the end of our journey we will
find the vast valley of Paris, the cradle of the new Europe,
the great laboratory where world history is formed and has
its ever fresh source. It is in Paris that we shall live our vic-
tories and our defeats. Even our philosophy, the field where
we are in advance of our time, will only be able to triumph
when proclaimed in Paris and impregnated with the French
spirit.

A. Ruge, *Zwei Jahre in Paris* (Leipzig, 1846) I 4 ff.

I. MARRIAGE AND HEGEL

WITH THE suppression of the *Rheinische Zeitung*, Marx found himself
once again an unemployed intellectual. His immediate preoccupations
were to find a secure job and get married. As far as journalism was
concerned, Marx's variety had become virtually impossible in Germany. The differences of opinion among the Young Hegelians, already
manifest over their attitude to the *Rheinische Zeitung*, provoked a complete split following the decision of the Prussian Government to
suppress the liberal Press. Those in Berlin, led by Bruno Bauer, tended
more and more to dissociate themselves from political action. They
had imagined their influence to be such that the suppression of their
views would lead to a strong protest among the liberal bourgeoisie.
When nothing of the sort happened, they confined themselves
increasingly to purely theoretical criticism that deliberately re-
nounced all hope of immediate political influence. The response of
the group around Ruge was different: they wished to continue the
political struggle – but in an even more effective manner. A review of
their own still seemed to them the most promising means of political
action, and their first ideas was to base themselves on Julius Froebel's

publishing house in Zürich. Froebel was a Professor of Mineralogy at Zürich who had started his business at the end of 1841 in order to publish the radical poems of Georg Herwegh; he also published a review, edited by Herwegh, which looked for a moment like a successor to the *Deutsche Jahrbücher*. With Herwegh's expulsion from Zürich in March 1843 an obvious gap was waiting to be filled. Ruge was all the more attracted to Zürich as it was (together with Paris) the main centre of German expatriates. Given that these exiles comprised both intellectuals and workers, it was sensible that any new review should combine the theory of the *Deutsche Jahrbücher* with the more immediately political ideas of the *Rheinische Zeitung*. Ruge had a great admiration for Marx and wrote to his brother, Ludwig: 'Marx has great intelligence. He is very worried about his future and particularly his immediate future. So in continuing with the *Jahrbücher* it is quite natural to ask for his assistance.'[1] So when Ruge proposed in January 1843 that he and Marx by co-editors, Marx accepted with enthusiasm.

Naturally Marx's conception of the review was conditioned by his estimate of Germany's political future which he regarded as revolutionary. In March 1843 he wrote: 'You could probably let a shipload of fools sail before the wind for a good while, but it would run into its fate just because the fools did not believe in it. This fate is the revolution which stands before us.'[2] In a letter to Ruge, written two months later for publication in the forthcoming review, Marx took him to task for his pessimistic view of Germany's future. 'It is true', he wrote, 'that the old world is in the possession of the philistine; but we should not treat him as a scarecrow and turn back frightened. Let the dead bury and mourn their dead. In contrast, it is enviable to be the first to go alive into the new life; and this shall be our lot.'[3] After a lengthy analysis of the 'Philistine' nature of contemporary Germany, Marx declared that 'it is only its own desperate situation that fills me with hope'. He was already beginning to envisage the possibility of revolution as consisting in an alliance of 'thinkers' and 'sufferers':

> The system of profit and commerce, of property and human exploitation, leads much more quickly than an increase of population to a rift inside contemporary society that the old society is incapable of healing, because it never heals or creates, but only

[1] A. Ruge, *Briefwechsel*, ed. P. Nerrlich (Berlin, 1886) I 295.
[2] Marx to A. Ruge, 'A Correspondence of 1843', *Early Texts*, p. 74.
[3] Ibid.

exists and enjoys. The existence of a suffering humanity which thinks and a thinking humanity which is oppressed must of necessity be disagreeable and unacceptable for the animal world of philistines who neither act nor think but merely enjoy.

On our side the old world must be brought right out into the light of day and the new one given a positive form. The longer that events allow thinking humanity time to recollect itself and suffering humanity time to assemble itself the more perfect will be the birth of the product that the present carries in its womb.[1]

In view of his revolutionary optimism Marx was definitely against simply continuing the *Deutsche Jahrbücher*. 'Even if the *Jahrbücher* were once again permitted, all we could achieve would be a pale imitation of the extinct review and that is no longer sufficient.'[2] Ruge had at first thought in terms of a series of pamphlets but Marx was strongly in favour of a monthly as a more effective means of propaganda. So he and Ruge decided to give practical expression to the idea of Franco-German co-operation that had been suggested by most of the Young Hegelians at some time or other during the previous two years. The influence of French thought had made the radicals very internationally-minded – in contrast to the liberals whom the crises of the 1840s forced into a narrow nationalism. Hess and Weitling had both learned their socialism in France and Feuerbach had forcefully expressed the idea that the 'new' philosophy, if it wished to be at all effective, would have to combine a German head with a French heart. Marx was extremely enthusiastic at the prospect: 'Franco-German annals – that would be a principle, an event of importance, an undertaking that fills one with enthusiasm.'[3] Froebel agreed to publish a review of this character and preparations began. In May, Marx and Froebel went to visit Ruge in Dresden; Ruge agreed to put up 6000 thalers, Froebel 3000, and the three of them decided on Strasbourg as the place of publication. Marx's immediate future was now guaranteed: as co-editor of the review he had a salary of 550 thalers, and earned a further 250 or so on royalties.

The way was now at last open for marriage. He had written to Ruge in March:

As soon as we have signed the contract I will go to Kreuznach and

---

[1] K. Marx, 'A Correspondence of 1843', *Early Texts*, p. 79.
[2] Marx to A. Ruge, *MEW* XXVII, 416.   [3] Ibid.

get married. . . . Without romanticising, I can tell you that I am head over heels in love and it is as serious as can be. I have been engaged for more than seven years and my fiancée has been involved on my behalf in the toughest of struggles that have ruined her health. These have been in part against her pietist and aristocratic relations, for whom the Lord in Heaven and the Lord in Berlin are the objects of an equal veneration, and in part against my own family where certain radicals and other sworn enemies have insinuated themselves. For years, my fiancée and I have been fighting more useless and exhausting battles than many other persons three times our age – who are for ever talking of their 'experience', a word particularly dear to our partisans of the *juste-milieu*.[1]

The difficulties with Jenny's family had been increased by the arrival of her step-brother Ferdinand, a career civil servant and later Prussian Minister of the Interior, who in 1838 had been appointed to an important post in Trier. It was possibly to avoid his influence that Jenny moved with her mother, probably as early as July 1842, to the spa of Kreuznach about fifty miles east of Trier. Marx paid a visit to her there in March to make plans for the marriage.

As soon as he left, Jenny wrote to him:

I think that you have never been as dear, as sweet, as charming. Every time we parted before I was certainly enraptured with you, and would have had you back to tell you once more how dear, how completely dear you are to me. But this last time you left triumphant; I did not know how dear you were to me in my deepest heart until I no longer saw you in the flesh; I have only the one faithful portrait of you standing so full of life before my soul in all its angelic mildness and goodness, heightened love and spiritual lustre. If you were back here again, my dear little Karl, what a capacity for happiness you would find in your brave little girl; and even if you showed a still worse tendency and even nastier intentions, I would still not take reactionary measures;[2] I would patiently lay down my head, sacrificing it to my naughty boy. . . . Do you still remember our twilight conversation, our beckoning

[1] Ibid.
[2] The language here is ironically borrowed from exchanges between the censorship authorities and the *Rheinische Zeitung*.

games, our hours of slumber. Dear heart, how good, how loving, how attentive, how joyful you were![1]

The letter also contained careful instructions as to what to buy and what not to buy for the wedding which took place in the Protestant Church and registry office in Kreuznach on 19 June 1843. The official registration described the couple as 'Herr Karl Marx, Doctor of Philosophy, residing in Cologne, and Fraulein Johanna Bertha Julie Jenny von Westphalen, no occupation, residing in Kreuznach'. From the two families, only Jenny's mother and brother Edgar were present, the witnesses being acquaintances from Kreuznach.

Marx and Jenny left immediately for a honeymoon of several weeks. They first went to Switzerland to see the Rhine Falls near Schaffhausen and then – travelling through the province of Baden – they took their time on the journey back to Kreuznach. Jenny later told a story that illustrated how extraordinarily irresponsible they both were (and continued to be) in their attitude to money. Jenny's mother had given them some money for the honeymoon and they took it with them, in a chest. They had it with them in the coach during their journey and took it into the different hotels. When they had visits from needy friends they left it open on the table in their room and anyone could take as much as he pleased. Needless to say, it was soon empty.[2]

On returning to Kreuznach, Marx and Jenny lived for three months in her mother's house – which enabled Marx to 'withdraw from the public stage into my study'[3] and get down to writing for the *Deutsch-französische Jahrbücher*. It was clear that the *Jahrbücher* would be a specifically political review. Although Marx had dealt with political subjects in his articles for the *Rheinische Zeitung*, his approach – as was normal in polemical articles – had been very eclectic with lines of argument drawn from Spinoza, Kant and Hegel. Now he felt the need for a more systematic framework of criticism and decided to try to come to terms with Hegel's political philosophy, particularly as expressed in *The Philosophy of Right*. All Hegel's disciples had sooner or later to do this when it became clear that the Prussian Government showed no possibility of becoming Hegel's 'rational state'. Marx had had the idea

[1] Jenny von Westphalen to Marx, *MEW*, Ergsbd. 1 644 f.
[2] Cf. F. Kugelmann, 'Small Traits of Marx's great Character', in *Reminiscences*, p. 279.
[3] K. Marx, 'Preface' to *A Critique of Political Economy*, *MEWS* 1 362.

for at least a year. In March 1842 he had written to Ruge: 'Another article that I also intend for the *Deutsche Jahrbücher* is a critique of the part of Hegel's natural right where he talks of the constitution. The essential part of it is the critique of constitutional monarchy, a bastard, contradictory and unjustifiable institution.'[1] He went on to say that the article was finished and only required rewriting. Six months later he was still talking about publishing it in the *Rheinische Zeitung*. The critique of Hegel's politics that Marx elaborated in the three months he spent at Kreuznach is much richer than the purely logical-political approach of the previous year.

Two factors shaped Marx's view of Hegel's politics. The first was his recent experience as editor of the *Rheinische Zeitung*. Many years later, in the preface to his *Critique of Political Economy*, Marx wrote:

The first work which I undertook for the solution of the doubts which assailed me was a critical review of the Hegelian philosophy of law. . . . My investigation led to the conclusion, firstly, that legal relations as well as forms of state are to be understood neither in themselves nor from the so-called general development of the human mind, but rather have their roots in the material conditions of life (the sum total of which Hegel, following the example of the Englishmen and Frenchmen of the eighteenth century, combines under the name of 'civil society'); but secondly that the anatomy of civil society is to be sought in political economy.[2]

Although this account is too simplified, his experience with the *Rheinische Zeitung* and the rejection of liberal politics by Heine and the socialists (including Hess) enabled his critique of Hegel to take socio-economic factors into account to a much greater extent.

The second factor was the impression made on Marx by his reading of Feuerbach's *Preliminary Theses for the Reform of Philosophy*. Marx had already read Feuerbach when composing his doctoral thesis, but Feuerbach's *magnum opus*, *The Essence of Christianity*, which claimed that religious beliefs were merely projections of alienated human desires and capacities, had not made as great an impression on him as it had on Ruge.[3] But the *Theses* had an immediate and important influence

[1] Marx to A. Ruge, *MEW* xxvii 397.

[2] K. Marx, 'Preface to *A Critique of Political Economy*', *MESW* i 362.

[3] See D. McLellan, *The Young Hegelians and Karl Marx*, pp. 92 ff. That Marx was very probably *not* the author of the article 'Luther as Judge between Strauss and Feuer-

on Marx: they had been published in Switzerland in February 1843 in a collection of essays that had been censored from Ruge's *Deutsche Jahrbücher*. In them Feuerbach applied to speculative philosophy the approach he had already used with regard to religion: theology had still not been completely destroyed; it had a last rational bulwark in Hegel's philosophy, which was as great a mystification as any theology. Since Hegel's dialectic started and ended with the infinite, the finite – namely, man – was only a phase in the evolution of a superhuman spirit: 'The essence of theology is transcendent and exteriorised human thought.'[1] But philosophy should not start from God or the Absolute, nor even from being as predicate of the Absolute; philosophy had to begin with the finite, the particular, the real, and acknowledge the primacy of the senses. Since this approach had been pioneered by the French, the true philosopher would have to be of 'Gallo-Germanic blood'. Hegel's philosophy was the last refuge of theology and as such had to be abolished. This would come about from a realisation that 'the true relationship of thought to being is this: being is the subject, thought the predicate. Thought arises from being – being does not arise from thought.'[2]

Marx read a copy of Feuerbach's *Theses* immediately after publication and wrote an enthusiastic letter to Ruge, who had sent it to him: 'The only point in Feuerbach's aphorisms that does not satisfy me is that he gives too much importance to nature and too little to politics. Yet an alliance with politics affords the only means for contemporary philosophy to become a truth. But what happened in the sixteenth century, when the state had followers as enthusiastic as those of Nature, will no doubt be repeated.'[3] For Marx, the way ahead lay though politics, but a politics which questioned current conceptions of the relationship of the state to society. It was Feuerbach's *Theses* that enabled him to effect his particular reversal of Hegel's dialectic. As far as Marx was concerned in 1843 (and this was true of most of his radical democratic contemporaries also) Feuerbach was *the* philosopher. Every page of the critique of Hegel's political philosophy that Marx elaborated during the summer of 1843 showed the influence of Feuerbach's method.

---

bach' has been shown by H. M. Sass 'Feuerbach Statt Marx', *International Review of Social History* (1967).

[1] L. Feuerbach, *Sämtliche Werke* (Stuttgart, 1959) ii 226.

[2] L. Feuerbach, op. cit., p. 239.

[3] Marx to Ruge, *MEGA* i i (2) 308.

True, Marx gave his criticism a social and historical dimension lacking in Feuerbach, but one point was central to both their approaches: the claim that Hegel had reversed the correct relation of subjects and predicates. Marx's fundamental idea was to take actual political institutions and demonstrate thereby that Hegel's conception of the relationship of ideas to reality was mistaken. Hegel had tried to reconcile the ideal and the real by showing that reality was the unfolding of an idea, and was thus rational. Marx, on the contrary, emphasised the opposition between ideals and reality in the secular world and categorised Hegel's whole enterprise as speculative, by which he meant that it was based on subjective conceptions that were at variance with empirical reality.[1]

Inspired by Feuerbachian philosophy and historical analysis, this manuscript was the first of many works by Marx (up to and including *Capital*) that were entitled 'Critique' – a term that had a great vogue among the Young Hegelians. The approach it represented – reflecting on and working over the ideas of others – was very congenial to Marx, who preferred to develop his own ideas by critically analysing those of other thinkers. Marx's method in his manuscript – which was obviously only a rough first draft – was to copy out a paragraph of Hegel's *The Philosophy of Right* and then add a critical paragraph of his own. He dealt only with the final part of *The Philosophy of Right* which was devoted to the state. According to Hegel's political philosophy – which was part of his general effort to reconcile philosophy with reality – human consciousness manifested itself objectively in man's juridical, moral, social and political institutions. These institutions permitted Spirit to attain full liberty, and the attainment of this liberty was made possible by the social morality present in the successive groups of the family, civil society and the state. The family educated a man for moral autonomy, whereas civil society organised the economic, professional and cultural life. Only the highest level of social organisation – the state, which Hegel called 'the reality of concrete liberty' – was capable of synthesising particular rights and universal

[1] There is an excellent edition of Marx's manuscript: K. Marx, *Critique of Hegel's 'Philosophy of Right'*, ed. J. O'Malley (Cambridge, 1970). See also L. Dupré, *The Philosophical Foundations of Marxism* (New York, 1966) pp. 87 ff.; S. Avineri, 'The Hegelian Origins of Marx's Political Thought', *Review of Metaphysics* (Sep 1967); H. Lefebvre, *The Sociology of Marx* (London, 1968) pp. 123 ff.; J. Hyppolite, 'La Conception hégélienne de l'État et sa critique par Karl Marx', *Études sur Marx et Hegel*, 2nd ed. (Paris, 1965); J. Barion, *Hegel und die marxistische Staatslehre* (Bonn, 1963).

reason into the final stage of the evolution of objective spirit. Thus Hegel rejected the view that man was free by nature and that the state curtailed this natural freedom; and because he believed that no philosopher could move outside his own times and thus rejected theorising about abstract ideals, he considered that the state he described was to some extent already present in Prussia.[1]

In his commentary Marx successively reviewed the monarchical, executive and legislative powers into which (according to Hegel) the state divided itself, and showed that the supposed harmony achieved in each case was in fact false.

With regard to monarchy, Marx's main criticism was that it viewed the people merely as an appendage to the political constitution; whereas in democracy (which was Marx's term at this time for his preferred form of government) the constitution was the self-expression of the people. To explain his view of the relationship of democracy to previous forms of constitution, he invoked a parallel with religion:

Just as religion does not make man but man makes religion, so the constitution does not make the people but the people make the constitution. In a certain respect democracy has the same relation to all the other forms of state as Christianity has to all other forms of religion. Christianity is the religion par excellence, the essence of religion, deified man as a particular religion. Similarly democracy is the essence of all constitutions of the state, socialized man as a particular constitution of the state.[2]

In Greece and the Middle Ages the political aspects of life had been intimately linked with the social ones; it was only in modern times that the political state had become abstracted from the life of society. The solution to this problem in which 'the political constitution was

---

[1] Hegel's political philosophy was undoubtedly rather ambivalent: on the one hand he described the French Revolution as a 'glorious dawn' and throughout his life drank a toast on the anniversary of the fall of the Bastille; on the other hand many of his pronouncements, particularly later in life, tended to a more conservative, not to say reactionary position. On the question of how liberal in politics Hegel really was, see Z. A. Pelczynski's introduction to *Hegel's Political Writings* (Oxford, 1964) and criticism of Pelczynski by Sidney Hook in his articles 'Hegel Re-habilitated', *Encounter* (Jan 1965), and 'Hegel and his Apologists', *Encounter* (May 1966), together with the replies by S. Avineri and Pelczynski, *Encounter* (Nov 1965 and Mar 1966). The two best books on Hegel's politics are S. Avineri, *Hegel's Theory of the Modern State* (Cambridge, 1972) and R. Plant, *Hegel* (London, 1973).

[2] K. Marx, 'Critique of Hegel's Philosophy of Right', *Early Texts*, p. 65.

formerly the religious sphere, the religion of the people's life, the heaven of its universality over against the earthly and real existence' was what Marx called 'true democracy'.[1] This conception could be summed up as a humanist form of government in which free socialised man was the one and only subject of the political process in which the state as such would have disappeared.

Turning to Hegel's views on executive power, Marx produced several interesting passages on bureaucracy which represented his first attempt to give a sociological definition of state power and reflected in part his own difficulties with officialdom when editor of the *Rheinische Zeitung*.[2] Hegel had said that the state mediated between conflicting elements within civil society by means of corporations and bureaucracy: the former grouped individual private interests in order to bring pressure to bear upon the state; the latter mediated between the state and private interests thus expressed. By bureaucracy Hegel meant a body of higher civil servants who were recruited by competition from the middle classes. To them were entrusted the formulation of common interests and the task of maintaining the unity of the state. Their decisions were prevented from being arbitrary by the monarch above them and the pressure of the corporations from below.

Marx began by denouncing this attempted mediation that did not resolve, and at best only masked, historically determined oppositions. Hegel had well understood the process of the dissolution of medieval estates, the growth of industry and the economic war of all against all. Indeed some of Marx's most striking characterisations of the capitalist ethic were taken almost directly from Hegel.[3] But in trying nevertheless to construct a formal state unity, Hegel only created a further alienation: man's being, which was already alienated in monarchy, was now even more alienated in the growing power of the executive, the bureaucracy. All that he offered was an empirical description of bureaucracy, partly as it was, and partly as it pretended to be. Marx rejected Hegel's claim that the bureaucracy was an impartial and thus

[1] K. Marx, *Early Texts*, p. 67.
[2] For later references to bureaucracy in Marx's writings, see Avineri, *The Social and Political Thought of Karl Marx*, pp. 48 ff.; K. Axelos, *Marx, Penseur de la technique* (Paris, 1961) pp. 97 ff.; I. Fetscher, 'Marxismus und Bürokratie', *International Review of Social History*, v (1960).
[3] See R. Heiss, 'Hegel und Marx', *Symposium, Jahrbuch für Philosophie*, i (1948).

'universal' class. He reversed the Hegelian dialectic by asserting that, though their function was in principle a universal one, the bureaucrats had in practice ended by turning it into their own private affair, by creating a group interest separate from society. Thus bureaucracy, being a particular, closed society within the state, appropriated the consciousness, will and power of the state. In the battle against the medieval corporations the bureaucracy was necessarily victorious as each corporation needed it to combat other corporations, whereas the bureaucracy was self-sufficient. Bureaucracy, which came into existence to solve problems and then engendered them in order to provide itself with a permanent *raison d'être*, became an end rather than a means and thus achieved nothing. It was this process that accounted for all the characteristics of bureaucracy: the formalism, the hierarchy, the mystique, the identification of its own ends with those of the state.

Marx summed up these characteristics in a passage whose insight and incisiveness merit lengthy quotation:

Bureaucracy counts in its own eyes as the final aim of the state. . . . The aims of the state are transformed into the aims of the bureaux and the aims of the bureaux into the aims of the state. Bureaucracy is a circle from which no one can escape. Its hierarchy is a hierarchy of knowledge. The apex entrusts the lower echelon with insight into the individual while the lower echelon leaves insight into the universal to the apex, and so each deceives the other.

Bureaucracy constitutes an imaginary state alongside the real state and is the spiritualism of the state. Thus every object has a dual meaning – a real one and a bureaucratic one, just as knowledge is dual – real and bureaucratic (and it is the same with the will). But the real thing is treated according to its bureaucratic essence, its other-worldly spiritual essence. Bureaucracy holds in its possession the essence of the state – the spiritual essence of society; the state is its private property. The general ethos of bureaucracy is secrecy, mystery, safeguarded within by hierarchy and without by its nature as a closed corporation. Thus public political spirit and also political mentality appear to bureaucracy as a betrayal of its secret. The principle of its knowledge is therefore authority, and its mentality is the idolatry of authority. But within bureaucracy the spiritualism turns into a crass materialism, the materialism of passive obedience, faith in authority, the mechanism of fixed and formal behaviour, fixed principles, attitudes, traditions. As far as the individual bureaucrat is concerned, the aim of the state becomes his private aim, in the form of competition for higher posts – careerism. He considers the real life as a material one, for the spirit of this life has its own separate existence in bureaucracy.[1]

Marx's fundamental criticism of Hegel was the same as that contained in the preceding sections: the attributes of humanity as a whole had been transferred to a particular individual or class, which thus represented the illusory universality of modern political life.

Finally Marx dealt with Hegel's discussion of legislative power and particularly the Prussian Estates which, according to Hegel, constituted a synthesis between the state and civil society. Marx objected that such a view in fact presupposed the separation of the state and civil society – regarding them as entities to be reconciled, and therein lay the whole problem since 'the separation of the political state from civil society appears necessarily as a separation of political man – the citizen – from civil society, from his own actual empirical reality'.[2] In order to give himself a historical perspective from which to criticise Hegel, during the summer of 1843 Marx had not only immersed himself in the political theories of Machiavelli, Montesquieu and Rousseau; he also took extensive notes on recent French, English, American and even Swedish history, and wrote a chronological table of the period A.D. 600–1589 that covered eighty pages. These readings led Marx to the conclusion that the French Revolution had completely destroyed any political significance that the Estates enjoyed in the Middle Ages: Hegel's idea of their being adequate representatives of civil society was archaic and indicative of German underdevelopment. Hegel's conceptual framework was based on the ideas of the French Revolution, but his solutions were still medieval; this was a mark of how far the political situation in Germany was retarded when compared with German philosophy. Indeed, the only estate in the medieval sense of the word that still remained was the bureaucracy itself. The enormous increase in social mobility had rendered obsolete the Old Estates as originally differentiated in terms of need and work. 'The only general difference, superficial and formal, is merely that between country and town. But in society itself, differences developed in spheres that were constantly in movement with arbitrariness as their

[1] K. Marx, *Early Texts*, p. 69.
[2] K. Marx, *Critique of Hegel's 'Philosophy of Right'*, p. 78.

principle. Money and education are the main distinguishing characteristics.'[1] Marx broke off here, noting that the proper place to discuss
this would be in later sections (never written) on Hegel's conception
of civil society. He did, however, go on to say, in a remark that fore-
shadowed the future importance of the proletariat in his thought,
that the most characteristic thing about contemporary civil society
was precisely that 'the property-less, the class that stands in immediate
need of work, the class of physical labour, formed not so much a class
of civil society as the basis on which society's components rest and
move'.[2] Marx summarised his objection to Hegel, as follows: 'As soon
as civil estates as such become political estates, then there is no need of
mediation, and as soon as mediation is necessary, they are no longer
political. . . . Hegel wishes to preserve the medieval system of estates
but in the modern context of legislative power; and he wants legislative power, but in the framework of a medieval system of estates! It
is the worst sort of syncretism.'[3]

Since the whole problem arose, in Hegel's view, from the separation
of the state from civil society, Marx saw two possibilities: if the state
and civil society continued to be separate, then all as individuals could
not participate in the legislature except through deputies, the 'expression of the separation and merely a dualistic unity'.[4] Secondly, if
civil society became political society, then the significance of legislative
power as representative disappeared, for it depended on a theological
kind of separation of the state from civil society. Hence, what the
people should aim for was not legislative power but governmental
power. Marx ended his discussion with a passage which makes clear
how, in the summer of 1843, he envisaged future political developments:

> . . . It is not a question of whether civil society should exercise legis-
> lative power through deputies or through all as individuals. Rather
> it is the question of the extent and greatest possible extension of the
> franchise, of active as well as passive suffrage. This is the real bone of
> contention of political reform, in France as well as in England. . . .
> Voting is the actual relationship of actual civil society to the civil
> society of the legislative power, to the representative element. Or,
> voting is the immediate, direct relationship of civil society to the
> political state, not only in appearance but in reality. . . . Only with

---

[1] Ibid., pp. 80f.   [2] Ibid., p. 81.   [3] Ibid., p. 96.   [4] Ibid., p. 119.

universal suffrage, active as well as passive, does civil society actually rise to an abstraction of itself, to political existence as its true universal and essential existence. But the realisation of this abstraction is also the transcendence of the abstraction. By making its political existence actual as its true existence, civil society also makes its civil existence unessential in contrast to its political existence. And with the one thing separated, the other – its opposite – falls. Within the abstract political state the reform of voting is a dissolution of the state, but likewise the dissolution of civil society.[1]

Thus Marx arrived here at the same conclusion as in his discussion of 'true democracy'. Democracy implied universal suffrage, and universal suffrage would lead to the dissolution of the state.

It is clear from this manuscript that Marx was adopting the fundamental humanism of Feuerbach and with it Feuerbach's reversal of subject and predicate in the Hegelian dialectic. Marx considered it evident that any future development was going to involve man's recovery of the social dimension that had been lost ever since the French Revolution levelled all citizens in the political state and thus accentuated the individualism of bourgeois society. Although he was convinced that social organisation had no longer to be based on private property, he was not here explicitly arguing for its abolition, nor did he make clear the various roles of classes in the social evolution. The imprecision of his positive ideas is not at all surprising since Marx's manuscript represented no more than a preliminary survey of Hegel's text; and it was written at a very transient stage in the intellectual evolution of both Marx and his colleagues. Moreover, the surviving manuscript is incomplete and there are references to projected elaborations either never undertaken or now lost.[2]

A letter from Marx to Ruge, written in September 1843 and later published in the Deutsch-französische Jahrbücher, gives a good impression of Marx's intellectual and political position immediately before leaving Germany, and of how much importance he attached to what he called the 'reform of consciousness'. The situation might not be very clear, he wrote, but 'that is just the advantage of the new line:

[1] Ibid., pp. 120f.
[2] Evidence for this is to be found in Marx's manuscript itself. For example, in a phrase about 'starting from self-conscious, real Spirit', he subsequently deleted the word 'self-conscious' which was, no doubt, too reminiscent of Bauer's idealism. See 'Critique of Hegel's Philosophy of the State', MEGA I i (1) 418.

that we do not dogmatically anticipate events but seek to discover the new world by criticism of the old'.[1] What was clear was that all dogmatism was unacceptable, and that included the various communist systems:

> Communism in particular is a dogmatic abstraction, though by this I do not mean any imaginable and possible communism but the really existing communism taught by Cabet, Dezamy, etc. This communism is itself only a peculiar presentation of the humanist principle infected by its opposite: private individualism. The abolition of private property is therefore by no means identical to communism; and it is no accident that communism has seen other socialist doctrines like those of Fourier, Proudhon, etc., necessarily arise in opposition to it, since it is itself only a particular, one-sided realisation of the socialist principle. Moreover, the whole socialist principle is only one facet of the true reality of the human essence.[2]

In Germany, the fulfiment of this human nature depended above all on a critique of religion and politics, for there it was these that were the focal points of interest; ready-made systems were no use; criticism had to take as its starting-point contemporary attitudes. In terms that recall Hegel's account of the progress of Reason in history, Marx asserted: 'Reason has always existed, but not always in rational form.'[3] In any form of practical or theoretical consciousness rational goals were already inherent and awaited the critic who would reveal them.

Thus Marx saw no objection to starting from actual political struggles and explaining why they took place. The point was to demystify religious and political problems by instilling an awareness of their exclusively human dimensions. He ended his letter:

> So our slogan must be: reform of consciousness not through dogmas, but through the analysis of mystical consciousness that is not clear to itself, whether it appears in a religious or political form. It will then be clear that the world has long dreamt of something of which it only needs a fully developed consciousness in order really to possess it. Clearly, the problem does not lie in filling some great void between past ideas and those of the future but in the completion of ideas of the past. Finally, it will be clear that humanity is not

---

[1] Marx to A. Ruge, *Early Texts*, p. 80.
[2] Ibid., pp. 80 f.   [3] Ibid., p. 81.

beginning a new work, but consciously bringing its old work to completion.

So we can summarise the purpose of our journal in one word: self-understanding (meaning critical philosophy) by our age of its struggles and desires. This is a task for the world and for us. It can only be achieved by united forces. What is at stake is a confession, nothing more. To have its sins forgiven, humanity needs only to recognise them as they are.[1]

This notion of salvation through a 'reform of consciousness' was, of course, very idealistic. But this was merely typical of German philosophy at this time. Marx himself was very mindful of the intellectual disarray among the radicals, and wrote to Ruge soon after finishing his critique of Hegel: 'even though the "whence" is not in doubt, yet all the more confusion reigns over the "whither". It is not only that a general anarchy has pervaded the reformers. Everyone will have to admit to himself that he has no exact view of what should happen'.[2] It was the intellectual climate of Paris that finally led Marx to make the transition from the realm of pure theory to the world of immediate, practical politics.

II. THE 'DEUTSCH-FRANZÖSISCHE JAHRBÜCHER'

While Marx in Kreuznach was writing his commentary on Hegel's politics, Ruge had been busy organising the administration of the *Deutsch-französische Jahrbücher*. To finance it, he tried to float a large loan in Germany: when this failed completely he bore virtually the whole cost of publication himself. As a place of publication Strasbourg (which they had previously favoured) was rejected, and Froebel proposed that he and Ruge together go to Brussels and Paris to see which city would be more suitable. At the end of July Ruge travelled west, stopped at Kreuznach to see Marx, and then, joining forces with Hess and Froebel at Cologne, went on to Belgium. Brussels also proved unsatisfactory, for – though its Press enjoyed comparative freedom – the city was too small and not politically-minded. So in August (1843) Hess and Ruge moved on to Paris with a view to establishing the *Deutsch-französische Jahrbücher* there.

It proved difficult to attract contributors – especially ones with a common viewpoint: both Ruge and Froebel were very active in trying

[1] Ibid., p. 82.   [2] Ibid., p. 80.

to get German participation but the liberal writers refused, and of the Berlin Young Hegelians only Bruno Bauer agreed (and in the end even he contributed nothing). So the contributors were reduced to those already associated with Froebel through his Zürich publications: Hess, Engels, Bakunin and Herwegh. Their views were diverse: Hess and Bakunin proclaimed their own brand of eclectic anarcho-communism, whereas Froebel, Herwegh and Ruge vaguely called themselves democrats and emphasised the importance of popular education. As French influence increased the political awareness of the Young Hegelians, the slogan 'radicalism' began to give way to the more specifically political term 'democracy'. But the unity of Ruge's group amounted to little more than a wish to further the political application of Feuerbach's philosophy; and their favourite term was 'humanism'. But Feuerbach himself was unwilling to co-operate. Marx considered that Schelling was enjoying a quite unjustified reputation among the French: just before leaving Kreuznach for Paris, he accordingly wrote to Feuerbach suggesting that he contribute a critique of him:

> These sincere youthful ideas which, with Schelling, remained an imaginative dream of his youth, have with you become truth, reality, and virile earnestness. Schelling is therefore an anticipatory caricature of you, and as soon as the reality appears opposite the caricature it must dissolve into dust or fog. Thus I consider you the necessary and natural opponent of Schelling – summoned by their majesties, Nature and History. Your struggle with him is the struggle of an imaginary philosophy with philosophy itself. . . .[1]

Feuerbach, however, replied that in his opinion the time was not yet ripe for a transition from theory to practice, for the theory had still to be perfected; he told Marx and Ruge bluntly: they were too impatient for action.

All the contributors to the *Deutsch-französische Jahrbücher* were at least united in regarding Paris as both a haven and an inspiration. Their expectations were justified in so far as the revolutions of 1789 and 1830 had made Paris the undisputed centre of socialist thought. The 'bourgeois monarchy' of Louis-Philippe was drawing to its close and becoming more conservative; the censorship laws had been tightened in 1835, and from 1840 onwards the anti-liberal Guizot dominated the Government. But political activity was none the less lively for being

[1] Marx to L. Feuerbach, *Early Texts*, p. 84.

semi-clandestine, and there was a bewildering variety of every conceivable kind of sect, salon and newspaper each proclaiming some form of socialism.[1] As soon as he had arrived in Paris Ruge set out to make contacts, guided by Hess who was familiar with the political scene from his days as French correspondent of the *Rheinische Zeitung*. Ruge's account of his tour of the salons is a catalogue of one misunderstanding after another.[2] Each group thought the other a century out of date. Amazed that he appeared so little versed in communism, the French were equally surprised by his being an advocate of atheism and materialism, watchwords of pre-1789 French thought. For his part, Ruge could not understand how the French could be so attached to religion, which German philosophy had spent such long and involved efforts in neutralising.

Lamartine at first described the conception of the *Deutsch-französische Jahrbücher* as 'holy' and sublime, but later declined to contribute on learning of its revolutionary nature. Leroux was occupied with inventing a new printing machine. Cabet was shocked by Ruge's atheism and lack of commitment to communism. Considérant was also alienated, suspecting that the review would advocate violence. Proudhon was not in Paris. Thus in spite of every effort the *Deutsch-Französische Jahrbücher* appeared without a single French contribution. By November, Ruge began to be anxious even about the number of his German contributors: Herwegh was honeymooning; and Bakunin was leading an errant life after expulsion from Zürich. Their absence was offset by Heine who (having been increasingly sympathetic to socialist ideas during his stay in Paris) agreed to contribute some poems, and also by Ferdinand Bernays (recently expelled from Bavaria after being the editor of the *Mannheimer Abend-Zeitung*).

Marx himself arrived in Paris at the end of October 1843. Jenny, already four months pregnant, came with him. They first lodged at 23 rue Vaneau, a quiet side-street in the St Germain area of the Left Bank where many other German immigrants were concentrated. The 'office' of the *Deutsch-französische Jahrbücher* was on the ground floor of No. 22 and Ruge had rented two floors of No. 23 where Germain Maurer, a leading German socialist writer, was already living. Ruge had written to Marx outlining his project of a 'phalanstery' along

---

[1] For an excellent account of current political groupings and publications, see
P. Kägi, *Genesis des historischen Materialismus* (Vienna, 1965) pp. 157 ff.
[2] G. A. Ruge, *Zwei Jahre in Paris*, I 69 ff.

Fourierist lines: he invited the Marxes, the Herweghs and the Maurers to join him and his wife in an experiment in community living. Each family would have separate living quarters, but there would be a shared kitchen and dining room; the women would take turns with the domestic duties.[1] Emma Herwegh summed up the situation at a glance and refused immediately: 'How could Ruge's wife, a little Saxon woman, nice but characterless, hit it off with Mrs Marx who was very intelligent and still more ambitious and far more knowledgeable than she? How could Mrs Herwegh, the youngest of the three women and so recently married, take to this communal life?'[2] Marx and Jenny did not stay long either: within two weeks they had moved to No. 31 and then in December finally settled at 38 rue Vaneau where they stayed for the rest of their time in Paris.

Marx had brought with him from Kreuznach an essay entitled 'On the Jewish Question', a distillation of his reading the previous summer on France and America. His central problem was still the contemporary separation of the state from civil society and the consequent failure of liberal politics to solve social questions. The question of Jewish emancipation was now of general interest in Prussia where, since 1816, the Jews had enjoyed rights far inferior to those of Christians. Marx himself had been thinking about this issue for some time. As early as August 1842 he had asked Oppenheim to send him all the anti-semitic articles of Hermes, editor of the *Kölnische Zeitung*, who favoured a sort of apartheid for Jews in Germany. Marx made little use of this material but in November 1842 Bauer published a series of articles on the problem in Ruge's *Deutsche Jahrbücher*. Marx considered that Bauer's view were 'too abstract',[3] and decided that a lengthy review would be a convenient peg on which to hang his criticism of the liberal state. In his articles Bauer had claimed that, in order to be able to live together, both Jews and Christians had to renounce what separated them. Neither Christians nor Jews as such could have human rights: so it was not only Jews but all men who needed emancipation. Civil rights were inconceivable under an absolute system. Religious prejudice and religious separation would vanish when civil and political castes and privileges were done away with and all men enjoyed equal rights in a liberal, secular state.

---

[1] Cf. A Ruge to Marx, *MEGA* i i (2) 315.
[2] Quoted in *Karl Marx: Dokumente seines Lebens*, p. 155.
[3] Marx to A. Ruge, *Early Texts*, p. 60.

Marx welcomed Bauer's critique of the Christian state, but attacked him for not calling into question the state as such – and thus failing to examine the relationship of political emancipation (that is, the granting of political rights) to human emancipation (the emancipation of man in all his faculties). Society could not be cured of its ills simply by emancipating the political sphere from religious influence. Marx quoted several authorities to show the extent of religious practice in North American and went on:

> The fact that even in the land of complete political emancipation we find not only the existence of religion but its living existence full of freshness and strength, demonstrates that the continuance of religion does not conflict with or impede the perfection of the state. But since the existence of religion entails the existence of a defect, the source of this defect can only be sought in the nature of the state itself. On this view, religion no longer has the force of a basis for secular deficiencies but only a symptom. Therefore we explain the religious prejudice of free citizens by their secular prejudice. We do not insist that they abolish their religious constraint in order to abolish secular constraints: we insist that they abolish their religious constraints as soon as they have abolished their secular constraints. We do not change secular questions into theological ones: we change theological questions into secular ones. History has for long enough been resolved into superstition: we now resolve superstition into history. The question of the relationship of political emancipation to religion becomes for us a question of the relationship of political emancipation to human emancipation. We criticize the religious weakness of the political state by criticising the secular construction of the political state without regard to its religious weaknesses.[1]

Thus political emancipation from religion did not free men from religious conceptions, for political emancipation was not the same as human emancipation. For example, citizens might still be constrained by a religion from which a state itself had broken free. What Bauer had not realised was that the political emancipation he advocated embodied an alienation similar to the religious alienation he had just criticised. Man's emancipation, because it passed through the intermediary of

[1] K. Marx, 'On the Jewish Question', *Early Texts*, p. 91.

the state, was still abstract, indirect and partial. 'Even when man proclaims himself an atheist through the intermediary of the state – i.e. when he proclaims the state to be atheistic – he still retains his religious prejudice, just because he recognizes himself only indirectly – through the medium of something else. Religion is precisely man's indirect recognition of himself through an intermediary. The state is the intermediary between man and his freedom.'[1]

Similarly with private property: in America it had been abolished as far as the constitution was concerned by declaring that no property qualification was necessary for voting. But this, far from really abolishing private property, actually presupposed it. The result was that man's being was profoundly divided:

> When the political state has achieved its true completion, man leads a double life, a heavenly one and an earthly one, not only in thought and consciousness but in reality, in life. He has a life both in the political community, where he is valued as a communal being, and in civil society where he is active as a private individual, treats other men as means, degrades himself to a means and becomes a tool of forces outside himself.[2]

Political democracy was not, however, to be decried. For it was a great step forward and 'the final form of human emancipation inside the present world order'.[3] Political democracy could be called Christian in that it had man as its principle and regarded him as sovereign and supreme. But unfortunately this meant

> man as he appears uncultivated and unsocial, man in his accidental existence, man as he comes and goes, man as he is corrupted by the whole organization of our society, lost to himself, sold, subjected to domination by inhuman conditions and elements – in a word, man who is no longer a real species-being. The fantasy, dream and postulate of Christianity, the sovereignty of man – but of man as an alien being separate from actual man, is present in democracy as a tangible reality and is its secular motto.[4]

Having shown that religion was more than compatible with *civil* rights, Marx now contested Bauer's refusal to acknowledge the Jewish claim to *human* rights, the rights of man. Bauer had said that neither the Jew nor the Christian could claim universal human rights because

[1] K. Marx, *Early Texts*, p. 92.   [2] Ibid., pp. 93 f.   [3] Ibid., p. 95.   [4] Ibid., p. 99.

their particular and exclusive religions necessarily invalidated any
such claims. Marx refuted Bauer's view by referring to the French and
American Constitutions. Firstly, he discussed the distinction between
the rights of the *citizen* and the rights of *man*. The rights of the citizen
were of a political order; they were expressed in man's participation in
the universality of the state and, as had been shown, by no means
presupposed the abolition of religion. These rights reflected the social
essence of man – though in a totally abstract form – and the reclaiming
of this essence would give rise to human emancipation. Not so the
rights of man in general: being expressions of the division of bourgeois
society they had nothing social about them. As exemplified in the
French Constitutions of 1791 and 1793 and in the Constitutions of
New Hampshire and Pennsylvania, the rights of man did not deny the
right to practise religion; on the contrary, they expressly recognised it,
and Marx quoted chapter and verse to prove it.

Marx then asked: Why are these rights called the rights of *man*?
Because they were the rights of man regarded as a member of civil
society. And why was the member of civil society identified with man?
Because the rights of man were egoistic and anti-social. This was the
case with all the constitutions in question, even the most radical; none
succeeded in subordinating 'man' to the 'citizen'. All the rights of
man that they proclaimed had the same character. Liberty, for
example, 'the right to do and perform what does not harm others',
was, according to Marx, 'not based on the union of man with man but
on the separation of man from man. It is the right to this separation,
the right of the limited individual who is limited to himself.'[1] Property, the right to dispose of one's possessions as one wills without
regard to others, was 'the right of selfishness . . . it leads man to see in
other men not the realisation, but the limitation of his own freedom'.[2] Equality was no more than the equal right to the liberty
described above, and security was the guarantee of egoism.

Thus none of the so-called rights of man went beyond the egoistic
man separated from the community as a member of civil society.
Summarising some of the more detailed analyses of his *Critique of
Hegel's Philosophy of Right*, Marx showed that political emancipation
involved the dissolution of the old feudal society. But the transition
from feudal to bourgeois society had not brought *human* emancipation:

[1] Ibid., p. 102 f.   [2] Ibid., p. 103.

'Man was not freed from religion; he was given religious freedom'.
Marx finished his review by declaring:

> The actual individual man must take back into himself the abstract
> citizen and, as an individual man in his empirical life, in his indivi-
> dual work and individual relationships become a species-being;
> man must recognise his own forces as social forces, organize them
> and thus no longer separate social forces from himself in the form of
> political forces. Only when this has been achieved will human
> emancipation be completed.[1]

In the same article Marx included a much shorter review of an essay
by Bauer entitled 'The Capacity of Present-Day Jews and Christians to
Become Free' which was published in Herwegh's *Twenty-one Sheets from
Switzerland*. Bauer's theme was that the Jew was further removed from
emancipation than the Christian: whereas the Christian had only to
break with his own religion, the Jew had also to break with the completion of his religion, that is, Christianity: the Christian had only one
step to make, the Jew two. Taking issue again with Bauer's theological
formulation of the problem, Marx developed a theme that he had
already touched on in the first part of his article: religion as the
spiritual façade of a sordid and egoistic world. For Marx, the question
of Jewish emancipation had become the question of what specific
social element needs to be overcome in order to abolish Judaism. He
defined the secular basis of Judaism as practical need and self-interest,
the Jew's worldly cult as barter, and his worldly god as money. He
stated in conclusion:

> An organization of society that abolished the presupposition of
> haggling and thus its possibility, would have made the Jew impos-
> sible. His religious consciousness would dissolve like an insipid
> vapour into the real live air of society. On the other hand: if the
> Jew recognises this practical essence of his as void and works for its
> abolition, he is working for human emancipation with his previous
> development as a basis, and turning himself against the highest
> practical expression of human self-alienation.[2]

The Jew had, however, already emancipated himself in a Jewish way.
This had been possible because the Christian world had become
impregnated with the practical Jewish spirit. Their deprivation of

[1] Ibid., p. 108.   [2] Ibid., p. 110.

nominal political rights mattered little to Jews, who in practice wielded
great financial power. 'The contradiction between the Jew's lack of
political rights and his practical political power, is the general contradiction between politics and the power of money. Whereas the first
ideally is superior to the second, in fact it is its bondsman.'[1] The basis
of civil society was practical need, and the god of this practical need
was money – the secularised god of the Jews:

> Money is the jealous god of Israel before whom no other god may
> stand. Money debases all the gods of man and turns them into com-
> modities. Money is the universal, self-constituted value of all things.
> It has therefore robbed the whole world, human as well as natural,
> of its own values. Money is the alienated essence of man's work and
> being; this alien essence dominates him; and he adores it.[2]

Judaism could not develop further as a religion, but had succeeded in
installing itself in practice at the heart of civil society and the Christian
world:

> Judaism reaches its apogee with the completion of civil society; but
> civil society first reaches its completion in the Christian world. Only
> under the domination of Christianity which made all national,
> natural, moral and theoretical relationships exterior to man, could
> civil society separate itself completely from the life of the state, tear
> asunder all the species-bonds of man, put egoism and selfish need
> in the place of these species-bonds and dissolve man into a world of
> atomised individuals hostile to one another.[3]

Thus Christianity, which arose out of Judaism, had now dissolved and
reverted to Judaism.

Marx's conclusion outlined the idea of alienated labour that he
would shortly develop at length:

> As long as man is imprisoned within religion, he only knows how to
> objectify his essence by making it into an alien, imaginary being.
> Similarly, under the domination of egoistic need he can only become
> practical, only create practical objects by putting his products and
> his activity under the domination of an alien entity and lending
> them the significance of this alien entity: money.[4]

[1] Ibid., p. 111.   [2] Ibid., p. 112.   [3] Ibid., p. 113.   [4] Ibid., p. 114.

It is largely this article that has given rise to the view that Marx was an anti-semite. It is true that a quick and unreflective reading of, particularly, the briefer second section leaves a nasty impression. It is also true that Marx indulged elsewhere in anti-Jewish remarks – though none as sustained as here. He was himself attacked as a Jew by many of his most prominent opponents – Ruge, Proudhon, Bakunin and Dühring; but there is virtually no trace of Jewish self-consciousness either in his published writings or in his private letters. An incident that occurred while Marx was in Cologne throws some light on his attitude:

> Just now [he wrote to Ruge in March 1843], the president of the Israelites here has paid me a visit and asked me to help with a parliamentary petition on behalf of the Jews; and I agreed. However obnoxious I find the Israelite beliefs, Bauer's view seems to me nevertheless to be too abstract. The point is to punch as many holes as possible in the Christian state and smuggle in rational views as far as we can. That must at least be our aim – and the bitterness grows with each rejected petition.[1]

Marx's willingness to help Jews of Cologne suggests that his article was aimed much more at the vulgar capitalism popularly associated with Jews than at Jewry as such – either as a religious body or (still less) as an ethnic group. Indeed, the German word for Jewry – *Judentum* – has the secondary sense of commerce and, to some extent, Marx played on this double meaning. It is significant, moreover, that some of the main points in the second section of Marx's article – including the attack on Judaism as the embodiment of a money fetishism – were taken over almost *verbatim* from an article by Hess – who was the very opposite of an anti-semite. (Hess's article, entitled 'On the Essence of Money', had been submitted for publication in the *Deutsch-französische Jahrbücher* but the journal collapsed before it could appear).[2]

The second of Marx's articles in the *Deutsch-französische Jahrbücher* was written after his arrival in Paris: it revealed the immense impact made on him by his discovery there of the class to whose emancipation he was to devote the rest of his life. Paris, the cultural capital of Europe, had a large population of German immigrant workers – almost

[1] Ibid., p. 60. Cf. H. Hirsch, 'Karl Marx and die Bittschriften für die Gleichberechtigung der Juden', *Archiv für Sozialgeschichte* (1968).
[2] Cf. D. McLellan, *The Young Hegelians and Karl Marx*, pp. 152 ff.

100,000. Some had come to perfect the techniques of their various trades; some had come simply because they could find no work in Germany. Marx was immediately impressed:

> When communist artisans form associations, education and propaganda are their first aims. But the very act of associating creates a new need – the need for society – and what appeared to be a means has become an end. The most striking results of this practical development are to be seen when French socialist workers meet together. Smoking, eating and drinking are no longer simply means of bringing people together. Company, association, entertainment which also has society as its aim, are sufficient for them; the brotherhood of man is no empty phrase but a reality, and the nobility of man shines forth upon us from their toil-worn bodies.[1]

Marx attended the meetings of most of the French workers' associations, but was naturally closer to the Germans – particularly to the League of the Just, the most radical of the German secret societies and composed of émigré artisans whose aim was to introduce a 'social republic' in Germany.[2] He knew intimately both its leaders: Ewerbeck, a doctor, and Maurer who had been a member of Ruge's short-lived phalanstery. But he did not actually join any of the societies.[3]

Although Marx's second article ended with the forthright proclamation of the proletariat's destiny, the first part was a reworking of old themes. It was written as an introduction to a proposed rewriting of his *Critique of Hegel's Philosophy of Right*; in fact, several of the arguments outlined in the *Critique* had already been developed in *The Jewish Question*. Being only an introduction, it was in the nature of a summary, ordering its themes in a way that reflected the different phases of Marx's own development: religious, philosophical, political, revolutionary. Taken as a whole, it formed a manifesto whose incisiveness and dogmatism anticipated the *Communist Manifesto* of 1848.

All the elements of the article were already contained in the *Critique of Hegel's Philosophy of Right*, but there was now a quite new emphasis on the proletariat as future emancipator of society. Although written in Paris, the whole article was orientated towards Germany and the

---

[1] K. Marx, *Early Writings*, ed. T. Bottomore (London, 1963) p. 176. There are similarly enthusiastic comments in a letter to Feuerbach, *Early Texts*, p. 185, and in *The Holy Family* (Moscow, 1956) p. 113.

[2] Cf. E. Schraepler, 'Der Bund der Gerechten', *Archiv für Sozialgeschichte* (1962).

[3] K. Marx, 'Herr Vogt', *MEW* xiv 439.

possibility of a German revolution; accordingly it started with religion and went on to politics – the two most pressing subjects in Germany (according to his programmatic letter to Ruge of September 1843).

Marx began with a brilliant passage on religion summarising the whole work of the Young Hegelian school from Strauss to Feuerbach. 'So far as Germany is concerned,' he wrote, 'the criticism of religion is essentially complete, and criticism of religion is the presupposition of all criticism.'[1] This latter assertion doubtless depended on two main factors: in Germany, religion was one of the chief pillars of the Prussian state and had to be knocked away before any fundamental political change could be contemplated; more generally, Marx believed that religion was the most extreme form of alienation and the point where any process of secularisation had to start, and this supplied him with a model for criticism of other forms of alienation. But he differed from Feuerbach in this: it was not simply a question of reduc-tion – of reducing religious elements to others that were more funda-mental Religion's false consciousness of man and the world existed as such because man and the world were radically vitiated: 'The founda-tion of irreligious criticism is this: man makes religion, religion does not make man. But man is no abstract being squatting outside the world. Man is the world of man, the state, society. This state and this society produce religion's inverted attitude to the world because they are an inverted world themselves.'[2] Religion was the necessary idealis-tic completion of a deficient material world and Marx heaped meta-phor on metaphor: 'Religion is the general theory of this world, its encyclopaedic compendium, its logic in popular form, its spiritual *point d'honneur*, its enthusiasm, its moral sanction, its solemn comple-ment, its universal basis for consolation and justification.'[3]

Marx continued with a series of brilliant metaphors to show that religion was at one and the same time both the symptom of a deep social malaise and a protest against it. Religion nevertheless stood in the way of any cure of social evil since it tended at the same time to justify them. Thus,

> the struggle against religion is indirectly the struggle against that world whose spiritual aroma is religion. Religious suffering is at the same time an expression of real suffering and a protest against real

[1] K. Marx, 'Introduction to *A Critique of Hegel's Philosophy of Right*', *Early Texts*, p. 115.
[2] K. Marx, *Early Texts*, pp. 115 f.
[3] Ibid., p. 116.

suffering. Religion is the sign of the oppressed creature, the feeling of a heartless world and the soul of soulless circumstances. It is the opium of the people. . . . The criticism of religion is therefore the germ of the criticism of the valley of tears whose halo is religion.[1]

Marx did not write much about religion (Engels wrote much more) and this is the most detailed passage in all his writings. What he said here – that religion is a fantasy of alienated man – is thoroughly in keeping with his early thought. (Later, the element of class ideology was to be much more dominant.) He thought religion at once important and unimportant: important, because the purely spiritual compensation that it afforded men detracted from efforts at material betterment; unimportant, because its true nature had been fully exposed, in his view, by his colleagues – particularly by Feuerbach. It was only a secondary phenomenon and, being dependent on socioeconomic circumstances, merited no independent criticism.

Attempts to characterise Marxism as a religion, although plausible within their own terms, confuse the issue, as also do attempts to claim that Marx was not really an atheist. This is the usual approach of writers who stress the parallel between Marxism and the Judaeo-Christian history of salvation[2] – though some say that Marx took over this tradition when already secularised by Schelling or Hegel into an aesthetic or philosophical revelation.[3] It is true that Marx had in mind the religion of contemporary Germany dominated by a dogmatic and over-spiritual Lutheranism, but he wrote about 'religion' in general and his rejection was absolute. Unlike so many early socialists (Weitling, Saint-Simon, Fourier), he would brook no compromise. Atheism was inseparable from humanism, he maintained; indeed, given the terms in which he posed the problem, this was undeniable. It is, of course, legitimate to change the meaning of 'atheism' in order to make Marx a believer *malgré lui*, but this tends to make the question senseless by blurring too many distinctions.[4]

Marx then turned from a summary of past criticism, and what it had achieved, to current developments:

Criticism has plucked the imaginary flowers from the chains not so

[1] Ibid.
[2] See, for example, R. Tucker, *Philosophy and Myth in Karl Marx* (Cambridge, 1961).
[3] See H. Popitz, *Der entfremdete Mensch* (Basel, 1953).
[4] The best general discussions of this topic are the two books by H. Desroches, *Marxisme et religions* (Paris, 1962); *Socialismes et sociologie religieuse* (Paris, 1965).

that man may bear chains without any imagination or comfort, but so that he may throw away the chains and pluck living flowers. The criticism of religion disillusions man so that he may think, act and fashion his own reality as a disillusioned man come to his senses; so that he may revolve around himself as his real sun. Religion is only the illusory sun which revolves around man as long as he does not revolve around himself.[1]

Criticism had, consequently, to turn to a deeper alienation, that of politics:

It is therefore the task of history, now the truth is no longer in the beyond, to establish the truth of the here and now. The first task of philosophy – which is in the service of history – once the holy form of human self-alienation has been discovered, is to discover self-alienation in its non-religious forms. The criticism of heaven is thus transformed into the criticism of earth, the criticism of religion into the criticism of law, and the criticism of theology into the criticism of politics.[2]

Following this introduction, the body of Marx's article consisted of two parts: an analysis of the gap between the reactionary nature of German politics and the progressive state of German philosophy; and the possibilities of revolution arising from this contrast. Marx began by pointing out that even the necessary negation of Germany's present was anachronistic and would still leave Germany fifty years behind France.

Indeed, German history can congratulate itself on following a path that no people in the historical firmament have taken before and none will take after it. For we have shared with modern peoples in restorations without sharing their revolutions. We have had restorations, firstly because other peoples dared to make a revolution, and then because they suffered a counter-revolution; because our masters were at the one moment afraid and at another not afraid. Without shepherds at our head, we always found ourselves in the company of freedom only once – on the day of its burial.[3]

But there was, Marx argued, one aspect in which Germany was actually in advance of other nations and which afforded her the

[1] K. Marx, *Early Texts*, p. 116.   [2] Ibid.,   [3] Ibid., p. 117.

opportunity for a radical revolution: her philosophy. This view, shared by all the contributors to the *Deutsch-Französische Jahrbücher*, made them appear to the French as some sort of missionaries; it had been current in the Young Hegelian movement since Heine (in his *History of Religion and Philosophy in Germany*, written in 1835) had drawn a parallel between German philosophy and French politics and prophesied a radical revolution for Germany as a consequence. To be at the heart of contemporary questions it was German philosophy that had to be criticised. In Germany it was only political philosophy that was abreast of modern conditions.

Marx then clarified his own position by pointing to two different attitudes both of which seemed to him to be inadequate. The first, which in some respects recalled the views of Feuerbach, Marx called the 'practical political party':

> This party is justified in demanding the negation of philosophy. Their error consists not in their demand, but in being content with a demand that they do not and cannot really meet. They believe that they can complete that negation by turning their back on philosophy. You ask that we start from the real seeds of life, but forget that until now the real seed of the German people has only flourished inside its skull. In a word: you cannot transcend philosophy without giving it practical effect.[1]

The second attitude, characteristic of the theoretical party – by which Marx meant Bruno Bauer and his followers – committed the same error but from the opposite direction:

> It sees in the present struggle nothing but the critical struggle of philosophy with the German world and does not reflect that earlier philosophy itself has belonged to this world and is its completion, albeit in ideas. Its principal fault can be summed up thus: it thought it could give practical expression to philosophy without transcending it.[2]

Bauer's philosophy, because it refused any mediation with the real, was undialectical and condemned to sterility. What Marx proposed was a synthesis of the two views he condemned: a mediation with the real that would abolish philosophy 'as philosophy' while giving it practical expression. This was akin to his later advocacy of the 'unity of

[1] Ibid., p. 121.   [2] Ibid., pp. 121 f.

theory and practice', and took up a theme that had been in his mind since his doctoral thesis (if not before): that of the secularisation of philosophy. From Cieszkowski's *praxis* in 1838 to Hess's 'Philosophy of Action' in 1843 this was a theme central to Hegel's disciples trying to break loose from their master's system so as to get to grips with contemporary events. It was along these lines that Marx saw the only possible way of solving Germany's political problems.

In the second part of his article, Marx then turned to an exploration of the possibility of a revolution that would not only eliminate Germany's backwardness, but also thrust her into the forefront of European nations by making her the first to have achieved emancipation that was not merely political. Thus he put the question: 'Can Germany achieve a *praxis* that will be equal to her principles, i.e. can she achieve a revolution that will not only raise her to the official level of modern peoples but to the human level that is the immediate future of these peoples?'[1] By way of a preliminary answer, Marx recapitulated his previous conclusion:

> The weapon of criticism cannot, of course, supplant the criticism of weapons; material force must be overthrown by material force. But theory, too, will become material force as soon as it seizes the masses. Theory is capable of seizing the masses as soon as its proofs are *ad hominem* and its proofs are *ad hominem* as soon as it is radical. To be radical is to grasp the matter by the root. But for man the root is man himself. The manifest proof of the radicalism of German theory and its practical energy is that it starts from the decisive and positive abolition of religion. The criticism of religion ends with the doctrine that man is for himself the highest being – that is, with the categorical imperative to overthrow all systems in which man is humiliated, enslaved, abandoned and despised.[2]

The importance of the 'weapon of criticism' for Germany was shown by Luther's revolution of theory – the Reformation. Of course this revolution was an incomplete one: Luther had merely internalised man's religious consciousness; he had 'destroyed faith in authority by restoring the authority of faith'.[3] But although Protestantism had not found the true solution, at least its formulation of the problem had been correct. The present situation of Germany was similar to that

---

[1] Ibid., p. 122.   [2] Ibid., pp. 122 f.   [3] Ibid., p. 123.

which preceded the Reformation; the only difference was that philosophy took the place of theology and the result would be a human
emancipation instead of one that took place entirely within the sphere
of religion.

In the final, pregnant pages of the article Marx drew from his sombre
review of the German scene the optimistic conclusion that the revolution in Germany, as opposed to France, could not be partial and had
to be radical; and only the proletariat, in alliance with philosophy,
would be capable of carrying it out. Marx began with the difficulties
that seemed to stand in the way of a radical German revolution.
'Revolutions need a passive element, a material basis. A theory will
only be implemented among a people in so far as it is the implementation of what it needs.'[1] And 'a radical revolution can only be a revolution of radical needs whose presuppositions and breeding-ground seem
precisely to be lacking'.[2] But the very fact that Germany was so
deficient politically indicated the sort of future that awaited her:
'Germany is the political deficiencies of the present constituted into a
world of their own and as such will not be able to break down specifically German barriers without breaking down the general barriers of
the political present.'[3] What was utopian for Germany was not a
radical revolution that would achieve the complete emancipation of
mankind but a partial revolution, a revolution that was merely
political, a revolution 'that leaves the pillars of the house still standing'.[4] Marx then characterised a purely political revolution, obviously
taking the French Revolution as his paradigm:

> A part of civil society emancipates itself and achieves universal
> domination, a particular class undertakes the general emancipation
> of society from its particular situation. This class frees the whole
> of society, but only on the supposition that the whole of society is
> in the same situation as this class – that it possesses, or can easily
> acquire (for example) money and education.[5]

No class could occupy this 'special situation' in society without

> arousing an impulse of enthusiasm in itself and among the masses.
> It is a moment when the class fraternizes with society in general and
> merges with society; it is identified with society and is felt and
> recognized as society's general representative. Its claims and rights

[1] Ibid., p. 124. [2] Ibid. [3] Ibid., p. 125. [4] Ibid. [5] Ibid.

are truly the claims and rights of society itself of which it is the real social head and heart.[1]

And for a class to be able to seize this emancipatory position, there had to be a polarisation of classes:

> One particular class must be a class that rouses universal reproba-
> tion and incorporates all deficiencies: one particular social sphere
> must be regarded as the notorious crime of the whole society, so
> that the liberation of this sphere appears as universal self-liberation.
> So that one class *par excellence* may appear as the class of liberation,
> another class must conversely be the manifest class of oppression.[2]

This, according to Marx, was the situation in France before 1789 when 'the universally negative significance of the French nobility and clergy determined the universally positive significance of the class nearest to them and opposed to them: the bourgeoisie'.[3]

In Germany, the situation was very different. For there every class lacked the cohesion and courage that could cast it in the role of the negative representative of society, and every class also lacked the imagination to identify itself with the people at large. Class-consciousness sprang from the oppression of a lower class rather than from defiant protest against oppression from above. Progress in Germany was thus impossible, for every class was engaged in a struggle on more than one front:

> Thus the princes are fighting against the king, the bureaucracy
> against the nobility, the bourgeoisie against all of them, while the
> proletariat is already beginning its fight against the bourgeoisie. The
> middle class scarcely dares to conceive of emancipation from its
> own point of view and already development in social circumstances
> and political theory make this point of view itself antiquated or at
> least problematical.[4]

Marx then summarised the contrast he had been elaborating between France and Germany:

> In France it is enough that one should be something in order to wish
> to be all. In Germany one must be nothing, if one is to avoid giving
> up everything. In France partial emancipation is the basis of univer-
> sal emancipation, in Germany universal emancipation is a *sine qua*

---

[1] Ibid.   [2] Ibid., p. 126.   [3] Ibid.   [4] Ibid., p. 127.

non of every partial emancipation. In France it is the reality, in Germany the impossibility, of a gradual liberation that must give birth to total freedom. In France every class of the people is politically idealistic and is not primarily conscious of itself as a particular class but as a representative of general social needs. The role of emancipator thus passes in a dramatic movement to different classes of the French people until it comes to the class which no longer brings about social freedom by presupposing certain conditions that lie outside mankind and are yet created by human society, but which organizes the conditions of human existence by presupposing social freedom. In Germany, on the contrary, where practical life is as unintellectual as intellectual life is unpractical, no class of civil society has the need for, or capability of, achieving universal emancipation until it is compelled by its immediate situation, by material necessity and its own chains.[1]

This passage shows the importance of Marx's study of the French Revolution in the formation of his views. The Rhineland – where he was born and spent his early life – had been French until 1814, and had enjoyed the benefits of the French Revolution where civil emancipation was a genuine experience and not a possession of foreigners only, to be envied from afar. To all German intellectuals the French Revolution was *the* revolution, and Marx and his Young Hegelian friends constantly compared themselves to the heroes of 1789. It was his reading of the history of the French Revolution in the summer of 1843 that showed him the role of class struggle in social development.[2]

Approaching the conclusion of his article, Marx introduced the *dénouement* with the question: 'So where is the real possibility of German emancipation?' His answer was:

... in the formation of a class with radical chains, a class in civil society that is not a class of civil society, the formation of a social group that is the dissolution of all social groups, the formation of a sphere that has a universal character because of its universal sufferings and lays claim to no particular right, because it is the object of no particular injustice but of injustice in general. This class can no

---

[1] Ibid.

[2] While at Kreuznach Marx had read, and took many extracts from, the works of Wachsmuth, Condorcet, Madame Roland, Madame de Staël, Mignet, Thiers, Buchez and Roux, Bailleul and Levasseur.

longer lay claim to a historical status, but only to a human one. It is not in a one-sided opposition to the consequences of the German political regime; it is in total opposition to its presuppositions. It is, finally, a sphere that cannot emancipate itself without emancipating itself from all other spheres of society and thereby emancipating these other spheres themselves. In a word it is the complete loss of humanity and this can only recover itself by a complete redemption of humanity. This dissolution of society, as a particular class, is the proletariat.[1]

This passage raises an obvious and crucial question as to the reasons for Marx's sudden adherence to the cause of the proletariat. Some have claimed that Marx's description of the proletariat is non-empirical and thus that its ultimate source is Hegel's philosophy. It has, for example, been maintained that 'The insight into the world-historical role of the proletariat is obtained in a purely speculative manner by a "reversal" of the connection that Hegel had established between different forms of objective spirit.'[2] Others have claimed that Hegel's insights were fundamentally those of a German Protestant and thus that Marx's underlying schema here was the Christian conception of salvation – the proletariat played the role of Isaiah's suffering servant:

Through Hegel, the young Marx links up, no doubt unconsciously, with the soteriological schema underlying the Judaeo-Christian tradition: the idea of the collective salvation obtained by a particular group, the theme of salvic destitution, the opposition of injustice that enslaves and generosity that frees. The proletariat, bringing universal salvation, plays a role analogous to that of the messianic community or personal saviour in biblical revelation.[3]

Or even more explicitly: 'That the universality of the proletariat echoes the claims of the universal Christ is confirmed by Marx's insistence that the proletariat will exist, precisely at the point when it becomes universal, in a scourged and emptied condition – and this, of course, is Marx's variant of the divine kenosis.'[4] Others have claimed that, since

---

[1] K. Marx, Early Texts, pp. 127 f.
[2] M. Friedrich, Philosophie und Oekonomie beim jungen Marx (Berlin, 1962) p. 81, following H. Popitz, Der entfremdete Mensch (Basel, 1967) p. 99.
[3] Wackenheim, La Faillite de la religion d'après Karl Marx (Paris, 1963) p. 200.
[4] E. Olssen, 'Marx and the Resurrection', Journal of the History of Ideas (1968) p. 136

Marx's views are not empirically based, this shows that they have their origin in a moral indignation at the condition of the proletariat.

All these interpretations are mistaken – at least as attempts at total explanation. Marx's proclamation of the key role of the proletariat was a contemporary application of the analysis of the French Revolution outlined earlier in his article, when he talked of a particular social sphere having 'to be regarded as the notorious crime of the whole society so that the liberation of this sphere appears as universal self-emancipation'.[1] The proletariat was now in the position the French bourgeoisie had occupied in 1789. It was now the proletariat which could echo the words of Siéyès, 'I am nothing and I should be everything'. The context thus shows that Marx's account of the role of the proletariat was drawn from his study of the French Revolution, however much his language may be that of Young Hegelian journalism.

To this historical base was added a distillation of contemporary French socialist ideas. For three months already Marx had lived and worked with prominent socialists in Paris. The view of the proletariat contained in his article was not unique even in Young Hegelian circles, but it was of course commonplace in Paris.[2]

Marx's sudden espousal of the proletarian cause can be directly attributed (as can that of other early Germany communists such as Weitling and Hess) to his first-hand contacts with socialist intellectuals in France. Instead of editing a paper for the Rhineland bourgeoisie or sitting in his study in Kreuznach, he was now at the heart of socialist thought and action. He was living in the same house as Germain Maurer, one of the leaders of the League of the Just whose meetings he frequented. From October 1843 Marx was breathing a socialist atmosphere. It is not surprising that his surroundings made a swift impact on him.[3]

---

[1] K. Marx, *Early Texts*, p. 126.

[2] It is surprising, then, that some have argued that Lorenz von Stein's book *Socialism and Communism in Contemporary France* was instrumental in his conversion. The book had first appeared eighteen months previously when Marx was not responsive to socialist ideas; though it had wide influence on the German radical circles in which he moved, it had apparently made no impact on him at that time. Further on Stein, see K. Mengelberg, 'Lorenz von Stein and his Contribution to Historical Sociology', *Journal of the History of Ideas*, XII (1961); and J. Weiss, 'Dialectical Idealism and the Work of Lorenz von Stein', *International Review of Social History*, VII (1963).

[3] On the immense interest in 'social questions' in Germany in the mid-1840s,

Marx admitted that the proletariat he described was only just beginning to exist in Germany – indeed, factory workers constituted no more than 4 per cent of the total male population over the age of fourteen.[1] What characterised it was not natural poverty (though this had a part to play) but poverty that was artificially produced and resulted particularly in the disintegration of the middle class. The proletariat would achieve the dissolution of the old older of society by the negation of private property, a negation of which it was itself the embodiment. This was the class in which philosophy could finally give itself practical expression: 'As philosophy finds its material weapons in the proletariat, so the proletariat finds its intellectual weapons in philosophy, and as soon as the lightning of thought has struck deep into the virgin soil of the people, the emancipation of the Germans into men will be completed.'[2] The signal for this revolution would come from France: 'When all internal conditions are fulfilled, the day of German resurrection will be heralded by the crowing of the Gallic cock.'[3]

The first double-number of the *Deutsch-französische Jahrbücher* was also the last. Having clamped down on the Press inside Prussia, the Government there was particularly anxious to avoid the importation of seditious literature. The propagation of communist ideas was explicitly forbidden in Prussia and several of the articles in the *Jahrbücher* had a distinctly socialist flavour. The German authorities acted swiftly: the journal was banned in Prussia, several hundred copies being seized on entry. Warrants were issued for the arrest of Marx, Heine and Ruge; and for the first time in his life Marx had become a political refugee. The *Jahrbücher* met with little success in France; there were no French contributors and it attracted virtually no comment in the French Press. Froebel withdrew from the enterprise, both because he was unwilling to risk losing more money and because he disliked the revolutionary tone of the first number. But the fate of the *Jahrbücher* was finally sealed by the increasing divergence in the views of the two

---

and the literature to which this gave rise, see K. Obermann, 'Die soziale Frage in den Anfängen der sozialistischen und kommunistischen Bewegung in Deutschland, 1843–45', *Annali* (1963).

[1] Cf. P. Noyes, *Organization and Revolution* (Princeton, 1966) pp. 15 ff., and for France in particular, R. Price, *The French Second Republic* (London, 1972) ch. 1.

[2] K. Marx, *Early Texts*, p. 128.

[3] Ibid., p. 129.

co-editors. Ruge had been ill during the weeks immediately preceding publication, and most of the crucial editorial work had fallen on Marx. Ruge was rather dismayed to see that the general impression left by the body of the *Jahrbücher* was considerably different from his own vaguely humanist Preface; he appreciated the articles by Marx but thought them too stylish and epigrammatic. There were also problems of finance: Ruge had paid Hess an advance for articles he in fact failed to write, and wanted it back immediately – which annoyed Hess who had no money (and knew anyway that Ruge had just made a considerable amount through lucky speculation in railway shares). Marx urged Ruge to continue publication: Ruge refused and by way of payment for Marx's contributions gave him copies of the single issue of the *Jahrbücher*. Marx's finances were, however, re-established by the receipt in mid-March 1844 of 1000 thalers (about twice his annual salary as co-editor), sent on the initiative of Jung by the former shareholders of the *Rheinische Zeitung*.[1]

During the spring of 1844 Marx and Ruge were still in close contact. What led to the final break between them was Marx's overt adoption of communism and his rather bohemian life-style. He had not used the term 'communism' in the *Jahrbücher* but by the spring of 1844 Marx had definitely adopted the term as a brief description of his views.[2] Ruge could not stand communists. 'They wish to liberate people', he wrote to his mother with the bitterness of one whose financial resources had been called on just once too often, 'by turning them into artisans and abolishing private property by a fair and communal repartition of goods; but for the moment they attach the utmost important to property and in particular to money. . . .'[3] Their ideas, he wrote further, 'lead to a police state and slavery. To free the proletariat intellectually and physically from the weight of its misery, they dream of an organisation that would generalise this misery and make all men bear its weight.'[4] Ruge had a strong puritan streak and was also exasperated by the sybaritic company Marx was keeping. The poet Herwegh had recently married a rich banker's daughter and was leading the life of a playboy: according to Ruge,

One evening our conversation turned to the relations of Herwegh

<hr>

[1] Cf. K. Marx: *Chronik seines Lebens in Einzeldaten* (Frankfurt, 1971) p. 21.
[2] On what Marx understood by the term at this date, see pp. 116 ff. below.
[3] A. Ruge, *Briefwechsel*, ed. P. Nerrlich (Berlin 1886) I 341.
[4] A. Ruge, op. cit., I 346.

with the Countess d'Agoult.[1] I was just at that time occupied in trying to restart the *Jahrbücher* and was outraged by Herwegh's style of life and laziness. I referred to him several times as a wanton and said that when someone got married he ought to know what he was doing. . . . Marx said nothing and took friendly leave of me. But the next day he wrote to me that Herwegh was a genius with a great future in front of him and that he had been angry to hear me treat him as a wanton, adding that I had a narrow-minded outlook lacking in humanity. . . . He could no longer work with me as I was only interested in politics, whereas he was a communist.[2]

Thereafter the break between the two men was complete. Marx publicised these disagreements later that summer by means of a sharp attack on an article Ruge had written concerning a weavers' revolt in Silesia. Several thousand weavers had smashed the newly introduced machinery that had driven down their wages, and had been repressed with great brutality. Ruge's article criticising the paternalistic attitude of Frederick William IV to social problems appeared in *Vorwärts*, a new twice-weekly publication that had become (largely owing to the flair of its editor, F. C. Bernays) the main forum for radical discussion among German émigrés. Bernays, who had recently fled from Baden, was a journalist of some resource: in order to make the conservative Press in Germany appear ridiculous he had once wagered that in one week he could get them to print fifty items of manifest stupidity; he won his bet and republished the items in book-form. In his article Ruge rightly denied that the weavers' rebellion was of any immediate importance: no social revolt, he said, could succeed in Germany since political consciousness was extremely underdeveloped and social reform sprang from political revolution.

Marx published his reply in *Vorwärts* at the end of July 1844. He attached a quite unrealistic weight to the weavers' actions and favourably contrasted the scale of their revolt with workers' revolts in England. A political consciousness was not sufficient to deal with social poverty: England had a very developed political consciousness, yet it was the country with the most extensive pauperism. The British Government had an enormous amount of information at its disposal

---

[1] Formerly mistress of the composer Liszt.

[2] A. Ruge, op. cit., I 350, and *Zwei Jahre in Paris* (Leipzig, 1946) II 140. See further F. Mehring's Introduction to *Aus dem literarischen Nachlass von K. Marx, F. Engels, F. Lassalle*, II 13 ff.

but, after two centuries of legislation on pauperism, could find nothing better than the workhouse. In France, too, the Convention and Napoleon had unsuccessfully tried to suppress beggary. Thus the fault was not in this or that form of the state – as Ruge believed – and the solution could not be found in this or that political programme. The fault lay in the very nature of political power:

> From the political point of view the state and any organisation of society are not two distinct things. The state is the organisation of society. In so far as the state admits the existence of social abuses, it seeks their origin either in natural laws that no human power can control or in the private sector which is independent of it or in the inadequacy of the administration that depends on the state. Thus, Britain sees misery as founded in the natural law according to which population must always outstrip the means of subsistence; on the other hand, it explains pauperism by the cussedness of the poor; whereas the King of Prussia explains it by the un-Christian spirit of the rich, and the Convention by the counter-revolutionary and suspicious attitude of the property-owners. Therefore, Britain punishes the poor, the King of Prussia exhorts the rich and the Convention beheads the property owners.[1]

Thus if the state wanted to transcend the impotence of its administration it would have to abolish itself, for the more powerful the state and the more developed the political consciousness of a nation, the less it was disposed to seek the cause of social ills in the state itself. Marx once again substantiated his point by reference to the French Revolution, whose heroes 'far from seeing the source of social defects in the state, see in social defects the source of political misfortunes'.[2]

Thus for Marx it was not 'political consciousness' that was important. The Silesian revolt was even more important than revolts in England and France because it showed a more developed class-consciousness. After favourably comparing Weitling's works with those of Proudhon and the German bourgeoisie, Marx repeated his prediction made in the Deutsch-Französische Jahrbücher of the role of the proletariat and the chances of a radical revolution:

The German proletariat is the theoretician of the European prole-

[1] K. Marx, 'Critical Remarks on the Article: The King of Prussia and Social Reform', Early Texts, p. 213.   [2] K. Marx, Early Texts, p. 220.

tariat, as the English proletariat is its economist and the French its politician. It must be admitted that Germany has a vocation for social revolution that is all the more classic in that it is incapable of political revolution. It is only in socialism that a philosophical people can find a corresponding activity, and thus only in the proletariat that it finds the active element of its freedom.[1]

Marx finished his article with a passage that gave a concise summary of his studies of social change:

A social revolution, even though it be limited to a single industrial district, affects the totality, because it is a human protest against a dehumanized life, because it starts from the standpoint of the single, real individual, because the collectivity against whose separation from himself the individual reacts is the true collectivity of man, the human essence. The political soul of revolution consists on the contrary in a tendency of the classes without political influence to end their isolation from the top positions in the state. Their standpoint is that of the state – an abstract whole, that only exists through a separation from real life. Thus a revolution with a political soul also organizes, in conformity with its limited and double nature, a ruling group in society to society's detriment.[2]

Thus Ruge's idea that social revolution necessarily had a political soul was the opposite of the truth:

Every revolution is social insofar as it destroys the old society. Every revolution is political insofar as it destroys the old power. . . . Revolution in general – the overthrow of the existing power and dissolution of previous relationships – is a political act. Socialism cannot be realized without a revolution. But when its organizing activity begins, when its particular aims are formulated, when its soul comes forward, then socialism casts aside its political cloak.[3]

This controversy marked the end of all contact with Ruge. Although Marx continued his friendship with Herwegh, this also did not last long, and Marx soon admitted that there was something after all in Ruge's strictures. Herwegh's sybaritic character and his sentimental version of communism could never harmonise with the temperament and ideas of Marx of whom Herwegh wrote at the time that 'he

---

[1] Ibid., p. 221.   [2] Ibid., p. 220.   [3] Ibid., p. 221.

would have been the perfect incarnation of the last scholastic. A tire-less worker and great *savant*, he knew the world more in theory than in practice. He was fully conscious of his own value. . . . The sarcasms with which he assailed his adversaries had the cold penetration of the executioner's axe.'[1] Disillusioned with Herwegh, Marx spent more and more time with Heine, the only person he declared himself sorry to leave behind on his expulsion from Paris.

Heine had made Paris his base immediately after the 1830 revolution there. As well as flourishing as a poet in a city which could boast Musset, Vigny, Sainte-Beuve, Ingres and Chopin among many other famous cultural figures, Heine was much attracted to the doctrines of Saint-Simon and the later French socialists. Embittered by the banning of his books in Prussia, he regarded the success of communism as inevitable, but feared the triumph of the masses and 'the time when these sombre inconoclasts will destroy my laurel groves and plant potatoes'.[2] His friendship with Marx coincided with much of his best satirical verse in which Marx is said to have encouraged him with the words: 'Leave your everlasting complaints of love and show the satiric poets the real way of going about it – with a whip!'[3] According to Eleanor:

> There was a period when Heine came daily to see Marx and his wife to read them his verse and hear their opinion of it. Marx and Heine could endlessly revise a little ten-line poem – weighing every word, correcting and polishing it until everything was perfect and every trace of their working-over had disappeared. Much patience was necessary as Heine was extremely sensitive to any sort of criticism. Sometimes he arrived at the Marxes literally in tears because an obscure writer had attacked him in a journal. Marx's best tactic then was to address him to his wife whose kindness and wit soon brought the despairing poet to reason.[4]

Heine also had the distinction of saving the life of the Marxes' first baby: he arrived one day to find the child having convulsions and

---

[1] G. Herwegh, *Briefwechsel*, ed. M. Herwegh (Munich, 1898) p. 328.

[2] H. Heine, *Lutèce*, 2nd ed. (Paris, 1855) p. xii. [3] A. Ruge, *Briefwechsel*, II 346.

[4] Eleanor Marx, in *Die neue Zeit*, XIV (1896) I 16 f. These reminiscences, and the following story which comes from the same source, are not, of course, entirely reliable. See L. Marcuse, 'Heine and Marx: A History and a Legend', *Germanic Review* (1955); W. Victor, *Marx und Heine* (Berlin, 1952); and especially N. Reeves, 'Heine and the Young Marx', *Oxford German Studies* (1972–3).

both parents at their wits' end; he immediately prescribed a hot bath, prepared it himself, and bathed the baby, who at once recovered.

Marx also spent a lot of his time in the company of Russian aristocratic émigrés who, he said later, 'fêted' him throughout his stay.[1] These included his later adversary Bakunin with whom Marx seems to have been on friendly terms. The same cannot be said of the Polish Count Cieszkowski, author of a seminal book at the beginning of the Young Hegelian movement, of whom Marx later recalled that 'he so bored me that I wouldn't and couldn't look at anything that he later perpetrated'.[2] Marx naturally passed much of his time with French socialists – such as Louis Blanc, and particularly Proudhon (also a subsequent adversary) whose unique brand of anarcho-socialism had already made him the most prominent left-wing thinker in Paris. Marx later claimed that he was responsible for teaching Proudhon about German idealism: 'In long discussions that often last the whole night, I injected him with large doses of Hegelianism; this was, moreover, to his great disadvantage as he did not know German and could not study the matter in depth.'[3] The most that can be said is that Marx shared this distinction with Bakunin.[4]

III. THE 'PARIS MANUSCRIPTS'

Marx thrived in this perfervid intellectual atmosphere. However much Ruge might disapprove of what he considered Marx's disorderly life, cynicism and arrogance, he could not but admire his capacity for hard work.

> He reads a lot. He works in an extrordinarily intense way. He has a critical talent that degenerates sometimes into something which is simply a dialectical game, but he never finishes anything – he interrupts every bit of research to plunge into a fresh ocean of books. . . .

[1] Marx to Kugelmann, MEW xxxII 567. Cf. D. Ryazanov, 'Marx and seine Bekannten in den vierzigen Jähren', Die neue Zeit, xxxI (1913).

[2] Marx to Engels, MEW xxxv 35.

[3] Marx to Schweitzer, MESW I 392. See also, F. Engels, Introduction to K. Marx, The Poverty of Philosophy (New York, 1963) p. 7.

[4] Herzen recalled in his Memoirs that Karl Vogt – against whom Marx later polemicised at extraordinary length – once got so bored during an evening at Bakunin's when Proudhon was there discussing Hegel's Phenomenology that he went home. He returned the next morning and 'was amazed to hear a loud conversation at that hour of the morning . . . on opening the door he saw Proudhon and Bakunin still sitting in the same places in front of the dead embers of the fire, concluding the discussion they had started the evening before'.

He is more excited and violent than ever, especially when his work
has made him ill and he has not been to bed for three or even four
nights on end.[1]

Marx intended to continue his critique of Hegel's politics, then he
intended to do a history of the Convention; 'he always wants to write
on what he has read last, yet continues to read incessantly, making
fresh excerpts'.[2] If Marx wrote anything substantial on Hegel's politics
or the Convention, it has not survived. During July and August,
however, Marx had a period of peace and quiet that he put to good use.
On 1 May their first child was born – a girl, called Jenny after her
mother. The baby was very sickly and Jenny took her away to Trier for
two months to show her to the family there and obtain the advice of
her old doctor. While his wife and baby were away Marx made volu-
minous notes on classical economics, communism and Hegel. Known
as the 'Economic and Philosophical Manuscripts' or '1884 Manuscripts',
these documents (when fully published in 1932) were hailed by some
as his most important single piece of work. Four of the manuscripts
which were to form the basis of this critique of political economy have
survived, though in an incomplete form. The first – twenty-seven
pages long – consists largely of excerpts from classical economists on
wages, profit and rent, followed by Marx's own reflections on alienated
labour. The second is a four-page fragment on the relationship of
capital to labour. The third is forty-five pages long and comprises a
discussion on private property, labour and communism; a critique of
Hegel's dialectic; a section on production and the division of labour;
and a short section on money. The fourth manuscript, four pages
long, is a summary of the final chapter of Hegel's *Phenomenology*.

The manuscripts as a whole were the first of a series of drafts for a
major work, part of which, much revised, appeared in 1867 as *Capital*.
In a preface sketched out for this work Marx explained why he could
not fulfil the promise (made in the *Deutsch-Französische Jarhbücher*) to
publish a critique of Hegel's philosophy of law:

While I was working on the manuscript for publication it became
clear that it was quite inappropriate to mix criticism directed purely
against speculation with that of other and different matters, and
that this mixture was an obstacle to the development of my line of

[1] Cf. A. Ruge, *Briefwechsel*, I 343.
[2] A. Ruge to Dunker, *Tägliche Rundschau*, 22 July 1921.

thought and to its intelligibility. Moreover, the condensation of such rich and varied subjects into a single work would have permitted only a very aphorisitic treatment; and furthermore such an aphorisitic presentation would have created the appearance of an arbitrary systematization.[1]

He therefore proposed to deal with the various subjects – among them law, morals, politics – in separate 'booklets', beginning with political economy and ending with a general treatise showing the interrelationship between the subjects, and criticising the speculative treatment of the material. In this project for a lifetime's work, Marx never got beyond the first stage: *Capital* and its predecessors.

Marx had been reading economics in a desultory manner since the autumn of 1843 and by the spring of 1844 he had read and excerpted all the main economists from Boisguillebert and Quesnay in the late seventeenth century to James Mill and Say. He also mentioned his debt to unspecified French and English socialists and, among his fellow countrymen, to Weitling, Hess and Engels. Marx had been much impressed by Engels' essay in the *Deutsch-Französische Jahrbücher* entitled 'Outlines of a Critique of Political Economy' and excerpts from it headed Marx's Paris notebooks. Central to the article was an indictment of private property and of the spirit of competition that it engendered. The recurrent crises were the result of anarchy in production; the growth and accumulation of capital involving a lowering of salaries and accentuated the class struggle. Science and technology, which could afford immense possibilities under communism, only served, in a capitalist society, to increase the oppression of the workers

Marx later called Engels' article a 'brilliant sketch'[2] and quoted from it several times in *Capital*. His reading it marked the real beginning of his lifelong interest in economic questions. Engels (like Hess) would have described himself as a disciple of Feuerbach; and certainly in all of Marx's Paris notes Feuerbach's humanism is quite central. Positive criticism, and thus also German positive criticism of political economy, was founded, Marx claimed, on Feuerbach's discoveries in his 'Thesen' and *Grundsätze*. 'The first positive humanist and naturalist criticism dates from Feuerbach. The less bombastic they are, the more sure, deep, comprehensive and lasting is the effect of Feuerbach's works,

[1] K. Marx, 'Paris Manuscripts', *Early Texts*, p. 131.
[2] K. Marx, 'Preface to *A Critique of Political Economy*', *MESW* I 364.

the only ones since Hegel's *Phenomenology* and *Logic* to embody a real theoretical revolution.'[1]

Marx's first manuscript was mainly economic and started with extracts or paraphrases from the books on economics that he was reading at that time.[2] He divided these extracts into three sections on wages, capital and rent, each occupying one of the three vertical columns into which Marx had divided his pages. In the first, drawing on Adam Smith, Marx noted that the bitter struggle between capitalist and worker which determined wages also reduced the worker to the status of a commodity. The worker could not win: if the wealth of society was diminishing, it was he who suffered most; if it was increasing, then this meant that capital was being accumulated and the product of labour was increasingly alienated from the worker.

Political economy, said Marx, dealt with man in much the same terms as it dealt with, say, a house. It did not deal with man 'in his free time, as a human being'; this aspect it left to other disciplines. And he continued:

Let us now rise above the level of political economy and seek from the foregoing argument, which was presented almost in the words of the economists, answers to two questions:

1. What is the significance, in the development of mankind, of this reduction of the greater part of mankind to abstract labour?

2. What errors are committed by the advocates of piecemeal reform, who either want to raise wages and thereby improve the conditions of the working class, or (like Proudhon) regard equality of wages as the aim of social revolution?[3]

To answer these two questions Marx amassed a series of quotations from three sources: firstly from the German writer Wilhelm Schulz on workers' pauperisation, the dehumanising effect of machinery and the number of women and children working;[4] secondly from Constantin Pecqueur on the dependence and degradation forced on

[1] K. Marx, 'Paris Manuscripts', *Early Texts*, p. 132.
[2] On the economic parts of the Manuscripts, see particularly, E. Mandel, *The Formation of the Economic Thought of Karl Marx* (London, 1971) ch. 2; J. Maguire, *Marx's Paris Writings* (Dublin, 1972) ch. 3.
[3] K. Marx, *Early Writings*, pp. 76 f.
[4] Cf. W. Schulz, *Die Bewegung der Produktion. Eine geschichtlich-statistische Abhandlung* (Zürich, 1843). The economic sections of the Manuscripts show the influence of Schulz more than any other writer.

workers under capitalism;[1] thirdly from Eugène Buret on the wretchedness and exploitation of the proletariat.[2]

In his second section Marx noted a number of passages under the heading 'Profit of Capital'. First, quoting Adam Smith, he defined capital as the power of command over labour and its products. He then described the means by which capitalists made a profit both from wages and from raw materials advanced; the motives that inspired the capitalist; and the accumulation of capital and competition among capitalists. Marx's third section was on rent and he outlined the similarities between landlord and capitalist: in the last analysis there was no distinction between them and society was divided into two classes only – workers and capitalists. The character of landed property had been utterly transformed since feudal times and neither the preservation of large estates nor their division into small properties could avoid precipitating a crisis. Later in the manuscript Marx offered his own trenchant critique of the 'Protestant ethic' enshrined in the classical economists:

> Thus, despite its worldly and pleasure-seeking appearance, it is a truly moral science and the most moral of all sciences. Its principal thesis is the renunciation of life and of human needs. The less you eat, drink, buy books, go to the theatre or to balls, or to the public house, and the less you think, love, theorise, sing, paint, fence, etc., the more you will be able to save and the greater will become your treasure which neither moth nor rust will corrupt – your capital. The less you are, the less you express your life, the more you have, the greater is your alienated life and the greater is the saving of your alienated being.[3]

At this point in his manuscript Marx broke off writing in three parallel columns and began to write straight across the page. He also changed his style, writing now without recourse to quotation from other writers. This passage on alienated labour is the best-written part

[1] C. Pecqueur, *Théorie nouvelle d'économie sociale et politique* (Paris, 1842). Pecqueur advocated a democratic, fairly centralised socialism and criticised capitalism as contrary to religion and morality.

[2] E. Buret, *De la misère des classes laborieuses en Angleterre et en France* (Paris, 1840). Buret's book is a well-documented account both of the horrors of the Industrial Revolution and of the positive possibilities it offers to men. For the influence of Buret on Marx's economic conceptions, see G. Cottier, *Du romantisme au marxisme* (Paris, 1961).

[3] K. Marx, *Early Writings*, p. 171.

of the manuscripts. In it Marx criticised the concept of labour found in the classical economists from whom he had just been quoting, on the general grounds that their conceptions were superficial and abstract whereas his own gave a coherent account of the essential nature of economics. Having started from their presuppositions Marx claimed to show that the more the worker produced the poorer he became. But this analysis remained superficial:

> Political economy starts with the fact of private property, it does not explain it to us. It conceives of the material process that private property in fact goes through in general abstract formulae which then have for it the value of laws. . . . But political economy tells us nothing about how far these external, apparently fortuitous circumstances are merely the expression of a necessary development. We have seen how it regards exchange itself as something fortuitous. The only wheels that political economy sets in motion are greed and war among the greedy: competition.[1]

But because the classical economists had failed to understand the necessary connection and development of different economic factors, they could give no coherent account of economics. He, on the contrary, aimed 'to understand the essential connection of private property, selfishness, the separation of labour, capital and landed property, of exchange and competition, of the value and degradation of man, of monopoly and competition, etc. – the connection of all this alienation with the money system'.[2] The usual method of the economist was to suppose a fictitious primordial state and to proceed from there; but this simply accepted as a fact what it was supposed to be explaining: 'Similarly the theologian explains the origin of evil through the fall, i.e. he presupposes as a historical fact what he should be explaining.'[3]

Before introducing his main point, Marx once more insisted on its empirical basis. 'We start', he says, 'with a contemporary fact of political economy.'[4] This fact was the general impoverishment and dehumanisation of the worker. Marx developed the implications of this, thus introducing the theme of this section:

> The object that labour produces, its product, confronts it as an

---

[1] K. Marx, 'Paris Manuscripts', *Early Texts*, pp. 133 f.
[2] K. Marx, *Early Texts*, p. 134. [3] Ibid. [4] Ibid.

alien being, as a power independent of the producer. The product of labour is labour that has solidified itself into an object, made itself into a thing, the objectification of labour. The realization of labour is its objectification. In political economy this realization of labour appears as a loss of reality for the worker, objectification as a loss of the object or slavery to it, and appropriation as alienation, as externalization.[1]

Simply stated, what Marx meant when he talked of alienation was this: it is man's nature to be his own creator; he forms and develops himself by working on and transforming the world outside him in co-operation with his fellow men. In this progressive interchange between man and the world, it is man's nature to be in control of this process, to be the initiator, the subject in which the process originates. However, this nature has become alien to man; that is, it is not longer his and belongs to another person or thing. In religion, for example, it is God who is the subject of the historical process. It is God who holds the initiative and man is in a state of dependence. In economics, according to Marx, it is money or the cash-nexus that manoeuvres men around as though they were objects instead of the reverse. The central point is that man has lost control of his own destiny and has seen this control invested in other entities. What is proper to man has become alien to him, being the attribute of something else.[2]

Having discussed this relationship of the worker to the objects of his production, Marx defined and analysed three further characteristics of alienated man. The second was his alienation in the act of production. 'How would the worker be able to confront the product of his work as an alien being if he did not alienate himself in the act of production itself?'[3] Marx distinguished three aspects of this type of alienation: firstly, labour was external to the worker and no part of his nature; secondly, it was not voluntary, but forced labour; and thirdly, man's activity here belonged to another, with once more the religious parallel: 'As in religion the human imagination's own activity, the

---

[1] Ibid., pp. 134 f.

[2] Marx used two German words to express his ideas of alienation: they were *Entäusserung* and *Entfremdung*. Strictly speaking, the first emphasises the idea of dispossession and the second the idea of something being strange and alien. Marx seemed to use the two terms indiscriminately, sometimes using both together for rhetorical emphasis.

[3] K. Marx, *Early Texts*, p. 137.

activity of man's head and his heart, reacts independently on the individual as an alien activity of gods or devils, so the activity of the worker is not his own spontaneous activity. It belongs to another and is the loss of himself.'[1] The result of this was to turn man into an animal, for he only felt at ease when performing the animal functions of eating, drinking and procreating – in his distinctly human functions he was made to feel like an animal.

Marx had analysed man as alienated from the product of his labour and also as alienated in the act of production (this second he also called 'self-alienation'). He then derived his third characteristic of alienated labour from the two previous ones: man was alienated from his species, from his fellow men. Marx then defined what he meant by 'species', a term he took over from Feuerbach. The two chief characteristics of a species-being were self-consciousness and universality: 'Man is a species-being not only in that practically and theoretically he makes both his own and other species into his objects, but also, and this is only another way of putting the same thing, he relates himself as to the present, living species, in that he relates to himself as to a universal and therefore free being.'[2] This universality consisted in the fact that man could appropriate for his own use the whole realm of inorganic nature. It was true that animals also produced – but only what was immediately necessary for them. It was man's nature, on the other hand, to produce universally and freely: he was able 'to produce according to the measure of every species and knows everywhere how to apply its inherent standard to the object; thus man also fashions things according to the laws of beauty'.[3]

Marx then completed his picture by drawing a fourth characteristic of alienation out of the first three: every man was alienated from his fellow men.

> In general, the statement that man is alienated from his species-being means that one man is alienated from another as each of them is alienated from the human essence. The alienation of man and generally of every relationship in which he stands is first realized and expressed in the relationship in which man stands to other men. Thus in the situation of alienated labour each man measures his relationship to other men by the relationship in which he finds himself placed as a worker.[4]

[1] Ibid.   [2] Ibid., p. 138.   [3] Ibid., p. 140.   [4] Ibid., p. 141.

The fact that both the product of man's labour and the activity of production had become alien to him meant that another man had to control his product and his activity.

> Every self-alienation of man from himself and nature appears in the relationship in which he places himself and nature to other men distinct from himself. Therefore religious self-alienation necessarily appears in the relationship of layman to priest, or, because here we are dealing with a spiritual world, to a mediator, etc. In the practical, real world, the self-alienation can only appear through the practical, real relationship to other men.[1]

Marx went on to point to practical consequences as regards private property and wages, which followed from his conclusion that social labour was the source of all value and thus of the distribution of wealth. He used his conclusion to resolve two contemporary problems. The first was the utter rejection of any system that involved the paying of wages. Wages only served to reinforce the notion of private property and thus even the proposal of Proudhon that all wages should be equal was quite misconceived. Secondly, Marx considered – extremely optimistically – that universal human emancipation could be achieved through the emancipation of the working class, since 'the whole of human slavery is involved in the relationship of the worker to his product'.[2]

He next planned to extend the entire discussion to all aspects of classical economics – barter, competition, capital, money – and also to a comparison of the relative alienations of the capitalist and the worker.[3] But the manuscript broke off, unfinished.

In spite of the incompleteness of the manuscript, it is possible to infer what the remaining portion would have contained. In his notebooks of this time, Marx set down his reflections on his reading of the classical economists. His note on James Mill's *Elements of Political Economy* is exceptionally long and rich: in it Marx dealt with the categories of classical economics he had planned to discuss in the unfinished part of his manuscript on alienated labour – barter, competition, capital and money. He concentrated on the dehumanising effect of money

---

[1] Ibid., p. 142.   [2] Ibid., p. 144.
[3] See further on this point G. Cohen, 'Bourgeois and Proletarians', *Journal of the History of Ideas* (Jan 1968).

and private property, finishing with an account of his conception of unalienated labour which was the positive side of his critique of alienated labour. Marx began his note by criticising Mill's attempt to formulate precise 'laws' in economics, a field so chaotic and open to constant fluctuation; and proceeded to comment on Mill's description of money as the medium of exchange. In capitalist society, Marx argued, money alone gave significance to man's relationship to his fellow men and even to his products.

The note-books deal extensively with the problem of credit. Credit only increased the dehumanising power of money:

> Credit is the economic judgement on the morality of a man. In credit, man himself, instead of metal or paper, has become the mediator of exchange but not as man, but as the existence of capital and interest. Human individuality, human morality, has itself become both an article of commerce and the form in which money exists. Instead of money, paper is my own personal being, my flesh and blood, my social value and status, the material body of the spirit of money.[1]

The credit system, according to Marx, had four main characteristics: it increased the power of the wealthy – for credit was more readily available to those who already had money; it added a moral judgement to an economic one, by implying that a man without credit was untrustworthy; it compelled people to try to obtain credit by lying and deceit; and finally, credit reached its perfection in the banking system. In a short section on money later in the manuscript Marx quoted extensively from Goethe's *Faust* and Shakespeare's *Timon of Athens* to show that money was the ruin of society. Since money could purchase anything, it could remedy all deficiences: it was 'the bond of all bonds'.[2] 'Since money is the existing and self-affirming concept of value and confounds and exchanges all things, it is the universal confusion and exchange of all things, the inverted world, the confusion and exchange of all natural and human qualities.'[3] In truly human society where man was man – then everything would have a definite, human value and only love could be exchanged for love, and so on.

[1] K. Marx, 'On James Mill', *Early Texts*, p. 192.
[2] K. Marx, 'Paris Manuscripts, *Early Texts*, p. 181.
[3] Ibid., p. 182.

It was in contrast to this society based on money and credit that Marx outlined his idea of man's authentic social existence:

> Since human nature is man's true communal nature, men create and develop their communal nature by their natural action; they develop their social being which is no abstract, universal power as opposed to single individuals, but the nature of each individual, his own activity, his own life, his own enjoyment, his own wealth. Therefore this true communal nature does not originate in reflection, it takes shape through the need and egoism of individuals, i.e. it is produced directly by the effect of their being. It is not dependent on man whether this communal being exists or not; but so long as man has not recognized himself as man and has not organized the world in a human way, this communal nature appears in the form of alienation – because its subject, man, is a self-alienated being. Men – not in the abstract, but as real, living, particular individuals -- are this nature.[1]

With the transformation of labour into wage-labour, this alienation was inevitable. In primitive barter men only exchanged the surplus of their own produce. But soon men produced with the sole object of exchanging and finally 'it becomes quite accidental and inessential whether the producer derives immediate satisfaction from a product that he personally needs, and equally whether the very activity of his labour enables him to fulfil his personality, realize his natural capacities and spiritual aims'.[2] This process was only accelerated by the division of labour that increased with civilisation and meant that 'you have no relationship to my object as a human being because I myself have no human relation to it'.[3]

Marx finished his note on money with a description of unalienated labour and this is one of the few passages where he described in any detail his picture of the future communist society. It is therefore worth quoting at length:

> Supposing that we had produced in a human manner; in his production each of us would have doubly affirmed himself and his fellow men. (1) I would have objectified in my production my

---

[1] K. Marx, 'On James Mill', *Early Texts*, pp. 193 f.
[2] Ibid., pp. 197 f.   [3] Ibid., p. 201.

individuality and its peculiarity, and would thus have enjoyed in my activity an individual expression of my life and would have also had – in looking at the object – the individual pleasure of realizing that my personality was objective, visible to the senses and therefore a power raised beyond all doubt; (2) in your enjoyment or use of my product I would have had the direct enjoyment of realizing that by my work I had both satisfied a human need and also objectified the human essence and therefore fashioned for another human being the object that met his need. (3) I would have been for you the mediator between you and the species and thus been felt by you and acknowledged as a completion of your own essence and a necessary part of yourself, and I would thereby have realized that I was confirmed both in your thought and in your love; (4) in my expression of my life I would have fashioned your expression of your life, and thus in my own activity have realized my own essence, my human, communal essence. In such a situation our products would be like so many mirrors, each one reflecting our essence. Thus, in this relationship what occurred on my side would also occur on yours. My work would be a free expression of my life, and therefore a free enjoyment of my life. In work the peculiarity of my individuality would have been affirmed since it is my individual life. Work would thus be genuine, active property. Presupposing private property, my individuality is so far externalised that I hate my activity: it is a torment to me and only the appearance of an activity and thus also merely a forced activity that is laid upon me through an external, arbitrary need – not an inner and necessary one.[1]

Marx's basic thesis was thus that man's objectification of himself in capitalist society denied his species-being instead of confirming it. He asserted that this was a judgement based purely on a study of economic facts; he claimed to be using the evidence presented by the classical economists themselves and only criticising their premises. Several times he claimed merely to be giving expression to economic facts; and in the introduction to the manuscripts as a whole, he wrote: 'I do not need to reassure the reader who is familiar with political economy that my results have been obtained through a completely empirical analysis founded on a conscientious and critical study of political

[1] Ibid., pp. 202 f.

economy.'[1] However, his use of terms like 'alienation' and 'the realisation of the human essence' plainly show that Marx's analysis was not a purely scientific one. Nor was it empirical, if this is taken to mean devoid of value judgements. For Marx's description was full of dramatically over-simplified pronouncements that bordered on the epigrammatic. And while the economic analysis was taken over from classical economics, the moral judgements were inspired by the reading (noted above) of Schulz, Pecqueur, Sismondi and Buret. In order to understand Marx's claims, it is important to realise that 'empirical' for him did not involve a fact-value distinction (an idea he would have rejected) but merely that the analysis (wherever it might lead) started in the right place – with man's material needs.[2]

The second of Marx's manuscripts provided the kernel to his 1844 writings and it is this one that has aroused most enthusiasm among later commentators. It is certainly a basic text for anyone interested in 'socialism with a human face'. In it Marx outlines in vivid and visionary language his positive counter-proposal to the alienation suffered by man under capitalism – a proposal he called 'communism'. His conceptions obviously reflected the first of many long debates with German workers and with French socialists whose deficiencies he remarked on at the outset. Proudhon, for example, had advocated the abolition of capital; and Fourier and Saint-Simon had traced the alienation of labour to a particular form of labour. Fourier had consequently advocated a return to agricultural labour; whereas Saint-Simon saw the essential solution in terms of the correct organisation of industrial labour. Communism, however, went further than these partial insights and represented 'the positive expression of the overcoming of private property'.[3] Naturally, the idea of communism had its own intellectual history and developed only by stages.

The first form to appear – what Marx called 'crude' communism – was merely the universalisation of private property. 'This sort of communism is faced with such a great domination of material property that it seeks to destroy everything that cannot be possessed by

[1] K. Marx, 'Paris Manuscripts', *Early Texts*, p. 131.

[2] For a closely argued analysis of the empirical features of Marx's doctrine of alienation, see D. Braybrooke, 'Diagnosis and Remedy in Marx's Doctrine of Alienation', in *Social Research* (Autumn 1958). There are several pieces of research that take Marx's doctrine as a basis. One of the best known is R. Blauner, *Alienation and Freedom* (Chicago, 1964).

[3] K. Marx, 'Paris Manuscripts', *Early Texts*, p. 146.

everybody as private property; it wishes to abstract forcibly from talent, etc. It considers immediate physical ownership as the sole aim of life and being.'[1] This conception of communism had its counterpart in the proposal to abolish marriage and substitute the community of women. For it was the relationship between the sexes that was 'the immediate, natural and necessary relationship of human being to human being. . . .'

> By systematically denying the personality of man this communism is merely the consistent expression of private property which is just this negation. Universal envy setting itself up as a power is the concealed form of greed which merely asserts itself and satisfies itself in another way. How little this abolition of private property constitutes a real appropriation is proved by the abstract negation of the whole world of culture and civilization, a regression to the unnatural simplicity of the poor man without any needs who has not even arrived at the stage of private property, let alone got beyond it.[2]

Here the only community was a community of (alienated) labour and the only equality was one of wages paid out by the community as universal capitalist.

The second form of communism that Marx branded as inadequate was of two sorts: the first he described as 'still political in nature, whether democratic or despotic', and the second as achieving 'the abolition of the state, but still incomplete and under the influence of private property, i.e., of the alienation of man'.[3] Of both these forms Marx commented (rather obscurely):

> Communism knows itself already to be the reintegration or return of man into himself, the abolition of man's self-alienation. But since it has not yet grasped the positive essence of private property nor the human nature of needs, it is still imprisoned and contaminated

[1] Ibid.

[2] Ibid., pp. 146 f. Marx seems here to be referring to two groups active in Paris at that time – the 'Travailleurs Égalitaires' and the 'Humanitaires'. The former were followers of Babeuf with strong anti-cultural tendencies; the latter were well known for their attacks on marriage and the family. See further, P. Kägi, Genesis des historischen Materialismus, pp. 328 ff.; E. Dolléans, Histoire du mouvement ouvrier (Paris, 1957) I 179.

[3] K. Marx, Early Texts, p. 148.

by private property. It has understood its concept, but not yet its essence.[1]

The 'democratic' communism that Marx mentioned here must have been the utopian, non-violent sort advocated by Étienne Cabet which was increasingly popular in Paris about this time, particularly in the League of the Just; the 'despotic' type probably alluded to the transitory dictatorship of the proletariat advocated by the followers of Babeuf. The second type of communism, involving the abolition of the state, was represented by Dezamy (who coined the famous phrase about an accountant and a register being all that was necessary to ensure the perfect functioning of the future communist society).

Thirdly, Marx described in a few tightly written and pregnant pages his own idea of communism – the culmination of previous inadequate conceptions:

> Communism is the positive abolition of private property and thus of human self-alienation and therefore the real reappropriation of the human essence by and for man. This is communism as the complete and conscious return of man – conserving all the riches of previous development for man himself as a social, i.e. human, being. Communism as completed naturalism is humanism and as completed humanism is naturalism. It is the genuine resolution of the antagonism between man and nature and between man and man. It is the true resolution of the struggle between existence and essence, between objectification and self-affirmation, between freedom and necessity, between individual and species. It is the solution to the riddle of history and knows itself to be this solution.[2]

Having thus outlined his own conception of communism, Marx went on to enlarge on three of its particular aspects: its historical bases, its social character, and its regard for the individual.

Dealing with the first aspect – the historical bases of communism – Marx drew a further distinction between his own communism and the 'underdeveloped' variety. The latter types (he cited as examples the utopian communism of Cabet and Villegardelle) tried to justify themselves by appealing to certain historical forms of community that were opposed to private property. For Marx, this choice of isolated aspects or epochs implied that the rest of history did *not* provide the case for

[1] Ibid.   [2] Ibid.

communism. In his own version, on the other hand, 'both as regards the real engendering of this communism – the birth of its empirical existence, and also as regards its consciousness and thought, the whole movement of history is the consciously comprehended process of its becoming'.[1] Thus the whole revolutionary movement 'finds not so much its empirical as its theoretical basis in the development of private property, and particularly of the economic system'.[2] This was so because the alienation of human life was expressed in the existence of private property, and it was in the movement of private property, in production and consumption, that man had hitherto attempted to realise himself.

> Religion, family, state, law, morality, science and art are only particular forms of production and fall under its general law. The positive abolition of private property and the appropriation of human life is therefore the positive abolition of all alienation, thus the return of man out of religion, family, state, etc., into his human, i.e. social, being.[3]

The basic alienation, Marx went on, took place in the economic sphere: religious alienation only occurred in the consciousness of man, whereas economic alienation occurred in his real life and thus its supersession involved the supersession of all alienations. Of course, the preaching of atheism might be important where religion was strong, but atheism was only a stage on the path to communism, and an abstract one at that; only communism proposed a doctrine of action that affected what was real.

Secondly, Marx emphasised the social character of communism and extended the reciprocal relation of man and society to man and nature:

> ... only to social man is nature available as a bond with other men, as the basis of his own existence for others and theirs for him, and as the vital element in human reality; only to social man is nature the foundation of his own human existence. Only as such has his natural existence become a human existence and nature itself become human. Thus society completes the essential unity of man and nature: it is the genuine ressurrection of nature, the accomplished naturalism of man and the accomplished humanism of nature.[4]

(This passage, and other similar ones, show Marx very much under

[1] Ibid. [2] Ibid., pp. 148 f. [3] Ibid., p. 149. [4] Ibid., p. 150.

the influence of Hegel, to such an extent that he almost said that nature was *created* by man).[1] As regards the social aspect, Marx showed that the capacities peculiar to man were evolved in social intercourse. Even when a man was working in isolation, he performed a social act simply by virtue of his being human. Even thought – since it used language – was a social activity.

But this emphasis on the social aspects of man's being did not destroy man's individuality (and this was Marx's third point): 'However much he is a particular individual (and it is precisely his particularity that makes him an individual and a truly individual communal being), man is just as much the totality – the ideal totality – and the subjective existence of society as something thought and felt'.[2]

Marx devoted most of the rest of this section to drawing a picture of unalienated man, man whom he called 'total' and 'multi-sided'. One should not, he said, have too narrow an idea about what the supersession of private property would achieve: just as the state of alienation totally vitiated all human faculties, so the supersession of this alienation would be a total liberation. It would not be limited to the enjoyment or possession of material objects. All human faculties – Marx listed seeing, hearing, smelling, tasting, touching, thinking, observing, feeling, desiring, acting, loving – would, in their different ways, become means of appopriating reality. This was difficult for alienated man to imagine, since private property had made men so stupid that they could only imagine an object to be theirs when they actually used it and even then it was only employed as a means of sustaining life which was understood as consisting of labour and the creation of capital.

Referring to Hess's work on this subject, Marx declared that all physical and mental senses had been dulled by a single alienation – that of *having*. But this absolute poverty would give birth to the inner wealth of human beings:

> The supersession of private property is therefore the complete emancipation of all human senses and qualities, but it is this emancipation precisely in that these senses and qualities have become

[1] See, for example, the interpretation of J.-Y. Calvez, *La Pensée de Karl Marx* (Paris, 1956) pp. 380 ff.

[2] K. Marx, *Early Texts*, p. 151. Marx added a (not very convincing) remark on death, which 'appears as the harsh victory of the species over the particular individual and seems to contradict their unity; but the particular individual is only a determinate species-being and thus mortal'.

human, both subjectively and objectively. The eye has become a human eye when its object has become a social, human object produced by man and destined for him. Thus in practice the senses have become direct theoreticians. They relate to the thing for its own sake, but the thing itself is an objective human relationship to itself and to man and vice versa. (I can in practice only relate myself humanly to an object if the object relates humanly to man.) Need and enjoyment have thus lost their egoistic nature and nature has lost its mere utility in that its utility has become human utility.[1]

This cultivation or creation of the faculties could be achieved only in certain surroundings.

> For it is not just a matter of the five senses, but also the so-called spiritual senses – the practical senses (desiring, loving, etc.) – in brief: human sensibility and the human character of the senses, which can only come into being through the existence of its object, through humanized nature. The cultivation of the five senses is the work of all previous history.[2]

For plainly a starving man appreciated food in a purely animal way; and a dealer in minerals saw only value, and not necessarily beauty, in his wares. For his faculties to become human faculties, man needed to be liberated from all external constraints.

It is passages such as this that have led some commentators to argue plausibly that Marx's model of human activity was an artistic one and that he drew much of his picture of man from romantic sources and particularly from Schiller. The idea of man's alienated senses finding objects appropriate to them, the attempt to form a connection between freedom and aesthetic activity, the picture of the all-round man – all these occurred in Schiller's *Briefe*.[3] It is also possible that there was a more contemporary and personal influence of the same nature, in

---

[1] K. Marx, *Early Texts*, p. 152.   [2] K. Marx, *Early Writings*, p. 161.

[3] The following passages show what Schiller was describing: '... Enjoyment was separated from labour, the means from the end, exertion from recompense. Eternally fettered only to a single little fragment of the whole, man fashions himself only as a fragment; ever hearing only the monotonous whirl of the wheel which he turns, he never displays the full harmony of his being. ... The aesthetic formative impulse establishes ... a joyous empire wherein it releases man from all the fetters of circumstance, and frees him both physically and morally, from all that can be called constraint.' F. Schiller, *Über die ästhetische Erziehung des Menschen*, ed. W. Henckmann (Munich, 1967) pp. 92 and 185, quoted in S. Lukes, 'Alienation and Anomie', in *Philosophy, Politics and Society*, 3rd series (Oxford, 1967).

that Marx spent a lot of his time in Paris in the company of Heine and Herwegh, two poets who did their best to embody the German romantic ideal. Marx's picture of the all-round, unalienated individual was drawn to some extent from models that were very present to him at the time.

Marx went on to sketch the importance of industry in the history of mankind. The passages anticipated his later, more detailed accounts of historical materialism. It was the history of industry, he maintained, that really revealed human capabilities and human psychology. Since human nature had been misunderstood in the past, history had been turned into the history of religion, politics and art. Industry, however, revealed man's essential faculties and was the basis for any science of man. In the past, natural science had been approached from a purely utilitarian angle. But its recent immense growth had enabled it, through industry, to transform the life of man. If industry were considered as the external expression of man's essential faculties, then natural science would be able to form the basis of human science. This science had to be based on sense-experience, as described by Feuerbach. But since this was *human* sense-experience, there would be a single, all-embracing science: 'Natural science will later comprise the science of man just as much as the science of man will embrace natural science: there will be one single science.'[1] Thus the reciprocal relationship that Marx had earlier outlined between man and nature was reflected here in his idea of a natural science of man.

The last part of his manuscript on communism consisted of a discussion, both digressive and uncharacteristic of his usual approach, on the question of whether the world was created or not. One of the key ideas in Marx's picture of man was that man was his own creator; any being that lived by the favour of another was a dependent being. Accordingly, Marx rejected the idea that the world was created, but got bogged down in an Aristotelian type of discussion about first causes in which he was defeated by his imaginary opponent until he broke off the argument and continued in a much more characteristic vein: 'But since for socialist man what is called world history is nothing but the creation of man by human labour and the development of nature for man, he has the observable and irrefutable proof of his self-creation and the process of his origin.'[2]

Thus for socialist man the question of an alien being beyond man

[1] K. Marx, *Early Texts*, p. 154.   [2] Ibid., p. 156.

and nature whose existence would imply their unreality had become impossible. For him the mutual interdependence of man and nature was what was essential and anything else seemed unreal. 'Atheism, as a denial of this unreality, has no longer any meaning, for atheism is a denial of God and tries to assert through this negation the existence of man; but socialism as such no longer needs this mediation; it starts from the theoretical and practical sense-perception of man and nature as the true reality.'[1] This perception, once established, no longer required the abolition of private property, no longer needed communism. Marx finished with a very Hegelian remark on the transitoriness of the communist phase:

> Communism represents the positive in the form of the negation of the negation and thus a phase in human emancipation and rehabilitation, both real and necessary at this juncture of human development. Communism is the necessary form and dynamic principle of the immediate future, but communism is not as such the goal of human development, the form of human society.[2]

Here communism seems to be viewed as merely a stage in the dialectical evolution, a stage that at a given moment would have served its purpose and be superseded. The picture, in the first part of the manuscript, of 'true communism' as 'the solution ot the riddle of history'[3] was much more static and unhistorical.

In the third and final section of the Manuscripts, Marx tried to come to grips definitively with the thought of the Master. He began by discussing the various attitudes of the young Hegelians to Hegel and singled out Feuerbach as the only constructive thinker; he then used Hegel to show up the weaknesses in Feuerbach's approach. Finally he settled down to a long analysis of Hegel's fundamental error, evident generally in the *Phenomenology* and particularly in the last chapter. Marx's style is here often obscure, involved and extremely repetitive, as he was constantly working over and reformulating his attitude to Hegel. In his doctoral thesis he had rejected the idea that Hegel was guilty of 'accommodation' and demanded that apparent contradictions be resolved by appeal to Hegel's 'essential consciousness'.[4] In his *Critique of Hegel's Philosophy of Right*, he showed by reference to particular examples that Hegel's principles inevitably involved accommodation. But it was not until he transferred his attention from Hegel's

[1] Ibid., p. 157.   [2] Ibid., p. 157.   [3] Ibid., p. 148.   [4]See above pp. 35f.

Philosophy of Right to his *Phenomenology* that he was able to formulate a general criticism of Hegel's dialectic. Here it was clear that Marx, although still at home with Hegel's concepts and terminology, did not confine himself to criticism on Hegel's own terms. At the same time he still respected Hegel as a great thinker and considered his dialectic a valuable instrument for investigating the world. He also credited Hegel with having discovered, though in a mystified form, the process of man's alienation and the means by which it could be overcome.[1]

According to Marx none of Hegel's disciples had even attempted to face the crucial question of the validity of their Master's dialectical method. The only exception to this was Feuerbach: 'Feuerbach is the only person to have a serious and critical relationship to the Hegelian dialectic and to have made real discoveries in this field; in short, he has overcome the old philosophy. The greatness of his achievement is in striking contrast to the unpretentious simplicity with which he presents it to the world.'[2] Feuerbach had shown that the Hegelian system was merely a philosophised form of religion and equally alienating; he had thus 'founded true materialism and real science by making the social relationship of "man to man" the basic principle of his theory'.[3] Marx briefly summarised Feuerbach's achievement in a letter he sent him in August 1844:

> In your writings you have given – whether intentionally I do not know – a philosophical basis to socialism, and the communists, too, have similarly understood these works in that sense. The unity of man with man based on the real differences between men, the concept of human species transferred from an abstract heaven to the real world: what is this other than the concept of society![4]

Continuing with the third and final section of the Manuscripts, Marx turned to look at Hegel's system. He began by copying out the table of contents of the *Phenomenology*, 'the true birth place and secret of his philosophy',[5] and accused Hegel of making all entities that in reality belonged objectively and sensuously to man into mental entities, since for him spirit alone was the genuine essence of man. This criticism was tempered, however, by an analysis of Hegel's achieve-

---

[1] For Marx's later assessment of his relationship to Hegel, see the Afterword to the Second German edition of *Capital*.

[2] K. Marx, 'Paris Manuscripts', *Early Texts*, p. 159.   [3] Ibid.

[4] 'Marx to L. Feuerbach', *Early Texts*, p. 184.

[5] K. Marx, 'Paris Manuscripts', *Early Texts*, p. 160.

ments that clearly showed how much (despite his critical comments) he owed to him. For Marx considered that, although the concept of criticism in the *Phenomenology* was still liable to mystify and was not sufficiently self-aware, it nevertheless went far beyond later developments; in other words, none of the disciples had as yet been able to surpass the Master. Indeed, Marx made the astonishing claim for the *Phenomenology* that:

> It contains all the elements of criticism – concealed but often already prepared and elaborated in a way that far surpasses Hegel's own point of view. The 'unhappy consciousness', the 'honest consciousness', the struggle of the 'noble and base consciousness', etc., etc., these single sections contain the elements (though still in an alienated form) of a criticism of whole spheres such as religion, the state, civil life, etc.[1]

This was because the *Phenomenology* had understood the alienation of man, contained insights into the process of man's development, and had seen that the objects which appeared to order men's lives – their religion, their wealth – in fact belonged to man and were the product of essential human capacities. Marx summed up his attitude to Hegel as follows:

> The greatness of Hegel's *Phenomenology* and its final product – the dialectic of negativity as the moving and creating principle, is on the one hand that Hegel conceives of the self-creation of man as a process, objectification as loss of the object, as externalization and the transcendence of this externalization. This means, therefore, that he grasps the nature of labour and understands objective man, true because real, man as the result of his own labour.[2]

Thus although Hegel did grasp labour as the self-confirming essence of man, yet 'the only labour Hegel knows and recognises is abstract, mental labour'.[3]

Although Marx's language was (as often) involved, and his arrangement somewhat haphazard, this is the passage where he gave his fullest and clearest account of his debt to, and disagreements with, Hegel. Hegel thought that reality was Spirit realising itself. In this process Spirit produced a world which it thought at first was external; only later did it realise that this world was its own creation. Spirit

[1] K. Marx, *Early Texts*, p. 163.   [2] Ibid., p. 164.   [3] Ibid.

was not something separate from this productive activity; it only existed in and through this activity. At the beginning of this process Spirit was not aware that it was externalising or alienating itself. Only gradually did Spirit realise that the world was not external to it. It was the failure to realise this that constituted, for Hegel, alienation. This alienation would cease when men became fully self-conscious and understood their environment and their culture to be emanations of Spirit. Freedom consisted in this understanding and freedom was the aim of history. In broad terms, what Marx did was to reject the notion of Spirit and retain only finite individual beings: thus the Hegelian relationships of Spirit to the world became the Marxian notion of the relationship of man to his social being. Marx said that Hegel only took account of man's mental activities – that is, of his ideas – and that these, though important, were by themselves insufficient to explain social and cultural change.

Turning to the final chapter of the *Phenomenology*, Marx opposed his view of man as an objective, natural being to Hegel's conception of man as self-consciousness. If man were reduced to self-consciousness, Marx objected, then he could establish outside himself only abstract objects that were constructs of his mind. These objects would have no independence *vis-à-vis* man's self-consciousness. Marx's own view of human nature was very different:

> When real man of flesh and blood, standing on the solid, round earth and breathing in and out all the powers of nature posits his real objective faculties, as a result of his externalisation, as alien objects, it is not the positing that is the subject; it is the subjectivity of objective faculties whose action must therefore be an objective one.[1]

Marx called his view 'naturalism' or 'humanism', and distinguished this from both idealism and materialism, claiming that it united what was essential both to idealism and to materialism.

Marx followed this with two concise paragraphs (very reminiscent of the previous section on private property and communism) on the meaning of naturalism and objectivity. Nature seemed to mean to Marx whatever was opposed to man, what afforded him scope for his activities and satisfied his needs. It was these needs and drives that made up man's nature. Marx called his view 'naturalism' because man

[1] Ibid., p. 167.

was orientated towards nature and fulfilled his needs in and through nature, but also, more fundamentally, because man was part of nature. Thus man as an active natural being was endowed with certain natural capacities, powers and drives. But he was no less a limited, dependent suffering creature. The objects of his drives were independent of him, yet he needed them to satisfy himself and express his objective nature. Thus, 'a being that does not have its nature outside itself is not a natural being and has no part in the natural world'.[1] Marx concluded: 'To be sentient is to suffer. Man as an objective, sentient being is therefore a suffering being and, since he is a being who reacts to his sufferings, a passionate being. Passion is man's faculties energetically striving after their object.'[2] This contained echoes of the eighteenth-century French materialists, Holbach and Helvetius, but the main source for Marx's ideas and terminology when discussing nature and objectivity was Feuerbach's *Philosophy of the Future*.[3]

Following this digression on his own concept of human nature, Marx continued with his critique of the *Phenomenology* by emphasising that Hegel seemed to equate alienation with any sort of objectivity and thus only transcended alienation in thought: the consequence was that, for Hegel, man was truly human only when he was engaging in philosophy and that, for example, the most authentically religious man was the philosopher of religion. The last few pages of the manuscript degenerate into absolute obscurity. Indeed, throughout this whole section where Marx was wrestling so tortuously with Hegel's dialectic, the modern reader must find the arguments rather diffcult to follow. In so far as the arguments can be grasped, 'common sense' would tend to agree with Marx as against Hegel – though it is, of course, a Hegel refracted through Marx himself.[4] What must be remembered, however, is the dense idealist fog (created particularly by Hegel's disciples) that Marx had to disperse in order to arrive at any sort of 'empirical' view.

Marx himself supplied no conclusion to the 'Paris Manuscripts' and

[1] Ibid., p. 168 on this whole passage; see further J. O'Neill, 'The Concept of Estrangement in the Early and Later Writings of Karl Marx', *Philosophy and Phenomenological Research* (Sep 1964), reprinted in *Sociology as a Skin Trade* (London, 1972) ch. 9.

[2] K. Marx, *Early Texts*, p. 168.

[3] A commentary that emphasises the French materialists is P. Kägi, *Genesis des historischen Materialismus*, pp. 262 ff. For the debt to Feuerbach, see D. McLellan, *The Young Hegelians and Karl Marx*, pp. 101 ff.

[4] On how fair Marx is to Hegel, see J. Maguire, *Marx's Paris Writings*, pp. 96 ff.

it is impossible to draw one from such a disjointed work which included discussions of economics, social criticism, philosophy, history, logic, dialectics and metaphysics. Although each section was dominated by a separate subject, to some extent all were approached in similar fashion. Here for the first time there appeared together, if not yet united, what Engels described as the three constituent elements in Marx's thought – German idealist philosophy, French socialism, and English economics. It is above all these Manuscripts which (in the West at least) reorientated many people's interpretation of Marx – to the extent of their even being considered as his major work. They were not published until the early 1930s and did not attract public attention until after the Second World War; certain facets of the Manuscripts were soon assimilated to the existentialism and humanism then so much in vogue and presented an altogether more attractive basis for non-Stalinist socialism than textbooks on dialectical materialism.

Seen in their proper perspective, these Manuscripts were in fact no more than a starting-point for Marx – an initial, exuberant outpouring of ideas to be taken up and developed in subsequent economic writings, particularly in the *Grundrisse* and in *Capital*. In these later works the themes of the '1844 Manuscripts' would certainly be pursued more systematically, in greater detail, and against a much more solid economic and historical background; but the central inspiration or vision was to remain unaltered: man's alienation in capitalist society, and the possibility of his emancipation – of his controlling his own destiny through communism.

IV. LAST MONTHS IN PARIS

While Marx had been feverishly composing his Manuscripts in Paris, Jenny was re-immersing herself in the provincial life of Trier. She was glad to be reunited with her mother for whom she had so often wept in France; but the genteel poverty in which the Westphalen household was compelled to live and the sponging of her spineless brother Edgar depressed her. The baby, now provided with a wet nurse, was soon out of danger, and was the subject of long paragraphs of loving description in Jenny's letters to Marx. When her old friends and acquaintances came to see her and view the baby, she felt as though she were holding court. She fended off as best she could inquiries about exactly what sort of a job Marx had acquired in Paris. In fact she was filled with misgivings which she confided to her husband:

Dear heart, I have too great an anxiety about our future, both in the long and the short term, and I think that I shall be punished for my present high spirits and exuberance. If you can, please calm my fears on this point. People talk far too much about a *steady* income. I then answer simply with my red cheeks, my white flesh, my velvet cloak, my feathered hat and my fine ribbons.[1]

Full of anxiety she made the difficult trip to her mother-in-law whose attitude, she was surprised to find, had quite changed since the marriage. Marx's mother and his three sisters still living at home received her with open arms, a change of heart she could only attribute to the impression made by their new prosperity with the 1000 thalers sent by Jung. She finished her first letter to Marx with a delightful admonition – unfortunately little-heeded – of his style:

Please do not write in such a bitter and irritated style!!! Either write factually and precisely or lightly and with humour. Please, dear heart, let the pen run over the page, and even if it should sometimes fall and stumble and cause a sentence to do likewise, yet your thoughts stand upright like Grenadiers of the old Guard, steadfast and brave. . . .What does it matter if their uniform hangs loosely and is not so tightly laced? How handsome the loose, light uniform looks on French soldiers. Think of our elaborate Prussians – doesn't it make you shudder? So let the participles run and put the words where they themselves want to go. Such a race of warriors must not march too regularly. Are your troops marching to field? Good luck to their general, my black master. Fare well, dear heart, darling and only life.[2]

A later letter, however (written from a Trier grown suddenly feverish with the influx of nearly a million pilgrims to see the Holy Coat), was more worried: she was anxious to return to Paris lest Marx be led astray by the temptations of the city; at the same time she feared – and the event proved her right – that a second baby would be on its way soon after her return. 'Though the exchequer may be full at the moment,' she wrote, 'reflect how easily it empties itself again, and how difficult it is to fill it!'[3] She returned to Paris in September 1844

[1] Jenny Marx to Marx, *MEW* Ergsbd. I 650.
[2] Ibid.   [3] Ibid., 654.

with the wet nurse and her four-tooth baby to find that Marx had just formed the most important friendship of his life – that with Friedrich Engels.

Engels was two years younger than Marx, born on 28 November 1820, the eldest child of a large family of rich industrialists in Barmen (now called Wuppertal), a few miles east of Düsseldorf, near the Ruhr. His great-grandfather had founded a lace factory which prospered sufficiently to enable the family to claim its own coat of arms. Friedrich Engels senior diversified the business by associating with Peter Ermen to found an extensive cotton-spinning enterprise based in Barmen and Manchester. Engels' mother came from a family of Dutch schoolteachers. Business and Church were the twin pillars of the Engels household and Engels senior expected his son to take both to heart. Young Engels was an excellent pupil at school, particularly in languages; but he left before his final year and entered his father's factory to gain practical experience. He spent all his spare time, however, writing large quantities of poetry – even more than Marx – and by the time he was dispatched to Bremen in 1838 to gain further business experience, he already had several small anonymous publications of his credit. Although he was lodged with a clergyman's family, the atmosphere in the city of Bremen was very different from the biblical, puritanical and intransigeant form of Christianity that imbued his family back in Prussia.

During his three years in Bremen he struggled hard to rid himself of his fundamentalist upbringing, and particularly of the notion of predestination.[1] Strauss's *Life of Jesus* made a strong impression on him and, through Schleiermacher, he made a swift progression to Young Hegelianism. Berlin was the obvious place to pursue his literary interests and he willingly underwent his military service – as an artilleryman in a barracks on the outskirts of the capital, arriving a few months after Marx had left. He gravitated quickly towards the *Freien*, composed a striking pamphlet against Schelling and wrote for the *Rheinische Zeitung*. When his year in the army was finished, his father sent him to work in the Manchester branch of the firm. On his way he passed through the Rhineland, had a lengthy meeting with Hess from which he emerged 'a first-class revolutionary'.[2] He also called on the editor of the *Rheinische Zeitung*; Marx, however, received Engels

[1] See his moving correspondence with the Gräber brothers, MEGA i i (2) 485 ff.
[2] M. Hess, *Briefwechsel*, p. 103.

'coldly', seeing in him an emissary of the *Freien* with whom he had just severed all contacts.[1]

In Manchester, Engels wrote for Owen's *New Moral World* and got to know several leading Chartists, particularly George Julian Harney. He also continued from Manchester to write for the *Rheinische Zeitung* and sent two pieces to the *Deutsch-französische Jahrbücher*: a critique of Carlyle's *Past and Present*; and the essay entitled *Outlines of a Critique of Political Economy*[2] whose stark and clear prediction of the impending doom of capitalism caused Marx to revise his opinion of Engels with whom he began to correspond. Already, from his observation of conditions in Manchester, Engels was beginning to collect material for his masterpiece, *The Situation of the Working Class in England*, probably the bitterest criticism of early capitalism over written.[3]

At the end of August 1844, Engels passed through Paris on his way back to Germany. His historic meeting with Marx occurred on 28 August in the Café de la Régence, one of the most famous Parisian cafés of the time, which had counted among its clients Voltaire, Benjamin Franklin, Diderot, Grimm, Louis Napoleon, Sainte-Beuve and Musset.[4] Their long, initial conversation persuaded them to spend the next ten days in each other's company in the rue Vaneau. 'Our complete agreement in all theoretical fields became obvious,' wrote Engels, 'and our joint work dates from that time.'[5] At the end of his life, looking back on this co-operation Engels summed up his view as follows:

> Both before and during my forty years' collaboration with Marx I had a certain independent share in laying the foundations of the theory, and more particularly in its elaboration. But the greater part of its leading basic principles – especially in the realm of economics and history, and, above all, their final trenchant formulation, belong to Marx. For all that I contributed – at any rate with the exception of my work in a few special fields – Marx could very well have done without me. What Marx accomplished I would not have achieved. Marx stood higher, saw farther, and took a wider and

[1] Cf. *Karl Marx: Chronik seines Lebens* (Frankfurt, 1971) p. 14.

[2] Translated in F. Engels, *Selected Writings*, ed. W. Henderson (Harmondsworth, 1967).

[3] Further on Engels, see the classical biography by G. Mayer, *Friedrich Engels, Eine Biographie*, 2 vols. (The Hague, 1934).

[4] Cf. K. Marx, *Dokumente seines Lebens*, p. 167.

[5] F. Engels, 'On the History of the Communist League', *MESW* II 311.

quicker view than all the rest of us. Marx was a genuis; we others were at best talented. Without him the theory would not, by a long way, be what it is today. It therefore rightly bears his name.[1]

Probably this passage presents an accurate account of their later relationship – though obviously Engels was indispensable to Marx financially. But so far as the theory is concerned, it has been argued (and with considerable justification), that during the thirteen years that he survived his friend, Engels managed – in his all too clear elucidations – to take much of the subtlety out of Marx's ideas.[2] Nevertheless, in the late summer of 1844 Engels, with his practical experience of capitalism, brought more to Marx than he received.

Thus began a friendship that ended only with Marx's death. In their similar origins in comfortable middle-class homes, their youthful enthusiasm for poetry and their transition through Young Hegelian liberalism to radical politics, Marx and Engels shared sufficient experiences to form a basis for lasting friendship. But it was a friendship more of contrasts than similarities: Marx's forte lay in his power of abstraction. He had throughly absorbed the Hegelian method and his dialectical approach managed to blend elements in a subtle synthesis. While Marx had been studying Hegel, Engels had been gaining practical experience and making first-hand observations as a professional business man; always quick at synthesis, he could write fast and clearly, and sometimes with a dogmatism foreign even to Marx. Their lifestyles, too, were very different. Engels was invariably immaculately dressed, his study was invariably tidy, and he was precise, business-like and responsible in money matters. Marx was careless about his clothing, had a very disorderly order in his study and had no notion of how to manage money. Marx was, moreover, very definitely a family man, however much he might sometimes regret it; Engels was a great womaniser and although capable of long attachments, always refused marriage.

During their first ten days together, the two men decided to publicise their newly agreed viewpoint by means of a pamphlet which finally disposed of Bruno Bauer. Jung particularly urged Marx to enter

[1] F. Engels, 'Ludwig Feuerbach and the End of Classical German Philosophy', *MESW* II 349.

[2] For two recent discussions of this question, see A. Schmidt, *The Concept Nature in Marx* (London, 1971) ch. 1; A. Gamble and P. Walton, *From Alienation to Surplus Value* (London, 1972) ch. 3.

the lists against Bauer, and Marx had already announced in the Preface to the 'Paris Manuscripts' his intention of dealing with the 'critical criticism' Bauer was propagating in a newly founded journal, the *Allgemeine Literatur-Zeitung*. Engels wrote the fifteen pages or so that he conceived to be his half of the pamphlet, and departed to propagandise with Hess in the Rhineland where interest in communism was growing fast. Marx took until the end of November to draft his contribution and (typically) soon found that the 'pamphlet' had grown to a book of almost 300 pages which was published in February 1845 under the ironic title (referring to the Bauer brothers) of *The Holy Family* (subtitled 'Critique of Critical Criticism').[1]

The modern reader is likely to share the view of Engels expressed when he learnt of the scope of the book, namely that 'the sovereign derision that we accord to the *Allgemeine Literatur-Zeitung* is in stark contrast to the considerable number of pages that we devote to its criticism'.[2] The book was extremely discursive, being a critique of random articles in the *Allgemeine Literatur-Zeitung*. Much of Mark's attack consisted of hair-splitting and deliberate misrepresentation which distorted their opponents' articles to the point of absurdity. This sort of approach had a particular vogue at that time and, more importantly, it was directed at precisely the kind of esoteric circle able to grasp some of the rather baroque points. There was little, indeed, of permanent interest. This was particularly so of the two long sections dealing with the comments made by Bauer's followers on Eugène Sue's enormous Gothic novel, *The Mysteries of Paris*. These comments endeavoured to show, in a Hegelian manner, that Sue's novel contained the key to the 'mysteries' of modern society. Marx criticised at great length both this vapourising interpretation and also the moralising tone of the novelist himself. The three sections of real interest in the book were Marx's replies to Bauer's attacks on Proudhon, on the role of the masses in history, and on materialism.

Marx praised Proudhon as the first thinker to have questioned the existence of private property and to have demonstrated the inhuman effects it had on society. He then summarised his own view of the relationship between private property and the proletariat:

The propertied class and the class of the proletariat present the

---

[1] 'Criticism' was the order of the day: one of the replies by a follower of Bauer was entitled *Critique of the Critique of Critical Criticism*.
[2] Engels to Marx, *MEW* xxvii 26.

same human self-alienation. But the former class finds in this self-alienation its confirmation and its good, its own power: it has in it a semblance of human existence. The class of the proletariat feels annihilated in its self-alienation; it sees in it its own powerlessness and the reality of an inhuman existence. The proletariat executes the sentence that private property pronounced on itself by begetting the proletariat, just as it carries out the sentence that wage-labour pronounced on itself by bringing forth wealth for others and misery for itself. When the proletariat is victorious, it by no means becomes the absolute side of society, for it is victorious only by abolishing itself and its opposite. The then proletariat disappears as well as the opposite which determines it, private property.[1]

In answer to the criticism that socialist writers, by attributing this historic role to the proletariat, seemed to consider it a god, Marx continued:

The question is not what this or that proletarian, or even the whole of the proletariat at the moment *considers* as its aim. The question is *what the proletariat is*, and what, consequent on that *being*, it will be compelled to do. Its aim and historical action are irrevocably and obviously demonstrated in its own life-situation as well as in the whole organisation of bourgeois society today.[2]

Bauer wished to dissociate his philosophy from the mass of the people and considered the operative force in society to be the idea of even a personalised history. Marx's view was the opposite: 'History ... does not use man to achieve its own ends, as though it were a particular person: it is merely the activity of man pursuing his own objectives.'[3] Or again: 'Ideas never lead beyond the established situation, they only lead beyond the ideas of the established situation. Ideas can accomplish absolutely nothing. To become real, ideas require men who apply practical force.'[4] For Bauer, the ideas of an intellectual élite were threatened by popular contact and he believed that the ideas of the French Revolution had been contaminated by the enthusiasm of the masses. For Marx, on the other hand, these ideas had not sufficiently penetrated the masses, and the bourgeoisie had consequently been able to turn the French Revolution to its own profit. Bauer made

---

[1] K. Marx and F. Engels, *The Holy Family*, pp. 51 f.   [2] Ibid., p. 52.
[3] Ibid., p. 125.   [4] Ibid., p. 160.

much of the 'human rights' embodied in the French Revolution, but Marx, pursuing the theme of his *On the Jewish Question*, declared that it was only a ruthless selfishness that had been really emancipated.

On the significance of French materialism, Marx also disagreed with Bauer who held that the materialist movement in France was a direct descendant of Spinoza's metaphysical monism. Marx wished to emphasise the anti-metaphysical humanist aspects of French materialists such as Helvetius and Holbach. He traced the influence on socialism and communism of the materialist doctrine of the eighteenth-century social philosophers:

> If man draws all his knowledge, sensation, etc., from the world of the senses and the experience gained in it, the empirical world must be arranged so that in it man experiences and gets used to what is really human and becomes aware of himself as man. If correctly-understood interest is the principle of all morals, man's private interest must be made to coincide with the interest of humanity. If man is unfree in the materialist sense, i.e., is free not through the negative power to avoid this or that, but through the positive power to assert his true individuality, crime must be not punished in the individual, but the anti-social source of crime must be destroyed, and each man must be given social scope for the vital manifestation of his being. If man is shaped by his surroundings, his surroundings must be made human. If man is social by nature, he will develop his true nature only in society, and the strength of his nature must be measured not by the strength of separate individuals but by the power of society.[1]

The Holy Family was little read at the time of its publication and was certainly not one of Marx's major works. But several of the themes of what was to become 'the materialistic conception of history' appeared there for the first time and Marx, re-reading the book after twelve years, was able to comment: 'I was pleasantly surprised to find that we do not need to be ashamed of our work, although the cult of Feuerbach strikes me as very amusing.'[2]

Before *The Holy Family* was published Marx had to leave Paris. The Prussian Government became more insistent in its complaints about *Vorwärts* and even Louis Philippe is said to have explained: 'We must purge Paris of German philosophers!' On 25 January 1845 Guizot, the

[1] Ibid., p. 176.   [2] Marx to Engels, *MEW* xxxi 290.

Minister of the Interior, closed down *Vorwärts* and issued an order expelling its leading personnel, including Marx, Heine and Ruge. Marx took a little longer than the twenty-four hours grace given him and he left for Liège and Brussels on 2 February taking with him Heinrich Bürgers, a young radical journalist from the *Vorwärts* staff. The two kept up their spirits by singing choruses throughout the journey. Jenny sold off the furniture and some of the linen, stayed two nights with the Herweghs, and followed Marx to Brussels a few days later.

3

Brussels

When in the spring of 1845 we met again, this time in
Brussels, Marx had already advanced to the main aspects of
his materialist theory of history. Now we set about the task
of elaborating the newly gained theory in the most different
directions.

F. Engels, 'History of the Communist League', *MEW* XXII 212.

I. THE MATERIALIST CONCEPTION OF HISTORY

BRUSSELS WAS to be Marx's home for the next three years. It was still
in many ways a provincial city, capital of a very rapidly industrialising
country independent only since 1830, with a Catholic-conservative
government and a vocal liberal opposition. Belgium was something of
a political haven for refugees as it enjoyed greater freedom of expression than any other country on the continent of Europe. Marx
arrived with a list of instructions written in his notebook by Jenny: the
children's room and his study were to be 'very simply furnished'; the
kitchen did not need to be furnished at all and Jenny would get the
utensils herself, as also the beds and linen. She finished: 'The rest I
leave to the wise judgement of my noble protector; my only remaining request is to have particular regard for some cupboards; they
play an important role in the life of a housewife and are extremely
valuable objects, never to be overlooked. How should the books best
be stored? And so amen!'[1] At first it was impossible to find a satisfactory
lodging. Jenny arrived about ten days after Marx and the family lived
for a month in the Bois Sauvage guest house. Then they moved into
Freiligrath's old lodging on his departure for Switzerland. Finally in
May they rented a small terraced house in the rue de l'Alliance in a
Flemish-speaking, countrified area at the eastern edge of the city,
where they stayed for more than a year.

[1] Jenny Marx to Marx, quoted in L. Dornemann, *Jenny Marx*, pp. 71 f.

Jenny found herself pregnant on her arrival in Brussels and her mother now sent her her own maid, Helene Demuth, a practical young baker's daughter from a village near Trier, then aged twenty-five, who had grown up in the Westphalen family from the age of eleven or twelve and who was to be the constant, if often unmentioned, companion to the family until Marx's death.[1] Marx at first found difficulty in obtaining a residence permit: the Belgian authorities were afraid that he would publish a resuscitated version of *Vorwärts* and also the Prussian police were applying pressure. Marx had to show the authorities the contract he had signed for a book on Economics and Politics and declared that he was living off his wife's money while waiting for the royalties. Only after signing a promise to abstain from all political activity did he finally obtain permission to stay. In October 1845 Marx thought of emigrating to the United States and even applied to the mayor of Trier for a permit. When the Prussian police continued to demand his extradition Marx abandoned Prussian nationality in December 1845.

Nevertheless, the years in Brussels were probably the happiest ever enjoyed by the Marx family. There was a comfortable source of income from the sale of the furniture and linen in Paris and the 1500 francs advance that Marx received for his forthcoming book. In addition, on learning of his expulsion from Paris, Engels, together with Hess and Jung, had organised a subscription for him 'in order to spread your extra expenses among us all communistically'.[2] This appeal yielded almost 1000 francs, mainly from friends in the Rhineland, and Engels also put at Marx's disposal the royalties from his own book *The Condition of the Working Classes in England*. When Engels moved to Brussels he rented a house next to the Marx family and Hess and his wife Sibylle soon moved in next door to Engels. Sibylle acted as an 'auntie' to the Marx children. They had an agreeable circle of friends, including the poet Ferdinand Freiligrath and a socialist journalist Karl Heinzen, and Jenny remembered with pleasure their evenings in the gay cafés of the city.[3] Joseph Weydemeyer, an artillery officer with socialist leanings, who was to become a lifelong friend of Marx, describing one of their outings in early 1846: 'To crown our folly,

---

[1] The date of her birth on the Highgate cemetery stone is mistaken. See H· Monz, *Karl Marx und Trier*, p. 171.

[2] Engels to Marx, *MEW* XXVII 19.

[3] Cf. Jenny Marx, 'Short Sketch of an Eventful Life', in *Reminiscences of Marx and Engels*, p. 222.

Marx, Weitling, Marx's brother-in-law and myself spent the night playing cards. Weitling was the first to tire. Marx and I spent some hours on a sofa and the next day, in the company of his wife and brother-in-law, we vagabonded in the most agreeable manner imaginable. Early in the morning we went to a café, then we took the train to Villeworde, a nearby village, where we had lunch. We were madly gay, and came back on the last train.'[1]

The sorties were only reliefs from long periods of intense intellectual activity. On the day he left Paris Marx had signed a contract with Karl Leske, a progressive Darmstadt publisher, for a book to be entitled *A Critique of Economics and Politics* to be finished by the summer of 1845. The economic side would no doubt have been a reworking of the 'Paris Manuscripts'. Marx got as far as sketching out a table of contents for the political half which shows that he intended to continue the themes of his *Critique of Hegel's Philosophy of Right* and essays *On the Jewish Question* by writing a detailed critique of the institutions of the liberal state viewed as a stage leading towards the abolition of both the state and of civil society.[2] Engels had urged Marx even before he left Paris to finish the book as 'people's minds are ripe and we must strike while the iron is hot'.[3] Marx received many letters of inquiry and encouragement and Engels even announced in the *New Moral World* that it was in print.[4] Engels, who was sitting in his parents' home in Barmen finishing off his *Condition of the Working Classes in England* and in close contact with the Rhineland socialists, produced a constant stream of publishing projects. On two of these Marx agreed to collaborate: a critique of Friedrich List as the chief proponent of protective tariffs as a means to ensure Germany's economic development; and a series of translations of utopian socialists with critical introductions, beginning with Fourier, Owen, Morelly and the Saint-Simonians. But neither of these projects came to anything. But Marx was never a man to be hurried in his researches; and during the first few months in Brussels he buried himself in the municipal library to read books in French on economic and social problems in an effort to understand more fully the workings of bourgeois society, the factors that determined the general historical process, and the possibilities of proletarian emancipation.

[1] Weydemeyer to Luise Lüning, *Münchner Post*, 30 April 1926.
[2] Cf. *MEW* III 537.
[3] Engels to Marx, *MEW* XXVII 16.
[4] Cf. *MEW* II 519.

Engels said later that when he moved to Brussels at the beginning of April Marx 'had already advanced from these principles [i.e. 'that politics and its history have to be explained from the economic conditions and their evolution and not vice versa'] to the main aspects of his materialist theory of history';[1] and in the Preface to the English edition of the *Communist Manifesto* he wrote that Marx had already worked out his theory in the spring of 1845 'and put it before me in terms almost as clear as those in which I have stated it here'.[2] The only writing of Marx's surviving from this period are the famous eleven *Theses on Feuerbach* rightly called by Engels 'the first document in which the brilliant kernel of the new world view is revealed'.[3] From his first reading of Feuerbach in the early 1840s Marx had never been entirely uncritical; but both in the 'Paris Manuscripts' and in the *Holy Family* Marx had nothing but praise for Feuerbach's 'real humanism'. Marx was now becoming identified too closely as a mere disciple of Feuerbach from whose static and unhistorical views Marx was bound to diverge owing to the growing attention he was paying to economics. In the *Theses on Feuerbach* Marx gave a very brief sketch of the ideas that he and Engels elaborated a few months later in *The German Ideology*. By any standard *The German Ideology* is one of Marx's major works. In it by criticising Feuerbach, the most 'secular' of the Young Hegelians, he and Engels completed the 'settling of accounts with our erstwhile philosophical consciousness',[4] a process which had lasted since the Doctoral Thesis of 1841.

The first thesis contained the essence of Marx's criticism of Feuerbach's materialism: 'The chief defect of all hitherto existing materialism (that of Feuerbach included) is that the things, reality, sensuousness, is conceived only in the form of the object or of contemplation, but not as sensuous human activity, practice, not subjectively'.[5] In the second thesis Marx outlined his ideas on the unity of theory and practice: 'The question whether objective truth can be achieved by human thinking is not a question of theory but is a *practical question*. Man must prove the truth, i.e., the reality and power, the this-

---

[1] *MEW* xxi 212. Engels' 'History of the Communist League' is translated in *The Birth of the Communist Manifesto*, ed. D. Struik (New York, 1971).

[2] *MESW* i 29.

[3] F. Engels, 'Ludwig Feuerbach und der Ausgang der klassischen Deutschen Philosophie', *MEW* xxi 264.

[4] K. Marx, 'Preface to *A Critique of Political Economy*', *MESW* i 364.

[5] K. Marx and F. Engels, *The German Ideology* (Moscow, 1968) p. 659.

sidedness of his thinking in practice. The dispute over the reality or non-reality of thinking that is isolated from practice is a purely *scholastic* question.'[1] And in the third thesis Marx pointed out the deficiencies of the French materialists of the previous century, who had not realised that their own thinking was just as much a part of

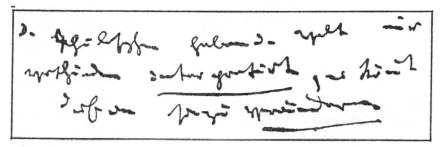

The famous eleventh thesis on Feuerbach. The text reads: '*Die Philosophen haben die Welt nur verschieden interpretiert, es kommt darauf an, sie zu verändern.*' Translation: 'The philosophers have only interpreted the world in different ways; the point is to change it.'

the historical process as anybody else's: 'The materialist doctrine concerning the changing of circumstances and upbringing forgets that circumstances are changed by men and that it is essential to educate the educator himself. This doctrine must, therefore, divide society into two parts, one of which is superior to society.'[2] In the following theses Marx declared that Feuerbach was correct in resolving religion into its secular basis: but he had failed to account for the existence of religion and this 'can only be explained by the cleavages and contradictions within this secular basis. The latter must, therefore, in itself be both understood in its contradiction and revolutionised in practice.'[3] The final, and the best known, thesis read: 'The philosophers have only interpreted the world in various ways; the point is to change it.'[4]

In the three months following Engels' arrival he and Marx 'set about the task of elaborating the newly gained theory in the most different directions'.[5] For Engels this took the form of a large-scale *History of English Society* and for Marx his *Critique of Economics and Politics*. In July 1845 they both undertook a six-week trip to England. According

---

[1] Ibid.   [2] Ibid., p. 660.   [3] Ibid.   [4] Ibid., p. 662.
[5] F. Engels, 'History of the Communist League', *MEW* xxi 212, in Struik, op. cit., p. 156.

to a subsequent letter from Marx to his publisher, this journey was undertaken exclusively for research on his book.[1] Most of the time they spent in Manchester reading economic works by writers such as Petty, Tooke, Cooper, Thomson and Cobbett in the Old Chetham Library. Much later Engels still recalled with pleasure 'the small alcove and the four-sided desk where we sat 24 years ago. I like the place a lot: because of the stained glass window it always seems fine and sunny there.'[2] On their return Marx and Engels stayed a few days in London where they met the Chartist leader George Julian Harney, editor of the most influential working-class paper, *The Northern Star*. Engels also introduced Marx to the leaders of the German workers' organisations in London – contacts that were to become the centre of Marx's preoccupations the following year – and together they attended a meeting of the leaders of various national groups to discuss the founding of some form of international democratic association. This took form as the Fraternal Democrats in September 1845.[3]

While Marx was away in England, Jenny went to stay with her mother in Trier for two months. Their second daughter, Laura, was to be born at the end of September and Jenny prolonged her stay as long as possible in order to keep her lonely mother company. She wrote to Marx on his return from England:

> The little house will have to do. Anyway, in winter a lot of room is not necessary. When I have finished the big business on the upper floor, I will move downstairs again. Then you can sleep in your present study and set up tent in the big lounge. That's fine. Then the children's noise is sealed off below. You are undisturbed above, I can join you in peaceful moments and we can keep the room in some sort of order. In any case, a good hot stove with accessories must be installed in the room as soon as possible. That is Breuer's[4] affair, since nobody rents a room that is impossible to heat. . . . Everything else I will see to later. . . .[5]

Once back from England Marx's socio-economic studies were interrupted by his decision to write a definitive critique of the Young

---

[1] Cf. Marx to Leske, *MEW* xxvii 450.   [2] Marx to Engels, *MEW* xxxii 510.
[3] On Harney and the Fraternal Democrats see further: A. Schoyen, *The Chartis Challenge* (London, 1958) pp. 143 ff; J. Braunthal, *History of the International* (London 1967) i 62 ff.
[4] The landlord.
[5] Jenny Marx to Marx, quoted in L. Dornemann, *Jenny Marx*, p. 81.

Hegelians. In a letter of explanation to Leske he wrote: 'It seemed to me very important that a work polemicising against German philosophy and current German socialism should precede my positive construction. This is necessary in order to prepare the public for the point of view of my *Economics* which is diametrically opposed to the previous German intellectual approach.'[1] *The Holy Family* had not accomplished this: it was written before Marx had developed his systematically materialist approach to history. Further, Bauer had published a reply to the *Holy Family* in which Marx and Engels were labelled as 'Feuerbachian dogmatists';[2] and in November 1844 another Young Hegelian, Max Stirner, had published *The Ego and its Own*, an anarcho-existentialist work of extraordinary power and fascination which branded all the forces that oppressed mankind, whether religion or liberalism or socialism, as illusions from which men should free themselves by refusing any form of self-sacrifice and indulging in conscious egoism.[3] And Marx and Engels had naturally been the object of strong criticism from Stirner as communist disciples of Feuerbach. *The German Ideology* was thus conceived primarily as a work to make clear the disagreements between Marx and Engels and Feuerbach, and also to deal finally with the latest – and last – manifestations of Young Hegelian idealism, Bauer's 'pure criticism' and Stirner's egoism.

The book was begun at the end of September 1845 with a lengthy criticism of Feuerbach – 'the only one who has at least made some progress'[4] – into which critiques of Bauer and Stirner were to be inserted. By April 1846 these critiques had grown to the size of a large book in its own right which was prepared for publication and taken to Germany by Weydemeyer who had been staying with the Marx family for the first few months of 1846. The section on Feuerbach, however, remained unfinished and, in fact, contained very little on Feuerbach himself. The second volume dealt with current socialist trends in Germany. It reached only a hundred or so pages and work on the manuscript was abandoned in August 1846.[5]

[1] Marx to Leske, *MEW* XXVII 448 f.

[2] B. Bauer, 'Charakteristik Ludwig Feuerbachs', *Wigandsvierteljahrschrift* (1845) III 138.

[3] On Stirner in general, see R. Paterson, *The Nihilistic Egoist – Max Stirner* (Oxford, 1971).

[4] K. Marx and F. Engels, *The German Ideology*, p. 28.

[5] On the circumstances surrounding the composition and fate of *The German Ideology*, see the exhaustive study, B. Andreas and W. Mönke, 'Neue Daten zur "Deutschen Ideologie",' *Archiv für Sozialgeschichte*, VIII (1968).

By far the most important part of *The German Ideology* is the unfinished section on Feuerbach. Marx and Engels began by making fun of the philosophical pretensions of the Young Hegelians which they described as 'the putrescence of Absolute Spirit' and characterised as follows:

> In the general chaos mighty empires have arisen only to meet with immediate doom, heroes have emerged momentarily only to be hurled back into obscurity by bolder and stronger rivals. It was a revolution beside which the French Revolution was child's play, a world struggle beside which the struggles of the Diadochi appear insignificant. Principles ousted one another, heroes of the mind overthrew each other with unheard-of rapidity, and in the three years 1842–45 more of the past was swept away in Germany than at other times in three centuries. All this is supposed to have taken place in the realm of pure thought.[1]

The main body of the section is then divided into three parts: a general statement of the historical and materialist approach in contrast to that of the Young Hegelians, a historical analysis employing this method, and an account of the present state of society and its immediate future – a communist revolution.

Marx and Engels began by stating their general position, which deserves lengthy quotations as it is the first concise statement of historical materialism:

> The premises from which we begin are not arbitrary ones, not dogmas, but real premises from which abstraction can only be made in the imagination. We begin with real individual men, their activity and the material conditions under which they live, both those which they find already existing and those produced by their activity. These premises can thus be verified in a purely empirical way.
>
> The first premise of all human history is, of course, the existence of living human beings. Thus the first fact to be established is the physical organisation of these individuals and their consequent relation to the rest of nature. . . .
>
> Men can be distinguished from animals by consciousness, by religion or anything else you like. They themselves begin to distin-

[1] K. Marx and F. Engels, *The German Ideology*, p. 27.

guish themselves from animals as soon as they begin to *produce* their means of subsistence, a step which is conditioned by their physical organisation. By producing their means of subsistence men are indirectly producing their actual material life.

The way in which men produce their means of subsistence depends first of all on the nature of the actual means of subsistence they find in existence and have to reproduce. This mode of production must not be considered simply as being the reproduction of the physical existence of the individuals. Rather it is a definite form of activity of these individuals, a definite form of expressing their life, a definite *mode of life* on their part. As individuals express their life, so they are. What they are, therefore, coincides with their production, both with *what* they produce and with *how* they produce. The nature of individuals thus depends on the material conditions determining their production.[1]

Marx and Engels went on to state that 'how far the productive forces of a nation are developed is shown most manifestly by the degree to which the division of labour has been carried'.[2] They showed how the division of labour led to the separation of town and country and then to the separation of industrial from commercial labour, and so on. Next they summarised the different stages of ownership that had corresponded to the stages in the division of labour: tribal ownership, communal and state ownership, feudal or estate ownership. Marx and Engels summarised their conclusions so far as follows:

The fact is, therefore, that definite individuals who are productively active in a definite way enter into these definite social and political relations. Empirical observation must in each separate instance bring out empirically, and without any mystification and speculation, the connection of the social and political structure with production. The social structure and the State are continually evolving out of the life-process of definite individuals, but of individuals, not as they may appear in their own or other people's imagination, but as they *really* are; i.e. as they operate, produce materially, and hence as they work under definite material limits, presuppositions and conditions independent of their will.[3]

Marx and Engels then reiterated their general approach, stating that

[1] Ibid., pp. 31 f. [2] Ibid., p. 32. [3] Ibid.

'consciousness does not determine life, but life determines consciousness',[1] and showed how the division of labour, leading to private property, created social inequality, class struggle and the erection of political structures:

> Out of this very contradiction between the interest of the individual and that of the community the latter takes an independent form as the *State*, divorced from the real interests of individuals and community, and at the same time as an illusory communal life, always based, however, on the real ties existing in every family and tribal conglomeration – such as flesh and blood, language, division of labour on a larger scale, and other interests – and especially, as we shall enlarge upon later, on the classes, already determined by the division of labour, which in every such mass of men separate out, and of which one dominates all the others. It follows from this that the struggles within the State, the struggle between democracy, aristocracy, and monarchy, the struggle for the franchise, etc., are merely the illusory forms in which the real struggles of the different classes are fought out among one another.[2]

Marx and Engels then took up the question of 'premises' and repeated their criticism of the Young Hegelians who considered that philosophical ideas were themselves productive of revolutions. On the contrary:

> These conditions of life, which different generations find in existence, decide also whether or not the periodically recurring revolutionary convulsion will be strong enough to overthrow the basis of the entire existing system. And if these material elements of a complete revolution are not present (namely on the one hand the existing productive forces, on the other the formulation of a revolutionary mass, which revolts not only against separate conditions of society up till then, but against the very 'production of life' till then, the 'total activity' on which it was based), then, as far as practical development is concerned, it is absolutely immaterial whether the *idea* of this revolution has been expressed a hundred times already, as the history of communism proves.[3]

Elaborating on Marx's *Theses*, the text continued with a passage specifically devoted to Feuerbach. Taking as an example the cherry

[1] Ibid., p. 38.   [2] Ibid., p. 45.   [3] Ibid.

tree (imported into Europe for commercial reasons) Marx and Engels pointed out that an increasing number of objects could not be grasped by mere 'observation' but had to be understood as a result of social development, industry and commerce. With Feuerbach, however, 'in as far as he is a materialist he does not deal with history and in as far as he considers history he is not a materialist'.[1] For no ideas could claim an eternal, objective validity. They changed in accordance with changing socio-economic relationships and it would be found that 'the ideas of the ruling class are in every epoch the ruling ideas'.[2]

There followed a lengthy section on the division of labour, particularly in the Middle Ages, and the transition to capitalism; then a section on the influence of the division of labour on the evolving forms of the state, the legal system and property relations. The final section was on communism. 'Communism', it had already been stated, 'is not for us a state of affairs which is to be established, an ideal to which reality will have to adjust itself. We call communism the real movement which abolishes the present state of things.'[3] This 'real movement' differed from all previous movements in that

> it overturns the basis of all earlier relations of production and intercourse, and for the first time consciously treats all natural premises as the creatures of hitherto existing men, strips them of their natural character and subjugates them to the power of the united individuals. Its organisation is, therefore, essentially economic, the material production of the conditions of this unity; it turns existing conditions into conditions of unity. The reality, which communism is creating, is precisely the true basis for rendering it impossible that anything should exist independently of individuals, insofar as reality is only a product of the preceding intercourse of individuals themselves.[4]

The key factor in the establishment of communism was the abolition of the division of labour. But the only example that Marx gave of this here was drawn from a rural community:

> In communist society, where nobody has one exclusive sphere of activity but each can become accomplished in any branch he wishes, society regulates the general production and thus makes it possible for me to do one thing today and another tomorrow, to

---

[1] Ibid., pp 59 ff.   [2] Ibid., p. 61.   [3] Ibid., p. 48.   [4] Ibid., pp. 87 f.

hunt in the morning, fish in the afternoon, rear cattle in the evening, criticise after dinner, just as I have a mind, without ever becoming hunter, fisherman, cowboy or critic. This fixation of social
activity, this consolidation of what we ourselves produce into an
objective power above us, growing out of our control, thwarting
our expectations, bringing to naught our calculations, is one of the
chief factors in historical development up till now.[1]

At least the means to the end was clear. The section finished with
the words:

If the proletarians are to assert themselves as individuals, they will
have to abolish the very condition of their existence hitherto (which
has, moreover, been that of all society up to the present), namely,
labour. Thus they find themselves directly opposed to the form in
which, hitherto, the individuals of which society consists have given
themselves collective expression, that is, the State. In order therefore
to assert themselves as individuals, they must overthrow the State.[2]

The section of *The German Ideology* dealing with Bruno Bauer is very
short: Marx had already dealt with Bauer's ideas at length in *The
Holy Family* and restricted himself here to reiterating in a few pages the
complete barrenness of 'critical criticism' and refuting Bauer's attacks
on Feuerbach.

The section on Stirner, on the other hand, is much longer than all
the other parts of *The German Ideology* put together. When Stirner's
book first appeared Engels considered that it contained several positive
elements that could serve as a basis for communist ideas, but Marx
soon disabused him of any such notion.[3] Marx's plans in December
1844 to write an article criticising Stirner had been upset up his expulsion from Paris and the banning of *Vorwärts*. In *The German Ideology* he
and Engels certainly spared no effort: their onslaught on 'Saint Max'
as they called him equals in length and easily surpasses in tedium
Stirner's own book.[4] There is the occasional flash of brilliance, but the
(quite correct) portrayal of Stirner as the final product of the Young
Hegelian school who carried to its logical extreme the subjective side
of the Hegelian dialectic too often degenerates into pages of mere

[1] Ibid., p. 45.   [2] Ibid., p. 36.
[3] Cf. Engels to Marx, Marx to Engels, *MEW* xxvii 11 ff.
[4] See further, N. Lobkowicz, 'Karl Marx and Max Stirner' in *Demythologising
Marxism*.

word-play and hair-splitting. The central criticism made by Marx and Engels is that Stirner's fundamental opposition of egoism to altruism is itself a superficial view:

> Communist theoreticians, the only ones who have time to devote to the study of history, are distinguished precisely because they alone have discovered that throughout history the 'general interest' is created by individuals who are defined as 'private persons'. They know that this contradiction is only a seeming one because one side of it, the so-called 'general', is constantly being produced by the other side, private interest, and by no means opposes the latter as an independent force with an independent history – so that this contradiction is in practice always being destroyed and reproduced. Hence it is not a question of the Hegelian 'negative unity' of two sides of a contradiction, but of the materially-determined destruction of the preceding materially-determined mode of life of individuals, with the disappearance of which this contradiction together with its unity also disappears.[1]

Equally, Stirner's view of might as right was not sufficient:

> If one regards power as the basis of right, as Hobbes and others do, then right, law, etc., are merely the symptoms – the expression – of other relations upon which State power rests. The material life of individuals, which by no means depends merely on their 'will', their mode of production and form of intercourse, which mutually determine each other – these are the real basis of the State and remain so at all the stages at which division of labour and private property are still necessary, quite independently of the will of individuals. These actual relations are in no way created by the State power; on the contrary they are the power creating it. The individuals who rule in these conditions, besides having to constitute their power in the form of the State, have to give their will, which is determined by these definite conditions, a universal expression as the will of the State, as law – an expression whose content is always determined by the relations of this class, as the civil and criminal law demonstrates in the clearest possible way.[2]

Towards the end of the book there were also some remarks on the organisation of labour which Stirner attacked as being authoritarian

---

[1] K. Marx and F. Engels, *The German Ideology*, p. 272.　　[2] Ibid., p. 366.

in proposals for a communist society, as true abolition of the division of labour implied that everyone would have to do everything. Marx and Engels replied that it was not their view 'that each should do the work of Raphael, but that anyone in whom there is a potential Raphael should be able to develop without hindrance'.[1]

> With a communist organisation of society [they continued] there disappears the subordination of the artist to local and national narrowness, which arises entirely from division of labour, and also the subordination of the artist to some definite art, thanks to which he is exclusively a painter, sculptor, etc., the very name of his activity adequately expressing the narrowness of his professional development and his dependence on division of labour. In a communist society there are no painters but, at most, people who engage in painting among other activities.[2]

But such passages are brief intervals of interest in an otherwise extremely turgid polemic.

The second volume of *The German Ideology* had a much more topical subject, Utopian German socialism – which Marx and Engels termed 'true' socialism and which at that time informed almost all socialist thinking in Germany. This section was a practical application of the discussion on Feuerbach – as most of the 'true' socialists were strongly influenced by his thinking as well as sharing in the anarchism of Stirner. On to elements of French socialism was grafted the Feuerbachian idea of a 'true', genuine human essence which consisted in the adoption of an altruistic attitude towards one's fellow men. The 'true' socialists considered that liberal ideas were already out of date and demanded the immediate realisation of 'true' human essence. Thus they rejected any participation in the struggle for 'bourgeois' rights. Their meetings contained a lot of moralising and sentiment – to the detriment, according to Marx and Engels, of sound historical analysis. 'True socialism', they said, 'is nothing but the transfiguration of proletarian communism, and of its kindred parties and sects in France and England, within the heaven of the German mind and . . . of true German sentiment.'[3] Inevitably in so stagnant a country as Germany, they replaced revolutionary enthusiasm with the universal love of mankind and relied mainly on the petty bourgeoisie. The comments of Marx and Engels on the 'true' socialists were contained in three

---

[1] Ibid., p. 441.   [2] Ibid., p. 443.   [3] Ibid., p. 514.

review articles. The first attacked an anonymous essay which advocated the German philosophical socialism of Feuerbach and Hess as opposed to the crudeness of French communism and regarded humanism as the synthesis of both. The second review attacked Karl Grün, a close disciple of Feuerbach and friend of Marx in his earliest university days, whom Marx referred to later as 'a teacher of German philosophy who had over me the advantage that he understood nothing about it himself'.[1] Grün had failed to grasp the essential points of French socialists (even when he plagiarised them) and concentrated on vague notions of 'human' consumption as opposed to studying real relationships of production. The third short essay dealt with a Dr Kühlmann, who was not a true socialist at all but a bogus Swiss preacher of messianic communism.

The section of *The German Ideology* on Feuerbach was one of the most central of Marx's works. It was a tremendous achievement in view of the low level of socialist writing and thought prevalent at the time. Marx never subsequently stated his materialist conception of history at such length and in detail. It remains a masterpiece today for the cogency and clarity of its presentation. Yet it remained unknown for almost a century.

From the beginning of 1846 Marx and Engels made great efforts to find a publisher for *The German Ideology*. Weydemeyer and Hess conducted lengthy negotiations with Rempel and Meyer, two Westphalian businessmen who sympathised with true socialism and had agreed to put up the necessary money; at least six other prospective publishers were approached; the manuscript was sent to Cologne and even split up into sections to be published separately. The authors continued their efforts up till the end of 1847, but only the short review of Grün was ever published. This failure was due to the strict censorship regulations and the serious financial risks incurred in publishing radical works, though Marx considered that the refusals were motivated by the publishers' opposition to his ideas.[2] Thus, as Marx wrote later, 'we abandoned the manuscript to the gnawing of the mice all the more willingly as we had achieved our main purpose – self-clarification'.[3] And, in fact, the manuscript as it survives does bear considerable traces of mice's teeth. Marx nevertheless continued to

[1] *MESW* I 392.
[2] Cf. Marx to Annenkov, in K. Marx, *The Poverty of Philosophy* (Moscow, 1956) p. 217.
[3] *MESW* I 364. The manuscript was not published until 1932.

work frantically on his *Economics and Politics*.[1] His publisher Leske had threatened to cancel the contract. Marx duly promised the first volume by the end of November. But he was distracted by his polemic with Proudhon. Leske accordingly cancelled the contract in February 1847 – though he was still trying to recover his advance in 1871!

II. WEITLING AND PROUDHON

With *The German Ideology*, Marx and Engels clarified their fundamental differences with the Young Hegelians and – more importantly – with contemporary German socialists. They now turned their attention to impress their newly acquired insights on the very varied existing left-wing groups, and 'to win over to our convictions the European proletariat in general and the German proletariat in particular'.[2] Brussels was an ideal vantagepoint from which to build up contacts among German socialists, for it was in the middle of a triangle formed by Paris and London (where the largest colonies of expatriate German workers had congregated) and Cologne (capital of the Rhineland, the German province by far the most receptive to communist ideas). In Brussels a colony of gifted German exiles soon began to form around Marx. He had been accompanied on his journey from Paris by Heinrich Bürgers, a young journalist who had contributed to the *Rheinische Zeitung* and become a communist in Paris. The morning after their arrival Marx insisted that they call on the poet Ferdinand Freiligrath who had been attacked by the *Rheinische Zeitung* for subservience to the Prussian Government which had none the less later exiled him for his radical writings.[3] Their meeting was a cordial one in which Freiligrath found Marx 'an interesting fellow – agreeable and unpretentious'.[4] Through Freiligrath and the German solicitor Karl Maynz, Marx met the leading Belgian democrats – in particular the lawyer Lucien Jottrand, and the leader of the Polish exiles Lelewel – and also Philippe Gigot, a young Belgian palaeographist in the Ministry of the Interior.[5] Among the Germans who were closely connected with Marx were Sebastian

[1] Cf. Georg Weerth to Wilhelm Weerth, *Sämtliche Werke* (1957) v 239. Marx told Weerth that he had never slept more than four hours a night for several years.
[2] *MEW* xxi 212. Translated in Struik, op. cit., pp. 15 f.
[3] Cf. H. Bürgers, 'Erinnerungen an F. Freiligrath', *Vossische Zeitung*, Sep–Dec 1870.
[4] Quoted in F. Mehring, 'Freiligrath und Marx in ihrem Briefwechsel', *Die neue Zeit*, no. 12 (April 1912) p. 7.
[5] For Gigot and other Belgians in Marx's circle, see J. Kuypers, 'Karl Marx' belgischer Freundeskreis', *International Review of Social History* (1962).

Seiler, a former Swiss contributor to the *Rheinische Zeitung* who ran a left-orientated news agency in Brussels; Karl Heinzen, a radical journalist then in the insurance business; Hermann Kriege, a journalist and disciple of Weitling; Wilhelm Wolff, who had arrived unheralded on the Marxes' doorstep in 1846 straight from Silesia where he had escaped from arrest for communist propaganda among the peasantry; and Georg Weerth, a representative for a German commercial firm who – though still in his early twenties – had already made a reputation as a poet. Jenny's unstable but likeable brother, Edgar, who had a temporary job in Seiler's agency, also formed part of the group. Marx was also visited by Stefan Born, a young typesetter who was to play a central role in the 1848 revolution.

After a brief stay in the Bois Sauvage guest house (for economy reasons, he told Weydemeyer[1]), the Marx family moved in October 1846 to Ixelles, a southern suburb of Brussels. Here, Marx's first son, the ill-fated Edgar was born. Marx's financial situation was becoming very difficult and he was forced to write begging letters to Herwegh and Annenkov. He managed to get a loan from Bürgers in Cologne and also from his brother-in-law, but the situation only improved when in early 1848 his mother granted him a sizeable advance on his inheritance.[2] Jenny was glad of the opportunities afforded by Brussels to extend her horizons beyond the household.

> In Germany [she wrote to Marx at the beginning of their stay] a child is still a very great honour, the cooking pot and needle still bring respect and moreover one still has the satisfaction of a duty fulfilled in return for all the days spent washing, sewing and minding the children. But when these old things no longer count as duties and honours and so on, when people progress so far that they even consider such old expressions to be obsolete... from then on one feels no more impulse to the small duties of life. One wants to enjoy, become active and experience in oneself the happiness of mankind.[3]

---

[1] Marx claimed that he had debts of more than 1000 francs and that it was cheaper to live in the guest house – which lodged many of the Brussels communists on and off – as he 'would have had to hire another maid as the smallest child is now weaned'. Marx to Weydemeyer, in B. Andreas and W. Mönke, 'Neue Daten zur "Deutschen Ideologie" ', *Archiv für Sozialgeschichte*, VIII 70.

[2] See below, pp. 189f.

[3] Jenny Marx to Marx, in L. Dornemann, *Jenny Marx*, p. 91.

In his memoirs written some fifty years later Stefan Born left the following account of his visit to Marx in late 1847:

> I found him in a very simple – I might almost say poor – little dwelling in a suburb of Brussels. He received me in a friendly fashion, asking me about the success of my propaganda trip, and complimented me on my pamphlet against Heinzen; his wife joined him in this and gave me a friendly welcome. . . . I have seldom known so happy a marriage in which joy and suffering – the latter in most abundant measure – were shared and all sorrow overcome in the consciousness of full and mutual dependency. Moreover I have seldom known a woman who in outward appearance as well as in spirit was so well balanced and so immediately captivating as Mrs Marx. She was fair-haired and the children (who were then still young) had their father's dark hair and eyes. Marx's mother, who lived in Trier, contributed to the expenses of the household, though the writer's pen no doubt had to find the greater part. . . .[1]

After his stay in Brussels Marx made very few close friendships; most of those he made or strengthened in Brussels remained so for life.

Even before *The German Ideology* was finished, Marx had started to establish a Communist Correspondence Committee in which Engels and Gigot were to take the most active part. This Committee was the embryo of all the subsequent Communist Internationals. It was designed as an instrument to harmonise and co-ordinate communist theory and practice in the European capitals. Marx described the aim as

> providing both a discussion of scientific questions and a critical appraisal of popular writings and socialist propaganda that can be conducted in Germany by these means. But the main aim of our correspondence will be to put German socialists in touch with English and French socialists, to keep foreigners informed of the socialist movements that will develop in Germany and to inform the Germans in Germany of the progress of socialism in France and England. In this way differences of opinion will be brought to light and we shall obtain an exchange of ideas and impartial criticism.[2]

This Correspondence Committee, and the subsequent Communist

---

[1] S. Born, *Erinnerungen eines Achtundvierzigers* (Leipzig, 1896) pp. 67 ff.
[2] Marx to Proudhon, *MEW* xxvii 442.

League which followed it, were Marx's first ventures into practical politics. The foundation of the Committee was to account for two controversies that raised questions central to the communist movement of that time. The first (with Weitling) carried into practical politics the polemic against 'true' socialism in *The German Ideology*; the second (with Proudhon) continued for the best part of the century – Proudhon's followers being particularly active in the First International.

Weitling was the illegitimate son of a French officer and a German laundry woman and earned his living as an itinerant tailor while absorbing the writings of the French socialists. His first book, *Mankind as it is and as it ought to be*, had been written in 1838 at the request of the League of the Just in Paris, and he had been very effective in his propaganda in Switzerland where his imprisonment had earned him the additional distinction of a martyr's halo. Thus he was widely welcomed on his arrival in London in 1844. During 1845, however, his preacher's style, the quasi-religious terms in which he expounded his ideas, his demands for immediate revolution, his proposals for a dictatorship à la Babeuf, and the marked psychological deterioration caused by his imprisonment: all these factors ended by alienating the majority of the London German communists who felt his approach to be impractical and unrealistic.[1] On his way back to the Continent in early 1846 Weitling stopped in Brussels and the newly founded Correspondence Committee invited him to a discussion in Marx's house. Among those present were Engels, Gigot, Edgar von Westphalen, Weydemeyer, Seiler, a journalist Heilberg, and a visitor by special invitation, Paul Annenkov, a well-to-do Russian tourist whom Marx had known in Paris.[2] Weitling struck him as 'a handsome fair-haired young man in a coat of elegant cut, a coquettishly trimmed small beard – someone more like a commercial traveller than the stern, embittered worker that I had expected to meet'. Annenkov continued:

We introduced ourselves to each other casually – with a touch of elaborate courtesy on Weitling's side, however – and took our places at the small green table. Marx sat at one end of it with a pencil in his

[1] Cf. M. Nettlau, 'Londoner deutsche kommunistische Diskussionen, 1845', *Grünberg-Archiv*, x (1925).
[2] See the passage quoted below p. 452 for the pungent characterisation of Marx as he appeared at the meeting.

hand and his leonine head bent over a sheet of paper, while Engels, his inseparable fellow-worker and comrade in propaganda, tall and erect and as dignified and serious as an Englishman, made the opening speech. He spoke of the necessity for people, who have devoted themselves to transforming labour, to explain their views to one another and agree on a single common doctrine that could be a banner for all their followers who lack the time and opportunity to study theory. Engels had not finished his speech when Marx raised his head, turned to Weitling and said: 'Tell us, Weitling, you who have made such a noise in Germany with your preaching: on what grounds do you justify your activity and what do you intend to base it on in the future?'

I remember quite well the form of the blunt question, because it was the beginning of a heated discussion, which, as we shall see, was very brief. Weitling apparently wanted to keep the conference within the bounds of common-place liberal talk. With a serious, somewhat worried face he started to explain that his aim was not to create new economic theories but to adopt those that were most appropriate, as experience in France had shown, to open the eyes of the workers to the horrors of their condition and all the injustices which it had become the motto of the rulers and societies to inflict on them, and to teach them never more to believe any promises of the latter, but to rely only upon themselves, and to organize in democratic and communist associations. He spoke for a long time, but – to my astonishment and in contrast to Engels – confusedly and not too well from the literary point of view, often repeating and correcting himself and arriving with difficulty at his conclusions, which either came too late or preceded his propositions. He now had quite different listeners from those who generally surrounded him at his work or read his newspaper and pamphlets on the contemporary economic system: he therefore lost his ease of thought and speech. Weitling would probably have gone on talking had not Marx checked him with an angry frown and started his reply.

Marx's sarcastic speech boiled down to this: to rouse the population without giving them any firm, well-thought-out reasons for their activity would be simply to deceive them. The raising of fantastic hopes just spoken of, Marx continued, led only to the final ruin and not to the saving of the sufferers. To call to the workers without any strictly scientific ideas or constructive doctrine, especially in Germany, was equivalent to vain dishonest play at preaching which assumed on the one side an inspired prophet and on the other only gaping asses. . . . Weitling's pale cheeks coloured and he regained his liveliness and ease of speech. In a voice trembling with emotion he started trying to prove that a man who had rallied hundreds of people under the same banner in the name of justice, solidarity and mutual brotherly assistance could not be called a completely vain and useless. Weitling consoled himself for the evening's attacks by remembering the hundreds of letters and declarations of gratitude that he had received from all parts of his native land and by the thought that his modest spadework was perhaps of greater weight for the common cause than criticism and armchair analysis of doctrines far from the world of the suffering and afflicted people.

On hearing these last words Marx finally lost control of himself and thumped so hard with his fist on the table that the lamp on it rung and shook. He jumped up saying: 'Ignorance never yet helped anybody!' We followed his example and left the table. The sitting ended, and as Marx paced up and down the room, extraordinarily irritated and angry, I hurriedly took leave of him and his interlocutors and went home, amazed at all I had seen and heard.[1]

The day after this discussion Weitling wrote to Hess that Marx had insisted on vetting party members; that for Marx the question of financial resources was all important (Weitling had the impression that Marx wished to exclude him from the Westphalian publishing project);[2] there was to be no propaganda based on emotional appeals; and lastly 'there can be no talk at present of achieving communism; the bourgeoisie must first come to the helm'. Weitling continued: 'I see in Marx's head only a good encylopaedia, but no genius. He owes his influence to other people. Rich men back him in journalism, that's all.'[3]

This was not the end of all contact between Weitling and Marx; for the next few weeks Weitling continued to accept a midday meal from Marx.[4] But Marx went on with his campaign by issuing a circular

---

[1] *Reminiscences of Marx and Engels*, pp. 270 ff.

[2] In Engels' letter to Bebel of 1888, this point is said to be the main reason for the break. See *MEW* xxxvii 118.

[3] M. Hess, *Briefwechsel*, p. 151.

[4] Cf. M. Hess, op. cit., p. 153. To speak of a 'purge' in this connection is to read

against Hermann Kriege, a young Westphalian journalist who had
been a member of the Brussels group before going to London and
finally emigrating to America where he published a weekly entitled
Volkstribun.[1] Kriege's views were much more representative of 'true
socialism' than Weitling's and this lengthy circular condemned
Kriege's ideas as 'not communism': they were 'childish and pompous'
an 'imaginary and sentimental exaltation' that 'compromised the
communist movement in America and demoralised the workers'.[2]
There followed sections in which derision was poured on Kriege's
metaphysical and religious phraseology, his use of the word 'love'
thirty-five times in a single article, and his naïve scheme of dividing up
the soil of America equally between all citizens which aimed at
'turning all men into owners of private property'.[3] Weitling was the
only member of the Correspondence Committee who voted against
the circular; he left Brussels immediately for Luxembourg and then
some months later moved to New York on Kriege's invitation. The
circular aroused a considerable volume of protest. Hess wrote to
Marx about Weitling: 'You have made him quite crazy and don't be
surprised. I want to have nothing more to do with the whole business;
it's enough to make one sick.'[4] And a week later he wrote that he
himself wished 'to have nothing more to do with your party'.[5] The
London communists also reacted strongly against the circular.

This attack on Kriege was apparently only one of many such pamphlets, for Marx wrote later:

> We published at the same time a series of pamphlets, partly printed,
> partly lithographed, in which we subjected to a merciless criticism
> the mixture of French-English socialism or communism and
> German philosophy, which at the time constituted the secret
> doctrine of the League. We established in its place the scientific
> understanding of the economic structure of bourgeois society as
> the only tenable theoretical foundation. We also explained in
> popular form that our task was not the fulfilment of some utopian

---

back post-1917 events quite inappropriately. There was, in any case, no 'party' in
the relevant sense.

[1] See further, H. Schlüter, *Die Anfänge der deutschen Arbeiterbewegung in Amerika*
(Stuttgart, 1907) pp. 19 ff.

[2] *MEW* IV 3.   [3] *Ibid.*, 10.

[4] M. Hess, *Briefwechsel*, p. 155.   [5] M. Hess, op. cit., p. 157.

system but the conscious participation in the historical process of social revolution that was taking place before our eyes.[1]

At the same time Marx tried to forge links with Paris where the most influential socialist was Proudhon. His position as a French thinker was peculiar in that he shared the atheistic approach to communism of the German Young Hegelians and rejected the patriotic Jacobinism that made Paris so impenetrable to German ideas. In early May 1846 Marx wrote to Proudhon describing the aims of the Correspondence Committee and inviting him to act as its Paris correspondent 'since as far as France is concerned we can find no better correspondent than yourself'.[2] In a postscript Marx warned Proudhon against Grün, whom he described as 'a charlatan ... who misuses his acquaintances'. Gigot and Engels also added postscripts saying how pleased they would be if Proudhon could accept the invitation. Proudhon's reply cannot have pleased Marx. He was willing to participate in Marx's project, but he had several reservations:

> Let us together seek, if you wish, the law of society, the manner in which these laws are realised, the process by which we shall succeed in discovering them; but, for God's sake, after having demolished all the *a priori* dogmatisms, do not let us in our turn dream of indoctrinating the people. . . . I applaud with all my heart your thought of inviting all shades of opinion; let us carry on a good and loyal polemic; let us give the world the example of an informed and far-sighted tolerance, but let us not – simply because we are at the head of a movement – make ourselves the leaders of a new intolerance, let us not pose as the apostles of a new religion, even if it be the religion of logic, the religion of reason. Let us gather together and encourage all dissent, let us outlaw all exclusiveness, all mysticism; let us never regard a question as exhausted, and when we have used our last argument, let us if necessary begin again – with eloquence and irony. On these conditions, I will gladly enter into your association. Otherwise – no![3]

Proudhon continued by saying that he was not in favour of immediate revolutionary action and preferred 'to burn property by a slow fire,

[1] K. Marx, 'Herr Vogt,' *MEW* xiv 439. Translated in D. Struik, op. cit., p. 149.
[2] Marx to Proudhon, *MEW* xxvii 442.
[3] Proudhon to Marx, in P. Haubtmann, *Marx et Proudhon* (Paris, 1947) pp. 63 f. For the relations of Proudhon and Marx, see further: J. Hoffman, *Revolutionary Justice* (Urbana, 1972) pp. 85 ff.

rather than give it new strength by making a St Bartholomew's Night of the property owners'. There followed an ironical paragraph: 'This, my dear philosopher, is where I am at the moment; unless, of course, I am mistaken and the occasion arises to receive a caning from you, to which I subject myself with good grace while awaiting for my revenge. . . .' Proudhon finished by excusing Grün on the grounds that he had been obliged to exploit 'modern ideas' in order to earn money for his family; he added, moreover, that it was at Grün's suggestion that he was hoping to insert a mention of Marx's works in his next book – The System of Economic Contradictions subtitled 'The Philosophy of Poverty'. Marx apparently made no reply to Proudhon's letter except in the form of his furious attack on Proudhon's book published a year later under the title of The Poverty of Philosophy. In his reply Marx accepted Proudhon's facetious invitation to 'administer the cane' with a vengeance.

Proudhon's book was a large sprawling two-volume work which bore the motto destruam et aedificabo – though there was much more of the former than the latter. With great vigour Proudhon attacked religion, academic economics and communism but did not provide any very clear solutions.[1] The book's ideas were very popular among French workers and in Germany three separate translations were arranged and two published in 1847, one being by Grün, whose ideas Engels had spent such a long time combating in Paris. Marx did not obtain Proudhon's book until Christmas 1846 and immediately wrote his impression of it in a long letter to Annenkov in which he clearly and succinctly applied to Proudhon's ideas his own materialist conception of history. The centre of Marx's criticism was that Proudhon did not grasp the historical development of humanity and thus had recourse to eternal concepts such as Reason and Justice. Marx wrote:

> What is society, whatever its form may be? The product of men's reciprocal action. Are men free to choose this or that form of society for themselves? By no means. Assume a particular state of development in the productive forces of man and you will get a particular form of commerce and consumption. Assume particular stages of development in production, commerce and consumption and you will have a corresponding social constitution, a corres-

[1] For Proudhon in general, see G. Woodcock, Proudhon (London, 1956). Probably the best account of Proudhon's ideas is J. Bancal, Proudhon: Pluralisme et Autogestion, 2 vols. (Paris, 1970).

ponding organisation of the family, or orders or of classes, in a word, a corresponding civil society. Assume a particular civil society and you will get particular political conditions which are only the official expression of civil society. M. Proudhon will never understand this because he thinks he is doing something great by appealing from the state to society – that is to say, from the official synopsis of society to official society.

It is superfluous to add that men are not free to choose their productive forces – which are the bases of all their history – for every productive force is an acquired force, the product of former activity. A coherence arises in human history, a history of humanity takes shape which is all the more a history of humanity as the productive forces of man and therefore his social relations have been more developed. Hence it necessarily follows that the social history of men is never anything but the history of their individual development, whether they are conscious of it or not. Their material relations are the basis of all their relations. These material relations are only the necessary forms in which their material and individual activity is realised.[1]

Marx did, however, grant that Proudhon, by trying to mediate between bourgeois economics and socialist ideas, had 'the merit of being the scientific interpreter of the French petty bourgeoisie – a genuine merit because the petty bourgeoisie will form an integral part of all the impending social revolutions'.[2]

These criticisms were elaborated on in his two-part book *The Poverty of Philosophy*. The first part dealt with the theory of value and the second began with an attack on Proudhon's method and ended with an important section on the working-class movement.

At the very outset Marx criticised Proudhon's lack of a precise starting point for his analysis. Proudhon's 'dialetic' merely consisted 'in the substitution for use-value and exchange-value and for supply and demand, of abstract and contradictory notions such as scarcity and abundance, utility and estimation, *one* producer and *one* consumer, both of them knights of free will'.[3] And Proudhon's purpose in this was to 'arrange for himself a means of introducing later on one of the elements he had set aside, the cost of production, as the synthesis of

---

[1] Marx to Annenkov, in K. Marx, *The Poverty of Philosophy* (Moscow, n.d.) pp. 202 f.
[2] K. Marx, op. cit., p. 217. [3] Ibid., p. 46

use-value and exchange-value. And it is thus that in his eyes the cost of production constitutes synthetic value or constituted value.'[1] By 'constituted value' of a product Proudhon meant 'the value which is constituted by the labour time incorporated in it'.[2] According to Marx this doctrine was no invention of Proudhon's (as he claimed) but was clearly to be found in Ricardo, the difference between them being that 'Ricardo takes his starting point from present-day society to demonstrate to us how it constitutes value – M. Proudhon takes constituted value as his starting point to construct a new social world with the aid of this value'.[3] So far from one's being able to draw 'egalitarian' consequences from this doctrine, it meant that wages always tended to a minimum.[4] For Proudhon had confused 'the two measures: measure by the labour time needed for the production of a commodity and measure by the value of the labour. "Any man's labour", he says, "can buy the value it represents". Thus, according to him, a certain quantity of labour embodied in a product is equivalent to the worker's payment, that is, to the value of labour. It is the same reasoning that makes him confuse cost of production with wages.'[5] Thus, 'in measuring the value of commodities by labour, M. Proudhon vaguely glimpses the impossiblity of excluding labour from this same measure, insofar as labour has a value, as labour is a commodity. He has a misgiving that it is turning the wage minimum into the natural and normal price of immediate labour, that it is accepting the existing state of society. So, to get away from this fatal consequence, he contradicts himself and asserts that labour is not a commodity, that it cannot have value. He forgets that he himself has taken the value of labour as a measure.'[6] Further, Proudhon set out to show that 'the labour time needed to create a product indicates its true proportional relation to needs, so that the things whose production costs the least time are the most immediately useful and so on, step by step'.[7] But the same argument would show that 'the wide use of spirits, because

---

[1] Ibid.   [2] Ibid., p. 47

[3] The big difference between *The Poverty of Philosophy* and Marx's 1844 writings is that Marx in 1847 accepted the labour theory of value that he had previously rejected. He had probably made this change during his visit to Manchester in 1845 where he read the English socialist economists who drew the radical conclusions that were obviously deducible from Ricardo's idea that labour was the source of all value. See further, E. Mandel, *The Formation of Marx's Economic Thought*, chs. 3 and 4.

[4] In 1847–8 Marx held a theory of absolute pauperisation that he later abandoned.

[5] K. Marx, *The Poverty of Philosophy* (Moscow, n.d.) p. 61.

[6] Ibid., p. 64.   [7] Ibid., p. 67.

of their low cost of production, is the most conclusive proof of their utility: it is telling the proletarian that potatoes are more wholesome for him than meat; it is accepting the present state of affairs; it is, in short, making an apology, with M. Proudhon, for a society without understanding it'.[1]

For Marx, on the other hand, 'In a future society, in which class antagonism will have ceased, in which there will no longer be any classes, use will no longer be determined by the minimum time of production; but the time of production devoted to different articles will be determined by the degree of their social utility.'[2] Proudhon's proposals abstracted from differences in demand, competition, etc., and he was inevitably forced into a dilemma: 'Either you want the genuine bartering process of past centuries with present-day means of production – in which case you are both reactionary and utopian; or you want progress without anarchy – in which case, in order to preserve the productive forces, you must abandon individual exchange.'[3] Anyway, Marx claimed, Proudhon was far from the first to think of 'reforming society by transforming all men into actual workers exchanging equal amounts of labour'.[4] To prove his point he quoted at great length from the English economist Bray, views which he nevertheless rejected on the grounds that 'individual exchange corresponds . . . to a definite mode of production which itself corresponds to class antagonism. There is thus no individual exchange without the antagonism of classes.'[5] Marx then finished the first half of the book with remarks on the impossibility of deducing the value of money from labour time, and on the way that Proudhon (in order to oppose the idea that labour produced a surplus) had to suppose existing social relations to be non-existent.

In the second part of the book, Marx attacked Proudhon's desire 'to frighten the French by flinging quasi-Hegelian phrases at them',[6] and his use of such pseudo-explanatory devices as thesis, antithesis and synthesis.[7] He then accused Proudhon of seeing 'in actual relations nothing but the incarnation of . . . principles' and continued in a well-known passage:

Social relations are closely bound up with productive forces. In

[1] Ibid., p. 70.   [2] Ibid.   [3] Ibid., p. 76.
[4] Ibid.   [5] Ibid., pp. 86 f.   [6] Ibid., p. 116
[7] Contrary to what is alleged in many books, Marx never employed these terms – nor, for that matter, did Hegel.

acquiring new productive forces men change their mode of production; and in changing their mode of production, in changing the way of earning their living, they change all their social relations. The hand-mill gives you society with the feudal lord: the steam-mill, society with the industrial capitalist.[1]

According to Marx, in the eyes of classical economists 'there are only two kinds of institutions, artificial and natural. The institutions of feudalism are artificial institutions, those of the bourgeoisie are natural institutions.'[2] But bourgeois doctrines were as relative as any other and were to be supplanted by proletarian economic doctrines. The theoreticians of such doctrines were, of course, merely utopian in the beginning of the proletarian movement;

> but to the extent that history moves forward and with it the struggle of the proletariat assumes clearer outlines, they no longer need to seek solutions by drawing on their imagination; they have only to take note of what is happening before their eyes and to become its mouthpiece. So long as they look for knowledge by merely constructing systems, so long as they are at the beginning of the struggle, they see in poverty nothing but poverty – without seeing in it the revolutionary, subversive aspect which will overthrow the old society. From this moment, knowledge which is a product of historical process will have associated itself consciously with it, ceased to be doctrinaire and become revolutionary.[3]

Proudhon was also deficient in his account of the division of labour which was not an economic category but a historical one; competition, equally, was above all an eighteenth-century product and no 'eternal' category; and landed property was no 'independent relation, a category apart, no abstract and eternal idea'. Finally Marx rejected Proudhon's view that strikes for higher wages were useless as their success only entailed a corresponding increase in prices. He dealt with this view in the last pages of his book which contained a sort of anarchist manifesto portraying the working class as essentially revolutionary:

> An oppressed class is the vital condition for every society founded on the antagonism of classes. The emancipation of the oppressed

---

[1] K. Marx, *The Poverty of Philosophy* (Moscow, n.d.) p. 122.
[2] Ibid., p. 135.
[3] Ibid., pp. 140 f.

class thus implies necessarily the creation of a new society. For the oppressed class to be able to emancipate itself it is necessary that the existing productive powers and social relations should no longer be capable of existing side by side. Of all the instruments of production, the greatest productive power is the revolutionary class itself. The organization of revolutionary elements as a class presupposes the existence of all the productive forces which could be brought to fruition within the framework of the old society.

Does this mean that after the collapse of the old society there will be a new dominant class culminating in a new political power? No. The condition for the emancipation of the working class is the abolition of every class, just as the condition for the liberation of the third estate, of the bourgeois order, was the abolition of all estates and all orders.

The working class, in the course of its development, will substitute for the old civil society an association which will exclude classes and their antagonism, and there will be no more political power as such, since political power is precisely the official expression of antagonism in civil society.

Meanwhile the antagonism between the proletariat and the bourgeoisie is a struggle of class against class – a struggle which, carried to its highest expression, is a total revolution. Indeed, is it at all surprising that a society founded on the opposition of classes should culminate in brutal contradiction, the shock of body against body, as its final *dénouement*?

Do not say that social movement excludes political movement. There is never a political movement which is not at the same time social. It is only in an order of things in which there are no more classes and class antagonisms that social evolutions will cease to be political revolutions. Till then, on the eve of every general restructuring of society, the last word of social science will always be: 'Le combat ou la mort, la lutte sanguinaire ou le néant. C'est ainsi que la question est invinciblement posée.' George Sand.[1]

Marx's book contained the first published and systematic statement of the materialist conception of history and he himself recommended it as an introduction to *Capital*. It also demonstrated Marx's great talent as a pamphleteer – though Proudhon's book was certainly an

[1] Ibid., pp. 196 ff.

easy target. However, in spite of its having been published in both Brussels and Paris, the total edition of 800 copies made little impression on Marx's contemporaries and he had to pay for the printing himself. Proudhon called the book 'a tissue of abuse, falsification and plagiarism'[1] and its author 'the tape-worm of socialism'.[2] He carefully annotated his own copy of *The Poverty of Philosophy* and probably intended to reply but was interrupted by family affairs and the 1848 revolution. Thus culminated the highly acrimonious debate between the two men.

Proudhon was only one of several Paris socialists that the Brussels Correspondence Committee sought to recruit. The others, however, were not much more fruitful. There was a brief exchange of letters with Louis Blanc; and Dr Ewerbeck, who espoused a sort of peaceful communist humanism based on Cabet's ideas, served as a rallying point for what remained of the League of the Just. Having persuaded the Marx family to spend a fortnight with him at Ostend, Engels himself went to Paris in August 1846. In the regular letters he sent back to the Brussels Correspondence Committee he reported on the progress of his propaganda among the German workers which he directed particularly against Grün and the disciples of Proudhon. Among the main craft unions in Paris, the tailors were still subject to the effect of Weitling's emotionally based communist propaganda (though he himself had left the city). Engels therefore attempted to recruit the remnants of the League of the Just (mostly members of joiners' unions) and instil into them some definite form of communism. By October he could report back to Brussels that his new recruits had now accepted a definition of communism comprising: a maintenance of the interests of the proletariat against those of the bourgeoisie; the abolition of private property; and, as a means, a violent democratic revolution. This ideological victory, however, was not of great moment for Engels continued in the same letter: 'The public in front of whom we played this face was composed of about twenty joiners. Apart from our meetings they organise discussions with all sorts of people in the outer boulevards, and outside their working association, they do not form any real group. . . .'[3] This letter showed Engels in a moment of uncharacteristic realism. In general it is clear that Engels was over-optimistic about the success of

---

[1] Proudhon to Fuillaumin, 19 Sep 1847, in P. Haubtmann, *Marx et Proudhon*, p. 92.
[2] P. Haubtmann, op. cit., p. 94.
[3] Engels to Marx, *MEW* xxvii 62

his propaganda. At the end of October the police intervened to stop even what small-scale activity existed and Engels thought it more prudent to turn his attention to the conquest of as many girls of as many different nationalities as possible before he left Paris.

Correspondence with Germany was established on a fairly regular basis: there were periodical reports from Silesia inspired by Wilhelm Wolff, from the Wuppertal where the painter Koettgen (a close friend of Hess) led a communist group, and from Kiel where Georg Weber, a doctor, led the movement. Marx, however, was impatient with Weydemeyer's failure in Westphalia to find a publisher for *The German Ideology* and relations became strained. The centre of communist activity was still Cologne. Hess was there for the second half of 1846 and declared himself 'to some extent reconciled to "the Party" ';[1] he recognised the necessity of basing communism on historical and economic presuppositions and was waiting with great interest for the appearance of Marx's book; his break with Marx did not become final until early 1848. But Marx's ideas seem to have had very little impact there, although the group there was organised by Roland Daniels (a close friend of Marx) with the support of d'Ester and Bürgers, and was very active in local politics.

The only letter that has survived from the Brussels communists to Germany is one to Koettgen written in June 1846. Marx, together with the other members of the committee, criticised 'illusions' about the efficacy of petitions to authorities – arguing that they could only carry weight 'when there is a strong and well-organised communist party in Germany – both elements being currently lacking'. Meanwhile the Wuppertal communists should act 'jesuitically' and support bourgeois demands for freedom of the Press, constitutional government, etc. Only later would specifically communist demands be possible: for the present 'it is necessary to support, in a single party, "everything" that helps the movement forward and not have any tiresome moral scruples about it'.[2]

III. THE FOUNDING OF THE COMMUNIST LEAGUE

The most important result of the Correspondence Committee was to create close ties between Marx and Engels and the London communists who at that time were the largest and best-organised colony of German workers. Until the late 1830s the most important centre had been

[1] M. Hess, *Briefwechsel*, p. 44.   [2] Marx to Koettgen, *MEW* IV 21 ff.

Paris where exiled German artisans had started in 1836 the League of the Just (a secret society with code names and passwords) which itself derived from an earlier League of Outlaws. Its original object was to introduce into Germany the Rights of Man and the Citizen, and very roughly half of its membership came from artisans and half from the professions. The League of the Just participated in the rising organised by Blanqui and Barbès in 1839 and on its failure the majority of its members fled to London where they founded a flourishing branch.[1] This in its turn created a 'front' organisation, the German Workers Educational Union, which had almost 1000 members by the end of 1847 and survived until the First World War.

The League was led by a triumvirate of Karl Schapper, Heinrich Bauer and Joseph Moll. Schapper was a veteran communist from Nassau, the son of a poor country pastor. As a forestry student he had joined the *Burschenschaft* movement and had worked with both Buchner and Mazzini while Marx was still a schoolboy. According to one of his colleagues in the League Schapper was a revolutionary 'more through enthusiasm than theoretical knowledge'.[2] Bauer was a shoemaker. Moll was a Cologne watchmaker, intellectually and diplomatically the most gifted of the three.[3] The Union organised courses four evenings a week in the Red Lion public house near Piccadilly. A German economics professor, Bruno Hildebrand, has left an account of one of these evenings which is worth extensive quotation as it vividly conveys the atmosphere in which was born the Communist League (and also the German Workers Educational Union, which remained peripheral to Marx's activities for many years). Hildebrand described an evening in April 1846 just at the time when Marx was beginning to establish regular contact with the London communists. He wrote:

> We went to the meeting place of the Association about half past eight in an atmosphere of tension and impatience. The ground floor seemed to be a beer shop. Porter and other fine beers were on sale but I did not notice any seats for consumers. We went through this shop and up a staircase into a room furnished with tables and

---

[1] Cf. E. Schraepler, 'Der Bund der Gerechten. Seine Tätigkeit in London 1840–1847', *Archiv für Sozialgeschichte* (1962).

[2] F. Lessner, 'Vor 1848 und nachher', *Deutsche Worte*, XVIII (1898) p. 103.

[3] For Schapper and Moll, see *Marx und Engels und die erste proletarischen Revolutionäre*, ed. E. Kandel (Berlin, 1965) pp. 42 ff.

benches which could accommodate about 200 people. Twenty or so men were seated in little groups eating a very simple dinner or smoking one of the pipes of honour (of which there was one on each table) with their pot of beer in front of them. Others were still standing and the door was always opening to admit new arrivals. It was clear that the meeting would not begin for some time. The clothes were very proper, the behaviour had a simplicity that did not exclude dignity, but most of the faces were evidently those of workers. The main language was German, but we could also hear French and English. At the end of the room there was a grand piano with some music books on it – and this, in a London that was so unmusical, showed us that we had come to the right place. We had been scarcely noticed and sat down at a table opposite the door. While waiting for Schapper, the friend who had invited us, we ordered porter and the traditional little penny packet of tobacco. Soon we saw a man enter who was tall and strong, a picture of health. He had a black moustache, a clear and penetrating look and an imperious manner. He seemed to be about thirty-six. He was introduced to me as Schapper. . . .

Schapper invited us to sit with him at the back of the room. On the way he showed me a poster with the heading, 'Statutes of the German Workers Educational Union'. . . . The main principle of the Union is that men can only come to liberty and self-consciousness by cultivating their intellectual faculties. Consequently all the evening meetings are devoted to instruction. On one evening, English is taught, on another geography, on the third history, on the fourth, drawing and physics, on the fifth, singing, on the sixth, dancing and on the seventh communist politics. . . .

We sat in the places allotted to us; meanwhile the room had filled up completely. The president, who was unknown to me – I was told he was a doctor, opened the meeting. When a solemn silence had been established and everyone had taken his pipe from his mouth, the secretary (a working tailor whose descriptive talent seemed to me to be truly enviable) declared that Citizen Schapper had invited Citizen Hildebrand and Citizen Diefenbach and asked if anyone had an objection to make. Then we went on to current politics and Citizen Schapper delivered a report on the week's events. His speech was eloquent, very detailed and full of interest. It was evident that he and the Association had many sources of information. . . .

Naturally a strong communist tendency was always plain and the proletariat was the constant theme and the one real thread running through the entire speech. I admit that I can stand a good dose of liberalism, but certain passages made my hair stand on end. . . .[1]

At first the German communists in London had been under the influence of Cabet's peaceful utopian communism following the failure of their attempt at a *putsch* in Paris in alliance with the Blanquists. Cabet had also persuaded them to give up their conspiratorial methods – though they necessarily remained a secret society. But they rejected Cabet's proposal to found a communist colony in America. By that time Weitling's influence had become important. But his notions of immediate revolution soon alienated the majority of the London communists who began to be much influenced by their personal experience of Owenite schemes, by Chartism and by the tangible success of the British trade unions. Weitling held the view that 'mankind is either always ripe or it never will be. . . . Revolutions arise like storms and no one can chart their operations beforehand. . . . The intellect has only a poor role to play and without emotion can do nothing . . . the greatest deeds are accomplished by the emotions that move the masses.'[2] Schapper's view, on the other hand, was that 'it is as easy to compel a tree to grow as to inculcate new ideas into mankind by force. Let us avoid physical violence: it is crude; and mankind does not need it. . . . Let us view ourselves as leaves on the great tree of humanity and posterity will reap what we with our calm activity have sown.'[3] This debate went on for several months in the meetings of the Association, and Weitling was ably supported by Kriege but the majority of the workers eventually sided with Schapper.

The London communists had broken off all contact with Weitling by the time that Marx, in mid-May 1846, suggested that they form a communist correspondence bureau in regular liaison with Brussels. As early as March Engels had formally asked Harney to act as correspondent with Brussels. But Harney, who had himself become a member of the League in February, insisted that Schapper and the

---

[1] C. Grünberg, 'Bruno Hildebrand über den Kommunistischen Arbeiterbildungsverein in London', *Archiv fär die Geschichte des Sozialismus und der Arbeiterbewegung*, (1925) pp. 455 ff.

[2] M. Nettlau, 'Londoner deutsche kommunistische Diskussionen, 1845', *Archiv für die Geschichte des Sozialismus und der Arbeiterbewegung*, x (1925) p. 371.

[3] Ibid., p. 368.

leaders of the League be consulted first – suggesting that they were mistrustful of the 'literary characters in Brussels';[1] and Marx's ideas were indeed far from popular with them. According to Schapper (and his letters reflected the views of the League leaders as a whole) revolutions could not be made to order, and a spiritual awakening would have to precede a physical uprising. The task of the League was seen by its leaders as one of 'enlightening the people and propaganda for the community of goods'.[2] They were also opposed to Marx's attitude to Kriege and complained of the 'intellectual arrogance' of the Brussels communists.[3] Schapper did agree, however, to Marx's proposal in July 1846 that a congress he held in London at some future date to hammer out differences and 'bring force and unity into our propaganda'.[4] As late as December 1846 Engels was suggesting to Marx – in a letter which is a good example of their 'intellectual arrogance' – that they might have to let the correspondence with the Londoners drop quietly and try to reach some agreement with Harney.[5] But it was clear that the German communists in London, in terms of numbers and organisation, represented for Marx and Engels by far the most promising entrée into working-class politics, particularly because Marx's various European Correspondence Committees never really got off the ground.

In November the Central Committee of the League of the Just, which had remained in Paris, was formally transferred to London. Together with the attempt at organisational reform that this implied, there was the growing feeling that, after the rejection of the communism of Cabet and Weitling, firmer theoretical foundations for the League were needed. On 20 January 1847, the London Correspondence Committee decided to send Moll (whose views were noticeably closer to Marx's than were Schapper's) to Brussels to solicit the help of Marx and invite him to join the League. Marx wrote later: 'Whatever objections we had against this proposal were met by Moll's statement that the Central Committee planned to call together a Congress of the League in London. There, the critical position we had taken would be

[1] Harney to Engels, *The Harney Papers* (Assen, 1969) pp. 242 f.
[2] Schapper to Marx, quoted in H. Gemkow, *Karl Marx, Eine Biographie* (Berlin, 1968) p. 100.
[3] K. Marx: *Chronik seines Lebens* (Moscow, 1934) p. 35.
[4] Schapper to Marx, quoted in *Karl Marx: Dokumente seines Lebens*, p. 190.
[5] Cf. Engels to Marx, *MEW* xxvii 70.

adopted in a public manifesto as the doctrine of the League. Antiquated and dissident views could only be counteracted by our personal collaboration, but this was only possible if we joined the League.'[1] Another condition that Marx laid down before joining was 'that everything that encouraged a supersititious attitude to authority be banished from the Statutes of the League'.[2] Several other Brussels communists joined the League at the same time, as did Engels, whom Moll went on to visit in Paris. The London Central Committee demonstrated its willingness to change its ideas by issuing an Address to members of the League in which they now called for a stricter definition of aims, rejected socialism based on pure sentiment and condemned conspiratorial approaches to revolution.

The promised congress, which had in fact been summoned by the London Central Committee as early as November 1846 along extremely democratic lines, assembled in London from 2 to 9 June 1847. Marx did not attend, pleading lack of money, so Wolff went as a delegate of the Brussels communists, and Engels represented the Parisians. It was decided to reorganise the democratic basis of the League, to change the name of the League to 'The Communist League', to emphasise the inappropriateness of the conspiratorial approach, and to issue a periodical. The first and last issue of this periodical, written mainly by Schapper and entitled *Kommunistische Zeitung*, appeared in September. In the new statutes, the previous slogan 'All Men are Brothers' was replaced by 'Proletarians of all Countries – Unite'. (Marx was said to have declared that there were many men whose brother he wished on no account to be.) Yet the statutes as a whole still represented a compromise between Marx's views and those of the London communists; their first article read: 'The League aims at the abolition of man's enslavement by propagating the theory of the community of goods and by its implementation as soon as possible.'[3] A three-tiered structure was now proposed for the League: the Commune, the Circle Committee (comprising the chair-

---

[1] K. Marx, 'Herr Vogt', *MEW* XXIV 439.

[2] Marx to Blos, *MEW* XXXIV 308.

[3] The documents relevant to this Congress have only recently been discovered and published as *Gründungsdokumente des Bundes der Kommunisten Juni bis September 1847*, ed. B. Andreas (Hamburg, 1969). This corrects the widespread view (e.g. Mehring, p. 139) that Marx's ideas were thoroughly accepted as early as the summer of 1847. The documents also show that the League had branches in a dozen German cities and even one in Stockholm.

man and treasurers of the relevant communes) and the Central Committee, together with an annual congress, all officials being elected for one year and subject to instant recall. A draft 'Confession of Faith', drawn up by Engels, was circulated to the branches to be discussed at a second Congress in the following November.

The success of the June Congress inspired Marx in early August formally to turn the Brussels Correspondence Committee into a branch of the Communist League with himself as President. It was the general practice of the League (which was a secret society) to set up non-clandestine 'Workers' Associations'. In late August a German Workers' Association was formed in Brussels with Karl Wallau (a typesetter) as President and Moses Hess as Vice-President. It had thirty-seven members to begin with and increased rapidly.[1] In addition to many social activities, there were lectures on Wednesdays – sometimes given by Marx – and a review of the week's politics on Sundays by Wilhelm Wolff. Marx was pleased with its 'quite parliamentary discussions' and found the public activity that it afforded him 'infinitely refreshing'.[2]

At the same time Marx managed to secure ready access to a newspaper as a vehicle for his views. The *Deutsche Brüsseler Zeitung* was published twice weekly from the beginning of 1847 by Adelbert von Bornstedt, who had previously edited *Vorwärts* in Paris. Bornstedt had been a spy for both the Prussians and the Austrians in the 1830s and early 1840s, and many in Brussels suspected that he was continuing those activities. However, the paper took on an increasingly radical and anti-Prussian tone. In April 1847 Wilhelm Wolff started contributing, and in September Marx began to write frequently – having come to an arrangement with Bornstedt that the paper would accept all contributions by himself and Engels. He complained bitterly to Herwegh of criticism of this step from Germans who 'always have a thousand words of wisdom up their sleeves to prove why they should once again let an opportunity slip by. An opportunity for doing something is nothing but a source of embarrassment for them.'[3]

Marx contributed two important essays to the *Deutsche Brüsseler Zeitung*. One was a reply to an unsigned article in the *Rheinischer Beobachter* whose author – Hermann Wagener, later the close associate of

[1] See the list in J. Kuypers, 'Karl Marx' belgischer Freundeskreis', *International Review of Social History* (1962).
[2] Marx to Engels, *MEW* XXVII 470.   [3] Marx to Herwegh, *MEW* XXVII 469.

Bismarck – had tried to give the impression that the Prussian Government was in favour of 'socialist' and even 'communist' measures, citing its recent proposals to shift the main tax burden from foodstuffs to incomes. Marx rejected the idea that the communists had anything to gain from supporting the Government against the bourgeoisie. And in so far as Wagener appealed to the social principles of Christianity, Marx claimed that they merely

> transferred to heaven the task of reparing all infamies and that this justified their continuation on earth. . . . The social principles of Christianity preach cowardice, self-abasement, resignation, submission and humility – in short, all the characteristics of the *canaille*; but the proletariat is not prepared to let itself be treated as *canaille*, and it needs its courage, confidence, pride and independence even more than it needs its daily bread. The social principles of Christianity are sneaking and hypocritical whilst the proletariat is revolutionary.[1]

In Germany, the proletariat had to ally itself with the bourgeoisie for 'the aristocracy can only be overthrown by an alliance of the bourgeoisie and the people'.[2] Wagener was quite mistaken in arguing that the proletariat would be well advised to ally itself with the royal Government which was in reality its most dangerous rival. 'The real people, the proletarians, the small peasants and the rabble are, as Hobbes said, *puer robustus sed malitiosus* and are not taken in by kings, whether they be fat or thin. This people would above all extract from His Majesty a constitution with universal suffrage, freedom of association, freedom of the press and other unpleasant things.'[3]

The second of Marx's articles was a polemic against Heinzen, who commented later that Marx was the sort of man who brought up heavy artillery in order to smash a window-pane. Heinzen had written for the *Rheinische Zeitung* in 1842 and spent much time in Marx's company in 1845, but he attacked not only communism but also 'true' socialism on his emigration to Switzerland, where he had become friendly with Ruge. Heinzen was a thoroughgoing republican who saw the monarchy as the foundation of all social evil to which the proclamation of a republic would put an end. In his reply to Heinzen Marx stated that 'the political relationships of men . . . are also social

---

[1] K. Marx, 'The Communism of the *Rheinischer Beobachter*', *MEW* iv 200.
[2] Ibid., 202.   [3] Ibid.

relationships',[1] and analysed the role played by the monarchy as a transitional institution between the old feudal classes and the nascent bourgeoisie. But the bourgeoisie was growing ever more powerful and already found itself in opposition to the proletariat. The solemn idea of 'humanity' would never, as Heinzen hoped, cause classes to melt away. The task of the proletariat was 'to overthrow the political power that the bourgeoisie already has in its hands. They must themselves become a power, and first of all a revolutionary power.'[2]

From 16 to 18 September 1847 a congress of professional economists – in effect, a pressure group for free trade – was held in Brussels. Marx attended by invitation. Georg Weerth was a dissident voice in declaring it a scandal that in all the eulogies they made of free trade there was no mention of the misery inflicted on the working class. Marx intended to deliver a speech in support of Weerth, but the list of speakers was closed to prevent his intervention. Marx at once circulated his speech to several newspapers in Belgium and abroad, but only the small Brussels *Atelier Démocratique* would publish it. After analysing the disastrous effect of free trade on the working class Marx declared himself nevertheless in favour of it 'because by Free Trade all economical laws, with their most astonishing contradictions, will act upon a larger scale, upon a greater extent of territory, upon the territory of the whole earth; and because from the unity of these contradictions into a single group, where they stand face to face, will result the struggle which will itself eventuate in the emancipation of the proletariat'.[3]

On 29 September a dinner was held in order to inaugurate in Brussels what was to become the International Democratic Association, a body modelled on the Fraternal Democrats in London. (At this time many political meetings were held under the guise of dinners as they were more difficult for the police to control.) The dinner had been arranged on the initiative of Bornstedt. Marx had briefly gone to Maastricht to see his brother-in-law on family business. Although Engels regarded the holding of the dinner as an anti-communist move, he managed to be chosen as one of its vice-presidents and also a

[1] K. Marx, 'Moralising Criticism and Critical Morality', *MEW* IV 340.
[2] Ibid., 338.
[3] K. Marx, *MEGA* I 6 431: this is taken from a summary of the speech published by Engels in the *Northern Star*. The beginning of the speech is published in *MEW* IV 296 ff. Apparently the continuation was taken up verbatim in Marx's lecture of 9 January 1848 to the Democratic Association. See below p. 177.

member of the committee that was to establish the Association. Engels promptly delegated his place to Marx and left for Paris where he renewed his contacts with French socialists and republican leaders; and Marx was duly chosen as Vice-President of the Association. The Association held meetings, established a number of branches in Belgium, and issued addresses on such subjects as the threat to freedom in Switzerland and the anniversary of the Polish revolution.[1]

But Marx had other and more pressing business to attend to: at the end of October he received a letter from the Central Committee of the Communist League in London telling him that the congress had been put off until the end of November and urging him to attend in person. On 27 November Marx left Brussels in the company of Weerth and Victor Tedesco; he met Engels at Ostend on the twenty-eighth and, with Tedesco, they crossed the Channel on the twenty-ninth. Ostensibly Marx went as a delegate of the Democratic Association to attend a meeting of the Fraternal Democrats in celebration of the Polish uprising of 1830. The evening after his arrival in London Marx duly delivered an 'energetic'[2] speech to the Fraternal Democrats, meeting in the headquarters of the German Workers' Educational Association at 20 Great Windmill Street, near Piccadilly.[3] The downfall of the established order, he told them, 'is no loss for those who have nothing to lose in the old society and this is the case in all countries for the great majority. They have, rather, everything to gain from the collapse of the old society which is the condition for the building of a new society no longer based on class opposition.'[4] Marx concluded by proposing Brussels as the venue for the following year's meeting, but this proposal was overtaken by events.

The next day, in the same building, the second congress of the Communist League began. According to Engels, 'Marx ... defended the new theory during fairly lengthy debates. All opposition and doubt was at last overcome and the new principles were unanimously accepted.'[5] The debates lasted a full ten days, during which new statutes were drawn up making it quite clear that the Communist League

[1] See further, W. Haenisch, 'Karl Marx and the Democratic Association of 1847', *Science and Society*, Winter 1937.

[2] Report in the *Northern Star*, quoted in Haenisch, op. cit., p. 88.

[3] There is a very full account of this meeting in E. Dolleans, *Le Chartisme* (Paris, 1949) pp. 296 ff.

[4] K. Marx, 'Speech on Poland', *MEW* IV 416 f.

[5] F. Engels, 'History of the Communist League', *MEW* XXI 215 f.

(although necessarily operating largely in secret) was to have a democratic structure ultimately dependent on an annual congress and have as its principal purpose the progapation of publicly declared doctrines. The statutes adopted in June with their somewhat utopian notions of 'community of goods' were set aside and the aims of the League were proclaimed as 'the overthrow of the bourgeoisie, the domination of the proletariat, the abolition of the old bourgeois society based on class antagonisms, and the establishment of a new society without classes and without private property'.[1] At the end of the congress Marx and Engels were given the task of writing a Manifesto to publicise the doctrines of the League. There are no surviving records of these discussions, but the following vivid description of the impression made by Marx at that time was written much later by Frederick Lessner:

Marx was then still a young man, about 28 years old, but he greatly impressed us all. He was of medium height, broad-shouldered, powerful in build, and vigorous in his movements. His forehead was high and finely shaped, his hair thick and pitch-black, his gaze piercing. His mouth already had the sarcastic curl that his opponents feared so much. Marx was a born leader of the people. His speech was brief, convincing and compelling in its logic. He never said a superfluous word; every sentence contained an idea and every idea was an essential link in the chain of his argument. Marx had nothing of the dreamer about him. The more I realized the difference between the communism of Weitling's time and that of the *Communist Manifesto*, the more clearly I saw that Marx represented the manhood of socialist thought.[2]

On his return to Brussels Marx had little time to compose his Manifesto. He immediately began to give a course of lectures on wages to the German Workers' Educational Association.[3] Here Marx was chiefly concerned to go beyond the idea of capital as simply composed of raw materials, instruments of production, and so forth. He insisted

---

[1] *MEW* IV 596. The structure adopted was, if anything, less democratic than that of the June Congress.

[2] F. Lessner, 'Before 1848 and After', in *Reminiscences of Marx and Engels*, p. 153.

[3] These were eventually published in 1849 in the *Neue Rheinische Zeitung*. See *MEW* VI 397 ff. Marx's notes for his lectures covering sixteen pages have been published in *MEGA* I 6 451 ff.

that it was only in given social conditions that such things constituted capital.

> Capital, also, is a social relation of production. It is a bourgeois production relation, a production relation of bourgeois society. Are not the means of subsistence, the instrument of labour, the raw materials of which capital consists, produced and accumulated under given social conditions, in definite social relations? Are they not utilised for new production under given social conditions, in definite social relations? And it is not just this definite social character which turns the products necessary to new production into capital?[1]

In order for capital to exist there had to be 'a class which possesses nothing but its capacity for labour'.[2] Capital and wage-labour were complementary in function and entirely opposed in interest. Although for a time working conditions might improve this only meant that the working class could consider itself 'content with forging for itself the golden chains by which the bourgeoisie drags it in its wake'.[3] And Marx went on to issue a categorical statement – to be revised in his later works – that with the increase in productive capacity and machinery wages would fall. In February Marx started writing up these lectures for publication, but was to be interrupted by his expulsion from Belgium.

Marx was also active in the Democratic Association to which, on his return to Brussels, he read the reply from the Fraternal Democrats that declared: 'Your representative, our friend and brother Marx, will tell you with what enthusiasm we welcomed his appearance and the reading of your address. All eyes shone with joy, all voices shouted a welcome and all hands stretched out fraternally to your representative. ... We accept with the liveliest feelings of satisfaction the alliance you have offered us.'[4] Marx helped to found a new branch in Ghent and was prominent in the meeting to celebrate the New Year where Jenny was complimented on her social capacity. It was on one of these occasions, too, that Jenny Marx refused categorically to be introduced to Mary Burns whom Engels had had the temerity to bring with him. Stefan Born recalled that 'in matters of honour and purity of morals

---

[1] K. Marx, 'Wage Labour and Capital', *MESW* I 90.
[2] Ibid., 91.   [3] Ibid., 98.   [4] *MEGA* I 6 635.

1 Marx's birthplace: Brückergasse 664 (not Brückerstrasse 10). The family lived here for only about eighteen months, occupying two rooms on the ground floor and three on the second floor.

2 Karl Marx, aged eighteen. Detail from a lithograph of the Trier Students' Club in 1836, made by D. Levy-Elkan.

3 Jenny von Westphalen.

4 Friedrich Engels, from a daguerrotype of 1845.

5 Helena Demuth.

6 Jenny Marx, soon after
her marriage.

7 Jenny Marx with her eldest daughter Jenny, about 1854.

8 28 Dean Street, where the Marx family lived from 1850 to 1856 (the GLC plaque is not quite accurate on the dates). The Marxs' large front room spanned three windows on the second floor. The photograph was taken in 1972.

9 The first known photograph of Marx, taken in 1861.

10 The younger Jenny, in the late 1860s.

11 Laura Marx.

12 Freddy Demuth in old age.

13 Eleanor Marx, taken about 1874, when she was aged eighteen.

14 Edgar Marx, from a contemporary drawing of the mid-1850s — possibly by Engels.

15 Marx and Engels with Jenny, Eleanor and Laura in 1864.

16 9 Grafton Terrace, where the Marx family
lived from 1856 to 1864, occupying all
four floors. Photograph taken in 1972.

17 Marx in 1872, the year of the collapse of the First International.

18 Marx and his daughter Jenny, taken in 1868.

chico →

19 Marx in 1867, the year of publication of *Capital*, Volume One.

← Harpo

20 The only known profile photograph of Marx, taken in 1867.

Groucho →

21 Marx in 1875: a photograph taken by Magall, who was also photographer to Disraeli and Queen Victoria.

22 Marx in 1882 in Algiers: the last photograph.

23 41 Maitland Park Road, the Marxs' house from 1875 to 1883.
Marx's study was on the first floor. It was here that he died.

24 The chair in the British Museum reputed to be Marx's favourite.

25 Marx's tomb in Highgate Cemetery.

26 Jenny Marx in the early 1880s, shortly before her death.

the noble lady was intransigent'.[1] He also introduced Bakunin and
d'Ester into the Democratic Association. Bakunin, however, would
have nothing to do with the League or even with the Workers' Association. In his view Marx was 'spoiling the workers by making logic-
choppers of them' and it was 'impossible to breathe freely'[2] in the
company of Marx and Engels. Nevertheless, Marx managed to get his
ideas across to the Democratic Association in a speech on Free Trade
he delivered on 9 January (it was along the same lines as one that he
would have delivered at the September economic Congress, had he
been allowed to speak). He summed up his thesis as follows: 'At the
present time the system of protection is conservative, whereas the
system of free trade is destructive: it dissolves old nationalities and
pushes to the extreme the antagonism between bourgeoisie and
proletariat. In a word, the system of commercial freedom hastens the
social revolution.'[3]

Meanwhile Marx had been working on the Manifesto. The London
communists had supplied him with a sheaf of material that included
at least three separate tentative drafts for the Manifesto. Engels had
composed a draft incorporating the views of the first League Congress
in June 1847 and this draft was discussed in the various groups in late
summer and autumn.[4] Moses Hess had proposed an alternative version which Engels ironically described as 'divinely improved'.[5] Hess's
version does not survive but two 'confessions of faith' that he composed around this time[6] show differences from Marx and Engels both
in ideas (in that Hess believed in appealing to eternal principles to
justify his policies) and in tactics (in that Hess considered that the next
revolution should be a proletarian one). On behalf of the League's
Paris branch Engels produced a third draft of which he wrote to Marx
just before they left for London:

> Think over the confession of faith a bit. I think it would be better
> to drop the catechistic form and call the thing a communist mani-
> festo. As a certain amount of history will have to be brought in, I

[1] S. Born, *Erinnerungen* (Berlin, 1898) p. 73.

[2] See E. H. Carr, *Michael Bakunin* (London and New York, 1937) pp. 153 ff.

[3] K. Marx, 'Discours sur le Libre-échange', *Oeuvres*, ed. M. Rubel, I (Paris, 1963)
p. 156.

[4] See the translation in D. Struik (ed.), *The Birth of the Communist Manifesto*, pp.
163 ff.

[5] Engels to Marx, *MEW* XXVII 98.

[6] See M. Hess, *Philosophische Aufsätze*, ed. A. Cornu and W. Monke (Berlin, 1961).

think the present form is unsuitable. I am bringing along what I have done here. It is in simple narrative form, but miserably edited and done in a terrible hurry.[1]

This draft, entitled 'Principles of Communism', a catechism of 25 questions and answers, was drawn on quite extensively by Marx. In places, however, there is a noticeable difference between the optimistic, determinist approach of Engels which stemmed from the Enlightenment and his experiences in industrial England, and the greater emphasis given by Marx to politics in the light of experiences of the French working class.[2] Engels said later that it was 'essentially Marx's work'[3] and that 'the basic thought . . . belongs solely and exclusively to Marx'.[4] Notwithstanding the appearance of their two names on the title page and the persistent assumption about joint authorship, the actual writing of the *Communist Manifesto* was done exclusively by Marx.

The *Communist Manifesto* has four sections. The first section gives a history of society as class society since the Middle Ages and ends with a prophecy of the victory of the proletariat over the present ruling class, the bourgeoisie. The second section describes the position of communists within the proletarian class, rejects bourgeois objections to communism and then characterises the communist revolution, the measures to be taken by the victorious proletariat and the nature of the future communist society. The third section contains an extended criticism of other types of socialism – reactionary, bourgeois and utopian. The final section contains a short description of communist tactics towards other opposition parties and finishes with an appeal for proletarian unity.

The opening words typify Marx's approach to history:

The history of all hitherto existing society is the history of class struggles.

Freeman and slave, patrician and plebeian, lord and serf, guildmaster and journeyman, in a word, oppressor and oppressed, stood in constant opposition to one another, carried on an uninterrupted, now hidden, now open fight, a fight that each time ended, either in

[1] Engels to Marx, *MEW* xxvii 107.
[2] Cf. H. Bollnow, 'Engels' Auffassung von Revolution und Entwicklung in seinen *Grundsätzen des Kommunismus*' in *Marxismusstudien*, i (1954) pp. 57 ff.
[3] F. Engels, 'Karl Marx', *MEW* xvi 363.
[4] F. Engels, Preface to 1883 edition, *MESW* i 25.

a revolutionary reconstitution of society at large, or in the common ruin of the contending classes.[1]

'The present age' he continued, in a passage that summarised conclusions reached in the first part of *The German Ideology*, was unique in that class antagonisms had been so simplified that there were now two hostile camps facing each other: bourgeoisie and proletariat. The bourgeoisie, from its origins in feudal society, helped by the discovery of America, the development of a world market and modern industry, had everywhere imposed the domination of its class and its ideas. In a well-known phrase that fitted contemporary France more than any other country, Marx described the modern state as merely 'a committee for managing the common affairs of the whole bourgeoisie'.[2] Historically, the bourgeoisie had been a most revolutionary class: 'it has accomplished wonders far surpassing Egyptian pyramids, Roman aqueducts and Gothic cathedrals; it has conducted expeditions that put in the shade all former Exoduses of nations and crusades'.[3] But this progress had to continue: the bourgeoisie could not exist without constantly revolutionising the means of production. And just as the bourgeoisie had caused the downfall of feudal society, so now they were preparing their own downfall 'like the sorcerer who is no longer able to control the powers of the nether world whom he has called up by his spells'.[4] For the bourgeoisie had not only forged the weapons of their destruction: they had also created in the proletariat the men who were to wield those weapons.

Marx then described the revolutionary nature of the proletariat. Workers had become mere appendages of machines. To the extent that the use of machinery and division of labour increased, so the wages of the workers got less in spite of the longer hours they worked. The lower middle class was forced down into the proletariat:

The lower strata of the middle-class – the small tradespeople, shop-keepers, and retired tradesmen generally, the handicraftsmen and peasants – all these sink gradually into the proletariat, partly because their diminutive capital does not suffice for the scale on which Modern Industry is carried on, and is swamped in the competition with the large capitalists, partly because their specialised skill is rendered worthless by new methods of production. Thus the proletariat is recruited from all classes of the population.[5]

[1] *MESW* 1 34.   [2] Ibid., 36.   [3] Ibid., 37.   [4] Ibid., 39.   [5] Ibid., 41.

The proletariat itself went through several stages: at first their principal aim had been to restore to the working man the status he had lost since the Middle Ages; with increase of numbers they began to form trade unions; finally the class struggle became a political struggle. As the struggle neared its decisive hour, a process of dissolution set in within the ruling class, and a small section (of bourgeois ideologists in particular) went over to the proletariat. No other class in society could fulfil the revolutionary role of the proletariat: the lower middle class were in fact reactionary in that they tried to roll back the wheel of history; and the 'dangerous class, the social scum, that passively rotting mass thrown off by the lower layers of society',[1] was ripe for bribery by reactionary intrigue. Marx summed up this section with the words:

> The advance of industry, whose involuntary promoter is the bourgeoisie, replaces the isolation of the labourers, due to competition, by their revolutionary combination, due to association. The development of Modern Industry, therefore, cuts from under its feet the very foundation on which the bourgeoisie produces and appropriates products. What the bourgeoisie, therefore, produces, above all, is its own grave-diggers. Its fall and the victory of the proletariat are equally inevitable.[2]

Obviously Marx was here projecting into the future tendencies he saw at work in the present. In Germany at that time the proletariat in fact comprised less than 5 per cent of the population, and even in England the rule of the bourgeoisie was far from being 'universal'.

In the second section Marx raised the question of the relationship of the communists to the proletariat as a whole. The communists were not opposed to other working-class parties; their interests were those of the proletariat as a whole. Two factors distinguished them from other working-class groups: they were international, and they understood the significance of the proletarian movement. Communist ideas were not invented or discovered: they merely expressed actual relations springing from an existing class struggle and could be summed up in a single sentence: abolition of private property.

Marx then dealt with objections.

The first objection was that communists desired to abolish 'the right of personally acquiring property as the fruit of a man's own labour'.[3]

[1] Ibid., 44.   [2] Ibid., 45.   [3] Ibid., 47. See further the exhaustive analysis of H. Draper, 'The concept of the *Lumpenproletariat* in Marx and Engels', *Economie et Sociétés* (Dec. 1972).

His reply was that the property of the petty artisan and small farmer was being abolished anyway by the power of capital; the proletariat did not *have* any property; and capital, being a collective product and the result of the united action of all members of society, should be owned collectively. Private property was bourgeois property and all arguments against its abolition were bourgeois arguments.

Similarly, in reply to a second criticism he argued that the abolition of the family meant the abolition of the bourgeois family – whose counterpart was the practical absence of family life among proletarians, and public prostitution.

To meet a third objection Marx maintained that the real point about the so-called 'community of women' was to do away with the status of women as mere instruments of production; the present system was merely public and private prostitution.

It was also said that communists wished to abolish countries and nationality. But working men had no country. Modern industry was abolishing national differences and, with the disappearance of class antagonisms, hostility between nations would also end.

Sweeping value-laden condemnation of communism was not worthy, in Marx's view, of serious consideration. In a passage which minimised to the point of caricature the role of ideas in society Marx asked:

> Does it require intuition to comprehend that man's ideas, views and conceptions, in one word, man's consciousness, changes with every change in the conditions of his material existence, in his social relations and in his social life?
>
> What else does the history of ideas prove, than that intellectual production changes its character in proportion as material production is changed? The ruling ideas of each age have ever been the ideas of its ruling class.[1]

Having dealt with these objections, Marx outlined the measures that would be taken by the proletariat once it had become the ruling class:

> The proletariat will use its political supremacy to wrest, by degrees, all capital from the bourgeoisie, to centralise all instruments of production in the hands of the State, i.e. of the proletariat organised as the ruling class; and to increase the total of productive forces as rapidly as possible.[2]

[1] Ibid. 52.   [2] Ibid. 53.

In a section that was very largely inspired by Engels' draft, there followed a programme which included the abolition of landed property and inheritance, the imposition of income tax, the centralisation of credit and communications, state ownership of factories, and free education. He concluded:

> When, in the course of development, class distinctions have disappeared and all production has been concentrated in the hands of a vast association of the whole nation, the public power will lose its political character. Political power, properly so called, is merely the organised power of one class for oppressing another. If the proletariat during its contest with the bourgeoisie is compelled, by the force of circumstances, to organise itself as a class, if, by means of a revolution, it makes itself the ruling class, and as such, sweeps away by force the old condition of production, then it will, along with these conditions, have swept away the conditions for the existence of class antagonisms and of classes generally, and will thereby have abolished its own supremacy as a class.
>
> In place of the old bourgeois society, with its classes and class antagonisms, we shall have an association, in which the free development of each is the condition for the free development of all.[1]

The third section of the *Communist Manifesto* contained criticism of three types of socialism – reactionary, bourgeois and utopian. The first was a feudal socialism preached by the aristocracy to revenge themselves on the bourgeoisie who had supplanted them as the ruling class. Hand-in-hand with feudal socialism went Christian socialism which Marx simply dismissed as 'the holy water with which the priest consecrates the heart-burnings of the aristocrat'.[2] The second type – petty-bourgeois socialism – was chiefly represented by the French economist Sismondi. This school had well analysed the contradictions inherent in modern methods of production; but in its positive proposals it was reactionary, wishing to restore corporate guilds in manufacture and patriarchal relations in agriculture. The third party,

---

[1] Ibid. 54. This programme is remarkable for its comparatively tentative and moderate nature. With an eye to an alliance with sections of the bourgeoisie, reform proposals were limited to circulating capital while production, for the time being, was to remain largely in private hands. See further, Y. Wagner and M. Strauss, 'The Programme of *The Communist Manifesto* and its Theoretical Implications', *Political Studies*, Dec 1969.

[2] *MESW* I.

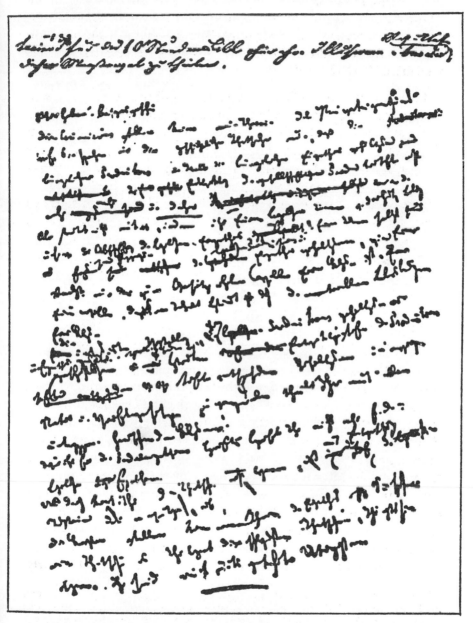

The only surviving page from a draft of the *Communist Manifesto*. The two lines at the top are in Jenny Marx's handwriting.

labelled by Marx reactionary socialists, were the 'true' socialists. These were the German philosophers (mainly the followers of Feuerbach) who had emasculated French socialism by turning it into a metaphysical system. This was inevitable in an economically backward country like Germany where ideas tended not to reflect the struggle of one class with another. These philosophers thus claimed to represent '. . . not true requirements, but the requirements of Truth; not the interests of the proletariat, but the interests of Human Nature, of Man in general, who belongs to no class, has no reality, who exists only in the misty realm of philosophical fantasy.'[1]

In the *Manifesto*'s review of socialist and communist literature the second section – devoted to bourgeois socialism – was short. Proudhon was the main representative of this tendency and Marx had already devoted considerable space to examining his theories. Here he confined himself to observing that 'the Socialistic bourgeois want all the advantages of modern social conditions without the struggles and dangers necessarily resulting therefrom. They desire the existing state of society minus its revolutionary and distintegrating elements. They wish for a bourgeoisie without a proletariat.'[2] Thus the reforms advocated by these socialists in no respect affected the relations between capital and labour, but they did at least lessen the cost and simplify the administrative work of bourgeois government.

The final school discussed was the 'critical-Utopian' school represented by such writers as Saint-Simon, Fourier and Owen. It originated during the early, inchoate period of the struggle between the bourgeoisie and the proletariat. These writers had perceived class antagonisms; but in their time the proletariat was still insufficiently developed to be a credible force for social change. Hence they wished to attain their ends by peaceful means and small-scale experiments, rejecting political – and in particular revolutionary – action. Their utopias, envisaged at a time when the proletariat was still underdeveloped, 'correspond with the first instinctive yearnings of that class for a general reconstruction of society'.[3] But at the same time these utopian writings also contained critical elements: since they attacked every principle of existing society, they were full of insights valuable to the enlightenment of the working class. But as the modern class-struggle gathered strength, these utopian solutions lost all practical value or theoretical justification. Thus 'although the originators of these

[1] Ibid. 58.   [2] Ibid. 60.   [3] Ibid. 62.

systems were, in many respects, revolutionary, their disciples have, in every case, formed mere reactionary sects'.[1]

The fourth and concluding section of the *Manifesto* dealt with the attitude of communists to various opposition parties: in France they supported the social democrats, in Switzerland the radicals, in Poland the peasant revolutionaries, in Germany the bourgeoisie. Nevertheless in Germany they never ceased to instil into the working class the clearest possible recognition of the inherent antagonism between bourgeoisie and proletariat. The communists directed their attention chiefly to Germany, which they believed to be on the eve of a bourgeois revolution. The *Manifesto* ended:

> The Communists disdain to conceal their views and aims. They openly declare that their ends can be attained only by the forcible overthrow of all existing social conditions. Let the ruling classes tremble at a communistic revolution. The Proletarians have nothing to lose but their chains. They have a world to win. Working men of all countries, unite![2]

In a sense, of course, virtually all the ideas contained in the *Communist Manifesto* had been enunciated before – particularly among French socialists in whose tradition the *Manifesto* is firmly situated.[3] Babeuf's ideas on revolution, Saint-Simon's periodisation of history and emphasis on industry, Considérant's *Manifeste*, all inspired aspects of Marx's work. And he himself was the first to admit that the concept he began with – that of class – was used long before by French bourgeois historians.[4] But the powerful, all-embracing synthesis and the consistently materialist approach were quite new.

The *Manifesto* was a propaganda document hurriedly issued on the eve of a revolution. Marx and Engels considered in 1872 that 'the general principles expounded in the document are on the whole as correct today as ever' though they would doubtless have modified

---

[1] Ibid. 63.   [2] Ibid. 65.

[3] For the commentary stressing Marx's debt to the French socialists, see C. Andler, *Le Manifeste Communiste. Introduction historique et commentaire* (Paris, 1901).

[4] In a letter to Weydemeyer, written in 1852, Marx said: 'What I did that was new was to prove: (1) that the existence of classes is only bound up with particular historical phases in the development of production; (2) that the class struggle necessarily leads to the dictatorship of the proletariat; and (3) that this dictatorship itself only constitutes the transition to the abolition of all classes and to a classless society'. K. Marx and F. Engels, *Selected Correspondence* (London, 1934) p. 69 (hereinafter referred to as *MESC*).

radically some of its ideas – particularly (in the light of the Paris Commune) those relating to the proletariat's taking over of the state apparatus and the rather simplistic statements on pauperisation and class polarisation.[1] For all the clarity and force that later made it a classic, the publication of the *Manifesto* went virtually unnoticed. Before it was off the presses, the 1848 revolutions had already begun.

[1] See particularly the Preface to the 1872 edition in *MESW* I 22.

4

Cologne

No German newspaper, before or since, has ever had the
same power and influence or been able to electrify the proletarian masses as effectively as the *Neue Rheinische Zeitung*.
And that it owed above all to Marx.

F. Engels, 'Marx and the *Neue Rheinische Zeitung*',
MESW ii 305.

I. FROM BRUSSELS TO PARIS

THE REVOLUTIONARY movement that swept over Europe in 1848–9
began in Switzerland in November 1847 when the unwillingness of
Austria to intervene in support of reactionary cantons against the
radicals severely diminished her prestige in Italy: shortly afterwards,
the Bourbon King Ferdinand of Naples was overthrown and republics
proclaimed in Naples, Turin and Florence. In France, Louis Philippe
continued complacently to believe that the Parisians never revolted in
winter, but when his troops fired on unarmed demonstrators a rash
of barricades sprang up; the King was exiled and a provisional republican government formed.

News of the revolution in Paris reached Brussels on 26 February. At
first the Belgian Government acted very cautiously and the King even
offered to abdicate. But once its forces had been concentrated, the
Government's policy became tougher. A mild demonstration on
28 February was broken up, Wilhelm Wolff was arrested and a list of
foreigners to be deported was drawn up, with Marx's name at the top.
The Democratic Association had already demanded that the Government arm the workers, and sent a congratulatory Address to the
provisional French Government. Two weeks earlier Marx had inherited 6000 francs from his mother (probably as much as his total
income for the three previous years) and the police suspected (there

was no evidence) that he was using it to finance the revolutionary movement. They even went as far as asking the authorities in Trier to question Marx's mother, who protested that the only reason she had for sending the money at that time was that 'her son had long been asking her for money for his family and this was an advance on his inheritance'.[1] On 3 March Marx received an order, signed by the King, to leave Belgium within twenty-four hours. The same day he received from Paris a reply to his request for the cancellation of the previous expulsion order:

> Brave and loyal Marx,
> The soil of the French Republic is a place of refuge for all friends of freedom. Tyranny has banished you, free France opens her doors to you and all those who fight for the holy cause, the fraternal cause of all peoples. Every officer of the French Government must interpret his mission in this sense. *Salut et Fraternité.*
> > Ferdinand Elocon
> > Member of the Provisional Government.[2]

Yet Marx was not left to depart in peace. The same evening the Central Committee of the Communist League met in the Bois Sauvage guest house where Marx had moved a week earlier on receipt of his inheritance, and decided to transfer the seat of the Central Committee to Paris and to give Marx discretionary powers over all the League's affairs.[3] At one o'clock in the morning the over-zealous local police commissioner broke into the guest house and arrested Marx. A week later in a letter of protest to the Paris paper *La Réforme*, he described the situation:

> I was occupied in preparing my departure when a police commissioner, accompanied by ten civil guards, penetrated into my home, searched the whole house and finally arrested me on the pretext of my having no papers. Leaving aside the very correct papers that Monsieur Duchatel gave me on my expulsion from France, I had in my hands the deportation pass that Belgium had issued to me only several hours before. . . .
> Immediately after my arrest, my wife had herself gone to M.

---

[1] Quoted in L. Somerhausen, *L'Humanisme agissant de Karl Marx* (Paris, 1946) p. 245.
[2] *MEW* xxiv 676.
[3] The decisions of the meeting are printed in *MEGA* i vii 587 ff. There was nothing in the statutes allowing for the transfer of such discretionary power.

Jottrand, President of the Belgian Democratic Association, to get him to take the necessary steps. On returning home, she found a policeman in front of the door who told her, with exquisite politeness, that if she wanted to talk to Monsieur Marx, she had only to follow him. My wife eagerly accepted the offer. She was taken to the police station and the commissioner told her at first that Monsieur Marx was not there; he brusquely asked her who she was, what she was doing at Monsieur Jottrand's house and whether she had any papers with her. . . . On the pretext of vagabondage my wife was taken to the prison of the Town Hall and locked in a dark room with lost women.[1] At eleven o'clock in the morning she was taken, in full daylight and with a whole escort of policemen, to the magistrate's office. For two hours she was put in a cell in spite of the most forceful protests that came from all quarters. She stayed there exposed to the rigours of the weather and the shameful propositions of the warders.

At length she appeared before the magistrate who was astonished that the police had not carried their attentions to the extent of arresting the small children too. The interrogation could only be a farce since the only crime of my wife consisted in the fact that, although she belonged to the Prussian aristocracy, she shared the democratic opinions of her husband. I will not enter into all the details of this revolting affair. I will only say that, on our release, the 24 hours had just expired and we had to leave without even being able to take away our most indispensable belongings.[2]

This whole affair caused widespread protests in Brussels which resulted in questions being asked in the Chamber of Deputies and the dismissal

[1] Marx's account is not quite accurate here: according to the evidence of the concierge: 'the prisoner having requested a separate room, he was going to take her there when there was a violent knocking at the door and as he had several doors to open, he temporarily shut Madame Marx in the common room where in fact there were three prostitutes. There were two further summons to the door and he only released Madame Marx when he had committed the prisoners which could have taken a maximum of a quarter of an hour. He found the prisoner very sad, tried to console her and in order to dispel her fears, offered to put her in a room with two beds, which he did in fact do. He immediately made up one bed for her; the other was occupied by a woman arrested for assault and battery' (quoted in L. Somerhausen, L'Humanisme agissant de Karl Marx, p. 241). In order to justify his actions the concierge pointed out that Jenny had given him a large tip on leaving. Jenny's own account (Reminiscences, pp. 223 f.) is fairly imaginative. Born's version (Erinnerungen, pp. 83 ff.) outstrips even Jenny.

[2] From the German version in MEW IV 536.

of the police commissioner concerned. On her release Jenny Marx sold what she could, left her silver plate and best linen in the charge of a friend, and the whole family was conducted, under police escort, to the frontier. Travelling was difficult since in Belgium there were large-scale troop movements while in France portions of the track had been torn up by those who had been put out of business by the railway. The Marx family eventually reached Paris the following day after a miserably cold journey.

In the city, charred ruins and the debris of recent barricades were still evident. The tricolour was everywhere, accompanied by the red flag. Marx settled his family in the Boulevard Beaumarchais, near the Place de la Bastille, and urged Engels (who had remained behind in Brussels) to collect his old debts and use them to bring his silver and other possessions over the frontier as far as Valenciennes. Revolutionary enthusiasm was still strong in Paris, and Marx took an active part in the meetings of the Society of the Rights of Man, one of the largest of the 147 political clubs in existence in Paris in early 1848. The club had been sponsored by Ledru-Rollin and Flocon, and Marx joined it the same day he arrived in the city. Later he is known to have spoken in favour of deferring the elections to the National Assembly and for the easier recruitment of working men into the National Guard.[1] Marx's main activities, however, were naturally among the expatriate Germans, many of whom were quite carried away by revolutionary enthusiasm. Before Marx's arrival the German Democratic Association had decided – as had the other main émigré groups – to form a German Legion. Recruits soon numbered several thousand and exercises were held on the Champ de Mars throughout March. The Provisional Government, by no means unwilling to see the departure of so many possible trouble-makers, placed barracks at the disposal of the Legion and granted them fifty centimes a day per man for the march to the frontier. Following the tradition of 1789, the leaders of the Legion – Bornstedt, who was a member of the Communist League, and Herwegh the poet – believed that a revolutionary war was inevitable after a successful revolution and this time proposed themselves to contribute the vanguard of liberating forces. Marx was utterly opposed to these adventures. Sebastian Seiler, a member of the Communist League, later wrote:

[1] On the period in general, see S. Bernstein, 'Marx in Paris, 1848: A Neglected Chapter', *Science and Society*, Vols. 3 and 4 (1938 and 1940).

The socialists and Communists declared themselves decidedly against any armed imposition of a German Republic from without. They held public sessions in the Rue St Denis attended by some of those who later became volunteers. In one of these sessions Marx developed in a long speech the theme that the February revolution should be viewed only as the superficial beginning of the European movement. In a short time here in Paris the open struggle between proletariat and bourgeoisie would break out, as did happen, in fact, in June. The victory or defeat of revolutionary Europe would depend on this struggle.[1]

In order to give their opposition strength, Marx and his friends organised a meeting based on the four Parisian sections of the Communist League[2] and founded a German Workers' Club (under the presidency first of Heinrich Bauer and then of Moses Hess) which by the end of March had 400 members – mainly drawn from tailors and bootmakers. It was also possible to reconstitute the Central Committee of the Communist League: the Fraternal Democrats in London had sent to Paris a deputation, including Harney and Jones, with an Address to the Provisional Government. Schapper and Moll were sent by the London German Workers' Association. At a meeting on 10 March Marx was elected President, Schapper Secretary, and Moll, Bauer, Engels, Wolff and Wallau committee members. Marx also enjoyed good relations with Ledru-Rollin and Flocon, both members of the Provisional Government. Flocon offered money to start a German-language newspaper, but Marx refused – as he wished to preserve his independence.

On 19 March news reached Paris which changed the situation radically: a week earlier Metternich had been driven out of Vienna and the Emperor was forced to grant the demands of the insurgents; and on the twentieth news came of revolution in Berlin. The Legion made immediate preparations for departure and marched out of Paris – appropriately on 1 April: at its first encounter with government troops after crossing the Rhine it was virtually annihilated. Marx and his followers also decided to return to Germany, but in a less spectacular manner. They, too, benefited from the Provisional Government's

[1] S. Seiler, *Das Complott vom 13 Juni 1849 oder der letzte Sieg der Bourgeoisie in Frankreich* (Hamburg, 1850) p. 21.

[2] See the Minutes of the Communist League meeting of 8 March reprinted in *MEGA* I vii 588 f.

subsidy, and most of the members of the Communist League left for various towns in Germany (either singly or in small groups) with the intention of establishing a national network. They carried with them two propaganda documents: one was the *Communist Manifesto* of which the first 1000 copies had just arrived from London; the other was a flysheet listing seventeen points elaborated by Marx and Engels in the last half of March and entitled *The Demands of the Communist Party in Germany*. Marx himself paid for the printing of the *Demands* which were an attempt to adapt the proposals of the *Communist Manifesto* to Germany. Only four of the ten points of the *Manifesto* were included: a state bank, nationalisation of transport, progressive income tax and free education. The right of inheritance was to be limited rather than abolished, and there was no proposal for nationalising land – but only the estates of the feudal princes.[1] The *Demands* were a plan of action for a bourgeois (and not socialist) revolution; they were designed to appeal to the petty bourgeoisie and peasants as well as to the workers, and were very similar to programmes proposed by radical republicans.

II. POLITICS IN COLOGNE

Marx himself, armed with a passport valid for one year only, left Paris at the beginning of April and travelled to Mainz. He was accompanied by his family, Engels, and Ernst Dronke (a young radical writer who had recently been brought into the Communist League). They stopped two days in Mainz where the Workers' Educational Association had shortly before issued an appeal for the organisation and unification of workers' unions throughout Germany. Marx arrived in Cologne on 10 April, and settled in the north of the city.[2] About three months later he was followed by Jenny and the children who had been waiting in Trier until he obtained a residence permit. They all moved into lodgings situated in the narrow streets of the Old City,[3] almost next door to the future offices of the *Neue Rheinische Zeitung*.

Cologne was an obvious base: it was the third biggest town in Prussia with nearly 100,000 inhabitants and was situated in the most industrialised region of Germany; Marx had many old contacts there and the Rhineland laws were known to be more liberal than those of any other German state. There was also a group of the Communist

[1] See the translation in D. Struik (ed.), *The Birth of the Communist Manifesto*, pp. 190 ff.
[2] Apostelnstrasse, no. 7.
[3] Cecilienstrasse, no. 7 (today Schreibweise).

League there which in mid-1847 met twice weekly for singing, discussion and propaganda[1] – though by the time of Marx's arrival in Cologne, Wolff reported it to be 'vegetating and disorganised'.[2] Its leading members had been Andreas Gottschalk, gifted son of a Jewish butcher who practised as a doctor among the poor of Cologne, and August Willich and Friedrich Anneke, both ex-Prussian officers. Cologne had also been the first city to witness mass action by the workers. On 3 March, two weeks before the outbreak of the revolution in Berlin, a crowd of several thousand assembled on the main square and invaded the session of the Town Council where Gottschalk and Willich presented their demands: universal suffrage, freedom of the Press and association, a people's militia, and state responsibility for work and education. The army was called in and, after some casualties, Gottschalk, Willich and Anneke were all arrested – to be released three weeks later after the successful revolution in Berlin. Four days before Marx's arrival, Gottschalk had founded a Workers' Association (which he viewed as an extension of the Communist League),[3] recruiting 8000 members in a few months. The current business was transacted in a Committee of fifty elected members. Gottschalk was immensely popular with the Cologne workers, more than a quarter of whom were unemployed. The Association, organised in sections according to the different professions, persuaded the municipality to initiate a public works programme and negotiated with employers on wages and hours. It is, of course, important to remember that factory workers were still only a small proportion of Cologne's working population: the number of artisans and traders was much greater.[4] Thus Marx entered a situation in Cologne in which the working-class movement was already well under way, and there were suggestions that he would do better to go on to Berlin or even run as a parliamentary candidate from Trier.[5]

[1] Gottschalk to Hess, in M. Hess, *Briefwechsel*, p. 174.
[2] Quoted in E. Czobel, 'Zur Geschichte des Kommunistenbundes', *Archiv für die Geschichte des Sozialismus und der Arbeiterbewegung* (1925).
[3] Cf. Gottschalk to Hess, in M. Hess, *Briefwechsel*, p. 177.
[4] For figures as precise as can be obtained on the socio-economic situation in Cologne at this time, see H. Stein, *Der Kölner Arbeiterverein 1848–49* (Cologne, 1921) pp. 9 ff.
[5] Cf. F. Engels, 'Marx und die *Neue Rheinische Zeitung* 1848–1849', *MEW* xxi 18; Gottschalk to Hess, in M. Hess, *Briefwechsel*, p. 176. On arrival Marx was also offered a post in the Press Bureau in Berlin by Claessen, a friend of Camphausen. See *MEW* xxx 510.

Differences between Marx and Gottschalk were inevitable. Gottschalk was a close friend of Moses Hess and a thoroughly 'true' socialist in his outlook, taking a conciliatory attitude to religion and rejecting notions of class struggle; he also supported a federalist solution to the problem of German unification. Soon after his arrival Marx attacked Gottschalk's organisation of the Workers' Association,[1] no doubt because he considered its activities too limited to purely economic demands. But the immediate quarrel between Marx and Gottschalk was over tactics: whether or not to participate in the elections (at the beginning of May) to the Prussian Assembly and the National Parliament at Frankfurt. Although Gottschalk's immediate demands were moderate (he thought that the workers should agitate on the basis of 'monarchy with a Chartist base'[2]) he could not approve of participation in elections based on an indirect voting system which in some states came near to disenfranchising the workers completely; he also thought that elections could only be successful when the working-class movement had developed considerably further, and wished to dissuade the workers from taking part in a struggle for a bourgeois republic in which the fruits of victory would not go to them. Marx strongly criticised this isolation of the workers from the political process, and himself helped to found and preside over a Democratic Society in Cologne which successfully sponsored Franz Raveau as candidate for the Frankfurt Parliament. There was a further open clash between the Democratic Society and Gottschalk's Workers' Association when Willich appealed to the Society for financial aid on behalf of the refugee remnants of Herwegh's Legion. The Society refused to help – fearing to be associated with the Legion; but Gottschalk's Association (although Gottchalk himself disagreed with the aims of the Legion) agreed to arrange payments.

On one thing Marx and Gottschalk did agree, and that was the increasing irrelevance of the Communist League. At a meeting of the Cologne branch in the middle of May, Gottschalk confirmed his decision to resign from the League declaring that its constitution needed reframing -- though he promised his future co-operation is required.[3] However, by this time the League had virtually ceased to

---

[1] Cf. W. Blumenberg, 'Zur Geschichte des Bundes der Kommunisten', *International Review of Social History* (1964) p. 89.

[2] Gottschalk to Hess, in M. Hess, *Briefwechsel*, p. 175.

[3] Cf. 'Minutes of the Cologne Section, etc.' *MEW* v 484.

exist. From Berlin Born wrote to Marx: 'The League has dissolved; it is everywhere and nowhere.'[1] It seems probable that Marx exercised the power granted him in Brussels in February to declare a formal dissolution in spite of the opposition of the former leaders of the League of the Just. According to Peter Röser, a member of the Cologne group who later turned King's evidence: 'because it was impossible to agree and Schapper and Moll insisted on the maintenance of the League, Marx used his discretionary power and dissolved the League. Marx considered the continuance of the League to be superfluous, since the aim of the League was not conspiracy but propaganda and under present circumstances propaganda could be conducted openly and secrecy was not necessary since a free Press and the right of association were guaranteed.'[2] Marx himself said later that the League's activities 'faded out of their own accord in that more effective means of carrying out its aims were available'.[3] And two years later in London Marx found the Communist League 'reconstituted'.[4] The reasons Marx gave for the dissolution seem implausible: they only argue for the continuance of an *open* Communist League. More likely, Marx considered the radical policies of the Communist League and the *Seventeen Demands* harmful to the more moderate line being pursued by the *Neue Rheinische Zeitung*.

III. THE 'NEUE RHEINISCHE ZEITUNG'

Marx's main energies throughout this period were concentrated on giving effect to an idea he had had since the outbreak of the German revolution: the founding of an influential radical newspaper. The Cologne communists had already planned a paper of which Hess was to be the editor. But Marx and Engels had laid their plans too. They had started collecting subscriptions while in Paris; and on arrival in Cologne, in Engels' words, 'in twenty-four hours, through Marx,

---

[1] Born to Marx, 11 May 1848, reprinted in K. Marx, *Enthüllungen über den Kommunistenprozess zu Köln* (Berlin, 1914) p. 19.

[2] Published in W. Blumenberg, 'Zur Geschichte des Bundes der Kommunisten,' *International Review of Social History* (1964) p. 89. This is supported by Born, *Erinnerungen*, p. 48. Röser's testimony has been discounted by Russian historians (particularly E. P. Kandel), who maintain that the Communist League was never dissolved. See further B. Nicolaievsky, 'Who is distorting history?' *Proceedings of the American Philosophical Society* (April 1961) and Kandel's reply, 'Eine schlechte Verteidigung einer schlechten Sache', *Beiträge zur Geschichte der Arbeiterbewegung* (1963).

[3] K. Marx, 'Herr Vogt', *MEW* XXIV 439 f.

[4] Ibid.

we had conquered the terrain and the paper was ours, though we had agreed to take Heinrich Bürgers on to the editorial committee'.[1] Money was their chief difficulty: Engels left to collect subscriptions in the Wuppertal but met with no success. Of his father, he wrote that 'he would sooner send us 1000 bullets than 1000 thaler'.[2] In the end they raised only 13,000 thaler out of the 30,000 which had been their aim, and Marx had to contribute substantially from his own pocket. The provenance of the share money was severely criticised in the paper of the Workers' Association, edited by Gottschalk: Marx's paper, it was said, had put itself in the hands of the 'money aristocracy' and its printer, Clouth, had lowered wages and tried to impose no-strike agreements on his workers. Clouth replied that he had merely refused to raise wages; and that the editorial board had no control over the printing workers. The editorial board was composed entirely of members of the Communist League with the exception of Bürgers, who was soon forced out. According to Engels, Marx exercised 'a dictatorship pure and simple' which was 'completely natural, uncontested and freely accepted. By the clarity of his vision and the resoluteness of his principles he made the paper into the most famous of the revolutionary period.'[3] The only criticism voiced was that Marx worked too slowly. 'Marx is no journalist and never will be,' wrote Born. 'He spends a whole day on a leading article that another would write in two hours, as though it was concerned with the solution of a deep philosophical problem. He changes and polishes and changes the changed and can never be ready in time.'[4]

From the start the *Neue Rheinische Zeitung* was conceived as a national paper containing little local news. Engels contributed most of the leading articles in the early period and followed developments in France and England, while Marx concentrated on internal politics. Its general character was factual and ironically descriptive rather than theoretical, and there was an attractive *Feuilleton* edited by Georg Weerth.

Marx had arrived in Germany with the hope of reproducing there

[1] F. Engels, 'Marx und die *Neue Rheinische Zeitung*', *MEW* xxi 18.

[2] Engels to Marx, *MEW* xxvii 125.

[3] F. Engels, 'Marx und die *Neue Rheinische Zeitung*', *MEW* xxi 19. According to Liebknecht, however, it was Engels who, in contradistinction to Marx, acted in a military fashion in the *Neue Rheinische Zeitung* office and caused many rows. Cf. *Engels-Bebel Briefwechsel*, ed. W. Blumenberg, p. xvii.

[4] S. Born, *Erinnerungen* (Berlin, 1898) pp. 198 f.

the sort of revolutionary situation that he had experienced in Paris, but he soon realised that this was beyond the bounds of possibility. The German 'revolution' had been a very partial one: only in Berlin and Vienna had there been any serious violence, and in the whole of Germany only one prince lost his throne – let alone his head. In 1848 it was only possible to modify autocratic structures: these did not entirely disappear until after the First World War. For the autocratic Government managed to retain control both of the army and of the administration that was more powerful than that in either France or England (since it controlled the development of the economy which at that time needed protection). There were two main reasons for this necessarily limited character of the 1848 revolution. Firstly, Prussia, the key to Germany, still had a social structure much more akin to that of Eastern Europe and Russia than to the states of Western Europe.[1] The land-owning aristocracy – the Junkers – still held the decisive power based on largely unemancipated serfs. The second reason lay in the nature of the opposition to the Government: once an all-German Assembly had been promised (it did not meet until mid-May), the opposition spent its time preparing for the elections, sending in petitions and indulging its hopes. This opposition was itself extremely diverse, and the various liberals, radicals and socialists of which it was composed could have very little common programme. Nor could working-class organisations make much impact: although now legalised and spreading very fast, they were mainly interested in improving wages and working conditions.

Faced with this situation the programme of *Neue Rheinische Zeitung* contained, as Engels said later, two main points: 'a single, indivisible, democratic German Republic, and war with Russia which would bring the restoration of Poland'.[2] In Prussia the events of March had forced Frederick William to form a ministry headed by Rudolf Camphausen, a prominent liberal businessman from the Rhineland. A new Prussian Assembly was elected to work out a constitution. This Assembly was far from radical: it summoned the King's brother-in-law, the Prince of Prussia, back from England where he had fled in March; and agreed that its task was to elaborate a constitution – the panacea of those times – 'in agreement with the King'. There was an abortive rising in Berlin in mid-June and Camphausen was replaced

[1] Cf. F. L. Carsten, *The Origins of Prussia* (Oxford, 1954).
[2] F. Engels, 'Marx und die *Neue Rheinische Zeitung*', *MEW* xxi 19.

by the slightly less liberal Hansemann who stayed in office until September. It was to sarcastic attacks on the vacillations and essential impotence of the Camphausen ministry that Marx devoted most of the few articles that he wrote on German politics in the first few months of the *Neue Rheinische Zeitung*'s existence.

According to Marx, 'the provisional political circumstances that follow a revolution always require a dictatorship and an energetic one at that. From the beginning we reproached Camphausen with not acting dictatorially, with not immediately breaking and abolishing the remains of the old institutions.'[1] One particular field in which Marx felt compelled to attack the Prussian Assembly was their decision that peasants could buy their freedom, but at a prohibitively high price. This was a serious mistake:

> The French bourgeoisie of 1789 did not for a moment forsake its allies, the peasants. It knew that the basis of its rule was the destruction of rural feudalism, and the creation of a free, landowning peasant class. The German bourgeoisie of 1848 without any hesitation betrays its peasants who are its most natural allies, flesh of its flesh, without whom it is powerless against the nobility.[2]

In an article on the Frankfurt Assembly published in the first issue of the paper Engels attacked the Assembly for not defending the sovereignty of the people and a corresponding constitution. This immediately cost the paper half its shareholders. And a week later Marx gave the Left in Frankfurt the following advice:

> We do not make the utopian demand that a single indivisible German Republic be proclaimed *a priori*, but we do demand of the so-called Radical Democratic party that it should not confuse the beginning of the struggle and revolutionary movement with its final aim. German unity and a German constitution can only be the end results of a movement in which both internal conflicts and war with the East can be pushed to a decisive point.[3]

But the paper in general paid very little attention to the Frankfurt Parliament which it rightly considered increasingly irrelevant to the

---

[1] K. Marx, 'The Crisis and the Counter-Revolution', *MEW* v 402.
[2] K. Marx, 'Draft Law on the Abolition of Feudal Dues', *MEW* v 283.
[3] K. Marx, 'Programme of the Radical-Democratic Party and the Left in Frankfurt', *MEW* v 42.

evolution of German affairs. Although it contained many highly gifted men, the method of election yielded a narrowly middle-class parliament and, bereft of any executive authority, it found itself discussing in a void. As the months went by, it also became aware of irreconcilable divisions between the 'big Germans' who wanted a united Germany to include Austria and the 'little Germans' who looked exclusively to Prussia for hegemony. And with the decline of the workers' movements from June onwards, the middle class found itself increasingly isolated and vulnerable in face of the Government.

With the Berlin and Frankfurt Assemblies so weak, where could the *Neue Rheinische Zeitung* look for support? Engels was quite clear:

> When we founded a wide-circulation paper in Germany, our slogan presented itself automatically. It could only be the slogan of democracy but one that emphasised everywhere and in detail its specifically proletarian character which it could not yet inscribe on its banner once and for all. If one refused this, if we were unwilling to join the movement on its most progressive and proletarian wing, there was nothing left for us but to preach Communism in a small corner magazine and found a small sect instead of a large party of action. But we were no good at crying in the wilderness; we had studied the utopians too well for that.[1]

The subtitle of the *Neue Rheinische Zeitung* was 'An Organ of Democracy' and it supported a 'united front' of all democratic forces. A mark of this was Marx's support for the Democratic Society in Cologne in spite of the fact that its newspaper condemned the June uprising of the Paris proletariat. Following the principles of the *Communist Manifesto* Marx considered it the workers' main task to aid the bourgeois revolution to achieve its aims by supporting the radical wing of the bourgeoisie. The *Neue Rheinische Zeitung* did not preach a socialist republic nor exclusively a workers' one. The programme was universal suffrage, direct elections, the abolition of all feudal dues and charges, the establishment of a state banking system, and the admission of state responsibility for unemployment. Capitalism (even state capitalism), private property and class antagonism would still exist and, indeed, expand. The essence of the programme was the emancipation of the bourgeoisie with some concessions to workers and peasants. This position implied a certain standing apart from the efforts of

[1] F. Engels, 'Marx and the *Neue Rheinische Zeitung*', *MEW* xxi 18.

workers' organisations for self-improvement, and lay behind Marx's criticism of Gottschalk's policies in Cologne and his lack of enthusiasm for Born's success in Berlin in founding an all-German workers' movement and various mutual-aid funds and co-operatives. Marx declared that, in this context, 'the proletariat has not the right to isolate itself; however hard it may seem, it must reject anything that could separate it from its allies'.[1] This policy was so carefully carried out in the *Neue Rheinische Zeitung* that, with one exception and notwithstanding the declaration of Engels above, neither Marx nor Engels published anything during 1848 that dealt with the situation or interests of the working class as such.

The one exception was Marx's impassioned article on the 'June days' in Paris. Finding conditions worse than they had been before the February revolution, the workers in Paris rose spontaneously only to be killed in their thousands by the troops of General Cavaignac in six days of bitter street fighting; those who survived were transported. Marx finished the article by saying:

> They will ask us whether we have no tears, no sighs and no words of regret for the victims in the ranks of the National Guard, the Mobile Guard, the Republican Guard and the Regiments of the Line who fell before the anger of the people. The State will look after their widows and orphans, pompous decrees will glorify them and solemn processions will bear their remains to the grave. The official press will declare them immortal and the European reaction from East to West will sing their praises. On the other hand, it is the privilege and right of the democratic press to place the laurel wreaths on the lowering brows of the plebeians tortured with the pangs of hunger, despised by the official press, abandoned by the doctors, abused as thieves, vandals and galley-slaves by all respectable citizens, their wives and children plunged into still greater misery and the best of their survivors deported overseas.[2]

The second plank in the *Neue Rheinische Zeitung*'s platform was a revolutionary war against Russia.[3] On the model of the French offensive against feudal Germany after 1789, it seemed to Marx that only an

---

[1] Quoted in S. Born, *Erinnerungen*, p. 102.

[2] K. Marx, 'The June Revolution', *MEW* v 136 f.

[3] The foreign policy of the *Neue Rheinische Zeitung* is fully discussed by F. Mehring in his *Introduction* to *Aus dem literarischen Nachlass von K. Marx, F. Engels, F. Lassalle*, III 3 ff.

attack on Russia could enable the revolution to survive. Russia was Germany's most dangerous enemy who, as the backbone of the Holy Alliance, would eventually crush any revolutionary movement unless crushed by it. Such a war would also achieve the otherwise impossible task of uniting Germany's democratic forces. A secondary consequence of a war against Russia would be the liberation of Poland which was at that time partitioned between Prussia, Russia and Austria. On the occasion of a debate in the Frankfurt Assembly on the situation in Poland, Engels published the longest series of articles over to appear in the paper. Their message was: 'The division that the three powers have effected in Poland is the band that holds them together; their common plunder has created their common solidarity . . . the creation of a democratic Poland is the first condition for the creation of a democratic Germany.'[1]

The remaining important issue of Prussian foreign policy was the notoriously complicated question of Schleswig-Holstein, two duchies whose loyalties were divided between Prussia and Denmark. The Danish King, largely supported by the bourgeoisie of Schleswig-Holstein, was making strenuous efforts to imbue them with a Scandinavian spirit, while the nobles felt more sympathetic to Germany. The Prussian military forces were, of course, vastly superior, but Denmark was supported diplomatically by Britain and Russia, and Prussia was forced to sign the armistice of Malmö at the end of August. The Neue Rheinische Zeitung, through the pen of Engels, was quite clear about the issue. Scandinavianism was merely 'enthusiasm for a brutal, dirty, piratical Old-Nordic nationality which is incapable of expressing its profound thoughts and feelings in words, but certainly can in deeds, namely, in brutality towards women, perpetual drunkenness and alternate tear-sodden sentimentality and berserk fury'.[2]

In addition to editing the newspaper, Marx also found time to be active in local politics. In mid-June a large congress with delegates from almost 100 democratic organisations met in Frankfurt; it urged a national organisation of democratic unions and created a central committee in Berlin, of which Kriege, Ruge and Weitling were members. The national organisation never got off the ground, but the congress bore fruit in the Rhineland where the three main Cologne organisations – the Workers' Association, the Democratic Society and

---

[1] F. Engels, 'The Frankfurt Debate on Poland', MEW v 332 f.
[2] F. Engels, 'The Danish-Prussian Armistice', MEW v 394.

the Union of Employees and Employers – decided to co-operate. The delegate of the Workers' Association at the Frankfurt Congress had been Gottschalk who had created the impression of a man 'made to be dictator, with an energy of iron and an intelligence as sharp as any guillotine: a living portrait of Robespierre'.[1] Gottschalk wanted a fusion of the three bodies which would have made his Workers' Association dominant; the Democratic Society suggested a steering committee. But before anything was decided the situation was drastically altered on 3 July by the arrest, on charges of incitement to violence, of Gottschalk and Anneke who were to remain in prison for the next six months. Moll became President of the Workers' Association with Schapper as Vice-President. The Association immediately began to devote more time to the discussion of social and political questions and less to practical economic demands, thereby losing a lot of its momentum during July and August. Moll also became editor of the Association's newspaper.

The collaboration of the three democratic organisations was now no problem: a Committee of Cologne Democratic Unions was formed with Moll and Schapper representing the Workers' Association, Marx and Schneider (a lawyer) representing the Democratic Society, and the young barrister Hermann Becker from the Union of Employees and Employers. This committee summoned a congress of Rhineland Democrats which met in Cologne in mid-August. At this congress, whose main conclusion was to increase agitation among factory workers and peasants, Marx emerged as one of the leading figures. Carl Schurz, a student at Bonn at the time who soon afterwards emigrated and made for himself a distinguished career as a United States Senator and Secretary of the Interior, wrote many years later in his memoirs of Marx's being 'already the recognised head of the advanced socialistic school' and 'attracting general attention', though what struck him most of all was Marx's sarcasm and extreme intolerance.[2] Albert Brisbane, an editor of the New York Daily Tribune for which Marx was later to write extensively, has a left slightly different picture of the Marx he met in the autumn of 1848:

> There I found Karl Marx, the leader in the popular movement. . . .
> He was just then rising into prominence: a man of some thirty

[1] Quoted in B. Nicolaievsky and O. Maenchen-Helfen, La Vie de Karl Marx, p. 198.
[2] The Reminiscences of Carl Schurz (London, 1909) I 138 f. See the full quotation on pp. 452 f. below.

years, short, solidly built, with a fine face and bushy black hair. His expression was that of great energy, and behind his self-contained reserve of manner were visible the fire and passion of a resolute soul.[1]

Meanwhile Marx had also had to defend his orthodoxy against the renewed intervention of Weitling who had returned from America to establish himself in Berlin on the outbreak of the revolution. At the same meeting which elected Marx to the six-man committee of the Cologne Democrats, Weitling gave a speech in favour of the separation of the political and social movements: in his view a democracy at the present time could only lead to chaos and he proposed a 'dictatorship of those with most insight'.[2] Marx replied in a plenary session two weeks later that only the interaction of social and political elements could achieve success for either, and that the solution to political problems was not to be found in a dictatorship but in a 'democratic government composed of the most heterogeneous elements' which by exchanging their ideas would have to evolve a suitable political programme.[3]

Although the *Neue Rheinische Zeitung* had achieved a circulation of around 5000 – which made it one of the largest in Germany – share-capital was no longer available to it: it had therefore to rely on its subscriptions. During July difficulties increased. The printer refused any more credit and one issue was lost before another printer could be found. Marx himself had to appear twice before a magistrate and the premises of the paper were searched following an article by Marx protesting at the brutality of the police when they arrested Anneke. More seriously, the Cologne authorities refused Marx's request for Prussian citizenship, a decision maintained despite energetic protests from the Democratic Society and a personal letter from Marx to the Prussian Minister of the Interior. This meant that his position in Cologne remained precarious as at any time he could be expelled as a 'foreigner'.

IV. THE WATERSHED

At the end of August 1848 Marx decided on a trip to Berlin and Vienna to meet the Democratic leaders there and try to raise funds for the

---

[1] A. Brisbane, *A Mental Biography*, ed. R. Brisbane (Boston, 1893) p. 273.
[2] Cf. H. Meyer, 'Karl Marx und die Deutsche Revolution von 1848', *Historische Zeitschrift*, Dec 1951.   [3] Ibid.

paper. He spent two days in Berlin where he saw his old friend Koep-
pen, Bakunin and leaders of the Left – such as the energetic d'Ester
who represented Cologne in the Prussian Assembly. In Vienna he
spent almost two weeks. A few days before his arrival, there had been a
bloody repression of the workers and the whole city was to pass under
democratic control for a short period at the end of October. Marx
took part in a meeting of the Democratic Club which, though agreed
on demanding the resignation of the Government, were debating
whether the demand should be made of the Emperor or of Parliament.
Marx is reported as intervening testily to say that Emperor and Parliament were largely irrelevant here: 'the greatest power of all has been
forgotten: the people. We must turn to the people and influence *them*
with all the means at our disposal, through the press, placards and
public meetings.'[1] Marx also gave two lectures in the Workers'Association, one on the development of the workers' movements in Europe
and the other a repeat of his Brussels talks on 'Wage-Labour and
Capital'. On his return to Berlin he attended a meeting of the Prussian
Assembly and succeeded in negotiating a gift of 2000 thalers from the
Polish community who were impressed by the *Neue Rheinische Zeitung*'s
defence of their cause. Another 2000 thalers he managed to collect
from other sources.

The Hansemann ministry, proving too recalcitrant for the Prussian
establishment, had fallen while Marx was in Berlin; the controversial
armistice with Denmark also contributed to the general feeling of
unrest throughout Germany. Marx hurried back to Cologne on
11 September to experience the most tempestuous month of that
turbulent year. Relations in Cologne between the citizens and the
soldiers (most of whom came from East Prussia) were tense in any
event; and on 13 September, after a particularly brutal provocation
and looting by the soldiers, Wolff and Bürgers summoned a public
meeting on Cologne's main square. Several thousands surrounded
the tribune draped in a black, red and gold flag; the flysheet with the
Seventeen Demands was distributed, and a Committee of Public
Safety of thirty members was elected 'to represent those portions of
the population not represented by the present authorities'.[2] The
Committee included Marx and most of the staff of the *Neue Rheinische*

[1] Quoted in E. Priester, 'Karl Marx in Wien', *Zeitschrift für Geschichtswissenschaft*
(1953) p. 723.
[2] *Neue Rheinische Zeitung*, 15 Sep 1848, in *MEW* v 493.

Zeitung; its five-man executive committee, of which Marx was not a member, was headed by Hermann Becker. The last act of the meeting was to send an Address, proposed by Engels, to the Prussian Assembly urging them to stand firm in the face of government pressure.

The Committee of Public Safety summoned a mass meeting at Worringen just outside Cologne for the following Sunday, 17 September, in order to support the Frankfurt Assembly against the Prussian Government over Denmark. It was also hoped that the choice of venue would help to draw into the revolutionary movement peasants and factory workers who lived in the villages. About 10,000 people arrived to hear a series of speeches in favour of a Social-Democratic Republic from, among others, Henry Brisbane (editor of the *New York Daily Tribune*) and Lassalle (whose championship of Countess von Hatzfeld in a *cause célèbre* had already provided him with a national reputation), representing the Düsseldorf radicals. On Engels' proposal a motion was carried that, if a conflict broke out between Prussia and the other German states, the participants 'would give life and limb for Germany'.[1] The news had not yet arrived that the Frankfurt Assembly (which had not even been previously consulted) had reluctantly agreed to the armistice of Malmö that Prussia had signed with Denmark. This aroused nation-wide protests, particularly from Democrats who considered that Prussia had merely dishonoured Germany and had rejected all aspirations towards national unity. Barricades were erected in Frankfurt and two conservative deputies were lynched. The momentum of protest in Cologne was continued on 20 September with a mass meeting called in support of the Frankfurt insurgents by the Democratic Society and the Workers' Association as well as the Committee of Public Safety. The *Neue Rheinische Zeitung* opened a subscription for them and their families.

But the movement had already passed its zenith: the Frankfurt uprising was suppressed and the King nominated General Pfuël to form an administration that could no longer be called liberal.

The second Congress of the Rhineland Democrats had been called for 25 September. But early in the morning of the same day, the authorities struck: Becker and Schapper were arrested and only the gathering of a hostile crowd gave Moll time to escape. Warrants were also issued for the arrest of Engels, Dronke, Wolff and Bürgers, the charge in every case being conspiracy to overthrow the regime. Marx

[1] *Neue Rheinische Zeitung*, 19 Sep 1848, in *MEW* v 497.

himself could not be prosecuted as he had taken no active part in the recent public meetings. A meeting of the Democratic Society that afternoon – which Marx attended – decided to do everything to avoid a confrontation with the soldiers. Marx wrote two weeks later:

> The democrats told ... the workers that under no circumstances did they want a *putsch*. At this moment, there was no burning question to bring the people as a whole into the struggle and every revolt must therefore fail; it was even more senseless since in a few days violent events could occur and we would have made ourselves incapable of fighting even before the day of decision.[1]

A few barricades were raised and although these were dismantled without violence (the authorities being thereby deprived of the clash that they had hoped to provoke) martial law was declared that evening. The Civil Guard was disbanded, all political organisations were forbidden, and the *Neue Rheinische Zeitung* (together with three smaller newspapers) was suppressed.

Martial law lasted for a week: it was lifted on 3 October on orders from Berlin following pressure from the Cologne City Council and the Prussian Assembly. The *Neue Rheinische Zeitung* had been hard hit: Marx had planned to bring out the newspaper in Düsseldorf had martial law continued, but even so it was impossible to put an issue together before 13 October. Engels and Dronke had gone to Belgium, Wolff to Pfalz, and Marx and Weerth were the only editors left. The one fresh recruit was the poet Ferdinand Freiligrath. Marx had to contribute yet more of his own and Jenny's money to get the paper restarted and it became legally his own property.

When it did reappear, the paper was full of reports on Vienna: the city had fallen under the control of the Democrats on 6 October, and the Emperor had been forced to flee for a second time; he was reinstated at the end of the month by loyalist troops under Prince Windischgratz who had struck the first blow for the counter-revolution as early as June when he suppressed the rising of the Czechs in Prague. Austria set the example for Prussia: on 2 November General Pfuël was replaced by Count Brandenburg, illegitimate son of Frederick William II and an energetic conservative, and on 9 November the Prussian Assembly was transferred to the small provincial town of Brandenburg. At first it refused to move and had to be hounded

[1] K. Marx, 'The Cologne Revolution', *MEW* v 421.

ignominiously from one hall to another; but finally it agreed, merely appealing to the people not to pay their taxes as a protest.

These events marked the definite end of any revolutionary prospect for Germany. In response to the new situation there was a sharp change in the content and editorial policies of the *Neue Rheinische Zeitung*: much less space was given to purely political questions and more to problems of direct concern to the working class; the notion of class struggle was much more to the fore and the whole tone became more radical. Owning to the depletion in the paper's staff Marx wrote more of the articles himself. He appears to have believed, for a moment at least, in the possible success of an armed uprising. On 1 November the paper carried an appeal, inserted independently of the editorial board, for arms and volunteers for Vienna. On 6 November Marx himself announced the fall of Vienna to a sombre meeting of the Workers' Association and laid the blame for Windischgratz's victory on 'the manifold treachery of the Viennese bourgeoisie'.[1] He elaborated this accusation in the article, 'Victory of the Counter-Revolution in Vienna', published in the *Neue Rheinische Zeitung* on 7 November. The article ended:

> Granted that the counter-revolution is alive throughout Europe thanks to weapons, it will die throughout Europe thanks to money. The destiny that will abolish victory is European bankruptcy, State bankruptcy. Bayonet tips break on economic 'points' like dry tinder. . . . The useless butcheries of the June and October days, the wearisome feast of victims since February and March, the cannibalism of the counter-revolution will itself convince the people that there is only one means to shorten, simplify and concentrate the death agony of the old society and the bloody birth pangs of the new, one means only – revolutionary terrorism.[2]

And when it seemed that the Civil Guard in Berlin might refuse to surrender their weapons and support the Assembly, Marx proclaimed: 'It is the duty of the Rhine Province to hasten to the aid of the Berlin National Assembly with men and arms.'[3]

On 18 November the Committee of Rhineland Democrats proclaimed a three-point programme signed by Marx, Schapper and

[1] Minutes of the General Meeting, etc., *MEW* v 502.
[2] K. Marx, 'Victory of the Counter-Revolution in Vienna' *MEW* v 457.
[3] K. Marx, 'The Counter-Revolution in Berlin', *MEW* vi 12.

Schneider. It was published in the *Neue Rheinische Zeitung* and led to Marx's subsequent prosecution. The programme consisted in: resistance to tax collection; the organisation of a popular levy 'for defence against the enemy' (and for those without resources 'weapons and munitions are to be procured at the expense of the communes and through voluntary subscription'); and, thirdly, any refusal to obey the National Assembly was to be answered by the creation of Committees of Public Safety.[1] A 'People's Committee' was set up in Cologne (Marx was not a member), but the feeble reactions of the Assembly precluded any recourse to arms and tax refusal was the only point in the programme that was implemented: from 19 November until mid-December the *Neue Rheinische Zeitung* carried the slogan 'No More Taxes' underneath its masthead and the paper devoted much space to reporting the progress of the campaign. Marx had already given the historical and economic background to this campaign a month earlier in a popular application of his materialist conceptions:

> After God had created the world and Kings by the grace of God, He left smaller-scale industry to men. Weapons and Lieutenants' uniforms are made in a profane manner and the profane way of production cannot, like heavenly industry, create out of nothing. It needs raw materials, tools and wages, weighty things that are categorised under the modest term of 'production costs'. These production costs are offset for the state through taxes and taxes are offset through the nation's work. From the economic point of view, therefore, it remains an enigma how any King can *give* any people anything. The people must first make weapons and give them to the King in order to be able to receive them from the King. The King can only give what has already been given to him. This from the economic point of view. However, constitutional Kings arise at precisely those moments when people are beginning to understand the economic mystery. Thus the first beginnings of the fall of Kings by the grace of God have always been *questions of taxes*. So too in Prussia.[2]

In spite of its vigorous campaigning, the *Neue Rheinische Zeitung* was getting more difficult to produce. At the end of October Marx wrote

[1] Cf. *MEW* vi 33.
[2] K. Marx, 'Reply of Frederick William IV to the Deputation of the Civil Guard', *MEW* v 431 f.

to Engels: 'I am up to my ears in work, and find it impossible to do anything detailed; moreover, the authorities do everything to steal my time.'[1] Engels had wandered through France during the month of October compiling a delightful travel-diary in which his admiration for the way of life of the French peasants was mingled with disgust at their political ignorance. Once he arrived in Switzerland Marx kept him supplied with money – a strange reversal of their later roles. The 'stupid reactionary shareholders' had thought that economies would be possible now that the editorial board had shrunk. But Marx replied 'it is up to me to pay as high a fee as I wish and thus they will get no financial advantage'.[2] He further admitted to his friend that: 'it was perhaps not wise to have advanced such a large sum for the paper, as I have 3 or 4 press prosecutions on my back and could be locked up any day – and then I could pant for money like the deer for cooling streams. But it was important to make progress under any conditions and not to give up our political position.'[3] He added that it was 'pure fantasy' to suppose that he could have left Engels in a fix for a single moment. 'You always remain my intimate friend, as I hope I do yours.'[4] Marx was much heartened by a demonstration of popular support on 14 November when he had to appear before the public prosecutor. According to a government report Marx was 'accompanied by several hundred people to the courtroom ... who on his return received him with a thundering cheer and made no secret of the fact that they would have freed him by force if he had been arrested'.[5] In reply to this demonstration Marx made a short speech – his only speech to a public meeting in Frankfurt – thanking the crowd for their sympathy and support. At the end of the month he wrote optimistically to Engels: 'Our paper is still conducting a policy of revolt and nevertheless steering clear of the *code penal* in spite of all the publication regulations. It is now very much *en vogue*. We also publish daily fly sheets. The Revolution goes on.'[6]

An increasing amount of Marx's time was taken up by the Workers' Association. On 12 October a delegation had asked him whether he would take over the presidency of the Association, both Moll and Schapper being unavailable. Marx pointed out that his situation in

---

[1] Marx to Engels, *MEW* xxvii 128.   [2] Ibid., 129.
[3] Ibid.   [4] Ibid. 130.
[5] Quoted in H. Gemkow, *Karl Marx*, p. 174, cf. also *MEW* vi 571.
[6] Marx to Engels, *MEW* xxvii 131.

Cologne was precarious as he had not managed to obtain Prussian citizenship and was liable to prosecution for the *Neue Rheinische Zeitung*, but he agreed to take on the job 'provisionally, until the release of Dr Gottschalk'.[1] Some modifications were introduced: half the time at meetings was regularly given to the study of social and political questions and from November a lengthy study of the *Seventeen Demands* was begun.

By December it was quite clear that the disturbances of the previous three months could have no revolutionary issue. On 5 December Frederick William took the decisive step of dismissing the Prussian Assembly and himself proclaiming a Constitution. Marx drew his conclusions in a series of articles in the *Neue Rheinische Zeitung* entitled 'The Bourgeoise and the Counter-Revolution' which marked a substantial revision of his earlier position. According to Marx, since the bourgeoisie had proved incapable of making its own revolution, the working class would have to rely exclusively on its own forces. 'The history of the Prussian bourgeoisie', he wrote, 'and that of the German bourgeoisie as a whole from March to December demonstrates that in Germany a purely bourgeois revolution and the establishment of bourgeois rule in the form of a constitutional monarchy is impossible and that the only possibility is either a feudal absolutist counter-revolution or a social-republican revolution.'[2] But Marx now despaired of the impetus for such a social-republican revolution arising from inside Germany: it could only be produced by an external shock. This was the programme for 1849 that he sketched out on 1 January:

> The liberation of Europe . . . is dependent on a successful uprising by the French working class. But every French social upheaval necessarily founders on the English bourgeoisie, on the industrial and commercial world-domination of Great Britain. Every partial social reform in France and on the European continent in general is and remains, in as far as it aims at being definitive, an empty pious hope. And old England will only be overthrown by a world war, which is the only thing that could provide the Chartists, the organised party of the English workers, with the conditions for a successful rising against their gigantic oppressors. The Chartists at the head of the English government – only at that moment does

[1] Minutes of the Committee Meeting, etc., *MEW* v 501.
[2] K. Marx, 'The Bourgeoisie and the Counter-Revolution', *MEW* vi 124.

the idea of a social revolution leave the realm of Utopia for that of reality. But every European war which involves England is a world war. And a European war will be the first result of a successful workers' revolution in France. As in Napoleon's time, England will be at the head of the counter-revolutionary armies, but will be precipitated to the front of the revolutionary movement by the war itself and thus redeem its guilt against the revolution of the 18th century. Revolutionary uprising of the French working class, world war – that is the programme for the year 1849.[1]

But however much Marx might see world war as the solution to Germany's problems, there was still the more immediate question of the elections to be held under the new Constitution at the end of February. The problems of the previous May arose again: to participate or not to participate. And Marx's answer, despite his drastically changed attitude to the bourgeoisie, was still the same. When Anneke proposed in the committee meeting of 15 January that the Workers' Association put up its own candidates, the minutes record Marx as saying that

the Workers' Association as such could not run any candidates at the present moment; nor was it a question for the present of maintaining certain principles, but of opposing the government, absolutism and feudal domination; and for this even simple democrats, so-called liberals, were sufficient as they were in any event far from satisfied with the present government. One had simply to take matters as they were. The important thing was to create as strong an opposition as possible to the present absolutist regime; it was therefore common sense, since they could not secure the victory of their own principles in the elections, to unite with another opposition party to prevent the victory of their common enemy, absolute monarchy.[2]

And, in the event, the two deputies whom Cologne sent to Berlin were both Democrats.

V. THE DEMISE OF THE 'NEUE RHEINISCHE ZEITUNG'
During January 1849 the staff of the *Neue Rheinische Zeitung* was strengthened by the return of Engels, who had written from Berne to inquire

[1] K. Marx, 'The Revolutionary Movement', *MEW* vi 149 f.
[2] Minutes of the Committee Meeting, etc., *MEW* vi 579.

of Marx whether it was safe to return: he did not mind standing trial but what he could not support was the no-smoking rule in preventive detention. Engels devoted many of his articles to affairs in Eastern Europe, but his contributions were not entirely felicitous: he published two articles, one in February and the other in May, which branded (in a way reminiscent of Hegel) whole Slav peoples as 'reactionary' and 'without a history'. In the first of these articles, written particularly in response to Bakunin's romantically revolutionary appeals, Engels talked of the treason to the revolution of the Czecks and Southern Slavs and 'promised a bloody revenge on the Slavs'. He finished his second article with these words:

> With the first successful revolt of the French proletariat . . . the Austrian Germans and Magyars will be free and exact a bloody revenge from the Slavic barbarians. The general war that will break out will break this Slavic union and annihilate all these small pigheaded nations right down to their very names. The next world war will cause to vanish from the face of the earth not only reactionary classes and dynasties but also whole reactionary peoples. And that, too, is progress.[1]

This view was typical of other correspondents of the paper: the *Neue Rheinische Zeitung* was misled by the role that certain sections of the Slavs played in 1848–9 into describing whole nations as being once and for all revolutionary or counter-revolutionary, as having a right to a history or not having a right to any history at all.[2]

During the electoral campaign the case against Marx for his incitement during the September troubles finally came up for trial. The previous day Marx had also had to appear in court, together with Engels and Korff (who was legally responsible for the paper), to answer

---

[1] F. Engels, 'The Hungarian Struggle', *MEW* VI 176.

[2] This matter is investigated in extraordinary detail by R. Rosdolsky, 'Friedrich Engels und das Problem der "Geschichtslosen Völker"', *Archiv für Sozialgeschichte*, IV (1964). See also F. Mehring, *Aus dem literarischen Nachlass*, III 18 ff.; G. Mayer, *Friedrich Engels*, II 345 ff. Two of Engels' essays are translated in K. Marx and F. Engels, *The Russian Menace to Europe*, ed. Blackstock and Hoselitz (London, 1953) pp. 56 ff. The *Neue Rheinische Zeitung* also contained a fair amount of anti-semitism whose generally anti-capitalist tone it facilely considered to be of a progressive nature. Many of these articles (as also some of those in the vein of Engels' quoted above) came from Müller-Tellering (the paper's Vienna correspondent) whose contributions Marx considered to be 'the best we have had, absolutely in keeping with our line'. (Marx to Müller-Tellering, *MEW* XXVII 485).

a charge of libel against state officials arising out of the article of the previous July protesting at the arrest of Anncke. Marx was defended by Schneider, his colleague in the Democratic Association, and also spoke lengthily himself. He defended his article by explicit reference to the *Code Napoléon* and by describing the subject of his article as 'tangible manifestation of the systematically counter-revolutionary tendency of the Hansemann ministry and the German government in general'.[1] He went on to say that it could not be judged in isolation from the general situation in Germany and the failure of the March revolution. He finished:

> Why did the March revolution fail? It reformed the political summit and left untouched all the foundations of this summit – the old bureaucracy, the old army, the old courts, the old judges born, educated and grown grey in the service of absolutism. The first duty of the press is now to undermine all the foundations of the present political situation.[2]

His speech was greeted with applause and all three defendants were acquitted.

The trial on the following day was a more serious affair. Marx, Schapper and Schneider, as signatories of the anti-tax proclamation of the Rhineland Democratic Committee, were accused of plotting to overthrow the regime. Marx again defended himself in a speech lasting almost an hour. He professed amazement at being prosecuted under laws that the Government itself had abrogated by its dissolution of the Assembly on 5 December. Furthermore, these laws were those passed by the pre-March Diet which was an outdated institution. Marx then gave the jurors an object lesson on the materialist conception of history.

> Society is not based on the law [he stated], that is a legal fiction, rather law must be based on society; it must be the expression of society's common interests and needs, as they arise from the various material methods of production, against the arbitrariness of the single individual. The *Code Napoléon*, which I have in my hand, did not produce modern bourgeois society. Bourgeois society, as it arose in the eighteenth century and developed in the nineteenth, merely finds its legal expression in the Code. As soon as it no longer

---

[1] K. Marx, Speech in his Defence, *MEW* vi 232.   [2] Ibid. 234.

corresponds to social relationships, it is worth no more than the paper it is written on. You cannot make old laws the foundation of a new social development any more than these old laws created the old social conditions. . . . Any attempted assertion of the eternal validity of laws continually clashes with present needs, it prevents commerce and industry, and paves the way for social crises that break out with political revolutions.[1]

Marx went on to explain that in this context the National Assembly represented modern bourgeois society against the feudal society of the United Diet and as such was incapable of coming to terms with the monarchy. Moreover, the Assembly merely derived its rights from the people and 'if the crown makes a counter-revolution then the people rightly answers with a revolution'. Marx concluded with a prophecy: 'Whatever way the new National Assembly may go, the necessary result can only be a complete victory of the counter-revolution or a fresh and successful revolution. Perhaps the victory of the revolution is only possible after a complete counter-revolution.'[2]

The three defendants were again acquitted and the foreman of the sympathetic jury thanked Marx for his instructive explanation. Marx's two speeches in his defence appeared shortly afterwards as a pamphlet.

One result of the February election was to provoke in the Workers' Association the serious split that had been imminent for some time. Gottschalk had eventually been acquitted and released from prison just before Christmas. He found the Workers' Association much changed since July and realising that it was impossible for him to be re-elected President on his own terms, he left Cologne of his own accord and went to Brussels. But he still continued to follow the affairs of the Association with interest and expressed his views through the Association's newspaper, whose editor, Prinz, was a close friend. Prinz launched a violent attack on the Democrats, and the committee meeting next day, 15 January, decided to appoint a commission to supervise Prinz in his editorial activities.[3] But Prinz would not be supervised and the Association was obliged to found a rival journal. On the proposal of Schapper, the organisation of the Association was tightened up 'in order that disunity should not arise through lack of rules'.[4] Schapper himself became President; Marx did not hold any

[1] Ibid. 245. [2] Ibid. 257.
[3] Cf. Minutes of the Committee Meeting, etc., MEW vi 578.
[4] Quoted in H. Stein, Der Kölner Arbeiterverein, p. 92.

official position, though he and Engels offered to give the members fortnightly lectures on social questions. At the end of February Gottschalk himself launched a violent attack on Marx in an unsigned article in Prinz's newspaper. Gottschalk took particular exception to an article by Marx in the *Neue Rheinische Zeitung* in which he had defended his position on the forthcoming elections. Marx had written:

> We are certainly the last to desire the rule of the bourgeoisie. . . . But our cry to the workers and petty-bourgeoisie is: you should prefer to suffer in modern bourgeois society whose industry creates the material condition for a new society that will free you all, rather than return to an obsolete form of society which, under the pretence of saving your classes, precipitates the whole nation into medieval barbarism.[1]

This did, in fact, seem to mark a change from the stark choice between social republican revolution and feudal reaction that Marx had proclaimed in December. Gottschalk was quick to attack this modified position in an unsigned open letter 'To Herr Karl Marx' which was typical of many attacks on Marx from the Left during (and after) the 1848 revolution:

> Why should we make a revolution? Why should we, men of the proletariat, spill our blood? Should we really, as you, Mr Preacher, proclaim to us, escape the hell of the Middle Ages by precipitating ourselves voluntarily into the purgatory of decrepit capitalist rule in order to arrive at the cloudy heaven of your Communist Credo? . . . . You are not serious about the liberation of the oppressed. For you the misery of the worker, the hunger of the poor has only a scientific and doctrinaire interest. You are elevated above such miseries and merely shine down upon the parties as a learned sun-god. You are not affected by what moves the heart of man. You have no belief in the cause that you pretend to represent. Yes, although every day you prune the revolution according to the pattern of accomplished facts, although you have a Communist Credo, you do not believe in the revolt of the working people whose rising flood is already beginning to prepare the downfall of capitalism; you do not believe in the permanence of the revolution, you do not even believe in the innate capacity for revolution. . . . And now that we, the

[1] K. Marx, Montesquieu LVI, *MEW* vi 195.

revolutionary party, have realised that we can expect nothing from any class except our own, and thus our only task is to make the revolution permanent, now you recommend to us people who are known to be weaklings and nonentities.[1]

Such was the tenor of Gottschalk's onslaught, echoing the previous views of Weitling. Marx did not reply to this attack of which the majority of the Association disapproved. Gottschalk returned to Cologne in the summer but died of cholera in September while coping with an epidemic in the poor quarters of the city.

It was not only Gottschalk who considered that Marx's policies were not radical enough. Moll and Schapper had never really approved of Marx's unilateral dissolution of the Communist League,[2] and the branches outside Germany had continued to lead a (rather shadowy) existence. On his flight from Cologne in September Moll had settled in London and reinvigorated the group there. It was decided to re-establish the League on a wider basis: a new Central Committee comprising Moll, Heinrich Bauer and Eccarius was elected, and Schapper was invited to found a group in Cologne 'even without Marx's agreement'.[3] Schapper called a meeting of selected persons to whom he suggested that, after the events of December 1848, the existence of the Communist League was once again a necessity. This meeting proved inconclusive and shortly afterwards Moll appeared in Cologne with the specific object of winning over Marx and Engels. A meeting was held on the premises of the Neue Rheinische Zeitung at which Marx resolutely opposed the idea. Firstly, he maintained that the relative freedom of speech and Press that still obtained rendered the League superfluous. He was further opposed to its re-creation 'since a "single, indivisible republic" was proclaimed as the goal to be achieved – and this made the proposed League statutes more socialist than communist – and also since the statutes had a conspiratorial tendency'.[4] The meeting agreed to disagree and Moll continued his trip to other German towns but with little success.

Meanwhile pressure on the Neue Rheinische Zeitung mounted. Marx's paper – and Marx himself – came in for attention from the military as well as the civil authorities. On 2 March two N.C.O.s called on

---

[1] Quoted in H. Stein, op. cit., p. 96.   [2] See p. 197 above.
[3] Evidence of P. Röser, in W. Blumenberg, 'Zur Geschichte des Kommunisten-bundes', Archiv für Sozialgeschichte (1964) p. 90.
[4] Evidence of P. Röser, op. cit., pp. 90 f.

Marx in his home to ask for the name of the author of an article reporting on the conviction of an officer for the illicit sale of army material. Marx described the encounter in a subsequent letter of complaint to the Cologne Commandant:

> I answered the gentlemen (1) that the article had nothing to do with me as it was an inscription in the non-editorial part of the paper; (2) that they could be provided with free space for a counter-statement; (3) that it was open to them to seek satisfaction in the courts. When the gentlemen pointed out that the whole of the Eighth Company felt itself slandered by the article, then I replied that only the signatures of the whole of the Eighth Company could convince me of the correctness of this statement which was, in any case, irrelevant. The NCOs then told me that if I did not name 'the man', if I did not 'hand him over', they could 'no longer hold their people back', and it would 'turn out badly'. I answered that the gentlemen's threats and intimidation would achieve absolutely nothing with me. They then left, muttering under their breath.[1]

Engels, in a much later letter, made it plain that it was not only Marx's bitter irony that made the soldiers leave so fast: 'Marx received them wearing a dressing gown in whose pocket he had placed an unloaded pistol with the handle showing. The sight of this was enough to make the NCOs stop asking for any further explanation. In spite of the sabre bayonets with which they were armed, they lost their self-possession and departed.'[2] Engels also recounted later that many wondered

> how we were able to conduct our business so unhampered in a Prussian fortress of the first rank in face of a garrison of 8000 men and right opposite the main guard post; but the eight bayonets and the 250 sharp cartridges in the editorial room and the red Jacobin hats of the typesetters made our building also look like a fortress to the officers and one that could not be taken by any mere surprise attack.[3]

But the days of the *Neue Rheinische Zeitung* were evidently numbered. One month before the end Marx took the most dramatic step of his

---

[1] Marx to Oberst Engels, *MEW* xxvii 496.
[2] Engels, to Kautsky, *MEW* xxxvi 399.
[3] F. Engels, 'Marx and the *Neue Rheinische Zeitung*', *MEW* xxi 23.

year in Cologne: he broke the ties with the Democrats that he had, till then, been so eager to foster. On 15 April the *Neue Rheinische Zeitung* carried the brief announcement, signed by Marx, Schapper, Anneke, Becker and Wolff:

> We consider that the present organisation of Democratic Associations contains too many heterogeneous elements to allow of an activity profitable to the aims of the Cause. We are rather of the opinion that a closer connexion between workers associations is preferable as their composition is homogeneous; therefore, as from today, we are resigning from the Rhineland Committee of Democratic Associations.[1]

The reasons for Marx's decision were probably complex. The Democratic Association had debated at length the question whether it should change its title to Democratic and Republican Association, but it had rejected the proposals and had in consequence been bitterly attacked by Anneke's *Neue Kölnische Zeitung*. Probably also the refounding of the Communist League and criticism from within the Workers' Association of his temporising attitude led Marx to break with the Democrats. The content of the *Neue Rheinische Zeitung* had been reaching towards this 'left turn' for some time: in March Wolff had started a series of articles on the misery of the Silesian peasantry and on 5 April Marx began to publish the lectures that he had given two years before to the German Workers' Association in Brussels on Wage Labour and Capital.[2] The articles were prefaced with a reference to the reproach addressed to the paper 'from various quarters' of 'not having presented the *economic relations* which constitute the material foundation of the present class struggle and national struggles'.[3] Three days before Marx left the Democratic Association, the Cologne Workers' Association had invited all the Rhineland Workers' Associations to unite on a regional basis; on 16 April the General Assembly decided to cease co-operating with Democratic Associations in the Rhineland; and on 26 April the leaders of the Workers' Association summoned a Congress of the Workers' Associations of the Rhineland and Westphalia to meet in Cologne on 6 May. One of the tasks of this Congress was to be to elect delegates to attend the all-German Workers' Congress in Leipzig the following month. This Congress was called by the *Verbrüderung*

---

[1] *MEW* VI 426.   [2] See pp. 177 f above.
[3] K. Marx, 'Wage Labour and Capital', *MESW* I 79.

(Brotherhood), the only national workers' organisation
This change of tactics further weakened the Colog
Association: a section of the members resigned and ser
Gottschalk asking him to return, saying that recent po
only showed that 'the present leaders of the Association w
are not, clear as to what they want'.[2]

All this, however, happened in Marx's absence. For the past two
months the *Neue Rheinische Zeitung* had been perpetually on the verge of
bankruptcy. Immediately on resigning from the Democratic Association Marx went on a three-week trip through North-West Germany
and Westphalia to collect money for the newspaper and also, no
doubt, in view of the policies just adopted, to make contacts with
workers' groups: he spent a fortnight in a first-class hotel in Hamburg
laying plans for further communist activity with Karl von Bruhn and
Konrad Schramm, both members of the Communist League.[3] While
Marx was in Hamburg, revolution broke out in Germany for the last
time for many years. The Frankfurt Assembly had at length drafted a
Constitution, but the King was in a strong enough position to reject it
and coined at this time the famous phrase: against Democrats the only
remedy is soldiers. In early May street fighting broke out in Dresden
and lasted for a week with such colourful figures as Bakunin and the
young Richard Wagner behind the barricades. There were also short-
lived revolts in the Ruhr, but it was only in Baden that there was any
extensive insurgency.

The renewed confidence of the authorities led to the expulsion of
Marx. The military authorities in Cologne had already in March applied
to the police for his expulsion. The request had gone so far as Man-
teuffel, the Minister of the Interior, but was not immediately implemented as the civil authorities in Cologne though it would be unduly
provocative to expel Marx without any particular reason. By May,
however, they felt strong enough to do just that: on his return to
Cologne on 9 May Marx learnt that he was to be expelled; the authorities in Hamburg had already issued him with a passport valid for Paris
only. On the sixteenth he received the order to leave Prussian soil

[1] On the achievements of workers' organisations in Germany during 1948–9,
see P. Noyes, *Organization and Revolution* passim.
[2] Quoted in H. Stein, op. cit., p. 99.
[3] Reference for Marx's Hamburg activities in H. Meyer, 'Karl Marx und die
deutsche Revolution von 1848', *Historische Zeitschrift* (1953) p. 533. See also Marx to
Engels, *MEW* xxxi 93 f.

within twenty-four hours 'because of his shameful violation of hospitality'.[1] All the other editors of the *Neue Rheinische Zeitung* were either expelled or threatened with arrest. The paper could not continue. The last number appeared on 18 May, printed in red. On the first page there appeared a poem by Freiligrath of which the first stanza ran:

> No open blow in an open fight,
>   But with quips and with quirks they arraign me,
> By creeping treacherous secret blight
>   The Western Kalmucks have slain me.
> The fatal shaft in the dark did fly;
>   I was struck by an ambushed knave;
> And here in the pride of my strength I lie,
>   Like the corpse of a rebel brave![2]

Also on the first page was a message to the workers of Cologne from the editors which warned them against any attempt at a *putsch* in Cologne and finished: 'the last word of the *Neue Rheinische Zeitung* will always and everywhere be: emancipation of the working class'.[3]

Marx himself contributed a defiant article claiming – rather implausibly – that the paper had always been revolutionary and had made no attempt to conceal its views:

> Of what use are your hypocritical phrases that strain after impossible subterfuges? We also are ruthless and we ask for no consideration from you. When our turn comes we will not excuse our terrorism. But royal terrorists, terrorists by the grace of God and the law are brutal, contemptible and vulgar in their practice, cowardly, secretive and double-faced in their theory, and in both respects entirely without honour.[4]

20,000 copies of the 'Red Number' were sold and were soon changing hands at ten times the original price. It was even rumoured that some copies had been expensively framed, to serve as ikons.

Marx was left with the task of winding up the affairs of the paper. All the plant and machinery – which belonged to Marx personally – had to be sold to pay the various debts to shareholders, employees and contributors: Marx later claimed to have sunk 7000 thalers of his own

---

[1] *MEW* vi 503.   [2] The translation is by the Chartist, Ernest Jones.
[3] K. Marx, 'To the Workers of Cologne', *MEW* vi 519.   [4] *MEW* vi 505.

money in the paper.[1] The circulation of the paper at the time of its demise was almost 6000, but its growth had merely increased the expenses without a corresponding increase in revenue. Everything that remained, including incoming articles, Marx gave over to the *Neue Kölnische Zeitung*. This left them only Jenny's silver. This was packed in a suitcase lent by one of Marx's creditors and the whole family left Cologne on 19 May 1849 and went down the Rhine to Bingen where Jenny stayed with friends for a few days. Marx and Engels went on to Frankfurt where, assisted by Wilhelm Wolff, they met the leaders of the Left in the Frankfurt Assembly to persuade them to assume leadership of the revolutionary movement in South-West Germany by summoning the revolutionary forces to Frankfurt. Meanwhile Jenny arranged, with the help of Weydemeyer, to pawn her silver in Frankfurt. She then took the children to stay with her mother in Kreuznach for a few days. She found her mother much changed: 'Straitened circumstances and old age have infiltrated into a soul that is otherwise so mild and loving the qualities of hardness and selfishness that deeply wound those near to her.' But she comforted herself with amusement at the provinciality of Trier and the confidence of Marx that 'all the pressures that we now feel are only the sign of an imminent and even more complete victory of our views'.[2]

When Marx and Engels could get no agreement from the Left in Frankfurt, they went south to Baden where they spent a week vainly urging the revolutionary leaders (who had established a provisional government) to march on Frankfurt. In Speyer Marx encountered Willich, still enthusiastic for campaigning, and in Kaiserslautern he met d'Ester who gave him a mandate on behalf of the Democratic Central Committee (of which Marx had recently been so severely critical) to liaise on their behalf with the Paris socialists. There was plainly no further role for Marx in Germany. The two friends decided to split up: Marx would go to Paris while Engels put his talents as a bombardier at the service of the Baden revolutionaries. However, on their way back from Kaiserslautern to Bingen they were both arrested by Hessian troops who took them to Darmstadt and Frankfurt where they were eventually released. Marx returned to Bingen and left for Paris on 2 June accompanied by Ferdinand Wolff.

[1] Cf. Marx to Cluss, *MEW* xxviii 733; also Jenny Marx to Weydemeyer, *MEW* xxvii 607.
[2] Jenny Marx to Lina Scholer, in L. Dornemann, *Jenny Marx*, p. 136.

VI. PARIS AGAIN

Marx arrived in Paris, where he was to spend the next three months, confident of an imminent revolutionary outbreak. In reality, following the crushing victory of Louis Napoleon at the Presidential election the previous December, a military autocracy was imminent. Marx settled in the rue de Lille near Les Invalides under the pseudonym of M. Ramboz. He found Paris 'dismal' – as indeed it must inevitably have seemed compared to the previous year. In addition a cholera epidemic was raging far and wide. Marx was nevertheless confident of an immediate uprising and set about fulfilling his mandate. On 7 June he wrote to Engels: 'A colossal eruption of the revolutionary crater was never more imminent than now in Paris. . . . I am in touch with the whole of the revolutionary party and in a few days will have *all* the revolutionary journals at my disposition.'[1] In fact, however, the situation was grim: the sporadic armed revolts in Germany were petering out, the Hungarian rebellion was crushed by Russian troops, and in Italy the French army was in the process of re-establishing papal authority. On 11 June, following a censure motion on the Government proposed by Ledru-Rollin and the radical Montagne, the workers' associations proposed an armed *coup d'état* by night, but the Montagne refused; and when the latter held a peaceful demonstration themselves two days later, it was easily dispersed by government troops. Thus the two parties 'mutually paralysed and deceived each other'.[2] The 'revolution' was finished.

At the beginning of July Jenny and the children had joined Marx in Paris to find themselves in a state of poverty that was to become chronic. Marx enlisted Weydemeyer's help to try and persuade a lady who had promised money for the *Neue Rheinische Zeitung* to give it to Marx personally so that he could purchase the copyright of the *Poverty of Philosophy* and make some money from a second edition. 'If help does not come from some quarter,' he wrote to Weydemeyer, 'I am lost . . . the last jewels of my wife have already gone to the pawn-shop.'[3] Marx also wrote to Lassalle, who responded promptly and generously, but he bitterly regretted his request when he learned from Freiligrath that Lassalle had made the affair the talk of the taverns.

---

[1] Marx to Engels, *MEW* xxvii 137.
[2] K. Marx, *MEW* vi 528.
[3] Marx to Weydemeyer, *MEW* xxvii 500.

On 19 July, however, as Jenny wrote, 'the familiar police sergeant came again and informed us that "Karl Marx and his wife had to leave Paris within 24 hours" '.[1] Marx was given the alternative of moving to the Morbihan district of Brittany. He described the area – rather ungenerously – as 'the pontine marshes of Brittany'[2] and the whole proposition was 'a disguised attempt at murder'.[3] He managed at least to obtain a delay by appealing to the Ministry of the Interior and writing to the Press that he had come to Paris with 'the general aim of adding to source-material for my work on the history of political economy that I began five years ago'.[4] Marx still declared himself 'satisfied' with the political situation. 'Things progress well', he wrote, 'and the Waterloo that the official democratic party has experienced is to be treated as a victory.'[5] He asked Weydemeyer to try to persuade Leske, despite the still outstanding debt, to publish his articles on 'Wage-Labour and Capital'; he had already put out feelers to Berlin in the hope of establishing a monthly on economics and politics. On 17 August Marx wrote to Engels that the increasingly reactionary nature of the French Government gave hope for an immediate revolutionary insurrection: 'We must start a literary and commercial enterprise: I await your propositions.'[6] A week later, he sailed for England.

[1] Jenny Marx, 'Short Sketch of an Eventful Life', *Reminiscences*, p. 225.
[2] Marx to Engels, *MEW* xxvii 139.
[3] Ibid. 142.
[4] K. Marx, 'To the Editor of *La Presse*', *MEW* vi 529.
[5] Marx to Weydemeyer, *MEW* xxvii 506.
[6] Marx to Engels, *MEW* xxvii 141.

5

London

One comes to see increasingly that the emigration must
turn everyone into a fool, an ass, and a common knave
unless he contrives to get completely away from it.

Engels to Marx, *MEW* XXVII 186.

I. THE FIRST YEAR IN LONDON

NOTHING, IT has been said, endures like the temporary. When Marx
came to England certainly he had no idea that he would make it his
permanent home. For years he shared the view of most of his fellow-
refugees that a new round of revolutions would soon break out on
the Continent. Like the early Christians awaiting the Second Coming,
they regarded their present life as of little importance compared to the
great event that was to come. This partly accounts for the *ad hoc* nature
of much of Marx's life during what was in fact to be a long and sleep-
less night of exile.

Leaving Jenny and the children behind in Paris, Marx crossed the
Channel on 24 August 1849 in the company of the Swiss communist
Seiler and Karl Blind, a young Democrat from Baden. Probably on his
arrival in London he temporarily stayed in Karl Blind's lodgings above
a coffee-house in Grosvenor Square: this, anyway, was the address he
used for correspondence. His prospects were bleak. 'I am in a really
difficult position,' he wrote soon after his arrival, 'my wife's preg-
nancy is far advanced. She must leave Paris by 15 September and I
don't know where I am to rake together the necessary money for her
travel and our settling here.'[1] Jenny had difficulty extending her visa
even to 15 September (when the lease on their Paris house expired),
and arrived in London on the seventeenth with her three small
children and the birth of her fourth less than three weeks away. She
was met by Georg Weerth, a wholesaler trader who was one of the

[1] Marx to Freiligrath, *MEW* XXVII 512.

founder members of the Communist League and had worked on the *Neue Rheinische Zeitung*. He found them a furnished room in a Leicester Square boarding house which they soon left, moving to a two-roomed flat in the fashionable area off the King's Road in Chelsea. The rent was high (about £6 a month[1]) but their own meagre resources were supplemented by money from Jenny's mother, and they managed for the time being. 'On 5 November,' Jenny wrote in her memoirs, 'while the people outside were shouting "Guy Fawkes for ever" and small masked boys were riding the streets on cleverly-made donkeys and all was in an uproar, my poor little Heinrich was born. We call him Little Fawkes in honour of the great conspirator.'[2] Thus, as Weerth remarked, Marx had four nations in his family, each of his children having been born in a different country.

The Marx family soon moved from the Chelsea flat. When they had been there scarcely more than six months, trouble with their landlady and a lack of ready cash caused their summary eviction. Jenny related what happened shortly afterwards in a letter to Weydemeyer:

> I shall describe to you just *one* day of that life, exactly as it was, and you will see that few emigrants, perhaps, have gone through anything like it. As wet-nurses here are too expensive I decided to feed my child myself in spite of continual terrible pains in the breast and back. But the poor little angel drank in so much worry and hushed-up anxiety that he was always poorly and suffered horribly day and night. Since he came into the world he has not slept a single night, two or three hours at the most and that rarely. Recently he has had violent convulsions, too, and has always been between life and death. In his pain he sucked so hard that my breast was chafed and the skin cracked and the blood often poured into his trembling little mouth. I was sitting with him like that one day when our landlady came in. We had paid her 250 thalers during the winter and had an agreement to give the money in the future not to her but to her own landlord, who had a bailiff's warrant against her. She denied the agreement and demanded five pounds that we still owed her. As we did not have the money at the time (Naut's letter did not arrive until later) two bailiffs came and sequestrated all my few possessions

---

[1] This would have to be multiplied by well over ten to get present-day sterling equivalents.
[2] Jenny Marx, 'Short Sketch of an Eventful Life', *Reminiscences*, p. 225.

– linen, beds, clothes – everything, even my poor child's cradle and the best toys of my daughters, who stood there weeping bitterly. They threatened to take everything away in two hours. I would then have to lie on the bare floor with my freezing children and my bad breast. Our friend Schramm hurried to town to get help for us. He got into a cab, but the horses bolted and he jumped out and was brought bleeding back to the house, where I was wailing with my poor shivering children.

We had to leave the house the next day. It was cold, rainy and dull. My husband looked for accommodation for us. When he mentioned the four children nobody would take us in. Finally a friend helped us, we paid our rent and I hastily sold all my beds to pay the chemist, the baker, the butcher and the milkman who, alarmed at the sight of the sequestration, suddenly besieged me with their bills. The beds which we had sold were taken out and put on a cart. What was happening? It was well after sunset. We were contravening English law. The landlord rushed up to us with two constables, maintaining that there might be some of his belongings among the things, and that we wanted to make away abroad. In less than five minutes there were two or three hundred persons loitering around our door – the whole Chelsea mob. The beds were brought in again – they could not be delivered to the buyer until after sunrise next day. When we had sold all our possessions we were in a position to pay what we owed to the last farthing. I went with my little darlings to the two small rooms we are now occupying in the German hotel, 1 Leicester St., Leicester Square. There for £5 per week we were given a humane reception.[1]

On expulsion from their house in Camberwell in April 1850 they found a permanent logding in two rooms in 64 Dean Street, a house belonging to a Jewish lace dealer where Heinrich Bauer, treasurer of the refugee committee, also lived. Jenny described the summer there with the four children as 'miserable'.[2] Prospects in London were so bleak that Marx considered emigrating to the United States together with Engels. He prepared the ground for a continuation of his publishing projects there and went as far as to find out the price of the ticket; but this was 'hellishly expensive'[3] and instead the Marx family

---

[1] Jenny Marx to Weydemeyer, *Reminiscences*, pp. 237 f.
[2] Jenny Marx, 'Short Sketch of an Eventful Life', *Reminiscences*, p. 226.
[3] Marx to Engels, *MEW* XXVII 55.

merely moved up the street to number 28, while Engels departed to work in his father's firm in Manchester. The move was prompted by the death of Guido, born just a year previously, who died suddenly from convulsions caused by meningitis – the first of the three children to die in Dean Street.

In spite of these difficulties, Marx was very active politically. His first few months in London were taken up by three interrelated activities: his work on behalf of refugees in the framework of the German Workers' Educational Association;[1] the reorganisation of the Communist League; and his efforts to start a monthly journal on the pattern of the *Neue Rheinische Zeitung*. He regarded all three as means of rebuilding the 'Marx party' as it had existed in Cologne in 1848.[2]

The day after Jenny's arrival in London, a Committee for the Assistance of German Political Refugees was elected by a general assembly of the Association to which it was to present monthly accounts. Marx was one of the chosen members along with Blind, Bauer, Pfänder and Fuster. The committee immediately began to collect money through personal contacts and newspaper appeals, both mainly in Germany. After only two months, however, the committee had to be reconstituted. For with the departure of Blind and Fuster and the arrival of Willich in London, the orientation of the committee became too extreme for radical republicans such as Struve and Heinzen who tried to form (separate from the Association) a new and politically more moderate committee. Although these efforts (which were renewed in the following April) failed, they did lead to the reconstitution of the original committee – with Engels and Willich elected to the two vacant seats and a change of name to the Social-Democratic Committee for the Assistance of German Refugees. (This disagreement was part of a wider split among the refugees, for the orthodox republicans, led by Struve and Heinzen, formed a Workers' League in opposition to the Association.) The new committee, of which Marx became President and Engels Secretary, was very active during the following year: It raised over £300 and helped more than 500 refugees, though the original generous donations decreased as numbers grew. A hostel was set up in the summer of 1850 to house eighteen refugees and feed about forty: the plan was to make the hostel self-supporting by turning it into a multi-purpose factory staffed by refugees. But these ideas never materialised: the committee

[1] See above pp. 168 ff.   [2] See above pp. 197 ff.

in fact ceased to function when the split in the Communist League occurred in September 1850.

Marx also participated in other activities of the Association: as well as attending the picnics and dances it organised and participating in its fencing and chess, he delivered a course of lectures entitled 'What is bourgeois property?'–beginning in November and continuing through the first half of 1850. He had started to give a few private lectures in his house to a small circle of friends, and was persuaded to make them available to a wider audience by addressing crowded meetings in the Association's first-storey premises in Great Windmill Street. A vivid description of Marx's pedagogical method is given by Wilhelm Lieb-knecht, the future founder of the German Socialist party who had become an unwavering disciple of Marx after their meeting at one of the Association's picnics:

> Marx proceeded methodically. He stated a proposition – the shorter the better, and then demonstrated it in a lengthier explanation, endeavouring with utmost care to avoid all expressions incomprehensible to the workers. Then he requested his audience to put questions to him. If this was not done he commenced to examine the workers, and he did this with such pedagogic skill that no flaw, no misunderstanding, escaped him. On expressing my surprise about his dexterity I learned that Marx had formerly given lectures on political economy in the workers' club in Brussels. At all events he had the qualities of a good teacher. He also made use of a blackboard, on which he wrote the formulas – among them those familiar to all of us from the beginning of *Capital*.[1]

Another account of more lurid discussions in Great Windmill Street is contained in the following description by a Prussian government spy which eventually found its way to the British Foreign Office via the British Ambassador in Berlin:

> One of the German Societies under Marx, Wolff, Engels, Vidil, meets at No. 20 Great Windmill Street on the first storey. It is divided again into three Sections. The Society B. is the most violent. The murder of Princes is formally taught and discussed in it. At a meeting held the day before yesterday at which I assisted and over which Wolff and Marx presided, I heard one of the Orators call out 'The Moon Calf

[1] W. Liebknecht, *Karl Marx, Biographical Memoirs* (Chicago, 1901) p. 69.

will likewise not escape its destiny. The English Steel Wares are the
best, the axes cut particularly sharp here, and the guillotine awaits
every Crowned Head.' Thus the murder of the Queen of England is
proclaimed by Germans a few hundred yards only from Bucking-
ham Palace. The secret committee is divided again into two Sections,
the one composed of the Leaders and the other of the so-called
'Blindmen' who are from 18 to 20 in number and are men of great
daring and courage. They are not to take part in disturbances, but
are reserved for great occasions and principally for the murder of
Princes.[1]

That this report is remarkable chiefly for the imaginative capacities
of its author is shown by the surviving minutes of such meetings.

In general the refugees were ignored by the British Government. In
March 1851, for example, the Prussian Minister of the Interior pressed
for a joint approach with Austria and Prussia to the British Government for 'decisive measures against the chief revolutionaries known
by name' and for 'rendering them innocuous by transportation to the
colonies'.[2] The previous year the Austrian ambassador had already
raised the question with Sir George Grey, the British Home Secretary,
pointing out that 'the members of the Communist League, whose
leaders were Marx, Engels, Bauer and Wolff, discussed even regicide',
but got the reply: 'under our laws, mere discussion of regicide, so
long as it does not concern the Queen of England and so long as there
is no definite plan, does not constitute sufficient grounds for the arrest
of the conspirators'.[3] The most the Home Office was prepared to do
in answer to these demands was to give financial assistance to those
refugees wishing to emigrate to the United States.[4]

Although when still in Cologne Marx had rejected the advances of
the London Central Committee of the Communist League (resur-
rected by Schapper and Moll early in 1849), he now began to devote
great energy to the League's work. It is not entirely clear how Marx
became a member of the Central Committee: official election is
unlikely; probably he was co-opted by Bauer and Eccarius as later were

[1] Quoted in R. Payne, *Karl Marx* (London, 1968) p. 235.
[2] Deutsches Zentral-Archiv, quoted in K. Obermann, *Zur Geschichte des Bundes der Kommunisten 1849-52* (Berlin, 1955) pp. 66 f.
[3] L. Brügel, 'Aus den Londoner Flüchtlingstagen von Karl Marx', *Der Kampf*, XVII (1924).
[4] See the bills submitted to the Home Office referred to in A. Schoyen, *The Chartist Challenge*, p. 230.

Engels and Willich. At any rate he attended its fortnightly meetings and eventually became its president. The League had been far from inactive during 1849, although the Central Committee's June Address[1] stated that '. . . the failure of the revolutionary party in the previous summer for a time practically dissolved the League's organisation. . . . The Central Committee was condemned to complete inactivity until the end of the previous year.' This was an exaggeration, and Marx stated later that on his arrival in London 'I found the operation of the Communist League there reconstituted and the links with the rebuilt groups in Germany renewed.'[2] But the general confusion and dispersion in late 1849 certainly diminished the League's activities. Ideologically, too, the 'secret propaganda society' (as Marx described it[3]) was far from homogeneous. Although it is true that not every applicant was admitted to membership and that there were sometimes even expulsions, there was no clear orthodoxy – nor would this have been possible so long as contact was simply by letter and by the occasional emissary bearing an Address from the Central Committee. In what Marx – now as later – called his 'party' he certainly *did* insist on ideological purity, but this 'party' was by no means coterminous with the League, nor was it composed exclusively of League members: it was made up of the comparatively few people who – to varying extents – knew Marx personally, understood his views and respected their overriding superiority.

In January 1850 Marx attempted to reorganise the League in Germany and sent a letter to the cigar-maker Röser, the future Chairman of the Cologne group who later turned King's evidence, urging him, in Röser's words, '. . . to found a group in Cologne and do my best to found similar ones in other Rhenish cities, since he too considered it necessary, now that freedom of speech and of the press had in fact been suppressed, to reorganise the League since future propaganda could only be carried on in secret.'[4] Röser responded by asking for official statutes that would preclude any conspiratorial tendencies. Marx replied that these would be ratified by a future congress, but that for the moment they should adopt the general guide-lines laid down in the *Communist Manifesto*.

[1] See below pp. 234 f.   [2] K. Marx, 'Herr Vogt', *MEW* xiv 440.
[3] *MEW* viii 414.
[4] W. Blumenberg, 'Zur Geschichte des Kommunistenbundes', *International Review of Social History* (1964) p. 91.

In an attempt to give some sort of unity to the League in Germany, the Central Committee sent Bauer on an inspection tour in March with a mandate signed by Marx and an instruction on tactics composed by Marx and Engels. This famous Address demonstrated how far Marx had changed his mind on tactics during the previous year. He now accepted the necessity for 'organising both secretly and publicly the workers' party alongside, but independent of, the official democrats'[1] and now approved of the Central Committee's previous attempts to reorganise the League in Germany. Marx attacked all types of 'democratic party' whose interests, because they represented the numerous German lower middle class, were bound in the long run to be opposed to those of the proletariat. Marx's advice here was this:

> ... While the democratic petty-bourgeois wish to bring the revolution to a conclusion as quickly as possible, and with the achievement, at most, of the above demands, it is our interest and our task to make the revolution permanent, until all more or less possessing classes have been forced out of their position of dominance, until the proletariat has conquered state power, and the association of proletarians, not only in one country but in all the dominant countries of the world, has advanced so far that competition among the proletarians of these countries has ceased and that at least the decisive productive forces are concentrated in the hands of the proletarians.[2]

Thus the workers should initially support any bourgeois democratic revolution while retaining their independent and, if possible, armed organisation; if this revolution were successful the workers should keep up the pressure by demanding nationalisation of land and a united and highly centralised Republic. The slogan that Marx proposed at the end of the Address – 'revolution in permanence' – did not imply that he believed in an imminent proletarian revolution in Germany, though he did think it likely in France and was much more sanguine now than later about the probability of an economic crisis. At the end of the Address Marx talked of a 'lengthy revolutionary development' and gave this final advice to the German workers:

> ... they themselves must do the utmost for their final victory by clarifying their minds as to what their class interests are, by taking

[1] *MESW* I 111.   [2] Ibid. 110.

up their position as an independent party as soon as possible and by not allowing themselves to be seduced for a single moment by the hypocritical phrases of the democratic petty-bourgeois into refraining from the independent organisation of the party of the proletariat.[1]

The Address was accepted and copied out by the Cologne group as they found no conspiratorial tendencies in it and Bauer proceeded to visit groups in all parts of Germany in a similar fashion. On his return he passed through Cologne where some criticism was expressed about the initiative taken by London, on the grounds that Marx had dissolved the League in 1848 and there had as yet been no official reconstitution. However, this was not the majority view of the Cologne group and Bauer's mission was in general deemed by the Central Committee to have been successful.

The precise influence of the Communist League in Germany is difficult to assess.[2] The membership seems to have been composed mainly of middle-class intellectuals who often had a rather idealised picture of the proletariat and whose only means of attaining practical influence was contact with workers' associations on the model of the London group. These associations – a response to direct social needs – held open elections, exerted strict control over elected representatives, and concentrated on practical activities such as mutual aid and formal education. Although in some towns – Cologne and Frankfurt, for example – the influence of League members on the associations was considerable, the grandiose claims made in the June Address of the London Central Committee should not be taken at their face value.

Although this second Address still stated 'that the early outbreak of a new revolution could not be far away',[3] its tone and purpose was different from that of the March Address: it asserted the supreme authority of the London Central Committee when confronted with the claims to a separate autonomy made, for example, by a German refugee organisation in Switzerland, as well as by other groups all of which were active in Germany itself. The Address gave a rather optimistic account of the state of the League in Belgium, Germany, France and England, and also postponed the General Congress which had been requested by Cologne. Its bombastic style, lack of realism

[1] Ibid. 117.

[2] On this question, see further, F. Balser, *Sozial-Demokratie 1848/49–1863* (Stuttgart, 1962) esp. ch. 3.   [3] *MEW* VII 312

and excessive optimism concerning contacts with workers' organisations and the army make it doubtful that Marx and Engels played a large part in drawing it up, though they must have acquiesced in its final form as they never disavowed it – and it was even reprinted by Engels. The Address did not entirely achieve its purpose for there were still disagreements between London and the Cologne group: the latter had always viewed itself as no more than a propaganda society and angrily accused Marx of 'unbrotherly conduct' when he charged them with 'lack of energetic activity'.[1] A General Congress was to be held in London in September, but the split in the Central Committee in September 1850 prevented it taking place.

The Address also announced to the German groups the Central Committee's contacts with French and English revolutionary parties. At the end of 1849 Marx had attended a dinner organised by the left wing of the disintegrating Chartist movement, known as the Fraternal Democrats, whose leader (George Harney) Marx knew from his previous stay in London. At this dinner Marx made the acquaintance of exiled leaders of Blanqui's party and in April 1850 the Universal Society of Communist Revolutionaries was formed. The signatories were Marx, Engels and Willich for the Germans, Harney for the English and Vidil and Adam for the French. The first of the six statutes, couched in the spirit of the March Address, read:

> The aim of the society is the overthrow of all the privileged classes, and to submit these classes to the dictatorship of the proletariat by maintaining the revolution in permanence until the realisation of communism, which will be the last organisational form of the human family.[2]

The statutes were written in French and drawn up by Willich. The Universal Society also began to issue revolutionary propaganda: Barthélemy, one of the most flamboyant of Blanqui's disciples, reported to his leader: 'We have begun, together with the German communists, to draw up a revolutionary manual containing a numbered list of all the measures that the people will have to take immediately after the revolution.'[3] The Society did not survive the split

[1] Cf. W. Schieder, 'Der Bund der Kommunisten im Sommer 1850', *International Review of Social History* (1968).

[2] N. Plotkin, 'Les Alliances des Blanquists dans la Proscription', *Revue des Révolutions Contemporaines*, LXV (1951) 120.

[3] Ibid.

in the Communist League when most of the Blanquists sided with
Willich. It did, however, achieve a temporary unification of the
European Left after 1848 and as such was a forerunner of the First
International.

A key factor in all Marx's political activities in 1849 and 1850 was his
effort to establish a newspaper that would continue the role played by
the *Neue Rheinische Zeitung* in the 1848–9 revolutions. Before he left
Paris he already had specific plans for a journal which would act as a
rallying point for his scattered 'party'. Its title of *Neue Rheinische Zeitung –
Politisch-Oekonomisch Revue* indicated, firstly, the continuity with the
previous paper, secondly, the intention to transform it into a daily as
soon as 'circumstances allow its return to Germany'[1] and, finally, the
close link that Marx saw between socio-economic investigation and
political activity.

The last months of 1849 were taken up in the search for contributors
and a publisher. In December Theodor Hagen, a member of the Communist League, informed Marx that the Hamburg publisher Schuberth
was willing to take on the review. Schuberth took fifty per cent of all
the income to defray the cost of publication while the rest of the
arrangements, including that of distribution (though agents who took
a commission), were left to Marx, who bore the cost of them. Shares
were advertised in the hope of raising £500 and Conrad Schramm was
to go to the United States with the support of the Chartists and Blanquists to raise money there: but neither scheme was realised. There
were also delays in publication: the intended date was 1 January, but
Schuberth received no manuscript at all during the whole of January,
partly owing to Marx's illness at the end of the month. The manuscript did arrive in early February but with the printer's lack of paper
and his difficulty in deciphering Marx's 'frightful handwriting'[2] publication was further delayed. In addition, Schuberth was also worried
by the possibility of prosecution and thought that Marx, as editor,
should tone down the articles for 'he can handle language like no
one else on earth'.[3] The issue intended for January with a printing of
2500 eventually appeared early in March and the three ensuing numbers followed fairly quickly until mid-May. However, relations with

---

[1] *MEW* vii 550.
[2] K. Bittel, *Karl Marx. Neue Rheinische Zeitung – Politisch-Oekonomisch Revue* (Berlin,
1955) p. 16.
[3] Ibid.

Schuberth swiftly deteriorated: he was slow in sending information about the sale of the journal; he altered the text without consultation; and did not distribute it according to instructions. The revenue from sales was very small and in May Jenny Marx wrote to Weydemeyer saying bitterly that it was impossible to tell which was the worst, 'the delays of the publisher or those of the managers and friends in Cologne or the whole general attitude of the democrats'.[1] The charges against Schuberth were certainly justified, but the tone of the Revue was too intellectual to have any wide impact. One of the leading members of the Cologne group, Roland Daniels, wrote to Marx: 'Only the more intelligent from this party and the few middle-class people who have some knowledge of history will be interested in the revolution by the publication of your monthly.'

During the summer the Revue was in abeyance and the final number (a double issue) appeared in November. Marx considered Schuberth to have been so negligent that he (unsuccessfully) took steps to prosecute him. He also had plans to continue the Revue as a quarterly in Cologne or, alternatively, to publish it in Switzerland. These plans came to nothing.

It is difficult to see how the Revue – or indeed the Communist League to which it was intended to give an intellectual orientation – could have been successful in the circumstances: both depended on the enthusiasm generated by the revolutions of 1848–49 and the expectation of the imminence of a similar wave of unrest. These hopes were common to all the refugees including Marx who, before he left Paris, had told Lassalle that he expected a fresh revolutionary outbreak there early in the following year. In fact Marx's contributions to the Revue (whose declared aim was 'to provide a complete and scientific treatment of the economic relationships that form the basis of the whole political movement'[2]) document his progressive realisation that the economic prerequisites for his political aims were just not there.

In the original publicity for the Revue Marx had stated that: '. . . a time of apparent truce like the present must be used to shed light on the period of revolution that we have lived through.'[3] This was the intention of one of Marx's main contributions to the Revue, a series of articles entitled '1848 to 1849'. These articles were republished later by Engels under the title The Class Struggles in France and described, with

[1] Jenny Marx to Weydemeyer, Reminiscences, pp. 236 f.
[2] MEW vii 5.   [3] Ibid.

justification, as 'Marx's first attempt to explain a section of contemporary history by means of his materialistic conception'.[1]

The Class Struggles in France was a brilliant and swift moving account of the changing political scene in France during 1848–49 against a background of class and economic interest. Marx's general judgement on the failure of the recent revolutionary upsurge was given to the opening words:

> With the exception of only a few chapters, every more important part of the annals of the revolution from 1848 to 1849 carries the heading: *Defeat of the revolution!*
>
> What succumbed in these defeats was not the revolution. It was the pre-revolutionary traditional appendages, results of social relationships which had not yet come to the point of sharp class antagonisms – persons, illusions, conceptions, projects from which the revolutionary party before the February Revolution was not free, from which it could be freed not by the victory of February, but only by a series of defeats.
>
> In a word: the revolution made progress, forged ahead, not by its immediate tragicomic achievements, but, on the contrary, by the creation of a powerful, united counter-revolution, by the creation of an opponent in combat with whom, only, the party of overthrow ripened into a really revolutionary party.[2]

Marx continued with an analysis of the July Monarchy, likening it to a joint-stock company with the state continually kept on the verge of bankruptcy so that the bankers and brokers could speculate on its debts to the ruin of the small investor.[3] The resulting general discontent erupted into revolution with the severe effect on French industry of the 1845–46 commercial and industrial crisis in England. But the provisional government set up after the February barricades could do no more than mirror the disagreements of the various classes that had created it. It was to some extent a criticism of his own past actions in Germany when Marx declared that it was an illusion for the workers to have hoped for emancipation alongside the bourgeoise or inside the national walls of France. The inevitable result of the May elections, he continued, was a bourgeois republic against which the workers

---

[1] *MESW* I 118.   [2] Ibid. 139.

[3] For a thorough evaluation of Marx's account in terms of the socio-economic background see R. Price, *The French Second Republic* (London, 1972).

could but revolt in vain. But their very defeat only prepared a future victory:

> . . . the June defeat has created all the conditions under which France can seize the initiative of the European revolution. Only after being dipped in the blood of the June insurgents did the tricolour become the flag of the European revolution – the red flag!
> And we exclaim: *The revolution is dead! – Long live the revolution!*[1]

Marx's second article discussed the contradictions of the new constitution promulgated in the autumn of 1848 and the opportunities this afforded Louis Napoleon, who won an overwhelming victory in the presidential elections in December. Napoleon was the only man who had captured the imagination of the peasants. To the proletariat his election meant the dismissal of bourgeois republicanism and revenge for the June defeat; to the petty bourgeoisie it meant the rule of the debtor over the creditor; while to big business Napoleon presented the opportunity of ridding itself of its forced alliance with potentially progressive elements. 'Thus it happened', said Marx, 'that the most simple-minded man in France acquired the most multifarious significance. Just because he was nothing, he could signify everything save himself.'[2]

The third and last article, written in March about the same time as the March Address and the creation of the London alliance with the Blanquists, analysed the different elements in the opposition party. Here Marx was concerned to emphasise the difference between *'petit-bourgeois'* or 'doctrinaire' socialism (he had Proudhon particularly in mind) and the revolutionary socialism of Blanqui:

> While this utopian, doctrinaire socialism, which subordinates the total movement to one of its moments, which puts in place of common, social production the brainwork of individual pedants and, above all, in fantasy does away with the revolutionary struggle of the classes and its requirements by small conjurers' tricks or great sentimentality; while this doctrinaire socialism, which at bottom only idealises present society, takes a picture of it without shadows and wants to achieve its ideal athwart the realities of present society; while the proletariat surrenders this socialism to the petty bourgeoisie; while the struggle of the different socialist leaders

[1] *MESW* I 163.   [2] Ibid. 174.

among themselves sets forth each of the so-called systems as a pretentious adherence to one of the transit points of the social revolution as against another – the proletariat rallies more and more round revolutionary socialism, round communism, for which the bourgeoisie has itself invented the name of Blanqui. This socialism is the declaration of the permanence of the revolution, the class dictatorship of the proletariat as the necessary transit point to the abolition of class distinction generally, to the abolition of all the relations of production on which they rest, to the abolition of all the social relations that correspond to these relations of production, to the revolutionising of all the ideas that result from these social relations.[1]

The article ended on a characteristically optimistic note by declaring the reactionary bourgeois republic to have been merely 'the hothouse of revolution'.[2]

This optimism was also reflected in the extended comments on current affairs written by Marx and Engels for the *Revue* during the first months of 1850. In France 'the strength of the revolutionary party naturally grows in proportion to the progress of reaction' and 'a hitherto politically dead class, the peasants, has been won for the revolution'.[3] As for Britain, the tremendous development of productive forces there would soon outstrip even the markets of the Americas and Australia: a panic would ensue 'at the latest in July or August' bringing with it a crisis which, 'because it must coincide with great clashes on the Continent, will produce results quite different from all previous ones'.[4] Marx was insistent, now as later, that the industrial crisis would bring revolution, not the other way round. He wrote to Weydemeyer in December 1849 that the outbreak of a revolution before the next crisis 'would in my opinion be a misfortune because just now, when business is still expanding, the working masses in France, Germany, etc., are perhaps revolutionary in word but certainly not in reality'.[5]

There followed far-sighted comment on the industrial potential of the United States inspired by an event 'more important than the February revolution' – the discovery of gold in California.[6] The flow of

---

[1] Ibid. 222 f.   [2] Ibid. 227.   [3] *MEW* VII 218   [4] Ibid. 220.   [5] *MEW* XXVII 516.
[6] *MEW* VII 220. Engels pointed out that this 'creation of large markets out of nothing' was 'not foreseen in the *Manifesto*' (*MEW* XXVIII 118).

population westwards and the incredible growth of the railway system showed that New York and San Francisco were usurping the place in world trade hitherto held by London and Liverpool. Marx continued:

> The fulcrum of world commerce, in the Middle Ages Italy, more recently England, is now the Southern half of the North American continent. . . . Thanks to the gold of California and to the tireless energy of the Yankees both coasts of the Pacific will soon be as thickly populated, as industrialized and as open to trade as the coast from Boston to New Orleans is now. The Pacific Ocean will then play the same role the Atlantic Ocean is playing now and the role that the Mediterranean played in the days of classical antiquity and in the Middle Ages – the role of the great water highway of world commerce – and the Atlantic Ocean will sink to the level of a great lake such as the Mediterranean is today.[1]

The only hope for Europe of avoiding industrial, commercial and political dependence on the United States was 'a revolution which would transform the mode of production and intercourse in accordance with the needs of production arising from the nature of modern productive forces, thus making possible the development of new forces of production which would maintain the superiority of European industry and counteract the disadvantages of geographical situation'.[2] Marx finished the article with a remark on the recent beginning of Chinese socialism and the social upheaval brought about by contact with the West, an upheaval that 'must have the most important results for civilization'.[3]

The second article on current affairs comment, written in April, dealt more specifically with the possibilities of revolution in Europe. Marx thought he saw an approaching crisis in Britain due to over-investment, particularly in the key wool industry. The interaction of this crisis with the imminent upheavals on the continent would give to the latter a 'pronounced socialist character'.[4] In Britain the crisis would drive from power both Whigs and Tories to be replaced by the industrial bourgeoisie, who would have to open Parliament to representatives of the proletariat, thus 'dragging England into the European revolution'.[5] A note added later just as the *Revue* was going to press

---

[1] *MEW* VII 221.   [2] Ibid.   [3] Ibid. 222.   [4] Ibid. 294.   [5] Ibid.

admitted that there had been a slight betterment in the economic situation in the early 1850s but declared, nevertheless, that 'the co-incidence of commercial crisis and revolution is becoming ever more unavoidable'.[1] As the months went by, however, this short-term optimism was more and more difficult to sustain. It was to be entirely dispelled by the systematic study of the economic history of the previous ten years that Marx undertook in the summer of 1850.

In June of that year Marx obtained the ticket to the Reading Room of the British Museum that he was to use so often in the years ahead. His reading there in July, August and September consisted mainly in back numbers of the London *Economist*. The main conclusion, as Engels put it later, was that 'the industrial prosperity, which has been returning gradually since the middle of 1848 and attained full bloom in 1848 and 1850, was the revitalising force of the newly-strengthened European reaction'.[2] The results of this study were set down in detail in the long current-affairs comment written in October for the last number of the *Revue*. Marx declared bluntly: 'The political agitation of the last six months is essentially different from that which immediately preceded it.'[3] The 'real basis' for this change was the period of prosperity that had begun in Britain in 1848. The crisis of 1845–46 had been due to overproduction and the accompanying overspeculation in railways, corn, potatoes and wool. With the economic stabilisation of 1848, additional capital tended to be invested, and speculation was less easy. The most striking evidence of this temporary prosperity were the plans for the 'Pantheon in the modern Rome',[4] the Great Exhibition of 1851. This prosperity was paralleled in the United States, which had profited from the European depression and the expanding market in California. Newly prosperous Britain and America had in turn influenced France and Germany, both of which were dependent on the economic situation in Britain, 'the demiurge of the bourgeois universe'.[5]

The conclusion of this detailed discussion was:

> With this general prosperity, in which the productive forces of bourgeois society develop as luxuriantly as is at all possible within bourgeois relationships, there can be no talk of a real revolution. Such a revolution is only possible in the periods when both these

[1] Ibid. 295.   [2] *MESW* I 120.   [3] *MEW* VII 421.
[4] Ibid. 431.   [5] Ibid. 440.

factors, the modern productive forces and the bourgeois productive forms, come into collision with each other. The various quarrels in which the representatives of the individual factions of the Continental party of Order now indulge and mutually compromise themselves, far from providing the occasion for new revolutions are, on the contrary, possible only because the basis of the relationships is momentarily so secure and, what the reaction does not know, so bourgeois. From it all attempts of the reaction to hold up bourgeois development will rebound just as certainly as all moral indignation and all enthusiastic proclamations of the democrats. A new revolution is possible only in consequence of a new crisis. It is, however, just as certain as this crisis.[1]

At the end of 1851, Louis Napoleon seized power in France as Emperor, thus consolidating the reaction that had followed the 1848 revolution. Marx immediately composed a series of articles which were published by his friend Weydemeyer, in a short-lived New York journal, under the title *The Eighteenth Brumaire of Louis Bonaparte*. They constitute his most brilliant political pamphlet. The title is an allusion to the date of the first Napoleon's *coup d'état* in 1799 and Marx was concerned to examine the socio-political background of Louis Napoleon's repeat performance in December 1851. In a preface to a second edition of his essay, Marx contrasted his own approach to that of two other well-known pamphleteers on the same subject, Victor Hugo and Proudhon: Hugo confined himself to bitter and witty invective; whereas Proudhon, seeking to represent the *coup d'état* as the result of antecedent historical development, ended up with a historical apologia for its hero. 'I, on the contrary,' wrote Marx, 'demonstrate how the class struggle in France created circumstances and relationships that made it possible for a grotesque mediocrity to play a hero's part.'[2]

Marx began his demonstration by referring to the remark of Hegel that all facts and personages of great importance in world history occurred twice and added that the first time was tragedy and the second, farce. So it was with the two Bonapartes. He continued:

> Men make their own history, but they do not make it just as they please; they do not make it under circumstances chosen by themselves, but under circumstances directly encountered, given and transmitted from the past. The tradition of all the dead generations

[1] *MESW* I 231.   [2] Ibid. 244.

weighs like a nightmare on the minds of the living. And just when they seem engaged in revolutionising themselves and things, in creating something that has never yet existed, precisely in such periods of revolutionary crisis they anxiously conjure up the spirits of the past to their service and borrow from them names, battle cries and costumes in order to present the new scene of world history in this time-honoured disguise and this borrowed language.[1]

Marx applied these considerations to the 1848 revolution and drew a distinction between eighteenth-century bourgeois revolutions whose very speed and brilliance made them short-lived, and nineteenth-century proletarian revolutions which possessed a slow thoroughness born of constant interruption and self-criticism. Turning to the recent *coup d'état*, Marx found unacceptable the excuse that the nation was taken unawares: 'A nation and a woman are not forgiven the unguarded hour in which the first adventurer that came along could violate them. The riddle is not solved by such turns of speech, but merely formulated differently. It remains to be explained how a nation of thirty-six millions can be surprised and delivered unresisting into captivity by three swindlers.'[2]

Marx then summarised the period dealt with in his *Class Struggles*. The success of Bonaparte was due to his having organised the Lumpen-proletariat of Paris under the cover of a 'benevolent society', with himself at their head. However, this immediate force had to be set against the long-term factors in Bonaparte's favour. The first of these was the old finance aristocracy who 'celebrated every victory of the President over its ostensible representatives as a victory of order'. And the reason for this was evident: 'If in every epoch the stability of the state power signified Moses and the prophets to the entire money-market and to the priests of this money-market, why not all the more so today, when every deluge threatens to sweep away the old states, and the old state debts with them?'[3]

The industrial bourgeoisie, too, saw in Louis Napoleon the man who could put an end to recent disorders. For this class, 'the struggle to maintain its public interests, its own class interests, its political power, only troubled and upset it, as it was a disturbance of private business'.[4] When trade was good, the commercial bourgeoisie raged

[1] Ibid. 247. On Marx's sources here, see B. Mazlish, 'The tragic Farce of Marx, Hegel and Engels', *History and Theory* (1972).
[2] *MESW* I 252.   [3] Ibid. 318.   [4] Ibid. 319.

against political squabbles for fear that trade might be upset; when trade was bad, they blamed it on the instability of the political situation. In 1851 France had indeed passed through a minor trade crisis and this, coupled with constant political ferment, had led the commercial bourgeoisie to cry 'Rather an end to terror than terror without end'[1] – a cry well understood by Bonaparte.

Marx devoted the last part of his article to a closer examination of the class basis of Bonaparte's power. To Marx this seemed to be non-existent: 'The struggle seems to be settled in such a way that all classes, equally impotent and equally remote, fall on their knees before the rifle-butt.'[2] The explanation was that, having perfected parliamentary power only to withdraw it, the revolution had now to perfect the executive power in order then to destroy it. Marx outlined the history of this bureaucracy:

> This executive power with its enormous bureaucratic and military organisation, with its ingenious state machinery, embracing wide strata, with a host of officials numbering half a million, besides an army of another half million, this appalling parasitic body, which enmeshes the body of French society like a net and chokes all its pores, sprang up in the days of the absolute monarchy, with the decay of the feudal system, which it helped to hasten.[3]

During and after the revolution of 1789 the bureaucracy had prepared the class rule of the bourgeoisie; under Louis Philippe and the parliamentary republic it had still been the instrument of the ruling class; under the second Bonaparte 'the state seems to have made itself completely independent'.[4] Marx then immediately qualified this by saying: 'and yet the state power is not suspended in mid-air. Bonaparte represents a class, and the most numerous class of French society at that, the small-holding peasants.'[5] The identity of interest of these peasants did not create a community, since they were physically so scattered. Thus they could not represent themselves, but had to be represented. But the peasants on whom Napoleon relied were burdened by a mortgage debt whose interest was equal to the annual interest on the entire British national debt. Finally the army had degenerated from the flower of the peasant youth into 'the swamp flower of the peasant Lumpenproletariat'.[6] Thus, according to Marx,

---

[1] Ibid. 324. [2] Ibid. 332. [3] Ibid.
[4] Ibid. 333. [5] Ibid. [6] Ibid. 339.

the three key ideas of Napoleon I – independent small-holdings for peasants, taxes to support strong central administration and a large army drawn from the peasants – had found their ultimate degeneration under Louis Napoleon. However, centralisation had been acquired and that would be an important feature of the future society:

> The demolition of the state machine will not endanger centralisation. Bureaucracy is only the low and brutal form of a centralisation that is still afflicted with its opposite, with feudalism. When he is disappointed in the Napoleonic Restoration, the French peasant will part with his belief in his small-holding, the entire state edifice erected on this small-holding will fall to the ground and the proletarian revolution will obtain that chorus without which its solo song becomes a swan-song in all peasant countries.[1]

It is interesting to note that this passage, with its emphasis on centralisation as a progressive factor, was omitted in the second edition of the *Eighteenth Brumaire* in 1869.

The conclusion that a new revolution was possible only as a result of a new crisis marked the end of Marx's first period of political activism and his return to the economic studies that had been interrupted by the events of the late 1840s. Inevitably the implications of Marx's views were quite unacceptable to many members of the Communist League. In London the chief spokesman for this opposition was Willich.

The differences between Marx and Willich were not only doctrinal. Willich came from an old and distinguished family. It was even said (and Willich did nothing to dispel the rumour) that he was descended from the Hohenzollerns. Since the age of twelve he had made his career that of a professional soldier, and he was a good one. Engels, his adjutant in the 1849 uprising in Baden, described him as 'brave, cold-blooded, skilful and of quick and sound perception in battle, but, when not fighting, something of a boring ideologist'.[2] Willich seems to have made an unfortunate impression on the Marx household on his arrival in London by bursting in on them very early in the morning with colourful attire and excessive bonhomie. Jenny even thought that Willich was out to seduce her: 'He would come to visit me', she wrote later, 'because he wanted to pursue the worm that lives in every

---

[1] Ibid. 340.   [2] *MEW* xxvii 502.

marriage and lure it out.'[1] At any rate it was natural that Marx should be jealous of Willich's flamboyant posturing just as Willich was outraged both by Marx's waning enthusiasm for immediate revolutionary struggle and by his autocratic tendency to (according to Willich) divide mankind into two parties: Marx and the rest. There was also an increasingly unfavourable contrast made by Willich's friends between 'intellectuals' such as Marx, who lived with his family, studied in the British Museum and lectured on economic theory, and 'practical' men like Willich, who lived a bachelor among the refugee workers, shared their hardships and thought that all problems were 'really so simple'.[2] Marx might command the distant respect of the workers, but it was Willich who won their devotion.

These differences soon caused dissension in the Central Committee of the Communist League, of which Willich had become a member on the suggestion of Marx himself. In the spring of 1850 Willich quarrelled violently with Engels and refused attempts by the Central Committee to mediate between them. In August Marx opposed Willich's suggestion to the Central Committee that they form a united front with other democratic refugee organisations. The same divergence of opinion occurred in the committee for refugees; here, when Willich found himself in a minority of one, he resigned and took the dispute to a general meeting of the Association where he gained the support of the majority. Marx found himself outflanked on the Left and called a 'reactionary' for his defence of the tactics advocated in the *Communist Manifesto*. Thus fortified, Willich returned to the attack in the Central Committee on 1 September and passions were so roused that Willich challenged Marx to a duel. Marx had moved a long way since his student days in Bonn and disdained the suggestion, but Conrad Schramm, whom Marx described as the Percy Hotspur of his group, challenged Willich in turn, despite Marx's dissuasions. Duelling was outlawed in England, so they took the night boat to Ostend, Willich being accompanied by Barthélemy. Liebknecht has left an account of what followed:

In the evening of the following day the door of Marx's house was opened – he was not at home, only Mrs Marx and Lenchen – and Barthélemy entered bowing stiffly and replying with a sepulchral

[1] Jenny Marx, *Kurze Umrisse eines bewegten Lebens, Mohr und General*, p. 212.
[2] Marx to Weydemeyer, *MEW* xxvii 560.

voice to the anxious question 'What news?' 'Schramm a une balle dans la tête!' – Schramm has a bullet in his head – whereupon bowing stiffly once more he turned and withdrew. You may imagine the fright of the half insensible lady; she knew now that her instinctive dislike had not deceived her.

One hour later she related the sad news to us. Of course, we gave up Schramm for lost. The next day, while we were just talking about him sadly, the door was opened and in came with a bandaged head but gaily laughing the sadly mourned one and related that he had received a glancing shot which had stunned him – when he recovered consciousness, he was alone on the sea coast with his second and his physician. Willich and Barthélemy had returned from Ostend on the steamer which they had just been able to reach. With the next boat Schramm followed.[1]

A split was unavoidable, particularly as Willich had, on his own authority, summoned a general meeting of the London members of the League. Marx therefore resigned from the refugee committee and opened the final meeting of the Central Committee, held on 15 September, with a long speech from the Chair containing three proposals. Firstly, he suggested that the Central Committee be transferred to Cologne; he had opposed the suggestion made previously by Schapper that Cologne be made responsible for Germany, but now the division in London was so great that effective leadership could no longer be given from Britain. Secondly, the new Central Committee should make new statutes since the original statutes of 1847 and the weakened ones of 1848 were neither up to date nor respected by large sections of the League. Thirdly, there should be two completely separate groups in London, both linked directly to the Central Committee in Cologne. This was necessary to preserve the unity of the League, for the views recently expressed by the minority showed that there were important differences of principle between the two groups. Marx continued:

A German national approach pandering to the nationalism of the German manual workers has replaced the universal approach of the *Manifesto*. *Will* is put forward as the chief factor in revolution, instead of real relationships. We say to the workers: 'You have 15, 20, 50 years of civil war to go through to change the circumstances and fit

[1] W. Liebknecht, *Karl Marx. Biographical Memoirs*, pp. 106 f.

yourselves for power!' You say instead: 'We must gain power *immediately* or we can go to sleep.' The word 'proletariat' is now used as an empty word, as is the word 'people' by the democrats. To give this phrase any reality all petty-bourgeois had to be declared proletarians which meant in fact that we were representing the petty-bourgeois and not the proletariat.[1]

Marx concluded by saying that the majority would be within its rights in expelling the minority from the League, but that this would be detrimental to the interests of the 'party' whose unity he had found a way of preserving while at the same time separating the two factions. There were at most twelve people he would like to see in his group and he would naturally resign from the Association.

Schapper followed with an impassioned and rather inarticulate speech. He declared himself in favour of Marx's first two proposals but disagreed with the third, which he regarded as far too subtle. They should split into two Leagues, 'one for those who work with the pen, the other for those who work differently'.[2] Finally, he could not accept that the bourgeoisie would come to power in Germany, as this robbed the proletarian movement of its whole purpose. Marx replied by insisting that his proposal ensured a complete separation while preserving the unity of the League. He then took up Schapper's point about the next revolution:

If the proletariat came to power, it would employ measures that were petty-bourgeois, not directly proletarian. Our party can only become the governing one when circumstances allow it to carry out its own views. Louis Blanc gives the best example of coming to power too soon. Moreover in France it is not the proletariat alone but also the peasants and petty-bourgeois who will come to power and the measures taken will have to be common to them all – not those of the proletariat alone.[3]

After Eccarius had supported Marx, Willich left the room without a word and Marx's proposals were adopted, being supported by six out of the ten possible votes.

The Cologne group, having now achieved (with Marx's agreement)

[1] Quoted in B. Nicolaievsky, 'Toward a History of the Communist League 1847–1852', *International Review of Social History*, I (1956) p. 249.
[2] B. Nicolaievsky, op. cit., p. 251.
[3] Ibid., pp. 251 f.

its ambition of being in charge of the League, was spurred to fresh activities – though the Willich–Schapper group probably commanded the loyalty of most of the League members in Germany. Marx duly got the new statutes accepted by a general assembly of the London members. Thereafter he seems to have lacked enthusiasm for the League's activities and devoted himself more to economic studies. In May 1851, however, widespread arrests in Germany – which meant the effective end of the League's activities – compelled Marx to demonstrate his solidarity. The Prussian Government had increased its campaign against subversive elements, following an attempted assassination of Frederick William IV in May 1850 and Kinkel's escape from prison the same year.[1] Peter Nothjung, a tailor's apprentice and a member of the Cologne Central Committee, was arrested in Leipzig while travelling on League business: on his person were found copies of the *Communist Manifesto*, Marx's *March Address*, the Cologne *Address* of December, the new statutes and a list of addresses which enabled the authorities to arrest the ten other members of the Cologne Committee. The prosecution was not at first successful: following the arrests, six months of investigation revealed no more than that the accused were members of a propaganda society and failed to show any conspiracy or plot to overthrow the regime; and the judicial authorities in the Rhineland (who retained from the French occupation a more liberal legal system and an antipathy to Prussia) duly declared that there was not enough evidence to justify a trial. The result, however, was not release but further imprisonment while the Government's agent, Stieber, attempted to secure the necessary evidence.

Marx set up a committee which collected money for the accused and organised letters from his friends to as many British newspapers as possible protesting against the imprisonment without trial. But public opinion was not impressed, *The Times* declaring that 'if the whole gang were treated as "sturdy beggars" instead of conspirators, they would be dealt with more according to their true characters'.[2] The trial was continually postponed during the summer of 1852 and when eventually it opened in October the prosecution revealed the evidence it had been so long accumulating; it amounted to nothing more than an attempt to associate Marx and the Cologne communists with some

[1] On the background, see further, R. Livingstone, Introduction to K. Marx, *The Cologne Communist Trial* (London and New York, 1971).
[2] *The Times*, 13 Oct 1852, p. 6.

of the more bizarre schemes of Willich's Paris friends – the principal exhibit being a notebook purporting to contain the minutes of meetings of the Communist League recently held in London under Marx's leadership. The notebook was a pure fabrication by one of Stieber's agents, helped by Hirsch, a former member of the League. No attempt had been made to imitiate the handwriting of Liebknecht and Rings, the two supposed minute writers. In fact, Rings was the one member of the group who hardly knew how to write; and Liebknecht's initial was wrong. Marx made two trips to the Police Court in Marlborough Street to authenticate a sample of Liebknecht's actual handwriting and corroborate the testimony of the owner of the public house where they met, who was willing to confirm that no minutes were ever taken and that the dates of the meetings were in any case in-inaccurate. This and other information had to be sent off to the defence counsel in Cologne in several copies through cover addresses. Jenny Marx described the scene in their household:

> My husband had to work the whole day right through into the night. The whole thing is now a battle between the police on one side and my husband on the other. He is credited with everything, the whole revolution, even the conduct of the trial. A whole office has been established in our house. Two or three do the writing, others run errands, others scrape together pennies so that the writers can continue to exist and bring against the old official world proof of the unheard-of scandal. In the middle of it all my three faithful children sing and pipe and often catch it from their dear father. Some business![1]

Their efforts succeeded in exposing the forgeries of the prosecution but the jury nevertheless convicted the majority of the accused. 'A degrading and completely unjust sentence',[2] wrote the Prussian diplomat Varnhagen von Ense, who had no love for communists.

The episode also had a frustrating sequel: during the trial Marx had begun to write an article putting the main facts of the case before the public. Typical of Marx's drafts, this had grown into a small book to which he gave the title *Revelations about the Communist Trial in Cologne*. As well as extensively documenting Prussian police methods, he publi-

---

[1] *MEW* XXVIII 640 ff.
[2] Varnhagen von Ense, *Tagebücher*, IX 411 quoted in K. Obermann, *Zur Geschichte des Bundes der Kommunisten 1849–52*, p. 125.

cised the split in the Communist League. For Marx felt compelled to dissociate himself from the plots and conspiracies of the Willich-Schapper faction. He explained that his group intended to build 'the opposition party of the future'[1] and would thus not have any part in conspiracies to produce immediate revolutionary overthrows. Two thousand copies, printed in Switzerland, were smuggled across the border into Prussia and stocked in a small village; but they were soon discovered and all confiscated by the police. The book was also published in America in a smaller edition but very few copies found their way back into Germany.

With the arrest of the Cologne Committee the League ceased to exist in Germany in an organised form. The fifteen–twenty strong London group had met regularly during 1851 – first in Soho on Tuesday evenings, then in Farrington Street in the City on Thursdays and finally (during 1852) in the Rose and Crown Tavern, Crown Street, Soho, on Wednesdays.[2] Marx presided and the group was referred to by its members as 'the Synagogue' or 'The Marx Society'.[3] Soon after the end of the Cologne trial, the League dissolved itself on Marx's suggestion with the declaration that its continued existence, both in London and on the Continent, was 'no longer opportune'.[4] Willich's branch of the League ceased to function shortly afterwards. For the next ten years Marx was a member of no political party.

II. REFUGEE POLITICS

Although the dissolution of the Communist League completed Marx's withdrawal from active politics, he continued throughout the 1850s to be an assiduous and often sarcastic observer of the various intrigues of the London refugees. Deprived of the possibility of engaging in national politics on their home ground, these refugees indulged in feverish political infighting in London, though the doctrinal differences between bourgeois republicans and socialists were real enough. The result was a constantly changing kaleidoscope of plans, committees and alliances, not the least among the largest group of refugees – the Germans, whose sects a bewildered Herzen compared in number to the forty times forty churches traditionally supposed to be found

---

[1] *MEW* viii 461.   [2] Ibid. 437.

[3] F. Freiligrath, *Briefwechsel mit Marx und Engels*, ed. M. Häckel (Berlin, 1968) i 31; *MEW* xxviii 170.

[4] *MEW* xxviii 195.

in Moscow. The feud in the Communist League only added to an already fragmented picture. Marx's supporters – with the exception of Liebknecht, who braved his anger – had withdrawn from the Association in Great Windmill Street, but it continued to function under Willich's leadership, as did also the Willich-Schapper group of the Communist League. This group, claiming to constitute the true Central Committee, expelled the Marx faction and declared in a circular to its members that 'we thought and still think that, given the right organisation, our party will be able to put through such measures in the next revolution as to lay the foundation for a workers' society'.[1] The split – made public by the unsuccessful prosecution of Bauer and Pfänder for the embezzlement of the Association's funds – was soon widened on the occasion of the 'Banquet of the Equals' held in the Highbury Barn Tavern, Islington, on 24 February 1851 to celebrate the anniversary of the 1848 February revolution.

This banquet was organised by the Socialist Louis Blanc in opposition to the 'radical' banquet of Ledru-Rollin. Blanc relied for support on the London communists, and Willich presided at the banquet. Marx sent two spies – Pieper and Schramm – but they were detected and thrown out with considerable violence, even losing in the process (according to Marx) several tufts of hair. This incident meant that, apart from the meetings of his group, Marx was isolated from the other refugees. 'Marx lives a very retired life,' wrote Pieper to Engels, 'his only friends are John Stuart Mill and Lloyd and when you visit him you are received with economic categories instead of with compliments.'[2] Marx, however, professed to be quite pleased with this situation and wrote to Engels the same month:

> I am very pleased with the public and genuine isolation in which we two, you and I, find ourselves. It entirely suits our position and principles. We have now finished with the system of mutual concessions, with half-truths admitted for reasons of propriety and with our duty of sharing in the public ridicule in the party with all these asses.[3]

Nevertheless, Marx became withdrawn and somewhat embittered, pouring a scorn on his fellow refugees that knew no bounds. Willich

---

[1] *Die kommunistischen Verschwörungen der neunzehnten Jahrhunderts*, ed. Wermuth and Stieber (Berlin, 1853) I 276.
[2] *MEW* xxvii 169.   [3] Ibid. 184.

in particular became the object of his biting irony and descriptions like 'cowardly, slandering, infamous, foul assassin'[1] were typical. At the same time Marx could not help seizing on every scrap of information concerning the refugees' activities and even occasionally personally indulging in the intrigues he so much despised. Late in 1850, for example, Schramm had written Willich a letter containing fantastic plans for revolution in Germany and inviting Willich to take charge. He signed it with the name of Hermann Becker of the Cologne group. Willich fell into the trap and replied with bold plans for immediate revolution. Marx foresaw an excellent opportunity to ridicule Willich and attempted to get the letters from Willich, but without success. Marx's bitterness was increased by Willich's alliance with 'Jesus-Christ' Kinkel (as Marx liked to call him) who had arrived in London at the end of 1850, his prestige as a young revolutionary writer even further enhanced by a remarkable escape from his Prussian gaol. Kinkel frequented the smart colony of German refugees in St John's Wood, gave public lectures at a guinea a head, and soon earned enough money to present his wife with an Evrard grand piano. More grandiose plans followed: in late 1851 Willich and Kinkel produced a scheme (inspired by Mazzini's highly successful 'shilling fund' for European democracy) for a German Revolutionary Loan to 'further the coming republican revolution', and Kinkel departed to America to publicise it. The target was two million dollars, but only a few thousands were actually lent which, after causing yet more dissension among the refugees, found their way into the vaults of the Westminster Bank in London – to be used (years later) to help found the German Social Democrat Party. A brief attempt made in August 1851 to unite the refugees was unsuccessful, and the split remained between the two main factions: the radical republicans led by Marx's old enemy Ruge, and the socialists led by Kinkel and Willich.

At the end of 1851 the arrival of more refugees from Germany coincided with a growing dissatisfaction within the Association over Willich's policies. The arrest of his Paris supporters and Napoleon's *coup d'état* made his revolutionary plans less and less plausible. Dissatisfaction was increased by Marx who, through Liebknecht, spread the rumour that Willich was concealing money destined for the refugees. In December some workers who, with Marx's approval, had formed an opposition group in the Great Windmill Street Association, seceded

[1] Ibid. 548.

and set up a new Association with statutes drawn up by Marx. Its leader was Gottlieb Stechan, a tablemaker who had been one of the leaders of the Communist League in Hanover. Marx wrote to Weyde-meyer:

> You can announce that a new Workers' Association has been formed in London under the presidency of Stechan that will steer clear of the 'émigrés', the 'agitators' and Great Windmill and pursue serious aims. You understand ... that this Association belongs to us, although we are only sending our young people there; I am only speaking of our 'educated people', not of our workers who all go.[1]

This Association contained about sixty members and the organising committee was in the hands of the members of the 'Marx Society'. It met twice weekly in the Bull's Head Tavern, New Oxford Street, to discuss such questions as the influence of pauperism on revolution, whether a general war was in the interests of revolution, the advisa-bility of co-operating with other revolutionary parties, and whether poverty could be abolished after the revolution. Pieper and Lieb-knecht took a leading part in the discussions, though their didactic views were occasionally challenged by some of the workers. The Association also provided English lessons and in June the political discussions were replaced by a course on medieval literature given by Wilhelm Wolff. The Association came to an end, however, in the late summer of 1852 when some of the workers, including Stechan him-self, returned to the Great Windmill Street Association.[2]

During 1852 Marx was also occupied in writing a diatribe against his fellow exiles. Its history illustrates the bizarreness of refugee politics at this time. In February 1852 Marx was approached by a Hungarian colonel named Bangya whose acquaintance he had made two years previously when the Communist League was trying to enter into alliance with other revolutionary bodies. Bangya came from a minor aristocratic family, had become an Austrian spy in 1850 and then went to Paris where he became vice-president of a committee uniting Hungarian, Austrian and German political exiles – a commit-tee of which five out of the seven members were professional spies! Bangya's contacts with Kinkel, Willich and Mazzini enabled him to

---

[1] *MEW* xxviii 478.

[2] See further, G. Becker, 'Der neue Arbeiter-Verein in London 1852', *Zeitschrift für Geisteswissenschaft* (1966).

keep Vienna very well informed and he was instrumental in the arrest of the Cologne communists. He was also involved in the arrest of Willich's Paris friends in the autumn of 1851, was later arrested himself and contrived an 'escape' to London. At his meeting with Marx there in February, Bangya avoided party politics and promised Hungarian help for Weydemeyer's paper. Marx was impressed and agreed to Bangya's request for some short biographical sketches of the German refugee leaders to be used by the Hungarians in Paris. At the end of May Bangya informed Marx that he had found a German publisher willing to pay £25 for extended versions of the sketches. Marx did not suspect any trap (Bangya had recently refused his invitation to attend a meeting of the Communist League) and set to work. At first he was helped by Ernst Dronke, a former member of the staff of the *Neue Rheinische Zeitung*, and later by Engels. Marx spent a month with Engels in Manchester in May when the final draft was composed. 'We are crying with laughter at the pickling of these blockheads,'[1] Marx wrote to Jenny. Once the manuscript had been delivered, however, the publication date was repeatedly delayed; Bangya's excuses sounded more and more implausible and inquiries revealed that the publisher Bangya had mentioned did not exist. Finally Marx came to the conclusion that the manuscript had been sold to the authorities in Germany.[2]

In August 1852 a further episode occurred which showed to what lengths Marx was prepared to go in his vendettas against the refugees. The rumour had reached Marx that on his American trip Kinkel had referred to Engels and himself as 'two down-and-outs who had been thrown out of the London pubs by the workers'.[3] He wrote to Kinkel: 'I await your explanation by return. Silence will be treated as an admission of guilt.'[4] Kinkel did reply by return that he wanted nothing more to do with Marx in view of Marx's article in the *Revue* attacking him while still in gaol. Marx should not, he continued, trust hearsay, but if he chose to do so, the due processes of law were open to him.

[1] *MEW* xxviii 257.
[2] Bangya, however, was not put off by the discovery of his activities: even in 1853 he was used by Kossuth to negotiate with the French Government. He then went to Constantinople, became a Muslim and an officer in the Turkish army, was condemned to death for treason with the Russians, but was freed and returned to Constantinople. Here he became press officer to the Grand Vizier Kiprisli Pascha and died in 1868 as a Turkish police lieutenant. The manuscript, entitled *Heroes of the Exile*, is translated in K. Marx, *The Cologne Communist Trial*, ed. R. Livingstone.
[3] *MEW* xxviii 100.   [4] Ibid.

Convinced that Kinkel would not look at anything with a Soho post-
mark, Marx 'got Lupus in Windsor to post a letter to him, written on
paper in the shape of a *billet doux* with a bunch of roses and forget-me-
nots printed on it in colour'.[1] The letter named Marx's sources of
information for the American venture and claimed that Kinkel's
letter provided 'a new and striking proof that the said Kinkel is a common and cowardly priest'.[2]

By the end of 1852 the feuds among the refugees began to cool off.
Engels wrote that when he was with Marx at Christmas 'we made a
point of going without any fuss into the middle of the crowds in the
Kinkel-Willich-Ruge pubs, which we would not have been able to risk
without a brawl six months previously'.[3] Kinkel's popularity was on
the decline since the relative failure of his American trip and the
squabbles over the money. Willich's reputation was destroyed more
swiftly: Baroness von Brüningk, who held a *salon* for the German
refugee leaders in St John's Wood, alleged that Willich had made
improper advances to her; he left for America very soon afterwards.
His quarrel with Marx did not immediatly cease, for Willich felt compelled to reply to the accusations against him in Marx's *Revelations*
with a long article entitled, 'Doctor Marx and his Revelations', to
which Marx responded with a sarcastic pamphlet, *The Knight of the Noble
Mind*. There the quarrel stopped. Willich became a journalist in
Cincinnati, reviewed Marx's later writings favourably and studied
Hegel. He was decorated during the Civil War, marched with Sherman
to Atlanta and left with the rank of Major General. He finally settled
in St Mary's, Ohio, where he became one of its most active and respected citizens, his funeral being attended by more than 2500 people.
Marx was not a man to pursue a quarrel interminably. He hesitated
before including the section on the Willich–Schapper faction in the
second edition of the *Revelations* in 1875, and wrote in the Preface that
'in the American Civil War Willich demonstrated that he was something more than a weaver of fantastic projects'.[4]

Although the leaders of the different national refugee groups did
(in contrast with the rank-and-file) mix quite freely with each other,
Marx's contacts with them were very sparse. He had been in close
touch with the Blanquists in 1850 but they sided with Willich when

---

[1] Ibid. 101.   [2] Ibid.   [3] Ibid. 596.
[4] *MEW* VIII 575. Further on Willich, see L. Easton, 'August Willich, Marx and
Left Hegelian Socialism', *Études de Marxologie* (1965).

the Communist League split. Louis Blanc, whom Marx considered more or less an ally after 1843, had also gone over to Willich on the occasion of the February banquet. Marx did receive an invitation to a similar banquet the following year, but sent Jenny in his place. He was not impressed by her report of the 'dry meeting with the trappings of tea and sandwiches'.[1] The Italian refugee leader Mazzini was dubbed by Marx 'the Pope of the Democratic Church *in partibus*'[2] and he criticised his policies in a letter to Engels as follows:

> Mazzini knows only the towns with their liberal aristocracy and their enlightened citizens. The material needs of the Italian agricultural population – as exploited and as systematically emasculated and held in stupidity as the Irish – are naturally too low for the phraseological heaven of his cosmopolitan, neo-Catholic ideological manifestos. It needs courage, however, to inform the bourgeoisie and the aristocracy that the first step towards the independence of Italy is the complete emancipation of the peasants and the transformation of their semi-tenant system into free bourgeois property.[3]

As for the other prominent refugee leader, the Hungarian Kossuth, Marx considered him a representative of 'an obscure and semi-barbarous people still stuck in the semi-civilisation of the sixteenth century'.[4]

The only national group with which Marx had any prolonged contact were the Chartists. By 1850 the slow process of disintegration that had affected the Chartist movement after its climax and failure in 1848 was already well advanced. At the same time repressive government measures had radicalised Chartism; and among the two most influential of its radical leaders in the early 1850s were George Julian Harney and Ernest Jones.

Harney was the orphaned son of a Kentish sailor and had been in Chartist journalism all his life. Engels had met him as early as 1843 when Harney was editing *The Northern Star*. He was the most internationally-minded of the Chartist leaders and this, together with his republicanism, led to his forced resignation from the *Star* in 1850. He then started his own paper, *The Red Republican*, later renamed *The Friend of the People*, which in November 1850 published the first English

[1] *MEW* xxviii 30. [2] Ibid. 43. [3] Quoted in F. Mehring, *Karl Marx*, p. 242.
[4] *MEW* xxvii 377.

translation of the *Communist Manifesto* of 'citizens Charles Marx and Frederic Engels'. A similarity in outlook, combined with the fact that Harney had a mass following and a newspaper, induced Marx to attempt a close collaboration with him. But Harney was above all a pragmatist and, while willing to join Marx and the Blanquists in the World Society of Communist Revolutionaries, he was at the same time embarking on a course that was bound to estrange him from Marx. By the summer of 1850 Harney had become convinced of the necessity of allying the National Charter Association with the expanding, but not so radical, Co-operatives and Trade Unions. The immediate cause of their estrangement was Harney's indiscriminate enthusiasm for the various refugee groups in London who could all rely on getting their views published in *The Friend of the People*. In February 1851 Harney's catholicity went further: he attended an international meeting to commemorate the Polish patriot Bem and gave the best speech of the evening. The meeting was supported by Louis Blanc and the Blanquists and held under the presidency of Schapper. Other incidents followed. On 24 February Harney contrived to be present at banquets organised by the rival French factions and failed to protest energetically enough when Schramm and Pieper, two of Marx's young hangers-on, were expelled from the one organised by Louis Blanc, a large affair with more than 700 present, mostly Germans. Marx professed to be tired of 'the public incense with which Harney indefatigably covers *les petits grands hommes*'[1] and described Harney, with that touch of snobbery which he sometimes found impossible to suppress, as 'a very impressionable plebeian'.[2] And concerning the 24 February banquet he wrote to Engels:

> Harney has got himself involved in this affair, first because of his need to have great men to admire, which we have often made fun of in the past. Then, he loves theatrical effects. He is stuck deeper in the democratic mud than he wishes to admit. He has a double spirit: one which Friedrich Engels made for him and another which is his own.[3]

This disagreement (which Engels partly ascribed to his own departure from London and Marx's poor command of English)[4] marked a definite estrangement between Marx and the Chartist movement as

[1] Ibid. 184.   [2] Ibid. 193.   [3] Ibid. 195 f.   [4] Ibid. 561.

a whole. Marx met Harney three months later at a tea party to celebrate the eightieth birthday of Robert Owen. Although they corresponded from time to time, a quarter of a century was to pass before
their next meeting (a brief encounter on Waterloo Station).[1] In 1852
Harney resigned from the Chartist executive, moved to the North of
England, thence to Jersey and eventually to the United States where
he continued a correspondence with Engels to whom he was always
more attached than to Marx.

As Marx's enthusiasm for Harney waned, so his relations with
Ernest Jones, the other leader of the Chartist Left, increased. Engels
wrote to Marx on Jones's death in 1869 that he had been 'the only
educated Englishman among the politicians who was, at bottom,
completely on our side'.[2] Jones, the son of a cavalry officer, was a
barrister by profession and a novelist and poet in his spare time. He
was born to wealth and high social standing, all of which he threw
away on his conversion to Chartism in 1846. He had been imprisoned
for two years in 1848 and on his release was tireless in trying to keep
the Chartist movement alive – through lecture tours (he was a very
effective speaker) and through the paper which he started in 1851 and
which continued until 1858, called originally *Notes to the People* and later
The People's Paper. In the early 1850s Jones, unlike Harney, emphasised
the doctrines of class struggle, the incompatibility of interests between
capital and labour, and the necessity of the conquest of political power
by the working class – views which his close association with Marx and
Engels did much to reinforce. Although he was the only notable
Chartist once Harney had retired from active politics, his influence
steadily declined. The workers did not welcome a doctrine of class
war and were more concerned to defend their own interests inside the
capitalist system. Marx kept up a regular contact with Jones during the
1850s and attended his public lectures, some of which he found 'great
stuff' (though Jenny Marx considered his lecture on the History of the
Popes to be 'very fine and advanced for the English, but for us Germans
who have run the gauntlet of Hegel, Feuerbach, etc., not quite *à la
hauteur*').[3]

Marx at first suspected Jones of siding with Harney; later, however,

---

[1] Marx's feelings were not reciprocated by Harney, who towards the end of his
life still considered Marx 'one of the most warm-hearted, genial and attractive of
men'.
[2] Engels to Marx, *MEW* xxxi 253.   [3] *MEW* xxvii 153.

he came to regard Jones as 'the most talented of the representatives of Chartism'[1] and approved of the tone of *The People's Paper*. This he contrasted favourably with Harney's criticism of Chartism as a 'class movement' which had not yet become 'a general and national movement',[2] expressions that particularly annoyed Marx in that they reminded him of Mazzini's phraseology. Nevertheless, by the autumn of 1852 Marx considered that Jones was making far too much use of him as a source of information on foreign affairs and for general editorial support. 'I told him', Marx wrote to Engels, 'that it was quite all right for him to be an egoist, but he should be one in a civilised manner.'[3] What especially riled Marx was Jones's failure to carry out his promise of publishing an English translation of the *Eighteenth Brumaire*. But Marx supported Jones against the less radical Chartists, was favourably impressed by the relative success of Jones's paper and his meetings in 1853, and eventually contributed some articles himself, though the number of printing errors made him very reluctant to continue. When invited by Jones to sit in the Labour Parliament in Manchester in 1854 Marx sent what he himself described as an ambivalent reply, declaring that 'the working class of Great Britain has shown itself more capable than any other of standing at the head of the great movement which, in the final analysis, must lead to the complete freedom of labour.... The organisation of its united forces, the organisation of the working class on a national scale – such I conceive to be the great aim which the Workers' Parliament has set for itself.'[4]

In February 1855 the same troubles as four years previously threatened to recur when Jones tried to organise another banquet to celebrate the 1848 revolution. Marx let himself be persuaded to attend a meeting of the Chartist International Committee to prepare the banquet, but 'the idle chatter of the Frenchmen, the staring of the Germans and the gesticulations of the Spaniards', not to mention the recent election of Herzen to the committee, impressed him merely as pure farce. He was a supercilious and silent observer at the meeting, smoking excessively to compensate.[5] He eventually declined the invitation to the banquet (though his name appeared on the handbill) on the grounds that all such meetings were 'humbug', that it could bring about renewed persecution of aliens, and finally that he had refused ever to appear in the company of Herzen 'because I have no intention

---

[1] Ibid. 591.   [2] *MEW* xxviii 523.   [3] Ibid. 125.
[4] *MEW* x 126.   [5] Cf. *MEW* xxviii 433.

of seeing old Europe renewed through Russian blood'.[1] In 1856, however, Marx did accept an invitation to attend a celebration of the
anniversary of the founding of *The People's Paper* 'because', as he put it,
'the times seem to me to be hotting up ... and even more because I
was the *only* one of the refugees to be invited'. The refugees were thereby convinced 'that we are the only "intimate" allies of the Chartists
and that, if we hold back from public demonstrations and leave it to
the Frenchmen openly to flirt with Chartism, it is always in our power
to reoccupy the position that history has already allotted us'.[2] Relations
between Marx and Jones became strained when, in 1857, Jones began
to co-operate with radical sections of the middle class in order to
get wide support for electoral reform; this failed however. In 1861 he
moved to Manchester to practise as a barrister, and maintained friendly
relations with Marx and Engels until his death in 1869.[3]

III. LIFE IN DEAN STREET

A hasty reading of Marx's correspondence gives the impression that
Marx's family difficulties were largely due to their living in the most
grinding poverty; and Marx's own descriptions of his lack of funds
appears to bear this out. 1852 seems to have been the worst year. In
February: 'Already for a week I have been in the pleasant position of
not going out because my coat is in the pawnshop and of not being
able to eat meat because of lack of credit.'[4] In the same month Jenny
wrote: 'Everything hangs on a hair, and 10/– at the right time can
often obviate a terrible situation.'[5] In April Marx had to borrow money
to bury his daughter. In September he gave a detailed description of
the situation:

> My wife is ill, little Jenny is ill, Lenchen has a sort of nervous fever,
> I cannot and could not call the doctor because I have no money
> for medicine. For 8–10 days I have fed the family on bread and
> potatoes of which it is still questionable whether I can rustle up
> any today. Naturally this diet was not recommended in the present
> climatic conditions. I did not write any articles for Dana, because I
> did not have the penny to go and read newspapers. ...
>   I had put off until the beginning of September all the creditors

[1] Ibid. 434.   [2] Ibid. 46 f.
[3] See further, J. Saville, *Ernest Jones Chartist* (London, 1952).
[4] *MEW* xxviii 30.   [5] *MEW* xxvii 608.

who, as you know, are only paid off in small sums. Now there is a general storm.

I have tried everything, but in vain. . . .

The best and most desirable thing that could happen would be that the landlady throw me out of the house. At least I would then be quit of the sum of £22. But I can scarcely trust her to be so obliging. Also baker, milkman, the man with the tea, greengrocer, old butcher's bills. How can I get clear of all this hellish muck? Finally in the last 8–10 days, I have borrowed some shillings and pence (this is the most fatal thing, but it was necessary to avoid perishing) from layabouts.[1]

In October, Marx had once more to pawn his coat in order to buy paper, and in December he wrote, in a letter to Cluss accompanying his *Revelations concerning the Cologne Communist Trial*: 'You will be able to appreciate the humour of the book when you consider that its author, through lack of sufficient covering for his back and feet, is as good as interned and also was and is threatened with seeing really nauseating poverty overwhelm his family at any moment.'[2]

The next year complaints were not so numerous, but still 'several valuable things must be renewed in the pawnshop if they are not to be forfeit and this is naturally not possible at a time when even the means for the most necessary things are not there'.[3] And in October: 'The burden of debt has risen so much, the most necessary things have so completely disappeared to the pawnshop that for ten days there has not been a penny in the house.'[4]

The pawnshop was an indispensable institution for the Marx household. It was also, on one occasion, a source of discomfort: Marx tried to pawn some of Jenny's family silver with the Argyll crest on it. The pawnbroker considered this so suspect that he informed the police and Marx had to spend the week-end in prison before he could establish his *bona fides*.[5] In the summer of 1855 more drastic measures were required, and Marx retired with his family to Imandt's house in Camberwell partly to avoid Dr Freund who was prosecuting him for non-payment of a bill; he spent from September to December *incognito* with Engels in Manchester for the same reason.

[1] *MEW* xxviii 128 f.   [2] Marx to Cluss, *MEW* xxviii 560.
[3] *MEW* xxviii 272.   [4] Ibid. 300.
[5] Cf. M. Kovalevsky, 'Meetings with Marx', *Reminiscences*, p. 298; H. M. Hyndman, *Record of an Adventurous Life* (London, 1911) pp. 277 f.

However, a closer examination of Marx's revenues gives the strong impression that his difficulties resulted less from real poverty than from a desire to preserve appearances, coupled with an inability to husband his financial resources. This is certainly what one would expect from Marx's incapacity to manage the large sums of money that he had previously received and was again to receive in the 1860s. On his arrival in London Marx was quite prepared to rent a flat in Chelsea that was very expensive – more than twice the rent Marx eventually paid for a house when he moved out of Dean Street. It was the failure of the *Neue Rheinische Zeitung – Revue* that finally reduced his income to nothing. He put a lot of his own money into the production of this journal, got virtually none of it back, and in October 1850 was obliged to ask Freiligrath to sell all the silver (apart from a few items belonging to little Jenny) that his wife had pawned a year previously in order to buy her ticket to Paris. Luckily he had some generous friends and a simple calculation seems to show that in the year previous to the arrival of the first cheque from the *New York Daily Tribune* – presumably the year in which his income was at its lowest – Marx received at least £150 in gifts. (Since this is only the money mentioned in surviving correspondence the total sum was probably considerably more.) It came from various sources: Engels, and Marx's Cologne friends through Daniels, were the chief contributors; Weerth and Lassalle also gave sums; one of Jenny's cousins sent Marx £15; and Freiligrath gave Marx £30 which he had obtained on the pretence of 'urgent party needs'[1] from 'some friends who willingly aid our cause'. Marx was insistent that this help should come only from his close friends. As Jenny said: 'my husband is very sensitive in these matters and would sooner sacrifice his last penny than be compelled to take to democratic beggary'.[2] Indeed, he even refused Lassalle's offer to open a public subscription to publish his work on economics. In the early 1850s the cost of living was in fact falling and £150 was considered quite an adequate income for a lower-middle-class family with three children. Freiligrath, whose family circumstances were similar to those of Marx, earned less than £200 a year and yet boasted that he had never been without 'the luscious beef-steak of exile'.[3]

By 1852 Marx's financial position improved in that he had a regular

---

[1] F. Freiligrath, *Briefwechsel mit Marx und Engels* I 34.
[2] Jenny Marx to Weydemeyer, *MEW* XXVII 607.
[3] Quoted in, F. Mehring, *Karl Marx*, p. 227.

income as London correspondent of the *New York Daily Tribune*. Although small in 1852, this amounted to £80 in 1853 and more than £160 in 1854. The revenue from the *New York Daily Tribune* dropped during 1855 and 1856, but Marx began corresponding for the *Neue Oder-Zeitung* at the end of 1854 for about £50 a year. This was, of course, supplemented by Engels and would – until the arrival of large sums in 1856 – have been a tolerable income, had it been carefully managed. But Marx was incapable of such management. He was, for example, quite unaware of what the *New York Daily Tribune* was paying him for months after he had agreed to write regularly for the paper. And for his biggest literary success in these years – his anti-Palmerston broadsheets which initially sold 15,000 copies and went into a second edition – he did not manage to get a single penny. What did not help financially, and reduced the family's morale, was the necessity of keeping up appearances. Writing to Engels in 1852 about his hardships, he stressed their unimportance when set beside his fear 'that the muck will sometime end in scandal'.[1] And in the same year he wrote of a visit by Weerth: 'It is painful when one sits in muck up to the neck to have so fine a gentleman opposite oneself from whom one must hide the too shameful things.'[2] Marx's creditors were quite naturally angry in 1854 when he spent considerable sums on Jenny's trip to Trier which 'necessitated all sorts of new outfits because naturally she could not go to Trier in tatters'.[3]

In May 1856 Jenny inherited about £150 from an uncle in Scotland[4] and went with her children to Trier to see her ailing mother, who died in July. She returned to London in Spetember with an inheritance of about £120 which allowed the family to leave 'the evil, frightful rooms which encompassed all our joy and all our pain' and move 'with joyful heart into a small house at the foot of romantic Hampstead Heath, not far from lovely Primrose Hill. When we slept in our own beds for the first time, sat on our own chairs and even had a parlour with second-hand furniture of a rococo style – or rather bric-à-brac, then we really thought that we were living in a magic castle....'[5] The house, 9 Grafton Terrace, which Marx rented for £36 a year, was a narrow, terraced building with three storeys and a basement making for eight rooms in all. It was three miles from the city-centre in a brand new

---

[1] *MEW* xxviii 30.   [2] Ibid. 147.   [3] Ibid. 377.
[4] Jenny Marx to Bertha Markheim, in B. Andreas, *Dokumente*, p. 176.   [5] Ibid.

development area that was in a few years to be built right over. All the money went to paying off old debts and setting up the house. Typically, Marx did not even have enough money to pay the first quarter's rent – a presage of difficulties to come.

The years spent in the Dean Street house were the most barren and frustrating of Marx's life. They would have embittered the most stoic of characters; and Marx, as he said himself, was usually not long-suffering. Soho was the district of London where most of the refugees congregated – being then as now very cosmopolitan and full of eating places, prostitutes and theatres. Dean Street was one of its main thoroughfares; long and narrow, it had once been fashionable but was now decidedly shabby. It was also in a quarter where there was much cholera, particularly in 1854, when Marx accounted for the outbreak 'because the sewers made in June, July and August were driven through the pits where those who died of the plague in 1688 (? I think) were buried'.[1] From 1851 to 1856 the Marx family lived in a flat on the second floor composed initially of two rooms until Marx rented a third for his study. There were always seven, and occasionally eight, people living in the two rooms. The first was a small bedroom and the other a large (15 ft by 18 ft) living-room with three windows looking out on the street.

By January 1851 Marx was already two weeks behind with the rent for his landlord – Morgan Kavanagh, an Irish author who sublet the rooms for £22 a year. A few months later Marx avoided eviction only by signing an IOU to his landlord, who the next year, after waiting for months for the rent, threatened to put the bailiffs in. There were no holidays until 1854 when Jenny and the children went to Seiler's villa in Edmonton for a fortnight before going on to Trier. Jenny did write – but without success – to one of the editors of the *New York Daily Tribune* in the hope that they might be able to provide a house for Marx, their London correspondent. It was only the death of Edgar, combined with the inheritance from Jenny's uncle, that enabled them eventually to move in 1856.

The family regularly managed to get out to Hampstead Heath on Sundays, a very popular excursion with Londoners at that time. The Heath – then still in its natural state – was about one and a half hours' walk from Dean Street, and they aimed to arrive there by lunchtime. Liebknecht has described the outing:

[1] *MEW* xxviii 393.

The lunch-basket of a volume unknown in London, which Lenchen had saved from their sojourn in Trier, contained the centrepiece – a mighty roast veal. Tea and fruit they brought with them; bread, cheese and beer could be bought on the Heath.

The march itself was generally accomplished in the following order: I led the van with the two girls – now telling stories, now executing callisthenics, now on the hunt after field flowers that were not so scarce then as they are now. Behind us some friends. Then the main body of the army: Marx with his wife and some Sunday guest requiring special attention. And behind these Lenchen with the hungriest of the guests who helped her carry the basket.

After the meal they 'produced the Sunday papers they had bought on the road, and now began the reading and discussing of politics – while the children, who rapidly found playmates, played hide and seek behind the heather bushes'. There followed games and donkey-riding at which Marx amused the company 'by his more than primitive art of riding and by the fanatical zeal with which he affirmed his skill in this art'.[1] They returned, with the children and Lenchen bringing up the rear, singing patriotic German songs and reciting Dante or Shakespeare.

Marx also liked to go out occasionally in the evenings.

Sometimes [wrote Liebknecht] it even happened that we relapsed into our old student's pranks. One evening Edgar Bauer, acquainted with Marx from their Berlin time and then not yet his personal enemy in spite of the 'Holy Family', had come to town from his hermitage in Highgate for the purpose of 'making a beer trip'. The problem was to 'take something' in every saloon between Oxford Street and Hampstead Road – making the 'something' a very difficult task, even by confining yourself to a minimum considering the enormous number of saloons in that part of the city. But we went to work undaunted and managed to reach the end of Tottenham Court Road without accident. There loud singing issued from a public house; we entered and learned that a club of Odd Fellows were celebrating a festival.[2]

Many toasts were exchanged, but when Liebknecht began to claim

[1] W. Liebknecht, *Karl Marx. Biographical Memoirs*, pp. 129 ff.
[2] Ibid., p. 146.

superior political intelligence for the Germans and Bauer alluded to English cant, 'fists were brandished in the air and we were sensible enough to choose the better part of valour and managed to effect, not wholly without difficulty, a passably dignified retreat'. However, the evening was not finished:

> ... in order to cool our heated blood, we started on a double quick march, until Edgar Bauer stumbled over a heap of paving stones. 'Hurrah, an idea!' And in memory of mad student's pranks he picked up a stone, and Clash! Clatter! a gas lantern went flying into splinters. Nonsense is contagious – Marx and I did not stay behind, and we broke four or five street lamps – it was, perhaps, 2 o'clock in the morning and the streets were deserted in consequence. But the noise nevertheless attracted the attention of a policeman who with quick resolution gave the signal to his colleagues on the same beat. And immediately counter-signals were given. The position became critical. Happily we took in the situation at a glance; and happily we knew the locality. We raced ahead, three or four policemen some distance behind us. Marx showed an activity that I should not have attributed to him. And after the wild chase had lasted some minutes, we succeeded in turning into a side street and there running through an alley – a back yard between two streets – whence we came behind the policemen who lost the trail. Now we were safe.[1]

When Engels was in London staying with Marx, the two of them used to go out together; once Engels wrote to Jenny apologising for having led her husband astray, and was informed that Marx's 'nocturnal wanderings' had brought him such a chill that he had had to stay in bed for a week.

Life in the three rooms in Dean Street was extremely irregular. The following vivid description, which seems to be largely accurate, was written by a Prussian government spy in 1852:

> As father and husband, Marx, in spite of his wild and restless character, is the gentlest and mildest of men. Marx lives in one of the worst, therefore one of the cheapest quarters of London. He occupies two rooms. The one looking out on the street is the salon, and the bedroom is at the back. In the whole apartment there is not one

---

[1] Ibid., pp. 149 ff.

clean and solid piece of furniture. Everything is broken, tattered and torn, with a half inch of dust over everything and the greatest disorder everywhere. In the middle of the salon there is a large old-fashioned table covered with an oilcloth, and on it there lie manuscripts, books and newspapers, as well as the children's toys, the rags and tatters of his wife's sewing basket, several cups with broken rims, knives, forks, lamps, an inkpot, tumblers, Dutch clay pipes, tobacco ash – in a word, everything topsy-turvy, and all on the same table. A seller of second-hand goods would be ashamed to give away such a remarkable collection of odds and ends.

When you enter Marx's room smoke and tobacco fumes make your eyes water so much that for a moment you seem to be groping about in a cavern, but gradually, as you grow accustomed to the fog, you can make out certain objects which distinguish themselves from the surrounding haze. Everything is dirty, and covered with dust, so that to sit down becomes a thoroughly dangerous business. Here is a chair with only three legs, on another chair the children are playing at cooking – this chair happens to have four legs. This is the one which is offered to the visitor, but the children's cooking has not been wiped away; and if you sit down, you risk a pair of trousers.[1]

Family accommodation was so restricted that when Franziska was born in the spring of 1851, she had to be given to a nurse, there being so little room in the house. A year later, she died.

At Easter, 1852 [wrote Jenny], our little Franziska had a severe bronchitis. For three days she was between life and death. She suffered terribly. When she died we left her lifeless little body in the back room, went into the front room and made our beds on the floor. Our three living children lay down by us and we all wept for the little angel whose livid, lifeless body was in the next room. Our beloved child's death occurred at the time of the hardest privations, our German friends being unable to help us just then. Ernest Jones, who paid us long and frequent visits about that time, promised to help us but he was unable to bring us anything. . . . Anguish in my heart, I hurried to a French emigrant who lived not far away and used to come to see us, and begged him to help us in our terrible necessity. He immediately gave me two pounds with the most

[1] *Archiv für die Geschichte des Sozialismus*, x (1922) pp. 56 ff.

friendly sympathy. That money was used to pay for the coffin in which my child now rests in peace. She had no cradle when she came into the world and for a long time was refused a last resting place. With what heavy hearts we saw her carried to her grave.[1]

In such circumstances it is not surprising that Jenny's physical and moral resources were quickly dissipated. In 1852, in many ways the worst of the Dean Street years, Jenny was frequently confined to bed. emaciated, coughing and, on doctor's orders, drinking a lot of port. Engels had tried to raise money to get her a holiday in the country but by the autumn she was in bed for days on end taking a spoonful of brandy hourly. Two years later she was again ill but cared for herself on the grounds that the doctor's prescription had only served to make her worse.

Since Jenny acted as his secretary, these illnesses hindered Marx in his work. Indeed, she participated to the full in all of Marx's activities. She attended meetings as an observer for him, picked out newspaper articles that she thought might interest him and looked after publishing details when he was away. She was at her most useful when acting as his secretary, writing letters, producing fair copies of his articles for newspapers (his handwriting being illegible) and keeping careful records of the dispatch of his journalism. She was proud of her role as secretary and wrote later: 'The memory of the days I spent in his little study copying his scrawled articles is among the happiest of my life.'[2] In financial matters, too, Jenny was active: she wrote innumerable begging letters, dealt with the creditors who besieged the house and even, in August 1850, 'desperate at the prospect of a fifth child and the future'[3] undertook a trip alone to Marx's uncle, a businessman in Holland. However, the recent revolutionary upheavals had not been good for trade and the old man was in no mood to help his eccentric nephew, so Jenny returned empty-handed.

Temperamentally, she was very unpredictable and liable to go to extremes. Marx wrote to her: 'I know how infinitely mercurial you are and how the least bit of good news gives you new life.'[4] 'Mercurial' was his favourite word in describing Jenny's character; but with the passage of years she found it increasingly difficult not to be submerged

[1] *Reminiscences of Marx and Engels*, p. 228.
[2] Jenny Marx, 'Short Sketch of an Eventful Life', *Reminiscences*, p. 228.
[3] *Reminiscences*, p. 227.
[4] *MEW* xxviii 527.

by her oppressive surroundings. In the summer of 1850 Marx wrote to Weydemeyer: 'You must not take amiss the excited letters of my wife. She is suckling, and our situation here is so extraordinarily miserable that it is pardonable to lose one's patience.'[1] At the death of her first child in November 1850 Jenny was quite 'beside herself' and 'dangerously overwrought'. The following year Marx described her as being ill' 'more from bourgeois than physical causes'. A few months later he wrote to Engels:

> Floods of tears the whole night long tire my patience and make me angry.... I feel pity for my wife. Most of the pressure falls on her and basically she is right. Industry must be more productive than marriage. In spite of everything you remember that by nature I am not at all patient and even a little hard so that from time to time my equanimity disappears.[2]

In 1854 Marx spoke of 'the dangerous condition of my wife';[3] the same year she retreated to bed 'partly from anger because good Dr Freund bombarded us once again with dunning letters'.[4] The following year 'for a week my wife has been more ill with nervous excitement than ever before'.[5]

Of course, much of the housework was taken over by Helene Demuth. Liebknecht wrote of her at this time: '27 years old, and while no beauty, she was nice looking with rather pleasing features. She had no lack of admirers and could have made a good match again and again.' She was in many ways the lynchpin of the Marx household: 'Lenchen was the dictator but Mrs Marx was the mistress. And Marx submitted as meekly as a lamb to that dictatorship.'[6]

'In the early summer of 1851', Jenny wrote in her autobiography, 'an event occurred that I do not wish to relate here in detail, although it greatly contributed to an increase in our worries, both personal and others.'[7] This event was the birth of Marx's illegitimate son Frederick; the mother was Helene Demuth. This fact was kept so well concealed and the surviving papers of the Marx family were so carefully sifted to eliminate all references to it that only the recent chance discovery of a letter brought it to light.[8] This letter, addressed to August Bebel, was

[1] Ibid. [2] *MEW* xxvii 536. [3] *MEW* xxviii 370. [4] Ibid. 410.
[5] *MEW* xxviii 442. [6] W. Liebknecht, *Karl Marx. Biographical Memoirs*, p. 123.
[7] *Reminiscences*, p. 227.
[8] There is a quite exceptional gap in the Marx–Engels correspondence of two weeks either side of Frederick's birth date.

written by Louis Freyberger (the first wife of Karl Kautsky) who had kept house for Engels on the death of Helene Demuth to whom she had been very close. According to her, Engels had accepted paternity for Frederick and thus 'saved Marx from a difficult domestic conflict.' But he gave Louise Freyberger the right to reveal the truth should he be accused of treating his 'son' shabbily. He even told the story to a distraught Eleanor on his deathbed, writing it on a slate as he had lost his voice. The secret was confined to the (Marx) family and one or two friends. The son was immediately sent to foster parents and had no contact at all with the Marx household, though he resumed contact with his mother after Marx's death. Louise Freyberger wrote:

> He came regularly every week to visit her; curiously enough, however, he never came in through the front door but always through the kitchen, and only when I came to General and he continued his visits, did I make sure that he had all the rights of a visitor. . . .
>
> For Marx separation from his wife, who was terribly jealous, was always before his eyes: he did not love the boy; he did not dare to do anything for him, the scandal would have been too great; he was sent as paying guest to a Mrs Louis (I think that is how she writes her name) and he took his name too from his foster-mother, and only after Nimm's[1] death adopted the name of Demuth.[2]

There is no doubt of the general credibility of this letter. The certificate of Frederick Demuth's birth in June 1851 is conserved in Somerset House; the space for the name of the father is left blank; the name of the mother is given as Helene Demuth and the place of birth as 28 Dean Street. Although so few details of this episode survive, it seems that the necessity of preserving appearances and the fear of the inevitable rumours only served to increase the strain on Jenny's nerves. Five weeks after the birth, and the day following its registration, Marx wrote to Weydemeyer concerning 'the unspeakable infamies that my enemies are spreading about me' and continued: '. . . my wife is ill, and she has to endure the most unpleasant bourgeois poverty from

[1] Nimm was Lenchen's nickname. The whole Marx family had a great attraction to nicknames: Marx himself was usually Mohr or Moor (from his dark complexion); Engels was General (from his military studies); and Eleanor was Tussy (to rhyme with pussy).

[2] The letter is quoted in full in A. Künzli, *Karl Marx, Eine Psychographie*, pp. 326 ff. Further on Frederick Demuth, see R. Payne, *Karl Marx*, final chapter; Y. Kapp, *Eleanor Marx* (London, 1972); D. Heisler, 'Ungeliebter Sohn', *Der Spiegel*, 23 Nov 1972.

morning to night. Her nervous system is undermined, and she gets none the better because every day some idiotic talebearers bring her all the vaporings of the democratic cesspools. The tactlessness of these people is sometimes colossal.'[1]

Marx described himself as having 'a hard nature';[2] and Jenny wrote of him in 1850: 'he has never, even at the most terrible moments, lost his confidence in the future or his cheerful good humour'.[3] But his correspondence with Engels shows that he did not always accept his troubles with so much serenity. In 1852 he wrote: 'When I see the sufferings of my wife and my own powerlessness I could rush into the devil's jaws.'[4] And two years later: 'I became wild from time to time that there is no end to the muck.'[5] One undated letter from Jenny to Marx in Manchester gives a glimpse of the state of mind to which she was sometimes reduced: 'Meanwhile I sit here and go to pieces. Karl, it is now at its worst pitch. . . . I sit here and almost weep my eyes out and can find no help. My head is disintegrating. For a week I have kept my strength up and now I can no more. . . .'[6]

In spite of all their difficulties, their basic sympathy and love for each other continued. While staying with Engels in Manchester in 1852, Marx wrote to her:

Dear Heart,
Your letter delighted me very much. You need never be embarrassed to tell me everything. If you, poor darling, have to go through the bitter reality, it is no more than reasonable than I should at least share the suffering in spirit. . . . I hope you will get another £5 this week, or at latest by Monday.[7]

From Manchester again in 1856 he wrote to Jenny (who was in Trier) a letter remarkable both for its sentiments and language and for its being one of the very few surviving from Marx to his wife. The letter is long and the following are some excerpts:

My dearest darling,
. . . I have the living image of you in front of me, I hold you in my arms, kiss you from head to foot, fall before you on my knees and

[1] *MEW* xxvii 566.   [2] *MEW* xxviii 54.
[3] *Reminiscences of Marx and Engels*, p. 239.
[4] *MEW* xxviii 161 f.   [5] Ibid. 329.
[6] Quoted in A. Künzli, *Karl Marx. Eine Psychographie*, pp. 320 f.
[7] *MEW* xxviii 527.

sigh 'Madam, I love you'. And I love you in fact more than the Moor of Venice ever loved. The false and corrupt world conceives of all men's characters as false and corrupt. Who of my many slanderers and snake-tonged enemies has ever accused me of having a vocation to play the principal role of lover in a second-class theatre? And yet it is true. Had the wretches had enough wit, they would have painted 'the relationships of production and exchange' on one side and myself at your feet on the other. 'Look to this picture and to that', they would have written beneath. But they are stupid wretches and stupid will they remain *in saeculum saeculorum*. . . .

But love – not of Feuerbachian man, not of Moleschott's metabolisms, not of the proletariat, but love of one's darling, namely you, makes a man into a man again. In fact there are many women in the world, and some of them are beautiful. But where can I find another face in which every trait, even every wrinkle brings back the greatest and sweetest memories of my life. Even my infinite sorrows, my irreplaceable losses I can read on your sweet countenance, and I kiss my sorrows away when I kiss your sweet face. 'Buried in your arms, awoken by your kisses' – that is, in your arms and by your kisses, and the Brahmins and Pythagoreans can keep their doctrine of reincarnation and Christianity its doctrine of resurrection.[1]

For both Marx and Jenny the final and hardest blow that they suffered in Dean Street was the death, at the age of eight, of their only son in April 1855. Edgar, whom they had nicknamed 'Musch' or 'little fly' was 'very gifted, but ailing from the day of his birth – a genuine, true child of sorrow this boy with the magnificent eyes and promising head that was, however, made too large for the weak body'.[2] His final illness – a sort of consumption – lasted all through March. By the beginning of April it seemed to be fatal and Marx wrote on the sixth to Engels: 'Poor Musch is no more. He went to sleep (literally) in my arms today between five and six.' Liebknecht described the scene:

> the mother silently weeping, bent over the dead child, Lenchen sobbing beside her, Marx in a terrible agitation vehemently, almost angrily, rejecting all consolation, the two girls clinging to their mother crying quietly, the mother clasping them convulsively as if

[1] Marx to Jenny Marx, *MEW* XXIX 532 ff. This letter is written in the semi-ironical tone typical of, for example, Heine.

[2] W. Liebknecht, *Karl Marx, Biographical Memoirs*, p. 132.

to hold them and defend them against Death that had robbed her of her boy.[1]

In spite of a holiday in Manchester and the new prospects opened up by Jenny's inheritance, the sorrow remained. At the end of July, Marx wrote to Lassalle:

Bacon says that really important men have so many relations with nature and the world that they recover easily from every loss. I do not belong to these important men. The death of my child has deeply shaken my heart and mind and I still feel the loss as freshly as on the first day. My poor wife is also completely broken down.[2]

Years later Marx still found a visit to the Soho area a shattering experience.[3]

Difficulties did not prevent Marx from holding what amounted to an open house:

You are received in the most friendly way [wrote one visitor] and cordially offered pipes and tobacco and whatever else there may happen to be; and eventually a spirited and agreeable conversation arises to make amends for all the domestic deficiencies, and this makes the discomfort tolerable. Finally you grow accustomed to the company, and find it interesting and original.[4]

No relations of either family seem to have come to the rooms in Dean Street – with the exception of Marx's sister Louise together with the South African she had just married in Trier. But there was a constant stream of other visitors; Harney and his wife, Ernest Jones, Freiligrath and his wife, and Wilhelm Wolff were all regular visitors. The most frequent was a group of young men whose company Marx liked and encouraged. One of this group was Ernst Dronke, a founder-member of the Communist League who had also worked on the *Neue Rheinische Zeitung*; he occasionally helped Marx with his secretarial work, but later went into commerce and retired from active politics. Another was Conrad Schramm who fought a duel with Willich – though Marx quarrelled with him in 1851 over Schramm's unwillingness to hand

[1] Ibid., p. 133.
[2] *MEW* xxviii 617.
[3] Cf. Marx to Engels, *MEW* xxx 325.
[4] *Archiv für die Geschichte des Sozialismus*, x (1922) pp. 56 ff.

over the Communist League's papers and lost touch when he emigrated to America soon afterwards. A more frequent – at times almost daily – visitor was Wilhelm Liebknecht, the young philology student who had fought in the Baden uprising of 1849 and escaped to England via Switzerland. He had a profound, if timid, admiration for Jenny (his own mother had died when he was three) and loved to run errands for her, look after the children and generally absorb Marx's ideas with much greater docility than he was later to show in the 1860s and 1870s as leader of the German Social Democrats. Finally there was Wilhelm Pieper, a young man in his middle twenties who had studied languages in Germany and in the early 1850s stayed with Marx sometimes for weeks on end (when he was not consorting with prostitutes or being employed as a tutor.) He acted as Marx's secretary for a time and translated *The Poverty of Philosophy* into execrable English. He was tactless enough to get on Jenny's nerves, and even to reduce Karl Blind's wife to tears during a discussion on Feuerbach in Marx's room. Marx referred to him as his 'doctrinaire echo', regretted his schoolmasterish tone and was pained by his attempts at playing 'modern' music. In spite of all this, he fed Pieper, housed him, helped him recover from illness, got Engels to lend him money and on several occasions even lent him some himself. However unwilling Marx might have been to accept intellectual or party-political opposition, in his relations with these younger friends he was usually amused, tolerant and even generous.

In his personal relationships Marx could exercise great tact and generosity. He would excuse the shortcomings of his friends to Engels and advise Weydemeyer on how to handle Freiligrath or Wolff. He showed great consideration for the wife of his friend Roland Daniels, one of the defendants in the Cologne trial, organised letters to her from Daniels's friends in England and on his death in 1855 wrote her a most moving tribute.[1] He even pawned Jenny's last coat to help Eccarius when he was ill.

The man whose friendship Marx valued most was, of course, Friedrich Engels. For the twenty years following his departure from London in late 1850, Marx and Engels kept up a regular correspondence, writing on the average every other day. Although this correspondence constitutes by far the most important source for any account of Marx's life during these years, it is not complete: the letters

[1] Cf. *MEW* xxviii 618.

were sifted after Engels' death to remove any (for example those concerning Frederick Demuth) which might embarrass family or friends. Thus the almost total absence in the surviving Marx-Engels correspondence of anything indicating a warm friendship between the two men may be attributable partly to this later sifting and partly also to the fact that both correspondents (particularly in the early 1850s) suspected that the authorities were intercepting their letters.

Engels' move to Manchester in 1850 meant taking up where he had left off eight years previously. The split in the Communist League and the failure of the *Neue Rheinische Zeitung-Revue* removed his chief reason for remaining in London; he had to earn his living; and his mother, to whom he was very attached, urged on him at least an outward reconciliation with his father. There was no representative of the Engels family in the Manchester branch of the firm of Ermen and Engels, and his father agreed to his acting in the family's interests there. The father's consent was reluctant at first, but it turned to enthusiasm after plans to send his son either to Calcutta or to America had failed, and after Engels had demonstrated in his reports back to Barmen his capacity to handle business. Early in 1851 his situation became more permanent, though some difficulties still remained:

> the problem is [he wrote to Marx], to have an official position as representative of my father vis-à-vis the Ermens, and yet have no official position inside the firm here entailing an obligation to work and a salary from the firm. However, I hope to achieve it; my business letters have enchanted my father and he considers my remaining here a great sacrifice on my part.[1]

When his father came over to Britain in July 1851 the matter was settled to the satisfaction of both: Engels was to stay in Manchester for at least three years. He later reckoned to have made more than £230 in his first year there. His father, during his annual inspection the following year, drew up a new contract with his partners that provided his son with an increasing proportion of the profits, and by the end of the decade Engels' income was over £1000 a year. Engels was, as Marx remarked, 'very exact'[2] in matters of money and this money enabled him to act as Dutch uncle to the entire 'Marx party'. Dronke received money from him, so did Pieper; Liebknecht was fitted out, at Engels' expense, with a new set of clothes in which to

[1] *MEW* xxvii 204 f.   [2] *MEW* xxix 540.

apply for a tutorship. But the lion's share went to Marx: in some years Engels seems to have given him more than he spent on himself. These sums of money – sometimes sent in postal orders, sometimes in £1 or £5 notes cut in half and sent in separate letters – often saved the unworldly Marx from complete disaster. 'Karl was frightfully happy', wrote Jenny on one occasion, 'when he heard the fateful double knock of the postman. "There's Frederic, £2, saved!" he cried out.'[1] As a result Engels found it difficult to make ends meet and wrote to Marx in 1853:

> Reorganisation of my personal expenses becomes urgent, and in a week or two I will move into cheaper lodgings and take to weaker drinks. . . . In the previous year, thank God, I got through half of my father's profits in the firm here. As soon as the arrival of my old man approaches, I will move into fine lodgings, produce fine cigars, wine, etc., so that we can create an impression. That's life.[2]

Although, as Engels had found previously, the centre of English free trade afforded a good vantage point from which to view economic developments, he would have preferred to be elsewhere. Harney declared that he would sooner be hanged in London than live in Manchester and Engels often complained of his loneliness and boredom. In spite of a plan early in 1852 to move to New Brighton with the entire Marx family, and another scheme in 1854 to move to London as military correspondent of the *Daily News*, he remained a prisoner in Manchester for twenty years. Several communist friends came to visit him: Weerth who travelled widely for his firm, Dronke who established himself in Bradford, and above all Marx who came once or even twice a year – sometimes for weeks on end. He was also able to renew his life with Mary Burns, though concern for 'respectability' prevented his living with her. His work for the Ermen and Engels business did not keep him from matters of more importance to himself: after a full day's work in his office he would regularly study languages, military science (hence his nickname 'General'), and write articles in Marx's stead.

Engels had a character that was in many ways the exact opposite of Marx's: he was warm, optimistic, well balanced, full of *joie de vivre*, and enjoyed the reputation of having a fine taste in all that concerned wine and women. Towards his friends he was loyal, patient and un-

---

[1] *MEW* xxviii 656. [2] Ibid. 217.

selfish; and intellectually he had a quick, clear mind, and an ability to simplify – sometimes oversimplify – deep and complex questions. In all his surviving correspondence with Marx, Engels only once seems to have reproached Marx – the occasion being Marx's cold reception of the news of Mary Burns's death. The whole correspondence is remarkably unemotional. Although Marx was sometimes angry at Engels' silences, there is only one really abusive letter: Marx had quarrelled with Wilhelm Wolff (nicknamed 'Lupus') over a book that Wolff claimed Marx had borrowed from him and not returned. When Engels' communications became a little less frequent, Marx implied that Engels was putting him in second place to Wolff and Dronke:

At least that is the method that you, since the arrival of Mr Lupus in Manchester, have observed with curious consistency in all matters concerning me and the two gentlemen. It is therefore better, so as not to reduce our correspondence to a purely telegraphic one, for us both to omit all references to your friends and protégés there.[1]

When Engels replied in a conciliatory manner, Marx wrote:

You know that everyone has his momentary moods and *nihil humani* etc. Naturally I never meant 'conspiracy' and such nonsense. You are accustomed to some jealousy and basically what annoys me is only that we cannot be together, work together, laugh together, while the 'protégés' have you comfortably in their neighbourhood.[2]

A great crisis was necessary for Marx to put his feelings on paper When his son was dying in 1855 he wrote to Engels: 'I cannot thank you enough for the friendship with which you work in my stead and the sympathy that you feel for the child.'[3] And soon afterwards: 'In all the frightful sorrows that I have been through in these days the thought of you and your friendship has always strengthened me, together with the hope that we have still something purposeful to do in the world together.'[4]

Engels was also on close terms with the rest of the Marx family: he wrote from time to time to Jenny and sent cotton goods as presents, and as 'Uncle Engels' he was very popular with the children. On occasion, however, Marx did criticise Engels – particularly to Jenny. After Marx's death his daughters Laura and Eleanor removed and

[1] Ibid. 313.   [2] Ibid. 314.   [3] Ibid. 441.   [4] Ibid. 444.

destroyed those parts of their parents' correspondence which contained passages that might have hurt Engels.[1]

IV. RESUMED ECONOMIC STUDIES

Considering his family circumstances, it is surprising that Marx got any serious work done at all. His one secure refuge was the British Museum; at home he would write up and collate the information he got there. His working habits were no more regular than they had been in Brussels – to judge by the report of a Prussian government spy:

> In private life he is an extremely disorderly, cynical human being, and a bad host. He leads a real gypsy existence. Washing, grooming and changing his linen are things he does rarely, and he is often drunk. Though he is often idle for days on end, he will work day and night with tireless endurance when he has a great deal of work to do. He has no fixed times for going to sleep and waking up. He often stays up all night, and then lies down fully clothed on the sofa at midday and sleeps till evening, untroubled by the whole world coming and going through the room.[2]

Eleanor wrote that she had heard tell how, in the front room in Dean Street, 'the children would pile up the chairs behind him to represent a coach to which he was harnessed as horse and would "whip him up" even as he sat at his desk writing'.[3]

In spite of all these impediments, Marx began to lay the foundation of his economic work and produce a considerable amount of high-quality journalism. During 1850–51 Marx spent long periods in the British Museum, resuming the economic studies that he had been forced to neglect since his Paris days of 1844. In his articles in the *Neue Rheinische Zeitung – Revue* he had already analysed the historical and political conclusions to be drawn from the failure of the 1848 revolutions, the cyclical process of overproduction and consequent overspeculation of 1843–45, the financial panic of 1846–47, and the recovery in England and France during 1848–50. The result of the analyses of the

[1] G. Mayer, *Friedrich Engels*, II 356. For an example which his daughters failed to destroy see Marx to Jenny, *MEW* XXXIV 344, where, on the death of Lizzie Burns, Engels' second wife, he makes fun of her illiteracy and speaks in a derogatory tone of Engels himself.

[2] *Archiv für die Geschichte des Sozialismus*, X (1922) pp. 56 f.

[3] Eleanor Marx, Preface to K. Marx (*sic*), *Revolution and Counter-Revolution* (London, 1971) p. vii.

1848 revolutions was not to make Marx any less sanguine about the next outbreak but only the circumstances in which it would occur. During the early 1850s Marx did not differ from the other German refugees in London in his belief that a revolution was imminent. He outlined his views in December 1849 in a letter to Weydermeyer:

> Another event on the continent – as yet unperceived – is the approach of a tremendous industrial, productive and commercial crisis. If the Continent puts off its revolution until the outbreak of this crisis, England will perhaps be forced from the start to be a companion, albeit a reluctant one, of the revolutionary continent. An earlier outbreak of the revolution – if not motivated directly by Russian intervention – would in my opinion be a misfortune.[1]

What Marx did become convinced of in late 1850 was that a commercial and financial crisis would be the inevitable precondition of any revolution. He was therefore constantly on the look-out for signs of this approaching crisis – and he found them in great number. Already in 1850 he had calculated that 'If the new cycle of industrial development that began in 1848 follows the same path as that of 1843–47, the crisis will break out in the year 1852';[2] and he duly produced indications that this would be the case. In December 1851: 'According to what Engels tells me, the city merchants also share our view that the crisis, held back by all sorts of chance events. . . . must erupt by next autumn at the latest.'[3] In February 1852 he spoke of 'the ever more imminent crisis in trade whose first signs are already bursting forth on all sides'.[4] A few weeks later: 'Through exceptional circumstances – California, Australia, commercial progress of the British in the Punjab, Sind and other newly conquered parts of East India – it could be that the crisis is postponed until 1853. But then its outbreak will be frightful.'[5] In September 1853: 'I think that the commercial crash, as in 1847, will begin early next year.'[6] Marx expected this movement, like the last, to occur first in France 'where' (he was saying in Octboer 1853) 'the catastrophe will still break out'.[7] The Hyde Park demonstration of 1855 led him to think that the Crimean War might precipitate a crisis in England, where 'the situation is bubbling and boiling publicly'.[8] He tended to be cautious as regards Germany, fearing that a revolt in

---

[1] *MEW* xxvii 516.   [2] *MEW* vii 432 f.   [3] *MEW* xxvii 598.
[4] *MEW* xxviii 498.   [5] Ibid. 520.   [6] Ibid. 542.
[7] Ibid. 302.   [8] Ibid. 452.

the Rhineland might have to turn to foreign help and so appear unpatriotic. 'The whole thing', he wrote to Engels in the spring of 1856, 'will depend on the possibility of backing the proletarian revolution by some second edition of the Peasants' War.'[1] His predictions in this field caused amusement to his friends: Wilhelm Wolff actually took bets on them. 'Only on the subject of industrial crises', wrote Liebknecht, '. . . did he fall victim to the prophesying imp, and in consequence was subject to our hearty derision which made him grimly mad.'[2]

In one respect Marx was not unhappy to see the crisis for ever receding before him: it would enable him to finish his *magnum opus* on economics. In August 1852 he wrote to Engels: 'the revolution could come sooner than we wish',[3] and Engels agreed that the uneasy calm 'could last until 1854. I confess I wish to have time to slog away for another year.'[4]

Marx's first studies in the British Museum were concerned with the two problems of currency and rent, subjects to which he was led by his view that in France the chief beneficiary of the 1848 revolution had been the financial aristocracy and that in Britain the key to the future development lay in the struggle between the industrial bourgeoisie and the large landowners. Marx noted the accumulation of precious metals by the Bank of France and the consequent expansion of credit controlled by the Bank. As regards Britain he was concerned to refute Ricardo's theory that income from land necessarily declined unless there was an increase in the price of corn. He considered that this was demonstrably untrue in the case of Britain during the previous fifty years and that the progress of science and industry could reverse the natural tendencies that would lessen incomes.

During the whole of 1851 Marx read voraciously. In January he was studying books on precious metals, money and credit; in February, the economic writings of Hume and Locke, and more books on money; in March, Ricardo, Adam Smith and books on currencies; in April, Ricardo again and books on money; in May, Carey, Malthus, and principles of economics; in June, value, wealth and economics; in July, literature on the factory system and agricultural incomes; in August, population, colonisation and the economics of the Roman

---

[1] *MEW* xxix 47.
[2] W. Liebknecht, *Karl Marx, Biographical Memoirs*, p. 59. For Wolff, cf. *MEW* xxix 225.
[3] *MEW* xxviii 116.   [4] Ibid. 118.

world; in the autumn, books on banking, agronomy and technology. In all, Marx filled his notebooks with long passages from about eighty authors and read many more. This study was directed towards the completion of his work on economics. Already in January 1851 Engels was urging Marx to 'hurry up with the completion and publication of your Economics'.[1] By April Marx wrote:

> I am so far advanced that in five weeks I will be through with the whole economic shit. And that done, I will work over my Economics at home and throw myself into another science in the Museum. I am beginning to be tired of it. Basically, this science has made no further progress since A. Smith and D. Ricardo, however much has been done in individual and often very subtle researches.[2]

The book was eagerly awaited by Marx's friends. In May Lassalle wrote: 'I have heard that your Economics will at last see the light of day. . . . I am burning to contemplate on my desk the giant three-volume work of the Ricardo-turned-socialist and Hegel-turned economist.'[3] Engels, however, who knew his friend well, declared that 'as long as you still have not read a book that you think important, you do not get down to writing'.[4] In June, however, Marx was as sanguine as ever, writing to Weydemeyer: 'I am slogging away mostly from nine in the morning until seven in the evening. The stuff I am working on has so many damned ramifications that with every effort I shall not be able to finish for 6–8 weeks.'[5] Although he realised that 'one must at some point break off forcibly',[6] in July 1851 Proudhon's new book *The General Idea of Revolution in the Nineteenth Century* came into his hands and he immediately diverted his energies into criticising its contents. Despite its anti-Jacobinism, Proudhon's book appeared to Marx to deal only with the symptoms of capitalism and not with its essence.

However, by October Freiligrath and Pieper (who was travelling in Germany at the time) had interested the publisher Löwenthal in Marx's work. Marx's scheme comprised three volumes: 'A Critique of Economics', 'Socialism', and a 'History of Economic Thought'. Löwenthal wished to begin with the last volume and see how it sold.

[1] *MEW* xxvii 171.   [2] Ibid. 228.
[3] F. Lassalle, *Nachgelassene Briefe und Schriften*, ed. G. Mayer (Stuttgart, 1921) iii 23f.
[4] *MEW* xxvii 233 f.   [5] Ibid. 560.   [6] Ibid.

Engels urged Marx to accept this proposal, but to expand the History into two volumes:

> After this would come the Socialists as the third volume – the fourth being the Critique – what would be left of it – and the famous Positive, what you 'really' want. . . . For people of sufficient intelligence, the indications in the first volumes – the Anti-Proudhon and the *Manifesto* – will suffice to put them on the right track. The mass of buyers and readers will lose any interest in the 'History' if the great mystery is already revealed in the first volume. They will say, like Hegel in the Phenomenology: I have read the 'Preface' and that's where the general idea can be found.[1]

Advising Marx to make the book a long one by padding out the 'History', Engels told him bluntly: 'Show a little commercial sense this time.'[2] In early December came Bonaparte's *coup d'état* which made Engels anticipate difficulties with Löwenthal, and though Marx stayed in contact with the publisher until well into the following year, nothing came of the negotiations. Even Kinkel was eager to get a 'positive foundation' from Marx's 'Economics' and Lassalle proposed the founding of a company that would issue shares to finance the publication; but Marx doubted the success of the venture and anyway did not wish to make public his lack of resources. In January 1852 he wrote asking Weydemeyer to find him a publisher in America 'because of the failure in Germany'.[3] By this time he had already abandoned work on his 'Economics'. He worked on his notebooks for a short period in the summer of 1852 and, as a last hope, submitted to the publisher Brockhaus the project of a book to be entitled *Modern Economic Literature in England from 1830 to 1852*. Brockhaus rejected it; and Marx, under the pressures of poverty, work for the Cologne Communist Trial and increasing journalistic commitments, abandoned his 'Economics' for several years.

V. JOURNALISM

'The continual newspaper muck annoys me. It takes a lot of time, disperses my efforts and in the final analysis is nothing. However independent one wishes to be, one is still dependent on the paper and its public especially if, as I do, one receives cash payment. Purely scientific works are something completely different. . . .'[4] This was

---

[1] *MEW* xxvii 373 f.   [2] Ibid. 375.   [3] *MEW* xxviii 486.   [4] Ibid. 592.

Marx's view of his journalism in October 1853 when he had already
been writing for the *New York Daily Tribune* for a year. The invitation to
write for the newspaper had come from its managing editor, Charles
Dana. Dana had a strong and independent personality: brought up by
uncles on the bankruptcy of his father and the death of his mother, he
entered Harvard on his own merits, but was forced by lack of means to
leave after a year. In 1841 he joined the colony at Brook Farm, which
adopted Fourierism and became a 'phalanstery' while he was there,
and was one of its most effective members. When the 'phalanstery' was
destroyed by fire, Dana was engaged by Horace Greeley as editor of the
New York Daily Tribune. The *Tribune*, founded in 1841, was an extraordinarily influential paper and the *Weekly Tribune*, composed of selections
from the daily editions, had a circulation of 200,000 throughout
America. The policies advocated by the paper and inspired by Greeley
were surprisingly radical: it gave much space to Fourierist ideas,
favoured prohibition and protection (at least as a short-time measure)
and opposed the death penalty and slavery. This rather curious mixture of causes often aroused Marx's contempt:

> The *Tribune* is of course trumpeting Carey's book with all its might.
> Both indeed have this in common, that under the guise of Sismon-
> dian philantrhopic socialistic anti-industrialism they represent the
> Protectionists, i.e., the industrial bourgeoisie of America. This also
> explains the secret of why the *Tribune* in spite of all its 'isms' and
> socialistic humbug can be the 'leading journal' in the United States.[1]

Dana had met Marx in Cologne in 1848 and been very impressed. In
August 1851 he asked Marx to become one of the *Tribune*'s eighteen
foreign correspondents and write a series of articles on contemporary
events in Germany. Marx, who was still thinking of finishing his
'Economics' and could not yet write good English, wrote to Engels in
the same letter that told him of the *Tribune*'s offer: 'If you can manage
to let me have an article on the German situation written in English
by Friday morning, that would be a great beginning.'[2] A week later
he wrote: 'In the matter of the *New York Tribune*, you must help me
now as I have my hands full with my "Economics". Write a series of
articles on Germany, from 1848 onwards. Witty and straightforward.
The gentlemen in the foreign department are very outspoken.'[3]
Engels complied and the first article appeared in the *Tribune* in October.

[1] Ibid., 226.   [2] *MEW* xxvii 296.   [3] Ibid. 314.

In all, eighteen articles (all by Engels) were published and were a great success. 'It may perhaps give you pleasure to know that [your articles] are read with satisfaction by a considerable number of persons, and are widely reproduced.'[1] The secret of the authorship was very well kept and for years the articles were reprinted, under the title *Revolution and Counter-Revolution in Germany*, with Marx as their author.[2]

In April 1852 Dana asked Marx to write regularly for the *Tribune* on English affairs. Marx wrote in German and sent the manuscript to Engels to be translated. In January 1853, however, he wrote to Engels: 'For the first time I've risked writing an article for Dana in English.' During the same year, as relations with Russia became tense, Marx enlarged his subject-matter and was soon writing about all aspects of world politics. His articles were highly appreciated and in January 1853 his fee was increased to £2 per article. A contemporary writer described Dana as regularly 'plunged in the reading of "Karl Marx" or "An American in Paris"'. At the beginning of 1854 Marx received through Dana an offer from an American magazine for articles on the history of German philosophy from Kant onwards. The articles were to be 'sarcastic and amusing' and yet to contain 'nothing which would hurt the religious feelings of the country'.[3] Marx wrote to Engels that if they were together it might be possible but 'alone I would not wish it',[4] and the matter was not pursued. In the same year, relations between Marx and the *Tribune* became strained: Dana often altered Marx's articles and sometimes took the first paragraphs of an article to serve as an editorial, printing the rest as a separate and anonymous article. In all, 165 of the *Tribune*'s editorials were taken from Marx's articles, though in fact Dana preferred the articles that (unknown to him) had been written by Engels. Marx insisted that either all or none of the articles should be signed and after 1855 they were all printed anonymously. During 1853 the *Tribune* printed eighty of Marx's articles and about the same number in 1854, but only forty in 1855 and twenty-four in 1856. At the beginning of 1857, Marx threatened to

[1] For the references of Marx's correspondence with Dana, see H. Draper, 'Marx, Engels and the *New American Cyclopaedia*', *Études de Marxologie* (1968).

[2] The articles have been republished under Marx's name by Allen & Unwin as recently as 1971. The back of the book has a quotation from a review which reads: 'Excellent specimens of that marvellous gift of Marx . . . of apprehending clearly the character, the significance and the necessary consequences of great historical events at a time when these events are actually in the course of taking place.' The author of the quotation is given as Engels.

[3] *MEW* xxviii 323.   [4] Ibid.

write for another paper since the *Tribune*, whose panslavist tendencies were becoming more pronounced, was printing so few of his articles: Dana thereupon agreed to pay him for one article a week, whether printed or not.

In April 1857 Dana invited Marx to contribute to the *New American Cyclopaedia*. The *Cyclopaedia* was the idea of George Ripley, a friend of Dana's since Brook Farm and literary editor of the *Tribune*. It eventually comprised sixteen volumes, had more than 300 contributors and was a tremendous success. A strict objectivity was aimed at, and Dana wrote to Marx that his articles should not give evidence of any partiality, either on political, religious or philosophical questions. Although Engels saw in Dana's proposition 'the opportunity we have been waiting for for so long to get your head above water'[1] and constructed schemes for getting a number of collaborators together, this proved impossible. Marx was asked to do articles mainly on military history and was severely handicapped when Engels fell ill with glandular trouble. He could give no plausible explanation for the embarrassing delays and was reduced to pretending that the articles had been lost in the post. Most of his contributions were written in 1857–58, but he continued to send a few until the end of 1960. At two dollars a page it was a useful source of income. The reason for the end of Marx's collaboration is not known. In all, sixty-seven Marx-Engels articles were published in the *Cyclopaedia*, fifty-one of them written by Engels, though Marx did a certain amount of research for them in the British Museum.

By the end of 1857 the commercial crisis had compelled the *Tribune* to dismiss all its foreign correspondents apart from Marx and one other; and in 1861 Greeley, disturbed by Marx's views, asked Dana to sack him also. Dana refused, but the publication of further articles by him was suspended for several months. A few were published at the end of 1861 and the beginning of 1862, but in March 1862 Dana wrote to Marx that the Civil War had come to occupy all the space in the newspaper and asked him to send no more articles. In all the *Tribune* published 487 articles from Marx, 350 written by him, 125 written by Engels (mostly on military matters) and twelve written in collaboration.

Marx's articles were not merely a means of earning his living: in spite of his low opinion of his own work, he consistently produced

[1] *MEW* xix 126.

highly talented pieces of journalism and was, in the words of the *Tribune*'s editor, 'not only one of the most highly valued, but one of the best-paid contributors attached to the journal'.[1] Marx was far removed from the conventional sources of news and so made much more use of official reports, statistics, and so on, than the majority of journalists. In addition he managed to tie a large number of his articles in with his 'serious' research, which gave them added depth. Some of his press articles on India, for example, were incorporated almost verbatim into *Capital*. Considering the strong views he held, his articles were remarkably detached and objective. In many areas – opposition to reactionary European governments, for example – he saw eye to eye with the *Tribune* and could express himself forcefully, but where there was a divergence he contented himself with the straight facts.[2]

Although Marx started writing exclusively on England (about which he was exceptionally well informed), by 1853 he was dealing with Europe too, where the dominant topic was the approach of the Crimean War. Here he was concerned broadly to defend the values of Western European civilisation, as expressed in the 'bourgeois' revolutionary movements of 1789 and later, against the 'asiatic barbarism' of Russia. His almost pathological hatred of Russia led him to his bizarre view of Palmerston as a tool of Russian diplomacy and prompted an 'exposure', in a series of articles, of Palmerstonian duplicity.[3] Some of these articles were written for the *Free Press*, run by David Urquhart, a romantic conservative politician whose Russophobe views Marx characterised as 'subjectively reactionary' but 'objectively revolutionary'.[4] In writing for the Press, Marx was particularly anxious to combat Herzen's faith in the socialist vocation of Russia and the writings of his old friend and colleague Bruno Bauer who saw Russian absolutism as the rebirth of Roman statecraft, the incarnation of a living religious principle as opposed to the hollow democracies of the West. This was the one point on which Dana was critical of Marx, considering his attitude to France and Russia as exhibiting 'too German a tone of feeling for an American newspaper'.[5]

---

[1] C. Dana to Marx, *MEW* xxiv 479.

[2] See, in general, H. Christman, *The American Journalism of Marx and Engels* (New York, 1966).

[3] See K. Marx, *Secret Diplomatic History of the Eighteenth Century*, ed. L. Hutchison (London, 1970).

[4] Marx to Lassalle, *MEW* xxx 547.

[5] C. Dana to Marx, *MEW* xiv 679. See further K. Marx and F. Engels, *The Russian*

Marx also devoted a considerable number of articles to the Far East and particularly India. In general he regarded the phenomenon of colonialism as inevitable since capitalism had to encompass the whole world before it could be overthrown. Like industrialisation in the West, it was both progressive and immensely destructive. He wrote: 'Britain has to fulfil a double mission in India: one destructive, the other regenerating – the annihilation of old Asiatic Society, and the laying of the material foundation of Western Society in Asia.'[1] This was particularly since, in Marx's view, Asia had no history of its own. The reason for this lay in a mode of production different to that of the West:[2] the necessity of providing vast public works to achieve satisfactory irrigation had led to a highly centralised government built on a substructure of self-contained villages and the entire absence of private property in land. The only changes brought about in India were those caused by invaders, the most recent and fundamental changes being those wrought by British capital, and these, although of no benefit to Britain, would bring India under the general laws of capitalist development.[3]

Menace to Europe, ed. Blackstock and Hoselitz (London, 1953); K. Marx and F. Engels, *Die Russische Kommune*, ed. M. Rubel (Munich, 1972).

[1] K. Marx, 'The Future of British Rule in India', *MESW* I 352.

[2] For Marx's views on this 'Asiatic' mode of production, see G. Lichtheim, 'Marx and the Asiatic Mode of Production', *St Anthony's Papers* (1963), and the literature there referred to.

[3] See further, *Karl Marx on Colonialism and Modernization*, ed. S. Avineri (New York, 1968). The excellent edition K. Marx and F. Engels, *The Collected Writings in the New York Daily Tribune*, ed. Ferguson and O'Neil (New York 1973), contains a wealth of detail on the publishing history.

6

The 'Economics'

> You can believe me that seldom has a book been written
> under more difficult circumstances, and I could write a
> secret history that would uncover an infinite amount of
> worry, trouble and anxiety.
>
> Jenny Marx to Kugelmann, Andreas, *Briefe*, p. 193

I. THE 'GRUNDRISSE' AND 'CRITIQUE OF POLITICAL ECONOMY'

IN 1857 the economic crisis that Marx had so often predicted did in
fact occur and moved him to a frantic attempt to bring his economic
studies to some sort of conclusion. The first mention of this in his
correspondence is in a letter to Engels of December 1857 where he
says: 'I am working madly through the nights on a synthesis of my
economic studies so that, before the deluge, I shall at least have the
outlines clear.'[1] A month later he was driven to taking a long course
of medicine and admitted that 'I had overdone my night-time labours,
which were accompanied on the one side only by a glass of lemonade
but on the other by an immense amount of tobacco.'[2]

He was also composing an extremely detailed day-to-day diary on
events during the crisis. In fact the 'synthesis' that Marx speaks of had
already been begun in August 1857 with the composition of a General
Introduction. This Introduction, some thirty pages in length, tentative in tone and incomplete, discussed the problem of method in the
study of economics and attempted to justify the unhistorical order of
the sections in the work that was to follow. The *Introduction* was left
unpublished because, as Marx said two years later, 'on closer reflection
any anticipation of results still to be proved appears to me to be dis-

---

[1] Marx to Engels, *MEW* XXIX 225. The title, *Grundrisse* (which was to be one of
Marx's major works), is no more than the German term for 'outlines'.
[2] Marx to Engels, *MEW* XXIX 259 f.

turbing, and the reader who on the whole desires to follow me must be resolved to ascend from the particular to the general.[1]

In the first of its three sections – entitled 'Production in General' – Marx defined the subject of his inquiry as 'the socially-determined production of individuals'.[2] He rejected the starting point of Smith, Ricardo and Rousseau who began with isolated individuals outside society: 'production by isolated individuals outside society . . . is as great an absurdity as the idea of the development of language without individuals living together and talking to one another'.[3] Marx then pointed out that it was important to try to isolate the general factors common to all production in order not to ignore the essential differences between epochs. Modern economists – like J. S. Mill – were guilty of such ignorance when they tried to depict modern bourgeois relations of production as immutable laws of society. Marx cited two examples: thinkers such as Mill tended to jump from the tautology that there was no such thing as production without property to the presupposition that a particular form of property – *private* property – was basic; whereas history showed that it was common property that was basic. Secondly, there was a tendency to suppose that the legal system under which contemporary production took place was based on eternal principles without realising that 'every form of production creates its own legal relations'.[4] Marx summed up his first section with the words: 'All the stages of production have certain characteristics in common which we generalise in thought; but the so-called general conditions of production are nothing but abstract conceptions which do not go to make up any real stage in the history of production.'[5]

The second section bore the title 'The General Relation of Production to Distribution, Exchange and Consumption'. Here Marx was anxious to refute the view that the four economic activities – production, distribution, exchange and consumption – could be treated in isolation from each other. He began by claiming that production was, in a sense, identical to consumption in that one talked of productive consumption and consumptive production; that each was in fact a means of bringing the other about; and that each moulded the forms of existence of its counterpart. Marx similarly denied that distribution

[1] *MESW* I 360. This Introduction was first published by Kautsky in 1903.
[2] *Marx's Grundrisse*, ed. D. McLellan (London and New York, 1971) p. 16.
[3] Ibid., p. 18.   [4] Ibid., p. 21.   [5] Ibid., p. 22.

formed an independent sphere standing alongside, and outside, production. This view could not be maintained since 'distribution, as far as the individual is concerned, naturally appears as a law established by society determining his position in the sphere of production within which he produces, and thus antedating production'.[1] External aggression or internal revolution also seemed, by their distribution of property, to antedate and determine production. Similarly with exchange, which seemed to Marx to be a constituent part of production. 'The result we arrive at', Marx concluded, 'is not that production, distribution, exchange and consumption are identical, but that they are all members of one entity, different aspects of one unit.'[2]

The third section, entitled 'The Method of Political Economy', is even more abstract, yet very important for understanding Marx's approach. He wished to establish that the correct method of discussing economics was to start from simple theoretical concepts like value and labour and then to proceed from them to the more complex but observable entities such as population or classes. The reverse was the characteristic approach of the seventeenth century; but eighteenth-century thinkers had followed 'the method of advancing from the abstract to the concrete' – which was 'manifestly the scientifically correct method'.[3]

Marx then took money and labour as examples of the simple, abstract concepts with which he wished to start his analysis. He claimed that both these only attained their full complexity in bourgeois society; and thus only someone thinking in the context of bourgeois society could hope fully to understand pre-capitalist economics, just as 'the anatomy of the human being is the key to the anatomy of the ape'.[4] Marx continued: 'It would thus be impracticable and wrong to arrange the economic categories in the order in which they were the determining factors in the course of history. Their order of sequence is rather determined by the relations which they bear to one another in modern bourgeois society.'[5] He then outlined in five sections the provisional plan for an extensive work on Economics, and concluded with a fascinating discussion of an apparent difficulty in the materialist approach to history: why was Greek art so much appreciated in the nineteenth century when the socio-economic background which produced it was so different? Marx produced no direct answer. The

[1] Ibid., p. 29.   [2] Ibid., p. 33.   [3] Ibid., p. 34.
[4] Ibid., p. 39.   [5] Ibid., p. 42.

manuscript breaks off by simply posing the following question: 'Why should the childhood of human society, where it has obtained its most beautiful development, not exert an eternal charm as an age that will never return?'[1]

The plan of the proposed book was outlined at the end of the Introduction:

1. The general abstract characterisations that can more or less be applied to all types of society.
2. The categories that constitute the internal structure of bourgeois society and which serve as a basis for the fundamental classes. Capital, wage-labour, landed property. Their relationship to each other. Town and country. The three large social classes. The exchange between them. Circulation. Credit (private).
3. Synthesis of bourgeois society in the shape of the state. The state considered in itself. 'Unproductive' classes. Taxes. Public debt. Public credit. Population. Colonies. Emigration.
4. The international relations of production. International division of labour. International exchange. Exports and imports. Exchange rates.
5. The world market and crises.[2]

The same plan, in a simpler form, was reiterated in the *Preface* (published in 1859) to his *Critique of Political Economy*: 'Capital, landed property, wage-labour; state, foreign trade, world market'.[3]

The surviving manuscripts (written in the six months from October 1857 to March 1858) have become known as the *Grundrisse* from the first word of their German title *Grundrisse der Kritik der politischen Oekonomie* ('Outlines of a Critique of Political Economy').[4] They do not cover at all equally the sections of the above table of contents. They are obviously for the most part a draft of the first section of the work. The whole is divided into two parts: the first on money, and the second, much longer, part on capital; the latter is divided into three sections on the production of capital, circulation and conversion of surplus-value into profit. However, these economic discussions are

[1] Ibid., p. 45. Further on the Introduction, see the excellent commentary in K. Marx, *Texts on Method*, ed. T. Carver (Oxford, 1974).   [2] Ibid., pp. 42 f.

[3] K. Marx, 'Preface to Critique of Political Economy', *MESW* I 361.

[4] It should be noted that this title is not Marx's, but stems from the first editors of his manuscripts. It could be misleading in that 'Critique of Political Economy' was the subtitle of *Capital* and, as is shown later, the *Grundrisse* is much more than a rough draft of *Capital*.

intertwined with wide-ranging digressions on such subjects as the individual and society, the nature of labour, the influence of automation on society, problems of increasing leisure and the abolition of the division of labour, the nature of alienation in the higher stages of capitalist society, the revolutionary nature of capitalism and its inherent universality, and so on. It is these digressions that give the *Grundrisse* its primary importance by showing that it is a rough draft for a work of enormous proportions; what Marx later presented to the world in his volume *Capital* covered only a fraction of the ground that had been marked out in the *Grundrisse*. Sections devoted to such topics as foreign trade and the world market show that Marx was led to sketch out to some extent the fundamental themes of the other five books of his 'Economics'. In Marx's own words: 'In the manuscript (which would make a thick book if printed) everything is topsy-turvy and there is much that is intended for later parts.'[1]

Like virtually all of Marx's major writings, the *Grundrisse* begins with a critique of someone else's ideas: he evidently found it easier to work out his own views by attacking those of others. Thus the first few pages contain a critique of the reformist economists, Carey and Bastiat, brilliantly portrayed as respectively embodying the vices (and virtues) of the mid-nineteenth-century 'Yankees' and the disciples of Proudhon. After ten pages or so there was no further discussion of the theories of Carey and Bastiat – Marx commenting acidly: 'It is impossible to pursue this nonsense further.'[2] Having sharpened his critical faculties by these attacks on minor theorists, he then proceeded to carve out his own path. The jumbled nature of these manuscript notes, the variety of subjects discussed and the tremendous compression of style – all make it difficult to give a satisfactory brief account of their contents and virtually impossible to paraphrase them. The

---

[1] Marx to Engels, *MEW* xxix 330. The schema in six parts given in the *General Introduction* and the *Preface* is plainly not the same as that of *Capital*, Book I, published in 1867. Karl Kautsky concluded that Marx must have changed the plan of his projected work on Economics. This was certainly the received opinion until the publication of the *Grundrisse*, which only emerged from the Moscow archives in 1939–41. However, Marx's correspondence with Lassalle and the Index to the first volume of his 'Economics' contained in the *Grundrisse* shows that Marx had in mind the plan of the three volumes of *Capital* as early as 1857. The change was not one of methodology but merely one of size. This point is amplified in the rest of this chapter. See further the Basel dissertation of O. Morf, *Das Verhältnis von Wissenschaftstheorie und Wirtschaftsgeschichte* (1951) pp. 75 ff.; also M. Rubel's Introduction to K. Marx, *Oeuvres*, II (Paris, 1968). See the diagram on p. 458.

[2] *Marx's Grundrisse*, p. 58.

Grundrisse is a vast uncharted terrain: as yet the explorers have been few and even they have only penetrated the periphery. However, some things stand out at first glance.

Firstly, there is in both thought and style a continuity with the 1844 Manuscripts most noticeable in the influence of Hegel on both writings. The concepts of alienation, objectification, appropriation, man's dialectical relationship to nature and his generic or social nature all recur in the *Grundrisse*. Early in these 1858 manuscripts Marx offered the following comments on the economic ideas of his day, comments entirely reminiscent of his remarks on the 'reification' of money in 1844: 'The economists themselves say that men accord to the object (money) a trust that they would not accord to each other as persons. ... Money can only possess a social property because individuals have alienated their own social relationships by embodying them in a thing.'[1] Or later, and more generally:

> But if capital appears as the product of labour, the product of labour also appears as capital – no more as a simple product, not as exchangeable goods, but as *capital*; objectified labour becomes mastery, has command over living labour. It appears equally to be the result of labour, that its product appears as alien property, an independent mode of existence opposed to living labour, an equally autonomous value; that the product of labour, objectified labour, has acquired its own soul from living labour and has established itself opposite living labour as an *alien force*. Considered from the standpoint of labour, labour thus appears to be active in the production process in such a way that it seems to reject its realisation in objective contradictions as alien reality, and that it puts itself in the position of an unsubstantial labour capacity endowed only with needs against this reality which is estranged from it and which belongs, not to it, but to others; that it establishes its own reality not as an entity of its own, but merely as an entity for others, and thus also as a mere entity of others, or other entity, against itself.[2]

In this respect, the most striking passage of the *Grundrisse* is the draft plan for Marx's projected 'Economics' which is couched in language that might have come straight out of Hegel's *Logic*.[3]

---

[1] *Grundrisse* (1953 ed.) p. 78.   [2] *Marx's Grundrisse*, p. 100.
[3] See *Grundrisse* (1953 ed.) pp. 162 ff. and particularly the schema on pp. 186 ff. Since these sections are typical of large parts of the *Grundrisse*, several of the accounts

Yet, there is also a striking difference. In 1844 Marx had read some classical economists but had not yet integrated this knowledge into his critique of Hegel. As a result, the '1844 Manuscripts' (otherwise known as the 'Paris Manuscripts') fall into two separate halves as illustrated by the title given them by their first editors: the 'Economic and Philosophical Manuscripts'. By 1857–58 Marx had assimilated both Ricardo and Hegel (there are, interestingly, no references to Feuerbach in the *Grundrisse*), and he was in a position to make his own synthesis. In Lassalle's words, he was 'a Hegel turned economist, a Ricardo turned socialist'.[1] The much richer content in terms of economic history means that the *Grundrisse*, while continuing the themes central to the '1844 Manuscripts', treats them in a much more sophisticated way than was possible before Marx had achieved a synthesis of his ideas on philosophy and economics. Thus to take the '1844 Manuscripts' as his central work – as many interpreters have done – is to exaggerate their significance.

As regards economics, the *Grundrisse* contains the first elaboration of Marx's mature theory. There are two key changes of emphasis. Firstly, instead of analysing the market mechanisms of exchange (as he had done in 1844), he now started from a consideration of *production*. Secondly, he now said that what the worker sold is not his labour, but his *labour-power*. It was a combination of these two views that gave rise to the doctrine of surplus-value. For, according to Marx, surplus-value was not created by exchange but by the fact that the development of the means of production under capitalism enabled the capitalist to enjoy the use-value of the worker's labour-power and with it to make products that far exceeded the mere exchange-value of labour-power which amounted to no more than what was minimal for the worker's subsistence. In fact, virtually all the elements of Marx's economic theory were elaborated in the *Grundrisse*. Since, however, these elements were to be dealt with at greater length in *Capital*, the *Grundrisse* is more

---

of Marx's thought produced by scholars of the older generation – Daniel Bell, 'The Debate on Alienation', in *Revisionism* (1962); Sidney Hook, *From Hegel to Marx* (2nd ed. 1962); Lewis Feuer, 'What is alienation? The career of a concept', *New Politics* (1962) – are in a need of revision. It was the thesis of these writers that there was a radical break between the Young and the Old Marx; and the major proof of this was held to be the absence in the later writings of the concept of alienation so central to the earlier works. In addition, the writers who have wished to minimise the influence of Hegel on Marx will have to revise their ideas.

[1] Lassalle to Marx, 12 May 1851.

interesting for the discussions that were not taken up again in the completed fragments of his vast enterprise.

These discussions took place around the central theme of man's alienation in capitalist society and the possibilities of creating an unalienated – communist – society. What was new in Marx's picture of alienation in the *Grundrisse* was that it attempted to be firmly rooted in history. Capital, as well as being obviously an 'alienating' force, had fulfilled a very *positive* function. Within a short space of time it had developed the productive forces enormously, had replaced natural needs by ones historically created and had given birth to a world market. After the limitations of the past, capital was the turning point to untold riches in the future:

> The universal nature of this production with its generality creates an estrangement of the individual from himself and others, but also for the first time the general and universal nature of his relationships and capacities. At early stages of development the single individual appears to be more complete, since he has not yet elaborated the wealth of his relationships, and has not established them as powers and autonomous social relationships, that are opposed to himself. It is as ridiculous to wish to return to that primitive abundance as it is to believe in the necessity of its complete depletion. The bourgeois view has never got beyond opposition to this romantic outlook and thus will be accompanied by it, as a legitimate antithesis, right up to its blessed end.[1]

The ideas produced by capitalism were as transitory as capitalism itself: here Marx formulated his most succinct critique of 'classical' liberal principles. Pointing out that free competition was bound eventually to hamper the development of capitalism – however necessary it might have been at the outset, Marx alluded to

> the absurdity of considering free competition as being the final development of human liberty.... The development of what free competition is, is the only rational answer to the deification of it by the middle-class prophets, or its bedevilment by the socialists. If it is said that, within the limits of free competition, individuals by following their pure self-interest realise their social or rather their general interest, this means merely that they exert pressure upon one

[1] *Marx's Grundrisse*, p. 71.

another under the conditions of capitalist production and that collision between them can only again give rise to the conditions under which their interaction took place. Moreover, once the illusion that competition is the ostensible absolute form of free individuality disappears, this proves that the conditions of competition, i.e. production founded on capital, are already felt and thought of as a barrier, as indeed they already are and will increasingly become so. The assertion that free competition is the final form of the development of productive forces, and thus of human freedom, means only that the domination of the middle class is the end of the world's history – of course quite a pleasant thought for yesterday's parvenus![1]

The key to the understanding of this ambivalent nature of capitalism – and the possibilities it contained for an unalienated society – was the notion of *time*. 'All economics', said Marx, 'can be reduced in the last analysis to the economics of time.'[2] The profits of capitalism were built on the creation of surplus work-time, yet on the other hand the wealth of capitalism emancipated man from manual labour and gave him increasing access to free time. Capital was itself a 'permanent revolution':

> Pursuing this tendency, capital has pushed beyond national boundaries and prejudices, beyond deification of nature and the inherited, self-sufficient satisfaction of existing needs confined within well-defined bounds, and the reproduction of the traditional way of life.
>
> It is destructive of all this, and permanently revolutionary, tearing down all obstacles that impede the development of productive forces, the expansion of needs, the diversity of production and the exploitation and exchange of natural and intellectual forces.[3]

But in Marx's eyes, these very characteristics of capitalism entailed its dissolution. Its wealth was based on the introduction of machinery followed by that of automation (Marx's foresight here is extraordinary); and this in turn led to an ever-growing contradiction between the decreasing role played by labour in the production of social wealth and the necessity for capital to appropriate surplus labour. Capital was was thus both hugely creative and hugely wasteful:

> On the one hand it calls into life all the forces of science and nature,

[1] Ibid., p. 31.   [2] Ibid. p. 76.   [3] Ibid., pp. 94 f.

as well as those of social co-operation and commerce, in order to create wealth which is relatively independent of the labour time utilised. On the other hand, it attempts to measure the vast social forces thus created in terms of labour time, and imprisons them within the narrow limits that are required in order to retain the value already created *as* value. Productive forces and social relationships – the two different sides of the development of social individuality – appear only as a means for capital, and are for it only a means to enable it to produce from its own cramped foundation. But in fact they are the material conditions that will shatter this foundation.[1]

Passages like this show clearly enough that what seem to be purely economic doctrines (such as the labour theory of value) are not economic doctrines in the sense that, say, Keynes or Schumpeter would understand them. Inevitably, then, to regard Marx as just one among several economists is somewhat to falsify and misunderstand his intentions. For, as Marx himself proclaimed as early as 1844, economics and ethics were inextricably linked. The *Grundrisse* shows that this is as true of his later writings as it is of the earlier work.

With the immense growth in the productive forces created by capitalism, there was, according to Marx, a danger that the forces guiding human development would be taken over entirely by machines to the exclusion of human beings: 'Science thus appears, in the machine, as something alien and exterior to the worker; and living labour is subsumed under objectified labour which acts independently. The worker appears to be superfluous insofar as his action is not determined by the needs of capital.'[2] In the age of automation, science itself could become the biggest factor making for alienation:

The worker's activity, limited to a mere abstraction, is determined and regulated on all sides by the movement of the machinery, not the other way round. The knowledge that obliges the inanimate

---

[1] Ibid., p. 143.
[2] Ibid., p. 135. In his correspondence with Engels, Marx says that he considered the primitive model of an automatic machine to be a clock. Marx derived a lot of his information on automatic spinning machinery (as well as other aspects of factory life) from Engels to whom he often turned for help in these practical questions. He confessed to his friend: 'I understand the mathematical laws, but the simplest technical reality, where observation is necessary, is as difficult for me as for the greatest ignoramus. . . .' (*MEW* xxx 320).

parts of the machine, through their construction, to work appropriately as an automaton, does not exist in the consciousness of the worker, but acts through the machine upon him as an alien force, as the power of the machine itself.[1]

Yet this enormous expansion of the productive forces did not necessarily bring with it the alienation of the individual: it afforded the opportunity for society to become composed of 'social' or 'universal' individuals – beings very similar to the 'all-round' individuals referred to in the '1844 Manuscripts'. This is how Marx describes the transition from individual to social production:

> Production based on exchange value therefore falls apart, and the immediate material productive process finds itself stripped of its impoverished, antagonistic form. Individuals are then in a position to develop freely. It is no longer a question of reducing the necessary labour time of society to a minimum. The counterpart of this reduction is that all members of society can develop their artistic, scientific, etc., education, thanks to the free time now available to all. . . .
> Bourgeois economists are so bogged down in their traditional ideas of the historical development of society in a single stage, that the necessity of the *objectification* of the social forces of labour seems to them inseparable from the necessity of its *alienation* in relation to living labour.[2]

It is noteworthy that here (as throughout the *Grundrisse*) there is no allusion to the agent of this transformation – namely, the revolutionary activity of the proletariat.

The 'universal' individual – a notion that Marx returns to almost *ad nauseam* in the *Grundrisse* – is at the centre of his vision of utopia; the millennial strain is no less clear here than in the passage in the '1844 Manuscripts' describing communism as 'the solution to the riddle of history'. The universal tendency inherent in capital, said Marx, created

> as a basis, a development of productive forces – of wealth in general – whose powers and tendencies are of a general nature, and at the same time a universal commerce, and thus world trade as a basis. The basis as the possibility of the universal development of indivi-

[1] *Marx's Grundrisse*, p. 133.   [2] Ibid., p. 151.

duals; the real development of individuals from this basis as the constant abolition of each limitation conceived of *as* a limitation and not as a sacred boundary. The universality of the individual not as thought or imagined, but as the universality of his real and ideal relationships. Man therefore becomes able to understand his own history as a *process*, and to conceive of nature (involving also practical control over it) as his own real body. The process of development is itself established and understood as a prerequisite. But it is necessary also and above all that full development of the productive forces should have become a *condition of production*, not that determined *conditions of production* should be set up as a boundary beyond which productive forces cannot develop.[1]

Marx very rarely discussed the form of the future communist society: in his own terms this was reasonably enough – for he would thereby have laid himself open to the charge of 'idealism', the spinning of ideas that had no foundation in reality. But certain passages in the *Grundrisse* give an even better idea than the well-known accounts in the *Communist Manifesto* and the *Critique of the Gotha Programme* of what lay at the heart of Marx's vision. One of the central factors was, of course, time – since the development of the 'universal' individual depended above all on the free time he had at his disposal. Time was of the essence in Marx's ideal of future society:

If we suppose communal production, the determination of time remains, of course, essential. The less time society requires in order to produce wheat, cattle, etc., the more time it gains for other forms of production, material or intellectual. As with a single individual, the universality of its development, its enjoyment and its activity depends on saving time. . . .[2]

Only by the extensive use of machinery was this free time possible. Whereas in the past machinery had been a factor hostile to the worker, in the future its function could be radically altered:

No special sagacity is required in order to understand that, beginning with free labour or wage-labour for example, which arose after the abolition of slavery, machines can only develop in opposition to living labour, as a hostile power and alien property, i.e. they must, as capital, oppose the worker.

[1] Ibid., pp. 121 f.   [2] Ibid., p. 75.

It is equally easy to see that machines do not cease to be agents of social production, once they become, for example, the property of associated workers. But in the first case, their means of distribution (the fact that they do not belong to the workers) is itself a condition of the means of production that is founded on wage-labour. In the second case, an altered means of distribution will derive from an altered new basis of production emerging from the historical process.[1]

Marx rejected Adam Smith's view of work as necessarily an imposition. Nor did he subscribe to Fourier's idea that work could become a sort of game. According to Marx, Smith's view was valid for the labour

which has not yet created the subjective and objective conditions (which it lost when it abandoned pastoral conditions) which make of it attractive labour and individual self-realisation. This does not mean that labour can be made merely a joke, or amusement, as Fourier naïvely expressed it in shop-girl terms. Really free labour, the composing of music for example, is at the same time damned serious and demands the greatest effort. The labour concerned with material production can only have this character if (1) it is of a social nature, (2) it has a scientific character and at the same time is general work, i.e. if it becomes the activity of a subject controlling all the forces of nature in the production process.[2]

Marx envisaged a time when production would depend not on the amount of labour employed but on the general level of science and technology, when wealth would be measured by an increase in production quite disproportionate to the labour-time employed, and when 'man behaves as the supervisor and regulator of the process of production'. Then the true emancipation of mankind would take place:

In this re-orientation what appears as the mainstay of production and wealth is neither the immediate labour performed by the worker nor the time that he works – but the appropriation of his general productive force, his understanding of nature and the mastery of it as a special force; in a word, the development of the social individual.

The theft of others' labour-time upon which wealth depends

[1] Ibid., p. 124.   [2] Ibid.

today seems to be a miserable basis compared with the newly-developed foundation that has been created by heavy industry itself.

As soon as labour, in its direct form, has ceased to be the main source of wealth, then labour-time ceases, and must cease, to be its standard of measurement, and thus exchange-value must cease to be the measurement of use-value. The surplus labour of the masses has ceased to be a condition for the development of wealth in general; in the same way that the non-labour of the few has ceased to be a condition for the development of the powers of the human mind in general.[1]

These extracts obviously cannot give a full picture of the contents of the *Grundrisse*; but they do give a clear impression of Marx's thought at its richest. The nature of the vision that inspired Marx is at least adumbrated: communal production in which the quality of work determined its value; the disappearance of money along with that of exchange value; and an increase in free time affording opportunities for the universal development of the individual. The *Grundrisse* is important not only as a vital element for the understanding and interpretation of Marx's thought. The contemporary relevance of Marx's views on the ambivalent nature of technology is sufficiently obvious.

Thus Marx's thought is best viewed as a continuing meditation on central themes first explored in 1844 – this process culminating in his writings of 1857–58. The continuity between the Manuscripts and the *Grundrisse* is evident. In correspondence Marx himself wrote of the *Grundrisse* as the result of fifteen years of research, 'the best period of my life'.[2] (This particular letter was written in November 1858, exactly fifteen years after Marx's arrival in Paris in November 1843.) He also said in the *Preface* in 1859: 'the total material lies before me in the form of monographs, which were written at widely separated periods, for self-clarification, not for publication, and whose coherent elaboration according to the plan indicated will be dependent on external circumstances'.[3] This can only refer to the 'Paris Manuscripts' of 1844 and the London notebooks of 1850–52. Marx constantly used, and at the same time revised, material from an earlier date (*Capital*, for instance, was written with the aid of his 1843–45 notebooks).

The beginning of the *Grundrisse*'s chapter on capital reproduces

[1] Ibid., p. 142.   [2] Marx to Lassalle, *MEW* xxix 566.
[3] K. Marx, 'Preface to Critique of Political Economy', *MESW* i 361.

almost word for word the passages in the Manuscripts on human need, man as a species-being, the individual as a social being, the idea of nature as (in a sense) man's body, the parallels between religious alienation and economic alienation, and so on. The two works also have in common a utopian and almost millennial strain. One point in particular emphasises this continuity: the *Grundrisse* is as 'Hegelian' as the '1844 Manuscripts'. This is sometimes said to have been a superficial Hegelianism, and a letter from Marx to Engels in January 1858 has often been quoted to justify this: 'In the method it has been of great use to me that by mere accident I have leafed through Hegel's *Logic* – Freiligrath found some volumes that belonged originally to Bakunin and sent me them as a present.'[1] Marx's reading of Hegel may have been accidental; but certainly Hegel's influence on him was profound. Some of the most Hegelian parts of the *Grundrisse* – and particularly the index of the part on capital – were written *before* the receipt of Freiligrath's present. In a note in the *Grundrisse* Marx himself wrote in November 1857, 'later, before going on to another problem, it is necessary to correct the idealist manner of this analysis'.[2] Moreover, while finishing the *Grundrisse* he wrote to Lassalle that Hegel's dialectic was 'without a doubt the last word in all philosophy' but that just because this was so 'it is necessary to free it from the mystical side it has in Hegel'.[3] (A justifiable parallel has sometimes been drawn between the renewal of Marx's interest in Hegel and Lenin's reading of Hegel that preceded the writing of his *Imperialism* and *The State and Revolution*.) To give a further example of the continuity of Marx's thought, reference may be made to the term 'alienation' (which occurs much more in *Capital* than some writers appear to think). In the *Grundrisse* the concept is central to most of the more important passages.

Marx never disowned any of his writings. It is, of course, true that he wrote of his embarrassment when re-reading the *Holy Family*. But this was characteristic: 'it is self-evident', he commented in 1846, 'that an author, if he pursues his research, cannot publish *literally* what he has written six months previously'.[4] Again in 1862, he remarked: 'I find unsatisfactory a work written four weeks before and rewrite it completely.'[5] He stated that even the *Communist Manifesto* was in need of emendation as time went on. Nevertheless he was, for instance,

---

[1] Marx to Engels, *MEW* xxix 260.   [2] *Grundrisse* (1953 ed.) p. 69.
[3] Marx to Lassalle, *MEW* xix 561.   [4] Marx to C. Leske, *MEW* xxvii 449.
[5] Marx to Lassalle, *MEW* xxx 622.

quite willing in 1851 to see reprinted his essays from as long ago as the *Rheinische Zeitung* of 1842. His intellectual development was a process of 'clarifying my own ideas' (to use his own expression),[1] which can neither be split into periods nor treated as a monolith.

By the end of February 1858, Marx's burst of creative effort had come to an end, and he was faced with the (for him) more difficult problem of how to get his 800 manuscript pages into publishable form. Lassalle had offered to act as Marx's literary agent in Berlin. Marx hit upon the idea of publishing his work in several short volumes giving as his reasons that he had neither the time nor the means to work up the whole of his material, that it would thus reach a wider audience, and that it would be easier to find a publisher. At the same time he informed Lassalle of the stage he had reached in his proposed 'Economics' which he described as a 'critique of economic categories or, if you like, a critical description of the system of bourgeois economics'.[2] Three weeks later he informed Lassalle that he was ready to forgo a royalty on the first part if that would make it easier to find a publisher. The first part, he went on, would have to be 'a relative whole' and would contain '1. Value, 2. Money, 3. Capital (Productive Process of Capital; Circulation Process of Capital; the unity of both Capital and Profit, Interest)' – material which in fact comprised the whole of the eventual three volumes of *Capital*. This part would deal in particular with the contradictions between Ricardo's correct treatment of value and his theory of profit, a contradiction which economists would find on closer inspection 'altogether a dirty business'.[3]

By the end of March 1858 Lassalle had found a publisher, Franz Duncker, who was ready to pay Marx a royalty that was – according to Lassalle – considerably better than that obtained by Berlin professors. But in spite of his promise to have the part ready 'by about the end of May'[4] Marx made little progress: he sent Engels a long synopsis of the sections on value and money, but could not manage to complete the one on capital although it was 'the most important thing in this first part'.[5] Marx's liver was again giving him trouble and Jenny wrote to Engels that 'his state is made much worse by mental stress and excitement which, with the signing of the publisher's contract, is naturally daily increasing as it is simply impossible for him to bring his work to a

---

[1] K. Marx, 'Preface to Critique of Political Economy', *MESW* I 364.
[2] Marx to Lassalle, *MEW* xxix 550.   [3] Ibid. 554.   [4] Ibid.
[5] Marx to Engels, *MEW* xxix 318.

finish'.[1] He made no more than a start before retiring to Manchester for the whole of May. On his return he was still looking through his manuscript trying to decide on what to include, but a combination of anxiety and physical illness prevented him doing anything for the next two months.

The chief difficulty that impeded Marx was once again financial. Engels had supposed that Marx's problems were solved once he was installed in the Haverstock Hill house, and he was therefore taken by surprise when Marx wrote that the move had actually worsened the situation: 'I am living a precarious existence and am in a house in which I have invested my little ready cash and where it is impossible to piss one's way through from day to day as in Dean Street; I have no prospects and growing family expenses ... In fact I am in a more parlous situation than five years ago. I'd thought I'd already had all the shit that was coming my way. But no. And the worst is, that this crisis is not temporary.'[2] Engels guaranteed a minimum contribution of £5 a month and Marx struggled on with the income from the *New York Daily Tribune* – to which his contributions were in fact declining as he was so occupied with the *Grundrisse*. He was also contributing regularly to the *New American Cyclopaedia* but – typically – overcalculated his fees and soon found himself in his publisher's debt. His only recourse was to the pawnshop, with the expectation of a crisis at the end of every quarter and the fear of the approach of winter when the coats and other clothes would have to be redeemed. But by July 1858 his financial crisis erupted in full force. He wrote to Engels: 'The situation is now absolutely unbearable.... I am completely disabled as far as work goes, partly because I lose most of my time in useless running around trying to make money and partly (perhaps a result of my feeble physical condition) because my power of intellectual concentration is undermined by domestic problems. My wife's nerves are quite ruined by the filth....'[3] The doctor predicted an inflammation of the brain and recommended that Jenny be sent to the seaside, but even that would not help 'if the spectre of an inevitable and ultimate catastrophe pursues her'.[4] Marx had applied to a loan society but all he had got out of it was a bill for £2 in fees. He enclosed a careful list of his debts compiled by Jenny, who was the one who dealt with the pawnbrokers, and including some still owed to Soho tradesmen, and

---

[1] Jenny Marx to Engels, *MEW* xxix 648.   [2] Marx to Engels, *MEW* xxix 97.
[3] Ibid. 340.   [4] Ibid.

finished: 'I have now made a clean breast of it and I can assure you that it has cost me no little effort. But I must be able to talk at least to one person. I would not wish upon my bitterest enemy to wade through the quagmire in which I have been sitting for the last eight weeks enraged by the additional fact that my intellect has been wrecked by the lousiest of situations and my work capacity completely broken.'[1] Engels came to the rescue once again with a £60 advance and by August Marx had got down to work again.

By mid-September he could say to Engels that his manuscript for the two parts would go off 'in two weeks'.[2] By the end of October he informed Engels curtly that the manuscript would not be ready 'for weeks'. The 'real reason' for this delay, he explained to Lassalle in November, was that 'the material lay before me; it was only a question of the form. But in everything that I wrote I could detect an illness of the liver.'[3] It was important for the style to be good for it represented the result of fifteen years' research and 'the first attempts at a scientific presentation of an important view of social relationships'.[4] By the end of November, however, Jenny was copying a manuscript to which Marx had added a chapter on commodities which was not in his original draft and expanded the section on money. By mid-December that manuscript would soon be ready but 'devil take me if anyone else could have been ready so early with such a lousy liver'.[5] By the end of January the manuscript was in fact ready but could not be sent off 'because I have not even a farthing to buy a stamp and register it'.[6] Marx's previous letter to Engels had continued the shocking *dénouement* to the whole affair: 'The manuscript is about 12 printer's sheets long and – take a grip on yourself – in spite of its title . . . contains NOTHING on Capital.'[7] In other words, Marx had dropped the idea of publishing the second part on Capital simultaneously in spite of his previous insistence to Lassalle that 'this second part must appear simultaneously. The inner consistency makes it necessary and the whole effect depends on it.'[8] Even when the manuscript was despatched, Marx's worries were not at an end: he suspected the authorities in Berlin of having confiscated his parcel and, when Lassalle still had not informed him of its arrival after two weeks, he was 'sick with anxiety'.[1] When

---

[1] Ibid. 343.   [2] Ibid. 355.   [3] Marx to Lassalle, *MEW* XXIX 566.
[4] Ibid.   [5] Marx to Engels, *MEW* XXIX 375.   [6] Ibid. 385.
[7] Ibid. 383.   [8] Marx to Lassalle, *MEW* XXIX 567.
[9] Marx to Engels, *MEW* XXIX 392.

eventually it did arrive, the printing was much too slow for Marx: it took Duncker six weeks to produce the proofs. Even worse, two weeks after Marx had sent off the last corrected proof sheets, the arrival of an unfranked pamphlet by Lassalle, obviously given priority by Duncker, compelled Marx to pawn his last respectable coat to pay the necessary two shillings excess postal charge.

In the manuscript, which was finally published in early June, by far the most valuable part was the Preface which contained as succinct an account of the materialist conception of history as Marx ever produced. Marx opened the Preface with a statement of the scope of his 'Economics' and his progress to date. There followed a short piece of intellectual autobiography in which Marx stressed the importance of his journalistic work for the *Rheinische Zeitung* in giving him an insight into the importance of 'material interests' and 'economic questions'. He then withdrew into his study to examine Hegel's political philosophy. The conclusion of this retreat was that

> legal relations as well as forms of state are to be grasped neither from themselves nor from the so-called general development of the human mind, but rather have their roots in the material conditions of life, the sum total of which Hegel, following the example of the Englishmen and Frenchmen of the eighteenth century, combines under the name of 'civil society', that, however, the anatomy of civil society is to be sought in political economy.[1]

Marx then, in a famous and often quoted passage, summed up the 'guiding thread' of his subsequent studies of political economy. This summary contained four main points:

1. The sum total of relations of production – the way men organised their social production as well as the instruments they used – constituted the real basis of society on which there arose a legal and political superstructure and to which corresponded definite forms of social consciousness. Thus the way men produced their means of subsistence conditioned their whole social, political and intellectual life.
2. At a certain stage in their evolution the forces of production would develop beyond the relations of production and these would act as a fetter. Such a stage inaugurated a period of social revolution.

[1] *MESW* I 362.

3. These productive forces had to develop to the fullest extent possible under the existing relations of production before the old social order would perish.

4. It was possible to pick out the Asiatic, ancient, feudal and modern bourgeois modes of production as progressive epochs in the economic formation of society. There bourgeois relations of production were the last ones to create a divided society and with their end the pre-history of human society would be brought to a close.

Marx added a few more biographical details, described his views as 'the result of conscientious investigation lasting many years'[1] and finished with a quotation from Dante against any intellectual compromise.

The most striking thing about the *Critique of Political Economy* itself – particularly after the alarms and excursions accompanying its writing – is how little substance it contains. Almost half the book consists of a critical exposition, with much quotation, of previous theorists on value and money. The rest is in two sections, the first on commodities and the second on money. Both were rewritten several years later in the first three chapters of *Capital*, the first section being expanded and the second condensed. The first section was the more important, but broke off after enunciating a few basic propositions. Marx began by defining a commodity as 'a means of existence in the broadest sense of the word'[2] and, quoting Aristotle, explained that a commodity had both a use-value and an exchange-value. The concept of use-value was not difficult but there was a problem as to how objects could be made equivalent to each other as exchange-values. The key to this problem was labour: 'Since the exchange-value of commodities, is in fact, nothing but a mutual relation of the exchange-value of individuals – labours which are similar and universal – nothing but a material expression of a specific form of labour, it is a tautology to say that labour is the *only* source of exchange-value and consequently of wealth, insofar as the latter consists of exchange-values.'[3] Marx left unanswered (for the moment) the key question that he himself formulated: 'How does production, based on the determination of exchange-value by labour-time only, lead to the result that the exchange-value

[1] *MESW* I 365.
[2] K. Marx, *Critique of Political Economy*, trans. Stone (Chicago, 1904) p. 20.
[3] Ibid., p. 34.

of labour is less than the exchange-value of its product?'[1] In the second section, on money, Marx went on to investigate 'the particular commodity which ... appears as the specially adopted expression of the exchange-value of all other commodities, the exchange-value of commodities as a particular exclusive commodity'[2] – money; the second section was devoted to examining money as a measure of value and a medium of circulation, with sections on coins, symbols and precious metals. Marx investigated the process of commodities being turned into money to buy further commodities, but there was nothing on capital as such. In the long sections on the history of theories of value, money and circulation, Marx incorporated much of the material that he had collected for the third, 'historical' volume of his 'Economics' in the early 1850s.

In view of its extremely fragmentary nature, it is not surprising that the book had a poor reception. Liebknecht declared that he had never been so disappointed by a book before and even Engels told Marx that the synopsis that he had given him was 'a very abstract abstract'.[3] The Preface was reprinted in *Das Volk*, a small-circulation newspaper for German workers in England that Marx was supporting with his own money, and the paper also carried a review by Engels, the main points in which had been dictated by Marx. These two pieces were reprinted in a few American newspapers, but this hardly justified Marx's euphoric claim to Lassalle that 'the first part has been thoroughly reviewed by the whole German press from New York to New Orleans'.[4] In Germany itself, however, Marx admitted that he had 'expected attacks or criticisms, anything but complete ignoring'.[5] And Jenny spoke of the 'silent, long-nourished hopes for Karl's book which have all been destroyed by the German conspiracy of silence'.[6] Marx had also entertained hopes for an English translation which he thought might make a *coup* if the book went well in Berlin. He wrote to Dana for an American edition and entered into negotiation with an English publisher, but nothing came of it – according to Marx owing to the late appearance of the German edition.

II. 'HERR VOGT'

Immediately after sending off the manuscript of the first part, Marx

---

[1] Ibid., p. 72.   [2] Ibid., p. 51.   [3] Engels to Marx, *MEW* xxix 319.
[4] Marx to Lassalle, *MEW* xxix 618.   [5] Ibid.
[6] Jenny Marx to Engels, *MEW* xxix 653.

had set to work on the chapter on capital. Duncker declared himself willing to continue with the publication, but the whole project was engulfed by the enormous dimensions taken on by Marx's quarrel with Karl Vogt.[1] This quarrel, which occupied Marx for eighteen months, is a striking example both of Marx's ability to expend tremendous labour on essentially trivial matters and also of his talent for vituperation. Vogt had been a leader of the left wing in the Frankfurt Assembly – though not left enough to avoid being attacked by the *Neue Rheinische Zeitung* – and on the dissolution of the Assembly he had emigrated to Switzerland where he taught geography at the University of Berne. He was the author of several works preaching a crude materialism and was a member of the Swiss diet. On the outbreak of the Franco-Austrian war, which had been engineered by Bonaparte and Cavour to loosen Austria's hold on North Italy, Vogt started a paper in Switzerland whose main editorial line was that Germany would benefit from Austria's defeat and ought to support Bonaparte. In early May 1859 Marx was on the platform of an Urquhartite meeting to protest at the supposed Russian menace caused by the war. Also on the platform was Karl Blind who informed Marx that Vogt was being subsidised by Bonaparte, that he had attempted to bribe printers in Germany and London, and that he had recently been in secret conclave with Prince Jerome Bonaparte to forward the establishment of the Tsar's brother on the throne of Hungary.

Marx mentioned these accusations to Elard Biskamp, editor of *Das Volk*, who promptly printed them and even sent a copy to Vogt. *Das Volk* was the successor to a small paper edited by Edgar Bauer on behalf of the German Workers' Education Association which collapsed when Kinkel offered its printer a more lucrative contract to print his own paper. When asked by the association to accept a commission to step into the breach, Marx informed Engels that he had replied that 'no one but ourselves had bestowed on us our position as representatives of the proletarian party; but this position had been countersigned by the exclusive and universal hatred accorded us by all factions and parties of the old world'.[2] But in spite of his decision ten years previously to have nothing more to do with the Association,

---

[1] On this question see further, H. Cunow, 'Zum Streit zwischen K. Marx und K. Vogt', *Die Neue Zeit* (1918); F. Mehring, Introduction to *Aus dem literarischen Nachlass*, vol. 3.

[2] Marx to Engels, *MEW* xxix 436.

Marx let himself be persuaded to support the paper, partly from compassion for the honest but incompetent Biskamp and partly from a desire to get at Kinkel. He refused at first to contribute directly to any paper he did not edit, but became increasingly involved, spent a lot of time and energy in organising support for the paper and, when it finally collapsed after little more than three months, had to meet the outstanding printer's bill himself in order to avoid a scandal.[1]

Thus Vogt had no difficulty in identifying Marx as the source of the attack on him and replied in kind in his own paper. The matter would have rested there had not Liebknecht discovered the galleys of an anonymous pamphlet repeating the accusations against Vogt which was being printed on the same press as *Das Volk* and had, according to the typesetter, been handed in by Blind whose handwriting he also claimed to have recognised in the proof corrections. Liebknecht sent off a copy to the *Augsburger Allgemeine Zeitung*, one of the leading conservative papers, for which he was London correspondent. On publication, Vogt prosecuted the *Augsburger*, which turned to Liebknecht for justification, who turned to Marx, who turned to Blind. Blind, however, refused to admit authorship of the pamphlet. Vogt's case against the *Augsburger* was dismissed on a legal technicality, though the fact that the defence had been unable to substantiate the accusations constituted a moral victory for him. This victory was enhanced by the publication in the *Augsburger* of a statement by Blind denying authorship of the pamphlet and supporting this with statements from the printer and typesetter whom he had suborned. Marx managed to secure an affidavit from the typesetter to the effect that the pamphlet really *was* in Blind's handwriting, and threatened Blind with prosecution. This produced a declaration in the *Daily Telegraph* that a friend of Blind's family, named Schaible, had been the author of the pamphlet; and at least Marx was exonerated.

There, too, the matter might have rested had not Vogt produced a book entitled *My Action against the Allgemeine Zeitung*. This included all the proceedings and documents of the trial followed by a commentary that branded Marx as a forger and a blackmailer who lived off the contributions of the proletariat while only having respect for purebred aristocrats like his brother-in-law Ferdinand von Westphalen. The book sold all its first printing of 3000 copies and immediately went

---

[1] See I. Bach, 'Karl Marx und die Londoner Zeitung "Das Volk" (1859)', in *Aus der Geschichte des Kampfes von Marx and Engels für die proletarische Partei* (Berlin, 1961).

into a second edition. The Berlin *National Zeitung* published two long leading articles drawn from Vogt's assertions, the arrival of which in London towards the end of January 1960 sent Marx into a panic. He tried to keep the news from Jenny but of course she found out and was in a 'truly shattering state'.[1] Marx also quarrelled violently with Freiligrath with whom his relations had become increasingly strained: Freiligrath had refused to heed his warning not to participate in the Schiller festival organised by Kinkel in November 1859; and he had dissociated himself abruptly from *Das Volk* when Liebknecht had mistakenly alleged that he was one of its collaborators. Marx's rage boiled over when he was informed – again mistakenly – that Vogt's book reprinted letters from Freiligrath that showed his intimacy with Vogt. When Marx realised how mistaken he was, he wrote to Freiligrath one of his most attractive letters. He claimed that his struggle against Vogt was 'decisive for the historical vindication of the party and its subsequent position in Germany', and continued:

I tell you frankly that I cannot decide to let irrelevant misunderstandings lose me one of the few men whom I have loved as a friend in the eminent sense of the word. If I am guilty of anything towards you, I am willing to make amends. *Nihil humani a me alienum puto*. . . .

We both know that each of us in his own way, putting aside all private interest and from the purest motives, has held aloft for years over the heads of the philistines the banner of the *classe la plus laborieuse et la plus misérable*; and I would consider it a petty crime against history if we were to break up because of trifles that are all explainable as misunderstandings.[2]

Freiligrath accepted Marx's explanations, but replied: 'My nature, like the nature of any poet, needs freedom. The party is also a cage, and it is easier to sing outside it, even for the party, than inside it.'[3] Marx was pleased with Freiligrath's reply: 'Your letter pleased me a lot, for I give my friendship to only a very few men, but then I hold fast to it. My friends of 1844 are still the same.' But he thought Freiligrath's interpretation of the party was much too narrow:

After the 'League' was dissolved in November 1852 on my proposition, I no longer belonged to any Society whether secret or public,

---

[1] Marx to Freiligrath, *MEW* xxx 460.   [2] Ibid. 459 ff.
[3] F. Freiligrath, *Briefwechsel mit Marx und Engels*, I 138.

nor do I; thus the party in this completely ephemeral sense ceased
to exist for me eight years ago . . . thus I know nothing of the party,
in the sense of your letter, since 1852. If you are a poet, then I am a
critic and had more than enough with the experiences of 1849–1852.
The 'League' . . . like a hundred other societies, was only an episode
in the history of the party which grows everywhere spontaneously
from the soil of modern society.[1]

Thus Marx and Freiligrath repaired their friendship; but it never
became as intimate as previously and all contact between the families
was broken off by Jenny who was, as Marx admitted, 'of an energetic
nature'.[2]

Meanwhile Marx had begun a forlorn prosecution of the *National
Zeitung* in Berlin and the *Daily Telegraph* in London, both dismissed for
lack of evidence, and began to collect material for a refutation of Vogt.
Vogt's attack, thought Marx, had been on a large scale and a large-
scale reply was needed, a reply which Marx also saw as a revenge for
the Cologne trial of 1853. In March he went to Manchester for six
weeks to check the archives of the Communist League in Engels'
possession as Vogt had stirred up all the 'foggy gossip of the refugees'.[3]
He caused affidavits to be made left, right and centre, fired off at least
fifty letters (that to his lawyer in Berlin alone is twenty printed pages)
and entered into a 'secret and confidential'[4] correspondence with the
Daily Telegraph to try to get them to make amends. He started on the
book in August but did not finish it until mid-November; both Jenny
and Engels disapproved of the delay and considered Marx's approach
much too thorough. It proved impossible to find a publisher in Germany and – despite Engels' warnings – Marx decided on a London
publisher for whom Marx's book was his first commercial enterprise;
Marx even optimistically persuaded him to agree to share the profits.
What with the cost of the lawsuits, gathering material and printing,
Marx found that he had spent about £100 to which Engels and Lassalle
had to contribute heavily.

It took Marx a long time to decide on the title: he himself, supported
by Jenny, favoured *Da-Da Vogt*, apparently on the grounds that it
would 'puzzle the philistines',[5] but Engels persuaded him to settle for
the simpler *Herr Vogt*. The book was very long and described by Marx

---

[1] Marx to Freiligrath, *MEW* xxx 488 ff.   [2] Marx to Lassalle, *MEW* xxx 563.
[3] Marx to Engels, *MEW* xxx 17.   [4] Ibid. 29.   [5] Ibid. 101 f.

himself as 'a system of mockery and contempt'.[1] Vogt, pillaried as a reincarnation of Sir John Falstaff, was pursued through two hundred closely printed pages whose style was so allusive that Engels recommended a résumé after each chapter 'in order to present the general impression clearly to the Philistines'.[2] Marx was at his most vituperative:

By means of an artificially hidden sewer system all the lavatories of London spew their physical filth into the Thames. By means of the systematic pushing of goose quills the world capital spews out all its social filth into the great papered central sewer called the *Daily Telegraph*.

Having transformed the social filth of London into newspaper articles, Levy transforms the articles into copper, and finally the copper into gold. Over the gate leading to this central sewer made of paper there can be read these words written *di colore oscuro*: 'hic . . . quisquam faxit oletum', or as Byron so poetically translated it: 'Wanderer, stop and – piss!'[3]

Marx read passages aloud to Jenny and she found them highly amusing. Engels thought it better than the *Eighteenth Brumaire* and Lassalle called it 'a masterpiece in all respects'. However, few copies sold and subsequent generations have not shared the taste for vituperation so characteristic of mid-Victorian polemics. *Herr Vogt* remains the only one of Marx's works never to have been reissued in a separate edition. Disappointment at the book's failure was enhanced when the publisher went bankrupt and Marx was saddled with all the printing costs. Ten years later, following the abdication of Napoleon III, the final stroke was added to the tragi-comedy: the French provisional Government of 1870 published papers found in the Tuileries showing, almost beyond doubt, that Vogt did in fact receive subsidies from Napoleon and that Marx, for once in his career as a polemicist, was wholly justified.

III. MARX AND LASSALLE

During the early 1860s Marx's relationship to working-class politics in Germany was dominated by his relationship to Lassalle which was

---

[1] Ibid. 102.   [2] Ibid. 120.   [3] K. Marx, 'Herr Vogt', *MEW* xiv 599 ff.

typical of the ambivalence that characterised all Marx's personal relationships. The son of a self-made Jewish tailor and seven years younger
than Marx, Lassalle had become intimate with him during the 1848
troubles. Throughout the 1850s Lassalle had been extremely accom-
modating to Marx: he had offered to raise subscriptions to publish
Marx's 'Economics' and also got him his job as London correspondent
of the *Neue Oder Zeitung*. But Marx was not the man to appreciate
favours and lent a ready ear to a series of accusations against Lassalle
delivered by one Levy, a self-styled representative of the Düsseldorf
workers who had already tried to convince Marx in late 1853 that a
revolution was imminent in the Rhineland and paid him a second
visit in 1856. According to Levy, Lassalle was only using the working-
class movement for his personal affairs; he had compromised himself
with the liberals, betrayed the workers and embezzled from friends.
Engels was even readier than Marx to give credit to these accusations
(although they were not supported by a shred of evidence) and
recommended the breaking off of relations, declaring of Lassalle that
'his desire to push his way into polite society, to *parvenir*, to gloss over,
if only for appearance's sake, the dirty Breslaw Jew with all kinds of
pomade and greasepaint, was always disgusting'.[1] Marx refused to
reply to Lassalle's letters thereafter and only gave him a 'short and
cool' answer when Lassalle offered him the possibility of writing articles
for the *Wiener Presse* whose editor was Lassalle's cousin. Marx was also
looking for a publisher for his 'Economics' and it was Lassalle again
who acted as a very competent literary agent in the negotiations with
Franz Duncker whose wife was Lassalle's mistress. Thus relations were
temporarily restored: Marx complimented Lassalle on his recent
publication *Heraclitus* (though he expressed himself differently to
Engels) and Lassalle even turned to Marx for advice on the problem of
duelling. Marx's curious reply was that, although duelling was irrational and 'a relic of a bygone culture, bourgeois society was so one-
sided that, in opposition to it, certain feudal forms of expressing individuality are justified'.[2]

This co-operation was, however, soon disturbed by differences of
opinion on the Franco-Austrian War of 1859. Immediately on its
outbreak Engels had – again through the agency of Lassalle – published
a pamphlet entitled *Po and Rhine* in which he declared that Bonaparte
was interfering in his own interests in North Italy preliminary to an

[1] Engels to Marx, *MEW* xxix 31.   [2] Marx to Lassalle, *MEW* xxix 562.

attack on the Rhine. Lassalle also published a pamplet, but his views were noticeably different: he considered that any purely nationalistic German war against France could only serve the cause of the reaction which would be increased enormously by an Austrian victory; Bonaparte was a bad man, but the cause he was supporting was good and anyway he was too weak to pose a serious threat to Germany; if it became plain that he had serious territorial designs in Italy, Prussia should retaliate with a war of liberation in Schleswig Holstein. Marx, who enthusiastically approved Engels' pamphlet and was obsessed by the fear of a Russian alliance with France and by the urgent necessity to unseat Bonaparte, called Lassalle's pamphlet 'an enormous blunder'.[1] He wrote to Engels: 'we must now absolutely insist on party discipline or everything will be in the soup',[2] and delivered Lassalle a long lecture on publishing his views without prior consultation. Events, however, showed that Lassalle had the more realistic view of the situation.

What made Marx even more annoyed was that he thought that Lassalle's pamphlet had been given priority by Duncker over his own *Critique of Political Economy*. And when Lassalle informed him of his intention to publish a two-volume work on economics, he attributed the ignoring of his *Critique* to Lassalle's influence, though he comforted himself with the thought that, to judge from Lassalle's *Heraclitus*, he would 'find to his cost that it is one thing to construct a critique of a science and thus for the first time to bring it to a point where a dialectic presentation is possible, and quite another to apply intimations of an abstract, ready-made system of logic'.[3] Lassalle had not replied to Marx's lecture on party discipline, but by January 1860 Marx felt the urgent need for assistance in his battle of words with Vogt and asked Engels to write Lassalle a diplomatic letter excusing his roughness. However, Lassalle refused to let himself be persuaded that Vogt was a Bonapartist agent: although he sympathised with Marx's case, he thought it unwise to have attacked Vogt without firm proof; he also reproached Marx with his 'mistrust', whereupon Marx sent him – from Manchester where he was staying with Engels – an anonymous denunciation of Lassalle that he had received from Baltimore and also informed him that 'official complaints' from Düsseldorf were now in the party archives.[4] Lassalle replied in a justified outburst:

---

[1] Marx to Engels, *MEW* xxix 432.   [2] Ibid.   [3] Ibid. 275.
[4] Cf. Marx to Lassalle, *MEW* xxx 463 f.

Why do you send me this stuff with so triumphant a mien, so proud a gesture? In order to prove to me how little you at least are mistrustful of me!

Heavens! NOT to believe such a cut-purse slander behind a man's back – but that is the most elementary of moral duties of man to man. To believe such slanders and such fatuities of me must be for any person of understanding, for any one who knows the least thing about me, a physical impossibility! ! ! And you think that, by not believing it, you are doing me a favour? You want to impute that to yourself as a merit?

The only conclusion I draw is a firm proof of your inclination to believe all possible evil of every man without evidence, if you *count it as a merit, and think it proves something*, that in this case you did not believe.[1]

Marx realised that he had gone too far and for the rest of 1861 he and Lassalle corresponded regularly and good-humouredly.

At the beginning of 1861, when Marx was at last rid of *Herr Vogt*, he began to toy with the idea of a definitive return to Prussia. In January 1861 Frederick William IV, who had been certified insane for the previous two years, died and was succeeded by his brother Wilhelm I who immediately declared a political amnesty. The conditions of the amnesty were not good: it only applied to those who had been convicted by Prussian courts and refugees had to rely on vague assurances. When Lassalle first proposed a renewal of the *Neue Rheinische Zeitung* backed by the money of his wealthy patron, the Countess von Hatzfeld, Marx was sceptical, thinking that 'the waves in Germany are not yet riding high enough to carry our ship'.[2] Engels suggested that Lassalle launch a weekly and that Marx co-operate if the money were good enough. Although chary of collaborating in anything under Lassalle's control, Marx's income from the *New York Daily Tribune* was decreasing dramatically owing to the Civil War and he decided to go to Berlin to investigate possibilities. His financial straits obliged him in any case to go to Holland to see his uncle. Borrowing money for the trip from Lassalle he spent two weeks in Zaltbommel with the Philips – 'I have never known a better family in my life'[3] he wrote afterwards to his uncle – and managed to borrow £160 as an advance on his mother's estate. His

[1] F. Lassalle, *Nachgelassene Briefs und Schriften*, III 263.
[2] Marx to Engels, *MEW* xxx 148 f.
[3] Marx to Lion Philips, *MEW* xxx 600.

uncle was, according to Marx, 'stubborn but very proud of my being an author'[1] and Marx got Lassalle to write him the sort of letter that he could 'confidentially'[2] show to his uncle to increase his reputation.

On his proceeding to Berlin, he was magnificently entertained for three weeks by Lassalle. He lived in 'a very beautiful house on one of the most beautiful streets of Berlin' and the countess, too, made a favourable impression on Marx: 'She is a very distinguished lady, no blue stocking, of great natural intellect, much vivacity, deeply interested in the revolutionary movement, and of an aristocratic *laissez-aller* very superior to the pedantic grimaces of professional *femmes d'ésprit*.'[3] There were visits to the theatre and the ballet (which bored Marx to death) and a dinner in Marx's honour where he was placed between the countess and the niece of Varnhagen von Ense. 'This Fraülein', he wrote to Antoinette Philips, 'is the most ugly creature I ever saw in my life, a nastily Jewish physiognomy, a sharply protruding thin nose, eternally smiling and grinning, always speaking poetical prose, playing at false enthusiasm, and spitting at her auditory during the trances of her ecstasis.'[4] Marx did, however, manage to persuade the countess to start a press campaign against Blanqui's ill-treatment by the French police. The visit was prolonged since Marx was applying, with Lassalle's active assistance, for the recovery of his Prussian citizenship and the bureaucracy moved slowly. But Marx began to tire of Berlin society very quickly: 'I am treated as a sort of lion and compelled to meet many professionally "intellectual" ladies and gentleman.'[5] He found the whole of Berlin engulfed in ennui: bickering with the police and the antipathy between civil and military authorities constituted the the sum of Berlin politics. Marx attended a session in the Prussian Chamber of Deputies and found it 'a curious mixture of bureaucracy and the school room';[6] there was a general spirit of dissolution in the city: people of every rank thought a catastrophe inevitable and the next elections would yield a parliament in opposition to the King.

In these circumstances, Marx considered the time ripe for the foundation of a new paper, but he and Lassalle could not agree upon terms. Lassalle insisted that if Engels joined the editorial board in addition to

---

[1] Marx to Lassalle, *MEW* xxx 588.   [2] Ibid.
[3] Marx to Antoinette Philips in W. Blumenberg, 'Ein Unbekanntes Kapital aus Marx' Leben', *International Review of Social History* (1956) p. 83.
[4] Marx to Antoinette Philips, op. cit., p. 84.
[5] Marx to Carl Siebel, *MEW* xxx 593.
[6] Marx to Engels, *MEW* xxx 167.

himself and Marx, then Marx and Engels should have only one vote against his own. But, although Lassalle was supplying the money, Marx considered that he could only supply a useful service if he were kept 'under strong discipline'. He wrote to Engels:

> Dazzled by the reputation that he has gained in certain learned circles through his 'Heraclitus' and in another circle of spongers through wine and cuisine, Lassalle is naturally unaware that he is discredited in the public at large. There is also his dogmatism, his obsession with the 'speculative concept' (the fellow even dreams of his writing a new Hegelian philosophy, raised to the second power), his infection with old French liberalism, his arrogant pen, importunity, tactlessness, etc.[1]

In the end, Marx left Berlin without receiving his Prussian nationality (in spite of a personal interview with the Prussian Chief of Police, again arranged by Lassalle) and without a definite decision one way or another on the paper. Marx at least had the satisfaction of finding his old friend Köppen unchanged: the drinking session with Köppen did him 'a power of good'[2] and Köppen presented him with his two-volume study on the Buddha. Marx also visited old friends in the Rhineland and spent two days with his mother. She interested him with her 'subtle *esprit* and indestructible stability of character'[3] – and she cancelled some of his old debts into the bargain. Marx defined his attitude towards a return to Germany as follows: 'Germany is so fine a country that one is better living outside its boundaries. I for my part, if I were quite free and not burdened with something that you might call "political conscience", would never leave England for Germany, still less for Prussia and least of all for this frightful Berlin with its dust and culture and over-clever people.'[4] And Jenny's views were even sharper: 'My wife is particularly against a move to Berlin', Marx informed his uncle, 'since she does not wish our daughters to be introduced to the Hatzfeld circle, and it would be difficult to keep them away from it.'[5]

The whole family was, however, enchanted by the gifts from Lassalle that Marx brought back with him. There was an atlas for Engels and

[1] Ibid. 163.   [2] Ibid. 166.
[3] Marx to Lassalle, *MEW* xxx 602.
[4] Marx to Antoinette Philips, *MEW* xxx 594.
[5] Marx to Lion Philips, *MEW* xxx 601. See also Jenny Marx to Lassalle, F. Lassalle, *Nachgelassene Briefe und Schriften*, III 295.

cloaks for the girls and for Jenny who strutted up and down so proudly in hers that Eleanor called after her: 'Just like a peacock!' Jenny was grateful for other reasons, too, as 'anything like this makes an impression on the philistines of the neighbourhood and earns us respect and credit'.[1]

On his return to London Marx failed to pursue any co-operation with Lassalle. He was too busy working on his 'Economics' and trying to spin out his meagre earnings from journalism: the New York Daily Tribune had anyway cut Marx's quota of articles by half owing to the Civil War and most of what Marx wrote was for the Viennese paper Die Presse which praised his contributions highly but only printed – and paid for – one out of every four or five. Many of these articles dealt with the American Civil War. Unlike Engels, Marx was confident that the North, being industrially more developed, would win in the end in spite of early setbacks.[2] 'In this struggle', he wrote in the Tribune, 'the highest form that the self-government of a people has so far attained is giving battle to the lowest and most shameful form of human slavery yet seen in the annals of history.'[3] Marx was particularly pleased that the English working class, although their interests were damaged by the blockade of the south, were staunchly opposed to intervention.

In July of the following year Lassalle reciprocated by visiting London at a time when Marx had just returned from several weeks' refuge in Manchester to find a mass of debts. Lassalle stayed in the Marx household for three weeks and spent a lot of time at the International Exhibition. The strain that he imposed on his finances, working time and nerves made Marx extremely bitter. 'In order to preserve a certain façade', Marx wrote to Engels, 'my wife had to take to the pawnbrokers everything that was not actually nailed down.'[4] It was all the more galling, therefore, that Lassalle had just thrown away almost £100 in speculation and to see him spend more than £1 daily just on cabs and cigars. Marx was even more riled when Lassalle offered to obtain the protection of a London Jewish banker for him and take one of his daughters as a 'companion' to the countess. Marx wanted nothing more than to get on with his 'Economics', but Lassalle coolly

[1] Jenny Marx to Lassalle, F. Lassalle, op. cit., II 359.
[2] Cf. Marx to Engels, MEW xxx 270.
[3] Cf. MEW xv 327.
[4] Marx to Engels, MEW xxx 257.

assumed that since the lack of a market for his articles meant that he had 'no job' and was only doing 'theoretical' work, then Marx had all the time in the world to kill with him.[1] As annoying as Lassalle's flamboyant display of wealth was his boastfulness. In Marx's view he had changed much since the previous year in Berlin. Lassalle's success had turned his head and 'he is now not only confirmed as the greatest scholar, profoundest thinker, a genius in research, etc.; he is also Don Juan and a revolutionary Cardinal Richelieu. And there is also his continual chatter in an unnatural falsetto voice, his ugly demonstrative gestures and didactic tone.'[2] And it must indeed have been difficult for Marx to tolerate long the company of a man who could, with complete self-assurance, begin a speech with the words: 'Working men! Before I leave for the Spas of Switzerland . . .'[3] After three weeks of this Marx gave vent to his pent-up frustration in a letter to Engels: 'It is now quite clear to me that, as shown by the shape of his head and the growth of his hair, that he is descended from the negroes who joined the flight of Moses from Egypt (unless his mother or grandmother on his father's side were crossed with a nigger). This union of Jew and German on a negro foundation was bound to produce something out of the ordinary. The importunity of the fellow is also negroid.'[4] Jenny's comment on Lassalle's visit is also worth quoting as her touch is a little lighter than Marx's:

In July 1862 we had a visit from Ferdinand Lassalle. He was almost crushed under the weight of the fame he had achieved as a scholar, thinker, poet and politician. The laurel wreath was fresh on his Olympian brow and ambrosian head or rather on his stiff bristling Negro hair. He had just victoriously ended the Italian campaign – a new political *coup* was being contrived by the great man of action – and fierce battles were going on in his soul. There were still fields of science that he had not explored! Egyptology lay fallow: 'Should I astonish the world as an Egyptologist or show my versatility as a man of action, as a politician, as a fighter, or as a soldier?' It was a splendid dilemma. He wavered between the thoughts and sentiments of his heart and often expressed that struggle in really stentorian accents. As on the wings of the wind he swept through our

[1] Ibid.   [2] Ibid. 258.
[3] Quoted in R. Morgan, *The German Social Democrats and the First International* (Cambridge, 1965) p. 6.
[4] Marx to Engels, *MEW* xxx 259.

rooms, perorating so loudly, gesticulating and raising his voice to such a pitch that our neighbours were scared by the terrible shouting and asked us what was the matter. It was the inner struggle of the 'great' man bursting forth in shrill discords.[1]

On the day of Lassalle's departure the landlord, tax collector and most of the shopkeepers all threatened Marx with immediate reprisals if he did not pay his debts. Lassalle noticed that something was amiss and lent Marx £15 until the end of the year and anything more that Marx might require provided that Engels would guarantee the loan. Marx drew a cheque for £60 on Lassalle. However, Lassalle wished first to be assured that Engels was in agreement and this angered Marx so much that he returned a very rough answer for which he half apologised in November: 'I think that the substance of our friendship is strong enough to stand such a shock. I confess to you quite unequivocally that, as a man sitting on a volcano, I allow circumstances to dominate me in a manner unfitting for a rational animal. But in any case it was ungenerous of you to turn this state of mind, in which I would as soon have put a bullet through my head, against me like some prosecutor in a law court. So I hope that "in spite of everything" our old relationship can continue untroubled.'[2] Thereafter the correspondence ceased though Lassalle continued to sent Marx his numerous publications.

In April 1864 Lassalle stated that he had not written to Marx for two years as their relationship was strained 'for financial reasons'. Marx, however, attributed the break to Lassalle's political views – with greater reason. In the early 1860s the prosperity of Germany produced strong liberal forces that considerably diminished the strength of the reaction that had dominated the country throughout the 1850s. This opposition was brought to a head by the refusal of the *Landtag* to vote the budget necessary for a reform of the army, a refusal which led to elections in May 1862. Lassalle campaigned hard and the radicals had considerable success. During his stay in London Lassalle wished to obtain Marx's backing for his programme of universal suffrage and state aid to workers' co-operatives. Combined with his radicalism Lassalle remained in many respects an Old Hegelian with an Old Hegelian's view of the state; he had never been through the traumatically secularising experience of the Young Hegelians. Thus his

---

[1] Jenny Marx, 'Short Sketch of an Eventful Life', in *Reminiscences*, p. 234.
[2] Marx to Lassalle, *MEW* xxx 637.

proposals could never be acceptable to Marx who summed up his attitude to them in two letters written after Lassalle's death.[1] Most importantly, Marx considered that any reliance on state aid would enfeeble the proletariat's struggle for political supremacy. Lassalle's ideas, according to Marx, were not based on any coherent economic theory and involved a compromise with feudalism 'whereas in the nature of things, the working class must be genuinely "revolutionary"'.[2] Lassalle, however, who was in many ways in closer contact with the situation in Germany than was Marx, might with justice have claimed that Marx overestimated the revolutionary potential of the Prussian bourgeoisie and that his own programme represented the only way forward for the working-class movement. Marx was equally opposed to the idea of universal suffrage in Germany: Lassalle had learnt none of the lessons of the manipulation of this political device in France by Louis Napoleon. He also claimed that Lassalle did not base himself enough on previous working-class movements in Germany (though in fact many of his collaborators were former members of the Communist League);[3] and that Lassalle had no international dimension to his political agitation. This last observation was certainly justified: Lassalle had never lived outside Germany and both his theory and his practice were strictly limited to German conditions.

Even after his visit to London, Lassalle still hankered after the idea of editing a newspaper in co-operation with Marx. But Marx's criticisms became even more pronounced during Lassalle's last year of feverish political activity. In May 1863 Lassalle's agitation culminated in a request from the Leipzig workers to attend a conference where the *Allgemeine Deutsche Arbeiterverein* (General Union of German Workers), the first effective German socialist party, was formed. Eleven days before the conference Lassalle had had an interview with Bismarck with whom he had already been in secret negotiation. Although Lassalle claimed that he was 'eating cherries with Bismarck, but Bismarck was getting only the stones', Lassalle did not live long enough for it to be clear whether he was right.[4] Marx himself very quickly

---

[1] Cf. Marx to J. von Schweitzer, *MEW* XXXII 568 ff.; Marx to Kugelmann, *MESC*, pp. 167 ff.

[2] Marx to Kugelmann, *MESC*, p. 169.

[3] Cf. B. Andreas, 'Zur Agitation und Propaganda des ADAV 1863/64', *Archiv für Sozialgeschichte* (1963).

[1] On this, see W. Mommsen, 'Lassalle und Bismarck', *Archiv für Sozialgeschichte* (1963).

came to the conclusion that Lassalle had sold out to Bismarck and complained even more strongly of his plagiarising the *Communist Manifesto* and *Wage Labour and Capital*. But Lassalle's sudden death intervened: on 28 August 1864 he was mortally wounded in a duel by a Wallachian Count, the fiancé of Helen von Dönniges, a seventeen-year-old girl to whom Lassalle had got himself engaged barely four weeks before. Engels received the news fairly coolly; Marx showed more humanity. He wrote:

> Lassalle's misfortune has been going damnably round in my head these last days. He was after all one of the old stock and the enemy of our enemies. Also the thing came so surprisingly that it is difficult to believe that so noisy, stirring, pushing a man is now as dead as a mouse and must shut his mouth altogether. About the cause of his death you are quite right. It is one of the many tactlessnesses which he performed in his life. For all that, I'm sorry that our relationship was troubled during the last years, of course through his fault. . . .
>
> The devil knows, the crowd is getting ever smaller and no new blood is being added.[1]

And to the countess, he wrote:

> You will understand how the quite unforeseen news of Lassalle's death has astonished, shocked and shattered me. He was one of those for whom I had a great affection. . . . Be convinced that no one can feel deeper grief than I at his being torn away. And above all I feel for you. I know what the departed was to you, what his loss means to you. Rejoice over one thing. He died young, in triumph, like Achilles.[2]

Although Marx was obviously over-generous here to his own past sentiments, yet his relationship to Lassalle was ambivalent, resentment and hate always being tempered by a grudging admiration.

IV. LIFE IN GRAFTON TERRACE

The years 1860–63 had marked a fresh – but final – low in Marx's domestic affairs. He touched the depth of 'bourgeois misery' and could manage no more in three years than research on the historical portions of his 'Economics'. In 1864, however, the situation changed: two

---

[1] Marx to Engels, *MEW* xxx 432.   [2] Marx to Sophie von Hatzfeld, *MEW* xxx 673. Further on Lassalle, see S. Na'aman, *Lassalle* (Hanover, 1970).

legacies gave the Marx household enough security for Marx to be able to devote himself to the spread of the First International (which had been founded just four weeks after Lassalle's death) and also to start drafting the vital chapters of his 'Economics' on capital.

As Marx had foreseen, the poverty that the family experienced in Grafton Terrace was in many ways worse than that of Dean Street. The building had, according to Jenny, 'the four characteristics the English like in a house: airy, sunny, dry, and built in gravely soil';[1] and on a fine day there was a clear view right down to St Paul's. But the Marxes lived a very isolated life as their house was, initially, very difficult of access: building was going on all round, there was no made-up road leading to it, and in rainy weather the sticky red soil turned into a quagmire. This particularly affected Jenny who wrote that

> it was a long time before I could get used to the complete solitude. I often missed the long walks I had been in the habit of making in the crowded West-End streets, the meetings, the clubs and our favourite public-house and homely conversations which had so often helped me to forget the worries of life for a time. Luckily I still had the article for the *Tribune* to copy out twice a week and that kept me in touch with world events.[2]

Even worse, there were more appearances to be kept up and expenditure much increased particularly with the elder children going to school – a 'ladies seminary'[3] – and having private lessons in French, Italian, drawing and music. A piano, too, had to be rented. From 1857 there was a second servant, Helene Demuth's younger sister, Marianne, who stayed until her death in 1862. Marx was as resolved as ever 'to pursue my aim through thick and thin and not let bourgeois society turn me into a money-making machine',[4] but was often rather naïvely surprised at the financial difficulties that his attitude entailed. In 1859 he hoped to double his revenue by an offer that Lassale had negotiated on his behalf to write for the *Wiener Presse* and announced to Engels that he would bother him no more for money. Jenny – who was always much more hard-headed about money – warned him that he could count on £2 a week maximum and should not believe Engels

[1] Jenny Marx to Wilhelm von Florencourt, in *Vier Briefe von Jenny Marx* (Trier, 1970) p. 6.
[2] Jenny Marx, 'Short Sketch of an Eventful Life', *Reminiscences,* p. 230.
[3] Marx to Engels, *MEW* XXIX 130.
[4] Marx to Weydemeyer, XXIX 570.

with his airy talk of £10. The following September his affairs were in a crisis. Engels, who was being prosecuted for assaulting someone in a pub with his umbrella, had to find about £50 to settle the case and Marx turned to Lassalle, assuring him that he would be able to recoup from the royalties of the *Critique of Political Economy*. At the end of the year things were so bad that Jenny had to write secretly to her brother Ferdinand, with whom she had kept on fairly friendly terms, though all she gained was a feeling that she had compromised her principles as he refused her request, saying that he had only his pension to live on. 1860 was slightly better as Engels' financial position was improving and he was able to sent Marx £100 in a lump sum. But a lot of money went on the quarrel with Karl Vogt and by the end of the year Engels was having to borrow money to bail Marx out, though his own income was diminished by the American Civil War.

In February 1861 Marx decided, on his way to see Lassalle in Berlin, to visit his uncle in Holland and try to anticipate his inheritance. This trip was preceded by two weeks in which Marx spent his whole time in avoiding 'the complete break up of the house'.[1] He could only keep sane by reading in the evenings Appian on the Roman Civil War. His favourite figure was Spartacus, 'the finest fellow produced by the whole of classical history ... a real representative of the ancient proletariat'. This admiration was matched by a complete contempt for Pompey, 'a pure louse of a man', into whose character Shakespeare in *Love's Labour's Lost* had some real insights.[2] By the summer the £160 that he had got from his uncle was gone. He felt the situation to be 'in every respect unsettled' and was reading Thucydides to shake off his ill humour. 'At least these ancients remain for ever new', he remarked to Lassalle.[3] In the autumn he renewed his correspondence with the *New York Daily Tribune* and at last obtained terms that enabled him to start writing for the *Wiener Presse*. This work for New York and Vienna would give him enough to live on, he considered, but his debts still amounted to £100. 'It is astonishing', he remarked naïvely to Engels, 'how lack of income together with debts that are never completely cleared blows up the old shit in spite of all assistance in minor matters.'[4]

The year 1862 marked the nadir of Marx's fortunes. He had to pretend not to have returned from a trip to Manchester in order to avoid

---

[1] Marx to Engels, *MEW* xxx 160. [2] Ibid.
[3] Marx to Lassalle, *MEW* xxx 606. [4] Marx to Engels, *MEW* xxx 206.

creditors, and Jenny even tried to sell his books. In such circumstances Lassalle's visit in July could only be excruciating. Lassalle had come to the rescue with £60 but by the autumn Marx was thinking of taking a job in a railway office. He went as far as getting an interview but was turned down owing to his appalling handwriting.[1] In January 1863 he wrote to Engels that the recent trouble had

> at last brought my wife to agree to a suggestion that I made a long time ago and which, with all its inconveniences, is not only the sole solution, but is also preferable to the life of the last three years, and particularly the last, as well as restoring our self-esteem.
>
> I will write to all my creditors (with the exception of the landlord) and say that, if they do not leave me in peace I will declare myself bankrupt. . . . My two eldest daughters will get positions as governesses through the Cunningham family. Lenchen will enter another service and I, with my wife and Tussy, will go and live in the same City Model Lodging House in which red Wolff and his family lived previously.[2]

It is not clear how serious Marx really was, but Engels read the letter as a cry for help and responded immediately by borrowing £100 at great risk to himself. Marx still had to go off to the British Museum to avoid his creditors, but in the summer Ernst Dronke lent Engels £250 for Marx which lasted until December when he received the telegram that presaged substantial relief: his mother was dead.

Borrowing the money from Engels, Marx rushed to Trier, but the administrative measures concerning the execution of the will took so long that Marx left to visit his uncle in Zaltbommel. During the week he spent in Trier, he wrote to Jenny, he went back to the old house of the Westphalens 'that was of more interest to me than all the Roman antiquities because it reminds me of the happiest time of my youth and housed my greatest treasure. Moreover, I was asked daily, left and right, after the former "prettiest girl in Trier" and the "queen of the ball". It is damned pleasant for a man when his wife lives on like that in the imagination of a whole city as an "enchanted princess".'[3] Most of the money (of which Marx's share was about £1000) was in the

[1] Cf. Marx to Kugelmann, *MEW* xxx 640.

[2] Marx to Engels, *MEW* xxx 315. The gap between the life-styles of the working class and middle class at this time was so great that this really *was* the stark alternative that faced Marx if he wished to escape from 'bourgeois respectability'.

[3] Marx to Jenny Marx, *MEW* xxx 643.

hands of Marx's uncle who was the executor of the will as well as being his chief creditor. Here also the legal processes were long but Marx only had time to visit two of his aunts in Frankfurt before he was struck down by a monster carbuncle which kept him in Zaltbommel for six weeks nursed by his uncle and cousin Antoinette Philips. Engels meanwhile paid the bills for Grafton Terrace. Marx considered the stay in Holland as 'one of the happiest episodes of my life',[1] and returned to London on 19 February, after visits to more relations in Amsterdam and Rotterdam, in possession of the residue of the money left him by his mother: some additional money was sent later as a result of the sale of objects in Trier.

In early May 1864 Marx obtained another windfall. On 9 May Wilhelm Wolff died. Marx felt that he had lost 'one of our few friends and fellow fighters, a man in the best sense of the word'.[2] Marx was at his bedside during the days before his death and gave a brief speech at his graveside. As one of the executors of Wolff's will he stayed on in Manchester for some days and was as surprised as anyone when it was discovered that Wolff had painstakingly accumulated a small fortune and left the bulk of it – £843 and some £50 worth of effects – to Marx. This put a stop to begging letters to Engels – for just over one year.

These continued financial disasters weighed upon the whole household, but most of all on the sensitive and houseproud Jenny whose health became seriously undermined. In late 1856 she was again pregnant (at the age of 42) and needed the doctor's attention throughout the nine months during which her nervous state neared what Marx described as 'catastrophe'.[3] The child was born dead. The following year Jenny went to Ramsgate with Lenchen and the children for several weeks to recuperate and this eventually became an annual occurrence: the Marx family had great faith in the health of sea air, and at one time or another visited practically every resort on the south-east coast. In Ramsgate Jenny had, so Marx informed Engels, 'made acquaintance with refined and, *horribile dictu*, intelligent English ladies. After the experience of bad society, or none at all, for years on end, the society of her equals seems to suit her.'[4] With her health, Jenny's optimism also declined: at the end of 1858, when she had no money for the Christmas festivities and was busy copying out the *Critique of Political Economy*, she informed Marx that 'after all the misery

---

[1] Marx to Lion Philips, *MEW* xxx 648.   [2] Marx to Jenny Marx, *MEW* xxx 655.
[3] Marx to Engels, *MEW* xxx 132.   [4] Ibid. 353.

that she would have had to endure, it would be even worse in the revolution and she would experience the pleasure of seeing all the present-day humbugs again celebrate their triumphs'.[1]

In November 1860, the year that Marx spent in his fruitless campaign against Karl Vogt, Jenny contracted the disease that was to mark a watershed in her life. Hardly had she finished copying the manuscript of *Herr Vogt* than she was struck down by a fever. Diagnosis was delayed as Jenny refused at first to call a doctor. After two visits the 'very nasty nervous fever' was declared to be smallpox contracted in spite of a double vaccination. The children had to go and stay with the Liebknechts for several weeks – they would not go to a boarding school 'because of the religious rites'.[2] Marx hired a nurse to look after Jenny, who had lost the use of her senses. She wrote later: 'I lay constantly by the open window so that the cold November air would blow over me, while there was a raging fire in the stove and burning ice on my lips, and I was given drops of claret from time to time. I could hardly swallow, my hearing was getting weaker, and finally my eyes closed, so that I did not know whether I would remain enveloped in eternal night.'[3] In these circumstances Marx could only preserve his 'quietness of mind' by absorbing himself in the study of mathematics.

Eventually the crisis passed and by Christmas the children were allowed back in the house. But the illness had after-effects: Jenny remained fairly deaf and her skin was marked with red pocks that took a long time to heal. In March of the following year she wrote to Louise Weydemeyer that before her illness she 'had had no grey hair and my teeth and figure were good, and therefore people used to class me among well-preserved women. But that was all a thing of the past now and I seemed to myself now a kind of cross between a rhinoceros and hippopotamus whose place was in the zoo rather than among the members of the Caucasian race.'[4] Her nervous state also continued to frighten the doctor particularly in times of financial trouble.

Marx found that his financial difficulties and Jenny's increasing irritability made family life very difficult. By the end of December 1857 when he was well into the *Grundrisse*, Jenny reported the return of his 'freshness and cheerfulness'[5] which he had lost with the death of Edgar. But two months later he declared to Engels: 'There is no greater

---

[1] Ibid. xxix 374.   [2] Ibid. xxx 113.
[3] Jenny Marx to Louise Weydemeyer, *Reminiscences*, p. 247.   [4] Ibid.
[5] Jenny Marx to Conrad Schramm, *MEW* xxix 645.

stupidity than for people of general aspirations to marry and so surrender themselves to the small miseries of domestic and private life.'[1] The life in Grafton Terrace was a very isolated one, with only the Freiligraths as close friends and very few family visitors, and Marx felt that Engels was the only person he could talk to frankly as at home he had to play the role of a silent stoic. This was necessary to combat Jenny's increasing pessimism. Marx's own health was seriously suffering: he continually complained to Engels that his liver bothered him for weeks on end (his father had died from a liver complaint) and he consumed enormous quantities of medicine to heal the toothache, headaches and disorders of his eyes and nerves. The boils were to follow shortly.

After Jenny's illness domestic troubles were aggravated. Marx tried to keep bad news from Jenny as 'such news always induces a sort of paroxysm'.[2] The year 1862 he could only wish to the devil since 'such a lousy life is not worth while living'.[3] Jenny's feelings were much the same: 'My wife tells me every day that she wishes she were in the grave with the children and I really cannot blame her.'[4] In January 1863, as a result of pressing money problems and Jenny's reaction to them, there occurred the only serious quarrel between Marx and Engels. On 6 January Mary Burns died. She had been living with Engels for nearly twenty years and he regarded her as his wife. On hearing of her death Marx wrote simply that 'the news of Mary's death both surprised and shocked me very much. She was very good-natured, witty and devoted to you', and then continued immediately to give Engels a lengthy description of his financial troubles.[5] Engels replied after a few days: 'You will find it natural that my own trouble and your frosty reception of it made it positively impossible for me to answer you earlier. All my friends, including philistine acquaintances, have shown me on this occasion, which was bound to touch me very nearly, more sympathy and friendship than I could expect. You found the moment suitable to enforce the superiority of your cold thought processes.'[6] Marx waited ten days before replying:

I thought it good to let some time pass before I answered you. Your situation on the one hand and mine on the other made it difficult to take a 'cool' look at the situation.

[1] Marx to Engels, *MEW* xxix 285. [2] Ibid. 210. [3] Ibid. 214.
[4] Ibid. 248. [5] Ibid. 310. [6] Engels to Marx, *MEW* xxx 312.

It was very wrong of me to write you the letter, and I regretted it as soon as it was posted. But it did not happen out of heartlessness. My wife and children will bear me witness that when your letter came (it was early in the morning) I was as much shattered as by the death of one of those nearest to me. But when I wrote to you in the evening, it was under the impression of very desperate conditions. I had the landlord's broker in the house, the butcher protesting at my cheque, shortage of coals and food, and little Jenny in bed. In such circumstances, I can generally save myself only by cynicism.[1]

This in turn led to a quarrel between Marx and Jenny. Marx had written in the same letter of excuse to Engels that 'what made me particularly wild was the fact that my wife believed that *I* had not sufficiently accurately communicated the true state of affairs to you'.[2] Marx considered that Jenny had forced him into a false position with regard to Engels.

I can now tell you without further ceremony [he wrote to Engels] that, in spite of all the pressure I have endured during the last weeks, nothing burdened me – even relatively speaking – as much as this fear that our friendship should now break up. I repeatedly told my wife that nothing in the whole mess was important to me compared with the fact that, owing to our lousy bourgeois situation and her eccentric excitement, I was not in a position to comfort you at such a time, but only to burden you with my private needs.

Consequently domestic peace was much disturbed and the poor woman had to face the music although it was no fault of hers in as much as women are accustomed to demand the impossible. Naturally she had no idea of what I wrote but her own reflexion could have told her what the outcome would be. Women are funny creatures – even those endowed with much intelligence.[3]

The children were also a cause of much concern to Marx and Jenny. In 1860, the year of Jenny's smallpox, the three girls were aged sixteen, fifteen and four years old. Jenny found their poverty all the harder to bear as 'the sweet girls, now blooming so lovelily, have to suffer it as well'.[4] At the beginning of 1863 Jenny gave the following description of her daughters to one of her friends:

Even if the word 'beautiful' is not fitting for them, I must still say,

---

[1] Marx to Engels, *MEW* xxx 314.   [2] Ibid.   [3] Ibid. 319.
[4] Jenny Marx to Engels, *MEW* xxix 653.

even at the risk of being laughed at for my maternal pride, that all three of them look very neat and interesting. Jennychen is strikingly dark in hair, eyes and complexion and, with her childishly rosy cheeks and deep, sweet eyes, has a very attractive appearance. Laura, who is in everything a few degrees lighter and clearer, is in fact prettier than the eldest sister as her features are more regular and her green eyes under her dark brows and long lashes shine with a continual fire of joy.... We have made every effort we could towards their education. Unfortunately we could not do so much for them in music as we would have hoped, and their musical accomplishments are not distinguished, although they both have particularly pleasant voices and sing with a very pretty expressiveness. But Jenny's real strong point is elocution; and because the child has a very beautiful voice, low and sweet, and from childhood had studied Shakespeare with fanaticism, she would in fact long ago have been on the stage had not regard for the family etc. held her back.... Neither would we have placed any obstacle in her way if her health were sounder.... The third one, the baby, is a true bundle of sweetness, charm and childish frenzy. She is the light and life of the house. All three children are attached body and soul to London and have become fully English in customs, manners, tastes, needs and habits, – and nothing frightens them more than the thought of having to exchange England for Germany ... and I myself would find the prospect frightening.... Above all London is so colossal that one can disappear into nothing....[1]

But things were not always so sunny. Marx had to ask Engels urgently to spend some days with them as 'it is absolutely necessary that my daughters see a "man" again in the house. The poor children have been shaken too early by the bourgeois shit.'[2] Jenny's health was particularly bad as she suffered continually from chest ailments. This, too, Marx considered was attributable to their poverty: 'Jenny is now old enough to feel the whole pressure and hastiness of our situation and that, I think, is one of the principal causes of her ill health.'[3]

[1] Jenny Marx to Bertha Markheim, in B. Andreas, 'Die Familie Marx in Briefen und Dokumenten', *Archiv für Sozialgeschichte* (1962) pp. 177 f. Bertha Markheim, to whom Jenny wrote this account, had been a close friend of the family since 1854. She had helped Jenny with small gifts of money but Jenny had had to warn against organising more help as 'you cannot imagine how proud my husband is even in such matters' (Andreas, *Briefe*, p. 173).

[2] Marx to Engels, *MEW* XXIX 521.   [3] Ibid., XXX 214.

v. 'CAPITAL'

In the summer of 1861, with the Vogt affair at last behind him, Marx began to work in earnest on the '3rd chapter' on Capital in General. For a year progress was very slow, though Marx considered that he had managed to popularise his style. By April 1862 he felt in a position to tell Lassalle that his book would not be ready for two months and added revealingly: 'I have the peculiar characteristic that when I see something that I have written out four weeks later, I find it unsatisfactory and re-work the whole thing. In any case the work doesn't lose anything thereby.'[1]

Two months later he was 'working like the devil',[2] not on the third chapter, but on the history of economic theory – and particularly theories of surplus-value – that he wished to add to the chapter on Capital just as he had added a historical account of theories of money and circulation to the *Critique of Political Economy*. He was padding his work out as 'the German wretches measure the value of a book by its cubic content'.[3] It was Marx's usual practice when domestic worries disturbed his concentration – and 1862 and 1863 were among the most troubled years of Marx's life – to turn to the historical part of his work. By the end of the summer he was getting depressed and expressed the wish to Engels to engage in some line of business: 'Grey, dear friend, is all theory and only business is green. Unfortunately, I have come too late to this insight.'[4] He reread Engels' *Condition of the Working Classes in England* and was filled with nostalgia for the past: 'How freshly, passionately and boldly is the matter dealt with here, without learned and scientific considerations! And even the illusion that tomorrow or the day after history will bring to light the result gives the whole a warmth and lively humour, compared with which the later "grey in grey" is damned unpleasant.'[5] A few years later he told one of his daughters that he felt himself to be 'a machine condemned to devour books and then throw them, in a changed form, on the dunghill of history'.[6] By the end of 1862 he told Kugelmann that 'the second part is now at last finished', though with the inevitable qualification that this was 'apart from the copying out and final polishing for the printer'. It would contain, he continued, 'only what was intended as the third

[1] Marx to Lassalle, *MEW* xxx 622.   [2] Marx to Engels, *MEW* xxx 243.
[3] Ibid. 248.   [4] Ibid. 280.   [5] Ibid. 343.
[6] Quoted in Y. Kapp, *Eleanor Marx* I 88.

chapter of the first part, i.e. "Capital in General". . . . . It is (together with the first bit) the quintessence and the development of what follows would be easy to complete, even by others, on the basis of what exists – with the exception perhaps of the relationship of different forms of the state to the different economic structures of society.'[1] But illness prevented any creative work for three months during the spring of 1863 and Marx concentrated on trying to give the historical part its final shape. He was, however, still confident that he could 'copy out' the remainder very quickly.[2] The possibility of competition from Lassalle spurred him on and by the summer he was regularly working ten hours a day and doing differential calculus in his spare time. In mid-August he reported to Engels that he was working on the manuscript for the printers which would be '100% easier to under-stand' than the *Critique of Political Economy*. He added that the ease with which Lassalle produced his works on economics made him laugh 'when I look at my colossal work and see how I have had to shift everything round and even construct the historical part from material that was in part totally unknown'.[3]

A certain number of the manuscripts from this period have either been lost or are inaccessible, so it is not possible to determine exactly how far Marx had got with with his '2nd part'. The main manuscript to have survived – from what Marx in 1837–58 conceived of as simply a third chapter – would amount to about 3000 printed pages and com-prises the 'historical stuff' that Marx in the summer of 1863 seems to have decided to incorporate into volume one as 'the Germans only have faith in fat books'.[4] Some of this contained material later incor-porated into the three volumes of *Capital*, but the major part was the historical section later published by Kautsky as the fourth volume of *Capital* under the title *Theories of Surplus Value*.

The *Theories of Surplus Value* comprises three large printed volumes of which a large part is simply extracts from previous theorists.[5] Marx began with Stewart and the economists of the mercantile system who tried to explain the origin of surplus-value simply from circula-tion. He then went on to the physiocrats who concentrated – rightly

[1] Marx to Kugelmann, *MEW* xxx 639.
[2] Cf. Marx to Engels, *MEW* xxx 359.
[3] Marx to Engels, *MEW* xxx 368.
[4] Jenny Marx to Bertha Markheim, in Andreas, *Briefe*, pp. 181 f.
[5] The manuscript was first published by Karl Kautsky in 1905–10 as the fourth volume of *Capital*. There is an English translation published in 1969.

in Marx's view – on the sphere of production, albeit mainly agricultural production. Most of the first volume was taken up with extracts from Adam Smith and an attempt to separate scientific from ideological elements in his theories, particularly focusing on his distinction between productive and unproductive labour. The second volume dealt mainly with Ricardo, who was blamed for reliance on certain faulty premisses taken over from Adam Smith. The discussion centred mainly round Ricardo's theories of profit and rent and particularly his confusion of surplus-value with profit. The third volume dealt with the Ricardian School and particularly the English socialists whom Marx called 'the proletarian opposition based on Ricardo'.[1] He also attacked Malthus as 'a shameless sycophant of the ruling classes'[2] for advocating extravagant expenditure by them as a remedy for overproduction. Marx regarded Ricardo as the high point of bourgeois economic theory. Thereafter, as the class struggle sharpened, 'in place of disinterested inquirers, there were hired prize-fighters; in place of genuine scientific research, the bad conscience and evil intent of apologetic'.[3] Those who tried to harmonise the principles of capitalism with the interests of the proletariat merely produced 'a shallow syncretism of which John Stuart Mill is the best representative'.[4] The English socialists, Ravenstone, Hodgskin and others, at least had the merit of drawing from Ricardo's labour theory of value the correct notion of capitalist exploitation. But they lacked the requisite theoretical insights to accomplish the necessary total reconstruction of his system.

The *Theories of Surplus Value* show how firmly Marx's ideas are situated in the tradition of classical economics.[5] As in other fields, Marx evolved his own ideas by a critique and elaboration of his predecessors. The volumes also contain a number of digressions such as one on alienation[6] and another on the growth of the middle class where he reproaches Ricardo with forgetting to emphasise 'the constantly growing number of the middle classes, those who stand between the workman on the one hand and the capitalist and landlord on the other'.[7]

From the summer of 1863 to the summer of 1865 there is a virtually

[1] Karl Marx, *Theories of Surplus Value* (London, 1969) I 30.   [2] Ibid.
[3] K. Marx, *Capital* I (London, 1954) p. 15.   [4] Ibid.
[5] Two accessible books on this tradition are: J. Schumpeter, *History of Economic Analysis* (New York, 1954); E. Heimann, *History of Economic Doctrines* (New York, 1964).
[6] Cf. K. Marx, *Theories of Surplus Value*, I 390 ff.   [7] Ibid., II 573.

complete silence in Marx's correspondence concerning his economic work. According to Engels, he spent 1864 and 1865 in drafting out Volume 3 of *Capital*. At the beginning of 1864 the finances improved but another obstacle immediately arose: carbuncles. When Marx began sending off the final manuscript of *Capital* to the publisher, he wrote to Engels: 'It is now three years since the first carbuncle was operated on. Since that time the thing has only let up in short intervals and, of all types of work, the purely theoretical is the most unsuitable when you have this devilish mess in your body.'[1] The boils started very suddenly in the autumn of 1863 and almost proved fatal. 'On 10 November,' wrote Jenny, 'a terrible abscess was opened and he was in danger for a fairly long time afterwards. The disease lasted a good four weeks and caused severe physical sufferings. These were accompanied by rankling moral tortures of all kinds.'[2] Jenny was ushered from the room for the operation during which Lenchen held Marx down and Allen wondered at the stoicism of German philosophers. The boils, however, continually reappeared; they usually started in the autumn and came to full bloom (so to speak) in January. There were times when Marx's body was so covered with them that he could only stand upright or lie on his side on the sofa. He took lots of advice, seldom followed it very long, and after some years claimed to know more about boils than any doctor; certainly he pursued widespread researches in the British Museum on the subject. At various times he took such extraordinary medicines as creosote, opium and arsenic (this for years on end), gave up smoking for months and took daily cold baths. He wished that the boils had been given to a good Christian who would have been able to turn his suffering to some account; but at the same time he comforted himself with the idea that the bourgeoisie would have good cause to remember his sufferings from this 'truly proletarian disease'.[3] On extreme occasions he would even operate on himself. 'Today', he wrote to Engels, 'I took a sharp razor (a relic of dear Lupus) and cut the wretch in my own person.' He was proud to think that 'I am one of the best subjects to be operated upon. I always recognise what is necessary.'[4] When the boils approached his penis he lightened the occasion by copying out and

[1] Marx to Engels, *MEW* xxx 263.
[2] Jenny Marx, 'Short Sketch of an Eventful Life', *Reminiscences*, p. 233.
[3] Marx to Kugelmann, *MEW* xxxii 573.
[4] Marx to Engels, *MEW* xxxi 182.

sending to Engels specimens of sixteenth-century French porno-
graphic verse – a field in which he considered himself 'well-read'.[1] He
found his only relief in occasional visits to the seaside. In March 1866,
for instance, he spent four weeks convalescing in Margate where he
was glad to find so little company that he felt he could sing with the
miller of the Dee: 'I care for nobody and nobody cares for me.'[2] One
day he walked the seventeen miles to Canterbury, 'an old, ugly
mediaeval sort of town, not mended by large modern English barracks
at the one end and a dismal dry Railway Station at the other end of the
oldish thing. There is no trace of poetry about it. . . . Happily I was too
tired, and it was too late, to look out for the celebrated cathedral.'[3]

In March 1865 Marx had signed a contract with the Hamburg
publishers Meissner and Behre. Meissner's was a medium-sized publishing house, one of the few in Germany with democratic leanings,
dealing mainly in school textbooks and works on history and medicine. This contract, which had been negotiated through Wilhelm
Strohn, a former member of the Communist League who often visited
Hamburg on business from England, gave May 1865 as the limit for the
delivery of the manuscript, though this had to be amended in a later
version. The terms of the agreement were not particularly advantage-
ous to Marx and he remarked to his future son-in-law Lafargue that
'*Capital* will not even pay for the cigars I smoked writing it'.[4] By July
1865, in spite of illness and work for the incipient International, Marx
was able to write to Engels that

> there are still three chapters to write to complete the theoretical
> part (the first three books). Then there is still the fourth book to
> write – the historico-literary one. This is relatively the easiest for me
> as all the problems are solved in the first three books and thus
> this last one is more of a repetition in historical form. But I cannot
> make up my mind to send anything off until I have the whole thing
> in front of me. Whatever shortcomings they may have, my writings
> do have *this* advantage that they are an artistic whole and that is
> only attainable through my habit of not letting them be printed
> until they lie before me complete.[5]

Marx was in a particular hurry to finish as 'the thing weighs on me

[1] Ibid. 369.   [2] Ibid. 193.

[3] Marx to Laura Marx, in *Karl Marx Privat*, ed. W. Schwerbrock (Frankfurt, 1962)
p. 112.

[4] Paul Lafargue, in *Reminiscences*, p. 73.   [5] Marx to Engels, *MEW* XXXI 132.

like a mountain'; also his friends – Liebknecht, for example – were spreading oversimplified versions of his ideas; and, as ever, Marx was haunted by the idea of not being able to complete his work before a revolutionary outbreak.[1]

In February 1866, being seriously ill and under pressure from Engels, Marx at last agreed to complete Volume One before drafting out the others. 'If I had enough money, that is more > -0, for my family and if my book were ready, it would be a matter of complete indifference to me whether I was thrown on the scrap heap today or tomorrow.' And he continued with the following report on his progress:

> As far as this 'damned' book goes, this is the situation: it was *ready* at the end of December. The discussion of ground rent alone is, in its present form, almost book length. I went to the museum in the day and wrote at night. I had to work through the new agricultural chemistry in Germany, especially Leibig and Schonbein, who are more important for this thing than all the economists put together and also the enormous material that the French have given us since I was last occupied with this point. . . . Although ready, the manuscript is gigantic in its present form and no one else apart from me can edit it – not even you. I began the copying out and stylising on the first of January and the thing went on very briskly since I was naturally delighted to lick the child smooth after so many birth pangs. But then once again the carbuncle broke it off. . . .[2]

By November 1866 he was able to send off the first batch of manuscript and the following April the whole was at last completed. Marx insisted on going to Germany himself with the manuscript and tactfully informed Engels of his clothes and watch that needed to be redeemed from the pawnshop before his trip. Engels sent by return the halves of seven £5 notes: the other halves, as was their usual practice, followed when Marx telegraphed the safe arrival of the first batch. Marx sailed for Hamburg in mid-April, proved to be one of the few passengers who kept upright in the storm, and deposited his manuscript in Meissner's safe. Since there was a possibility of printing the manuscript immediately (the printing was eventually done by Wigand who had published so much Young Hegelian material in the 1840s), Marx decided to stay on in Germany and went to Hanover at the invitation of Dr Kugelmann, a former member of the Communist

[1] Cf. Ibid. 134.   [2] Ibid. 178.

League and now a much respected gynaecologist, with whom Marx had been in correspondence since 1862. Marx described him as 'a fanatical adherent of our doctrine and our two persons. He bores me sometimes with his enthusiasm which is the opposite of his cold style in medical matters. But he understands, and he is upright, reckless, unselfish, and – what is most important – convinced.'[1]

While in Hanover, Marx was amused to be invited by a messenger from Bismarck to 'put his great talents to the service of the German people'.[2] Two years previously Marx had received a similar invitation, transmitted via Lothar Bucher, to write financial articles for the Prussian Government's official journal. Marx subsequently published his correspondence with Bucher, to Bismarck's embarrassment, at the height of the anti-socialist agitation in 1878. The visit to Germany had a strange sequel, which is worth telling in Marx's own words:

The crossing from Hamburg to London, was ... in general fair. Some hours before London a German girl whom I had already noticed for her military stance, explained to me that she wanted to go on the same evening to Weston Supra Mare and did not know how to deal with her large amount of luggage. The situation was all the worse since on the sabbath helpful hands are few in England. I got the girl to show me the railway station that she had to go to in London; her friends had written it on a card. It was the North Western, which I too would have to pass by. So, as a good knight, I offered to drop the girl off there. Accepted. On thinking it over, however, it occurred to me that Weston Supra Mare was South West of London whereas the station that I would pass by and that the girl had written on her card was North West. I consulted the Sea Captain. Correct. The upshot was that she was to be set down in quite the other end of London from myself. Yet I had committed myself and had to put a good face on it. At two o'clock in the afternoon we arrived. I brought *la donna errante* to her station where I learnt that her train left only at eight in the evening. So I was in for it and had to kill six hours with mademoiselle walking in Hyde Park, sitting in ice-cream shops, and so on. It came out that she was called Elizabeth von Puttkamer, *Bismarck's niece*, with whom she had just spent some weeks in Berlin. She had the whole army list with her. ... She was a spirited, cultured girl, but aristocratic and black and

[1] Ibid. 290.   [2] Ibid.

white to the tip of her nose. She was not a little astonished to learn
that she had fallen into 'red' hands. I comforted her, however, with
the assurance that our rendezvous would pass off without 'loss of
blood' and saw her off safe and sound to the place of her destination.
You can imagine what an uproar this would cause with Blind or
other vulgar democrats – my conspiracy with Bismarck.[1]

Whether the meeting was really pure chance or a 'plant' is impossible
to say.

The printing went slowly and, although Marx was able to correct
the first proof sheet on 5 May, his forty-ninth birthday, he had to
return to London in mid-May. It was a return that he feared. 'the
debts there are important and the Manichees are waiting "insistently"
for my return. Then there is the family moaning, the inner collisions,
the rush, instead of being able to approach my work fresh and untroubled.'[2] Throughout the summer Marx continued to be worried
by his creditors and only had time to correct the proofs sheet sent to
him by Meissner. He forwarded them regularly to Engels for his
opinion. (It is interesting to note that Marx had not shown any of his
drafts to Engels before they were sent to press.) Engels considered that
some of the more abstract first part bore 'the trace of the carbuncle'.[3]
He also wished that Marx had introduced many more subtitles and
had had his excursuses printed in a different type. Although the sharp-
ness of the dialectical development was improved in *Capital*, Engels
found the *Critique of Political Economy* easier to grasp. His opinion must
have improved, for Marx wrote soon after that 'your satisfaction up
till now is more important to me than anything that the rest of the
world may say of it'.[4] By the end of August the last galley was sent off
and Marx wrote jubilantly to Engels: 'To you alone I owe it that this
was possible: Without your sacrifice for me I could not have got
through the enormous labours of the three volumes. I embrace you,
full of thanks!'[5] In the third week of September 1867 *Capital: Critique of
Political Economy*, Volume I, Book 1: *The Production Process of Capital* appeared in an edition of 1000 copies.

Volume One of *Capital* is by no means the indigestible and virtually
unreadable book that it has the reputation of being. It consists of two
very distinct parts. The first nine chapters are, indeed, of an extremely

---

[1] Marx to Kugelmann, *MEW* xxxi 550 f.   [2] Marx to Engels, *MEW* xxxi 297.
[3] Engels to Marx, *MEW* xxxi 303.   [4] Marx to Engels, *MEW* xxxi 305.
[5] Ibid. 323.

abstract theoretical nature, whereas the rest of the book contains a
description of the historical genesis of capitalism which is at times
extremely vivid and readable.

The first nine chapters contain what Marx called in his 1857 Introduction 'the general abstract definitions which are more or less applic-
able to all forms of society'.[1] It is not only this abstract method that
makes these chapters difficult; there is also the Hegelian cast of the
book. In his Afterword to the second German edition of the book
Marx explained that he was employing the Hegelian dialectic of which
he had discovered the 'rational kernel' inside the 'mystical shell' by
'turning it right side up again'.[2] He even, as he said in the same Afterword, went as far as 'coquetting with modes of expression peculiar to
Hegel'. A third factor which makes the beginning of *Capital* difficult
is the fact that the concepts used by Marx are ones quite familiar to

[1] Marx's *Grundrisse*, p. 42. The argument of these nine chapters is summarised in
Marx's short *Wages, Prices and Profit* which, since it was delivered to British trade
unionists (see pp. 369 f. below), can serve as an admirable introduction to the more
abstract parts of *Capital*.
[2] K. Marx, *Capital* (Moscow, 1954) I 19 f.

Marx's letter to Engels on completing *Capital*, Volume One. The text reads:

2 Uhr Nacht, 16 Aug. 1867

Dear Fred,
Eben den *letzten Bogen* (49.) des Buchs fertig korrigiert. Der Anhang – *Wertform* –
kleingedruckt, umfaßt 1¼ Bogen.
Vorrede ditto gestern korrigiert zurückgeschickt. Also *dieser Band ist fertig*. Bloß
Dir verdanke ich es, daß dies möglich war! Ohne Deine Aufopferung für mich
konnte ich unmöglich die ungeheuren Arbeiten zu den 3 Bänden machen. I
embrace you, full of thanks!
Beiliegend 2 Bogen Reinabzug.
Die 15 £ mit bestem Dank erhalten.
Salut, mein lieber, teurer Freund!

Dein
K. Marx

Translation:

August 16, 1867, 2 o'clock in the night

Dear Fred,
Have just finished correcting the last galley proof (49th) of the book. The
appendix, on the form of value – is in small print and takes up 1¼ galleys.
The Preface likewise was corrected and sent back yesterday. So this volume is
finished. It is you alone that I have to thank for this being possible. Without
your self-sacrifice for me, I could never possibly have accomplished the enor-
mous labour for the three volumes. I embrace you, full of thanks!
Enclosed are two corrected galley proofs.
I got the £15. Many thanks.
Greetings, my dear, beloved friend.

Yours
K. Marx

economists in the mid-nineteenth century but thereafter abandoned by the orthodox schools of economics. Since the third quarter of the nineteenth century, economists in Western Europe and America have tended to look at the capitalist system as given, construct models of it, assuming private property, profit and a more or less free market, and to discuss the functionings of this model, concentrating particularly on prices. This 'marginalist' school of economics has no concept of value apart from price. To Marx, this procedure seemed superficial for two reasons: firstly, he considered it superficial in a literal sense, in that it was only a description of phenomena lying on the surface of capitalist society without an analysis of the mode of production that gave rise to these phenomena. Secondly, this approach took the capitalist system for granted whereas Marx wished to analyse 'the birth, life and death of a given social organism and its replacement by another, superior order'.

In order to achieve these two aims, Marx took over the concepts of the 'classical' economists that were still the generally accepted tool of economic analysis, and used them to draw very different conclusions. Ricardo had made a distinction between use-value and exchange-value. The exchange-value of an object was something separate from its price and consisted of the amount of labour embodied in the objects of production, though Ricardo thought that the price in fact tended to approximate to the exchange-value. Thus – in contradistinction to later analyses – the value of an object was determined by the circumstances of production rather than those of demand. Marx took over these concepts, but, in his attempt to show that capitalism was not static but a historically relative system of class exploitation, supplemented Ricardo's views by introducing the idea of surplus-value. Surplus-value was defined as the difference between the value of the products of labour and the cost of producing that labour-power, i.e. the labourer's subsistence; for the exchange-value of labour-power was equal to the amount of labour necessary to reproduce that labour-power and this was normally much lower than the exchange-value of the products of that labour-power.

The theoretical part of Volume One divides very easily into three sections. The first section is a rewriting of the Critique of Political Economy of 1859 and analyses commodities, in the sense of external objects that satisfy human needs, and their value. Marx established two sorts of value – use value, or the utility of something, and exchange value

THE 'ECONOMICS' 345

which was determined by the amount of labour incorporated in the object. Labour was also of a twofold nature according to whether it created use values or exchange values. Since 'the exchange values of commodities must be capable of being expressed in terms of something common to them all,'[1] and the only thing they shared was labour, then labour must be the source of value. But since evidently some people worked faster or more skilfully than others, this labour must be a sort of average 'socially necessary' labour time. There followed a difficult section on the form of value and the first chapter ended with an account of commodities as exchange values which he described as the 'fetishism of commodities' in a passage that recalls the account of alienation in the 'Paris Manuscripts' and (even more) the *Note on James Mill*. 'In order', said Marx here, 'to find an analogy, we must have recourse to the mist-enveloped regions of the religious world. In that world the productions of the human brain appear as independent beings endowed with life, and entering into relation both with one another and the human race. So it is in the world of commodities with the products of men's hands.'[2]

The section ended with a chapter on exchange and an account of money as the means for the circulation of commodities, the material expression for their values and the universal measure of value.

The second section is a small one on the transformation of money into capital. Before the capitalist era people had sold commodities for money in order to buy more commodities. In the capitalist era, instead of selling to buy, people had bought to sell dearer: they had bought commodities with their money in order, by means of those commodities, to increase their money.

In the third section Marx introduced his key notion of surplus value, the idea that Engels characterised as Marx's principal 'discovery' in economics.[3] Marx made a distinction between *constant* capital which was 'that part of capital which is represented by the means of production, by the raw material, auxiliary material and instruments of labour, and does not, in the process of production, undergo any quantitative alteration of value' and *variable* capital. Of this Marx said: 'That part of capital, represented by labour power, does, in the process of production, undergo an alteration of value. It both reproduces the equivalent of its own value, and also produces an excess, a surplus value, which

---

[1] K. Marx, op. cit. I 37.   [2] Ibid., 72.
[3] Cf. F. Engels, *Anti-Dühring* (Moscow, n.d.) p. 281.

may itself vary, may be more or less according to the circumstances.'[1] This variation was the rate of surplus value around which the struggle between workers and capitalists centred. The essential point was that the capitalist got the worker to work longer than was merely sufficient to embody in his product the value of his labour power: if the labour power of the worker (roughly what it cost to keep him alive and fit) was £3 a day and the worker could embody £3 of value in the product on which he was working in eight hours; then, if he worked ten hours, the last two hours would yield surplus value – in this case £1·

A little further on Marx expanded on the nature of this surplus value as follows:

> During the second period of the labour-process, that in which his labour is no longer necessary labour, the workman, it is true, labours, expends labour-power; but his labour being no longer necessary labour, he creates no value for himself. He creates surplus-value which, for the capitalist, has all the charms of a creation out of nothing. This portion of the working-day, I name surplus labour-time, and to the labour expended during that time, I give the name of surplus-labour. It is every bit as important, for a correct under-standing of surplus-value, to conceive it as a mere congelation of surplus labour-time, as nothing but materialised surplus-labour, as it is, for a proper comprehension of value, to conceive it as a mere congelation of so many hours of labour, as nothing but materialised labour. The essential difference between the various economic forms of society, between, for instance, a society based on slave-labour, and one based on wage-labour, lies only in the mode in which this surplus-labour is in each case extracted from the actual producer, the labourer.[2]

Thus surplus value could only arise from variable capital, not from constant capital, as labour alone created value. Put very simply, Marx's reason for thinking that the rate of profit would decrease was that, with the introduction of machinery, labour time would become less and thus yield less surplus value. Of course, machinery would increase production and colonial markets would absorb some of the surplus, but these were only palliatives and an eventual crisis was inevitable.

---

[1] K. Marx, *Capital* (Moscow, 1954) I 209.
[2] Ibid., 217. Cf. also vol I, ch. 19.

These first nine chapters were complemented by a masterly historical account of the genesis of capitalism which illustrates better than any other writing Marx's approach and method. Marx particularly made pioneering use of official statistical information that came to be available from the middle of the nineteenth century onwards. A reader who finds the beginning of *Capital* too arid would do well to follow Marx's advice to Mrs Kugelmann[1] and begin by reading the chapters on 'The Working Day', 'Machinery and Modern Industry' and 'Capitalist Accumulation'. In the chapter on 'The Working Day', Marx described in detail the 'physical and mental degradation'[2] forced on men, women and children by working long hours in unhealthy conditions and related the bitter struggle to gain some relief by legal limits on the number of hours worked and the passing of factory acts. Although, Marx concluded, it might seem as though the capitalist and worker exchanged contracts in a free market, the bargain was, in fact, one-sided:

> The bargain concluded, it is discovered that he was no 'free agent' that the time for which he is free to sell his labour-power is the time for which he is forced to sell it, that in fact the vampire will not loose its hold on him 'so long as there is a muscle, a nerve, a drop of blood to be exploited'. For 'protection' against 'the serpent of their agonies', the labourers must put their heads together, and, as a class, compel the passing of a law, an all-powerful social barrier that shall prevent the very workers from selling, by voluntary contract with capital, themselves and their families into slavery and death. In place of the pompous catalogue of the 'inalienable rights of man' comes the modest Magna Charta of a legally limited working-day, which shall make clear 'when the time which the worker sells is ended, and when his own begins'.[3]

Marx continued his indictment of capitalism in the chapter on 'Machinery and Modern Industry', describing the crippling effect of machinery on workers and the environmental effects of capitalist exploitation of agriculture.[4] Summing up his conclusions, however,

---

[1] K. Marx to L. Kugelmann, *MEW* xxxi 575 f.
[2] K. Marx, *Capital* (Moscow, 1954) i 269.
[3] Ibid., 302.
[4] Cf. on this topical point, K. Marx, op. cit., i 506.

Marx showed that his view of technological progress under capitalism was not wholly negative:

> We have seen how this absolute contradiction between the technical necessities of Modern Industry, and the social character inherent in its capitalistic form, dispels all fixity and security in the situation of the labourer; how it constantly threatens, by taking away the instruments of labour, to snatch from his hands his means of subsistence, and, by suppressing his detail-function, to make him superfluous. We have seen, too, how this antagonism vents its rage in the creation of that monstrosity, an industrial reserve army, kept in misery in order to be always at the disposal of capital; in the incessant human sacrifices from among the working-class, in the most reckless squandering of labour-power, and in the devastation caused by a social anarchy which turns every economical progress into a social calamity. This is the negative side. But if, on the one hand, variation of work at present imposes itself after the manner of an overpowering natural law, and with the blindly destructive action of a natural law that meets with resistance at all points, Modern Industry, on the other hand, through its catastrophes imposes the necessity of recognising, as a fundamental law of production, variation of work, consequently fitness of the labourer for varied work, consequently the greatest possible development of his varied aptitudes. It becomes a question of life and death for society to adapt the mode of production to the normal functioning of this law. Modern Industry, indeed, compels society, under penalty of death, to replace the detail-worker of today, crippled by life-long repetition of one and the same trivial operation, and thus reduced to the mere fragment of a man, by the fully developed individual, fit for a variety of labours, ready to face any change of production, and to whom the different social functions he performs, are but so many modes of giving free scope to his own natural and acquired powers.[1]

Volume One ended with a long section on 'Capitalist Accumulation' – the finest chapter in the book. The capitalist, being a prey to 'a Faustian conflict between the passion for accumulation and the desire for enjoyment', was forced to create an 'industrial reserve army' or vast pool of temporarily unemployed workers to serve the fluctua-

[1] Ibid., 487 f.

tions of the market. Marx synthesised his analyses in the thundering denunciation:

> We saw, when analysing the production of relative surplus-value: within the capitalist system all methods for raising the social produc- tiveness of labour are brought about at the cost of the individual labourer; all means for the development of production transform themselves into means of domination over, and exploitation of, the producers; they mutilate the labourer into a fragment of a man, degrade him to the level of an appendage of a machine, destroy every remnant of charm in his work and turn it into a hated toil; they estrange from him the intellectual potentialities of the labour- process in the same proportion as science is incorporated in it as an independent power; they distort the conditions under which he works, subject him during the labour-process to a despotism the more hateful for its meanness; they transform his life-time into working-time, and drag his wife and child beneath the wheels of the Juggernaut of capital. But all methods for the production of surplus- value are at the same time methods of accumulation; and every extension of accumulation becomes again a means for the develop- ment of those methods. It follows therefore that in proportion as capital accumulates, the lot of the labourer, be his payment high or low, must grow worse. The law, finally, that always equilibrates the the relative surplus-population, or industrial reserve army, to the extent and energy of accumulation, this law rivets the labourer to capital more firmly than the wedges of Vulcan did Prometheus to the rock. It establishes an accumulation of misery, corresponding with accumulation of capital. Accumulation of wealth at one pole is, therefore, at the same time accumulation of misery, agony of toil, slavery, ignorance, brutality, mental degradation, at the oppo- site pole, *i.e.*, on the side of the class that produces its own product in the form of capital.[1]

This judgement was supported by a series of detailed studies, moving yet objective, on the condition of the British working classes over the previous twenty years, the British agricultural proletariat, and the misery of Ireland. The book was rounded off with the following famous passage:

> Along with the constantly diminishing number of the magnates of

[1] Ibid., 645.

capital, who usurp and monopolise all advantages of this process of transformation, grows the mass of misery, oppression, slavery, degradation, exploitation; but with this too grows the revolt of the working class, a class always increasing in numbers, and disciplined, united, organised by the very mechanism of the process of capitalist production itself. The monopoly of capital becomes a fetter upon the mode of production, which has sprung up and flourished along with, and under it. Centralisation of the means of production and socialisation of labour at last reach a point where they become incompatible with their capitalist integument. This integument is burst asunder. The knell of capitalist private property sounds. The expropriators are expropriated.[1]

The subsequent two volumes, being only in draft form, have none of the polished verve of Volume One. There was, however, a long chapter entitled 'Results of the Immediate Process of Production' that Marx seems to have intended to put at the end of Volume One but left out at the last minute.[2] In this chapter Marx discussed how capitalist production reproduced the relationship of capitalist to worker in the total process. There are particularly interesting comments on the alienation involved in the relationship of capitalist to worker[3] and on the tendency of capitalism to 'reduce as much as possible the number of those working for a wage' in the production sphere and increase the number of workers in purely service industries.[4]

Whereas Volume One had dealt with production, Two and Three investigated what happened outside the factory when the capitalist came to sell his products for cash. In Volume Two Marx traced the circular movement of sale, profit and the ploughing back of resources for the next cycle of production and the complex factors underlying economic crises. This volume is far less interesting, due to its technical theoretical nature.

The first part of Volume Three appears to be in a more or less final

---

[1] K. Marx, op. cit., II 763. The fact that this passage is followed by a short section on colonisation is probably due to a desire not to attract the attention of the censor by finishing on too resounding a note.

[2] It is a sufficient indication of the disorder of the Marx archives that this chapter – some 200 pages long – was only published in 1933. It is still not translated into English, though there is a French translation (ed. R. Dangeville, Paris, 1971).

[3] See the passages translated in D. McLellan, *The Thought of Karl Marx* (London, 1971) pp. 118 ff.

[4] P. 245 of the French edition.

draft, but thereafter the book tails off without any final conclusion. It begins with a discussion of the conversion of surplus value into profit and thus the relationship between values and prices. Many people on reading Volume One had asked how it came about that, if values were measured by socially necessary labour, they should be so very different from market prices. The only answer that Marx provided to this problem was to assert that value was 'the centre of gravity around which prices fluctuate and around which their rise and fall tends to an equilibrium'.[1] He continued: 'No matter what may be the way in which prices are regulated, the result always is the following: the law of value dominates the movement of prices, since a reduction or increase of the labour-time required for production causes the prices of production to fall or to rise.'[2] Marx then enunciated in detail than in Volume One the falling tendency of the rate of profit which forms the centrepiece of the third volume. This law is expressed most succinctly by Marx as follows:

> ... it is the nature of the capitalist mode of production, and a logical necessity of its development, to give expression to the average rate of surplus-value by a falling rate of average profit. Since the mass of the employed living labour is continually on the decline compared to the mass of materialised labour incorporated in productively consumed means of production, it follows that that portion of living labour, which is unpaid and represents surplus-value, must also be continually on the decrease compared to the volume and value of the invested total capital. Seeing that the proportion of the mass of surplus-value to the value of the invested total capital forms the rate of profit, this rate must fall continuously.[3]

Marx then went further into the nature of economic crises which he traced to the basic contradiction between the necessity of a capitalist economy to expand its production without taking into account the level of consumption that alone could make it feasible:

> The *real barrier* of capitalist production is *capital itself*. It is that capital and its self-expansion appear as the starting and the closing point, the motive and the purpose of production; that production is only production for *capital* and not vice versa, the means of production

[1] K. Marx, *Capital* (Chicago, 1909) III 210.   [2] Ibid., 211
[3] Ibid., 249.

are not mere means for a constant expansion of the living process of the *society* of producers. The limits within which the preservation or self-expansion of the value of capital resting on the expropriation and pauperisation of the great mass of producers can alone move – these limits come continually into conflict with the methods of production employed by capital for its purposes, which drive towards unlimited extension of production as an end in itself, towards unconditional development of the social productivity of labour. The means – unconditional development of the productive forces of society – comes continually into conflict with the limited purpose, the self-expansion of the existing capital.[1]

The conclusion was:

The last cause of all real crises always remains the poverty and restricted consumption of the masses as compared to the tendency of capitalist production to develop the productive forces in such a way that only the absolute power of consumption of the entire society would be their limit.[2]

Marx then dealt with the factors that could slow down the fall in profits – principally increased production and foreign trade – and attempted to show that they can only be short-term palliatives. There followed two sections on interest-bearing capital and ground rent and the volume ended with the dramatically incomplete section on classes.

Even today, *Capital*, particularly Volume One, remains a masterpiece. Its historical analyses present an effectively damning picture of at least one aspect of nineteenth-century England composed with an attention to detail and a superb style that make it a permanent contribution both to history and to literature. Nor have its theoretical presuppositions or long-term predictions been 'disproved' – if only because they are not susceptible of ultimate refutation: the labour theory of value is not a 'scientific' theory[3] but a theory to be judged by the insights that it gives into the workings of the capitalist system.

[1] K. Marx, *Capital* (Moscow, 1954) III 245.   [2] Ibid., 260.
[3] Recent attempts to show that Marx's ideas *are* scientific have centred around the work of L. Althusser, e.g. *Reading Capital* (London, 1970). A lot of the debate will seem, particularly to the uninitiated, to be peculiarly Byzantine. For two substantial contributions, see N. Geras, 'Marx and the *Critique of Political Economy*' and M. Godelier, 'Structure and Contradiction in *Capital*', both in *Ideology in Social Science*, ed. R. Blackburn (London, 1972).

And Marx's famous predictions are only based on his abstract 'model' of capitalist society, a model capable of almost infinite variation in given circumstances and, like all models, it must be assessed by its fruitfulness.[1]

Capital did not immediately have the success that it later enjoyed. It was eagerly received in Marx's small circle and even his old allies Feuerbach and Ruge passed favourable comments on it. But there were disturbingly few reviews in German and most of them were hostile, though Engels' future adversary Dühring wrote favourably. Engels himself was the most assiduous review writer and managed to place seven, each carefully tailored to the nature of the paper in which it appeared. Kugelmann also acted as a very effective Public Relations Officer in Germany. Engels tried hard to get some publicity in England but the only result was a small notice in the *Saturday Review* of January 1868 which said: 'The author's views may be as pernicious as we conceive them to be, but there can be no question as to the plausibility of his logic, the vigour of his rhetoric, and the charm with which he invests the driest problems of political economy.' The general attitude of Marx's trade union colleagues was summed up by Peter Fox who, on being sent a copy by Marx, replied that he felt like a man who had been given an elephant and did not know what to do with it. The reception was indeed disappointing and Jenny wrote to Kugelmann: 'You can believe me that seldom has a book been written under more difficult circumstances, and I could write a secret history that would uncover an infinite amount of worry, trouble and anxiety. If the workers had an inkling of the sacrifice that was necessary to complete this work, written only for them and in their interest, they would perhaps show a bit more interest.'[2] But it took four long years before the 1000 copies were sold.

VI. LIFE IN MODENA VILLAS

Although the double inheritance of 1864 undoubtedly gave Marx the relative security that enabled him to finish Volume One of *Capital*, it had by no means been the final solution. In April 1864 the Marxes

[1] For a short and clear claim for the continued relevance of Marx's ideas, see A. Gamble and P. Walton, *From Alienation to Surplus Value*, ch. 7. Also, E. Hunt and J. Schwartz, *Critique of Economic Theory* (London, 1972).

[2] Jenny Marx to Kugelmann, *Briefe und Dokumente*, ed. B. Andreas, *Archiv für Sozialgeschichte* (1962) p. 193. Cf. also the letter of Jenny Marx (daughter) to Kugelmann in the same collection, p. 240.

moved to a considerably larger house in Maitland Park Road, a few hundred yards south of Grafton Terrace, where they remained for the next eleven years. To Jenny in her memoirs 1 Modena Villas (the postal address was changed to 1 Maitland Park Road in 1868) was 'a very attractive and healthy dwelling which we fitted out very comfortably and relatively smartly.... A new, sunnily placed, friendly house with airy light rooms.'[1] Indeed, later it seemed to her to be 'a veritable palace and, to my mind, far too large and expensive a house'.[2] It was one of two detached houses at the entrance to the Park with a flower garden in front, a well-stocked conservatory and plenty of space for their two dogs, three cats and two birds. Each of the girls had her own room and Marx himself had a fine study overlooking the Park, the room in which Marx wrote Volume One of *Capital* and which served as a focal point for the First International. Paul Lafargue has left the following description of Marx's study:

It was on the first floor, flooded by light from a broad window that looked out on to the park. Opposite the window and on either side of the fireplace the walls were lined with bookcases filled with books and stacked up to the ceiling with newspapers and manuscripts. Opposite the fireplace on one side of the window were two tables piled up with papers, books and newspapers; in the middle of the room, well in the light, stood a small, plain desk (three foot by two) and a wooden armchair; between the armchair and the bookcase, opposite the window, was a leather sofa on which Marx used to lie down for a rest from time to time. On the mantelpiece were more books, cigars, matches, tobacco boxes, paperweights and photographs of Marx's daughters and wife, Wilhelm Wolff and Frederick Engels.[3]

The books were arranged according to their contents, not their size, and were full of pages with corners turned down, marginal comments and underlinings. 'They are my slaves', Marx would say, 'and they must serve me as I will.'[4] Two features of the study that were added later were gifts from his friend and admirer, Dr Kugelmann. One was a bust of Zeus of Otricoli which had arrived – to the great consternation of the household – while the Christmas pudding was being pre-

---

[1] Jenny Marx, in *Reminiscences*, p. 233.   [2] Jenny Marx to Engels, *MEW* xxx 679.
[3] Paul Lafargue, in *Reminiscences*, p. 73.   [4] Cf. Ibid.

pared at the end of 1867; the other was a piece of tapestry that Leibniz (for whom Marx had a great admiration) had had in his study.

The money spent on furnishings (together with the repayment of debts) amounted to £500, its rent and rates were almost double those of Grafton Terrace, and, in general, it was a house whose inhabitants would be expected to have an income of around £500 p.a. – which is, in fact, about the sum of money that Marx did get through annually.[1] In addition Marx and the girls took three weeks' holiday at Ramsgate and Jenny had a fortnight by herself at Brighton. In October, the girls – who before had had to decline invitations as they had no money to return the hospitality – gave a ball for fifty of their friends. The financial situation was not helped by the arrival, in May 1865, of Edgar von Westphalen. He had just returned from America where – para-doxically – he had fought for the South in the Civil War. Despite his hypochondriac tendencies, he had an enormous appetite and even the amused tolerance of Marx, who described him as 'an egoist, but a kind natured one',[2] grew more and more strained during the six months of Edgar's stay.

A few months after the move, and in spite of his having made £400 by speculating in American funds,[3] Marx was obliged to write to Engels yet another begging letter:

> It is duly crushing, to remain dependent for half one's life. The one thought that sustains me here is that we two are executing a com-bined task in which I give my time to the theoretical and party political side of the business. Of course I live too expensively for my circumstances and moreover we have lived better this year than ever. But that is the one means by which the children, apart from all that they have suffered and for which they have been recom-pensed at least for a short time, can make connections and relation-ships that can assure them a future. I believe that you yourself will be of the opinion that, even looked at commercially, a purely proletarian set-up would be unsuitable here, however fine it might have been when my wife and I were alone or when the children were young.[4]

[1] Marx to Kugelmann, *MEW* xxxii 540.   [2] Marx to Engels, *MEW* xxxi 126.
[3] Marx to Lion Philips, *MEW* xxx 665. Marx may just have been boasting here. But he certainly gave Engels good advice on how to play the Stock Market (see *MEW* xxxiii 23, 29).
[4] Marx to Engels, *MEW* xxxi 131.

Engels duly came to the rescue and went as far as guaranteeing Marx £200 p.a., with the possibility of another £50. In November 1866 Marx's hopes were momentarily raised by the death of an aunt in Frankfurt but the result was only a meagre £12. The family was soon threatened with eviction and Marx had to get small loans from acquaintances 'as in the worst refugee period'.[1] The situation was made even worse by the necessity of keeping up appearances in front of Paul Lafargue, who was then paying court to Laura. Marx once again expressed a desire to go bankrupt – but instead ordered champagne and gymnastic lessons for Laura on the doctor's advice. During 1867 Marx recognised that Engels had given him 'an enormous sum of money'[2] but claimed that its effect was negated by his previous debts which amounted to £200. The next year, on his fiftieth birthday, he bitterly recalled his mother's words, 'if only Karl had *made* Capital, instead of just *writing* about it'.[3] Things were so bad that Marx seriously considered moving to Geneva. The poverty was all the more glaring as Marx had become a respected figure in the neighbourhood, culminating in his election to the prestigious sinecure of Constable of the vestry of St Pancras. Marx would not accept the office, agreeing with one of his neighbours that 'I should tell them that I was a foreigner and that they should kiss me on the arse.'[4]

In November 1868 the financial situation became intolerable and Engels asked Marx to let him know firstly how much he needed to clear *all* his debts and secondly whether he could live thereafter on £350 p.a. (Engels himself enjoyed an income from 1860 onwards of never less than £1100.)[5] Marx described himself as 'quite knocked down', asked Jenny to calculate their total debts and discovered that they were 'much larger' than he had imagined.[6] Engels let himself be bought out of Ermen and Engels earlier than he had anticipated and left the firm – to his immense jubilation and the popping of champagne corks – on 1 July 1869. Three weeks later, however, Marx noticed that Jenny was still not managing with the weekly allowance that he gave her. On pressing her about it, 'the stupidity of women emerged. In the list of debts that she had drawn up for you, she had suppressed about £75 which she was now trying to pay off little by little from the house allowance. When I asked why, she replied that

[1] Ibid. 262.   [2] Ibid. 321.   [3] Ibid. 75.   [4] Ibid. 108.
[5] Cf. K. Marx, *Dokumente seines Lebens*, p. 350.
[6] Marx to Engels, *MEW* xxxi 217.

she was frightened to come out with the vast total. Women plainly always need to be controlled!'[1] Engels accepted this with good grace and Marx's financial troubles were, at last, finished. It has been calculated from their correspondence that from 1865 to 1869 Engels gave Marx no less than £1862.[2]

The period of the composition of *Capital*, Volume One, also saw Marx take on the role of father-in-law and eventually grandfather. The chief event of the late 1860s was Laura's courtship and marriage. As early as 1865, at Jenny's twenty-first birthday party, she had received a passionate proposal of marriage from Charles Manning, a rich South American with an English father. However, according to Marx, Laura didn't 'care a pin for him' and was well experienced in 'dampening down Southern passions'.[3] The same year she met Paul Lafargue, then aged twenty-three, the only son of a well-to-do planter in Cuba whose parents had returned to France to enter the wine trade in Bordeaux. Paul was a (not very enthusiastic) medical student. As a follower of Proudhon, he was active in student politics and had been sent as a French delegate to the General Council of the International in London where he remained owing to his exclusion from the French university on political grounds. By August 1866 he was 'half-engaged' to Laura.[4] Marx was not entirely happy. Laura seemed to have little real affection for Lafargue whom he described to Engels as 'handsome, intelligent, energetic and gymnastically developed lad'.[5] Nevertheless, he went very carefully into his prospective son-in-laws' position: he wrote to Lafargue's old professor in Paris for a reference and sent Lafargue himself a rather heavy letter of which the first paragraph read:

If you wish to continue your relations with my daughter, you will have to discard your manner of 'paying court' to her. You are well aware that no engagement has been entered into, that as yet everything is provisional. And even if she were formally your bretrothed, you should not forget that this concerns a long-term affair. An all

[1] Ibid. xxxii 344.

[2] K. Marx, *Dokumente seines Lebens*, p. 352. Any conversion into present-day values must be approximate. Very roughly these figures should be multiplied between ten and twenty times to get present-day equivalents. For comparison, an unskilled worker in London in 1870 could earn around £50 p.a. The classical work on this subject is A. Bowley, *Wages in the United Kingdom in the Nineteenth Century* (Cambridge, 1900).

[3] Marx to Engels, *MEW* xxxi 110.   [4] Ibid. 247.   [5] Ibid.

too intimate deportment is the more unbecoming in so far as the two lovers will be living in the same place for a necessarily prolonged period of purgatory and of severe test. I have observed with dismay your change of conduct from day to day over the geologic epoch of a single week. To my mind, true love expresses itself in the lover's restraint, modest bearing, even diffidence regarding the adored one, and certainly not in unconstrained passion and manifestations of premature familiarity. Should you plead in defence your Creole temperament, it becomes my duty to interpose my sound sense between your temperament and my daughter. If in her presence you are unable to love her in a manner that conforms with the latitude of London, you will have to resign yourself to loving her from a distance. I am sure you take my meaning.[1]

Marx went on to explain that he himself had 'sacrificed all my fortune to the revolutionary struggle'; this he did not regret, but had he the choice again he would not have married. 'As far as it is in my power, I intend to save my daughter from the rocks on which her mother's life has been wrecked.'[2] He finished by insisting on economic guarantees for Lafargue's future as 'observation has convinced me that you are not by nature very diligent, for all your bouts of feverish activity and good will'.[3] Jenny, too, was rather dubious of French medical students but Lafargue must have been able to allay their fears for the engagement was announced in Spetember 1866 on Laura's twenty-first birthday. Jenny Marx became enthusiastic: his parents had promised Paul around £4000 on marriage and she admired his 'fine character, his kindheartedness, generosity and his devotion to Laura'.[4] Particularly fortunate was the fact that Paul and Laura shared the same views on religion. Bitterly remembering her own courtship, she wrote: 'thus Laura will be spared the inevitable conflicts and sufferings to which any girl with her opinions is exposed in society. For how rare it is nowadays to find a man who shares such views and at the same time has culture and a social position.'[5] The friendship between the families was cemented by the visit of all the Marx daughters to Bordeaux for three weeks.

Jenny, in particular, was keen on the civil marriage taking place as

[1] Marx to Paul Lafargue, *MEW* xxxi 518. The full letter is translated in Y. Kapp, *Eleanor Marx*, i 298 f.
[2] Marx to Paul Lafargue, *MEW* xxxi 519.   [3] Ibid.
[4] W. Liebknecht, *Briefwechsel mit Marx und Engels*, p. 80.   [5] Ibid.

privately as possible to avoid the neighbours' gossiping, and Engels obligingly suggested that the reason given for it should be that Laura was a Protestant and Paul a Catholic.[1] The publication of the banns was put off until the last possible moment as Jenny was not in a position to prepare Laura's trousseau, and Marx did not want 'to send her into the world like a beggar'.[2] Jenny was still preparing an extensive wardrobe for Laura four months after her marriage. This took place on 2 April 1868 in St Pancras' Registry Office and was followed by lunch at Modena Villas where Engels cracked so many jokes at Laura's expense that he reduced her to tears.[3] The couple honeymooned in Paris and returned to London where Paul completed his medical studies.

Meanwhile, her sister, too, began to establish her independence. Without asking her parents' permission, Jenny took a job as a governess five mornings a week to the children of a near-by doctor named Monroe. Marx, in fact, disapproved strongly and only agreed after insisting on stringent conditions. Jenny enjoyed her job, in spite of the difficulty she experienced in actually getting her employers to pay her, and it lasted almost three years until the Monroes made 'the terrible discovery that I am the daughter of the petroleur chief who defended the iniquitous communal movements'.[4] She began, too, to write articles on Ireland for French newspapers, being, like Eleanor, passionately attached to the cause of Home Rule. Marx confessed to Engels that he was glad at least 'that Jenny is distracted by something to do and particularly got outside the four walls of this house'. He continued: 'My wife has completely lost her temper for years. It is quite explicable in the circumstances but none the less pleasant for that. She wears the children to death with her complaints and irritability and ill humour, though no children bear everything in a more jolly way. But there are certain limits.'[5] And Jenny herself found Marx's temper scarcely any better.[6] The situation only improved with the move of Engels to London and the galvanising effect of the Paris Commune.

[1] Engels to Marx, *MEW* xxxi 409.
[2] Ibid. xxxii 33.
[3] *Engels–Lafargue Correspondence* (Moscow, 1959) i 111.
[4] Jenny Marx to Kugelmann, in B. Andreas, 'Briefe und Dokumente der Familie Marx', *Archiv für Sozialgeschichte* (1962) p. 263.
[5] Marx to Engels, *MEW* xxxii 217 ff.
[6] See her remarks to Engels on his irritability, *MEW* xxxii 705.

7

The International

The International belonged to the period of the Second
Empire during which the oppression reigning throughout
Europe prescribed unity and abstention from all internal
polemics to the workers' movement, then just reawakening.

Engels to Sorge (1874), *MESC*, p. 288

I. ORIGINS OF THE INTERNATIONAL

ONE OF the main reasons why Volume One of *Capital* was so long in
appearing and why the subsequent volumes never appeared at all is
that Marx's time was taken up by the work forced on him as the
leading figure in the International.

After the dissolution of the Communist League in 1852, Marx had
carefully avoided any party political commitment; for one thing, the
1850s were a period of reaction and left-wing activism was inoppor-
tune. But by the early 1860s political and economic conditions were
encouraging a revival of working-class activity in Europe. In England
the successful struggle of the building workers for a nine-hour day
encouraged the growth of organised trade unions and the establishment in 1860 of the London Trades Council. In France, Napoleon III
had begun to relax the anti-trade union laws in the hope of using the
workers as a counterweight to the increasing liberal opposition. As for
Central Europe, Lassalle (who died just a few weeks before the founding of the International) had 'reawakened the working-class movement in Germany after a sleep of fifteen years'.[1]

This revival coincided with a growing spirit of internationalism,
particularly strong in England. The cause of Italian independence had
long been popular among the British working class; Garibaldi was
fêted when he came to London and Mazzini was personally known to

[1] Marx to Schweitzer *MEW* XXXII 568 f.

many of the working-class leaders. Lincoln's proclamation abolishing slavery rallied trade unionists to the side of the North in the Civil War and Marx was very impressed by the 'monster meeting' organised by the trade unions in March 1863 which – exceptionally – he attended. However, the event which directly gave rise to the founding of the International was the Polish insurrection of 1863. A representative delegation of French workers – subsidised by Napoleon – had already visited London in the Exhibition year of 1862 and it was natural that the French should send a delegation to the mass meeting on Poland called in London in July 1863. These links were further strengthened by French and English workers contributing to each others' strike funds. Following the Polish meeting, George Odger, Secretary of the London Trades Council, was deputed to draw up an address, 'To the Workmen of France from the Working Men of England', which proposed the foundation of an international association to promote peace and foster the common interests of the working classes of all countries. The French drafted a reply and a meeting was called at St Martin's Hall near Covent Garden on 28 September 1864 to hear the exchange of addresses. It was at this meeting that the International was founded.[1]

Although Marx was in no way instrumental in summoning this meeting, he had a long-standing interest in the Polish cause.[2] In 1856 he had taken up the study of Polish history since 'the intensity and vitality of all revolutions since 1789 can be measured more or less accurately by their attitude to Poland'.[3] The insurrection of 1863 filled Marx with great hope: 'This much at least is certain,' he wrote to Engels, 'that the era of revolution has once more fairly opened in Europe. . . . Let us hope that this time the lava will flow from East to West and not the other way, so that we will be spared the "honour" of a French initiative.'[4] To give vent to his views, Marx conceived the idea

---

[1] It is obviously impossible to give anything but a very sketchy history of the International here. Two good general books are, G. D. H. Cole, *History of Socialist Thought*, II (London, 1954) 88 ff., and J. Braunthal, *History of the International*, I 75 ff. The British side of the International, and Marx's part in it, are exhaustively covered in H. Collins and C. Abramsky, *Karl Marx and the British Labour Movement* (London, 1965). For details on the early history of the International, see D. Rjazanoff, 'Zur Geschichte der Ersten Internationale', *Marx–Engels Archiv*, I (1925), and the documentary record in L. E. Mins (ed.), *The Founding of the First International* (New York, 1937).

[2] See further, A. Ciolkosz, 'Karl Marx and the Polish Insurrection of 1863', *The Polish Review*, X (1966).

[3] Marx to Engels, *MEW* XXVIII 88.   [4] Ibid. XXX 324.

of a pamphlet – the military half written by Engels, the political by himself – to be published by the German Workers' Educational Association. The dimension of the project grew and Marx worked steadily at it from February to May 1863, when his liver forced him to stop. These manuscripts, which remained unpublished until 1961,[1] form an integrated whole. Curiously enough, these historical tracts are of an exclusively political nature with no mention of economic influences, and their mainspring is Marx's Russophobia. According to him, the partition of Poland led to the dependence of the rest of Germany on Prussia, and Prussia's anti-Polish policy led in turn to Prussia's complete dominance by Russia. Thus 'the restoration of Poland means ... the thwarting of Russia's bid to dominate the world'.[2] In spite of his inability to finish this pamphlet, Marx took an active part in discussions with a Colonel Lapinski on the formation of a German legion to fight against Russia in Poland.[3] In October 1863 the German Workers' Educational Association did in fact publish a short pamphlet of which Marx was probably author.

Marx was thus actively interested in the immediate occasion for the St Martin's Hall meeting. His own account of his being invited (written some weeks later to Engels) is as follows:

> A Public Meeting was summoned for 28 September 1864 in St Martin's Hall by Odger (shoemaker, President of the Council of all London Trades' Unions) and Cremer (a mason and secretary of the Masons' Union). .... A certain Le Lubez was sent to me to ask whether I would take part on behalf of the German workers and in particular whether I could supply a German worker to speak at the Meeting. I supplied Eccarius, who was a great success, and I was also there – as a silent figure on the platform. I knew that this time the real 'powers' from both the London and Paris sides were present, and so decided to waive my otherwise standing rule to decline any such invitations.[4]

[1] K. Marx, *Manuskripte über die Polnische Frage (1863–1864)*, ed. W. Conze and D. Hertz-Eichenrode (The Hague, 1961).

[2] K. Marx, op. cit., p. 93.

[3] There is a rather fanciful account in Lapinski's memoirs, published in 1878, in which Marx is said to have shared a cab with Lapinski back to his flat after an international meeting in Herzen's rooms. According to Lapinski, Marx himself suggested raising a legion of 1000 men and promised, through a friend, to interest Prince Charles of Brunswick in providing the money to equip them (see L. Wasilewski, 'Karl Marx und der polnische Aufstand von 1863', *Polen*, XXVII (1915).

[4] *MEW* XXXI 12 f. The letter incidentally shows how out of touch Marx was with the British trade union movement: Odger was Secretary, not President, of the

In fact, Marx's invitation seems to have been a very hurried affair, for he only received the formal note from Cremer asking him to attend a few hours before the meeting. The French, being largely followers of Proudhon, believed that workers should run their own organisations, and Eccarius was an obvious choice, having been one of the signatories of the German Workers' Educational Association's Manifesto in October 1863.

The meeting was 'packed to suffocation' with some 2000 present. Beesly, Professor of History at London University and a leading Positivist, made a brief speech from the chair, the German workers' choir sang, and Odger read out the Address he had written the previous December. Henri Tolain, the most influential socialist in France, and a member of the delegations that visited London in 1862 and 1863, read the French reply which was almost exclusively confined to advocating, in Proudhonist terms, a reform of the relation between capital and labour that would ensure the worker a fair return for his work. Le Lubez then outlined the French plan for a Central Committee in London which was to correspond with sub-committees in the European capitals with a view to drawing up a common policy. George Wheeler and William Dell, two British trade unionists, proposed the formation of an international association and the immediate formation of a committee to draw up its rules. After a debate in which Eccarius spoke for the Germans, the meeting closed with the election of a committee comprising thirty-four members: twenty-seven Englishmen (eleven of them from the building trade), three Frenchmen, two Italians and two Germans, Eccarius and Marx.

This General Committee (soon to be called General Council) met on 5 October and elected Odger as President and Cremer, on the proposal of Marx, as Secretary. Corresponding secretaries were elected for France and Poland. Marx suggested that the secretary for Germany be chosen by the German Workers' Educational Association and he was himself elected by them shortly afterwards. Turning to its main business, after 'a very long and animated discussion'[1] the Committee

---

London Trades Council and Cremer was a carpenter, not a mason. F. Lessner's account ('Vor und nach 1848. Erinnerungen eines alten Kommunisten', *Deutsche Worte*, 1898) differs from Marx's in that Lessner says that it was he who was deputed by the German Workers' Educational Association to invite Marx. But Lessner's account was written thirty years after the event.

[1] *The General Council of the First International, Minutes* (Moscow, 1964) I 37.

could not agree on a programme – not surprisingly in view of its size (over fifty when the co-options had been completed). Marx had already left the meeting when he was elected to a sub-committee of nine to draw up a declaration of principles. At the sub-committee meeting three days later, Weston, an old and agreeable but long-winded Owenite, read out a statement of principles; and Major Wolff, a former aide of Garibaldi and now secretary to Mazzini, proposed the Rules of the Italian Working Men's Association as a basis. Marx missed this meeting owing to illness and also the subsequent meeting of the General Committee at which the proposals of Weston and Wolff were referred back to the sub-committee. Eccarius anxiously wrote to Marx: 'You absolutely must impress the stamp of your terse yet pregnant style upon the first-born child of the European workmen's organisation.'[1] Odger and others, continued Eccarius, were very dissatisfied with the proposed drafts and had remarked that 'the right man in the right place would be Dr Marx'.[2] Cremer himself wrote urging Marx to attend. However, Marx also missed the next meeting of the sub-committee claiming that he was not informed of the rendezvous in time. At this meeting Le Lubez was deputed to synthesise the drafts made by Wolff and Weston.

Marx finally put in an appearance at the General Committee which met on 18 October to consider this synthesis. Marx wrote that he was 'really shocked when I heard the worthy Le Lubez read out an appallingly verbose, badly written and completely crude preamble pretending to be a declaration of principles in which Mazzini was everywhere evident, crusted over with the vaguest tags of French socialism'.[3] Marx managed to get the drafting once more referred back to the sub-committee, which met two days later in his own house. His aim was if possible 'not to let one single line of the thing stand' and, in order to buy time, he suggested that they begin by discussing the rules. The strategy worked: by one o'clock in the morning they were still on the first rule and were forced to postpone the meeting of the General Committee until they had had time for a further sub-committee meeting. The papers were left for Marx to work on. His brief was merely to give expression to the 'sentiments' of Le Lubez's draft which the General Committee had already approved. To justify what he himself admitted to be the 'extremely peculiar way' in which he went about this, he wrote an *Address to the Working Classes* which he described

[1] Ibid. I 374.   [2] Ibid. I 376.   [3] Marx to Engels, *MEW* xxxi 14.

as 'a sort of review of the fortunes of the working classes' since 1845.[1] He also reduced the number of rules to ten. At the sub-committee meeting Marx's draft was approved except that, as he wrote to Engels, 'I was obliged to accept into the preamble of the Statutes two phrases on "duty" and "right", and also on "truth, morality and justice"; but they are so placed that they cannot do harm.'[2] The General Committee then approved the Preamble, Address and Rules, though not without amendment: that Marx was not able to get his way completely is shown by the passage of a motion that his term 'profit-mongers' be deleted.

The *Address*, a piece of writing skilfully adapted to his audience, was produced within a week and included material that later appeared in *Capital*. Marx wrote to Engels: 'It was very difficult to arrange the thing in such a way that our view appeared in a form that made it acceptable to the present standpoint of the workers' movement. It will take time before the reawakening of the movement allows the plain speaking of the past. We must act *fortiter in re, suaviter in modo* (strong in content, soft in form).'[3] Thus, in contrast to the *Communist Manifesto*, there were no sweeping generalisations or appeals to revolutionary action. The *Address* began with the statement that 'It is a great fact that the misery of the working masses has not diminished from 1848 to 1864',[4] and proceeded to document this statement with quotations from official British publications describing the poverty that contrasted so glaringly with the optimistic pronouncements of the Chancellor of the Exchequer on the country's increasing wealth. Marx's reason for dwelling on England at length was the apparently rather naïve view that 'with appropriate changes in local colour and scale, the English facts reproduce themselves in all the industrial and progressive countries of the continent'.[5] Although, he admitted, 'a minority of the working class have obtained increases in their real wages', yet 'since 1848 the great mass of the working classes have been sinking down to a lower depth at the same rate at least as those above them have been rising in the social scale'.[6] His conclusion was:

In all countries of Europe it has become a truth demonstrable to every unprejudiced mind, and only denied by those whose interest it is to hedge other people in a fool's paradise, that no improvement

---

[1] Ibid. xxi 15.   [2] Ibid.   [3] Ibid. xxxi 16.
[4] *MESW* i 377.   [5] Ibid. 381.   [6] Ibid.

of machinery, no application of science to production, no contrivance of communication, no new colonies, no emigration, no opening of markets, no free trade, nor all these things put together, will do away with the miseries of the industrial masses; but that, on the present false basis, every fresh development of the productive powers of labour must tend to sharpen social contrasts and accentuate social antagonisms.[1]

This is one of the clearest formulations of Marx's doctrine of relative pauperisation. It is paradoxical that in England the International chiefly helped to benefit the better-off workers and thus served to increase the very disparity Marx mentioned.[2]

Turning to more political aspects, Marx noted the failure of working-class movements in Europe since 1848. This failure had, however, been relieved by two important events: the passing of the Ten Hours Bill ('the first time that in broad daylight the political economy of the middle class succumbed to the political economy of the working class'),[3] and the co-operative movement. But – and Marx had in mind here the French disciples of Proudhon – this movement could only succeed against the power of capital if developed 'to national dimensions'. Thus 'to conquer political power has therefore become the great duty of the working classes'.[4] Finally Marx sketched the achievements of the working classes in the abolition of slavery, the support of Poland, and the opposition to Russia – 'that barbarous power whose head is at St Petersburg and whose hands are in every cabinet of Europe'.[5] He closed with the traditional appeal: 'Proletarians of all countries, Unite!'

In the Preamble to the Rules Marx started from the principle that 'the emancipation of the working classes must be achieved by the working classes themselves' and that this struggle would eventually involve 'the abolition of all class rule'. Since economic subjection was

[1] Ibid. 381.

[2] Marx's statement of relative pauperisation here is largely accurate, though not the whole story: during the 1850s, real wages remained fairly steady, though they increased rapidly just before the *Address* was written and in general maintained this increase thereafter. The situation of the mass of working people did improve slightly in an absolute sense, although the gap separating them from the labour aristocracy grew. For reference to the sources of these statistics, see R. Harrison, *Before the Socialists* (London, 1965) pp. 3 ff.; on the 'labour aristocracy' see E. Hobsbawm, *Labouring Men* (London, 1964) pp. 272 ff.

[3] *MESW* I 383.   [4] Ibid. 384.   [5] Ibid.

at the bottom of all social and political ills, it followed that 'the economical emancipation of the working classes is therefore the great end to which every political movement ought to be subordinate as a means'.[1] These statements were interlarded with the various phrases – about 'truth, justice and morality', and so forth – that Marx could not avoid, and the document closed with ten rules, dealing with such questions as annual Congresses and the election of the General Council.

The *Address* shows the extent to which Marx was prepared to take the working-class movement as it was without imposing any blueprint. He carefully avoided anything that might jar on the susceptibilities of the English or French. In particular the majority of English trade unionists prevented Marx from alluding in any way to revolutionary aims. Indeed Beesly said of the audience in St Martin's Hall: 'only a few, perhaps not one amongst them, belonged to any socialistic school. Most of them, I think, would have hesitated to accept the name of Socialist.'[2] Equally, in spite of his guarded criticism of the co-operative movement, Marx had to avoid any mention of state centralisation, a policy anathema to the French.

II. GROWTH OF THE INTERNATIONAL

The atmosphere of unrest which had characterised Europe in the early 1860s and been responsible to some extent for the birth of the International continued to favour its growth in the middle years of the decade. The political instability leading up to the Franco-Prussia War and the increase in strikes generated by the economic crisis of 1866–67 inevitably enhanced the International's prestige, and in its first years it was able to grow steadily inside the fairly loose doctrinal framework set up by Marx.

In England, the International made good progress for the first few years. It secured the affiliation of, among other organisations, the important Union of Bricklayers and Cordwainers. Its activities were regularly reported in the most influential working-class newspaper, the *Beehive*. One of the first acts of the General Council was to send a bombastic Address (drawn up by Marx) to Lincoln, the 'single-minded son of the working class'. In April 1865 Edmund Beales and other

[1] Ibid. 386.
[2] Quoted in D. Rjazanov, 'Zur Geschichte der Ersten Internationale', *Marx–Engels Archiv*, I (1925) p. 192.

middle-class radicals joined six workers to create the Reform League to agitate for manhood suffrage. Marx, renewing contact with his old friend Ernest Jones, was active in getting the League formed. All six workers were members of the General Council and Marx wrote enthusiastically to Engels: 'The great success of the International Association is this: The Reform League is our doing.'[1] In reality, however, the League merely weakened the International, whose work many of its members considered of less immediate importance than the League's own programme.

Marx put into the International a tremendous amount of work – much of it evidently against his will. In March 1865, for instance, he explained to Engels how he had spent the previous week: on 28 February there had been a sitting of the General Council until midnight which had been followed by a further session in a public house where he had to sign more than 200 membership cards. The following day he had attended a public meeting to commemorate the Polish uprising. On the fourth and sixth of March there had been subcommittee meetings into the small hours, and on the seventh again a meeting of the General Council until midnight.[2] A few months later Marx had to pretend to be absent on a journey in order to snatch some time to work on *Capital* and by the end of the year he complained that 'the International and everything to do with it haunts me like a nightmare'.[3]

During 1866 the progress of the previous year was maintained and the International displayed for the first time what the English viewed as its chief asset: its ability to prevent the introduction of blackleg labour from the Continent. Marx emphasised to Liebknecht that 'this demonstration of the International's direct effectiveness has not failed to impress itself on the practical spirit of the English'.[4] The strike of the London Amalgamated Tailors was a success owing to the International's efforts in this field and they immediately applied for affiliation. Several small societies joined and in August there was a major breakthrough: the Sheffield Conference of Trades Delegates recommended that its members join the International. By the time the first Congress was held in Geneva in September 1866, it could be reported that seventeen unions had joined the International and thirteen were negotiating. In November the National Reform League, the sole sur-

---

[1] Marx to Engels, *MEW* xxxi 110.   [2] Cf. Ibid. 100.
[3] Marx to Engels, *MEW* 162.   [4] Marx to Liebknecht, *MEW* xxxi 516.

viving Chartist organisation, applied to join. If only the London Trades Council could be persuaded to affiliate, Marx felt, 'the control of the working class here will in a certain sense be transferred to us and we will really be able to push the movement forward'.[1] Engels, however, did not allow himself to be influenced by Marx's enthusiasm and for several years was distinctly reticent about the achievements of the International. He failed to form a six-member section in Manchester and refused even to become a correspondent.

During this period there was occasional friction on the General Council between Marx and the English – over, for example, admiration for Mazzini or their dislike of Eccarius, a staunch but tactless supporter of Marx. But Marx had no difficulty in establishing his ascendancy. This was in part due to the role of mediator between England and the Continent that he was able to play. As he explained to Engels concerning Mazzini's opposition: 'Le Lubez had tried to make them [the English] believe that I dominated other continental groups thanks to my position as leader of the English group; the English gentlemen have now understood that, on the contrary, it is themselves whom I control completely, thanks to the continental groups, as soon as they begin to to be stupid.'[2] Marx also attributed his dominance to German ideological superiority and the fact that the rest of the General Council felt 'German science' to be 'very useful and even indispensable'.[3]

Marx's interventions when the General Council discussed Poland in January 1865 provoked an unusually enthusiastic response: the normally matter-of-fact minutes record that 'the address of Dr Marx was pregnant with important historical facts which would be very valuable in a published form'.[4] In the summer of 1865 the General Council discussed the views of John Weston (which he had already set out in the *Beehive*) that wage increases would only result in higher prices and that producers' co-operatives were therefore the only method of raising the workers' standard of living. Marx considered this view extremely superficial and, despite his opinion that 'you can't

[1] Marx to Kugelmann, *MEW* xxxi 534.
[2] Marx to Engels, *MEW* xxxi 195.
[3] Marx to Bolte, *MEW* xxiii 330. One of the later members of the General Council, Townshend, said that Marx always behaved as a 'gentleman', Engels as a 'domineering German', cf. M. Beer, *Fifty Years of International Socialism* (London, 1937) p. 134.
[4] *The General Council of the First International, Minutes*, i 61.

compress a course of Political Economy into one hour',[1] adopted the model of his previous addresses to working-class audiences and lectured the General Council through two long sessions. He attempted to show that rises in wages did not, in general, affect the prices of commodities and, since the tendency of capitalist production was to lower the average standard of wages, trade union pressure was necessary to resist these encroachments; of course, trade unions should always have in mind 'the final emancipation of the working class, i.e. the ultimate abolition of the wages system'.[2] In his arguments Marx incorporated a great deal of material from his drafts of *Capital* and in particular his theory of surplus value, there stated publicly for the first time. Although some members of the Council wanted the lecture published, Marx hesitated, considering it not flattering to have Weston as an opponent and not wishing to detract from the impression that the publication of his *magnum opus* would eventually make.[3]

The first real threat to Marx's position on the General Council came at the end of 1865 from the followers of Mazzini who had never forgiven Marx for altering so drastically their first version of the Inaugural Address and who particularly objected to the 'class' character of Marx's ideas. Marx described the events in a letter to his cousin Nannette Philips:

> During my absence ... Mazzini took pains to ferment a revolt against my leadership. Leadership is never something agreeable nor something that I covet. I have always in my mind's eye your father who said: 'the asses always hate their keeper'. Mazzini, who does not conceal his hatred of free thought and socialism, is jealously watching the progress of our association.... He intrigued with certain English workers and aroused their jealousy against 'German' influence.... In doing this he was certainly acting sincerely, for he abhors my principles which are, for him, tainted by the most criminal 'materialism'.[4]

Marx counter-attacked by convoking all the foreign secretaries to his house for a concerted drive against Mazzini's followers who thereafter abandoned all co-operation with the International.[5] In September 1866

[1] Marx to Engels, *MEW* xxxi 123.   [2] *MESW* i 447.

[3] The lecture was found among Marx's papers and published by his daughter Eleanor under the title *Value, Price and Profit*. It occupies fifty pages in *MESW* i.

[4] Marx to Antoinette Philips, *MEW* xxxi 504 f.

[5] It is worth noting Mazzini's judgement of Marx, delivered just before the fall

Marx himself was proposed as President of the General Council but declined on the grounds that the position should be occupied by a manual worker, and Odger was elected. From the start Marx regarded England as the linchpin of the International. A few months after the founding of the International, he wrote to Kugelmann: 'I prefer a hundred times my action here via the International. The influence on the English proletariat is direct and of supreme importance.'[1]

On the General Council Marx's official responsibility was for Germany of which he was corresponding-secretary. But in spite of the importance he attached to spreading the influence of the International in Germany, Marx had little to show for his efforts during the first year. Lassalle had died a few weeks before the foundation of the International and his party, the ADAV (General Union of German Workers), the only existing labour organisation in Germany, was left with a leadership problem as well as disputes about the party's centralised organisation and its attitude to Bismarck's policies. The party did not become sufficiently united to adopt an attitude towards the International until J. B. von Schweitzer, a gifted lawyer of aristocratic descent and editor of the party's newspaper *Sozial-Demokrat*, gained control in 1866. Marx was to retain a deep, life-long antipathy to the legacy of Lassalle – the 'Richelieu of the proletariat', who had wanted to sell the working class to Bismarck.[2] 'It is beyond all doubt', he wrote to Schweitzer, 'that there will be a disappointment over Lassalle's unholy illusions about a socialist initiative on the part of the Prussian Government. The logic of things will tell. But the honour of the workers' party demands that it reject such phantasms itself before it discovers their emptiness from experience. The working class is revolutionary or it is nothing.'[3]

During the first year of the International Engels referred to Wilhelm Liebknecht in Berlin as 'the only reliable contact that we have in Germany'.[4] Although he got the Inaugural Address printed in the *Sozial-Demokrat*, Liebknecht was able to do little more, for he had difficulty supporting his family and was put in an ambiguous position by

---

of the commune: he spoke of Marx as 'a German, a man of acute but destructive intelligence, imperious, jealous of the influence of others, without any strong philosophical or religious convictions and, I fear, with a heart more full of hate, albeit justified, than of love' (*La Roma del Popolo*, no. xx, 13 July 1871).
[1] Marx to Kugelmann, *MEW* xxxi 455.   [2] Marx to Engels, *MEW* xxxi 48.
[3] Marx to Schweitzer, *MEW* xxxi 446.   [4] Engels to Marx, *MEW* xxxi 138.

having agreed to write a life of Lassalle (commissioned by the Countess von Hatzfeld). Liebknecht was expelled from Prussia in July 1866 and Marx wrote disapprovingly to Engels that 'he has not been able to found even a six-man branch of the International Association'.[1]

It would have been very difficult to implant the International in Berlin, for Marx's relations with the ADAV soon reached breaking point. Before the founding of the International both Liebknecht and Klings in Solingen suggested that Marx stand for the presidency of the ADAV. He at first refused, then agreed to stand, though he had decided to decline the office publicly if and when elected. This would be 'a good party demonstration, both against the Prussian Government and against the bourgeoisie'.[2] However, Lassalle's will, which nominated for President Bernhard Becker (who was already acting in that capacity), was made public a few days before the election and Marx's attempt failed completely: even in Solingen he got no votes at all. Marx nevertheless urged the few contacts he had in Germany to secure the affiliation of the ADAV to the International at its Congress in December. To Engels' cousin, Karl Siebel, he wrote: 'The adherence of the ADAV will only be of use at the beginning, against our opponents here. Later the whole institution of this Union, which rests on a false basis, must be destroyed.'[3]

In November Liebknecht passed on Schweitzer's invitation to Marx and Engels to write for the *Sozial-Demokrat*, and Marx's first contribution – apart from the Inaugural Address – was a long ambivalent obituary of Proudhon, in which he repeated the views of the *Poverty and Philosophy* and, with an eye on the position of the ADAV in Germany, criticised Proudhon's apparent 'compromise with the powers-that-be'.[4] However, relations between Marx and Schweitzer soon became strained: the *Sozial-Demokrat* was faithful to Lassalle's doctrines and it seemed to be directly attacking the International when it printed an article from Hess in Paris which repeated a rumour that Tolain and his friends were Bonapartist agents. Marx was furious and, although Schweitzer agreed to make Liebknecht responsible for all material concerning the International, Marx eventually withdrew his collaboration and vigorously criticised Schweitzer for his appeasement of Bismarck's Government. It would have been surprising if Marx's designs on the ADAV had come to anything: it was more than fifteen years since he had

[1] Marx to Engels, *MEW* xxxi 136. [2] Marx to Klings, *MEW* xxxi 417.
[3] Marx to Siebel, *MEW* xxxi 437. [4] *MESW* i 397.

been active in Germany[1] and his close friends and supporters there could be counted on the fingers of one hand.

At first, the International met with no greater success in South Germany. When Liebknecht arrived in Saxony, he could do no more for the International there than he had done in Berlin. The only political party in which action was possible was the *Verband Deutscher Arbeitervereine* (Association of German Workers' Unions) – a loose federation of liberal People's Parties, united mainly by opposition to Prussia, with no centralised leadership and very little socialism. Moreover, the political atmosphere was dominated by the approaching Austro-Prussian War. Liebknecht – to whom both Marx and Engels referred in their letters with the most scathing epithets – was willing to help the International (and, indeed, was obviously intimidated by Marx's personality), but the political situation just would not permit it. Marx, embarrassed by the lack of enthusiasm in the very area for which he was responsible, made greatly exaggerated, if not outright false, statements to the General Council on progress in Germany. By far the most effective person working for the International in Germany was the veteran socialist Johann Philipp Becker.[2] On the foundation of the International Becker had been very active in recruiting members in Switzerland from his base in Geneva. In late 1866 Becker, encouraged by Marx, founded active sections of the International in at least a dozen German cities and formed them, in 1867, into a well-organised 'Group of German-speaking Sections' centred on Geneva.

Even during these relatively lean years Marx retained his early faith in the vocation of the German proletariat to constitute the vanguard of the proletarian revolution owing, in particular, to its ability to curtail the 'bourgeois' stage of social evolution. Especially interesting in this context is the speech that Marx delivered on the twenty-seventh anniversary of the German Workers' Educational Association in February 1867. Here he is reported as attributing the Germans' revolutionary superiority to three factors: 'The Germans had achieved most freedom from religious nonsense; they did not need to undergo a lengthy bourgeois movement like the workers of other lands; their

[1] How much out of touch he was is shown by his certainty that Prussia could not win the war against Austria in 1866. He was, however, happy with the outcome as 'everything is good which centralises the bourgeoisie' (Marx to Engels, *MEW* XXXI 243).

[2] Cf. R. Morgan, *The German Social Democrats*, pp. 63 ff.

geographical situation would compel them to declare war on eastern barbarism since all reaction against the West had come from Asia.'[1]

In France, still the centre of European socialism, the International made fair progress, but was hampered by ideological disputes, both internal and with the General Council. There were two separate groups which had been represented at the International's foundation meeting: the followers of Proudhon led by Tolain, and the Radical Republicans led by Lefort and Le Lebuz. The Proudhonists wished to build up a purely trade union movement overwhelmingly working class, whereas the Radical Republicans were mainly middle class and had political objectives. Since the followers of the Proudhonists were mainly shopkeepers, peasants and artisans they attached most importance to the institution of co-operatives, credit facilities and protective tariffs and were extremely suspicious of all centralising tendencies and strike action. Dissensions began with the very translation of the Rules by the Proudhonists who, in the key sentence declaring that 'the economical emancipation of th working classes is therefore the great end to which every political movement ought to be subordinate as a means',[2] cut out the words 'as a means', thus giving the impression that political activity was something of quite secondary importance. The Republicans regarded this as tantamount to compromise with Bonapartism. The Proudhonists replied that only workers should hold positions of responsibility in workers' organisations and that Lefort, who was the International's Press agent in Paris, should resign. Le Lubez, as Secretary for France and prominent among the French workers in London who never accepted very easily the authority of the General Council, was sent to investigate and naturally produced a report favourable to Lefort. But Tolain came to London to put his case in person. The English members of the General Council were bewildered and bored by the ideological quarrels of the French, and Marx wished to keep both parties inside the International, seeing 'on the one side Lefort (a literary man and also wealthy, and thus "bourgeois", but with a spotless reputation and, as far as *la belle France* is concerned, the real founder of our society), and on the other side, Tolain, Fribourg, Limousin – the workers'.[3] However, when Tolain forced the issue the General Council was compelled to come down on the side of the workers after a long and stormy discussion which,

---

[1] Report of Eccarius in 'Der Vorbote', *MEW* xvi 524.   [2] *MESW* i 386.
[3] Marx to Engels, *MEW* xxxi 85.

according to Marx, 'created, particularly on the English, the impression that the Frenchmen really do stand in need of a Bonaparte'.[1] Lefort was removed from his post, Le Lubez resigned and Mazzini's followers, who were sympathetic to the French Republicans, also eventually withdrew.

It was these same French followers of Proudhon who were to be the main opponents of Marx and the General Council at the London Conference of 1865 and the Geneva and Lausanne Conferences of 1866 and 1867. It had been planned to hold the first congress of the International in Brussels in the autumn of 1865. But Marx was anxious about the prevailing doctrinal confusion and persuaded the General Council to call a private conference in London to prepare the agenda carefully for a full congress at Geneva the following year. At this conference the only two countries represented – other than England and France – were Belgium and Switzerland. The questions discussed were mainly organisational and here the French delegation proposed what they called 'universal suffrage' – that all members should have the right to attend and vote at conferences. This ultra-democratic proposal was vigorously opposed by the English and heavily defeated. The rest of the meeting was taken up with drafting the agenda for the future congress: here the most important debate was on the Polish question – which had been instrumental in starting the International and figured on the agenda of all the early congresses. Most of the French, led by the young Belgian delegate de Paepe, opposed the introduction of a resolution *for* Polish independence and *against* Russian tyranny on the grounds that it would only benefit the Polish working classes and that tyranny needed to be condemned in general. This objection was overruled by a considerable majority. The French, however, did manage to ensure that the agenda included resolutions on the formation of international credit societies and 'the religious idea'.[2]

The Polish question was raised again in the General Council early

---

[1] Ibid. 101.

[2] George Howell alleged in 1878 that Marx himself was responsible for 'sowing the seed of discord' by introducing the religious idea at this meeting. Marx just as vehemently denied that he had anything to do with it. Although Marx's reply to Howell is not quite accurate in some details, the Minutes contain no mention of Marx in connection with the motion: support for it was exclusively French. For reference to sources and discussion of this point, see H. Collins and C. Abramsky, *Karl Marx and the British Labour Movement*, pp. 110 ff.

in 1866 and an effort was made, aided by the recent establishment of a French section of the International in London, to get the decision of the London Conference reversed. Marx outmanoeuvred the attempt, and was supported by Engels (making his first appearance in connection with the International), who wrote three articles for the *Commonwealth* (the successor to the *Beehive* as the mouthpiece of the General Council) entitled 'What have the working classes to do with Poland?' The Austro-Prussian War also caused an outbreak of what Marx termed 'Proudhonised Stirnerism'[1] when Lafargue (soon to become Marx's son-in-law but then under the influence of Proudhon) suggested that all nationalities and even nations were 'antiquated prejudices'. In the view of the Proudhonists – and here they were in direct opposition to Napoleon's encouragement of national revival – all states were by nature centralised and therefore despotic and productive of wars as well as being contrary to the small-scale economic interests typical of Proudhon's followers. Marx had nothing but ridicule for such views and, as he informed Engels, 'the English laughed very much when I began my speech by saying that our friend Lafargue and others, who had done away with nationalities, had spoken "French" to us, i.e. a language which nine-tenths of the audience did not understand'.[2]

At the Geneva Congress the majority of delegates were Franco-Swiss – thirty-three out of about sixty – and there was a large French contingent also. To meet the inevitable challenge from the French, Marx – who personally attended only the final Hague Congress of the International (in 1872) – drew up detailed instructions for the General Council delegates which were confined 'to such points as permit the immediate agreement and co-operation of workers and provide direct force and impetus to the needs of the class struggle and the organisation of the workers into a class'.[3] Social questions occupied most of the agenda. Marx's instructions stressed the necessity of trade unions in the battle against capital and their future role as 'organising centres of the working class in the broad interest of its complete emancipation';[4] these proposals were modified by a French amendment on justice and 'reciprocity' as the final aim. The French also opposed unsuccessfully the General Council's resolution on the legal

---

[1] Marx to Engels, *MEW* xxxi 229.   [2] Ibid.
[3] Marx to Kugelmann, *MEW* xxxi 529.
[4] *The General Council of the First International, Minutes,* i 349.

enactment of the eight-hour working day as they did not believe in using the state as a reforming agency. Marx's statements on child labour as a 'progressive, sound and legitimate tendency' although under capital it was 'distorted into an abomination'[1] met with no opposition; but the Proudhonists got an amendment passed which prohibited female labour.

Marx's view that standing armies should eventually be replaced by 'the general arming of the people and their general instruction in the use of arms'[2] was also endorsed without opposition. He had instructed that the problems of international credit and religious ideas should 'be left to the initiative of the French'. Inevitably the Polish question figured again and Marx's views met with strong opposition as the French produced a remarkable counter-resolution which read: 'We, partisans of freedom, protest against all despotisms; we emphatically condemn and denounce the organisation and social tendencies of Russian despotism, as leading inevitably to the most brutalising form of communism; but, being delegates at an economic congress, we consider that we have nothing to say concerning the political reconstruction of Poland.'[3] The Proudhonists did not share what they considered to be Marx's 'Russophobia' and did not see why Russian despotism should be more specifically condemned than any other. The Congress eventually adopted a compromise resolution, proposed by Becker, which was nearer to the French proposal and implied a defeat for Marx. In the debate on organisation, Tolain again proposed that only workers should be admitted as delegates to congresses. Cremer, in reply, said that in Britain much was owed to middle-class members. 'Among those members', he added, 'I will mention only one, Citizen Marx, who has devoted all his life to the triumph of the working class.'[4] Marx had entertained great fears for the Geneva Congress: but, as he wrote to Kugelmann, 'on the whole, its outcome has been better than my expectations'.[5]

III. THE INTERNATIONAL AT ITS ZENITH

During the years 1867–69, with its three Congresses at Lausanne, Brussels, and Basle, the International moved to the height of its power and influence. The Lausanne Congress was once more a Franco-Swiss

---

[1] Op. cit., I 343 f.   [2] Op. cit. I 351.
[3] J. Freymond (ed.), *La Première Internationale* (Geneva, 1962) I 107.
[4] J. Freymond, op. cit., I 56.   [5] Marx to Kugelmann, *MEW* 529.

gathering. Marx was too absorbed in finishing *Capital* (Volume One) to give much time to the preparations and the large French delegation made a considerable impact: they succeeded in forcing a compromise resolution on state responsibility for education, and would only agree to the words 'social ownership' in connection with the Belgian resolution urging nationalisation of railways and other monopolies. The Proudhonists supported peasant ownership, and the discussion on the nationalisation of land had to be adjourned until the following year. Resolutions on co-operatives and credit schemes were also French-inspired. The one question that united Marx and the French was how to reply to an invitation from the League of Peace and Freedom – an international semi-pacifist organisation supported by such varied people as John Stuart Mill, Victor Hugo, Bright, Herzen, Garibaldi and Bakunin. The League was holding a conference in Switzerland at the same time as the International and had invited the attendance of representatives. In the General Council Marx had strongly opposed having anything to do with this group of 'impotent bourgeois ideologists'. The majority of delegates at Lausanne were in favour of co-operating with the League but Tolain managed to have included in the statement of acceptance the view that war could only be stopped by a new social system created by a just redistribution of wealth. So far from finding this unpalatable, the League accepted the statement with enthusiasm, but did not pursue co-operation with the International any further.

The current industrial unrest and the passage of the 1867 Reform Bill in Britain focused public attention on working-class movements, and the Lausanne Congress was widely reported in the British Press. Marx wrote optimistically to Engels:

> Things are moving forward, and in the next revolution, which is perhaps nearer than it seems, we (i.e. you and I) have this powerful machine in our hands. Compare this with the results of the activities of Mazzini and others over the past 30 years. All accomplished without financial support and despite the intrigues of the Proudhonists in Paris, Mazzini in Italy and the ambitious Odger, Cremer and Potter in London, with Schultz-Delitzsch and the Lassalleans in Germany. We can be very content.[1]

On the General Council, however, things were far from smooth.

---

[1] Marx to Engels, *MEW* xxxi 342 f.

Marx had once again to defend Eccarius against the English, who objected strongly to the condescending tone of his reports in *The Times* on the Lausanne Congress. Difficulties with Odger persisted, until Marx eliminated his influence by abolishing the office of President. The French section in London caused so much disturbance that Marx for a while seriously considered transferring the seat of the General Council to Geneva until he was dissuaded by Engels who reminded him of the disastrous results of transferring the Communist League's headquarters to Cologne in 1851.

In England the progress of the International lost momentum and, after 1867, was almost non-existent: there were few new trade union affiliations and no breakthrough into the workers in heavy industry. The General Council was even evicted from its premises for debt, and Marx's enthusiasm over the Reform League turned to disillusion when he realised that it merely distracted the English working-class leaders from the tasks of the International. Ireland was one question, however, which did engage the attention both of the English working-class leaders and also of Marx. It had captured the imagination of Marx's whole family. The Fenian terrorists had been active in the autumn of 1867 and had been dealt with in what appeared to be an arbitrary manner. On their behalf Marx drafted a resolution to the Home Secretary; he also delivered a speech in the General Council which went into the history of the destruction of Ireland's infant industries and the sacrifice of his agriculture to English interests. What the English members of the General Council failed to realise, Marx explained to Engels, was that since 1846 the English no longer wished to colonise Ireland in the Roman sense – as they had done since Elizabeth and Cromwell – but to replace the Irish by pigs, sheep and cows. The following year he described how his views had changed on this point:

> I believed for a long time that it would be possible that the rise of the English working class would be able to overthrow the Irish regime. I always argued this point of view in the *New York Tribune*. More profound study has convinced me of the contrary. The English proletariat will never achieve anything until they have got rid of Ireland. The lever must be applied in Ireland. That is why the Irish question is so important for the social movement as a whole.[1]

[1] Marx to Engels, *MEW* xxxii 414 f.

The solution lay in self-government for Ireland, agrarian revolution and protective tariffs. Marx also delivered the same speech in the German Workers' Education Association: he was happy to make it as long as possible, he wrote to Engels, for his carbuncles made standing the only tolerable position.

In contrast to its stagnation in England, the International made rapid progress on the Continent, particularly in its capacity as a liaison committee between the unions of the various countries to support each other's strikes – the activity which had led to its original success in England. The financial help given by British trade unions to the striking Paris bronze workers led to their victory and a great increase in the prestige of the International in France: a little later a Parisian group calling themselves 'positivist proletarians' applied for affiliation and were admitted on the condition, proposed by Marx to the General Council, that they call themselves simply 'proletarian' 'for the principles of positivism are directly opposed to our Statutes'.[1] The International was also instrumental in arranging help for the Geneva builders and the Basle silkweavers; and since this was a period of great strike activity, it gained publicity far beyond its actual effectiveness. In Germany Liebknecht was still unable to further the International's aims until the end of 1867: for apart from his lack of organisational ability, the *Verband* was not ready to accept socialist ideas, and anti-Prussianism was still its (and Liebknecht's) main concern. But by the beginning of 1868, things were already moving in the International's favour: Bebel, the *Verband*'s President and a gifted organiser, felt the need of a more solid programme; and Liebknecht saw himself threatened by Schweitzer's renewed overtures to Marx, made easier by the fact that the Lassallean ADAV was moving leftwards in the face of Bismarck's alliance with the liberals. Becker had laid a grass-roots foundation with his network of German-speaking groups.[2] The International was steadily gaining in size, success and prestige throughout the continent of Europe during 1867.

The result of the Lausanne Congress had convinced Marx that there had to be a showdown with the Proudhonists at Brussels. He wrote to Engels: 'I will personally make hay out of the asses of Proudhonists at the next Congress. I have managed the whole thing diplomatically

---

[1] Ibid. 463.
[2] Cf. R. Morgan, *The German Social Democrats*, pp. 63 ff.

and did not want to come out personally until my book was published and our society had struck roots.'[1] The Brussels Congress – the longest and best-attended Congress held by the International – did indeed mark the eclipse of Proudhonist ideas. The opening debate endorsed the proposal of a general strike in case of war, though Marx dismissed the idea as a piece of 'Belgian stupidity' as 'the working class is not sufficiently organised to throw any decisive weight into the scales'.[2] To a further approach by the League of Peace and Freedom, the Congress replied that its members would do better to disband their association and join the International. The Congress accepted strikes as a legitimate weapon of working-class pressure and also adopted a resolution – concerning the impact of machinery – proposed on behalf of the General Council by Eccarius with the help of a long quotation from *Capital*. The proposal was drafted by Marx and summarised the views on the ambivalent nature of machinery that he had already published in *Capital*. Marx had previously defended these views at length in the General Council when the Brussels agenda was being drawn up.[3] Proudhonist resolutions on free credit and exchange banks were referred back to individual sections for study. Most importantly the Congress adopted a resolution calling for the collective ownership of land, railways, mines and forests. Marx was especially pleased with the results of the Congress: a resolution had been passed paying particular tribute to *Capital*, saying that 'Karl Marx has the inestimable merit of being the first economist to have subjected capital to a scientific analysis'.[4] The instructions that Marx had given both before and during the Congress to the General Council delegates, Eccarius and Lessner, had set the tone – heightened by considerable support from the massive Belgian delegation. The two main points for which Marx's had been striving – the common ownership of the means of production and the necessity for political action by the working class – had both become part of the programme of the International. *The Times* published two lengthy reports from Eccarius, and Marx (in spite of his annoyance that Eccarius had omitted the references to *Capital* in the debate on machinery) wrote enthusiastically to Meyer in America that 'it's the first time that the paper has aban-

[1] Marx to Engels, *MEW* xxxi 342.
[2] Marx to Eccarius and Lessner, *MEW* xxxii 558.
[3] Cf. *General Council of the First International, Minutes*, ii 232 ff.
[4] J. Freymond (ed.), *La Première Internationale*, i 430.

doned its mocking tone concerning the working class and now takes it very seriously'.[1]

The Basle Congress of 1869 saw the International at its zenith: it confirmed the defeat of the Proudhonists, and the influence of Bakunin's anarchism was not yet dangerous; it was also the most representative of the congresses. For the first time there was a delegation from Germany. Schweitzer had renewed his correspondence with Marx, and the International and Marx had been warmly praised at the ADAV's Congress in Hamburg in the autumn of 1868. Thus forced to declare himself, Liebknecht persuaded the *Verband* at its Congress in September 1868 to adopt the first four paragraphs of the Preamble to the International's statutes. Basing himself on this, Liebknecht then tried to get Marx to declare in his favour and condemn Schweitzer. Marx refused – still regarding Liebknecht as unenthusiastic about the International. In fact, Becker's group of German-speaking sections was much more active on the International's behalf. Marx summed up his attitude to both Liebknecht and Schweitzer as follows: 'The role of the General Council is to act impartially. Would it not therefore be better to wait until (1) the nullity of the results of Schweitzer's game have become apparent; and (2) Liebknecht and co. have really organised something?'[2] This ambiguous situation was brought to an end when Schweitzer found himself compelled, in order to safeguard his leadership, to reunite with the Hatzfeld faction – a move which provoked the exodus of the more liberal-minded members of the ADAV. These members joined with the *Verband* at a Congress at Eisenach in August 1869 to found the Social Democratic Workers' Party and sent a twelve-man delegation, including Liebknecht, to the Basle Congress.

The Congress reaffirmed the Brussels resolution on the nationalisation of land, this time by a decisive majority. This point was vital to Marx as land nationalisation was the 'prime condition' of the Irish emancipation to which he attached particular importance.[3] The resolution was supported by Bakunin, making his first appearance at a congress, who also supported a proposal of the General Council, soon to be used against himself, that the General Council should have power, pending a decision by the next congress, to suspend any section

---

[1] Marx to Meyer, *MEW* xxxii 560.　　[2] Marx to Engels, *MEW* xxxii 169.
[3] See in particular Marx's letter in Kugelmann in *MEW* xxxii 638. Also to Meyer and Vogt, *MESC* pp. 236 ff.

which acted against the interests of the International. He also tried to persuade the General Council to abolish the right of inheritance. Marx's view, as expressed in the General Council, was that the first task was to change the economic organisation of society of which the inheritance laws were a product and not the cause. A measure of the general support for Bakunin's ideas was the majority which he had on his side against the General Council on this specific question (although this did not amount to the necessary two-thirds).

The right of inheritance was only one of the many views for which Bakunin had been agitating in Italy and Switzerland, where he had been working for the last few years following his romantic escape from Siberia in 1861. Bakunin did not have a very orderly mind, but when he did formulate his ideas, they were usually the opposite of Marx's: he was opposed to any and all manifestations of state power (Marx's views he referred to as 'authoritarian communism'); he was against any centralisation of the International, and he opposed all co-operation with bourgeois political parties. Whereas Marx believed that the new society was being nurtured in the womb of the old and that there was thus a certain continuity between them, Bakunin believed in the thorough destruction of every facet of contemporary society. Marx saw the history of the International as 'a continual struggle against sects' – the chief of these being the Proudhonists, the Lassalleans and eventually the followers of Bakunin. 'The development of socialist sects', he declared, 'and that of the real workers' movement are in inverse relationship. As long as the sects are historically justified, the working class is not yet ripe to develop as an independent historical movement. . . . Here the history of the International has merely repeated the general lesson of history that the obsolete tries to reinstate and confirm itself inside the newly achieved form.'[1]

It is significant that Bakunin evolved his ideas against the background of Russia and Italy, where no organised working-class movement was possible, whereas Marx was thinking primarily of Germany, Britain and France. At the beginning of the International, nevertheless, relations between Marx and Bakunin were amicable. Bakunin had visited Marx in London in 1864 and Marx had found him 'very agreeable and better than before . . . one of the few people who, after sixteen years, have progressed instead of going backwards'.[2] Up to the end of

[1] Marx to Bolte, MEW xxxiii 328.   [2] Marx to Engels, MEW xxxi 16.

1868 Bakunin had been active in the League of Peace and Freedom and only seceded from it when it would not accept his ideas on the abolition of the right of inheritance; on leaving, he founded the Alliance of Social Democracy which then applied to join the International. When he first heard of the alliance Marx considered it 'stillborn'[1] – though Engels was much more disturbed by this attempt to create 'a state within a state'.[2] The General Council refused the application of the Alliance, and so the Alliance disbanded and urged its individual sections to join the International. Although Marx was extremely scornful of the Alliance's programme as drawn up by Bakunin,[3] the General Council approved the projected affiliation on condition that the Alliance replace 'equalisation of classes' by 'abolition of classes' in its programme. Even so, there were constant squabbles in Geneva where the local section of the International refused to accept the Alliance as an affiliated body.

Bakunin's idea had most influence in Italy and Spain; they made some impact in French Switzerland and the South of France, and on many questions the Belgian delegation to the Congress tended more to Bakunin's position than to Marx's. It would, however, be quite untrue to suppose that Bakunin actually organised opposition within the International. The Alliance was not a close-knit party; it was much nearer to being merely a name that Bakunin applied to the totality of his friends, acquaintances and correspondents. Bakunin had no wish to challenge Marx despite vicious accusations that he was a Russian spy made by Marx's associates Liebknecht and Hess. When Herzen urged him to do this, he replied by referring to Marx as a 'giant' who had rendered 'tremendous services in the cause of socialism which he has served for practically twenty-five years with insight, energy and disinterestedness, in which he has undoubtedly surpassed us all'.

He went on:

Marx's influence in the International is undoubtedly very useful. He has exercised a wise influence on his party down to the present day and he is the strongest support of socialism and the firmest bulwark against the invasion of bourgeois ideas and intentions.

[1] Ibid. xxxii 234.   [2] Engels to Marx, *MEW* xxxii 235.
[3] See Marx's marginal notes reproduced in *Documents of the First International* (Moscow, 1964) ii, 273 ff. Marx referred generally to Bakunin's ideas about this time as 'a grotesque programme . . . thoughtless babblings . . . insipid improvisations'.

I should never forgive myself if I had ever tried to destroy or even weaken his beneficial influence merely in order to revenge myself on him.[1]

Shortly afterwards he wrote to Marx himself that 'my fatherland is now the International of which you are one of the principal founders. You therefore see, dear friend, that I am your disciple and proud of being so.'[2]

Nevertheless, the Geneva paper *Egalité*, which was controlled by followers of Bakunin, began to attack the General Council and suggested its removal from London to Geneva. The General Council's reply, drafted by Marx, was addressed to the French-speaking Federal Councils, and emphasised how necessary it was for the General Council to be in charge of the revolutionary movement in England: this was vital for the success of the movement on the Continent, and the English movement would lack all momentum if left to its own resources. In the following March Marx (who always put more emphasis on Bakunin's alleged machinations than on his ideas) sent this same circular to the Brunswick Committee of the Eisenach party with a rider denouncing Bakunin as a downright intriguer and an obsequious sponger. But although this dispute was to dominate the later years of the International, it was not for the moment a major factor.

If 1869 was the year of the International's maximum power and influence, just how important was it and how vital was the part that Marx played?[3] Many contemporaries considered the influence and resources of the International to be gigantic: *The Times* put the number of its adherents at two-and-a-half million and some even doubled that figure. The paper also stated that the financial resources of the International ran to millions of pounds. These were, of course, wild exaggerations. For the year 1869–70 the total income of the General Council was about £50. The General Council did negotiate loans from the trade unions of one country to those of another, particularly to support strikes, but the Council was itself continually harassed for small debts.

As for membership figures, it is important to remember that (unlike its successors) the First International had an individual membmership

[1] M. Bakunin, *Correspondance avec Herzen et Ogareff* (Paris, 1896) pp. 290 f.
[2] Quoted in F. Mehring, *Karl Marx*, p. 404.
[3] On the strength of the International, see further J. Braunthal, *History of the International*, I 106 ff.

forming local sections which in their turn joined together in national federations. In Britain, the total number of individual members by the end of 1870 was no more than 254. In Germany, by the end of 1871 there were 58 branches with a total membership of 385. In France in 1870 there were 36 local sections. In Italy, the International increased its membership after the Paris Commune, but it had no formal organisation and its numbers cannot have exceeded a few thousand. The Spanish delegate at Basle claimed 20,000 members and there were said to be 30 sections in America with 500 members. However, anyone familiar with loose organisations of this kind knows how prone leaders are to exaggerate the number of their followers, and even the figures quoted cannot have been fee-paying members: otherwise the General Council would have been saved all financial embarrassment.

Some basis for the larger figures can be found in a different form of membership of the International – affiliation of trade union and political parties.[1] In Britain the total affiliated membership of trade unions was around 50,000 – out of a potential membership of around 800,000. In France as a result of the help given by the International during strikes, the number may well have been as large. In Germany, both the ADAV and the *Verband* eventually declared their adherence to the principles of the International, though affiliation was forbidden by German Law. In the United States the National Labour Union, which had some claim to speak for almost a million workers, declared its adherence to the principles of the International. Nevertheless, in all these countries, this commitment was an emotional one unsupported by close organisational, doctrinal, or – except in Britain – financial links.

Even in Britain, where many of the important trade union leaders sat on the General Council and were in close contact with Marx, they evolved working-class policies without reference to the International. The trade union leaders were immensely impressed by Marx's intellectual qualities and their backing gave Marx and the General Council great prestige in dealing with the continent of Europe in which the British had only a marginal interest. But when it came to home affairs, the influence of the International was peripheral. This was particularly so after 1867 when, with the disappearance of the Fenian menace, any hope of altering the *status quo* in Ireland seemed lost and

---

[1] See further, J. Rougerie, 'Sur l'Histoire de la Ière Internationale', *Le Mouvement Social*, May–June 1965, pp. 30 ff.

the success of the Reform movement made the trade union leaders less revolutionary in their demands. Marx was still convinced, as he had been since 1849, that no revolution in Europe could succeed without a similar movement in England. However, to his growing inability to infuse the affiliated British trade unionists with 'socialist theory and a revolutionary temper' was added the lack of success of the International in even recruiting trade unions. After 1867 only three more trade unions affiliated to the International. This loss of momentum by the International was due to its inability to attract the workers in heavy industry – this being true of all countries with the exception of Belgium. In Britain it was at a disadvantage since its seat was in London, whereas most of the heavy industry was concentrated in the North; and the industrial workers, secure in their technical superiority, did not feel as threatened by the Continent as did the craft workers. And in general the membership of the International tended to be composed more of artisans than of the industrial proletariat.

In Germany, in spite of the adherence of the Eisenach party to the principles of the International, the German political situation prevented any serious co-operation with the General Council. The Combination Laws began to be more strictly applied and in any case both the party's Executive Committee in Brunswick and Liebknecht in Leipzig were more concerned to build up the Eisenach party in opposition to the Lassalleans. Marx sent several hundred membership cards to Germany for free distribution, but that was about as far as it went. Moreover, Becker, who had been in many ways the International's most reliable contact in Germany, had ceased to have much influence on the formation of the Eisenach party. Summing up the situation later, Engels explained: 'The German labour movement's attitude to the International never became clear. It remained a purely platonic relationship; there was no real membership of individuals (with isolated exceptions) and the founding of sections was illegal. In fact, Liebknecht and company ... wanted to subordinante the International to their specifically German aims.'[1] Marx's correspondence shows how completely incapable he was of influencing Liebknecht, and *a fortiori* the other Social Democratic leaders, in favour of the International. Certainly his advice on tactics was valued and his approval sought (particularly when his prestige increased following the publication of *Capital* and the demand for a second edition of some of

[1] Engels to Cuno, *MEW* xxxiii 461 f.

his earlier works) but his specific ideas made very little impact in Germany until well after his death.[1]

Although the French were among the founding members of the International and were by far the strongest national group, they were almost impervious to the influence of Marx and the General Council; they never paid any regular subscriptions and their instinctive reaction to London was one of mistrust. Marx could not oppose the Proudhonism of men like Tolain, and even when Tolain began to be superseded by Varlin as the most influential leader of the International in France, there were still too many anarchist elements in Varlin's thought for easy co-operation with the General Council.

Nevertheless, although the International had proved to be a very loose federation of national groups, each of whose policies were dictated much more by local interests than by reference to the General Council, Marx could be reasonably pleased with the work of the first five years; most importantly, Proudhonism had been decisively defeated with the resolution on land nationalisation; the challenge of the League of Peace and Freedom had been beaten off; the International had grown enormously in prestige, if not in resources, as a result of help negotiated for strikers; in Germany, the Social Democrats had at last declared their adherence to the principles of the International; and finally, the General Council had had its authority over local sections enhanced, at least in principle, by the Basle Congress. Even so the International was too fragile a construction to be able to withstand the storm of the Franco-Prussian War.

IV. THE FRANCO-PRUSSIAN WAR AND THE DECLINE OF THE INTERNATIONAL

The General Council decided to hold the 1870 Congress in Paris, but growing persecution of the International by the French Government persuaded them to change the meeting-place to Mainz. But two weeks before the Congress was due to meet, Napoleon III (outmanoeuvred by Bismarck's deliberate editing of the Ems telegram into a calculated insult) declared war on Germany. The Paris section of the International immediately denounced the war; in Germany opinion was divided but the great majority of socialists considered the war to be a defensive one: the Lassalleans in the Reichstag voted for war credits and Liebknecht and Bebel were isolated in their decision to abstain. Marx

[1] See comment on pp. 430 ff. below.

seems at first to have approved of Liebknecht's stand – although he saw the advantages of a German victory since he considered Germany 'much riper for a social movement' than France. Before the abstention of Liebknecht, he wrote to Engels:

> The French need a drubbing. If the Prussians are victorious then the centralisation of the State power will give help to the centralisation of the working class. German preponderance will shift the centre of the working-class movement in Western Europe from France to Germany, and one has only to compare the movement of 1866 until now in both countries to see that the German working-class is theoretically and organisationally superior to the French. The superiority of the Germans over the French in the world arena would mean at the same time the superiority of *our* theory over Proudhon's and so on.[1]

On 23 July 1870, four days after the outbreak of war, the General Council endorsed the first of the Addresses drafted by Marx. It began by quoting from manifestos of the French section declaring the war to be purely dynastic. After predicting that 'whatever may be the incidents of Louis Bonaparte's war with Prussia, the death knell of the Second Empire has already sounded at Paris',[2] Marx pronounced the war to be, so far as Germany was concerned, a war of defence but castigated Prussia for encouraging the war by constructing a counterfeit Bonapartist regime in Germany. The Address warned: 'if the German working class allow the present war to lose its strictly defensive character and degenerate into a war against the French people, victory or defeat will prove alike disastrous'.[3] However, Marx continued optimistically, 'the principles of the International are too widely spread and too firmly rooted amongst the German working class to apprehend such a sad consummation'. There was the inevitable reference to the 'dark figure of Russia' and the Address concluded with the assertion that the exchange of good-will messages between the French and German workers proved that 'in contrast to the old society, with its economic miseries and political delirium, a new society is springing up, whose International rule will be Peace, because its

[1] Marx to Engels, *MEW* xxiii 5.

[2] 'First Address on the Franco-Prussian War', *MESW*, i 488. The sometimes peculiar English of the three Addresses is accounted for by the fact that they were drafted by Marx in English of which his command was never perfect.

[3] Op. cit., i 489.

national ruler will be everywhere the same – Labour'.[1] The General Council could have no material influence on the course of events, but the Address was very well received in Britain: John Stuart Mill sent a message of congratulation to the General Council, even Morley expressed his approval, and the Peace Society financed a print order of 30,000 copies.

Engels was more firmly on the German side than Marx and wrote to him in mid-August:

> If Germany wins, then French Bonapartism has had it in any case, the eternal squabbling about the esbtalishment of German unity will be ended at last, the German workers will be able to organise themselves on a far broader national basis than previously, and the French workers will also have much greater freedom of movement than under Bonapartism, no matter what sort of a government may follow there.[2]

Marx, too, had the impression that 'the definitive defeat of Bonaparte will probably provoke a revolution in France, whereas the definitive defeat of Germany would only perpetuate the present situation for another twenty years'.[3] Events followed quickly: the French Emperor was completely outmanoeuvred and forced to surrender at Sedan. On the night of 4 September a republic had been proclaimed in Paris. The Brunswick Committee issued an appeal for an honourable peace, and against the annexation of Alsace and Lorraine, but were immediately arrested and put in chains.

With Germany's adopting a less 'defensive' military posture, the General Council issued a Second Address, also drafted by Marx. After noting that the prophecy of the First Address about the end of the Second Empire had been fulfilled, Marx protested that the defensive war had now become a war of aggression as envisaged by the demand for the annexation of Alsace and Lorraine. Borrowing from Engels' military expertise, Marx pointed out that there were no good military reasons for supposing that the possession of Alsace and Lorraine would enhance the safety of a united Germany and that such an annexation would only sow the seed of fresh wars. With great prescience Marx continued:

> If the fortune of her arms, the arrogance of success, and dynastic

---

[1] Op. cit., I 450.   [2] Engels to Marx, *MEW* xxxiii 39.
[3] Marx to Paul and Laura Lafargue, *MEW* xxxiii 125 f.

intrigue lead Germany to a dismemberment of France, there will then only remain two courses open to her. She must at all risks become the avowed tool of Russian aggrandisement, or, after some short respite, make again ready for another 'defensive' war, not one of those new-fangled 'localised' wars, but a *war of races* – a war with the combined Slavonian and Roman races.[1]

And even more remarkably Marx told an émigré German communist: 'The present war will lead to one between Germany and Russia. . . . The specific characteristics of Prussianism have never existed and can never exist other than in alliance with and submission to Russia. Moreover, this second war will bring to birth the inevitable social revolution in Russia.'[2] Somewhat more realistically than in the First Address, Marx admitted the impotence of the working class. 'If the French workmen amid peace failed to stop the aggressor, are German workmen more likely to stop the victor amidst the clangour of arms?'[3] In spite of the dubious alliance of Orleanists and professed Republicans in the provisional Government, he continued, 'any attempt to upset the new government in the present crisis, when the army is almost knocking at the doors of Paris, would be a desperate folly'.[4]

Following Sedan and the declaration of the Republic in France, Marx decided that the International had two immediate aims: to campaign for the recognition of the Republican Government by Britain and to prevent any revolutionary outbreak by the French working class. The first aim had widespread support among the workers in England, though Marx totally misjudged the situation when he talked of 'a powerful movement among the working class over here against Gladstone . . . which will probably bring about his downfall'.[5] The General Council sent an emissary to Paris to prevent the London French committing 'stupidities there in the name of the International';[6] and a government newspaper in Paris went as far as publishing, on the day of the proclamation of the Commune, a letter (purporting to have come from Marx but in fact a complete forgery) which urged the Parisians to abstain from all political activity and confine themselves to the social aims of the International. Marx was exceedingly scornful of Bakunin's short-lived *coup* in Lyons when he

---

[1] *MESW* I 495. [2] Marx to Sorge, *MEW* XXXIII 140. [3] *MESW* I 490.
[4] Ibid. 492. [5] Marx to Meyer, *Letters to Americans* (New York, 1953) p. 81.
[6] Marx to Engels, *MEW* XXXIII 54.

seized the town hall and immediately proclaimed the abolition of the state. Engels wrote to Marx in September 1870 that if the workers attempted a revolutionary rising they 'would be needlessly crushed by the German armies and set back another 20 years'.[1] Nevertheless, as the Provisional Government grew more reactionary Marx began to modify his views as to the advisability of revolt. In any case the General Council was once again reduced to the role of helpless spectator. Marx considered the outbreak of the Commune to be largely the result of the 'accident' that the Prussians were at the gates of Paris. 'History', he wrote to Kugelmann, 'would be of a very mystifying nature if "accidents" played no part in it.' But he was optimistic enough to think that 'with the struggle in Paris the struggle of the working class with the capitalist class and its state has entered a new phase. Whatever the immediate result of the affair, a new starting point of world-historical importance has been achieved.'[2]

Contrary to widespread public opinion after the fall of the Commune, the International had very little influence either on its origins or on its policies; and when Marx referred to the Commune as 'the greatest achievement of our party since the June revolt',[3] he was using the word 'party' very loosely; and Engels was speaking even more loosely when he called the Commune 'the child of the International intellectually',[4] and also referred to it as 'the dictatorship of the proletariat'.[5] The establishment of the Commune was not the result of any preconceived plan, but of the void left in Paris when Thiers withdrew all government officials, local and central, to Versailles. This left the Central Committee of the National Guard as the only body capable of exercising effective control. The Central Committee immediately instituted direct elections by manhood suffrage to create a popular assembly which on 28 March 1871 assumed the title *Commune de Paris* after the title of the Council set up during the French Revolution in 1792.[6]

The Paris section of the International could not play a great part in the Commune; it had been crushed by Napoleon's police shortly

---

[1] Engels to Marx, *MEW* xxxiii 61.   [2] Marx to Kugelmann, *MEW* xxxiii 209.
[3] Ibid.   [4] Engels to Sorge, *MESC*, p. 288.   [5] *MESW* i 485.
[6] Probably the best overall historical view is S. Edwards, *The Paris Commune* (London, 1971). Marx's own writings are most easily available in K. Marx and F. Engels, *On the Paris Commune*; see also K. Marx and F. Engels, *Writings on the Paris Commune*, ed. H. Draper (New York, 1971).

before the outbreak of the Franco-Prussian War and was only just beginning to reorganise itself. Of the ninety-two members on the Council of the Commune only seventeen were members of the International. Contact between Paris and the General Council was difficult, though Marx received letters from some of the leaders of the Commune. Lafargue even suggested that Engels go over to help.[1] Nor was the social and political structure of the Commune of a nature to favour the policies of the International: two thirds of its members were of *petit-bourgeois* origins and the key positions went either to Blanquists or to old-style Jacobins. The actual measures passed by the Commune were reformist rather than revolutionary, with no attack on private property: employers were forbidden on the penalty of fines to reduce wages; there was to be no more night-working in bakeries, rents were suspended, and all abandoned businesses were transferred to co-operative associations. These measures were far from being socialist. In fact the Commune had such a short life, was composed of such disparate elements and operated under such exceptional circumstances that it is difficult to ascribe any coherent policy to it.

Virtually from the outset Marx was pessimistic about the success of the Commune. According to the Austrian socialist Oberwinder, 'two days after the beginning of the insurrection, Marx wrote to Vienna that it had no chance of success'.[2] 'It looks as though the Parisians are succumbing', he wrote to Liebknecht on 6 April. 'It is their own fault, that in fact comes from their being too decent.'[3] By their unwillingness to start a civil war and by their taking time to elect and organise the Commune, he considered that they had allowed Thiers to regain the initiative and concentrate his forces. A few days later Marx expressed to Kugelmann his admiration for the boldness of the Communards:

What resilience, what historic initiative and what self-sacrifice these Parisians are showing! After six months of starvation and ruin brought about more by internal treachery than by external enemies, they rise in revolt under Prussian bayonets as though there had never been a war between France and Germany, as though the

[1] Engels had constructed a plan for the defence of Paris against the Prussians. This plan was destroyed by his executors, Bebel and Bernstein, in order to remove evidence of his 'treason against the fatherland'.
[2] H. Oberwinder, *Sozialismus und Sozialpolitik* (Berlin, 1887) p. 55.
[3] Marx to Liebknecht, *MEW* xxxiii 200.

enemy were not still at the gates. History can show no similar example of such magnificence.[1]

But he repeated his views that they should have marched on Versailles immediately and that the Central Committee of the National Guard gave up its power too soon. And in 1881 he declared that 'with a modicum of common sense the Commune could have reached a compromise with Versailles useful to the whole mass of the people – the only thing that could have been reached at the time'.[2] There are only two surviving letters from Marx to the leaders of the Commune. He had been asked for specific advice by Frankel who was in charge of labour and commerce, but his reply has been lost; in the letters that survive Marx offered no specific advice, confining himself to the observation that 'the Commune seems to me to waste too much of its time with trivialities and personal rivalries'.[3]

Marx's personal ambivalence to the Commune goes a long way to explaining the otherwise curious fact that, throughout the two months of the Commune's existence, the General Council remained absolutely silent. On 28 March, the day after the establishment of the Commune, Marx himself had proposed that an Address to the People of Paris be drawn up and the Council had charged him with the drafting. A week later he stated in the Council that an Address 'would now be out of place'.[4] On 18 April he declared that an Address to the International about the struggle in France might be appropriate; but the members of the General Council agreed that since the only information to date was based on false newspaper reports, no detailed comment was possible. Marx was very assiduous in collating different press reports, though it is a pity that he does not seem to have used *The Times* correspondent who was, in fact, the best placed. Marx wrote to Frankel at the end of April: 'The General Council will publish shortly an address on the Commune. It has till now postponed the publication of this because it counted from day to day on receiving more precise information from the Paris Section.'[5] Marx had to apologise to the three subsequent meetings for not having completed the Address; at the last two sessions Engels explained Marx's absence on

[1] Marx to Kugelmann, *MEW* xxxiii 205.
[2] Marx to Domela Nieuwenhuis, *MESC* p. 226.
[3] Marx to Frankel and Varlin, *MEW* xxxiii 216.
[4] *The General Council of the First International, Minutes,* iv 169.
[5] Marx to Frankel, *MEW* xxiii 265.

the grounds of ill health. However, this did not prevent Marx from telling Frankel in mid-May that he had written 'several hundred letters . . . . to every corner of the world'.[1] Subsequent deadlines were again broken and the Address was not presented to the Council until 30 May, three days after the collapse of the Commune.

The Address, subtitled 'The Civil War in France', that Marx did eventually present to the General Council was some forty pages long and had been preceded by at least two full-length drafts that were noticeably different. These drafts, among other things, show how little sympathy Marx had for the Jacobin violence of some of the Communards. In the first of the four sections of the final and published version, Marx analysed the Republican Government under Thiers and concluded that it was more concerned to suppress working-class activities than to defeat the Prussians. Since 'Paris armed was the revolution armed', the first priority of the so-called Government of National Defence was capitulation. Marx characterised the leading members of the Government in a series of vicious sketches. Of Jules Favre, the Foreign Minister, for example, Marx wrote:

Living in concubinage with the wife of a drunkard resident in Algiers, he had, by a most daring concoction of forgeries, spread over many years, contrived to grasp, in the name of the children of his adultery, a large succession, which made him a rich man. In a lawsuit undertaken by the legitimate heirs, he only escaped exposure by the connivance of the Bonapartist tribunals.[2]

And of Thiers, the President:

A master in small state roguery, a virtuoso in perjury and treason, a craftsman in all the petty stratagems, cunning devices, and base perfidies of parliamentary party-warfare; never scrupling, when out of office, to fan a revolution, and to stifle it in blood when at the helm of the state; with class prejudices standing him in the place of ideas, and vanity in the place of a heart; his private life as infamous as his public life is odious – even now when playing the part of a French Sulla, he cannot help setting off the abomination of his deeds by the ridicule of his ostentation.[3]

The second section dealt with the events immediately preceding the

[1] Marx to Frankel, *MESC*, p. 265.   [2] 'The Civil War in France', *MESW* I 501.
[3] *MESW* I 506.

establishment of the Commune. The only obstacle to Thiers' counter-revolutionary conspiracy was armed Paris. To overcome this, Thiers had invented the lie that the cannon of the National Guard were the property of the state. It was Thiers who had begun the Civil War by sending soldiers to remove the cannon. The only violence practised by the Commune was the shooting of the two generals Lecomte and Thomas by their troops and the dispersal of an armed demonstration in the Place Vendôme, which was as nothing compared to the atrocities of the Versailles Government with their wholesale shooting of prisoners.

The most interesting part of the Address is its third section, where Marx described the political organisation of the Commune – both actual and potential. His organisational model was noticeably less centralised than that in the parallel passage at the end of the *Communist Manifesto*. This change of emphasis was marked right at the beginning of the section: 'the working class cannot simply lay hold of the ready-made state machinery, and wield it for its own purposes'.[1] Marx then defined the organs of state power as being the 'standing army, police, bureaucracy, clergy, and judicature' and gave a history of its developments in France up to the Second Empire which

> professed to save the working class by breaking down Parliamentarism, and, with it, the undisguised subservience of Government to the propertied classes. It professed to save the propertied classes by upholding their economic supremacy over the working class; and, finally, it professed to unite all classes by reviving for all the chimera of national glory. In reality, the Empire was the only form of government possible at a time when the bourgeoisie had already lost, and the working class had not yet acquired, the faculty of ruling the nation.[2]

The Commune was the 'direct antithesis' to the Empire and was the 'positive form' of the Republic of 1848. Marx then described the election of the Commune (he exaggerated the working-class nature of its composition) and the transformation of the standing army, police, administration and judicature into elected, responsible and revocable agents of the Commune:

> The Paris Commune was, of course, to serve as a model to all the great industrial centres of France. The communal *regime* once

[1] Ibid. 516.   [2] Ibid. 518.

established in Paris and the secondary centres, the old centralised Government would in the provinces, too, have to give way to the self-government of the producers. . . . The Commune was to be the political form of even the smallest country hamlet, and in the rural districts the standing army was to be replaced by a national militia, with an extremely short term of service. The rural communes of every district were to administer their common affairs by an assembly of delegates in the central town, and these district assemblies were again to send deputies to the National Delegation in Paris, each delegate to be at any time revocable and bound by the *mandat impératif* (formal instructions) of his constituents. The few but important functions which still would remain for a central government were not to be suppressed, as has been intentionally mis-stated, but were to be discharged by Communal, and therefore strictly responsible agents. The unity of the nation was not to be broken, but, on the contrary, to be organised by the Communal Constitution and to become a reality by the destruction of the State power which claimed to be the embodiment of that unity independent of, and superior to, the nation itself, from which it was but a parasitic excrescence. . . . Instead of deciding once in three or six years which member of the ruling class was to misrepresent the people in Parliament, universal suffrage was to serve the people, constituted in Communes, as individual suffrage serves every other employer in the search for the workmen and managers in his business. And it is well known that companies, like individuals, in matters of real business, generally know how to put the right man in the right place, and, if they for once make a mistake, to redress it promptly. On the other hand, nothing could be more foreign to the spirit of the Commune than to supersede universal suffrage by hierarchic investiture.[1]

This passage reveals much more about Marx's view of the shape of the future communist society after the revolution than it does about the plans of the Communards, a majority of whom would probably not have agreed with Marx's projects.[2]

Marx then mentioned some misconceptions about the Commune:

[1] *MESW* I 520 f.

[2] Engels wrote later of Marx's ascribing 'the unconscious tendencies of the Commune . . . to its credit as more or less conscious plans'. Engels to Bernstein, *MESC*, p. 366.

it was not a throw-back to the Middle Ages; it was not aimed at the breaking up of the nation; and it was not the sort of self-sufficient economic unit advocated by the Proudhonists.

Marx wrote of 'the multiplicity of interpretations, to which the Commune has been subjected, and the multiplicity of interests which construed it in their favour', but claimed that the Commune was nevertheless 'the political form at last discovered under which to work out the economic emancipation of labour'.[1] He elaborated on the character of this 'economic emancipation' by accepting the charge that the Commune intended to abolish class property and expropriate the expropriators by setting up 'united co-operative societies' which would 'regulate national production upon a common plan'. At the same time he declared:

> The working class have no ready-made utopias to introduce *par décret du peuple*. They know that in order to work out their own emancipation, and along with it that higher form to which present society is irresistibly tending by its own economical agencies, they will have to pass through long struggles, through a series of historic processes, transforming circumstances and men. They have no ideals to realise, but to set free the elements of the new society with which old collapsing bourgeois society itself is pregnant. In the full consciousness of their historic mission, and with the heroic resolve to act up to it, the working class can afford to smile at the coarse invective of the gentlemen's gentlemen with the pen and the ink-horn, and at the didactic patronage of well-wishing bourgeois doctrinaires, pouring forth their ignorant platitudes and sectarian crotchets in the oracular tone of scientific infallibility.[2]

Marx further proclaimed that the measures of the Commune also benefited the lower middle classes (which was true) and the peasantry (though this was less evident) – 'all the healthy elements of French society' – at the same time as being emphatically international. He admitted that the specific measures of the Commune 'could but betoken a tendency' and that is greatest social measure was its own existence. The proof of this was in the change that had overtaken Paris:

> No longer was Paris the rendezvous of British landlords, Irish absentees, American ex-slaveholders and shoddy men, Russian ex-

---

[1] *MESW* I 522.   [2] Ibid. 523.

serfowners, and Wallachian boyards. No more corpses at the morgue, no nocturnal burglaries, scarcely any robberies; in fact, for the first time since the days of February 1848, the streets of Paris were safe, and that without Police of any kind.[1]

This was very different from:

the Paris of the *francs-fileurs*, the Paris of the Boulevards, male and female – the rich, the capitalist, the gilded, the idle Paris, now thronging with its lackeys, its blacklegs, its literary *bohème*, and its *cocottes* at Versailles, Saint-Denis, Rueil, and Saint-Germain; considering the Civil War but an agreeable diversion, eyeing the battle going on through telescopes, counting the rounds of cannon, and swearing by their own honour and that of their prostitutes, that the performance was far better got up than it used to be at the Porte St Martin. The men who fell were really dead; the cries of the wounded were cries in good earnest; and, besides, the whole thing was so intensely historical.[2]

In the fourth and final section, Marx described Thiers's feeble attempts to raise an army against Paris and his reliance on prisoners released by Bismarck once the peace was signed. When eventually the final battle for Paris began, the atrocities of the Versailles were monstrous:

To find a parallel for the conduct of Thiers and his bloodhounds we must go back to the times of Sulla and the two Triumvirates of Rome. The same wholesale slaughter in cold blood, the same disregard, in massacre, of age and sex; the same system of torturing prisoners; the same proscriptions, but this time of a whole class; the same savage hunt after concealed leaders, lest one might escape; the same denunciations of political and private enemies; the same indifference for the butchery of entire strangers to the feud. There is but this difference, that the Romans had no *mitrailleuses* for the despatch, in the lump, of the prescribed, and that they had not 'the law in their hands' nor on their lips the cry of civilisation.[3]

To the charge of incendiarism Marx replied that in war fire was an arm as legitimate as any. A few hostages had also been killed, but their lives had also been forfeit many times by the shooting of prisoners by

---

[1] Ibid. 529.　　[2] Ibid. 530.　　[3] Ibid. 536.

the Versailles Government. The result of the Commune was that class antagonisms had been sharpened:

> But the battle must break out again and again and in ever-growing dimensions, and there can be no doubt as to who will be the victor in the end, – the appropriating few, or the immense working majority. And the French working class is only the advance guard of the modern proletariat. . . . Wherever, in whatever shape, and under whatever conditions the class struggle obtains any consistency, it is but natural that members of our association should stand in the foreground. The soil out of which it grows is modern society itself. It cannot be stamped out by any amount of carnage. To stamp it out the Governments would have to stamp out the despotism of capital over labour – the condition of their own parasitical existence.
>
> Working men's Paris, with its Commune, will be for ever celebrated as the glorious harbinger of a new society. The martyrs are enshrined in the great heart of the working class. Its exterminators history has already nailed to that eternal pillory from which all the prayers of their priests will not avail to redeem them.[1]

The *Civil War in France* (the title given to the Address) was the most brilliant of Marx's polemics, and had an immediate success unknown to any of the previous pronouncements of the General Council. It ran through three editions in two months, sold 8000 copies in the second edition and was translated into most European languages. In an overall study of Marx's views it is important for its emphasis on decentralisation as a goal of future socialist society. In the general context of socialist thought it is important in providing Lenin with a basis for the Bolshevik view of the dictatorship of the proletariat. (In the third chapter of his *State and Revolution*, Lenin put great emphasis on Marx's remark that the proletariat 'cannot simply lay hold of the ready-made state machinery and use it for its own purposes'[2] – though in fact Lenin's view of the Party as the vanguard of the proletariat is more akin to Blanqui's conceptions; and Lenin strained the facts of the Commune even further than Marx.) The *Civil War in France* is only one interpretation of the Commune: there were Proudhonist, Blanquist and anarchist interpretations that were as justified as Marx's in that their views were similarly represented to the Commune. It must also

---

[1] Ibid. 541.   [2] 'The Civil War in France', *MESW* I 516.

be remembered that the *Civil War* was an obituary[1] and scarcely the place to offer a critical assessment: Marx's letters show him much more reticent about the achievements of the Commune, and later he even went as far as to say (in a letter to the Dutch socialist Domela Nieuwenhuis) that the Commune 'was not socialist, nor could it have been'.[2]

Nevertheless, amid the reaction that swept over Europe following the defeat of the Commune, the very success of the *Civil War*, with its somewhat inaccurate claim that 'wherever ... the class struggle obtains any consistency, it is but natural that members of our Association should stand in the foreground',[3] helped to brand the International as the greatest threat to society and civilisation. The most incredible rumours were published as fact in the Press: the International had conspired with Napoleon; it had conspired with Bismarck; Marx had even been Bismarck's private secretary and was now dead. The charge of incendiarism was so often repeated that even the great Chicago fire of 1871 was attributed to the International. Favre, Foreign Minister in the Thiers Goverment, not content with stifling the remnants of the Commune in France, issued a circular to all European governments declaring the International a menace to established order. This circular was itself a catalogue of inaccuracies; it quoted, for example, a statement put out by Bakunin's *Alliance* as if it had been made by the International.

Although European governments tightened their laws, Spain was the only country that agreed to the extradition of the French refugees. In spite of the almost universal condemnation of the Commune in the British Press (complete with the wildest inaccuracies which Marx spent a lot of time trying to rebut) the British Government refused to co-operate with Favre: in reply to a Spanish request for extradition the foreign minister (Granville) said the British Government had no right to expel refugees who had not contravened any British law or committed any of the crimes specified in the treaty of extradition.

It soon became known that Marx was the author of the infamous Address; from being virtually unknown in England, except to a very small circle, he quickly became notorious. He wrote to Kugelmann

---

[1] According to the estimates of the Versailles Government 17,000 people were killed during the final *'semaine sanglante'* and recent research puts the figure even higher.

[2] Marx to Domela Nieuwenhuis, *MESW*, p. 338.

[3] 'The Civil War in France', *MESW* I 541.

on 28 June 1871 that his Address 'is making the devil of a noise and I have the honour to be at this moment the most abused and threatened man in London. That really does me good after the tedious twenty-year idyll in my den!'[1] The New York *World* sent a correspondent to interview him at the beginning of July. In the interview Marx refuted convincingly the more lurid of the rumours about the Commune. He said that the International 'does not impose any particular form on political movements; it only demands that these movements respect its aims'.[2] The London *Daily Telegraph* and the *New York Herald* also interviewed Marx; and he claimed to be under police surveillance even when he spent a few days at Brighton. On the Marx household the Commune had a profoundly depressing effect: many of their closest friends were involved in the slaughter and soon they had to cope with floods of refugees and 'all the nameless misery and unending suffering'[3] that they brought with them. Inevitably the burden of relief fell on the International. The refugees, wrote Jenny, 'were literally starving in the streets' and 'for more than five months the International supported, that is to say held between life and death, the great mass of the exiles'.[4] In addition to all the business of the International, Marx found that he 'not only had to fight against all the governments of the ruling classes, but also wage hand-to-hand battles with fat, forty-year-old landladies who attacked him when one or other communard would be late with his rent'.[5]

For all its notoriety, the International after the Commune was a spent force: with the arrival of an apparently durable peace and the tendency of European nations to become more interested in their internal affairs, the impetus towards internationalism declined. Reaction could only be met by better political organisation, and this could only be carried on within national boundaries. The hope of revolution in France had been destroyed and, with it, all chance of revolution in Europe. Moreover, although men like Varlin had helped defeat Proudhonist views in the International, their syndicalist opposition to political action was soon to bring them into conflict with the General Council. The General Council itself was much weakened

[1] Marx to Kugelmann, *MEW* xxxiii 238.
[2] *The World*, New York, 18 July 1871. The text is most readily available in 'An interview with Karl Marx', *Labour Monthly*, June 1972.
[3] Jenny Marx in *Liebknechts Briefwechsel*, ed. G. Eckert (The Hague, 1963) p. 169.
[4] Jenny Marx (daughter) to Kugelmann, Andreas, *Dokumente*, p. 263.
[5] Ibid.

by co-opting a large number of French refugees who soon began to bicker among themselves in the same way as after 1848.

All three Marx daughters were intimately involved in the aftermath of the Commune. Laura and Paul had just got out of Paris before it was encircled by the Prussians. They went to Bordeaux where their third child, a boy, was born in February 1871. Paul was active in the cause of the Commune and both Jenny and Eleanor set off to help Laura, arriving on 1 May. On the fall of the Commune the four adults and two children (Laura's second child had died the previous year) retired to the small resort of Bagnères-de-Luchon, suitably near the Spanish frontier. The baby died at the end of July and Paul, fearing imminent arrest, crossed into Spain. Laura joined him there, her only remaining child ill with dysentery. Jenny and Eleanor left to return to London but were arrested on the frontier, submitted to a lengthy interrogation and spent the night in jail. Jenny only just managed to get rid of an incriminating letter from Flourens, one of the Commune leaders. They were deported to Spain, and after further difficulties with the Spanish police managed to sail from St Sebastian, with Laura, at the end of August.[1]

In Germany, now the main centre of European socialism, the Eisenach party could not associate itself publicly with the International and anyway no longer needed its support against the ADAV with whom the old rivalry was beginning to decline. Although the Eisenach leaders were still loyal to Marx and Engels, appeals from London showed that (unlike the pre-1871 years) the General Council needed the support of the Germans more than they needed it. In fact, Lassalleanism continued to be the main force in German socialism; and though Marx's prestige remained high, it was more for personal than doctrinal reasons. In Britain, the publication of the *Civil War* occasioned the resignation of Odger and Lucraft from the General Council, but no trade union disaffiliated and the General Council continued to be active in assisting strikers. Nevertheless, British trade unions generally were becoming less radical: since the Reform Bill of 1867 and the failure of their candidates in 1868, they were looking to an alliance with the Liberals as the most effective means of securing their ends; and their support for Gladstone's pro-Russian policy made them even less congenial to Marx. Apart from Belgium, the only areas where the

[1] Cf. Eleanor Marx to Liebknecht, *Leibknechts Briefwechsel*, pp. 413 ff.

International made progress after the Commune were strongholds of anarchism: Spain and Italy.

But this situation was only slowly perceived by Marx who, for almost a year after the Commune, was imbued with a thoroughgoing revolutionary optimism and saw a parallel between the harassment of the International and the persecutions suffered by the first Christians which had failed to save the Roman Empire.[1] By the autumn of 1871 there had been no congress of the International for two years. On the General Council Marx was instrumental in changing a proposal to hold a congress in Amsterdam into a decision to convene a private conference in London similar to the one held in 1865. The conference was to concern itself solely with organisational questions, and Marx's intention was that it should check the growing influence of Bakunin; indeed, he had already proposed a conference to this end a year earlier, in August 1870. Bakunin's influence was centred mainly on Switzerland where the Geneva section had split and his supporters had set up a Jura Federation – with a Bakuninist group in Geneva in vehement opposition to the International's section there. The political situation in Europe after the Commune tended to sharpen the differences between Bakunin and Marx: Marx gradually gave up expecting a quick revolution and was unwilling to have the International committed to the support of spasmodic risings in Italy, Spain and Russia (the countries chiefly susceptible to anarchist doctrines). The anarchists considered any revolutionary uprising to be justified as a step towards the total destruction of contemporary society. To them, the General Council was an authoritarian irrelevance.[2]

The inevitable clash provoked by divergent assessments of the political situation was aggravated by more personal factors: extraordinary though it seems, Bakunin had undertaken in 1869 to translate *Capital* into Russian. About the same time Bakunin had had the misfortune to meet and trust a young psychopathic revolutionary, named Netchayev, who had just escaped from Russia with fabricated stories of widespread revolutionary activities among the students. Netchayev was utterly ruthless in his methods and when Bakunin – predictably in one who never completed any of his own works let alone the

---

[1] Cf. 'Speech on the Seventh Anniversary of the International', *MEW* xvii 432.
[2] See further, A. Lehning, *From Buonarotti to Bakunin* (Leiden, 1970) ch. vii. On Bakunin, see E. H. Carr, *Michael Bakunin* (London and New York, 1937). Also P. Ansart, *Marx et l'Anarchisme* (Paris, 1969).

translation of those of others – wished to suspend his labours on *Capital* and pay back the advance, Netchayev wrote to Bakunin's agent threatening him with death if so much as asked for the money back. Marx attributed Netchayev's reported activities to Bakunin's hatred for him, and his unreasonable suspicion of Bakunin was fed by his russophobe friend Borkheim and by Nicholas Utin, both of whom continually worked on Marx with tales of Bakunin's intrigues. Utin, a Russian exile who had collaborated and then quarrelled with Bakunin in Switzerland, had started a Russian section of the International in Geneva in opposition to Bakunin.[1] This section – which numbered only half-a-dozen members and was purely ephemeral – asked Marx to represent them on the General Council – a tribute which Marx accepted, remarking to Engels:

> A funny position for me, functioning as a representative of young Russia! A man can never tell what he is capable of and what strange bedfellows he may have to accept. In the official reply I praise Flerowski and emphasise that the main task of the Russian branch is to work for Poland (i.e. help Europe dispense with having Russia as a neighbour). I considered it safer to say no word about Bakunin, either in the official or in the confidential reply.[2]

The London Conference, held in an inn just off Tottenham Court Road in mid-September 1871, was not a very representative gathering: no Germans; only two Britishers; from France, only refugees; and from Switzerland simply two ex-supporters of Bakunin, including Utin.[3] The only strong delegation was the six-man group from Belgium where the International was flourishing. This group mediated between Marx, strongly supported by the Blanquist refugees on the Council, and the pro-Bakunin forces. The Conference, in which Marx was the most active and dominant participant, began by recommending the General Council to limit its numbers and not to take its members too exclusively from one nationality. It then forbad the use of the title General Council by national committees, renewed the

---

[1] See further, W. D. McClellan, 'Marxist or Populist? The Russian section of the First International', *Études de Marxologie*, No. 8 (Paris, 1964).

[2] Marx to Engels, *MEW* xxxii 466.

[3] On the London Conference there is a wealth of detail and interpretation in M. Molnar, 'Die Londoner Konferenz der Internationale in 1871', *Archiv für Sozialgeschichte* (1964).

efforts of the Geneva Congress to obtain comprehensive working-class statistics, discussed ways of attracting peasants to membership of the International, and in general attempted to tighten discipline and make the International more of a political party than a forum for discussion: the London Conference resolutions are the first documents of the International to speak specifically of a 'worker's party'. But the main business was the dispute with the Bakunists. The Conference re-emphasised the commitment to political action by declaring that 'in the militant state of the working class, its economic movement and its political action are indissolubly united'. This political action might well be within the framework of parliamentary democracy, for Marx decleared: 'the governments are opposed to us: we must answer them with all the means that are at our disposal. To get workers into parliament is equivalent to a victory over the governments, but one must choose the right man.'[1] Yet the onus of deciding whether the revolution would be violent or not lay with those who held power: 'we must declare to the governments: we will proceed against you peaceably where it is possible and by force of arms when it may be necessary'.[2] The Conference dissociated itself from the activities of Netchayev, though Marx did not manage to implicate Bakunin. Marx also wished to get a condemnation of Bakunin's Alliance, but Belgian mediation persuaded the conference to consider the matter of the Alliance closed by remarking that it appeared to have dissolved itself and that the International would henceforth only admit sections or federations to membership. In Swtizerland the dissident Bakuninists were invited to join the Swiss Federation or, if they found this impossible, to call themselves the Jura Federation. The Conference also agreed to set up an English Federal Council. Marx moved this motion himself: he had at last given up his opposition to its establishment, realising that it was impossible for the General Council to infuse the English workers with internationalism and the revolutionary spirit. Marx also criticised the trade unions for being an 'aristocratic minority'[3] and not involving lower-paid workers, to whom, together with the Irish, Marx increasingly looked for support.

In spite of Marx's view that it had 'achieved more than all the earlier

---

[1] Speech at London Conference, *MEW* cvii 651. Marx expressed very similar sentiments in his speech in Amsterdam after the Hague Congress in 1872; also in his interview with the New York *World* in July 1871.
[2] *MEW* xvii 652.   [3] Ibid.

Congresses put together',[1] the London Conference rendered more acute the divisions in the International, and there was almost immediate opposition to its decisions – opposition that very soon quenched for ever the optimism that Marx enjoyed throughout 1871.[2] The Germans were as apathetic as ever (they had paid no financial contributions since September 1869) and Marx took the unprecedented step of asking all their sections to correspond directly with him.[3] The French section in London opposed the decisions of the Conference, as did the followers of Victoria Woodhull in America and the sections in Italy and Spain. This opposition was voiced by the Jura Federation which in November 1871 issued a circular denouncing authoritarianism and hierarchy in the International, accusing the General Council of being a kind of government and proposing that it be replaced by a correspondence bureau linking a free association of national sections. Marx wrote a reply for the General Council entitled *The Alleged Splits in the International*. Here he rightly exposed the futility of many of the anarchist doctrines, but also repeated the charges against Bakunin arising out of the Netchayev affair, made much of the fact that two of Bakunin's followers had turned out to be Bonapartist spies, and finally dismissed the followers of both Lassalle and Bakunin as sects which

> have a justifiable existence at a time when the proletariat is not sufficiently developed to act as a class. Individual thinkers begin to critize social contradictions and seek to overcome them by fantastic solutions which the masses of the workers have only to accept, propagate and carry out. By their very nature the sects which form around such pioneers are exclusive and hold themselves aloof from all practical activities, from politics, strikes, trade unions, in a word from every form of mass movement. The masses of the workers remain indifferent, or even hostile to their propaganda. Originally one of the levers of the working-class movement, they become a hindrance and reactionary immediately the movement overtakes them. Examples of this are the sects in France and England, and later on the Lassalleans in Germany, who, after having hampered

[1] Marx to Jenny Marx, *MEW* xxxiii 286.
[2] As late as March 1872 Marx could talk of 'the excellent progress made since the London Conference' (Marx to Lafargue, *MEW* xxxiii 436).
[3] Marx to Kwasniewski, *MEW* xxxiii 287.

the organization of the proletariat for years, have finally become simply tools in the hands of the police.[1]

What finally destroyed Marx's influence in the International were the increasing difficulties he had to face even in the bastion of Britain. At first the establishment of the English Federal Council created no problems: Hales, its Secretary, continued to support Marx and it managed to create numerous branches. The first sign of revolt came over the groups in America, known as Section 12, founded by Victoria Woodhull and Tennie Claflin whose membership was middle class (and whose main energies were devoted to such causes as free love and spiritualism) in contrast to the more working-class and immigrant groups led by Frederick Sorge and Richard Bolte. Section 12 was supported on the General Council by followers of O'Brien, whom Marx nevertheless wished to see on the Council as they were 'an often necessary counterweight to the trade unions on the Council. They are more revolutionary, firmer on the land question, less nationalistic and not susceptible to bourgeois bribery in one form or another. Otherwise they would have been kicked out long ago.'[2]

However, Marx's position was further undermined by defections in his own ranks. There had been tension before between Marx and Eccarius who, in his reporting to *The Times*, seems to have tried to claim for himself the credit of some of Marx's ideas. Eccarius, as corresponding secretary for America, had been communicating with Section 12 and Marx charged him with abusing his position. Both Eccarius and Hermann Jung disliked the presence of Blanquists on the Council and favoured co-operation with working-class radicals: they considered that Marx's tactics could only result in splitting the International irretrievably. In spite of Marx's plea to Eccarius that 'the day after tomorrow is my birthday and I should not like to start it conscious that I was deprived of one of my oldest friends and adherents',[3] the breach this time was final. A second blow to Marx's position was the opposition of Hales who had up till then been a staunch supporter of Marx, except on the question of Ireland and an independent English Federal Council. In July he had attacked the General Council in private correspondence and had been suspended from his

---

[1] 'The Alleged Splits in the International', *La Première Internationale*, ed. J. Freymond, II 284.
[2] Marx to Bolte, *MEW* XXXIII 328.
[3] Marx to Eccarius, *MEW* XXXIII 454.

post as secretary. At the Nottingham Conference of the English Federal Council, he had proposed that the English branch correspond with foreign sections. The dispute was taken to the General Council, where Hales was with great difficulty persuaded to return its documents.

Thus disintegration in England was already apparent on the eve of the Congress which opened at the Hague in early September 1872. It was to be the last full meeting of the International and also its most representative one: only the Italian sections refused to participate. Jung and Eccarius did not come from England as they objected to what they considered to be Marx's moves to pack the Congress and also to his vindictiveness against the Bakuninists and his attacks on the British trade unionists. The Hague was the only Congress ever attended by Marx. According to Maltman Barry, who was reporting the Congress for the *Standard*, children had been warned 'not to go into the streets with articles of value upon them' as 'the International is coming and will steal them'.[1] Vast crowds followed the delegates from their station to the hotel, 'the figure of Karl Marx attracting special attention, his name on every lip'.[2] In the sessions, too, Marx was a prominent figure: his black broadcloth suit contrasted with his white hair and beard and he would screw a monocle into his eye when he wanted to scrutinise his audience. The Congress opened with a three-day examination of credentials behind closed doors. All that the public could hear was the tinkling of the President's bell, rising now and again above a storm of angry voices. Marx himself was so tense that he scarcely slept at all throughout the Congress. After the acceptance of the General Council's report, there was a debate on a motion to increase the powers of the General Council. Some wished the powers of the General Council to be drastically curtailed. In reply, Marx said that it would be more sensible to abolish the General Council than to turn it into a mere letter-box; its authority could in any case be only a moral one and only existed with the agreement of the members. The motion was carried by 32 to 6, with 16 abstentions, the English delegation splitting its vote.

After the vote, reported Barry, 'there was a slight pause. It was the lull before the storm. Knowing what was coming, and whom it would

[1] *The First International: Minutes of the Hague Congress with Related Documents*, ed. H. Gerth (Madison, 1958) p. 529.
[2] Ibid., p. 260.

most effect, I stood up and watched the operation. Up got Engels, Marx's right hand, and said he would make a communication to the Congress. It was a recommendation from a number of members of the General Council respecting the seat of the Council for next year.'[1] Engels proposed that the seat of the General Council be transferred to New York. 'Consternation and discomfiture stood plainly written on the faces of the party of dissension as he uttered the last words. . . . It was some time before anyone rose to speak. It was a *coup d'état* and each one looked to his neighbour to break the spell.'[2] The Blanquists who on other issues had, together with the Germans, ensured a substantial majority for Marx, opposed the proposal; and when the vote on whether the General Council should move its seat at all was taken, the result was very narrow: 26 for, 23 against, and 9 abstentions. Finally there came the report of the five man-commission of inquiry which had been set up following Marx's motion at the beginning of the Congress to expel the Alliance from the International. The commission found that Bakunin had tried to establish a secret society within the International and was also guilty of fraud. On the motion of the commission he was expelled from the International. This marked the end of the Congress and Marx retired to Scheveningen where he celebrated by entertaining the delegates to a seaside dinner.

There can be little doubt that Marx realised the impracticability of New York as a seat for the General Council. The arguments advanced by Engels for the transfer were remarkably unconvincing. Before the Congress Marx had written to Kugelmann: 'It will be a matter of life and death for the International; and, before I retire, I want at least to protect it from disintegrating elements.'[3] He wished at all costs to ensure that the Bakuninists would not get a majority at the next congress and that the General Council (on which an uncomfortable number of Blanquists were sitting) would still be subject to his influence; and neither of these was certain if the Council continued to sit in London. Marx felt increasingly frustrated by his inability to spend time on *Capital* and seemed to have seriously considered retiring as early as September 1871, a decision which he had made definite by May 1872.[4]

The International did not die immediately. Marx and Engels were very busy broadcasting the resolutions of the Hague Congress and for

---

[1] Op. cit., pp. 279 f.   [2] Ibid.   [3] Marx to Kugelmann, *MEW* xxxiii 565.
[4] Cf. Marx to de Paepe, *MEW* xxxiii 338.

some time kept up a regular correspondence with New York. In the International as a whole the anti-Marxian forces were now much stronger, and only in Germany did Marx retain substantial personal following. The anarchists held a rival congress immediately following the Hague: the Italians, Spaniards and Swiss alone were represented, but they soon contacted the Belgians and the Dutch, all of whom were represented at a congress in 1873. There was also a strong contingent from England present. After the Hague the English branches of the International continued functioning very effectively, but the Federal Council split, with a majority of its members (led by Hales) seceding. Both branches of the Federal Council then declined rapidly and by 1874 Marx wrote to Sorge: 'In England the International is for the time being as good as dead and the Federal Council in London still exists as such only in name, although some of its members are active individually.'[1] The General Council in New York attempted to organise a congress in Geneva in 1873, but it was a fiasco: the Council could not send even one representative and Marx discouraged his supporters from attending. A congress was held in 1874, with Eccarius as the only delegate from England. Sorge resigned from the General Council in the same year. In Philadelphia in 1876 the International was formally dissolved. The rival International of the anarchists struggled on for longer: functioning as a federation of autonomous national branches with no General Council it held its last Congress in 1877, after which it split into its anarchist and social-democratic elements.

[1] Marx to Sorge, *MEW* XXXIII 635.

8

The Last Decade

The more one lives, as I do, cut off from the outside world,
the more one is involved in the emotions of one's closest
circle.

Marx to Kugelmann, 1874

I. MARX AT HOME

DURING THE 1870s Marx's life became much calmer. His house was
no longer the venue for refugees from the Commune or British trade
union officials. Although he was increasingly wary of strangers – and
any German had to produce written evidence of legitimate business
before being let through the door by Helene Demuth – Marx was still
interested to receive visits from foreigners sympathetic to socialism.
Regular visits, however, were limited to those made by his family and
by the small circle of what Marx liked to call his 'scientific friends'.
He steadfastly refused the numerous invitations to give public
lectures.[1] His temper, too, was much more equable and his appetite
for public controversy considerably dampened.

> Even in London [he wrote in 1881] I have not taken the slightest
> notice of such literary yelping. If I didn't adopt this position, I would
> have to waste most of my time putting people right from Cali-
> fornia to Moscow. When I was younger, I often waded violently
> in but old age brings wisdom at least in so far as one avoids useless
> dissipation of energy.[2]

Marx's routine was fairly regular now: he liked to work during the
morning, walk after lunch, have his dinner at six and receive friends

[1] Cf. J. Verdes, 'Marx vu par la police française (1871–1883)', *Cahiers de l'ISEA*
(Aug 1966) p. 110.
[2] Marx to D. Nieuwenhuis, *MEW* xxxv 160. This was not always Marx's view:
when the English socialist leader Hyndman remarked to him that he grew more
tolerant as he grew older, Marx replied with a surprised: 'Do you? *Do* you?'

at nine.[1] His most frequent visitor was Engels who had moved to London in 1870 and lived in a fine house in Regent's Park Road less than ten minutes' walk away. He would come regularly to Marx at 1.00 p.m., and the two friends would either pace up and down in Marx's study, both wearing a beaten track in the carpet diagonally from corner to corner, or, if the weather was fine, go for a walk on Hampstead Heath. Jenny, however, could not face the last ten years of her life with much optimism: 'Now I am too old', she wrote to Liebknecht in 1872, 'to have much hope any more and the latest unhappy events have completely shattered me. I fear that we old ones will not be experiencing much more good and I only hope that our children will get through their lives more easily.'[2] In 1875, the Marx family moved for the last time, into a smaller elegant terraced house in the same road; and, although Marx still had to apply to Engels fairly regularly to supplement his allowance,[3] the financial worries of the past two decades were at an end.

The daughters married and the family consequently grew larger and less close-knit. Laura and Paul Lafargue settled in London after their return from Madrid following the Hague Congress. None of their children survived: a son and a daughter, born in 1870 and 1871, died while small babies; and Charles-Étienne, Marx's first grandchild and named after him, died in Madrid barely three years old. Disillusioned with medicine, Paul set up a photo-engraving firm in London. Competition from larger firms and Paul's utter lack of business sense meant that the undertaking had no chance of success, and throughout the 1870s the Lafargues lived (in very fair style) off Engels' contributions.[4]

Lafargue was also responsible for Marx's one venture into practical capitalist life. Lafargue had gone into partnership with Le Moussu, a refugee from the Commune and an expert engraver, who had invented a new copying machine. Together they intended to exploit the patent. There was a third partner, George Moore, also an engraver. Lafargue quarrelled with Le Moussu and his place was taken by Marx, whose share was paid by Engels. Early in 1874 Marx and Le Moussu also quarrelled about the ownership of the patent and in order to avoid an open law suit, decided to submit their case to an arbitrator, Frederic

[1] Cf. K. Kautsky, 'Hours with Karl Marx', *The Modern Thinker* (1933) p. 107.
[2] Jenny Marx to Liebknecht, *MEW* XXXIII 702.
[3] Cf., for example, *MEW* XXXV 11, 31, 81, 98.
[4] Cf. *Engels–Lafargue Correspondence*, I, where almost every letter of this period is a begging one.

Harrison, the Positivist friend of Beesly, then practising as a barrister. Harrison related in his memoirs what followed:

> Before they gave evidence I required them in due form to be sworn on the Bible, as the law then required for legal testimony. This filled both of them with horror. Karl Marx protested that he would never so degrade himself. Le Moussu said that no man should ever accuse him of such an act of meanness. For half an hour they argued and protested, each refusing to be sworn first in the presence of the other. At last I obtained a compromise, that the witnesses should simultaneously 'touch the book', without uttering a word. Both seemed to me to shrink from the pollution of handling the sacred volume, much as Mephistopheles in the Opera shrinks from the Cross. When they got to argue the case, the ingenious Le Moussu won, for Karl Marx floundered about in utter confusion.[1]

Jenny, who was as fervently francophile as Tussy was pro-Irish, had followed Laura's example by becoming engaged to a Frenchman, Charles Longuet, in the spring of 1872. She had already been a little in love with Gustave Flourens, the communard general killed in the siege. Longuet had been active in the International, where he enjoyed good relations with Marx in spite of his Proudhonism, and had been member of the Commune and editor of its official newspaper. There was as much amusement at the 'sheep's eyes' of the lovers as there had been with Laura's engagement. Longuet tried out several French dishes on the family, and everyone was happy except for Jenny Marx who wished that her daughter's choice could, for a change, have been an Englishman or a German, 'instead of a Frenchman, who naturally together with all the charming qualities of his nation is also not without its weaknesses and insufficiencies. . . . I can't help being afraid that Jenny's fate as a political wife is exposed to all the cares and troubles that are inseparable from it.'[2]

Longuet was as penniless as most of the French refugees. He had been a medical student and managed to get a temporary job lecturing at King's College. After their marriage in the St Pancras Registry Office in mid-October 1872, they moved to Oxford where Longuet tried to establish himself as a private tutor in French. Soon, however, they were back in London: Jenny did not like the 'orthodox and arrogant

---

[1] F. Harrison, *Autobiographic Memoirs* (London, 1911) II 33 f.
[2] Jenny Marx to Liebknecht, *MEW* XXXIII 703.

'atmosphere of Oxford ... that sham seat of science' and, as she wrote wrote to Kugelmann,

> London contains Modena Villas, and in the front room first floor of Modena Villas I can always find my dear Mohr. I cannot express to you how lonely I feel when separated from him and he tells me that he also missed me very much and that during my absence he buried himself altogether in his den ... Though married, my heart is as chained as it ever was to the spot where my Papa is, and life elsewhere would not be life to me.[1]

Jenny became governess to a local businessman's family and tried to give singing and elocution lessons, while Longuet eventually obtained a permanent post lecturing in French at King's College. Although Longuet was never as close to the Marx family as Lafargue, Jenny remained Marx's preferred companion. Her first child died in infancy, but she gave birth to five more children before her death in 1883. Marx was particularly attached to the eldest, Jean or Johnny, whom he referred to as 'the apple of my eye', and with whom he loved to play for hours on end the same boisterous games that he had enjoyed with his own children.[2]

Of the three daughters, therefore, only Eleanor was left unmarried.[3] At the same time as Longuet was courting Jenny, Eleanor was developing a deep attachment to Hippolyte-Prosper-Olivier Lissagaray, a flamboyant French Basque who, at thirty-four, was exactly twice her age.[4] He was a journalist, had been active in the Commune, and defended single-handed the last barricade to be manned. But he was too much of an individualist to be an adherent of any one school of political thought. The Lafargues tried to snub the persistent Lissagaray.

> Last night Lissa came again [wrote Eleanor to her sister Jenny] ... again Laura and Lafargue shook hands with everybody ... and not with him! Altogether they behave most oddly. Either Lissagaray is the perfect gentleman that Paul's letter and his own behaviour proclaim him to be, and then he should be treated as such, or else

[1] Jenny Marx to Kugelmann, in Andreas, *Briefe*, pp. 286, 291.
[2] Cf. W. Licbknecht, in *Reminiscences of Marx and Engels*, p. 116.
[3] Eleanor has been well served by biographers. See C. Tzuzuki, *The Life of Eleanor Marx* (Oxford, 1967); Y. Kapp, *Eleanor Marx*, I. The latter is full of well-researched information about the Marx family in general.
[4] On Lissagaray, see Preface to *Histoire de la Commune de 1871* (Paris, 1929).

he is no gentleman, and then he ought not to be received by us – one or the other – but this really unladylike behaviour on Laura's part is very disagreeable. I only wonder Lissagaray comes at all.[1]

Marx, too, disapproved of the association, and refused to allude to any 'engagement'. Eleanor claimed that he was unjust towards Lissagaray but, as he wrote to Engels,

> I require nothing of him except that he furnish proofs instead of phrases, that he be better than his reputation, that one has some reason for relying on him. You see from the reply what effect the man continues to have. The damnable thing is that, for the child's sake I must proceed with great consideration and care.[2]

He was sure that his intervention would force Lissagaray 'to put a good face on a bad situation'.[3] Jenny Marx, however, strongly disapproved of her husband's attitude when Engels tactlessly showed her Marx's letter.[4] She claimed to be the only one to understand her daughter's position and connived at Lissagaray's visits to Eleanor at Brighton, while keeping up a continual correspondence with her and sending her hampers of special food and clothes.

Meanwhile, Eleanor was trying to establish her financial independence. In the summer of 1873, aided by two clergymen and old Arnold Ruge (Marx's colleague of the 1840s) she got a teaching job in a ladies' boarding school run by the Misses Hall in Brighton. But she still pined for Lissagaray. Her health broke down and she had to return to London. Throughout 1874 she was the constant companion of her father, both at home and on his journeys to Harrogate and Carlsbad. Marx had forbidden her to see Lissagaray and she appealed to him, probably some time during 1874:

> I want to know, dear Mohr, when I may see L again. It is so *very* hard *never* to see him. I have been doing my best to be patient, but it is so difficult, and I don't feel as if I could be much longer. – I do not expect you to say that he can come here – I should not even wish it, but could I not, now and then, go for a little walk with him? You let me go out with Outine, with Frankel, why not with him? – No one

---

[1] Eleanor Marx to Jenny Marx, Bottigelli Collection, quoted in Tzuzuki, op. cit., p. 32.
[2] Marx to Engels, *MEW* xxxiii 84.   [3] Marx to Engels, *MEW* xxxiii 75.
[4] Cf. Engels to Marx, *MEW* xxxiii 78.

moreover will be astonished to see us together, as everybody knows we are engaged. . . .

When I was so very ill at Brighton (during the week I fainted 2 or 3 times a day) L came to see me, each time left me stronger and happier, and more able to bear the rather heavy load laid on my shoulders. It is *so* long since I saw him, and I am beginning to feel so very miserable notwithstanding all my efforts to be merry and cheerful. I cannot much longer. – Believe me, dear Mohr, if I could see him now and then it could do me more good than all Mrs Anderson's[1] prescriptions put together – I know that by experience.[2]

By the end of the year she had recovered from her ill health (which Marx attributed in large part to hysteria[3]), and continued a lively correspondence with Lissagaray who liked to address her as '*ma petite femme*'.[4] Marx seems later to have relaxed his restrictions on Eleanor, for in 1875 and 1876 she was assisting Lissagaray with his journalism and publishing projects. She translated into English the whole of Lissagaray's classic *History of the Commune*, which had been published in French in 1876; Marx himself helped considerably in revising the translation. But when an amnesty enabled Lissagaray to return to Paris in 1880, Eleanor did not follow him. During these years, the affair estranged Eleanor from her father; with her mother it was even worse:

For long miserable years there was a shadow between myself and my father. . . . yet our love was always the same, and despite everything, our faith and trust in each other. My mother and I loved each other passionately, but she did not know me as father did. One of the bitterest of many bitter sorrows in my life is that my mother died, thinking, despite all our love, that I had been hard and cruel, and never guessing that to save her and father sorrow I had sacrificed the best, freshest years of my life. But father, though he did not *know* till just before the end, felt he must trust me – our natures were so exactly alike! . . . Father was talking of my eldest sister and of me, and said: 'Jenny is most like me, but Tussy . . . is me'.[5]

[1] Elizabeth Garrett Anderson, the first woman in England to qualify as a doctor.
[2] Eleanor Marx to Marx, Bottigelli Collection, quoted in Tzuzuki, op. cit., p. 35.
[3] Cf. Marx to Engels, *MEW* xxxiii 110.
[4] Cf. F. Kugelmann, in *Reminiscences*, p. 285.
[5] Eleanor Marx to Olive Schreiner, quoted in Havelock Ellis, 'Eleanor Marx', *Adelphi* (Sep 1935) pp. 348 f.

For distraction, Eleanor threw herself into political activities: writing articles – particularly on Russia; and canvassing for free-thinking candidates in the London School Board elections. She also undertook translation and précis work and spent long hours in the British Museum where she met George Bernard Shaw. And as her mother moved more and more into the background, Eleanor began to act as hostess to the visitors, several of whom have left admiring accounts of her appearance, vivacity and political understanding. Hyndman, the founder of the Social Democratic Federation, wrote of her that:

> Eleanor herself was the favourite of her father, whom she resembled in appearance as much as a young woman could. A broad, low forehead, dark bright eyes, with glowing cheeks, and a brisk, humorous smile, she inherited in her nose and mouth the Jewish type from Marx himself, while she possessed a physical energy and determination fully equal to his own, and an intelligence which never achieved the literary or political success – for she was a keen politician as well as sociologist – of which she was capable. Possibly, she felt herself somewhat overshadowed by her father's genius, whose defects she was unable to see.[1]

In the late 1870s Eleanor made an effort to build a career on the interest in drama that she had inherited from her parents. The Marx family had always been intensely interested in Shakespeare and became fervent admirers of the new interpretation given to the tragedies by Henry Irving: Jenny Marx, aided by Eleanor, had a series of articles published in the *Frankfurter Zeitung* defending Irving and his 'peculiar, faithful and original picture of Shakespeare'.[2] Eleanor was a keen member of Furnivall's New Shakespeare Society and a friend of actors and actresses like Ernest Radford and Dolly Maitland. She was also a member of a Shakespeare reading club which often met at the Marxes' house. One of its members, Mrs Marian Comyn, gave the following description of Marx at one of the meetings:

> As an audience he was delightful, never criticising, always entering into the spirit of any fun that was going on, laughing when anything struck him as particularly comic, until the tears ran down his cheeks

[1] H. M. Hyndman, *Further Reminiscences* (London, 1912) p. 139.
[2] Quoted in L. Dornemann, *Jenny Marx*, p. 300.

– the oldest in years, but in spirit as young as any of us. And his friend, the faithful Frederic Engels, was equally spontaneous.[1]

But however much he may have enjoyed the club meetings, Marx did not favour acting as a career for his daughter and Eleanor did not perform publicly until July 1881 (when she appeared in two one-act French plays). Engels was in the audience and reported to Marx: 'Tussy was very good in the passionate scenes, though it was somewhat noticeable that she took Ellen Terry as a model, as Radford took Irving, but she will soon get out of that habit; if she wishes to have an effect on the public, she must absolutely strike out a line of her own, and I'm sure she will.'[2] Although interrupted by the illnesses and deaths of her parents, Eleanor persisted in her ambition and eventually, together with her future husband Edward Aveling, made a significant contribution to the theatre of the time.

II. WORK

During the years of the International Marx had little time for pursuing his economic studies. At the end of November 1871 Meissner informed him that the first edition of *Capital* was almost completely sold out and asked him – for a royalty of 500 thalers – to prepare a second and cheaper edition which he intended to issue in a dozen separate booklets. Marx worked on it for eighteen months; and the last instalment did not appear until June 1873, mainly because of a long printers' strike in Leipzig. He made substantial changes in the first chapter with which, as his daughter Jenny said, 'he is himself pleased – which is rare'.[3] The first foreign translation was the Russian one which appeared in March 1872. It was begun by a young Populist called Lopatin who moved to London in the summer of 1870 to work under Marx's direction in the British Museum while taking English lessons from Eleanor. Lopatin did not complete the translation (he returned to Russia on an unsuccessful mission to liberate Chernyshevsky from prison). The work was taken over by Danielson, a shy Populist scholar, who translated the book in the evenings on his return from the bank where he worked for fifty years. There was some fear that the Tsarist censors might ban the book but they found it so 'difficult and hardly

[1] *The Nineteenth Century and After* (Jan 1922), quoted in Y. Kapp, *Eleanor Marx*, p. 193.
[2] Engels to Marx, *MEW* xxxv 5.
[3] Jenny Marx to Mrs Kugelmann, *MEW* xxxiii 695.

comprehensible' that they concluded that 'few would read it and still
fewer understand it'.[1] Here they were wrong: the Russian edition sold
better than any other, and copies of it passed avidly from hand to
hand – sometimes inside the covers of the New Testament. Marx did
not even have time to rewrite the first chapter as he would have liked;
he wrote to Danielson complaining about the demands made on him
by the International: 'Certainly I shall one fine morning put a stop
to all this, but there are circumstances in which you are in duty bound
to occupy yourself with things much less attractive than theoretical
study and research.'[2]

Even after the removal of the General Council to New York in 1872
Marx spent most of the following year tying up the loose ends in
London. Then in the autumn of 1873 he suffered a serious breakdown
of health. What little time he did have during the years 1873–75 was
spent working on the French edition. As far back as 1867 there had
been plans to translate *Capital* into French and Elie Reclus (brother of
the famous anarchist geographer) had made a start, assisted by Marx's
old mentor, Moses Hess. He soon gave up, however, and it was not
until 1871 (after no fewer than five other translators had attempted the
task) that Marx opened negotiations with Roy, who had acquired a
considerable reputation as a translator of Feuerbach. Roy was a school
teacher in Bordeaux; mailing the various chapters and sections to and
from London naturally made for new delays, which were further
increased by Roy's difficulty in reading Marx's handwriting (he translated from the manuscript of the second German edition). Marx was
lucky to have been introduced (by Lafargue) to an extremely energetic
Parisian publisher, Maurice Lachâtre, who had recently been exiled to
Switzerland. Marx welcomed Lachâtre's proposal to publish in separate
instalments as 'in this form the work will be more easily accessible to
the working class, and this consideration is more important to me
than any other'.[3]

In February 1872 the contract with Lachâtre was signed. But the
book was to be published at the author's expense. Applying to his
cousin August Philips for financial help, Marx received the answer that,
'if necessary, I am ready to assist you, as a friend and relation, even
with money; but I'm not doing it for your political and revolutionary

---

[1] Quoted in A. Uroyeva, *For all Time and Men* (Moscow, 1967). This book contains
much detail about the publishing history of *Capital*.
[2] Marx to Danielson, *MEW* xxxiii 311.   [3] Marx to Lachâtre xxxiv 434.

aims'.[1] Roy's work, however, did not come up to Marx's high expectations and he found himself having to rewrite whole sentences and even pages. In the event the first instalment did not appear until May 1875 – owing to delays caused partly by Marx's health, partly by Roy's slowness, and partly by Lachâtre's desire to publish a photo of Marx in his edition (thus stealing a march on the Russian publishers who had had their photo banned by the Government, on the grounds that it would imply too much respect for Marx's personality). It had cost him, said Marx, 'more trouble than a whole fresh composition of the book in French';[2] and he wrote in the postscript to this edition: 'it possesses a scientific value independent of the original and should be used even by readers who are competent in German'.[3]

Even before the French edition was finished Marx received urgent letters from his German and Russian publishers asking for Volume Two. Engels assured Kugelmann in October 1876 that 'Volume Two will be tackled in a few days'.[4] Two years later Marx could only vaguely hope that it might be finished 'by the end of 1879'.[5] In April 1879 Marx explained the situation in a long letter to Danielson. He had just received information that the worsening political situation would prevent his second volume from being published in Germany. He almost welcomed the news, for there were grounds other than health reasons that compelled delay. Firstly, England was going through an economic crisis that differed interestingly from previous ones and 'it is therefore necessary to watch the present course of things until they are ripe before I can "digest" them "productively", I mean "theoretically"'.[6] Secondly, as Marx frankly explained, 'the mass of materials that I have, not only from Russia, but also from the United States, etc., make it pleasant for me to have a "pretext" for continuing my studies instead of winding them up finally for the public'.[7]

Danielson himself had been supplying Marx with numerous books on Russian agricultural economics since the freeing of the serfs – books that both Engels and Jenny sometimes felt like burning. This was a subject that occupied Marx's mind particularly in the years 1876 and 1877. As Engels wrote, Marx after 1870 'studied agronomics,

---

[1] A. Philips to Marx, W. Blumenberg, 'Ein unbekanntes Kapitel aus Marx' Leben', *International Review of Social History*, I (1956) p. 111.
[2] Marx to Mathilda Betham-Edwards, *MEW* xxxiv 146.
[3] *Oeuvres*, ed. M. Rubel, I 546.   [4] Engels to Kugelmann, *MEW* xxxiv 217.
[5] Marx to Danielson, *MEW* xxxiv 358.   [6] Marx to Danielson, *MESC*, p. 315.
[7] Ibid. p. 317.

agricultural conditions in America and especially Russia, the money market and banking institutions, and finally natural sciences, such as geology and physiology. Independent mathematical studies also form a large part of the numerous manuscripts of this period.'[1]

A study of the evolution of agriculture in Russia was intended to illuminate Marx's ideas on ground-rent in Volume Three of *Capital* in the same way as English industrial development provided the practical examples to the ideas expounded in Volume One. Marx had learnt Russian specifically to be able to study the original sources. As in the 1850s and 1860s, Marx amassed a huge amount of material but he now lacked the power of synthesis and the driving force to make something of it. After his death Engels was amazed to find among Marx's papers more than two cubic metres of documents containing nothing but Russian statistics. During these years Marx filled in his microscopic handwriting almost three thousand pages – these manuscripts comprising almost exclusively notes on his reading. In his later years this reading became obsessional: he no longer had the power to create, but at least he could absorb. Thus the manuscripts for Volume Three of *Capital* remained virtually in the state in which they had been since 1864–65. Marx had rewritten almost half of Volume Two in 1870, but thereafter made only minor additions and revisions – realising, as he said to Eleanor shortly before his death, that it would be up to Engels 'to make something of it'.[2] Marx kept the state of his manuscripts a secret from everyone, including Engels, who wrote later to Bebel that 'if I had been aware of this, I would not have let him rest day or night until everything had been finished and printed. Marx himself knew this better than anyone. . . .'[3] In fact, the state of the manuscripts was so chaotic that Engels could publish Volume Three of *Capital* only eleven years after Marx's death.

Marx's inherent reluctance to complete any of his economic work was abetted by other distracting tasks imposed on him during the 1870s. He collaborated on two shortened versions of *Capital*, Volume One, in German by Johannes Most and in Dutch by Domela Nieuwenhuis. Not only did he help Eleanor translate Lissagaray's book into English but he also supervised in great detail the German translation. His aversion to Lissagaray as a possible son-in-law was more than

---

[1] F. Engels, Preface to *Capital* (Chicago, 1909) II 10.
[2] Ibid., 11.
[3] Engels to Bebel, *MEW* xxxvi 56.

balanced by his admiration for his *History of the Commune*. During the mid-1870s Marx gave some of his time to assisting Engels write *Anti-Dühring* which, by virtue of its systematisation and clarity, was to become the best-known textbook in Marxist circles with a circulation much wider than *Capital*.[1] In the Preface to the second edition, written after Marx's death, Engels says that he read all the manuscript to Marx and that Marx actually wrote a chapter consisting of a review of Dühring's *Critical History of Political Economy*.

Towards the end of his life Marx moved nearer to the positivism then so fashionable in intellectual circles. This tendency, begun in *Anti-Dühring* and continued by Engels in his *Ludwig Feuerbach* and *Dialectics of Nature*, reached its apogee in Soviet textbooks on dialectical materialism. It was this trend which presented Marxism as a philosophical world-view or *Weltanschauung* consisting of objective laws and particularly laws of the dialectical movement of matter taken in a metaphysical sense as the basic constituent of reality. This was obviously very different from the 'unity of theory and practice' as exemplified in, for instance, the *Theses on Feuerbach*. This preference for the model of the natural sciences had always been with Engels, though not with Marx, who had, for example, a much more reserved attitude to Darwinism.

Marx had always had a great admiration for Darwin's work. He had read *On the Origin of Species* in 1860, a year after its publication, and had at once written to Engels that it contained 'the natural-history basis for our view'.[2] He considered that the book had finally disposed of religious teleology, but he regretted 'the crude English manner of the presentation'.[3] Two years later, however, his view was slightly different:

> It is remarkable how Darwin recognizes among beasts and plants his English society with its division of labour, competition, opening up of new markets, 'inventions', and the Malthusian 'struggle for existence'. It is Hobbes's 'bellum omnium contra omnes', and one is reminded of Hegel's *Phenomenology*, where civil society is described as a 'spiritual animal kingdom', while in Darwin the animal kingdom figures as civil society.[4]

In 1866 Marx wrote – again to Engels – and even more critically: 'in Darwin progress is merely accidental' and the book did not yield much

[1] On the circumstances giving rise to Dühring's criticism of Marx, see pp. 435 f. below.
[2] Marx to Engels, *MEW* xxx 131.　　　[3] Marx to Lassalle, *MEW* xxx 578.
[4] Marx to Engels, *MESC*, pp. 156 f.

'in connection with history and politics'.[1] Although he admitted that Darwin's book might have 'an unconscious socialist tendency', anyone who wanted to subsume the whole of history under the Darwinian expression 'struggle for survival' merely demonstrated his 'feebleness of thought'.[2] Marx certainly used biological metaphors to express his ideas and considered his method in the study of economic formations more akin to biology than to physics or chemistry. The only place where Marx drew a direct parallel between himself and Darwin was in an ironical review of his own work for the Stuttgart newspaper *Der Beobachter*.[3] Marx certainly wished to dedicate the Second Volume of *Capital* to Darwin. (Darwin refused the honour, apparently because he had the impression that it was an overtly atheistic book and did not wish to hurt the feelings of his family.) But this suggests no more than that Marx appreciated Darwin's work – and not that he approached history in the same way as Darwin had approached nature. Thus Engels' equating the views of Marx and Darwin in his famous speech at Marx's graveside is highly misleading.[4]

It is nevertheless true that Marx paid more attention to the natural sciences (physiology, geology and, above all, mathematics) during the last decade of his life than he ever did before. He was also much interested in the beginnings of anthropology and enthused about the work of Lewis Morgan, a once much-respected writer whose scholarly reputation has not survived subsequent research. In the winter of 1880–81 Marx drew up with great care a hundred pages of excerpts from Morgan's *Primitive Society*, excerpts later used by Engels in his *Origin of the Family*. What particularly interested Marx in Morgan's book was the democratic political organisation of primitive tribes together with their communal property. Marx was uninfluenced by the Victorian value judgements that permeate Morgan's work nor does he seem to have shared Engels' great admiration for his achievements. In particular, he did not see any close parallel between primitive communism and a future communist society.[5]

[1] Marx to Engels, *MEW* xxxi 248.

[2] Marx to Kugelmann, *MEW* xxxii 685 f.

[3] See S. Avineri, 'From Hoax to Dogma: A footnote on Marx and Darwin', *Encounter* (Mar 1967). See also the exhaustive article by E. Lucas, 'Marx' and Engels' Auseinandersetzung mit Darwin', *International Review of Social History* (1964).

[4] Cf. F. Engels, 'Speech at the Graveside of Karl Marx', *MESW* i 153 ff.

[5] See, further, E. Lucas, 'Die Rezeption Lewis H. Morgans durch Marx und Engels', *Saeculum* (1964) and the excellent edition by L. Krader, *The Ethnological Notebooks of Karl Marx* (Assen, 1972).

III. HEALTH

What prevented Marx from finishing his life's work was his illness. By the early 1870s his earlier life-style and privations had irredeemably impaired his health. Throughout the last ten years of his life the pathetic search for soundness of body, which drove him from one health resort to another, played an increasingly central role. In April 1871 Engels reported to Kugelmann that Marx had begun to live 'fairly rationally' since giving up his theoretical work with the outbreak of the Franco-Prussian War: he went for two-hour walks up to Hampstead most days and laid off beer for weeks on end if he felt unwell.[1] But scarcely had he returned to his theoretical work (continuing with the French translation of Volume One) than he had a serious relapse: there was pressure on the brain with an attendant insomnia that even strong doeses of chloral could not relieve. A stroke was feared. Engels persuaded him to go to Manchester at the end of May 1873 to consult Gumpert, Engels' own doctor and the only one in whom Marx had complete confidence. Gumpert gave him a strict regimen to follow and absolutely forbad him to work more than four hours a day. This considerably improved his health but there was a renewal of the headaches in the autumn and Marx again went north to see Gumpert. At the same time he took a three-week water cure in Harrogate in the company of Eleanor, who was near to a nervous breakdown. Marx occupied his time reading Sainte-Beuve's *Chateaubriand* which he found full of 'newfangled forms of expression, false profundity, Byzantine exaggerations, sentimental coquetry, garish tints, word painting, theatrical, sublime – in a word, a mish-mash of lies never before achieved in form and content'.[2] Gumpert detected a swollen liver and strongly advised Marx to take the Carlsbad cure. Harrogate certainly brought no relief; even the carbuncles returned in the winter, Marx was still plagued by insomnia and unable to do any serious writing or work – a situation he described as 'a judgement of death on any man who is not a beast'.[3] In April 1874 he was in Ramsgate for three weeks and in July visited the Isle of Wight, whose inhabitants amazed him by their religiosity. He had to leave the Isle of Wight to look after Eleanor, whose nerves had once again brought her to a state of collapse, and to attend the funeral of his grandson Charles

[1] Cf. Engels to Kugelmann, *MEW* xxxiii 218 f.
[2] Marx to Engels, *MEW* xxxiii 96.   [3] Marx to Sorge, *MEW* xxxiii 634.

who had lived a little less than a year. Thus Marx was temporarily left without grandchildren – the four born so far all having died in infancy.

At the end of June 1874 Marx finally decided to take Gumpert's advice and go to Carlsbad, the fashionable spa built on the steeply sloping banks of the river Egen in Bohemia (now Western Czechoslovakia). As early as 1869 Kugelmann had tried to persuade Marx to go there with his daughter Jenny, and Marx had flatly rejected the place as 'boring and expensive'.[1] Now, with more money and less health, he decided to go and took Eleanor with him. The trip was arranged by Kugelmann who booked them rooms at the Germania, one of the more modest hotels. The entry in the official list of visitors reads: 'Herr Charles Marx, private gentleman, with his daughter Eleanor, from London.' As a private person, Marx had to pay double bath tax, but hoped that the self-description would 'avoid the suspicion that I am the notorious Karl Marx'.[2] In anticipation of difficulties with the police Marx had applied for naturalisation as a British subject before his departure. At the beginning of August, his solicitor had forwarded the application to the Home Office together with the necessary references from four respectable householders. The Home Office, however, rejected his request and refused to give a reason when pressed. In fact, the information passed from Scotland Yard to the Home Office was that the applicant was 'the notorious German agitator' and 'had not been loyal to his own King and Country'.[3] Nor did Marx escape constant police surveillance in Carlsbad, though it was merely reported that his conduct 'did not give rise to any suspicion'.[4]

Marx took his cure very seriously and let himself be turned, as he put it, into a sort of machine. He would be up at 5.30 at the latest and travel round six different springs drinking a glass of water at each at fifteen-minute intervals. After a breakfast of special medicinal bread, there would be an hour's walk and mid-morning coffee in one of the cafés outside the town. Then a further walking tour among the surrounding hills, then back to the hotel to change and have a nap before lunch, which was preceded every other day by a bath. After lunch there was further walking or longer organised tours followed by a light meal and early bed, all entertainments ending at 9.00 p.m. Marx enjoyed the life very much, particularly the long walks among

---

[1] Marx to Engels, *MEW* xxxii 355.   [2] Ibid. xxxiii 112.
[3] Public Record Office, quoted in R. Payne, *Karl Marx*, p. 460.
[4] E. Kisch, *Karl Marx in Karlsbad* (Berlin, 1953) p. 20.

the pine-clad granite foothills of the Erzgebirge. He also liked to pursue his habit of conferring witty nicknames on the more conspicuous passers-by. Franziska Kugelmann recalled a visit to a porcelain works at which they observed a man supervising an intricate turning machine.

'Is this always your job?' Marx asked him, 'or have you some other?' 'No,' the man answered, 'I have not done anything else for years. It is only by practice that one learns to work the machine so as to get the difficult shape smooth and faultless.' 'Thus division of labour makes man an appendage of the machine,' Marx said to my father as we went on. 'His power of thinking is changed into muscular memory.'[1]

In the afternoon and evening, in general company, Marx preferred light conversation with such men as Otto Knille (a well-known painter) and Simon Deutsch (an Austrian journalist whom Marx remembered from his Paris days). Father and daughter were inseparable whether on walks or writing letters on the terrace behind their hotel. According to Eleanor, still embarrassingly forthright in her reactions to people and smoking almost continuously, she and her father got on very well in Carlsbad and 'his immense knowledge of history made every place we went to more alive and present in the past than in the present itself'.[2]

For Marx, the only drawback to Carlsbad was Kugelmann. From the start of his stay he annoyed Marx by his 'carping criticisms with which he quite needlessly embitters his own life and that of his family'.[3] Unfortunately, Kugelmann had chosen for Marx a room between his own and Eleanor's. The upshot was that

I had the pleasure of his company not only when I was with him, but also when I was alone. I put up patiently with the continual flow of his solemn chatter uttered in a deep voice ... but my patience at last broke down when he began to bore me too utterly with domestic scenes. This arch-pedant, this *bourgeois* hair-splitting philistine, imagines that his wife does not understand or comprehend his Faust-like nature, which is struggling to some higher conception of the world; and he torments the poor woman, who is in all respects

[1] F. Kugelmann, in *Reminiscences of Marx and Engels*, p. 286.
[2] Eleanor Marx, in *Reminiscences*, p. 126.　　[3] Marx to Engels, *MEW* xxxiii 113.

his superior, in the most revolting manner. It came to an open quarrel between us. I moved to a higher floor and so was completely quit of him (he had seriously spoiled the cure for me). We were only reconciled just before his departure, which took place last Sunday. But I said positively that I would not visit his house in Hanover.[1]

According to Eleanor, Mrs Kugelmann (for whom she had a great affection) was always being told by her husband that she was not sufficiently grateful for the benefits he conferred on her and 'the grand scene began because Mrs K. didn't lift up her dress on a dusty day'.[2] Franziska wrote later that there was another point at issue: Marx and Kugelmann quarrelled violently during a long walk in which Kugelmann 'tried to persuade Marx to refrain from all political propaganda and complete the third book of *Capital* before anything else'[3] – a subject on which Marx was always touchy. Marx and Eleanor left Carlsbad on 21 September and studiously avoided Hanover. They went first to Leipzig to see Liebknecht, who took them to welcome Wilhelm Blos on his release from prison. Blos, then a social-democratic journalist and later Prime Minister of Württemberg, wrote later:

> Excited and happy I walked through the prison doors. Outside stood Liebknecht with one of his small sons.[4] And near him there stood, with a beautiful young lady on his arm, a tall, thin man in his fifties with a long white beard, the moustache alone being really black. His complexion was fresh and he could have been taken for a jovial old Englishman. But I recognised him immediately from his photo. . . .[5]

They then went on to Berlin to see Marx's brother-in-law Edgar, who earned his living as a minor functionary while still preserving his sympathy for communism. After a trip to Hamburg to see Meissner they returned to London at the beginning of October.

The following year Marx went alone to Carlsbad. His journey out was enlivened by a discussion with a Catholic priest whose reserve Marx managed to break down by the production of a bottle of Cognac.

[1] Ibid. 117.

[2] Eleanor Marx to Jenny Longuet, Bottigelli Collection, quoted in Tzuzuki, op. cit., p. 37.

[3] F. Kugelmann, in *Reminiscences*, p. 286.

[4] Possibly Karl Liebknecht, Marx's godson, who played a leading role in the abortive German revolution of 1919.

[5] W. Blos, *Denkwürdigkeiten eines Sozial-demokraten* (Munich, 1914) I 163 f.

On arrival he announced in letters home that the absence of Kugelmann was a great help to his health, and set about enjoying the long walks and the Pilsener beer. He spent much time in the company of Maxim Kovalevsky, a liberal Russian aristocrat who shared his interest in the history of land ownership in Russia, and was later a frequent visitor in London. Kovalevsky was no socialist but admired Marx profoundly and came to occupy the position in Marx's life so recently vacated by Kugelmann.

The police continued to watch Marx closely but could only report back to Prague that 'he lives quietly, has very little intercourse with the other guests and frequently goes on long walks alone'. The cure was very beneficial: Engels reported in October 1875 that 'Marx has come back from Carlsbad quite changed, strong, fresh, confident and healthy, and can now once more take up his work in earnest.'[1]

In 1876, for the third year in succession, Marx returned to Carlsbad. This time he took Eleanor with him, saying that he had missed her too much the previous year. They stayed the regulation month and moved a little more in society – mostly among German university professors – where the question everyone wished to discuss was: what do you think of Wagner? Marx's thoughts were extremely sarcastic ones. Eleanor's health gave Marx much cause for anxiety and she narrowly avoided serious pneumonia at the end of their stay. On their return they spent some time in Prague with Kugelmann's brother-in-law, the businessman Max Oppenheim, and then made a detour via Bingen and Kreuznach as Marx wanted to show his daughter the places where he had married and spent his honeymoon.

In 1877 Marx did not go to Carlsbad; he went instead to the minor spa of Neuenahr in the Rhineland. In a lengthy justification to Engels, he explained that Carlsbad would be extremely expensive, as Jenny would not agree to be left behind this year; and also that a change of regime might be beneficial. Engels responded by presenting Marx with the detailed maps of the Black Forest he had used in the 1849 campaigns. Bismarck's anti-socialist laws of 1878 deprived Marx of the opportunity of travelling to German or Austrian spas and that year he had to make do with the English equivalent at Malvern. He went with his wife, his daughter Jenny and his grandson, all of whom were seriously ill. While they were there Lizzie Burns (with whom Engels had been living since the death of Mary) died of a tumour of the bladder

[1] Engels to Bracke, MEW xxxiv 157.

after long suffering. Engels married her on her deathbed according to the rites of the Church of England. The following year Marx went to Jersey, but had to return to Ramsgate to be with his daughter Jenny after the birth of Edgar, his third grandchild. During this time the family was preoccupied with Jenny Marx's illness, an incurable cancer of the liver. In 1880 Marx took his wife first to Manchester to see Gumpert and then for an extended stay in Ramsgate. Confined to her bed for long periods and mistrustful of doctors, she needed constant family attention. By the turn of the decade the topics of sickness and climate pervaded Marx's letters to the virtual exclusion of all else; understandably enough, in view of his own illnesses and the tragedies that had occurred within his family, he was now mentally and physically exhausted: in a word, his public career was over.

IV. THE EUROPEAN SCENE

The death of the International and the fragmentation of the European working-class movement meant that the 1870s saw the growth of autonomous national parties. As often, Marx looked to war as the catalyst of revolution. 'The general situation of Europe', he wrote to Sorge in 1874, 'is such that it moves to a general European war. We must go through this war before we can think of any decisive external effectiveness of the European working class.'[1] The only country in which there existed a proletarian party was Germany, to which, as Marx had foreseen, the centre of gravity of the workers' movement shifted after the Franco-Prussian War. It was Germany that occupied most of Marx's attention during the 1870s. More accurately, there were two proletarian parties in Germany, the Eisenach party and the followers of Lassalle, and the early 1870s saw attempts to bring about a union between them. This was aided by the unification of Germany under Prussian leadership, the resignation of Schweitzer from the presidency of the Lassallean party, and the increasing pressure which Bismarck applied to both parties in the aftermath of the Paris Commune. When their first big electoral success showed that the two parties polled an almost identical number of votes, negotiations were opened and agreement reached in principle at the end of 1874. A united programme was to be adopted at Gotha, a small town in central Germany, in May 1875.

Marx and Engels were somewhat out of touch with the situation

---

[1] Marx to Sorge, MEW xxxiii 635.

inside Germany,[1] and were enraged both with the content of the programme and with the fact that they had not been consulted. Engels composed a long letter to Bebel in March 1875 in which he recapitulated the unacceptable Lassallean propositions incorporated in the programme: the rejection of all non-proletarian parties as a 'reactionary mass', the lack of international spirit, the talk of the 'iron laws' of wages and the lack of consideration given to trade unions. And he predicted that they would have to break with Liebknecht if the programme were adopted.[2] Marx himself wrote to Bracke in May that 'every step of real movement is more important than a dozen programmes'.[3] In Marx's view the Eisenach party should have confined itself to concluding some sort of practical agreement for combined action. As it was, he and Engels would dissociate themselves from the programme immediately after the Congress. The letter accompanied a manuscript entitled 'Marginal Notes on the Programme of the German Workers' Party' which he asked Bracke to circulate among the Eisenach leaders. Liebknecht, who considered that the negotiations were too far advanced to be suspended, only allowed a few Eisenach leaders to see the document – and not, for example, Bebel. It was published only in 1891 and became known as the *Critique of the Gotha Programme*, one of the most important of Marx's theoretical writings.

The *Critique of the Gotha Programme* took the form of marginal notes notes and contained two main points: one being a criticism of the programme's proposals for distributing the national product, the other being a criticism of its views on the state. On the first point, Marx objected to the attempt to reintroduce into the party 'dogmas, ideas which in a certain period had some meaning but which have now become obsolete verbal rubbish'.[4] He did not find very revolutionary the opening declaration that the proceeds of labour belonged to society as a whole since it was a proposition that had 'at all times been made use of by the champions of the state of society prevailing at any given time'.[5] Further, he criticised the programme for not attacking landowners along with capitalists. Talk about 'fair distribution' and 'equal rights' was vague; proposals that the workers should receive the 'undiminished proceeds of their labour' showed a complete disregard

---

[1] Cf. F. Mehring, *Karl Marx*, pp. 507 f.
[2] Cf. Engels to Bebel, *MEW* xxxiv 125 ff.   [3] Marx to Bracke, *MEW* xxxiv 137.
[4] K. Marx, 'Critique of the Gotha Programme', *MESW* ii 25.
[5] K. Marx, *MESW* ii 19.

for necessary expenditure on capital replacement, administration of social services, poor relief, etc. In terms of the future communist society the phrase 'proceeds of labour' was meaningless, for

> within the co-operative society based on common ownership of the means of production, the producers do not exchange their products; just as little does the labour expended on the products appear here as the value of these products, as a material quality possessed by them, since now, in contrast to capitalist society, individual labour no longer exists in an indirect fashion but directly as a component part of the total labour.[1]

Marx then offered a description of the distribution of the social product in the first stage of communist society 'as it emerges from capitalist society, which is thus in every respect, economically, morally and intellectually, still stamped with the birthmarks of the old society from whose womb it emerges'.[2] In this society the individual producer would receive a certificate from society that he had furnished such and such an amount of labour (after deducting his labour for the common funds), and with this certificate he would draw from the social stock of means of consumption the cost of the equivalent amount of labour. The same amount of labour which he had given to society in one form he would receive back in another.[3]

Of course, Marx continued, this equality was, in effect, unequal. Measurement was made with an equal standard – that of labour: whereas men's capacities, family situations, etc., were not the same and thus inequality would arise.

> But [continued Marx in a famous passage] these defects are inevitable in the first phase of communist society as it is when it has just emerged after prolonged birth pangs from capitalist society. Right can never be higher than the economic structure of society and its cultural development conditioned thereby.
>
> In a higher phase of communist society, after the enslaving subordination of the individual to the division of labour, and therewith also the antithesis between mental and physical labour, has vanished; after labour has become not only a means of life but life's prime want; after the productive forces have also increased with the

---

[1] Ibid. 22 f.   [2] Ibid. 23.   [3] Ibid.

all-round development of the individual, and all the springs of co-operative wealth flow more abundantly – only then can the narrow horizon of bourgeois right be crossed in its entirety and society inscribe on its banners: from each according to his ability, to each according to his needs![1]

Marx summed up his criticism of this section of the programme by saying:

Vulgar socialism (and from it in turn a section of the democracy) has taken over from the bourgeois economists the consideration and treatment of distribution as independent of the mode of production and hence the presentation of socialism as turning principally on distribution. After the real relation has long been made clear, why retrogress again?[2]

Marx's second basic criticism was of the section where the programme called for a 'free state' and 'the abolition of the wage system together with the iron law of wages'. Marx replied that wages were not the value of labour, but the value of labour power. This fact made it clear that

the whole capitalist system of production turns on the increase of this *gratis* labour by extending the working day or by developing the productivity, that is, increasing the intensity of labour power, etc.; that, consequently, the system of wage-labour is a system of slavery, and indeed of a slavery which becomes more severe proportionate to the development of the social productive forces of labour, whether the worker receives better or worse payment.[3]

The programme's solution to the problem was as misguided as its formulation: it proposed state-aided workers' co-operatives instead of the revolutionary transformation of society.

Turning to the proposal for a 'free state' Marx roundly declared that this could not be an aim of workers worthy of the name 'socialist'. Marx put the question: 'What transformation will the state undergo in communist society? What social functions will remain in existence that are analogous to present functions of the state?' He did not answer this question specifically, but said: 'Between capitalist and communist society lies the period of the revolutionary transformation of the one

---

[1] Ibid. 24.   [2] Ibid. 25.   [3] Ibid. 27.

into the other. There corresponds to this also a political transition period in which the state can be nothing but *the revolutionary dictatorship of the proletariat*.'[1] In fact, the programme contained, according to Marx, nothing but the 'old familiar democratic litany' – universal suffrage, direct legislation, popular rights, a people's militia, etc., many of which had already been achieved in progressive bourgeois republics.

In spite of his threats, Marx did not dissociate himself from the programme; and Engels' assertion that a split in the new party was absolutely certain proved quite mistaken. Bismarck's growing opposition to the socialists made the Lassalleans' policy of co-operation with the state more and more implausible, and the Eisenachers soon gained the upper hand. As the industrialisation of Germany increased at a gigantic rate, the new Social Democratic Workers' Party polled an ever larger number of votes. Nevertheless Marx was still far from happy with the policies of his colleagues and disciples. As even Bebel – whom Marx and Engels regarded as the only completely reliable member of the Party – commented: 'It was no easy matter to arrive at an understanding with the two old men in London.'[2]

Although Marx was keen to have a theoretical journal in which to expose 'the absolute ignorance of professors and lecturers'[3] he could not welcome the appearance in August 1877 of *Die Zukunft*, a theoretical fortnightly designed to supplement the Party's newspaper *Vorwärts*. It was financed by Karl Hochberg, the rich son of a Frankfurt bookmaker who had the best of intentions but, as Marx said, 'I do not give a damn for intentions.'[4] He refused to write for the journal and felt more than justified when he read the phrases about justice and the phantasies of the future communist society that were reminiscent of the 'true socialism' of the 1840s. The result of 'bringing a bourgeois into the party'[5] had not been a success. Marx summed up his general opinion of the situation in Germany as follows:

> ... A rotten spirit is making itself felt in our Party in Germany, not so much among the masses as among the leaders (upper-class and 'workers'). The compromise with the Lassalleans has led to a compromise with other halfway elements too: in Berlin (like *Most*) with Dühring and his 'admirers', but also with a whole gang of half-mature students and super-wise diplomaed doctors who want to

---

[1] Ibid. 30.   [2] A. Bebel, *Aus Meinem Leben* (Stuttgart, 1910) II 138.
[3] Marx to Engels, *MEW* xxxiv 48.   [4] Marx to Sorge, *MESC*, p. 309.
[5] Marx to Bracke, *MEW* xxxiv 305.

give socialism a 'higher, idealistic' orientation, that is to say, to re-place its materialistic basis (which demands serious objective study from anyone who tries to use it) by modern mythology with its goddesses of Justice, Liberty, Equality and Fraternity. Dr Hochberg, who publishes *Die Zukunft*, is a representative of this tendency and has 'bought his way' into the Party – with the 'noblest' intentions, I assume, but I do not give a damn for 'intentions'. Anything more miserable than his programme of *Die Zukunft* has seldom seen the light of day with more 'modest presumption'.

The workers themselves, when, like Herr Most & Co., they give up work and become *professional literary men*, always breed 'theoretical' mischief and are always ready to join muddleheads from the allegedly 'learned' caste. *Utopian* socialism, especially, which for decades we have been clearing out of the German workers' heads with so much effort and labour – their freedom from it having made them theoretically (and therefore also practically) superior to the French and English – *utopian* socialism, playing with fantastic pictures of the future structure of society, is again spreading like wildfire, and in a much more futile form, not only compared with the great French and English utopians, but even with – Weitling. It is natural that utopianism, which *before* the era of materialistically critical socialism concealed the latter within itself in embryo, can now, coming belatedly, only be silly, stale, and reactionary from the roots up....[1]

The Social-Democratic Workers' Party set up at the Gotha Congress certainly embraced many different sorts of socialism: Johannes Most advocated something very near anarchism, 'philanthropic' socialists were legion, and Dühring's decentralised and highly egalitarian communes were very attractive to the Eisenach wing of the Party. Dühring's struggle to overcome the difficulties caused by the disability of his blindness together with his outspoken radicalism in the face of university authority gave him a popularity in Berlin (where he taught) that only later would be tarnished by developing megalomania and violent anti-semitism. In general, Dühring considered his attack on Marx to be 'from the left' and criticised what he called Marx's Hegelian scholasticism, his economic determinism, his dependence on Ricardo and the vagueness of his ideas on the future communist society.

[1] Marx to Sorge, *MESC*, pp. 309 ff.

Nevertheless, in spite of his witty characterisation of Marx as an 'old Young Hegelian', he rated him very high and held his works in considerable esteem. In 1877 the Party Congress almost passed a resolution to stop the publication of Engels' anti-Dühring articles. Johannes Most proposed the resolution, declaring that Engels' articles were 'without interest for the majority of readers of *Vorwärts*'.[1] Bebel managed to carry a compromise resolution that they be published in a scientific supplement. In view of the 'demoralisation of the Party' caused by Liebknecht's opening the door to all-comers, Marx welcomed the anti-socialist laws passed by Bismarck in October 1878. In the summer two attempts on the life of Wilhelm I had naturally infuriated Marx[2] as they at once gave Bismarck the excuse to ban all Social-Democratic organisations, meetings and publications, a ban that was to be maintained for twelve years.

Marx's displeasure at the situation in Germany centred once again around a new publication. In August 1879 there appeared the first number of a *Jahrbuch* edited by three exiles in Zürich: the same Hochberg who had started *Die Zukunft*, Karl Schramm (a Social-Democratic journalist), and Eduard Bernstein, the future exponent of Revisionism and a recent convert from the ideas of Dühring to those of Marx. The Party obviously needed a rallying point: Johannes Most had begun to issue the anarchist *Die Freiheit*; and Karl Hirsch, a socialist journalist living in Paris, had started a new paper called *Die Laterne*, published in Brussels. Hirsch was persuaded to take up the editorship of the proposed *Jahrbuch*, preparation of which was left to the three in Zürich: the first issue, however, contained such a quietist and reformist attitude that Marx and Engels felt bound to protest. What angered them also was the hostile attitude of the Zürich editors to Hirsch for having attacked in his paper a Social-Democrat named Kayser who had voted in favour of protecting the German iron industry. Kayser had in fact consulted his colleagues beforehand and secured their permission to vote as he did. Marx, however, dismissed this manoeuvring as so much 'parliamentary cretinism'.[3]

In a long letter sent to Bebel, Liebknecht and other Party leaders, Marx and Engels summed up their grievances. They rejected the

---

[1] Quoted in R. Adamiak, 'Marx, Engels and Dühring', *Journal of the History of Ideas* (1973). This is an admirably researched article on the background to the whole controversy.

[2] Cf. M. Kovalevsky, in *Reminiscences of Marx and Engels*, p. 299.

[3] Marx to Sorge, *MEW* xxxiv 413.

Zürich group's view that the working class was incapable of emancipating itself, that reform alone should be the aim of the Party, and that its programme should be postponed. This sort of attitude, they said, reminded them of 1848; and such men were

> the representatives of the petty bourgeoisie ... full of anxiety that the proletariat, under the pressure of its revolutionary position, may 'go too far'. Instead of determined political opposition, general mediation; instead of struggle against government and bourgeoisie, an attempt to win over and persuade them; instead of defiant resistance to ill-treatment from above, humble submission and confession that the punishment was deserved. Historically necessary conflicts are all interpreted as misunderstandings, and all discussion ends with the assurance that after all we are all agreed on the main point.[1]

It was of course necessary that the proletariat should be reinforced by bourgeois converts. But these had first of all to be able to make a valuable contribution to the proletarian cause and had secondly to abandon completely their *petit-bourgeois* prejudices. Marx and Engels ended:

> As for ourselves, in view of our whole past there is only one road open to us. For almost forty years we have stressed the class-struggle as the immediate driving power of history, and in particular the class-struggle between bourgeoisie and proletariat as the great lever of the modern social revolution; it is, therefore, impossible for us to co-operate with people who wish to expunge this class-struggle from the movement. When the International was formed we expressly formulated the battle-cry: The emancipation of the working classes must be achieved by the working classes themselves. We cannot therefore co-operate with people who openly state that the workers are too uneducated to emancipate themselves and must be freed from above by philanthropic big bourgeois and petit-bourgeois. If the new Party organ adopts a line which corresponds to the views of these gentlemen and which is bourgeois and not proletarian, then nothing remains for us (much though we should regret it) but publicly to declare our opposition to it, and to break the bonds of solidarity which we have hitherto maintained in our

[1] Marx and Engels to Bebel, etc., *MESC*, p. 325.

representation of the German Party abroad. But it is to be hoped that things will not come to *such* a pass. . . .[1]

However, the *Jahrbuch* only lasted for two issues and in September 1879 the *Sozial-Demokrat* was founded. According to Marx the new paper was 'not worth much'.[2] There were still complaints about the infiltration of *petit-bourgeois* ideas and relations continued to be strained. This was owing more to the military tone of Engels than to Marx, whom Liebknecht (for one) found much easier to deal with.[3] But the whole quarrel was patched up at the end of 1880 when Bebel and Bernstein undertook what they described as a 'journey to Canossa' to visit Marx and Engels. It was agreed that Bernstein should take over the editorship of the *Sozial-Demokrat* and, somewhat to the surprise of all, he made a success of it. (Marx's view of Bernstein is not recorded.) But for all his optimism about the future, Marx was very caustic about the rising generation. To take two examples: he remarked to Engels that Dietzgen's work was deteriorating and that he found the man's case 'quite incurable';[4] Kautsky (soon to become the leading Marxist theoretician in Germany) was stigmatised by Marx as 'a small-minded mediocrity, too clever by half (he is only twenty-six), industrious in a certain way, busies himself with statistics but does not derive anything intelligent from them, belonging by nature to the tribe of Philistines'.[5]

V. RUSSIA, FRANCE AND BRITAIN

Until 1875 Marx was extremely sceptical about the possibilities of revolution in Russia: his optimism immediately after the emancipation of the serfs in 1861 had been short-lived. In spite of the success of *Capital* in Russia and his admiration for individual thinkers such as Chernyshevsky, he continued to think of that country as the mainstay of European reaction more amenable to outside pressure than to internal subversion. By the beginning of 1877 – with the growing tension between Russia and Turkey – Marx predicted that the 'Eastern Question' would 'lead to revolution in Russia, whatever the outcome of the war'.[6] He and Engels followed with great attention the Russo-Turkish War (which occupied the second half of 1877) though they were not accurate in predicting its outcome. Marx was 'highly elated

---

[1] Ibid., p. 327.   [2] Marx to Sorge, *MEW* xxxiv 422.
[3] See Engels–Bebel, *Briefwechsel*, ed. W. Blumenberg, p. xvii.
[4] Marx to Engels, *MEW* xxv 31.   [5] Marx to Jenny Longuet, *MEW* xxxv 178.
[6] Marx to W. Freund, *MEW* xxxiv 245.

over the strong and noble performance of the sons of Mahomet'.[1]
Both Engels and himself gave full support to the Turks on the grounds
that 'we have studied the Turkish peasant – i.e. the mass of the Turkish
people – and got to know him as unconditionally one of the bravest
and most moral representatives of the European peasantry',[2] and that
'the defeat of the Russians in European Turkey will lead directly to
revolution in Russia'.[3] For Marx

> this new crisis is a turning point in European history. Russia – and I
> have studied her circumstances from original Russian sources, both
> official and unofficial – was already on the threshold of a revolution
> with all the elements ready. It will duly begin with constitutional
> games and then there will be a fine explosion! Unless mother
> Nature is particularly unkind to us then we will still experience this
> joy.[4]

The eventual defeat of the Turks he blamed on the treachery of Britain
and of Austria (whose dissolution he correctly saw as inevitable),[5] and
on the failure of the Turks to produce their own revolution.

After the failure of the Turkish war to shake the Tsarist system,
Marx pinned his hopes more and more on the possibilities of some
revolutionary movement inside Russia. He had studied conditions in
Russia in great detail – particularly in preparing Volume Three of
Capital; with the success there of the first volume of *Capital*, it was
natural that the growing Russian resistance movements should turn
to him for advice – advice that he readily gave them. Extensive political
activity was made possible by the liberal policies of Alexander II
following the emancipation of the serfs in 1861. The most radical types
of activity were various branches of Populism – their essential characteristics being a will to act as the catalyst of a revolution based on the
broad masses of the peasantry, and a desire to check the development
of capitalism by finding a specifically Russian alternative.[6]

This question had been opened in 1874 by an open letter from
Tkatchev, a Populist follower of Blanqui, which accused Engels of
underestimating the revolutionary potential of the *obchtchina*, the

---

[1] Jenny Marx to Sorge, *MEW* xxxiv 525.
[2] Marx to Liebknecht, *MEW* xxiv 317.   [3] Marx to Engels, *MEW* xxxiv 48.
[4] Marx to Sorge, *MEW* xxxiv 296.   [5] Marx to Liebknecht, *MEW* xxxiv 318.
[6] On the concept of Populism, see R. Pipes, 'Narodnichestvo: A Semantic
Inquiry', *Slavic Review* (Sep 1964). The fundamental work on Russian populism in
F. Venturi, *Roots of Revolution* (London, 1960).

traditional peasant commune. Engels' reply gave the impression that he considered a capitalist stage of development absolutely necessary for Russia: one of the leading Populist theoreticians, Mikhailovsky, attacked this position in 1877 – claiming that *Capital* involved a condemnation of the efforts of Russians who worked for a development in their country which would by-pass the capitalist stage. Marx, whose views were more subtle and more ambivalent than Engels', replied himself in a letter to the journal *Notes on the Fatherland*. He rejected Mikhailovsky's charge: 'If Russia continues to move along the path she has followed since 1861 she will lose the finest chance history has ever offered to a people and will undergo all the fatal developments of the capitalist regime.' And defending the chapter on 'Primitive Accumulation' in *Capital* he continued:

> If Russia is tending to become a capitalist nation after the example of the West European countries – and during the last few years she has been taking a lot of trouble in this direction – she will not succeed without having first transformed a good part of her peasants into proletarians; and after that, once taken to the bosom of the capitalist regime, she will experience its pitiless laws like other profane peoples.[1]

In some marginal notes which he wrote on Bakunin's *Statism and Anarchy* at the end of 1874, Marx had already come to the conclusion that

> Where the mass of the peasants are still owners of private property, where they even form a more or less important majority of the population ... the following situation arises: either the peasantry hinders every workers' revolution and causes it to fail, as it has done in France up till now; or the proletariat ... must as a government inaugurate measures which directly improve the situation of the peasant and which thus win him for the revolution; measures which in essence facilitate the transition from private to collective property in land so that the peasant himself is converted for economic reasons; the proletariat must not, however, come into open collision with the peasantry by, for example, proclaiming the abolition of inheritance or the abolition of property.[2]

Thus Marx did not rule out completely the possibility of Russia's by-

---

[1] K. Marx, *Oeuvres*, II (Paris, 1968) p. 1554.
[2] K. Marx, 'Marginal Notes on Bakunin's *Statism and Anarchy*, MEW XVIII 633.

passing the capitalist stage of development and expressed great admiration for *Narodnaia Volya* ('The People's Will'), the terrorist wing of the Populist movement, whose express aim this was. Following the assassination of Alexander II in 1881 by the *Narodnaia Volya*, Marx described the terrorists as 'brave people with no melodramatic poses, straightforward, realistic and heroic'. They were attempting to teach Europe that 'their method of operation is specifically Russian and historically unavoidable and that there is as little point in moralising argument for or against it as there is in the case of the earthquake in Chios'.[1]

Marx had much less respect for the populist exiles in Geneva (among them Plekhanov and Axelrod) who were opposed to terrorism and preferred to concentrate on propaganda: 'in order to make propaganda in Russia – they go away to Geneva! What a *quid pro quo*! These gentlemen are against all politico-revolutionary action. Russia must leap with a *salto mortale* into a anarchist-communist-atheist millennium! Meanwhile they prepare this leap with a boring cult of doctrine. . . .'[2] It was one of the members of this group, Vera Sassoulitch, who wrote to Marx in February 1881, asking him specifically to clarify his attitude to Russian economic development.

> Lately [she wrote] we often hear it said that the rural commune is an archaic form condemned to perish by history, scientific socialism and all that is least subject to debate. The people who preach this call themselves your disciples *par excellence*: 'Marxists'. The strongest of their arguments is often: 'Marx has said it'. 'But how do you deduce it from his *Capital*? He does not discuss the agrarian problem nor Russia,' was the objection. Your disciples reply: 'he would have said it had he talked of our country.'[3]

Marx's short reply to this *cri de cœur* was sibylline:

> The analysis given in *Capital* does not offer any reasons either for or against the vitality of the rural commune, but the special study that I have made of it, for which I have researched the material in its original sources, has convinced me that this commune is the starting point for the social regeneration of Russia, but that, in order for

[1] Marx to Jenny Longuet, *MEW* xxxv 179. There had been a serious earthquake in this region of Greece the previous week.
[2] Marx to Sorge, *MEW* xxxiv 477.
[3] V. Sassoulitch to Marx, in K. Marx, *Oeuvres*, ii 1556 f.

it to function as such, it would be necessary first of all to eliminate the deleterious influences that assail it on all sides and then to assure it the normal conditions for a spontaneous development.[1]

Brief though Marx's reply was, it was based on three very lengthy drafts which thoroughly analysed the development of the peasant commune and contained the more optimistic conclusion that:

> To save the Russian commune, a Russian revolution is necessary. Moreover, the Russian Government and the 'new pillars of society' are doing their best to prepare the masses for such a catastrophe. If the revolution comes at an opportune moment, if it concentrates all its forces to ensure the free development of the rural commune, this commune will soon develop into an element that regenerates Russian society and guarantees superiority over countries enslaved by the capitalist regime.[2]

In his last pronouncement on this question, the Preface to the 1882 translation of the *Communist Manifesto*. Marx reiterated this position: 'if the Russian Revolution becomes a signal for a proletarian revolution in the West, so that both complement each other, the present Russian common ownership of land may serve as the starting point for a communist development'.[3] Thus Marx's doctrinal legacy on this vital question was fatefully ambivalent.[4]

In France socialism was slow to revive after the shattering experience of the Commune. By 1877 Workers' Congresses began to reconvene and the future leaders Guesde and Malon, both with former anarchist leanings, moved nearer to a sort of Marxism which they proclaimed in their newspaper *L'Egalité*. In October 1879 the *Fédération du Parti des Travailleurs Socialistes* was formed; and the amnesty of 1880 strengthened the socialists by permitting the return of exiles, among them Marx's two sons-in-law. In May 1880 Guesde came to London to discuss an electoral programme with Marx, Engels and Lafargue. Marx was by and large happy with the programme – to which he wrote the preamble – as it embodied 'demands that have really sprung spontaneously from the workers' movement itself',[5] but he protested at the demand for a statutory minimum wage (which Guesde insisted on

---

[1] K. Marx, *Oeuvres*, II 1558.   [2] K. Marx, op. cit. II 1573.
[3] K. Marx, *MESW* I 24.
[4] See, in general, A. Walicki, *The Controversy over Capitalism* (Oxford, 1969).
[5] Marx to Sorge, *MEW* xxxiv 476.

including). 'If the French proletariat is still so childish that it needs such bait, then it is not worth while drawing up any programme whatever.'[1] He also drew up an extended questionnaire to be distributed among French workers, thus reviving an idea broached at the 1866 Geneva Congress of the International. The questionnaire was published in Malon's *Revue Socialiste* in April 1880 and 25,000 copies were off-printed.[2] The introduction insisted that 'it is the workers alone who can describe with thorough knowledge the evils that they suffer, it is they alone – and not some providential saviours – who can energetically apply remedies to the social miseries that they undergo'.[3]

Marx conceived the enterprise as primarily educative in the sense of inculcating a class consciousness, though there is no evidence of its having achieved any result. He doubted whether the new party could long remain united and this time he was quite justified: at the Congress of St-Etienne in September 1882 the party split into reformist and revolutionary wings – the latter led by Guesde, who found himself under attack on the grounds that he received orders from the 'Prussian' Marx in London.[4] In reality, the relationship between Marx and Guesde was a very tenuous one, and Marx's opinion of some of his would-be disciples in France was so low that he declared to Lafargue: 'what is certain is that I am no Marxist'.[5] Both his sons-in-law in fact disappointed him by their lack of political sense. He contemptuously dismissed 'Longuet as the last Proudhonist and Lafargue as the last Bakuninist! Devil take them!'[6]

Britain was still the country where Marx's ideas made the least impact. Even the United States gave him more encouragement. He closely followed America's 'chronic crisis' of 1873-78 and was particularly interested in the economic progress of the newest states such as California. He considered that there was a good possibility of 'establishing a serious workers' party'[7] and thought that the government

[1] Ibid.
[2] The questionnaire is reprinted in K. Marx, *Oeuvres*, I 1527 ff. See also H. Weiss, 'Die Enquête Ouvrière von Karl Marx', *Zeitschrift für Sozialforschung* (1936); M. Rubel, *Karl Marx, Essai de biographie Intellectuelle* (Paris, 1957) pp. 416 ff.
[3] K. Marx, *Oeuvres* I 1527.
[4] See in general, G. Lefranc, *Le Mouvement Socialiste sous la Troisième Republique* (Paris, 1963) pp. 33 ff.
[5] Engels to Bernstein, *MEW* xxxv 388. Cf. a similar remark retailed by Liebknecht, quoted in *K. Marx, Dokumente seines Lebens*, p. 363.
[6] Marx to Engels, *MEW* xxxv 110, see further, M. Dommanget, *L'Introduction du Marxisme en France* (Lausanne, 1969).   [7] Marx to Engels, *MEW* xxxiv 59.

policies of land appropriation would ally the Negroes and farmers with the working class. Even the transfer of the seat of the International to New York might turn out to have been opportune.[1] The British working class, however, had (according to Marx) now sunk so low that they were no more than 'the tail of the great liberal party, i.e. their enslavers, the capitalists'.[2] And Engels, in spite of his temporary enthusiasm for working-class radicals such as Joseph Cowen, had to warn Liebknecht that 'there is here at the moment no real working-class movement in the continental sense'.[3] Nevertheless, Marx persisted in his view that in Britain a peaceful transition to socialism was possible.

> My party [he wrote in 1880] considers an English revolution not
> *necessary*, but – according to historic precedents – *possible*. If the
> unavoidable evolution turn into a revolution, it would not only
> be the fault of the ruling classes, but also of the working class.
> Every pacific concession of the former has been wrung from them
> by 'pressure from without'. Their action kept pace with that pressure and if the latter has more and more weakened, it is only because
> the English working class know not how to wield their power and
> use their liberties, both of which they possess legally.[4]

Particularly after the Commune, Marx began to be better known in English society. During the Eastern crisis of 1877, he claimed to have placed many unsigned pieces in 'the fashionable London press' attacking Gladstone's Russian policy, all through the agency of Maltman Barry, his old acquaintance from the International. He was also using Barry to work on Members of Parliament who 'would hold up their hands in horror if they knew that it was really the "Red-Terror-Doctor", as they like to call me, who was whispering in their ears'.[5] In early 1879, the 'Red-Terror-Doctor' attracted the attention of no less a person than Queen Victoria's eldest daughter, who was married to the German Crown Prince. She requested Sir Mountstuart Grant Duff, a liberal M.P. who had been Under-Secretary for India, to meet Marx and give her his opinion of him; accordingly, he arranged a lunch with Marx at the Devonshire Club in St James's Street. Grant

[1] Cf. Ibid.   [2] Marx to Liebknecht, *MEW* xxxiv 320.
[3] Engels to Bernstein, *MEW* xxxiv 378.
[4] Marx to Hyndman, in H. Hyndman, *Record of an Adventurous Life*, p. 283. See also *MEW* xxxiv 498.
[5] Marx to Sorge, *MEW* xxxiv 296.

Duff's general impressions, as he related them to the Crown Princess, were as follows:

> He is a short, rather small man with grey hair and beard which contrasts strangely with a still dark moustache. The face is some- what round; the forehead well shaped and filled up – the eye rather hard but the whole expression rather pleasant than not, by no means that of a gentleman who is in the habit of eating babies in their cradles – which is I daresay the view which the police take of him. His talk was that of a well-informed, nay learned man – much interested in Comparative Grammar which had led him into the Old Slavonic and other out-of-the-way studies and was varied by many quaint turns and little bits of dry humour, as when speaking of Hezechiall's 'Life of Prince Bismarck' he always referred to it, by way of contrast to Dr Busch's book, as the *Old* Testament.
>
> It was all very *positif*, slightly cynical – without any appearance of enthusiasm – interesting, and often, as I thought, showing very correct ideas when conversing on the past and the present, but vague and unsatisfactory when he turned to the future.[1]

They talked for three hours – of Russia where Marx expected 'a great but not distant crash' and of Germany where there seemed to him a strong possibility of mutiny in the army. Marx further explained that the socialist revolution could be a very long-term affair and expressed his relief that the German Emperor's would-be assassin, Nobiling, had not, as he planned, visited him in London beforehand. Grant Duff's general conclusion was: 'It will not be Marx who, whether he wishes it or not, will turn the world upside down.'[2]

The English socialist with whom Marx had the closest contact in his later years was H. M. Hyndman, the founder of the Social Demo- cratic Federation, and a man of considerable private means.[3] Having read the French version of *Capital* on a voyage to America he was eager to meet Marx, to whom he was duly introduced by Karl Hirsch early in 1880.[4] Regularly during the following year Marx, accompanied by Eleanor, would go to dine with Hyndman in his elegant house in Devonshire Place; and Hyndman would in turn call on him (revering

[1] 'A Meeting with Karl Marx', *Times Literary Supplement* (15 July 1949) p. 464.
[2] Ibid.
[3] See C. Tzuzuki, *Hyndman and British Socialism* (Oxford, 1962).
[4] H. M. Hyndman, *Record of an Adventurous Life*, pp. 269 f.

him as 'The Aristotle of the nineteenth century')[1] and talk for hours –
both men striding up and down in Marx's study. Hyndman believed
in a peaceful revolution in England and some of his views were distinctly jingoistic; but at least he understood (to some extent) the
labour theory of value; and he was also violently anti-Russian, which
provided one of the most powerful links between the two men. The
friendship ended, however, with a violent quarrel in June 1881.
Hyndman had just published *The Text Book of Democracy: England for All*,
which advocated a decentralised self-governing Empire in which
reform would preferably be introduced by the rich and the powerful.
The two chapters in the book dealing with labour and capital drew
extensively on *Capital* and he duly acknowledged in the Preface his
debt here 'to the work of a great thinker and original writer'[2] – but
did not mention Marx by name. The book was distributed at the
foundation meeting of the Democratic Federation. Marx was angry
that Hyndman had not made more specific acknowledgement of his
work and was also annoyed that his ideas had appeared in a book with
whose general approach he found himself out of sympathy. When
Hyndman excused himself on the grounds that many Englishmen
would have less sympathy for the ideas if they knew they were Marx's
and that anyway Englishmen did not learn easily from foreigners,
Marx was even angrier and wrote – with great pleasure – a stinging
rebuke which ended their association.[3]

Marx was cheered, however, by the appearance in December 1881
of a pamphlet in the *Leaders of Modern Thought* series devoted to himself
and written by Ernest Belfort Bax, a Positivist and journalistic friend
of Hyndman's. There were many mistakes in Marx's biography and in
the account of his economic ideas but it was nevertheless 'the first
English publication imbued with real enthusiasm for the new ideas
and boldly presenting them to the British philistines'.[4] And he was
pleased with the publicity given to it on the placards of London's
West End and the joy it brought to Jenny two days before her death.
Yet paradoxically Mark remained little known in the country where
he had lived and worked most of his life. His obituary in *The Times*

---

[1] Ibid., p. 271.   [2] Ibid., p. 285.

[3] Cf. Marx to Eleanor Marx, *MEW* xxxv 422. The correspondence is reprinted,
and further details given, in E. Bottigelli, 'La Rupture Marx-Hyndman', *Annali*
(1960) pp. 636 f. Marx seems to have fallen out with J. S. Stuart-Glennie, another
'Tory' socialist, for the same reasons. See C. Tzuzuki, *The Life of Eleanor Marx*, pp. 53 f.

[4] Marx to Sorge, *MEW* xxxv 248. See further, S. Pierson, *Marxism and the origins
of British Socialism* (Ithaca and London, 1973), pp. 59 ff.

contained the most ridiculous mistakes and when the English edition of *Capital* did eventually appear in 1894 its combined sale in Britain and the United States for the first few years was extremely meagre. It is not surprising that Marx's last recorded words on Britain were: 'To the devil with the British'.[1]

With the departure of the Longuet family in February 1881, Marx began the lonely last two years of his life. The separation was extremely painful: for Marx his grandchildren were 'inexhaustible sources of life and joy'[2] and for weeks after their departure, so he wrote to Jenny, 'I often run to the window when I hear the voices of children ... unaware, for a moment, that they are the other side of the Channel.'[3] He had less and less time for outside company and felt that 'it is awful to be so "old" that we can only foresee instead of see', particularly when the newborn 'have before them the most revolutionary period with which men were ever confronted'.[4] Jenny's health continued to deteriorate although Marx called in the best doctors in London. She still had the strength to go to the theatre occasionally but spent long periods in bed clinging despairingly to a life she knew to be ebbing. In July Marx took her to Eastbourne for three weeks where she was wheeled about in a bathchair. The following month they decided to leave for Argenteuil, a western suburb of Paris, to pay a long visit to Jenny, who was herself suffering from asthma. After three weeks, however, news reached Marx that Eleanor was suffering from a serious nervous depression and he returned immediately to London, followed a few days later by Jenny and Lenchen.

VI. THE LAST YEARS

A full six months before her death in December 1881 it was clear that Marx's wife was dying. He himself had a serious setback in October. For two months he lay in bed with bronchitis. Engels feared he might die and Eleanor sat by his bedside through many nights. Jenny was in the adjacent room but for three weeks Marx could not visit her. Eleanor wrote later:

> It was a terrible time. Our dear mother lay in the big front room, Moor in the small room behind. And the two of them, who were so used to one another, so close to one another, could not even be

[1] Marx to Eleanor Marx, *MEW* xxxv 422.
[2] Marx to Danielson, *MEW* xxxv 154.   [3] Marx to Jenny Marx, *MEW* xxxv 177.
[4] Ibid. 186.

together in the same room. Our good old Lenchen ... and I had to nurse them both. . . . Never shall I forget the morning when he felt strong enough to go into Mother's room. When they were together they were young again – she a young girl and he a loving youth, both on the threshold of life, not an old man devastated by illness and an old dying woman parting from each other for ever.[1]

The unbearable pains characteristic of cancer only came in the last few days and were treated with morphia. When she died on 2 December it was 'a gentle going to sleep, her eyes fuller, more beautiful, lighter than ever'.[2] The last word she spoke to her husband was: Good. His doctor forbad Marx to attend the funeral, but he comforted himself with the fact that the day before her death, Jenny had remarked concerning funeral ceremonies 'we are no such *external* people'.[3] Marx never recovered from Jenny's death. On seeing him immediately afterwards, Engels remarked to Eleanor that 'Moor is dead, too'. Marx could only take refuge in the problems of his own health since 'the only effective antidote for sorrows of the spirit is bodily pain'.[4] Meissner wrote that a third edition of *Capital*, Volume One, was necessary, but Marx no longer had the heart to work on it.

On partially recovering from his illness, Marx felt himself to be doubly crippled, 'morally through the loss of my wife, and physically through a thickening of the pleura'.[5] He decided to go once more to the seaside and in January 1882 took Eleanor with him to Ventnor. His coughing and bronchial catarrh continued unabated and Eleanor proved a poor companion: she had been on the verge of a nervous breakdown since the previous summer following a proposal of marriage from the Russian Populist Leo Hartmann. She was in the throes of breaking off her engagement to Lissagaray and despairing of ever having the chance to establish herself on the stage. When her friends in London learnt of her state, Dollie Maitland rushed to Ventnor to assist. It was not a success. Apart from being quite unable to amuse herself alone, Dollie fed unending gossip to Marx, who was hurt that his daughter should have turned to others for help and anxious that she should not 'be sacrificed on the family altar as the "companion" of an old man'.[6] Eleanor certainly got the impression that her father

---

[1] Eleanor Marx to Liebknecht, *Reminiscences*, p. 127.
[2] Marx to Jenny Marx, *MEW* xxxv 241.
[3] Ibid. 240.   [4] Ibid.   [5] Marx to Sorge, *MEW* xxxv 247.
[6] Marx to Engels, *MEW* xxxv 35.

did not appreciate her mental stress and considered her to be indulging her illness at the expense of her family.

Disillusioned by Eleanor and Ventnor, with Jenny too busy with her babies to help him and Laura too selfish, Marx gave in to the pressure of Engels and his doctor and went to Algiers. He was the readier to leave London as he found Engels' boisterous company intolerable. 'Good old Fred', he wrote to his daughter Jenny, 'may easily kill someone out of love.'[1] Marx spent two and a half lonely months in Algiers in a small hotel overlooking the bay. The season was exceptionally cold and wet; his thoughts were 'to a great part absorbed by reminiscence of my wife, such a part of my best part of life!'[2]; and all his letters to Engels and his daughters are full of elaborate details about his health and the weather which (towards the end of his stay) became hot enough to persuade him to crop his hair and shave his beard. His letters began to contain faults of orthography and grammar – a result of the 'clouding of the mind'[3] produced by Jenny's death and his illness. Marx left Algiers in May 1882 and went to Monte Carlo where he stayed a month, but his pleurisy and bronchitis showed no signs of abating.

On 6 June he left for Argenteuil to stay with Jenny for the next three months, seeking rest in 'the noise of children, this "microscopic world" that is much more interesting than the "macroscopic"'.[4] Jenny's household, however, was far from being able to provide the peace for which Marx was looking. She was expecting yet another baby in mid-September and found no support in her husband, whom she bitterly criticised: the little time that Longuet spent at home he spent in bed, being preoccupied with his political activities in Paris which Marx considered as futile as those of Lafargue. Longuet was also tactless enough to invite to Argenteuil Roy (the French translator of *Capital*); in view of Marx's opinion of his capacities, this naturally caused great embarrassment.

During the summer of 1882 the other members of the Marx family gravitated towards Paris: Lenchen came in June to help Jenny, and both Eleanor and Laura came shortly afterwards. While Laura was still in London, Marx had written telling her it was her 'duty to accompany the old man of the mountains' when he went to Vevey in Switzerland in September. Laura consented and while there Marx promised

---

[1] Marx to Jenny Marx, *MEW* xxxv 289.   [2] Marx to Engels, *MEW* xxxv 46.
[3] Ibid. 105.   [4] Marx to Jenny Marx, *MEW* xxxv 330.

her all his documents of the International for her to write its history and broached the possibility of her undertaking the translation into English of *Capital*.[1] They returned to Argenteuil after Jenny had given birth to her only daughter. Quite unlike her relations with Laura, Eleanor got on well with Jenny and developed in Argenteuil capacities that had lain quite dormant in London. But she, too, left at the end of August and took Jenny's eldest son, Johnny, back to England where for several months she acted with exemplary firmness as a second mother to him.

On his return from Switzerland Marx felt that he could burden Jenny no longer and returned to London – only to depart once again for Ventnor, alone, at the end of October. He was feeling in slightly better health and sat drinking rum with Engels till one o'clock in the morning on the eve of his departure. In the Isle of Wight he spent long hours wandering over the downs. His increasing loneliness drove him to beg Laura to come and live with him. Only very occasionally now was the spark of the old fiery Marx rekindled – such as when he was suddenly notified of the success of his theories in Russia; he commented excitedly: 'I damage a power which, together with England, is the true bulwark of the old society.'[2] Meanwhile in Argenteuil Jenny's condition was deteriorating. From as early as April she was continuously suffering severe pains from what seems to have been cancer of the bladder. She had four young children to look after in addition to a husband who only shouted at her and did nothing at all to help. Her mother-in-law blamed her for the debts of the Longuet household and continually urged her to go out to work. When the Lafargues came to see her in early January they found her 'sunk in a torpor broken by nightmares and fantastic dreams'. She soon became delirious and died on 11 January 1883, aged 38. It fell to Eleanor to inform her father. 'I have lived many a sad hour', she wrote, 'but none so bad as that. I felt that I was bringing my father his death sentence. I racked my brain all the long anxious way to find how I could break the news to him. But I did not need to, my face gave me away. Moor said at once "our Jennychen is dead".'[3]

Irredeemably shattered by the death of his 'first born, the daughter he loved most',[4] Marx returned to London to die.

On his return to London, hoarseness as a result of laryngitis pre-

---

[1] Cf. *Engels-Lafargue Correspondence*, I 142.   [2] Marx to Laura Marx, *MEW* xxxv 408.
[3] Eleanor Marx to Liebknecht, *Reminiscences*, p. 128.   [4] Ibid.

vented Marx from speaking much. Lenchen cooked him the tastiest meals to try and restore his appetite and he was given constant mustard baths to warm his cold feet. He was drinking a pint of milk a day and got through a bottle of brandy in four. His reading alternated between publishers' catalogues when he was feeling low and French novels when his intellectual interest was aroused. An ulcer in the lung complicated his bronchitis. By the end of February he was confined to his room with a north-east wind bringing constant frost and snow. On 10 March Engels reported to Laura that the doctor considered Marx's health to be actually improving slightly and that all would be well if he could get through the next two months. On the morning of the thirteenth he had taken wine, milk and soup. But when Engels came on his daily visit early in the afternoon he found the scene he had so often feared:

> The house was in tears, it seemed that the end had come. I asked for information, tried to get a realistic view of the situation and to offer comfort. There had been a small haemorrhage and a sudden deterioration had set in. Our good old Lenchen who cared for him as no mother ever did for her child, went up and then came down again: he was half-asleep, would I come with her? When we entered, he sat there sleeping, but never to wake any more. In two minutes he had quietly and painlessly passed away.[1]

Epitomising his contempt for bourgeois society and his internationalism, Marx died both intestate and stateless. His papers were sifted by his daughters and Engels before being divided between the German Social-Democrats and the Moscow communists. Marx was buried in Highgate Cemetery on 17 March 1883. His ill-kept grave remained in a far corner of the cemetery until 1956 when a large marble block surmounted by a cast-iron head was erected.

[1] Engels to Sorge, *MEW* xxxv 460.

9

Epilogue

HERE, to conclude, are descriptions from seven people who knew Marx personally. They are interesting both in their divergence and in the insight that each presents. They are followed by Marx's own account of himself as given in the Victorian parlour game of 'Confessions'.

The Russian Aristocrat

Marx himself was the type of man who is made up of energy, will and unshakable conviction. He was most remarkable in his appearance. He had a shock of deep black hair and hairy hands and his coat was buttoned wrong; but he looked like a man with the right and power to demand respect, no matter how he appeared before you and no matter what he did. His movements were clumsy but confident and self-reliant, his ways defied the usual conventions in human relations, but they were dignified and somewhat disdainful; his sharp metallic voice was wonderfully adapted to the radical judgements that he passed on persons and things. He always spoke in imperative words that would brook no contradiction and were made all the sharper by the almost painful impression of the tone which ran through everything he said. This tone expressed the firm conviction of his mission to dominate men's minds and prescribe them their laws. Before me stood the embodiment of a democratic dictator such as one might imagine in a day dream.

P. Annenkov, 'Eine russische Stimme über
Karl Marx', *Die neue Zeit* (1883)

The American Senator

He could not have been much more than thirty years old at that time, but he was already the recognised head of the advanced socialistic school. The somewhat thick-set man, with broad forehead, very black hair and beard and dark sparkling eyes, at once attracted general attention. He enjoyed the reputation of having acquired great learning.... Marx's utterances were indeed full of meaning, logical and clear, but I have never seen a man whose bearing was so provoking and intolerable. To no opinion which differed from his own did he accord the honour of even condescending consideration. Everyone who contradicted him he treated with abject contempt; every argument that he did not like he treated either with biting scorn at the unfathomable ignorance that had prompted it, or with opprobrious aspersions on the motives of him who advanced it. I remember most distinctly the cutting disdain with which he pronounced the word *bourgeois*: and as a bourgeois – that is, as a detestable example of the deepest mental and moral degeneracy – he denounced everyone who dared oppose his opinions.

The Reminiscences of Karl Schurz
(London, 1909) I 138 f.

The Down-and-out Prussian Lieutenant

First we drank port, then claret which is red Boreaux, then champagne. After the red wine Marx became completely drunk. That was exactly what I wanted, because he became at the same time much more open-hearted than he probably would have been otherwise. I found out the truth about certain things which would otherwise have remained mere suppositions. In spite of his drunkenness Marx dominated the conversation up to the last moment.

The impression he made on me was that of someone who possessed a rare intellectual superiority, and he was evidently a man of outstanding personality. If his heart had matched his intellect, and if he had possessed as much love as hate, I would have gone through fire for him, even though at the end he expressed his complete and candid contempt for me, and had previously indicated his contempt in passing. He was the first and only one among us all to whom I would entrust leadership, for he was a man who never lost himself in small matters when dealing with great events.

Yet it is a matter for regret in view of our aims that this man with his fine intellect is lacking in nobility of soul. I am convinced that a most dangerous personal ambition has eaten away all the good in him. He laughs at the fools who parrot his proletarian catechism, just as he laughs over the communists à la Willich and over the bourgeoise. The only people he respects are the aristocrats, the genuine ones, those who are well aware of their aristocracy. In order to prevent them from governing, he needs his own source of strength, which he can find only in the proletariat. Accordingly he has tailored his system to them. In spite of all his assurances to the contrary, personal domination was the aim of all his endeavours.

E[ngels] and all his old associates, in spite of their very real gifts, are all far behind and beneath him; and if they should dare to forget it for a moment, he puts them back in their place with a shameless impudence worthy of a Napoleon.

Techow to Schimmelpfennig, in K. Vogt
Mein Prozess (Geneva, 1859) pp. 151 f.

The Faithful Disciple

No one could be kinder and fairer than Marx in giving others their due. He was too great to be envious, jealous or vain. But he had as deadly a hatred for the false greatness and pretended fame of swaggering incapacity and vulgarity as for any kind of deceit and pretence.

Of all the great, little or average men that I have known, Marx is one of the few who was free from vanity. He was too great and too strong to be vain, and too proud as well. He never struck an attitude, he was always himself. He was as incapable as a child of wearing a mask or pretending. As long as social or political grounds did not make it undesirable, he always spoke his mind completely and without any reserve and his face was the mirror of his heart. And when circumstances demanded restraint he showed a sort of childlike awkwardness that often amused his friends.

No man could be more truthful than Marx - he was truthfulness incarnate. Merely by looking at him you knew who it was you were dealing with. In our 'civilised' society with its perpetual state of war one cannot always tell the truth, that would be playing into the enemy's hands or risking being sent to Coventry. But even if it is often inadvisable to say the truth, it is not always necessary to say an untruth. I must not always say what I think or feel, but that does not mean that I must say what I do not feel or think. The former is wisdom, the latter hypocrisy. Marx was never a hypocrite. He was absolutely incapable of it, just like an unsophisticated child. His wife often called him 'my big baby', and nobody, not even Engels, knew or understood him better than she did. Indeed, when he was in what is generally termed society, where everything is judged by appearances and one must do violence to one's feelings, our 'Moor' was like a big boy and he could be embarrassed and blush like a child.

W. Liebknecht, *Karl Marx. Biographical Memoirs* (Chicago, 1901) pp. 93 f.

The Anarchist Opponent

We saw each other fairly often and I very much admired him for his knowledge and for his passionate and earnest devotion to the cause of the proletariat, although it always had in it an admixture of personal vanity; and I eagerly sought his conversation, which was instructive and witty so long as it was not inspired by petty spite – which, unfortunately, happened too often. But there was never real intimacy between us. Our temperaments did not harmonise. He called me a sentimental idealist; and he was right. I called him vain, treacherous and morose; and I too was right.

M. Bakunin, in M. Nettlau, *M. Bakounine, Esquisse biographique avec extraits de ses oeuvres*, in fol. Bibl. Nationale (Paris, 1901) p. 71.

The Adoring Daughter

To those who knew Karl Marx no legend is funnier than the common one which pictures him a morose, bitter, unbending, unapproachable man, a sort of Jupiter Tonans, ever hurling thunder, never known to smile, sitting aloof and alone in Olympus. This picture of the cheeriest, gayest soul that ever breathed, of a man brimming over with humour and good-humour, whose hearty laugh was infectious and irresistible, of the kindliest, gentlest, most sympathetic of companions, is a standing wonder – and amusement – to those who knew him.

In his home life, as in his intercourse with friends, and even with mere acquaintances, I think one might say that Karl Marx's main characteristics were his unbounded good-humour and his unlimited sympathy His kindness and patience were really sublime. A less sweet-tempered man would have often been driven frantic by the constant interruptions, the continual demands made upon him by all sorts of people. . . .

To those who are students of human nature, it will not seem strange that this man, who was such a fighter, should at the same time be the kindliest and gentlest of men. They will understand that he could hate so fiercely only because he could love so profoundly; that if his trenchant pen could as surely imprison a soul in hell as Dante himself it was because he was so true and tender; that if his sarcastic humour could bite like a corrosive acid, that same humour could be as balm to those in trouble and afflicted.

Eleanor Marx, in Reminiscences of Marx and
Engels (Moscow, n.d.) pp. 205 f.

The English Gentleman

The first impression of Marx as I saw him was that of a powerful, shaggy, untamed old man, ready, not to say eager, to enter into conflict and rather suspicious himself of immediate attack.

When speaking with fierce indignation of the policy of the Liberal Party, especially in regard to Ireland, the old warrior's small deep-sunk eyes lighted up, his heavy brows wrinkled, the broad, strong nose and face were obviously moved by passion, and he poured out a stream of vigorous denunciation, which displayed alike the heat of his temperament and the marvellous command he possessed over our language. The contrast between his manner and utterance when thus deeply stirred by anger and his attitude when giving his views on the economic events of the period was very marked. He turned from the role of prophet and vehement denunciator to that of the calm philosopher without any apparent effort, and I felt from the first that on this latter ground many a long year might pass before I ceased to be a student in the presence of a master.

H. M. Hyndman, Record of an Adventurous Life
(London, 1911) pp. 269 f.

Marx's Confession

Your favourite virtue	Simplicity
Your favourite virtue in man	Strength
Your favourite virtue in woman	Weakness

Your chief characteristic	Singleness of purpose
Your idea of happiness	To fight
Your idea of misery	Submission
The vice you excuse most	Gullibility
The vice you detest most	Servility
Your aversion	Martin Tupper[1]
Favourite occupation	Book-worming
Favourite poet	Shakespeare, Aeschylus, Goethe
Favourite prose-writer	Diderot
Favourite hero	Spartacus, Kepler
Favourite heroine	Gretchen
Favourite flower	Daphne
Favourite colour	Red
Favourite name	Laura, Jenny
Favourite dish	Fish
Favourite maxim	*Nihil humani a me alienum puto*[2]
Favourite motto	*De omnibus dubitandum*[3]

[1] Victorian popular writer.
[2] 'I consider that nothing human is alien to me.'
[3] 'You must have doubts about everything.'

Appendixes

CHRONOLOGICAL TABLE

Marx's writings, whether books or articles, which were not published in his lifetime, are in bold type: those which were are in capitals.

	HISTORICAL	WRITINGS	PERSONAL
1818			Birth
1824			Baptism
1830	Great Reform Bill		Entered grammar school
1835	Zollverein in Germany		Began at University of Bonn
1836			Began at University of Berlin
1837	Victoria's reign began	**Letter to his Father**	
1838	Rise of Chartism	**Doctoral Thesis**	Death of Heinrich Marx
1839		**Doctoral Thesis**	
1840	Accession of Frederick William IV	**Doctoral Thesis**	
1841		**Poems**	Obtained Doctorate; moved to Bonn
1842		ARTICLES for *Rheinische Zeitung*	Death of Baron von Westphalen; moved to Cologne as editor of *Rheinische Zeitung*

	HISTORICAL	WRITINGS	PERSONAL
1843		**Critique of Hegel's Philosophy of Right;** ON THE JEWISH QUESTION	Marriage; left for Paris (October)
1844		CRITIQUE OF HEGEL'S PHILOSOPHY OF RIGHT: INTRODUCTION; **Economic and Philosophical Manuscripts;** CRITICAL NOTES on 'The King of Prussia and Social Reform'; THE HOLY FAMILY	Birth of Jenny (May); met Engels (September)
1845		**Theses on Feuerbach**	Moved to Brussels (February); visited England (July); birth of Laura
1846	Repeal of Corn Laws	**The German Ideology;** CIRCULAR AGAINST KRIEGE; **Letter to Annenkov**	Set up correspondence committee (January); quarrelled with Weitling (March); birth of Edgar (December)
1847		THE POVERTY OF PHILOSOPHY	Joined Communist League (January)
1848	Year of Revolutions; Californian Gold Rush	SPEECH ON FREE TRADE; THE COMMUNIST MANIFESTO; DEMANDS OF THE COMMUNIST PARTY IN GER-	Moved to Paris (March) and Cologne (June) as editor of *Neue Rheinische Zeitung*

	HISTORICAL	WRITINGS	PERSONAL
		MANY; about 80 ARTICLES for *Neue Rheinische Zeitung*	
1849		WAGE, LABOUR AND CAPITAL; about 20 ARTICLES for *Neue Rheinische Zeitung*	Left for Paris (May) and London (August); birth of Guido (November)
1850	Ten Hours Act	ADDRESSES OF THE CENTRAL COMMITTEE TO THE COMMUNIST LEAGUE; ARTICLES in *Neue Rheinische Zeitung–Revue*; THE CLASS STRUGGLES IN FRANCE	Death of Guido (September); settled in Dean Street (December)
1851	Great Exhibition		Birth of Franziska (March); birth of Frederick Demuth (June)
1852 [1852/62]	Beginning of Second Empire in France	[ARTICLES for *New York Herald Tribune*.] THE EIGHTEENTH BRUMAIRE OF LOUIS BONAPARTE; THE GREAT MEN OF EXILE	Death of Franziska (April); dissolved Communist League (November)
1853		THE COLOGNE COMMUNIST TRIAL; PALMERSTON; THE KNIGHT OF THE NOBLE CONSCIENCE	
1854	Crimean War	PALMERSTON AND RUSSIA	
1855		About 100 ARTICLES for *Neue Oder Zeitung*	Birth of Eleanor (January); death of Edgar (April)

	HISTORICAL	WRITINGS	PERSONAL
1856		REVELATIONS ABOUT THE DIPLO-MATIC HISTORY OF THE EIGHTEENTH CENTURY; ARTICLES for *People's Paper* and *Free Press*	Death of Baroness von Westphalen (July); moved to Grafton Terrace
1857	Indian Mutiny	**General Introduction**	
1857/8		**Outlines of a Critique of Political Economy (Grundrisse)**	
1858		ARTICLES for *New American Encyclo-paedia*	
1859	Darwin's *Origin of Species*; Mill's *On Liberty*	PREFACE TO A CRI-TIQUE OF POLITI-CAL ECONOMY; CRITIQUE OF POLI-TICAL ECONOMY; ARTICLES for *Das Volk*	
1860	Kingdom of Italy established	HERR VOGT	
1861	American Civil War began	15 ARTICLES for *Die Priesse*	Visit to Holland and Germany to see Lassalle (April–February)
1862	Serfdom abolished in Russia; Bismarck Minister-President in Germany		Lassalle visited London (July)
1862/3		**Theories of Sur-plus Value;** 30 ARTICLES for *Die Priesse*; **Manuscripts**	

	HISTORICAL	WRITINGS on Polish Question	PERSONAL
1863	Lassallean Socialist Party (ADAV) founded	Capital vol. II (until 1877)	Death of Mary Burns (January); death of Marx's mother (November); Marx to Trier (December)
1864	First International	INAUGURAL AD-DRESS OF FIRST INTERNATIONAL Capital vol. III	Moved to Modena Villas (March); death of Wolff (May); death of Lassalle (August)
1865		Value, Price and Profit; ON PROUDHON	
1866	Austro-Prussian War	PROGRAMME FOR FIRST CONGRESS OF INTERNATIONAL	
1867		CAPITAL vol. I	Marx to Hamburg for *Capital* (April/May)
1868	First Gladstone Ministry		Marriage of Laura
1869	Social Democratic Party founded in Germany		Retirement of Engels; Marx visited Kugelman (September–October)
1870	Franco-Prussian War	TWO ADDRESSES ON FRANCO-PRUSSIAN WAR	Engels moved to London (September)
1871	Paris Commune; German Empire	THE CIVIL WAR IN FRANCE	
1872	Hague Congress of International	ALLEGED SPLITS IN INTERNATIONAL; PREFACE TO SECOND EDITION	Marriage of Jenny

	HISTORICAL	WRITINGS	PERSONAL
		OF COMMUNIST MANIFESTO; AMSTERDAM SPEECH	
1873		PREFACE TO SECOND GERMAN EDITION OF CAPITAL vol. I	
1874		**Remarks on Bakunin's Statism and Anarchy**	Marx to Karlsbad (August–October)
1875	Gotha Congress	CRITIQUE OF THE GOTHA PROGRAMME; FRENCH EDITION OF CAPITAL vol. I	Marx to Karlsbad (August–September); moved to Maitland Park Road
1876			Death of Bakunin; Marx to Karlsbad (August–September)
1877	Russo-Turkish War	CONTRIBUTION TO ANTI-DÜHRING; LETTER TO MIKHAILOVSKY	Marx to Neuenahr (August–September)
1878	Anti-Socialist laws in Germany		
1879		**Circular Letter**	
1880		QUESTIONNAIRE; INTRODUCTION TO FRENCH WORKERS' PROGRAMME; **Remarks on Wagner**	
1881		**Letter to Vera Sassoulitch; Notes on Morgan's Primitive Society**	Marx to Argenteuil (August–September); death of Jenny Marx (December)

	HISTORICAL	WRITINGS	PERSONAL
1882		PREFACE TO SECOND RUSSIAN EDITION OF COMMUNIST MANIFESTO	Marx to Algiers, Monte Carlo etc. (February–June)
1883	Nietzsche's *Thus Spake Zarathustra*		Death of Jenny Longuet (January); death of Marx (March)

GENEALOGICAL TREE

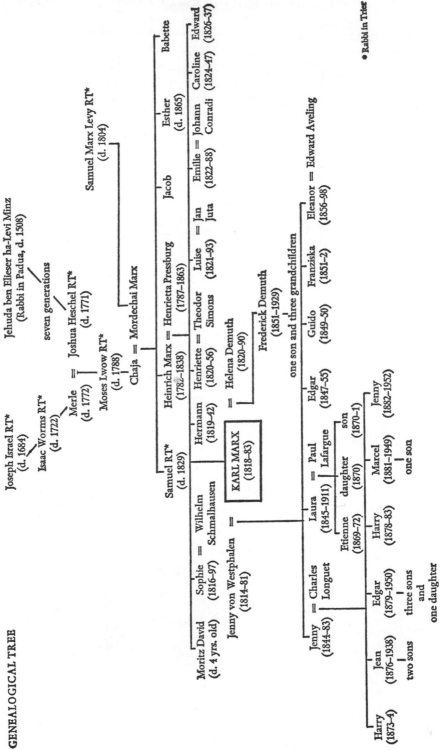

• Rabbi in Trier

DIAGRAM OF MARX'S 'ECONOMICS'

Works planned are in italics; works written but not published in Marx's lifetime are in bold type; works published in Marx's lifetime are in capitals.

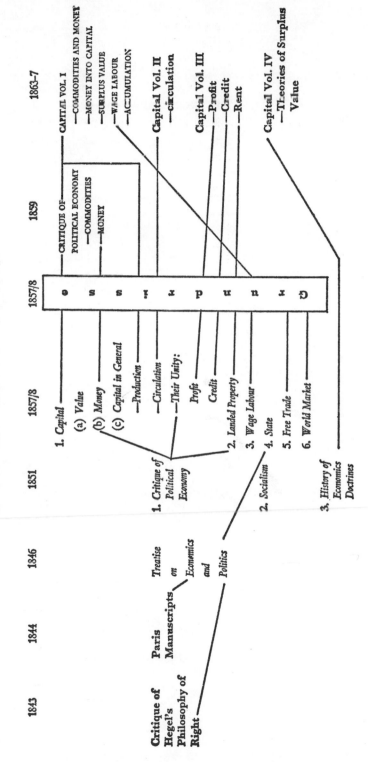

Select Critical Bibliography

I ENGLISH

A. Collected Texts

K. Marx, *Selected Essays*, ed. H. Stenning (London and New York, 1926, reprinted 1968). Abbreviation: Stenning. A collection of seven essays from the early Marx, most of them minor.

K. Marx, F. Engels, *Selected Works* (Moscow, 1935, several reprints). Abbreviation: *MESW*. The 'classical' anthology. None of the early writings are included and less than half the material is by Marx. Nevertheless provides complete and faithful translations of many of Marx's works.

K. Marx, *Capital, The Communist Manifesto and Other Writings*, ed. M. Eastman (New York, 1932). Concentrates on *Capital* to the complete exclusion of early writings.

K. Marx, F. Engels, *Basic Writings on Politics and Philosophy*, ed. L. Feuer (New York, 1959). Concentrates on Marx's historical writings, with a useful selection of letters and essays at the end.

K. Marx, *Selected Writings in Sociology and Social Philosophy*, ed. T. Bottomore and M. Rubel (London, 1956). In many ways the best anthology, drawing on all Marx's writings whether available in English or not.

K. Marx, *Early Writings*, ed. T. Bottomore (London, 1963). Abbreviation: Bottomore. Contains the essays in the *Deutsch-Französische Jahbücher* and the complete text of the 'Paris Manuscripts'.

Writings of the Young Marx on Philosophy and Society, ed. L. Easton and K. Guddat (New York, 1967). Abbreviation: EG. A comprehensive collection of Marx's writings from 1841 to 1847. Contains extracts from *The Holy Family* and *The German Ideology*.

The Essential Writings of Karl Marx, ed. D. Caute (London and New York, 1967). Small excerpts with emphasis on the philosophical and revolutionary aspects of Marx.

Marxist Social Thought, ed. R. Freedman (New York, 1968). Fairly comprehensive on the sociological aspects of Marx's later works. Little reference to economics or to Marx's early writings.

K. Marx, *The Early Texts*, ed. D. McLellan (Oxford, 1971). Abbreviation: *ET*. A comprehensive selection of writings up to and including 1844, with letters.

The Portable Marx, ed. E. Kamenka (New York, 1971). A selection containing longer extracts and some newly translated material.

Karl Marx on Economy, Class and Social Revolution, ed. Z. Jordan (London, 1971). A comprehensive collection, aimed at the sociologist.

Marx-Engels Reader, ed. R. Tucker (New York, 1971). A more balanced, but shorter, version of the Moscow edition above.

K. Marx, *The Essential Writings*, ed. R. Bender (New York, 1972). A large collection, well put together, with due emphasis on the economic writings.

There are also collections of texts, mostly newspaper articles, on the following specific themes:

On Britain (London, 1953).

On Ireland (London, 1970).

Marx on China (London, 1968).

First Indian War of Independence (Moscow, 1960).

Revolution in Spain (London, 1939).

On Colonialism (Moscow, 1960).

Karl Marx on Colonialism and Modernization, ed. S. Avineri (New York, 1968).

On Malthus (London, 1953).

On Literature and Art (Bombay, 1956).

On Religion (Moscow, 1957).

On Revolution, ed. S. Padover (New York, 1971).

There is no comprehensive English translation of Marx's works. Penguin books are currently bringing out an eight-volume selection. The translation of the Collected Works of Marx and Engels to comprise fifty-one volumes is being undertaken by Lawrence and Wishart in London and International Publishers New York in conjunction with the Institute for Marxism-Leninism in Moscow. The first three volumes will be published early in 1974 and the whole completed in the following ten or twelve years.

B. Collected Letters

K. Marx, F. Engels, *Selected Correspondence* (London, 1934). Abbreviation: *MESC.*

K. Marx, *Letters to Kugelmann* (London, 1934).

K. Marx, F. Engels, *Letters to Americans* (New York, 1963).

K. Marx, *On the Eastern Question* (London, 1899)

C. Individual Works

N.B. Where there is no English translation available, there is a reference to the original German (or French) edition.

1. *School Leaving Essays*. Partial translation in EG.
2. *Letter to his Father*. EG, ET.
3. *Doctoral Thesis*. The thesis itself is translated in N. Livergood, *Activity in Marx's Philosophy* (The Hague, 1967). Appendices partially translated in EG, ET.
4. *Poems 1836–1841*. Partially translated in R. Payne (ed.), *The Unknown Marx* (London, 1972).
5. *Articles for Rheinische Zeitung*. Selections in EG, ET.
6. *Critique of Hegel's Philosophy of Right*. Translated and edited by J. O'Malley (Cambridge, 1970).
7. *A Correspondence of 1843*. EG, ET.
8. *On the Jewish Question*. Bottomore, EG, ET; *A World without Jews*, ed D. Runes (New York, 1959).
9. *Critique of Hegel's Philosophy of Right: Introduction*. Bottomore, EG, ET.
10. *1844 Manuscripts*. Complete translation in Bottomore; also by M. Milligan (Moscow, 1959). Large selections in EG, ET.
11. *Critical Notes on 'The King of Prussia and Social Reform'*. EG, ET.
12. *The Holy Family* (Moscow, 1956).
13. *Theses on Feuerbach*. Appendix to *The German Ideology* (Moscow, 1968).
14. *The German Ideology* (Moscow, 1968). Selections in an edition, with introduction, by C. Arthur (London, 1970).
15. *Circular against Kriege*. *MEW* iv.
16. *Letter to Annenkov*. Appendix to *The Poverty of Philosophy* (Moscow, 1956).
17. *The Poverty of Philosophy* (Moscow, 1956).
18. *Karl Grün: The Social Movement in France and Belgium*. *MEW* iii.
19. *The Communism of the 'Rheinischer Beobachter'*. *MEW* v.

20 *Moralising Criticism and Criticising Moralism.* Stenning.

21. *Speech on Free Trade* (Boston, 1888).

22. *The Communist Manifesto. MESW* I; also separate editions by D. Ryazanow (London, 1936); H. Laski (London, 1948); A. Taylor (Harmondsworth, 1967).

23 *Demands of the Communist Party in Germany. The Birth of his Communist League*, ed. D. Struik (New York, 1971).

24. *Articles for Neue Rheinische Zeitung. MEW* v and vi.

25. *Wage-Labour and Capital. MESW* I.

26. *Addresses of the Central Committee to the Communist League.* March Address: *MESW* I; June Address: *MEW* vii.

27. *Articles for Neue Rheinische Zeitung-Revue. MEW* vii.

28. *The Class Struggles in France. MESW* I.

29. *Articles for New York Herald Tribune.* Selections in: H. Christman (ed.), *The American Journalism of Marx and Engels* (New York, 1966); *Marx on India*, ed. R. Dutt (London, 1934); *Revolution in Spain* (London, 1939); *Marx on China* (London, 1968); *The Eastern Question*, ed. E. and E. Aveling (London, 1897). Also the collections on Britain, Ireland and Colonialism above. Complete edition, ed. Ferguson and O'Neil (New York, 1973).

30. *The Eighteenth Brumaire of Louis Bonaparte. MESW* I.

31. *The Great Men of Exile. The Cologne Communist Trial*, ed. R. Livingstone (London, 1970).

32. *The Cologne Communist Trial*, ed. R. Livingstone (London, 1970).

33. *Palmerston*, ed. L. Hutchinson (London, 1970).

34. *The Knight of the Noble Conscience. The Cologne Communist Trial*, ed. R. Livingstone (London, 1970).

35. *Palmerston and Russia*, ed. L. Hutchinson (London, 1970).

36. *Articles for Neue Oder Zeitung. MEW* xi.

37. *Secret Diplomatic History of the Eighteenth Century*, ed. L. Hutchinson (London, 1970).

38. *Articles for The Peoples Paper and The Free Press. MEW* xii.

39. *General Introduction to Grundrisse.* Appendix to *A Contribution to the Critique of Political Economy*, trans. I. Stone (Chicago, 1904); *Marx's Grundrisse*, ed. D. McLellan (London, 1971).

40. *Grundrisse.* Selection in *Marx's Grundrisse*, ed. D. McLellan (London, 1971); *Pre-Capitalist Economic Formations*, ed. E. Hobsbawm (London, 1964). Full translation (London and New York, 1973).

41. *Articles for New American Cyclopaedia. MEW* xiv.

42. *Preface to A Critique of Political Economy. MESW* I.
43. *A Critique of Political Economy.* Translated by I. Stone (Chicago, 1904); re-edition with Introduction by M. Dobb (London, 1970).
44. *Articles for Das Volk. MEW* XIII.
45. *Herr Vogt. MEW* XIV.
46. *Articles for Die Presse. MEW* XV.
47. *Theories of Surplus Value,* 3 vols (Moscow, 1968; London, 1969).
48. *Manuscripts on the Polish Question* (The Hague, 1963). No English translation.
49. *Inaugural Address and Rules for First International. MESW* I.
50. *Capital,* Vol. 3. Translated by E. Untermann (Chicago, 1909); Moscow, 1972.
51. *Value, Price and Profit. MESW* I.
52. *On Proudhon. MESW* I.
53. *Results of the Immediate Process of Production.* German in *Archiv Marksa i Engelsa* (Moscow, 1934).
54. *Capital,* Vol. 1. Translated by S. Moore and E. Aveling (London, 1887); E. Untermann (Chicago, 1906); E. and C. Paul (London, 1928); Moscow, 1968.
55. *Capital,* Vol. 2. E. Untermann (Chicago, 1907); Moscow, 1971.
56. *Two Addresses on the Franco-Prussian War. MESW* I.
57. *On the Civil War in France. MESW* I; ed. C. Hitchens (London, 1971); *The Drafts* are also contained in K. Marx and F. Engels, *On the Paris Commune* (Moscow, 1971); *Writings of Marx and Engels on the Paris Commune,* ed. H. Draper (New York, 1971).
58. *The Alleged Splits in the International,* ed. Freymond (Geneva, 1962).
59. *Preface to Second German edition of Communist Manifesto. MESW* I and other editions.
60. *Speech at Amsterdam, 1872. MEW* XVIII.
61. *Afterword to Second German edition of Capital.* See editions of *Capital* above.
62. *Remarks on Bakunin's Statism and Anarchy.* H. Mayer, 'Marx on Bakunin: A neglected text', *Cahiers de l'ISEA.* 1959.
63. *Critique of the Gotha Programme. MESW* II.
64. *French edition of Capital,* Vol. 1. *Oeuvres,* ed. M. Rubel, II (Paris, 1968).
65. *Letter to Mikhailovsky. Basic Writings on Politics and Philosophy,* ed. L. Feuer (New York, 1959).
66. *Circular Letter. MESC.*
67. *A Workers' Enquiry.* C.P.G.B. (London, 1933).

68. *Introduction to French Workers' Programme. Oeuvres* (Paris, 1963) I.
69. *Letter to Vera Sassoulitch (and preliminary drafts).* Selections in Marx and Engels, *The Russian Menace to Europe,* ed. P. Blackstock and B. Hoselitz (London, 1953).
70. *Notes on Wagner's Textbook of Political Economy. MEW* XIX. *Texts on Method,* ed. T. Carver (Oxford, 1924).
71. *Preface to Second Russian edition of Communist Manifesto. MESW* I and other editions.

D. Commentaries

H. B. Acton, *The Illusion of the Epoch* (London, 1955). A critique of Marxism-Leninism as a philosophical creed.

H. B. Acton, *What Marx Really Said* (London, 1967). A short critical exposition, concentrating on Marx's ideas of historical materialism.

H. P. Adams, *Karl Marx in His Early Writings,* 2nd ed. (London, 1965). The first examination in English of Marx's early writings up to, and including, *The Holy Family.* Slightly dated.

L. Althusser, *For Marx* (London, 1970). A controversial interpretation of Marx using structuralist and Freudian concepts. Supports the idea of a radical break between the young and the old Marx.

L. Althusser, *Reading Capital* (London, 1971). An attempt to analyse *Capital* in a scientific manner and give an account of the philosophy underlying it.

W. Ash, *Marxism and Moral Concepts* (New York, 1964). A good introduction to the question.

S. Avineri, *The Social and Political Thought of Karl Marx* (Cambridge, 1968). An important and interesting book which emphasises the continuity of Marx's thought from its earliest formulations and the influence of Hegel.

J. Barzun, *Darwin, Marx and Wagner* (Boston, 1946). Good in placing Marx in an intellectual tradition.

M. Beer, *The Life and Teaching of Karl Marx* (London and Manchester, 1921). A small book; necessarily dated.

I. Berlin, *Karl Marx. His Life and Environment* (Oxford, 1939). A very readable short biography.

S. F. Bloom, *The World of Nations. A Study of the National Implications in the Work of Marx* (New York, 1941). An exposition of Marx's views on the position of nation states in the development of communism.

W. Blumenberg, *Karl Marx* (London, 1971). An excellent short biography mainly using Marx's own words with a varied selection of photographs.

M. M. Bober, *Karl Marx's Interpretation of History*, 2nd ed. (New York, 1965; original ed., 1927). The oldest and fullest discussion of historical materialism in English.

L. V. Böhm-Bawerk, *Karl Marx and the Close of his System* (London, 1890). The 'classical' critique of Marx's *Capital*.

T. Bottomore (ed.), *Karl Marx* (New York, 1971). A collection of commentaries on Marx, with an introduction, in the 'Makers of Modern Social Science' series.

T. Bottomore, *The Sociological Theory of Marxism* (London, 1973). Contains an analysis of Marx's theories on classes, the state, revolution, and so on.

L. B. Boudin, *The Theoretical System of Karl Marx in the Light of Recent Criticism* (Chicago 1907; reprinted New York, 1967). A defence of Marx's materialist conception of history and economic doctrine in face of the criticisms of Revisionists.

E. R. Browder, *Marx and America* (London, 1959). A useful brief overview of the position of America in Marx's thought.

B. Delfgaauw, *The Young Marx* (London, 1967). A short account of the ideas of the young Marx and their relevance today.

R. N. Carew-Hunt, *The Theory and Practice of Communism* (London, 1963). Contains a rather over-schematised and unreliable section on Marx.

J. Carmichael, *Karl Marx. The Passionate Logician* (London, 1968). A shortish biography.

E. H. Carr, *Karl Marx. A Study in Fanaticism* (London, 1943). A well-written critical biography of medium length.

S. Chang, *The Marxian Theory of the State* (Philadelphia 1931; new ed. 1965). A good exposition, but one which conflates the ideas of Marx and Lenin.

G. D. H. Cole, *What Marx Really Meant* (London, 1934). A sympathetic and systematic exposition of Marx's ideas.

G. D. H. Cole, *History of Socialist Thought* (London, 1953, vols 1 and 2). A measured and well-researched placing of Marx in the history of socialist thought.

H. Collins and C. Abramsky, *Karl Marx and the British Labour Movement. Years of the First International* (London, 1965). A very well-documented account of Marx's part in the First International with special reference to Britain.

R. Cooper, *The Logical Influence of Hegel on Marx* (Seattle, 1925). An interesting, though dated, comparison of the dialectics of Hegel and Marx.

A. Cornu, *The Origins of Marxian Thought* (Springfield, 1957). Deals with the development of Marx's ideas up to the mid 1840s.

M. Curtis (ed.), *Marxism* (New York, 1970). A wide-ranging reprint of articles on Marx's thought.

P. Demetz, *Marx, Engels and the Poets* (Chicago, 1967). An assessment of the views of Marx and Engels as literary critics.

M. Dobb, *Marx as an Economist* (London, 1943). One of the best short introductions to Marx as an economist.

R. Dunayevskaya, *Marxism and Freedom* (New York, 1958). Contains sections on the philosophical aspects of the *1844 Manuscripts* and *Capital*.

L. Dupré, *The Philosophical Foundations of Marxism* (New York, 1966). A straightforward discussion of Marx's thought up to the *Communist Manifesto*, with some preliminary chapters on Hegel.

I. Fetscher, *Marx and Marxism* (New York, 1971). Contains articles on the continuity in Marx's thought, bureaucracy, future communist society, and so on.

E. Fischer, *Marx in His Own Words* (London, 1970). A slight, but faithful, run-through of Marx's main ideas.

E. Fromm, *Marx's Concept of Man* (New York, 1963). This introduction to selections from the '1844 Manuscripts' portrays Marx as a humanist and existentialist thinker.

A. Gamble and P. Walton, *From Alienation to Surplus Value* (London, 1972). Concentrates on labour and surplus value as unifying themes in Marx's works with special attention paid to the *Grundrisse* and *Theories of Surplus Value*.

R. Garaudy, *Karl Marx: The Evolution of His Thought* (London, 1967). A reliable and readable account by (at the time of writing) an orthodox communist.

H. Gemkow and others, *Karl Marx. A Biography* (Berlin, 1970). A well-documented, but quite uncritical, piece of hagiography.

J. M. Gillman, *The Falling Rate of Profit. Marx's Law and Its Significance to 20th Century Capitalism* (London, 1958). An examination of the limitations of Marx's law when applied to monopoly capitalism.

G. Girardi, *Marxism and Christianity* (Dublin, 1968). An examination of the possibilities of dialogue between Marxism and Christianity.

M. Godelier, *Rationality and Irrationality in Economics* (London, 1972). Examines the basic structures of Marx's economic views.

A. J. Gregor, *A Survey of Marxism* (New York, 1965). The first few chapters discuss the philosophical aspects of Marx.

S. Hook, *Towards the Understanding of Karl Marx* (New York, 1933). Still a good introduction to the more systematic parts of Marx's thought.

S. Hook, *From Hegel to Marx*, 2nd ed. (Ann Arbor, 1962). A study of the relationships of Hegel and Marx and the young Hegelians.

D. Horowitz (ed.), *Marx and Modern Economics* (London, 1968). Contains essays examining the relevance today of particularly the more abstract of Marx's economic theories.

D. Howard, *The Development of the Marxian Dialectic* (Chicago, 1972). A reliable treatment of Marx's early thought.

J. Hyppolite, *Studies on Marx and Hegel* (London, 1969). Contains profound assessments of Marx's critique of Hegel's *Philosophy of Right* and of *Capital*.

J. Hampden Jackson, *Marx, Proudhon and European Socialism* (New York, 1962). A reliable short account of the relations between the two men.

Z. Jordan, *The Evolution of Dialectical Materialism* (London, 1967). The early chapters contain a good account of naturalism and materialism in Marx.

H. W. B. Joseph, *The Labour Theory of Value in Karl Marx* (London, 1923). A careful criticism by an Oxford philosopher.

E. Kamenka, *The Ethical Foundation of Marxism*, 2nd ed. (London, 1972). A description and critique of Marx's ethics from an analytical philosophical position.

E. Kamenka, *Marxist Ethics* (London, 1969). A brief analysis of the Marxian ethical tradition.

E. P. Kandel, *Marx and Engels. The Organizers of the Communist League* (Moscow, 1953). Contains much information on Marx in the late 1840s.

K. J. Kenafick, *Michael Bakunin and Karl Marx* (Melbourne, 1948: privately printed). A lengthy account of their relationship by a disciple of Bakunin.

A. C. Kettle, *Karl Marx, Founder of Modern Communism* (London, 1963). A good short biography by a communist.

L. Kolakowski, *Marxism and Beyond* (London, 1968). Contains essays highlighting the relationship between the individual and history in Marx's thought.

H. Koren, *Marx and the Authentic Man* (Duquesne, 1967). A short description of Marx's 'humanist' conception of man.

K. Korsch, *Karl Marx* (New York, 1936). An insightful biography by an ex-communist.

K. Korsch, *Marxism and Philosophy* (London, 1971). A brilliant reassessment of the Hegelian elements in Marx.

H. Lefebvre, *The Sociology of Marx* (London, 1968). An excellent introduction to Marx's sociology.

G. Leff, *The Tyranny of Concepts* (London, 1961). An important critique of Marx's materialist conception of history.

J. Lewis, *The Life and Teaching of Karl Marx* (London, 1965). A good medium-length biography presenting Marx in a favourable light.

J. Lewis, *The Marxism of Marx* (London, 1972). A wise and humane commentary by a veteran communist.

G. Lichtheim, *Marxism, an Historical and Critical Study* (London, 1961). An excellent study of the development of Marxist doctrines from their origins up to 1917.

G. Lichtheim, *From Marx to Hegel* (New York, 1971). Contains a series of essays on the Hegelian-Marxist tradition up to the present day.

N. Lobkowicz, *Theory and Practice, The History of a Marxist Concept* (Notre Dame, 1967). An examination of Marx's concept of 'praxis' against a Young Hegelian background.

N. Lobkowicz (ed.), *Marx and the Western World* (Notre Dame, 1967). A large collection of articles on the relevance of Marx's thought today.

K. Löwith, *From Hegel to Nietzsche* (London, 1965). A wide-ranging account of nineteenth-century German philosophy: Marx is considered, among many others, in the Hegelian tradition.

G. Lukacs, *History and Class Consciousness* (London, 1970). An extremely influential re-emphasis of Hegel's influence on Marx.

E. Mandel, *The Formation of Marx's Economic Thought* (London, 1971). An excellent analysis of the development of Marx's economic thought up to and including the *Grundrisse*.

H. Marcuse, *Reason and Revolution* (London, 1941). Contains an account of Marx's notion of labour.

D. McLellan, *The Young Hegelians and Karl Marx* (London, 1969). An examination of the social and political thought of the Young Hegelians and its influence on the genesis of Marx's thought.

D. McLellan, *Marx Before Marxism* (London and New York, 1970).

A detailed description of the development of Marx's thought up to and including the *1844 Manuscripts*.

D. McLellan, *The Thought of Karl Marx* (London and New York, 1971). A chronological and thematic introduction to Marx's thought.

J. Maguire, *Marx's Paris Writings* (Dublin, 1972). A well-informed and thorough commentary on the writings of 1844.

R. L. Meek, *Studies in the Labour Theory of Value* (London, 1956). Best treatment in English of this subject.

F. Mehring, *Karl Marx* (London, 1936). The classical biography of Marx; somewhat out of date and slightly hagiographical.

A. G. Meyer, *Marxism: The Unity of Theory and Practice. A Critical Essay* (Cambridge, Mass., 1954). Presents a functional interpretation of Marx's sociology.

D. Mitrany, *Marx against the Peasant* (London, 1951). An attack on the views of Marx and his followers on the peasants.

A. C. MacIntyre, *Marxism: an Interpretation* (London, 1953). A short and sharp philosophical assessment of Marx.

M. Morishima, *Marx's Economics* (Cambridge, 1973). A complex examination of Marx's theoretical economics.

B. Nicolaievski and O. Maenchen-Helfen, *Karl Marx, Man and Fighter* (London, 1933; 3rd ed. 1973). An excellent biography emphasising Marx's political activities.

B. Ollman, *Alienation: Marx's critique of Man in Capitalist Society* (Cambridge, 1971). An original and well-documented study of alienation in Marx, paying close attention to the way Marx uses his concepts.

F. Pappenheim, *The Alienation of Modern Man* (New York, 1959). Puts Marx's concept of alienation in a modern context.

R. Payne, *Marx, A Biography* (London, 1968). A lot of information on Marx's private life, though the author's understanding of Marx's ideas is extremely deficient.

G. Petrovic, *Marx in the Mid-Twentieth Century* (Garden City, 1967). Emphasises the humanist relevance of Marx today.

J. Plamenatz, *German Marxism and Russian Communism* (London, 1954). Contains one of the classical discussions of historical materialism as outlined in Marx's *Preface*.

J. Plamenatz, *Man and Society*, Vol. 2 (London, 1963). A clear, critical analysis of the main social and political themes in Marx.

K. R. Popper, *The Open Society and its Enemies* Vol. 2 (London, 1952). An attack on Marx as a totalitarian thinker.

Joan Robinson, *An Essay in Marxian Economics* (London, 1942). An impressive attempt to revitalise Marx's main economic doctrines.

C. L. Rossiter, *Marxism: The View from America* (New York, 1960). Contrasts Marx's ideas – often more or less equated with those of his disciples – with the American way of life.

N. Rothenstreich, *Basic Problems of Marx's Philosophy* (New York, 1965). A philosophical commentary on Marx's Theses on Feuerbach.

D. Ryazanov, *Karl Marx, Man, Thinker and Revolutionist* (New York, 1927). A well-informed series of lectures on Marx's life.

G. Sabine, *Marxism* (New York, 1958). A rather over-schematised short discussion.

F. Salter, *Karl Marx and Modern Socialism* (London, 1921). Describes Marx's ideas and their influence on the growth of labour movements.

J. Sanderson. *An Interpretation of the Political Ideas of Marx and Engels* (London, 1969). A short book which seeks to put together the main texts of Marx and Engels on historical materialism, the state, revolution and future communist society.

R. Schlesinger. *Marx, His Time and Ours* (London, 1950). An important book investigating the continued relevance of Marx's ideas for the twentieth century.

A. Schmidt, *The Concept of Nature in Marx* (London, 1971). An important and well-documented consideration of the importance of Marx's materialism.

L. Schwartzchild, *Karl Marx: The Red Prussian* (New York, 1948). A strongly critical biography.

P. Sloan, *Marx and the Orthodox Economists* (Oxford, 1973). A defence of Marx against subsequent economic thinking.

J. Spargo. *Karl Marx, His Life and Works* (New York, 1910). The first biography of Marx in English.

C. J. S. Sprigge, *Karl Marx* (London, 1938; New York, 1962). A short biography.

Elena A. Stepanova, *Karl Marx* (Moscow, 1962). A short piece of pure hagiography.

P. M. Sweeney, *The Theory of Capitalist Development* (New York, 1942). The best modern continuation of Marx's economic ideas.

R. Tucker, *Philosophy and Myth in Karl Marx* (Cambridge, 1961). A highly original – though in places also highly dubious – interpretation of Marx's thought as a continuity based on certain eschatological assumptions.

R. Tucker, *The Marxian Revolutionary Idea* (London, 1970). A series of essays dealing with the state and revolution in Marx.

D. Turner, *On the Philosophy of Marx* (Dublin, 1968). A slight book, written mainly for philosophers.

V. Venables. *Human Nature, the Marxian View* (New York, 1945). One of the best statements of the Marxist view of man.

P. Walton and S. Hall, eds., *Situating Marx* (London, 1972). A series of essays centring on Marx's *Grundrisse*.

E. Wilson, *To the Finland Station* (London, 1940; latest ed. 1970). A very readable (though occasionally inaccurate) account of the ideas of Marx as well as those of his predecessors and successors.

B. Wolfe, *Marxism: 100 years in the Life of a Doctrine* (London, 1967). A study of the evolution of Marxist doctrines with sections on Marx's political ideas in 1848 and 1871.

M. Wolfson, *Karl Marx* (New York, 1971). A short critique of Marx's main economic doctrines.

D. Wright, *The Trouble with Marx* (New Rochelle, 1967). A 'no holds barred' attack on Marx's ideas of history and economics.

C. Wright Mills, *The Marxists* (New York, 1962). Contains an acute account of Marx's sociological ideas.

I. Zeitlin, *Marxism: A Re-examination* (New York, 1967). A short and interesting book presenting in a favourable light the sociological elements in Marx's thought.

II GERMAN

A. Collected Texts

K. Marx, F. Engels, *Gesamtausgabe* (= MEGA) (Frankfurt, 1927 ff.).

Aus dem Literarischen Nachlass von K. Marx, F. Engels, F. Lassalle, ed. F. Mehring (Stuttgart, 1902).

K. Marx, F. Engels, *Werke* (= MEW), 39 vols (Berlin, 1956 ff.).

K. Marx, *Werke – Schriften – Briefe* (ed. Lieber, Furth, Kautsky), 6 vols (Stuttgart, 1962 ff.).

K. Marx, F. Engels, *Ausgewählte Schriften in 2 Bänden* (Berlin, 1952).

K. Marx, F. Engels, *Studienausgabe in 4 Bänden*, ed. Fetscher (Frankfurt, 1966).

K. Marx, *Texte zu Methode und Praxis* ed., G. Hillmann 3 (Reinbek, 1966).
K. Marx, *Ausgewählte Schriften*, ed. B. Goldenburg (Munich, 1962).
K. Marx, *Auswahl*, ed. F. Borkenau (Frankfurt, 1956).
K. Marx, *Die Frühschriften*, ed. S. Landshut and J. Mayer (Stuttgart, 1932).

B. *Collections on Specific Themes*

K. Marx, *Bildung and Erziehung*, ed. H. Wittig (Paderborn, 1968).
K. Marx, F. Engels, *Über Literatur und Kunst* (Berlin, 1967).
K. Marx, *Dokumente seines Lebens* (Berlin, 1970).

C. *Collected Letters*

Freiligraths Briefwechsel mit Marx und Engels, 2 vols, ed. Manfred Haeckel (Berlin, 1968).
Karl Marx Privat, ed. Wolfgang Schwerbrock (Munich, 1962).
Familie Marx in Briefen, ed. Manfred Müller (Berlin, 1966).
Briefe und Dokumente der Familie Marx aus den Jahren 1862–1873, ed. B. Andreas (Hanover, 1962).
Liebknechts Briefwechsel mit Marx und Engels, ed. G. Eckert (The Hague, 1963).

D. *Commentaries*

K. Adamczyk, *Marx und Engels zur Koalitions- und Streikfrage* (Breslau, 1917).
G. Adler, *Die Grundlagen der Karl Marx' schen Kritik der bestehenden Volkswirtschaft* (Tübingen, 1887).
Max Adler, *Marx als Denker* (Vienna, 1921).
V. Adoratski, *Karl Marx, Eine Sammlung von Erinnerungen und Aufsätzen* (Moscow, 1934).
Edgar Alexander, *Europa und der russische Imperialismus. Karl Marx und das europäische Gewissen* (Recklinghausen, 1957).
Horst Bartel, *Marx und Engels in Kampf um ein revolutionäres deutsches Parteiorgan 1879–1890* (Berlin, 1961).
Gerhard Becker, *Karl Marx und Friedrich Engels in Köln 1848–1849* (Berlin, 1963).
W. Becker, *Kritik der Marxschen Wertlehre* (Hamburg, 1972).
Konrad Bekker, *Marx's philosophische Entwicklung, sein Verhältnis zu Hegel* (Zürich, 1940).
I. Berlin, *Karl Marx. Sein Leben und sein Werk* (Munich, 1959).
Eduard Bernstein, *Karl Marx und Michael Bakunin* (Tübingen, 1960).
E. Bloch, *Uber Karl Marx* (Frankfurt, 1968).

Werner Blumenberg, *Karl Marx in Selbstzeugnissen und Bilddokumenten* (Hamburg, 1962).

Celina Bobinska, *Marx und Engels über polnische Probleme* (Berlin, 1958).

K. Böckmühl, *Leiblichkeit und Gesellschaft, Studien zur Religionskritik und Anthropologie im Frühwerk von Ludwig Feuerbach und Karl Marx* (Göttingen, 1961).

J. Borchardt, *Die volkswirtschaftlichen Grundbegriffe nach der Lehre von K. Marx.* (Berlin, 1920).

W. Bracht, *Trier und K. Marx* (Trier, 1947).

F. Brupbacher, *Marx und Bakunin. Ein Beitrag zur Geschichte der Internationalen Arbeiterassoziation* (Berlin, 1922).

Fritz Bruegel and Benedict Kautsky, *Der deutsche Sozialismus von L. Gall bis K. Marx. Ein Lesebuch* (Vienna and Liepzig, 1931).

E. A. von Buggenhagen, *Die Stellung zur Wirklichkeit bei Hegel und Marx* (Radolfzell, 1933).

E. Busch, *Der Irrtum von K. Marx* (Basel, 1894).

J. Y. Calvez. *Karl Marx. Darstellung und Kritik seines Denkens* (Freiburg, 1964).

Wilhelm Cohnstaedt, *Die Agrarfrage in der deutschen Sozialdemokratie von Karl Marx bis zum Breslauer Parteitag* (München, 1903).

A. Cornu, *Karl Marx und Friedrich Engels*, vols 1–3 (Berlin, 1954–68).

Heinrich Cunow, *Die Marxsche Geschichts-, Gesellschafts- und Staatstheorie* (Berlin, 1920).

Ralf Dahrendorf, *Marx in Perspektive. Die Idee des Gerechten im Denken von Karl Marx* (Hanover, 1952).

Peter Demetz, *Marx, Engels und die Dichter* (Stuttgart, 1959).

Gerd Dicke, *Der Identitätsgedanke bei Feuerbach und Marx* (Köln and Opladen, 1960).

Luise Dornemann, *Jenny Marx. Der Lebensweg einer Sozialistin* (Berlin, 1968).

Ernst Drahn, *Marx – Bibliographie* (Charlottenburg, 1920).

I. Fetscher, *Karl Marx und der Marxismus* (Munich, 1967).

E. Fischer, *Was Marx wirklich sagte* (Vienna, 1968).

Hugo Fischer, *Karl Marx und sein Verhältnis zu Staat und Wirtschaft* (Jena, 1932).

H. Fleischer, *Marx und Engels* (Munich, 1970).

Herwig Förder, *Marx und Engels am Vorabend der Revolution* (Berlin, 1960).

Manfred Friedrich, *Philosophie und Okonomie beim jungen Marx* (Berlin, 1960).

B. Fritsch, *Die Geld – und Kredittheorie von Karl Marx* (Einsiedeln, 1954).

E. Fromm, *Das Menschenbild bei Marx* (Frankfurt, 1963).

H. Gemkow, *Karl Marx. Eine Biographie* (Berlin, 1968).

Irma Goitein, *Probleme der Gesellschaft und des Staates bei Moses Hess. Ein Beitrag zu dem Thema Hess und Marx mit bisher unveröffentlichtem Quellen-Material* (Leipzig, 1931).

H. Gollwitzer, *Die Marxistiche Religionskritik und der christliche Glaube* (Hamburg, 1967).

G. Gross, *Karl Marx. Eine Studie* (Leipzig and Berlin, 1885).

E. Hammacher, *Das philosophisch-ökonomische System des Marxismus* (Leipzig, 1909).

K. Hartmann, *Die Marxsche Theorie* (Berlin, 1970).

Alexander Havadtöy, *Arbeit und Eigentum in den Schriften des jungen Marx* (Basel, 1951).

P. Kägi, *Genesis des historischen Materialismus* (Vienna, 1965).

Bruno Kaiser, *Ex libris Karl Marx und Engels: Schichsal und Verzeichnis* (Berlin, 1967).

Hans Kelsen, *Sozialismus und Staat. Eine Untersuchung der politischen Theorie des Marxismus* (Leipzig, 1920).

August Koppel, *Für und wider Karl Marx. Prolegomena zu einer Biographie* (no place of publication, 1905).

K. Korsch, *Marxismus und Philosophie* (Leipzig, 1930).

K. Korsch, *Karl Marx* (Frankfurt, 1967).

H. Krause, *Marx und Engels und das zeitgenössische Russland* (Giessen, 1958).

J. Kuczynski, *Zurück zu Marx! Antikritische Studien zur Theorie des Marxismus* (Leipzig, 1926).

A. Künzli, *Karl Marx. Eine Psychographie* (Vienna, 1966).

E. Kux, *Karl Marx: Die revolutionäre Konfession* (Stuttgart, 1967).

K. Löwith, *Von Hegel zu Nietzsche* (Stuttgart, 1941).

Friedrich Lenz, *Staat und Marxismus: Grundlegung und Kritik der maxistischen Gesellschaftslehre* (Stuttgart and Berlin, 1921).

Wilhelm Liebknecht, *Karl Marx zum Gedächtnis* (Nuremburg, 1896).

M. Lifschitz, *Karl Marx und die Asthetik* (Dresden, 1967).

E. Mandel, *Entstehung und Entwicklung der ökonomischen Lehre von Karl Marx* (Frankfurt, 1968).

Karl Marx 1818–1968 (no editor) (Mainz, 1968).

Karl Marx als Denker, Mensch und Revolutionär. Ein Sammelbuch (Vienna and Berlin, 1928).

Karl Marx Album (Berlin, Dietz Verlag, 1953).

Karl Marx. Chronik seines Lebens in Einzeldaten (Frankfurt, 1971).

T. G. Masaryk, *Die philosophischen und soziologischen Grundlagen des Marxismus* (Vienna, 1899).

A. Massiczek, *Der menschliche Mensch. Karl Marx' jüdischer Humanismus* (Vienna, 1968).

Franz Mehring, *Karl Marx. Geschichte seines Lebens* (Stuttgart, 1918).

Georg Mende, *Karl Marx' Entwicklung vom revolutionären Demokraten zum Kommunisten* (Berlin, 1955).

Sepp Miller and Bruno Sawadzki, *Karl Marx in Berlin* (Berlin, no date).

Heinz Monz, *Karl Marx und Trier, Verhältnisse-Beziehungen-Einflüsse* (Trèves, 1964).

O. Morf, *Das Verhältnis von Wirtschaftstheorie und Wirtschaftsgeschichte bei Karl Marx* (Basel, 1951).

Walter Morgenthaler, *Der Mensch Karl Marx* (Berne, 1962).

N. Moskovskaya, *Das Marxsche System* (Berlin, 1929).

Carl Mutis, *Anti-Marx. Betrachtungen über dem Inneren der Marxschen Ökonomik* (Jena, 1927).

F. Oelssner. *Die ökonomische Theorie von Karl Marx als Anleitung für die sozialistische Wirtschaftsführung* (Berlin, 1959).

T. Oiserman, *Die Entstehung der Marxistischen Philosophie* (Berlin, 1962).

F. Oppenheimer, *Das Grundgesetz der Marxschen Gesellschaftslehre* (Berlin, 1903).

F. Oppenheimer, *Die soziale Frage und der Sozialismus. Eine kritische Auseinandersetzung mit der marxistischen Theorie* (Jena, 1913).

W. G. Oschilewski, *Grosse Sozialisten in Berlin* (Berlin and Grünewald, 1956).

Henrik Popitz, *Der entfremdete Mensch, Zeitkritik und Geschichtsphilosophie des jungen Marx* (Basel, 1953).

K. Popper, *Falsche Propheten. Hegel, Marx und die Folgen* (Berne, 1958).

W. Post, *Kritik der Religion bei Karl Marx* (Munich, 1969).

Heinz Roehr, *Pseudoreligiöse Motive in den Frühschriften von Karl Marx* (Tübingen, 1962).

R. Rosdolsky, *Zur Entstehungsgeschichte des 'Kapitals'* (Frankfurt, 1968).

M. Rubel, *Marx-Chronik. Daten zu Leben und Werk* (Munich, 1968).

M. Rubel (ed.), *Marx und Engels über die Russische Kommune* (Munich, 1972).

Otto Ruehle, *Karl Marx, Leben und Werk* (Helleran, 1928).

R. F. Sannwald, *Marx und die Antike* (Einsiedeln, 1956).

Werner Schuffenhauer, *Feuerbach und der junge Marx. Entstehungsgeschichte der marxistische Weltanschauung* (Berlin, 1965).

Hubert Schiel, *Die Umwelt des jungen Marx. Die Triere Wohnungen der Familie Marx. Ein unbekanntes Auswanderungsgesuch von Karl Marx* (Trèves, 1954).

Alfred Schmidt, *Der Begriff der Natur in der Lehre von Marx* (Frankfurt, 1962).

Walter Sens, *Karl Marx. Seine irreligiöse Entwicklung und antichristliche Einstellung* (Halle, 1936).

L. Z. Slonimsky. *Versuch einer Kritik der Karl Marx'schen ökonomischen Theorien* (Berlin, 1899).

P. Stadler, *Karl Marx* (Basel, 1966).

R. Stammler, *Die materialistische Geschichtsauffassung* (Gütersloh, 1921).

F. Stenberg, *Marx und die Gegenwart* (Köln, 1955).

H. Sultan, *Gesellschaft und Staat bei Karl Marx, Freidrich Engels* (Jena, 1922).

Erich Thier, *Das Menschenbild des jungen Marx* (Göttingen, 1957).

R. Tucker, *Karl Marx. Die Entwicklung seines Denkens von der Philosophie zum Mythos* (Munich, 1972).

Karl Vorländer, *Kant und Marx* (Tübingen, 1926).

K. Vorländer, *Karl Marx: Sein Leben und Sein Werk* (Leipzig, 1929).

Jakob Walcher, *Ford oder Marx. Die praktische Lösung der sozialen Frage* (Berlin, 1925).

Carl Walcker, *Karl Marx. Gemeinverständliche, kritische Darlegung seines Lebens und seiner Lehren* (Leipzig, 1897).

Paul Weisengrün, *Der Marxismus und das Wesen der sozialen Frage* (Leipzig, 1900).

W. Weryha, *Marx als Philosoph* (Berne and Leipzig, 1894).

A. Wildermuth, *Marx und die Verwirklichung der Philosophie* (The Hague, 1970).

III FRENCH

L. Woltmann, *Der historische Materialismus. Darstellung und Kritik der Marxistischen Weltanschauung* (Düsseldorf, 1900).

J. Zeleny, *Die Wissenschaftslogik bei Marx und das 'Kapital'* (Berlin, 1968).

Louis Althusser et al., *Lire le Capital* (Paris, 1966); *Pour Marx* (Paris, 1965).

Charles Andler, *Le Manifeste Communiste de K. Marx et F. Engels* (Paris, 1901).

Pierre Ansart, *Marx et l'anarchisme* (Paris, 1969).

Raymond Aron, Dandieu, H. Holstein, *De Marx au marxisme* (Paris, 1948).

Henri Arvon, *Le Marxisme* (Paris, 1955).

Kostas Axelos, *Marx, penseur de la technique* (Paris, 1961).

Émile Baas, *Introduction critique au marxisme* (Colmar and Paris, 1960).

Jean Baby, *Principes fondamentaux d'économie politique* (Paris, 1949).

Z. Barbu, *Le développement de la pensée dialectique* (Paris, 1947).

Henri Bartoli, *La doctrine économique et sociale de Karl Marx* (Paris, 1950).

Pierre Bayart, *Que Savez-vous du marxisme?* (Lille, 1948).

J. Benard, *Théorie marxiste du Capital* (Paris, 1953).

Nicolas Berdiaeff, *Problèmes du communisme* (Paris, 1933).

Pierre Bigo, *Marxisme et humanisme, introduction à l'œuvre économique de Karl Marx* (Paris, 1953).

W. Blumenberg, *Karl Marx* (Paris, 1967).

J. Boissonnet, *La misère par la surabondance. Karl Marx, père de la crise mondiale* (Paris, 1938).

J. Bruhat, *K. Marx et F. Engels. Essai biographique* (Paris, 1971).

J. Y. Calvez, *La Pensée de Karl Marx* (Paris).

Guy Caire, *L'Aliénation dans les œuvres de jeunesse de Karl Marx*, (Aix-en-Provence, 1957).

Roger Caillois, *Description du marxisme* (Paris, 1950).

Henri Chambre, *De Karl Marx à Mao Tse Toung* (Paris, 1954).

A. Cornu, *Karl Marx et la Révolution de 1848* (Panz, 1948).

Auguste Cornu, *Karl Marx, L'homme et l'œuvre. De l'hégélianisme au matérialisme historique (1818–1845)* (Paris, 1934).

A. Cornu, *Karl Marx et Friedrich Engels* 3 vols (Paris, 1954 ff.).

Georges M. M. Cottier, *L'Athéisme du jeune Marx et ses origines hégéliennes* (Paris, 1959). *Du romantisme au marxisme* (Paris, 1961).

V. Dave, *Michel Bakounine et Karl Marx* (Paris, 1900).

H. Desroches, *Signification du marxisme* (Paris, 1949); *Marxisme et religions,* (Paris, 1962); *Socialisme et sociologie religieuse* (1965).

J. Diner-Dénes, *Karl Marx. L'homme et son génie* (Paris, 1933).

Pierre Fougeyrollas, *Le marxisme en question* (Paris, 1959).

Roger Garandy, *Karl Marx* (Paris, 1950).

H. Gollwitzer, *Atheisme marxiste et foi chrétienne* (Paris, 1965).

Antonio Graziadei, *La Théorie de la valeur. Critique aux doctrines de Marx* (Paris and Turin, 1935).

Franz Gregoire, *Aux sources de la pensée de Marx: Hegel, Feuerbach* (Louvain, 1947).

Daniel Guérin, *Pour un marxisme libertaire* (Paris, 1968).

Guiheneuf, *La théorie marxiste de la valeur* (Paris, 1951).

James Guillamme, *Karl Marx, pangermaniste, et l'Association Internationale des Travailleurs de 1864 á 1870* (Paris, 1915).

N. Gutermaun and H. Lefebvre, *La Conscience Mystifiée* (Paris, 1936).

J. B. S. Haldane, *La Philosophie Marxiste et les sciences* (Paris, 1936).

Pierre Haubtmann, *Marx et Proudhon, leurs rapports personnels 1844–47* (Paris, 1947).

Benoit P. Hepner, *Karl Marx: La Russie et l'Europe* (Paris, 1954).

Jean Hyppolite, *Logique et existence* (Paris, 1953); *Etudes sur Hegel et Marx* (Paris, 1955).

N. Klugmann and M. Dumesnil de Gramont, *Le Prophète rouge. Essai sur Marx et marxisme* (Paris, 1938).

Antonio Labriola, *Karl Marx, l'économiste et le socialiste* (Paris, 1910).

Jean Lacroix, *Marxisme, existentialisme et personnalisme* (Paris, 1950).

Henri Lefebvre, *Karl Marx, sa vie, son œuvre, avec un exposé de sa philosophie* (Paris, 1964); *Le Marxisme* (Paris); *Pour connaître la pensée de Karl Marx* (Paris, 1947); *Sociologie de Marx* (Paris, 1966); *Le matérialisme dialectique* (Paris, 1961).

Ignace Lepp, *Le Marxisme. Philosophie ambigue et efficace* (Paris, 1949).

G. Lukacs, *Historie et conscience de classe. Essai de dialectique marxiste* (Paris, 1964).

H. de Man, *Au-delà du marxisme* (Paris, 1929).

Ernest Mandel, *La formation de la pensée économique de Karl Marx, de 1843 jusqu'à la rédaction du Capital* (Paris, 1967); *Traité d'économie marxiste*, 2 vols (Paris, 1962).

A. Marc, *Marx et Hegel* (Paris, 1939).

J. Marchal. *Deux essais sur le marxisme* (Paris, 1954).

Dyonis Mascolo, *Le communisme (dialectique de besoins et de valeurs)* (Paris, 1953).

R. Maublanc, *Le marxisme et la liberté* (Paris, 1945).

M. Merlean-Ponty, *Les aventures de la dialectique* (Paris, 1955).

Miklos Molnar, *Le Déclin de la Première Internationale. Le Conférence de Londres de 1871* (Geneva, 1963).

Miklos Molnar, *La Politique d'Alliances du Marxisme 1848–1889* (Budapest, 1967).

Jules Monnerot, *Sociologie du communisme* (Paris, 1949).

Eliane Mosse, *Marx et le problème de la croissance dans une économie capitaliste* (Paris, 1957).

Pierre Naville, *Psychologie, marxisme et matérialisme* (Paris, 1946); *Le nouveau Leviathan*, i. *De l'aliénation à la jouissance. La genèse de la sociologie du travail chez Marx et Engels* (Paris, 1957).

C. Van Overbergh, *Karl Marx, sa vie et son oeuvre, Bilan du marxisme* (2nd ed.,

Bruxelles, 1948); *Karl Marx, critique de son économie politique* (Bruxelles' 1949); *Karl Marx, critique de sa guerre des classes* (3rd ed., Bruxelles, 1950); *Le marxisme. Critique de ses huit caractères fondamentaux* (2nd ed., Bruxelles, 1950).

L. Perchik, *Karl Marx, Notice biographique* (Paris, 1933).

André Piettre, *Marx et le marxisme* (Paris, 1957).

Max Raphael, *La théorie marxiste de la connaissance* (Paris, 1934).

Recherches internationales à la lumière du marxisme: le Jeune Marx (articles by various authors, Paris, 1960).

J. Rennes, *Exposé du marxisme* (Paris, 1934).

M. Rozenthal, *Les problèmes de la dialectique dans le Capital de Marx* (Paris and Moscow, 1959).

Maximilien Rubel, *Karl Marx. Essai de biographie intellectuelle* (Paris, 1957); *Karl Marx devant le bonapartisme* (Paris and The Hague, 1960); *Bibliographie des œuvres de Karl Marx* (Paris, 1956).

Josef Schumpeter, *Capitalisme, socialisme et démocratie* (Payot, 1950).

H. Sée, *Matérialisme historique et interprétation économique de l'histoire* (Paris, 1947).

Segal, *Principes d'économie politique* (Paris, 1936).

Lucien Sève, *Marxisme et théorie de la personnalité* (Paris, 1969).

Luc Somerhausen, *L'Humanisme agissant de Karl Marx* (Paris, 1946).

Thierry–Maulnier, *La pensée marxiste* (Paris, 1948).

Tran Duc Thao, *Phénoménologie et matérialisme dialectique* (Paris, 1952).

Leon Trotsky, *Le Marxisme à notre époque* (Paris, 1946).

M. Trumer, *Le Matérialisme historique chez Karl Marx et Friedrich Engels* (Paris, 1933).

R. Vancourt, *Marxisme et pensée chrétienne* (Paris, 1948).

André Vène, *Vie et doctrine de Karl Marx* (Paris, 1946).

Charles Wackenheim, *La faillite de la religion d'après Karl Marx* (Paris, 1963).

Index